ENCYCLOPEDIA OF

WORLD

POLITICAL

SYSTEMS

Volume 2

ENCYCLOPEDIA OF

WORLD

POLITICAL

SYSTEMS

Volume 2

J DENIS DERBYSHIRE

IAN DERBYSHIRE

SHARPE REFERENCE

an imprint of M.E. Sharpe. Inc.

SHARPE REFERENCE

Sharpe Reference is an imprint of M.E. Sharpe, INC.

M.E. Sharpe, INC.
80 Business Park Drive
Armonk, NY 10504

© 2000 by **M.E. Sharpe**, INC.

Library of Congress Cataloging in Publication Data
Derbyshire, J. Denis.
Encyclopedia of world political systems / J. Denis Derbyshire, Ian Derbyshire.
p. cm.
Includes bibliographic references and index.
Summary: Describes systems of government from throughout the
world, relates them to unique social and economic influences,
identifies particular features common to all or most, and makes
objective comparisons.
ISBN 0-7656-8025-4 (alk. paper)
1. Comparative government. [1. Comparative government.]
I. Derbyshire, Ian. II. Title.
JF51.D465 2000
320.3—dc21
99-34093
CIP

Printed and bound by De Agostini, Novara, Italy

DA (c) 10 9 8 7 6 5 4 3 2 1

M.E. Sharpe, INC.
Vice President and Publisher: Evelyn M. Fazio
Vice President and Production Director: Carmen P. Chetti
Editorial Coordinator: Aud Thiessen

Helicon Publishing Ltd
Managing Editor: Katie Emblem
Editors: Clare Colinson, Sue Donaldson, Denise Dresner,
Francis Gobey, Kate O'Leary, Stephen Pavlovich. Joseph Spooner
Index: Jane Martin
Production: Tony Ballsdon
Design: Terence Caven **Cartography:** Olive Pearson

Contents

Part 2: Political Systems of the World's Nation-states

Part 3: Towards One World

Chapter 8 The Relics of Empire —Colonies, Dependencies and Semi-Sovereign States

Chapter 9 The World Grows Smaller: International Cooperation

Preface

There are 192 sovereign nations in the world today, each with its own unique ethnic and social composition and its own unique history. The interplay of these, and other factors, has created, in turn, a unique system of government.

In this book we describe these systems and try to relate them to the social and economic influences which, over the years, have fashioned them. At the same time, we have identified particular features which are common to all, or most, countries and have classified them in an attempt to make objective comparisons.

In our classification we have sought to distinguish between those nations whose citizens have a completely free choice of which people should control the levers of political power and those where that choice is limited. The first we have called multiparty, or pluralistic, states and the second one-party, or monistic. This is an important distinction but it is not the only criterion for deciding whether or not a political system can be said to be democratic.

When the first edition of this book was written, some six years ago, there were 165 independent, sovereign states. Of these, 83, or just under half, could be classified as truly democratic. By 1995 the number had grown to 145 and remained at this figure in 1999, which was some three-quarters of the total.

As we said in our first study of the international political scene, the accession to power in the Soviet Union of Mikhail Gorbachev, in 1985, had the effect of casting a stone into the apparently static pond of Eastern European politics and we predicted that its ripples would spread to other regions. That prediction has come to pass, within a shorter time than we envisaged, and now one-party, monistic states are very much in a minority in most regions of the world. However, reconstructed communist parties have returned to power in several of the recently democratized states in Eastern Europe, with Lech Wałesa, so instrumental in the downfall of communism, being replaced as Polish president in November 1995 by the communist leader, Alexander Kwasniewski.

In the pages that follow we have tried to provide a better understanding of political institutions and events in the contemporary world and have addressed ourselves not just to academics and professional observers of the political landscape but also to the more general reader who is looking for a serious, but not over-technical, account of global politics.

When we embarked on this task we believed that our approach was new in a number of ways. First, we have considered all the contemporary states and not just the well-known and obvious. Second, we have attempted to identify connections between a country's political system and its historical, social, and economic background. Third, we have looked in some detail at the dynamics of political systems, including the activities of parties and similar groupings, as well as the formal institutions that states have created. Fourth, partly to make the material more manageable, but also to provide a better understanding of geographical and demographic influences, we have adopted a regional approach to our exposition of political systems. Finally, we have looked at examples of how sovereign states, either by choice or necessity, have found it increasingly profitable to co-operate with each other rather than just compete. Six years later, we believe that this approach is still unique and has been justified by recent events.

Although the task has been enjoyable, there have been inevitable frustrations resulting from the almost impossible task of ensuring that the information about each state is still valid in a world where change tends to be the rule rather than the exception.

'To understand others is a certain way of understanding ourselves' might well be the motto for this book. If we have succeeded in this task of creating a better understanding of politics throughout the world we will be well content.

Acknowledgments

We would like to record our appreciation for the encouragement and support we have received from our publishers for their faith in us and our project, and for keeping us to our task and ensuring the accuracy of our work. Having said this, we accept that any consequential errors or omissions are ours.

Finally, nearer home, we are particularly grateful to Joyce for her patient encouragement and support.

JDD and IDD
July 1999

Tables

Regional maps

Readers' note

Continuation of part 2 from volume 1 (page 463)

Central and Southern Africa

The region we have defined as Central and Southern Africa covers, as Table 54 shows, an area of more than 24 million square kilometres, nearly seven times larger than Northern and Western Europe, and comparable in size to Asia. It has a comparatively low population density, however: less than a quarter of that of Northern and Western Europe and less than a fifth of that of Asia. Lying mostly between the Tropic of Cancer and the Tropic of Capricorn it enjoys a mainly tropical or subtropical climate, although marked variations can be found between the Atlantic and Indian Ocean coasts and between the mountainous and low-lying areas. The great majority of the inhabitants of the region are indigenous black Africans. Even in South Africa only about 21% of the population is not of black ethnic stock.

As Table 1 in Part I reveals, 45 of the 48 states in Central and Southern Africa, or over 93%, are of post-1945 origin. Before that time virtually the entire region was controlled by one or other of the major European powers, yet the 'scramble for Africa', as it has been described, began comparatively late in the 19th century, the big 'share out' taking place between 1870 and 1914. Table 55, below, gives the distribution of 46 of the current 48 states between the European colonial powers during this period. This distribution does not necessarily indicate the European power which was the first to exploit a particular country, but the settlement finally agreed after much bargaining by the major powers during the late 19th and early 20th centuries.

Ethiopia and Eritrea, which were then one state, and Liberia were the exceptions to the rule. Ethiopia managed to retain its independence from the 11th century, and Eritrea was only briefly occupied by Italy between 1882 and 1923. Liberia was created by the American Colonization Society, as a home for liberated American slaves, and formally recognized as the Free and Independent Republic of Liberia by Britain and France in 1847.

Historically and culturally the most arresting aspect of Central and Southern Africa is its tribal nature. This has resulted in a great variety in its political systems and considerable social and political disunity. Although most of the European powers, initially at any rate, attempted to export their own tried and tested systems of democratic government, as civilizing and unifying devices, after independence most were significantly changed and adapted to suit local conditions, or were replaced with something much more authoritarian.

For example, of the 17 countries which were under British control during the first half of this century, only four, Botswana, Gambia, Mauritius, and, tentatively, Uganda, had pluralistic, democratic systems before the 1990s. The rest were either one-party states or under military rule. None of the 16 states which were part of the French colonial empire had, before the 1990s, succeeded, or even attempted, to fashion a pluralist democracy.

There are some good and valid reasons for this pattern of political systems and it would be unwise to compare them with contemporaneous states in other parts of the world in any censorious fashion. The need to cohere tribal loyalties into a sense of national identity and pride was clearly a major imperative. Examples of what can happen if tribal feelings are allowed to run completely free are to be found in the civil wars in Nigeria and the Congo in the early 1960s, and the more recent civil wars in Angola, Ethiopia, Somalia, Sudan, and the Democratic Republic of Congo, and in the killings by Hutus and Tutsis in Burundi and Rwanda.

It should also be remembered that the cultural histories of the people of Central and Southern Africa are much different from those of many of their counterparts in other parts of the world. Tribal decision-making was conducted on the basis of discussion, leading to a consensus enunciated by the chief, and the proliferation of one-party systems is, to a great extent, a modern manifestation of this approach.

Furthermore, the comparative sophistication of Western-style political systems was not necessarily appropriate for communities where levels of literacy were still comparatively low. For example, Table 47 shows adult literacy levels of less than 40% for 47% of the states in Central and Southern Africa, compared with under 5% of the states in Central America and the Caribbean, under 11% of those in the Middle East and North Africa, and under 18% of Asian countries. Within this overall picture there are, however, considerable variations, with literacy rates ranging from under 20% in Burkina Faso, Djibouti, Gabon, and Republic of Congo to over 60% in Botswana, Democratic Republic of Congo, Ethiopia, Kenya, Mauritius, South Africa, Zambia, and Zimbabwe. The high literacy level of 83% in Mauritius has contributed to the establishment, and maintenance, of a sophisticated, multiparty political system.

The 'scramble for Africa' in the 19th century has been matched by the 'scramble for democracy' in that continent during the last decade of the 20th century. The break-up of the Soviet Union in 1991, and the demise of

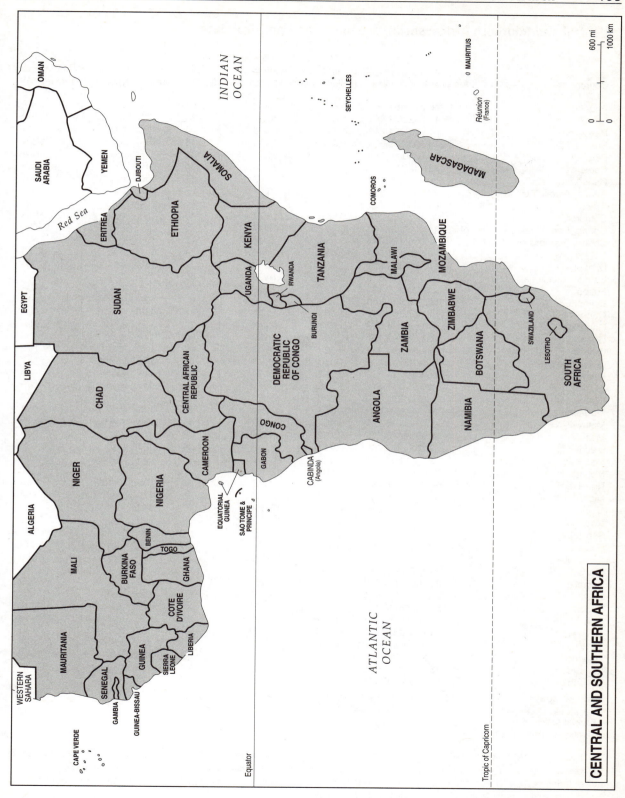

CENTRAL AND SOUTHERN AFRICA

OMAN

SAUDI ARABIA

YEMEN

Red Sea

INDIAN OCEAN

DJIBOUTI

ERITREA

ETHIOPIA

SOMALIA

KENYA

UGANDA

RWANDA

BURUNDI

TANZANIA

SEYCHELLES

COMOROS

MADAGASCAR

MAURITIUS

Réunion (France)

600 mi

1000 km

MOZAMBIQUE

MALAWI

ZIMBABWE

ZAMBIA

SWAZILAND

LESOTHO

SOUTH AFRICA

BOTSWANA

NAMIBIA

ANGOLA

DEMOCRATIC REPUBLIC OF CONGO

CONGO

GABON

CABINDA (Angola)

CAMEROON

EQUATORIAL GUINEA

SAO TOME & PRINCIPE

CENTRAL AFRICAN REPUBLIC

SUDAN

EGYPT

LIBYA

CHAD

NIGER

NIGERIA

BENIN

TOGO

GHANA

COTE D'IVOIRE

LIBERIA

SIERRA LEONE

GUINEA

GUINEA-BISSAU

GAMBIA

SENEGAL

BURKINA FASO

MALI

MAURITANIA

WESTERN SAHARA

ALGERIA

CAPE VERDE

ATLANTIC OCEAN

Equator

Tropic of Capricorn

Central and Southern Africa: social, economic, and political data

Country	Area (sq km/sq miles)	c. 1995 Population (million)	c. 1995 Pop. density per sq km/sq mile	c. 1992 Adult literacy rate (%)	World ranking	Income type	c. 1991 Human rights rating (%)
Angola	1,246,700/481,353	10.674	9/22	42	160	low	27
Benin	112,622/43,484	5.387	48/124	23	184	low	90
Botswana	582,000/224,711	1.443	2/6	74	114	middle	79
Burkina Faso	274,200/105,869	9.889	36/93	18	186	low	N/A
Burundi	27,830/10,745	6.134	220/571	34	171	low	N/A
Cameroon	475,442/183,569	12.871	27/70	54	141	low	56
Cape Verde	4,033/1,557	0.417	103/268	37	166	low	N/A
Central African Republic	622,984/240,535	3.235	5/13	27	177	low	N/A
Chad	1,284,000/495,755	6.214	5/13	30	174	low	N/A
Comoros	1,860/718	0.630	339/677	48	153	low	N/A
Congo, Democratic Republic of	2,345,000/905,409	42.552	18/47	72	117	low	57
Congo, Republic of	342,000/132,047	2.516	7/19	16	188	low	N/A
Côte d'Ivoire	322,460/124,502	13.695	42/110	54	141	low	75
Djibouti	23,200/8,958	0.566	24/63	12	189	low	N/A
Equatorial Guinea	28,100/10,849	0.389	14/36	50	149	low	N/A
Eritrea	117,600/45,406	3.437	29/76	N/A	–	low	N/A
Ethiopia	1,106,200/427,106	54.938	50/129	62	129	low	13
Gabon	267,667/103,347	1.283	5/12	12	189	middle	N/A
Gambia	11,300/4,363	1.081	96/248	27	177	low	N/A
Ghana	238,540/92,101	17.434	73/189	60	131	low	53
Guinea	245,860/94,927	6.500	26/68	24	182	low	N/A
Guinea-Bissau	36,130/13,939	1.050	29/75	37	166	low	N/A
Kenya	580,646/224,189	29.292	50/131	69	119	low	46
Lesotho	30,350/11,718	1.996	66/170	59	134	low	N/A
Liberia	111,370/43,000	2.700	24/63	40	161	low	N/A
Madagascar	587,041/226,658	14.303	24/63	53	145	low	N/A
Malawi	118,480/45,745	9.461	80/207	48	153	low	33
Mali	1,240,000/478,766	10.462	8/22	32	173	low	N/A
Mauritania	1,030,700/397,955	2.211	2/6	34	171	low	N/A
Mauritius	1,865/720	1.142	612/1586	83	98	middle	N/A
Mozambique	799,380/308,642	16.500	21/53	27	177	low	53
Namibia	824,292/318,261	1.500	2/5	38	163	middle	N/A
Niger	1,267,000/489,191	8.846	7/18	28	176	low	N/A
Nigeria	923,768/356,669	108.467	117/304	51	147	low	49
Rwanda	26,340/10,170	7.750	294/762	50	149	low	48
São Tomé	964/372	0.125	130/336	57	136	low	N/A
Senegal	197,000/76,062	8.102	41/107	38	163	low	71
Seychelles	450/174	0.074	164/425	58	135	middle	N/A
Sierra Leone	71,740/27,699	4.402	61/159	21	185	low	67
Somalia	637,660/246,202	9.007	14/37	24	182	low	N/A
South Africa	1,222,037/471,831	40.436	33/86	80	105	middle	50
Sudan	2,505,800/967,494	28.947	12/30	27	177	low	18
Swaziland	17,400/6,718	0.832	48/124	55	140	middle	N/A
Tanzania	945,090/364,901	28.846	31/79	46	157	low	41
Togo	56,790/21,927	3.930	69/179	43	159	low	48
Uganda	241,139/93,104	20.620	86/221	48	153	low	46
Zambia	752,620/290,588	9.196	12/32	73	115	low	57
Zimbabwe	390,759/150,873	11.150	29/74	67	121	low	65
Total/average/range	*24,296,409/9,389,892*	*582.702*	*24/62*	*12–83*	–	–	*13–90*

* Federal system is inoperative
** Though dominated by one party.

A = appointed, AMS = additional member system, E = elected, F = Federal, PL = party list, PR = proportional representation, SB = second ballot, SP = simple plurality, Lib-dem = liberal democratic, Em-dem = emergent democratic, Auth-nat = authoritarian nationalist as a consequence of civil war, Nat-soc = Nationalistic socialist, Unlim-pres = unlimited presidential, Lim-pres = limited presidential, Trans = transitional, U = unitary.)

Table 54

World ranking	Date of state formation	State structure	State type	Executive type	Number of assembly chambers	Party structure	Lower house electoral system
97	1975	U	Em-dem	Lim-pres	1	two	PR-PL
21	1960	U	Em-dem	Lim-pres	1	multi	PR-PL
37	1966	U	Lib-dem	Lim-pres	2	two	SP
–	1960	U	Em-dem	Lim-pres	2	multi**	PR-PL
–	1962	U	military/trans	military/trans	1	two	PR-PL
66	1960	U	Em-dem	Lim-pres	1	multi**	PR-PL
–	1975	U	military	military	1	two	SP
–	1960	U	Em-dem	Lim-pres	2	multi	SB
–	1960	U	Em-dem	Dual	1	multi	SB
–	1975	F	Military	Military	1	multi	SB
88	1960	U	Military	Military	-	trans	-
–	1960	U	Nat-soc	Unlim-pres	1	multi (trans)	-
40	1960	U	Em-dem	Lim-pres	1	multi**	SB
–	1977	U	Auth-nat	Unlim-pres	1	multi**	SP
–	1968	U	Auth-nat	Unlim-pres	1	multi**	PR-PL
–	1993	U	Nat-soc	Unlim-pres	1	one	mixed-E/A
106	11th c	F	Em-dem	Parliamentary	2	multi**	SP
–	1960	U	Em-dem	Lim-pres	2	multi**	mixed-E/A
–	1965	U	Em-dem	Lim-pres	1	multi	mixed-E/A
72	1957	U	Em-dem	Lim-pres	1	two	SP
–	1958	U	Em-dem	Lim-pres	1	multi	PR-AMS
–	1974	U	Military	Military	1	multi	PR-LV
83	1963	U	Em-dem	Lim-pres	1	multi**	mixed-E/A
–	1966	U	Em-dem	Parliamentary	2	multi**	SP
–	1847	U	Em-dem	Lim-pres	2	multi	SP
–	1960	U	Em-dem	Lim-pres	2	multi	SP
90	1964	U	Em-dem	Lim-pres	1	multi	PR-STV
–	1960	U	Em-dem	Lim-pres	1	multi**	SB
–	1960	U	Em-dem	Lim-pres	2	multi**	SB
–	1968	U	Lib-dem	Parliamentary	1	multi	PR-LV
72	1975	U	Em-dem	Lim-pres	1	two	PR-PL
–	1990	U	Em-dem	Lim-pres	2	two	mixed-E/A
–	1960	U	Military	Military	1	multi	SP
77	1960	F	Em-dem	Lim-pres	2	multi	SP
80	1962	U	Auth-nat	Unlim-pres	1	multi	A
–	1975	U	Em-dem	Lim-pres	1	multi	PR-PL
45	1960	U	Nat-soc	Unlim-pres	2	multi**	PR-AMS
–	1976	U	Em-dem	Lim-pres	1	multi**	PR-AMS
51	1961	U	Em-dem	Lim-pres	1	multi	mixed-E/A
–	1960	F*	Military	Military	-	-	-
75	1910	U	Em-dem	Lim-pres	2	multi	PR-PL
103	1956	F	Military	Military	1	trans	mixed-E/I
–	1968	U	Absolutist	Absolutist	2	one	mixed-E/A
87	1961	U	Em-dem	Lim-pres	1	multi**	mixed-E/A
80	1960	U	Em-dem	Lim-pres	1	multi	SB
83	1962	U	Auth-nat	Unlim-pres	1	one	mixed E/I
65	1964	U	Em-dem	Lim-pres	2	multi**	SP
53	1980	U	Nat-soc	Unlim-pres	1	one	mixed-E/A
–	–	–	–	–	–	–	–

European control of Central and Southern Africa, 1870–1914 — Table 55

Great Britain	Botswana		Djibouti
	Gambia		Gabon
	Ghana		Guinea
	Kenya		Madagascar
	Lesotho		Mali
	Malawi		Mauritania
	Mauritius		Niger
	Namibia (then part of South Africa)		Senegal
	Nigeria		Somalia (part)
	Seychelles	Portugal	
	Sierra Leone		Angola
	Somalia (part)		Cape Verde
	South Africa		Guinea-Bissau
	Sudan		Mozambique
	Swaziland		São Tomé e Príncipe
	Uganda	Germany	Burundi
	Zambia		Cameroon
	Zimbabwe		Rwanda
France	Benin		Tanzania
	Burkina Faso		Togo
	Central African Republic	Spain	Equatorial Guinea
	Chad		
	Comoros	Belgium	Democratic Republic of Congo (formerly Zaire)
	Congo, Republic of		
	Côte d'Ivoire	Italy	Eritrea

communism as a 'model ideology' for post-colonial states, has dramatically changed the political map of Central and Southern Africa. Using the criterion of the establishment of a liberal democratic system in the past decade, the region now has among its political types the largest proportion of emergent democracies, nearly 64%, of any in the world. Indeed, 41% of the world's 70 emergent democracies are situated within this region. If the two well-established liberal democracies, in Botswana and Mauritius, are added, then Central and Southern Africa has been transformed from a continent dominated by one-party, authoritarian or militarist political systems to one which can begin to be compared with other regions with much stronger democratic heritages. However, as emphasized in Chapters 3 and 6, a strong caveat exists. The competitive element remains weak in many of Africa's fledgling democracies and the military remains an influental background force. However, it is hoped that, over time, stable multiparty systems will develop across the region.

The distribution of religions throughout Central and Southern Africa tends to reflect patterns of colonization based sometimes on trade and sometimes on missionary fervour. For example, the countries where Islam is the main, or a major, religion, which include Burkina Faso, Chad, Comoros, Djibouti, Eritrea, Gambia, Guinea, Mali, Mauritania, Niger, Nigeria, Senegal, Sierra Leone, Somalia, Sudan, and Tanzania, are found near the early Arab coastal or northern trading routes, which predate European exploitation. On the other hand, the countries where Christians are in the majority, such as Angola, Burundi, Cape Verde, the Central African Republic, the Republic of Congo, Equatorial Guinea, Gabon, Ghana, Guinea-Bissau, Kenya, Lesotho, Madagascar, Malawi, Namibia, Rwanda, São Tomé e Príncipe, the Seychelles, South Africa, Swaziland, Uganda, Democratic Republic of Congo, Zambia, and Zimbabwe, came under the influence of European missionaries.

Although comparably rich in natural resources in many areas, Central and Southern Africa is still economically poor in relation to most other regions, 85% of the states having low incomes, only seven in the middle-income category and none, including potentially wealthy countries such as Nigeria and South Africa, falling into the high-income group. The bulk of international aid, and particularly assistance in food supplies, is still directed to this region, which has 10% of the world's population but produces barely 1% of global GDP. Since the 1980s the region has found itself caught in the vice of a rapidly growing population, not withstanding serious famines in the precarious Sahel belt running between Senegal and Somalia, notably in Ethiopia, and an escalating AIDS epidemic in parts of Eastern and Central Africa, and a sluggish economy. The latter was not improved by the paucity of intra-regional cooperation. The dramatic political changes of recent years may, it is hoped, stimulate corresponding economic improvements, as skills are improved and resources directed away from the defense sector into more productive channels. It is possible also that, with the ending of apartheid in South Africa and the collapse of the Soviet Union removing two key sources of discord, intra-regional cooperation will improve. A hopeful sign was the decision in August 1995 of the leaders of the 12-nation Southern African Development Community (SADC) to work towards establishing a free-trading southern African economic community by the year 2000.

Recommended reading

Arnold, G (ed.) *Political and Economic Encyclopedia of Africa*, Longman, 1993

Balewa, B A T *Governing Nigeria*, Malthouse Press, 1994

Bayatt, J-F *The State in Africa: The Politics of the Belly*, Longman, 1993

Chazan, N, Mortimer, R, Ravenhill, J, and Rothchild, D *Politics and Society in Contemporary Africa*, Lynne Rienner, 1992

Diamond, L, Linz, J, and Lipset, S M (eds.) *Democracy in Developing Countries*, Vol. 2, *Africa*, Lynne Rienner, 1988

Hyden, G and Bratton, M (eds.) *Governance and Politics in Africa*, Lynne Rienner, 1992

Maguire, K *Politics in South Africa: From Vorster to de Klerk*, W & R Chambers, 1991

Pocket Africa:, Economist Books, 1997

ANGOLA

The Republic of Angola
A República de Angola

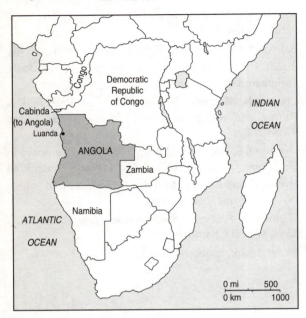

Capital: Luanda

Social and economic data
Area: 1,246,700 sq km/481,353 sq miles
Population: 10,674,000 *
Pop. density per sq km/sq mi: 9/22*
Urban population: 27%**
Literacy rate: 42%**
GDP: $4,440 million*; per-capita GDP: $415*
Government defense spending (% of GDP): 4.8*
Currency: new kwanza
Economy type: low income
Labor force in agriculture: 69%**
* 1995.
** 1992.

Head of state and government (executive)
President José Eduardo dos Santos, since 1979

Head of government
Prime Minister José Eduardo dos Santos, since 1999

Ethnic composition
There are eight main tribal groups, the Bakonga, the Mbunda, the Ovimbundu, the Lunda-Tchokwe, the Nganguela, the Nyaneka-Humbe, the Hiriro, and the Ambo, and about 100 subgroups. There was a major exodus of Europeans in the early 1970s and there are now about 30,000 left, mainly Portuguese. A 20-year insurgency in the northern enclave of Cabinda was ended in 1996 by a peace agreement with rebel guerrillas. The official language is still Portuguese.

Religions
Most of the population adheres to traditional, animist beliefs, but Roman Catholicism also attracts a following from around 60% of the people.

Political features
State type: emergent democratic
Date of state formation: 1975
Political structure: unitary
Executive: limited presidential
Assembly: one-chamber
Party structure: two-party
Human rights rating: 27%
International affiliations: ACP, CEEAC (observer), IBRD, IMF, Lusophone, NAM, OAU, SADC, UN, WTO

Local and regional government
The country is divided into 18 provinces, each governed by a Provincial Commissioner who is an *ex officio* member of the central government.

Political system
Formerly a one-party state, in 1991 a new constitution was adopted and this was amended in 1991 and 1992. It provided for an executive president, popularly elected for five years, renewable only twice, and a 220-member National Assembly. Presidential elections are by the second ballot majoritarian system. The Assembly has a life of four years, but a further constitutional amendment in November 1996 gave the national assembly a life of a minimum of two and a maximum of four years. The Assembly comprises 130 members elected by proportional representation and 90 elected in provincial districts. The president appoints a prime minister and Council of Ministers (cabinet). In 1995 two vice-presidential posts were created.

Political parties
There are over 40 political parties, the three most significant being the People's Movement for the Liberation of Angola (MPLA), the National Union for the Total Independence of Angola (UNITA), and the National Front for the Liberation of Angola (FNLA).

The MPLA was formed in 1956 as a 'liberation movement' with the specific aim of securing the country's independence from Portugal. When independence was obtained in 1975 it became the party of government and in 1977 it was reconstructed to become a Marxist–Leninist 'vanguard' party, adopting the title the People's Movement for the Liberation of Angola-Workers' Party (MPLA-PT). It was the only legally permitted party until 1991. In December 1990 it abandoned Marxism–Leninism for 'democratic socialism'.

UNITA, formed in 1966, was a rebel group, backed by South Africa, and is now the main opposition to the MPLA. It is authoritarian-conservative.

The center-right FNLA originated in 1962 as a rebel group which was to receive US backing. It is led today by Holden Roberto and is part of a 14-party Democratic Civilian Alliance, which was established in 1994.

Political leaders since 1970

1975–79 Agostinho Neto (MPLA), 1979– José Eduardo dos Santos (MPLA-PT)

Latest elections

Multiparty elections held in September 1992 resulted in a clear victory for the MPLA, which, with 53.7% of the national vote, won 129 National Assembly seats. UNITA, with 34.1% of the vote, captured 70 seats, and the FNLA, with 2.4% of the vote, 5 seats. Although the poll was viewed as generally fair by United Nations observers, the result was disputed by the UNITA leader, Jonas Savimbi, and the civil war resumed. In the concurrent presidential election, the incumbent president, dos Santos, won the first round, with 49.6% of the vote to the 40% cast for Savimbi, but narrowly fell short of the required first-round absolute majority. No date for the second round of the elections was announced. In November 1994 dos Santos and Savimbi signed a peace accord, providing for interim power sharing.

Political history

Angola had been colonized by Portugal as early as the 17th century and became an overseas province in 1951. A strong independence movement began in the 1950s, with guerrilla warfare organized by the People's Movement for the Liberation of Angola (MPLA), which was based in the Congo. Two other nationalist movements were formed, the National Front for the Liberation of Angola (FNLA) and the National Union for the Total Independence of Angola (UNITA) and the struggle for independence developed, in 1961, into a civil war. The MPLA attracted support from socialist and communist states, UNITA was helped by the Western powers, including the United States, and the FNLA was backed by the 'non-left' power groups of southern Africa, chiefly South Africa.

After the granting of full independence in 1975 there

was a return to a confused state of civil war, with the MPLA and UNITA the main contestants and foreign mercenaries helping the FNLA. By 1975 the MPLA, led by Dr Agostinho Neto and with the help of mainly Cuban forces, was in control of most of the country and the People's Republic of Angola was established, with Luanda as its capital and Neto as its first president. It soon won international recognition. In the meantime, the FNLA and UNITA had proclaimed their own People's Democratic Republic of Angola, based in Nova Lisboa, renamed Huambo, in the west-central area of the country.

President Neto died in 1979 and was succeeded by José Eduardo dos Santos (b. 1942), who maintained the policy of retaining strong links with the Soviet bloc. UNITA guerrillas, supported by South Africa, continued their guerrilla operations and in 1980 and 1981 South African forces made direct raids into Angola to attack bases of the South West Africa People's Organization (SWAPO), who were fighting for the independence of Namibia, whose claims Angola supported.

By 1982 there were international diplomatic moves to end the hostilities. In 1984 the FNLA surrendered to the MPLA and in 1983 South Africa proposed a complete withdrawal of its forces if it could be assured that the areas it vacated would not be filled by Cuban or SWAPO units. The Angolan government accepted the South African proposals and a settlement was concluded, known as the Lusaka Agreement, whereby a Joint Monitoring Commission (JMC) was set up to oversee the South African withdrawal. In 1985 South Africa announced that its withdrawal had been completed and the JMC was wound up. Relations between the two countries deteriorated however when, in 1986, new South African raids into Angola occurred. UNITA also continued to receive South African and US support.

By 1988 there was clear evidence that South Africa would welcome an opportunity of withdrawing from the conflict and secret talks between its country's representatives and those of Angola and Cuba were held in London under US auspices. The continued South African occupation of Namibia remained the main stumbling block to a lasting settlement. At the end of 1988, however, an agreement was eventually signed. This provided for the full withdrawal of South African and Cuban forces.

In May 1991 a US, Russian, and Portuguese-brokered peace accord between the Angolan government and UNITA was signed at Estoril, Portugal, and the rebel leader in exile, Jonas Savimbi (b. 1934), returned.

Multiparty elections held in September 1992 were disputed by Savimbi and, to avoid a renewal of the civil war, President dos Santos agreed to annul the result and hold fresh elections. At first this seemed to appease Savimbi but later fighting broke out again. During 1993 the actions of UNITA forfeited it of any remaining international support and, from September, a UN oil and arms embargo was imposed against the alternative UNITA regime, which controlled 70% of the country. International pressure forced Savimbi to agree to a provisional ceasefire in December 1993. This did not hold. However, in November 1994, after government forces captured the UNITA stronghold of Huambo, a definitive ceasefire accord was signed, with agreement at last reached on how the second round of the presidential elections would be conducted. In the interim, it was agreed to share power, with UNITA being given four full ministerial positions and Savimbi being offered the post of vice president in 1995. The formation of a government of national unity was repeatedly delayed until, following strong UN pressure on UNITA, it was established in April 1997, but the UNITA leader, Jonas Savimbi, refused to recognize it and rejected the offer of the post of vice president. Eventually in January 1998, UNITA agreed to demilitarization and was transformed into a political party. However, by June 1998 the build-up of government and UNITA forces threatened the peace process. Meanwhile, despite the introduction of a number of free-market reforms, the economic situation was serious, with hyperinflation and much infrastructure damaged.

In December 1998 fighting escalated between government forces and UNITA forces, which included mercenaries from Israel, Morocco, and South Africa. UNITA made advances in the central highlands, forcing the Angolan government to withdraw its troops from the Democratic Republic of Congo, where they had been supporting the regime of President Kabila in Congo's civil war. In February 1999 the UN Security Council voted unanimously to withdraw 1,000-strong UN Observer Mission in Angola (UNOMA), which had been established in mid-1997 to oversee the failed 1994 peace accords. The withdrawal came after two UN planes had been shot down. As the civil war intensified, President dos Santos assumed the post of prime minister in February 1999 and also took charge of the armed forces. In June 1999, with around one million displaced as refugees and with widespread starvation threatened, especially in the government-held besieged city of Huambo, the World Food Programme appealed for $40 million in aid.

BENIN

The Republic of Benin
La République du Bénin

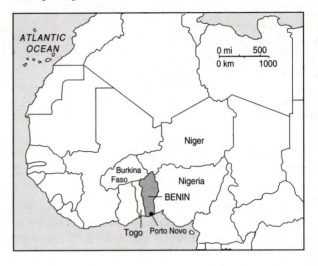

Capital: Porto Novo

Social and economic data
Area: 112,622 sq km/43,484 sq miles
Population: 5,387,000 *
Pop. density per sq km/sq mi: 48/124*
Urban population: 40%**
Literacy rate: 23%**
GDP: $2,035 million**; per-capita GDP: $380**
Government defense spending (% of GDP): 1.3 %**
Currency: franc CFA
Economy type: low income
Labor force in agriculture: 60%**
* 1995.
** 1992.

Head of state and head of government
President Mathieu Kerekou, since 1996

Ethnic composition
Ninety-nine per cent of the population is indigenous African, distributed among 42 tribes, the largest being the Fon, the Adja, the Yoruba, and the Bariba. There is a small European, mainly French, community. The official language is French.

Religions
Sixty-five per cent of the population follows traditional, animist beliefs, about 13% is Muslim, 12% Roman Catholic, and 3% Protestant.

Political features

State type: emergent democratic
Date of state formation: 1960
Political structure: unitary
Executive: limited presidential
Assembly: one-chamber
Party structure: multiparty
Human rights rating: 90%
International affiliations: ACP, BOAD, CEAO, ECOWAS, Francophone, FZ, IBRD, IMF, NAM, OAU, OIC, UEMOA, UN, WTO

Local and regional government

The country is divided into six provinces, which are further subdivided into 78 districts. A significant amount of general and financial policy-making has been devolved.

Political system

The former constitution was based on a Fundamental Law (Loi Fondamentale) of 1977 which made it a one-party state, dominated by the Benin People's Revolutionary Party (PRPB), committed to the path of 'scientific socialism'. In 1990 a new pluralist constitution was approved by referendum. It provides for an executive president, elected directly by the second-ballot majoritarian system for a five-year term, renewable once only. There is a single-chamber 83-member National Assembly, elected for a four-year term by proportional representation. The president appoints and heads a Council of Ministers (cabinet), although there is also a prime minister, and the president has decree powers. There is a Constitutional Court and an advisory Economic and Social Council.

Political parties

There are 88 registered parties, the most significant being the Benin Renaissance Party (PRB), the Party for Democratic Renewal (PRD), the Social Democratic Party (PSD), and the Action Front for Renewal and Development (FARD-Alafia). The general orientation of most parties is left-of-center. The PRB, led by Nicéphore Soglo, is centrist and in opposition to the other three parties mentioned above.

Political leaders since 1970

1970–72 Hubert Maga (civilian-military triumvirate), 1972 Justin Ahomadegbe (civilian-military triumvirate), 1972–91 Colonel Mathieu Kerekou (military/PRPB), 1991–96 Nicéphore Soglo (PRB-UTDR Coalition); 1996– Mathieu Kerekou (FARD)

Latest elections

The former president, Mathieu Kerekou, surprisingly defeated the incumbent Nicéphore Soglo in the run-off round of the March 1996 presidential election, attracting 52.5% of the vote.

The March 1999 National Assembly elections resulted in parties opposed to President Kerekou securing 42 of the 83 seats, with more than 10 securing representation. The results were as follows:

Benin latest election results

Party	Seats
PRB	27
PRD	11
FARD	10
PSD	9
Others*	26

* Minor parties.

Political history

Benin used to consist of a number of small, generally warring, principalities, the most powerful being the Kingdom of Dahomey, which was established in the 17th century. The area was conquered by the French in 1892 and became the French Protectorate of Dahomey. It was made part of French West Africa in 1904, and in 1958 became a self-governing dominion within the French Community. In 1960 it became a fully independent state.

For the next 12 years it went through a period of acute political instability, with swings from civilian to military rule, including five army coups, and with disputes between the inhabitants of the northern, central, and southern regions. In 1972 the deputy chief of the army, Colonel Mathieu Kerekou (b. 1933), established a military regime pledged to give fair representation to each region, governing through an appointed National Council of the Revolution (CNR). In 1974 he announced that the country would follow a path of 'scientific socialism', based on Marxism–Leninist principles, and the following year the nation's name was changed from Dahomey to Benin.

In 1977 the CNR was dissolved and a civilian government formed, with Kerekou elected as president and head of state. He was re-elected in 1984 and 1989. After some initial economic and social difficulties, the Kerekou government showed signs of growing stability and in 1987 the president resigned from the army to demonstrate his commitment to genuine democracy. In 1989 he disavowed Marxism–Leninism and embarked on a new course towards a market economy. In March 1990, following a constitutional confer-

ence, it became obvious that a transition to full democratic government would proceed at a faster pace than
Kerekou had anticipated. He appointed as prime minister Nicéphore Soglo (b. 1933), a former World Bank
administrator, and in the March 1991 free presidential
elections was defeated by his protégé. Soglo subsequently ruled with a ten-party coalition, known as Le
Renouveau, and attracted Western economic assistance.
In March 1996 Kerekou surprisingly defeated Soglo in
the elections for the presidency. He ruled with a nine-
party coalition, which had arisen from the inconclusive
parliamentary elections of March–April 1995. It was
built around Kerekou's Front for Renewal and
Development (FARD) and the Party for Democratic
Renewal (PRD), whose leader, Adrien Houngbédji, a
former Kerekou opponent who had been condemned
to death in 1975, became prime minister in 1996.
Houngbédji and PRD colleagues resigned from the
government in May 1998.

The March 1999 legislature elections saw voting
polarized on regional lines, with parties which supported President Kerekou polling strongly in the north,
and opposition parties, for example Nicéphore Soglo's
Benin Renaissance Party (PRB), making significant
gains in the south. The opposition parties gained a narrow single seat majority in the National Assembly.
However, after the election the president stated that he
looked forward to a new era of power-sharing, or 'cohabitation'.

BOTSWANA

The Republic of Botswana

Capital: Gaborone

Social and economic data
Area: 582,000 sq km/224,711 sq miles
Population: 1,443,000[*]
Pop. density per sq km/sq mi: 2/6[*]
Urban population: 27%[**]
Literacy rate: 74%[**]
GDP: $4,380 million[*]; per-capita GDP: $3,035[*]
Government defense spending (% of GDP): 7.1%[*]
Currency: franc CFA
Economy type: middle income
Labor force in agriculture: 26%[**]
[*] 1995.
[**] 1992.

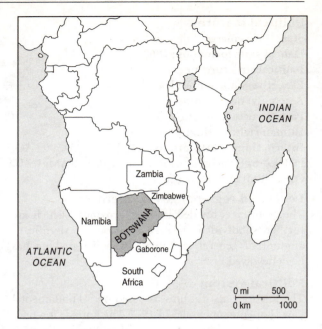

Head of state and head of government
President Festus Mogae, since 1998

Ethnic composition
About 94% of the population is Tswana, 5% Bushman,
and the rest is European. The official language is
English.

Religions
The majority of the population follows traditional, animist beliefs and about 30% is Christian.

Political features
State type: liberal democratic
Date of state formation: 1966
Political structure: unitary
Executive: limited presidential
Assembly: two-chamber
Party structure: two-party
Human rights rating: 79%
International affiliations: ACP, CW, IBRD, IMF, NAM,
OAU, SADC, UN, WTO

Local and regional government
The country is divided into nine districts, ranging in
popu-lation from under 20,000 to over 300,000 and six
independent townships. Each has an elected council
and is mainly responsible for primary education,
licensing, and collecting taxes in its own locality.

Political system
The 1966 constitution, amended in 1997, contains features which blend the British system of parliamentary

accountability with the distinctive tribal nature of the country. It provides for a National Assembly of 47 members, 40 directly elected in single-member constituencies, four elected by the Assembly itself, all through a simple plurality voting procedure, plus the speaker and the attorney general. It has a life of five years. The president, who must be at least 30 years old, is elected by the Assembly for its duration and is an *ex officio* member of it. From 1999 a president will be restricted to two terms of office. There is also a House of Chiefs of 15, consisting of the chiefs of the country's eight principal tribes, plus four members elected by the chiefs themselves and three elected by the House in general. The president is answerable to the Assembly. He or she may delay a bill for up to six months and then either sign it or dissolve the Assembly, putting both it and him or herself up for election. The House of Chiefs is consulted by the president and the Assembly in matters affecting them and alterations to the constitution. It may also make representations in other matters. The president chooses and appoints a cabinet which is answerable to the Assembly.

Political parties

The main political parties are the Botswana Democratic Party (BDP) and the Botswana National Front (BNF). There are ten other smaller parties or political groupings. The BDP was formed in 1962 and has a moderate center-right orientation. The BNF was formed in 1967 and its support comes mainly from the urban working class. Its stance is moderate left-of-center.

Political leaders since 1970

1966–80 Sir Seretse Khama (BDP), 1980–98 Sir Ketumile Masire (BDP), 1998– Festus Mogae (BDP)

Latest elections

In the October 1994 National Assembly elections the BDP won 27 of the 40 seats with a 53.1% share of the vote, the BNF winning 13 seats with a 37.7% vote.

In March 1998 Masire retired and Festus Mogae was elected by the National Assembly as his successor.

Political history

With South Africa to the south and east, Zimbabwe to the northeast, and Namibia to the west and north, Botswana occupies a delicate position geographically and politically. It was originally Bechuanaland and, at the request of local rulers who feared an invasion by Boer farmers, became a British protectorate in 1885. When the British Parliament passed the Union of South Africa Act in 1910, making South Africa independent, it made provision for the possibility of Bechuanaland eventually becoming part of South Africa, but stipulated that this would not happen without the consent of the local inhabitants. Successive South African governments requested the transfer but the chiefs always resisted it, preferring full independence to a South African takeover.

In 1960 a new constitution was agreed, providing for a Legislative Council but still under the control of a British high commissioner. In 1963 high commission rule was ended and in the Legislative Council elections the newly formed Bechuanaland Democratic Party (BDP) won a majority of seats. Its leader, the Oxford University-educated Seretse Khama (1921–80), had been deposed as chief of the Bangangwato tribe in 1950, following his marriage to an Englishwoman two years before. He was in exile in England and returned to lead his party as president. In 1966 the country, renamed Botswana, became an independent state within the Commonwealth and Sir Seretse Khama, as he had now become, was the new nation's first president.

He continued to be re-elected until his death in 1980, when he was succeeded by the vice president, Dr Quett Masire (b. 1925). Dr Masire was re-elected in 1984. Since independence Botswana has earned a reputation for political and economic stability and has successfully followed a path of nonalignment. From time to time it was provoked by South Africa, which accused it of providing bases for the African National Congress (ANC). This was always denied by both Botswana and the ANC itself. South Africa had also persistently pressed Botswana to sign a nonaggression pact, similar to the Nkomati Accord, agreed with Mozambique, but it always refused to do so. In 1985 South African forces raided the capital, Gaborone, allegedly in search of ANC guerrillas, killing 12 people, for which Botswana demanded compensation. The ending of apartheid in South Africa and the establishment of a multi-racial government from 1993 did much to normalize relations between the two countries.

Dr Masire was knighted and adopted the first name of Ketumile, in preference to Quett. In the 1994 elections the BDP retained power with a reduced majority, its share of the national vote falling by 12% compared to 1989, and he was re-elected for the third time. Since independence, the formerly impoverished economy of Botswana has been transformed by diamond mining, which first began in 1967. Annual GDP growth rates have averaged nearly 10% and diamonds currently account for 50% of GDP. However, the unemployment rate is 30% in Gaborone, prompting many to migrate to work in South Africa. In March 1998 Masire retired and was succeeded as president and leader of the BDP by Festus Mogae, who had been vice-president since 1992 and a former governor of the central bank. Lieutenant-General Ian Khama, the son of the country's first president, was appointed minister of presidential affairs and vice president designate.

BURKINA FASO

Republic of Burkina ('Land of Upright Men')
République de Burkina

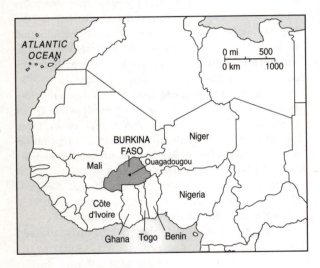

Capital: Ouagadougou

Social and economic data
Area: 274,200 sq km/105,869 sq miles
Population: 9,889,000*
Pop. density per sq km/sq mi: 36/93*
Urban population: 17%**
Literacy rate: 18%**
GDP: $2,420 million*; per-capita GDP: $245*
Government defense spending (% of GDP): 2.4%*
Currency: franc CFA
Economy type: low income
Labor force in agriculture: 84%**
* 1995.
** 1992.

Head of state (executive)
President Blaise Compaoré, since 1987

Head of government
Prime Minister Kadré Desiré Ouedraogo, since 1996

Ethnic composition
There are over 50 tribes in the country. They include the nomadic Mossi, 48% of the population, the Fulani, 10%, and the Gourma, 5%. The settled tribes include: in the north, the Lobi-Dagari, 7%, and the Mande, 7%; in the southeast, the Bobo, 7%; and in the southwest the Senoufo, 6%, and the Gourounsi, 5%. The official language is French.

Religions
Fifty-seven per cent of the population follows traditional, animist religions, about 40% is Sunni Muslim, and there are about 1 million Christians, the vast majority being Roman Catholics.

Political features
State type: emergent democratic
Date of state formation: 1960
Political structure: unitary
Executive: limited presidential
Assembly: two-chamber
Party structure: multiparty*
Human rights rating: N/A
International affiliations: ACP, BOAD, CEAO, CILISS, ECOWAS, Francophone, FZ, IBRD, IMF, NAM, OAU, OIC, UEMOA, UN, WTO

* But dominated by one party.

Local and regional government
For administrative purposes, the country is divided into 30 provinces, administered by governors, and subdivided into 300 departments.

Political system
The June 1991 constitution provides for an executive president, directly elected by universal adult suffrage for a seven-year term, renewable once only. There is a single-chamber, 111-member assembly, the Assembly of People's Deputies (ADP), which is elected by proportional representation for a five-year term. The president appoints a prime minister, subject to the ADP's veto, and a Council of Ministers (cabinet). Since December 1995, there has been a second, consultative chamber: the Chamber of Representatives, comprising 178 nominated members serving three-year terms. In June 1999 a 16-member College of Elders, which comprised those former heads of state, was formed by President Comporland and given the task of promoting national reconciliation and social peace.

Political parties

Of the more than 40 registered political parties the most significant is the Congress for Democracy and Progress (CDP), a left wing party which supports President Compaoré. It was formed in 1996 to succeed the Organization for Popular Democracy (ODP-MT). Other political parties include the centrist opposition Alliance for Democracy and Federation (ADF) and the center-left Party for Democracy and Progress (PDP).

Political leaders since 1970

1966–80 Colonel Sangoulé Lamizana (military), 1980–82 Colonel Zerbo (military), 1982–83 Major Jean-Baptiste Ouédraogo (military), 1983–87 Captain Thomas Sankara (military), 1987–92 Captain Blaise Compaoré (military), 1992– Captain Blaise Compaoré (ODP-MT/CDP-led coalition)

Latest elections

In the May 1997 assembly elections the CDP won 101 of the 111 seats and 69% of the vote, amid claims of fraud by its opponents. The PDP won 10% support and six seats and the ADF two seats. Turnout was 45%. In November 1998 President Compaoré was re-elected with a massive 87.5% of the vote, defeating candidates of the Green Party and the African Democratic Rally (ROA). Turnout was 56%. However, the main opposition parties boycotted the poll, claiming it was rigged.

Political history

Formerly known as Upper Volta, Burkina Faso was a province of French West Africa. In 1958 it became a self-governing republic and two years later achieved full independence, with Maurice Yaméogo as its first president. A military coup in 1966 removed Yaméogo and installed Colonel Sangoulé Lamizana as president and prime minister. He suspended the constitution, dissolved the National Assembly, put a ban on political activities, and set up a Supreme Council of the Armed Forces as the instrument of government. In 1969 the ban on political activities was lifted and in the following year a referendum approved a new constitution, based on civilian rule, which was to come into effect after a four-year transitional period.

However, General Lamizana announced, in 1974, a return to rule by the army and the dissolution of the National Assembly. Three years later political activities were again permitted and in the 1978 elections the Volta Democratic Union (UDV) won a majority in the National Assembly and Lamizana was elected president, but a deteriorating economy led to a wave of strikes and he was overthrown in a bloodless coup in 1980.

Colonel Zerbo, who had led the coup, formed a Government of National Recovery, suspended the constitution again and dissolved the National Assembly. In 1982 Zerbo was, in turn, ousted by junior officers and Major Jean-Baptiste Ouédraogo emerged as leader of a new military regime, with Captain Thomas Sankara as prime minister. In 1983 Sankara led another coup and seized supreme power, and a National Revolutionary Council (CNR) was set up.

In 1984 Sankara announced that the country would be known as Burkina Faso ('Land of Upright Men'), symbolizing a break with its colonial past, and launched literacy and afforestation programs in what was an immensely poor country. The government strengthened ties with neighboring Ghana and established links with Benin and Libya. In October 1987 President Sankara was killed, allegedly accidentally, in a coup led by a close colleague, Captain Blaise Compaoré, who then succeeded him.

An attempt to overthrow him in 1989 was foiled but public pressure grew for a more democratic form of government. Eventually a new multiparty constitution was approved, in a June 1991 national referendum, and provision was made for free elections. Compaoré was elected president in December 1991 and his ruling party group won the Assembly elections in May 1992, and increased its majority in May 1997, amid claims of widespread fraud and an opposition boycott.

Compaoré was re-elected president by a landslide margin in November 1998. Although, once again, candidates from the main opposition parties boycotted this poll, on the grounds that voter registration had been rigged, turnout, at 56%, remained relatively high and impartial outside observers from the EU and OAU declared that voting had been largely free and fair. However, political unrest flared up in May 1999, with four days of student rioting in the capital, Ougadougou, which was sparked by the report of an independent inquiry investigating the December 1998 assassination of the journalist Norbert Zongo which implicated presidential guards. Herbert Yaméogo, leader of the opposition Alliance for Democracy and Federation (ADF), was arrested and detained for several days.

BURUNDI

The Republic of Burundi
La République du Burundi

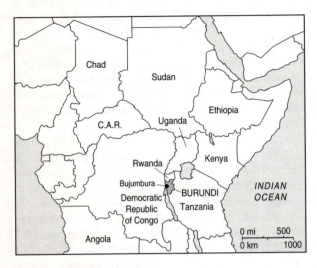

Capital: Bujumbura

Social and economic data

Area: 27,830 sq km/10,745 sq miles
Population: 6,134,000[*]
Pop. density per sq km/sq mi: 220/571[*]
Urban population: 6%[**]
Literacy rate: 34%[**]
GDP: $985million[*]; per-capita GDP: $160[*]
Government defense spending (% of GDP): 5.3%[*]
Currency: Burundi franc
Economy type: low income
Labor force in agriculture: 91%[**]
[*] 1995.
[**] 1992.

Head of state and government

President Pierre Buyoya, since 1996

Ethnic composition

There are two main tribes in the country: the agriculturalist Hutu, comprising about 85% of the population, and the predominantly pastoralist Tutsi, about 14%. A virtual tribal apartheid has been operated for many years by the traditionally Tutsi-controlled government and massive killings of Hutus were reported in 1988. Violence on an even greater scale occurred in 1993 and again in 1995. There is a small Pygmy minority, comprising about 1% of the population, and a few Europeans and Asians. The official languages are Kirundi and French.

Religions

About 60% of the population, mostly Hutus, are Roman Catholic, most of the other inhabitants following traditional beliefs, mainly in a God 'Imana'. There are also about 160,000 Pentecostalists and 60,000 Anglicans.

Political features

State type: military authoritarian[*]
Date of state formation: 1962
Political structure: unitary
Executive: military
Assembly: one-chamber
Party structure: two-party
Human rights rating: N/A
International affiliations: ACB, CEEAC, CEPGL, Francophone, IBRD, IMF, KBO, NAM, OAU, UN, WTO

[*] Transitional.

Local and regional government

For administrative purposes, the country is divided into 15 provinces, administered by governors. The provinces are further subdivided into districts and communes.

Political system

The March 1992 constitution provides for an executive president, directly elected for a five-year term, renewable once only, and a single-chamber 81-member National Assembly, elected by proportional representation, with a 5% barrier for representation, and serving a similar term. The National Assembly chooses a prime minister who, in turn, appoints a Council of Ministers, which he or she heads. The constitution specifically bans ethnically and regionally based parties, and requires party leaderships to be equally representative of the Hutu and Tutsi communities. The constitution was suspended, in mid-1996, as civil war broke out, but it was partially restored in June 1998.

Political parties

In 1997 the military government recognized 14 political parties. The two most significant are the Front for Burundian Democracy (Frodebu) and the Union for National Progress (UPRONA).

Frodebu was founded in 1992 and has a left-of-center orientation and receives strong Hutu support.

UPRONA was the only legally permitted party until 1992. It was founded in 1958, while the country was a monarchy, and given its monopoly position by royal decree in 1966. It is a socialist party with a strong authoritarian-nationalist orientation, and receives significant Tutsi support.

Political leaders since 1970

1966–76 Captain Michel Micombero (UPRONA), 1976–87 Colonel Jean-Baptiste Bagaza (military), 1987–93 Major Pierre Buyoya (military), 1993 Melchior Ndadye (Frodebu), 1993–94 Cyprien Ntaryamira (Frodebu), 1994–96 Sylvestre Ntibantunganya (Frodebu), 1996– Pierre Buyoya (military)

Latest elections

The June 1993 presidential election was won by Melchior Ndadye (Frodebu), a Hutu, defeating the incumbent president, Buyoya (UPRONA).

In the June 1993 National Assembly elections Frodebu won 65 seats, with a 71% vote share, and UPRONA the other 16 seats, with a 21% vote share.

Political history

The country now called Burundi was a semifeudal Tutsi kingdom known as Urundi which became part of the empire of German East Africa in 1899. During World War I it was occupied by Belgian forces and later, as part of Ruanda-Urundi, was administered by Belgium as a League of Nations, and later United Nations, trust territory.

As a prelude to full independence, elections in 1961 were supervised by the United Nations (UN), and won by the Union for National Progress (UPRONA), which had been formed by Louis, one of the sons of the reigning king, Mwambutsa IV. Louis became prime minister but was assassinated after only two weeks in office and succeeded by his brother-in-law, André Muhirwa.

In 1962 Urundi separated from Ruanda, and, as Burundi, was given internal self-government and then full independence. The minority Tutsi community were to dominate the government during the next 30 years. In 1966 King Mwambutsa IV, after a 50-year reign, was deposed by another son, Charles, with the assistance of the army, and the constitution was suspended. Later in the year Charles, now Ntare V, was himself deposed by his prime minister, Captain Michel Micombero, who declared Burundi a republic. Micombero was a member of the Tutsi tribe whose main rivals were the numerically superior Hutus. In 1972 the deposed Ntare V was killed, allegedly by Hutus, and this provided an excuse for the Tutsis to carry out a series of large-scale massacres of Hutus. An estimated 100,000 were killed and many also fled the country. In 1973 amendments to the constitution made Micombero president and prime minister and in the following year UPRONA was declared the only legal political party, with the president as its secretary general.

In 1976 Micombero was himself deposed in an army coup led by Colonel Jean-Baptiste Bagaza (b. 1946), who was appointed president by a Supreme Revolutionary Council. He was assisted by a prime minister. The following year the prime minister announced a return to civilian rule and a five-year plan to eliminate corruption and secure social justice. In 1978 the post of prime minister was abolished and in 1981 a new constitution, providing for a National Assembly, was adopted after a referendum. In the 1984 election Bagaza, as the only presidential candidate, secured over 99% of the votes cast.

In September 1987 another coup, led by Major Pierre Buyoya, ousted Bagaza and a Military Council for National Redemption was established. Despite Buyoya's promises to improve the human rights situation in Burundi, discrimination against the Hutus continued to be practised by the Tutsi minority and widespread killings were reported in 1988, many of them allegedly by Tutsi soldiers, and there was a large exodus of Hutu refugees to Rwanda. In October 1988 the appointment of the first Hutu prime minister provided a hint of rapprochement between the two tribes.

In March 1992 a new constitution was adopted and in the first ever multiparty presidential elections in June 1993 Buyoya, a Tutsi, was defeated by the Frodebu candidate, Melchior Ndadye, a Hutu. In the same month Frodebu won a majority in the National Assembly. Ndadye's new government included a mixture of Hutus and Tutsis.

In October 1993 President Ndadye was killed in a coup by the Tutsi-controlled army and was succeeded in January 1994 by a fellow Hutu, Cyprien Ntaryamira who was elected president by the National Assembly. Three months later, in April 1994, Ntaryamira was killed when an aircraft in which he was returning with the president of neighboring Rwanda was shot down, allegedly by dissident Tutsis. Their deaths unleashed ethnic killings on a scale never before experienced, with 500,000 (chiefly Hutus) fleeing to Rwanda, Tanzania, and the Democratic Republic of Congo, leading to a refugee crisis and 200,000 were also killed during 1993–95. The carnage escalated in Rwanda.

The speaker of the National Assembly, Sylvestre Ntibantunganya, another Hutu, became acting president and was confirmed in that post in September 1994. Meanwhile, in an effort to avoid the tribal violence in Rwanda, the leaders of all the main political parties signed a four-year power-sharing agreement and in February 1994 Anatole Kanyenkiko, a Tutsi with a Hutu mother and Hutu wife, was appointed prime minister. Twelve months later he was replaced by Antoine Nduwayo, another Tutsi.

In March 1995 there was another major outbreak of ethnic violence in the region, apparently initiated by dissident Tutsis. This time it was Burundi, and particularly the capital, Bujumbura, and not Rwanda, where most of the killings occurred. It was evident that, despite genuine attempts at democratic government and efforts to avoid ethnic clashes, the underlying tribal antipathies remained. In July 1996, as ethnic violence increased, the Tutsi-dominated army seized power and appointed Pierre Buyoya as president. Other African leaders criticized the coup and agreed to impose economic sanctions on Burundi. President Buyoya appointed a government of `national unity'. In June 1998 the warring factions agreed to a ceasefire. Buyoya was formally sworn in as president and a 22-member transitional government was formed, comprising 14 Hutus and eight Tutsis.

The economic sanctions imposed by seven central and east African states after the 1996 coup were suspended in February 1999, following signs of progress in peace talks, held in Tanzania, between the Burundi government and Hutu rebels. The government announced plans to apply for membership of the East African Co-operation (an economic association involving Kenya, Tanzania and Uganda) to underpin the peace process. Nevertheless, clashes continued between the Tutsi-dominanted government army and the National Liberation Forces (FNL), the armed wing of the Hutu-based Palipehutu movement, with innocent civilians massacred in inter-ethnic reprisals.

CAMEROON

The United Republic of Cameroon
La République unie du Cameroun

Capital: Yaoundé

Social and economic data
Area: 475,442 sq km/183,569 sq miles
Population: 12,871,000[*]
Pop. density per sq km/sq mi: 27/70[*]
Urban population: 42%[**]
Literacy rate: 54%[**]
GDP: $8,615 million[*]; per-capita GDP: $670[*]

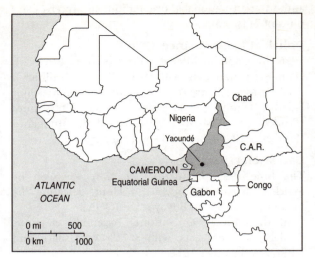

Government defense spending (% of GDP): 1.8%[**]
Currency: franc CFA
Economy type: low income
Labor force in agriculture: 60%[**]
[*] 1995.
[**] 1992.

Head of state (executive)
President Paul Biya, from 1982

Head of government
Prime Minister Peter Mafany Musonge, since 1996

Ethnic composition
The main ethnic groups include the Cameroon Highlanders, 31%, the Equatorial Bantu, 19%, the Kirdi, 11%, the Fulani, 10%, the Northwestern Bantu, 8%, and the Eastern Nigritic, 7%. A majority of the population are French speakers, but a fifth are English speakers who, claiming that they are discriminated against in public employment, seek autonomy. Both French and English have been designated as official languages.

Religions
About 40% of the population is Christian, mostly Roman Catholic, about 39% has traditional, animist beliefs, and about 21% is Muslim.

Political features
State type: emergent democratic
Date of state formation: 1960
Political structure: unitary
Executive: limited presidential
Assembly: one-chamber
Party structure: multiparty[*]

Human rights rating: 56%

International affiliations: ACP, BDEAC, CEEAC, CEMAC, CW, Francophone, FZ, IAEA, IBRD, IMF, LCBC, NAM, OAU, OIC, UN, WTO

* Though dominated by one party.

Local and regional government

The country is divided into ten provinces, ranging in popu-lation from under 400,000 to over 1.5 million. These are further subdivided into departments. A hierarchy of officials, responsible for regional and local administration, report to the president's representatives. Municipal elections took place in 1995.

Political system

Cameroon was a federal state until 1972 when a new constitution, revised in 1975, made it unitary. The constitution was further revised in 1991 and now provides for a president, who is head of state (and appoints a prime minister as head of government), directly elected by simple plurality for a five-year term, and a single-chamber 180-member National Assembly elected by proportional representation for the same term. Candidates for the presidency must be at least 35 years old. In 1995 a further amendment to the constitution extended the president's term of office to seven years and authorized a maximum of two terms. Provision was also made for a senate, but none was elected. However, there is an advisory Economic and Social Council.

Political parties

More than 40 parties officially registered in preparation for the first multiparty elections in 1992. Since then there has been considerable fluidity in party compositions and several have been constituted into allied groups or changed their names. The most significant of around 130 groups are the Cameroon People's Democratic Movement (RDPC), the center-left Social Democratic Front (SDF), the moderate Islamist National Union for Democracy and Progress (UNDP), and the Democratic Union of Cameroon (UDC).

The RDPC was formed in 1966, under the name of the Cameroon National Union (UNC), by a merger of the governing party of each state of the original federation and the four opposition parties. The name was changed to RDPC in 1985. Its orientation is nationalist left-of-center.

The SDF was formed in 1990, the UNDP in 1991, and the UDC in the same year. In February 1998 the SDF and UDF announced the formation of a united opposition front to the RDPC and its UNDP ally.

Political leaders since 1970

1960–82 Ahmadou Ahidjo (UNC), 1982–96 Paul Biya (RDPC), 1996– Peter Mafany Musonge

Latest elections

In the October 1997 presidential elections Paul Biya (RDPC) was re-elected by a massive majority. He secured 92.6% of the vote, defeating six challengers. However, the main opposition parties boycotted the poll after the government refused to establish an independent electoral commission. Turnout was around 80%, according to official sources.

The results of the May 1997 National Assembly elections are set out below. Seven parties secured representation, but the SDF, UNDP, and UDC opposition parties, which attracted half the vote, voiced claims of ballot-rigging in the RDPC's favor. Assembly elections are for 49 single-and multi-seat constituencies.

Cameroon latest election results

Party	Seats
RDPC	109
SDF	43
UNDP	13
UDC	5
Others	10

Political history

Although subject to slave trading by the Belgians, Cameroon avoided colonial rule until 1884 when it became the German protectorate of Kamerun. After World War I, the League of Nations gave France a mandate to govern about 80% of the area, mainly in the east and south, with Britain administering the remaining 20%. In 1946 both became United Nations trust territories.

In 1957 French Cameroon became a state within the French Community and three years later fully independent as the Republic of Cameroon. A 1961 plebiscite resulted in the northern part of British Cameroon deciding to merge with neighboring Nigeria, which had recently obtained its independence, and the southern part joining the Republic of Cameroon. Together they became the Federal Republic of Cameroon, with French and English as the official languages. The former French zone was called East Cameroon and the former British part West Cameroon.

Ahmadou Ahidjo (1924–89), who had been elected the first president of the original republic in 1960, became president of the new federal republic and was re-elected in 1965. In 1966 it became a one-party state, when the two government parties and most of the opposition parties merged into the Cameroon National Union (UNC). Extreme leftwing opposition to the single party was finally crushed in 1971. In 1972 a new constitution abolished the federal system and in 1973 a new National Assembly was elected. In 1982 Ahidjo resigned, nominating Paul Biya (b. 1933), the prime minister since 1975, as his successor. Soon after taking office in 1983 Biya began to remove supporters of his predecessor and Ahidjo accused him of trying to create a police state, resigning from the presidency of the UNC. Biya was, nevertheless, re-elected in 1984 while Ahidjo went into exile in France. Biya strengthened his personal control by abolishing the post of prime minister and reshuffling his cabinet. He also announced that the nation's name would be changed from the United Republic of Cameroon to the Republic of Cameroon. In 1985 the UNC changed its name to RDPC and Biya tightened his control still further by more cabinet changes. In 1988 he was re-elected for the second time.

Opposition to his autocratic regime grew, fuelled by a sharp decline in living standards, and at the end of 1991 he was forced to concede constitutional changes which would allow multiparty politics to operate.

He and a new National Assembly were elected under the revised constitution in 1992. However, the opposition claimed that there had been ballot-rigging. Pressure mounted during 1993 for further amendments to the constitution, including calls, from the English-speaking minority, for a return to the federal system. In November 1995 Cameroon was admitted to the Commonwealth.

Further amendments to the constitution in 1995 extended the president's term and provided for a second chamber (the latter proposal was not followed up). President Biya was re-elected in October 1997, after disputed Assembly elections in May 1997. The new government, formed in December 1997, was dominated by Biya's RDPC, but also included, as trade and industry minister, Maigari Bello Boubo, leader of the National Union for Democracy and Progress (UNDP), one of the leading opposition parties.

CAPE VERDE

The Republic of Cape Verde
A República de Cabo Verde

Capital: Praia

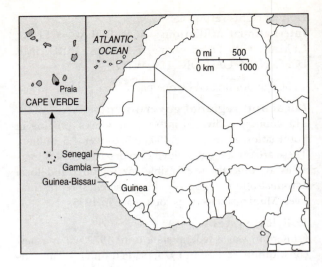

Social and economic data
Area: 4,033 sq km/1,557 sq miles
Population: 417,000[*]
Pop. density per sq km/sq mi: 105/268[*]
Urban population: 30%[**]
Literacy rate: 37%[**]
GDP: $365 million[*]; per-capita GDP: $875[*]
Government defense spending (% of GDP): 1.8%[**]
Currency: escudo
Economy type: low income
Labor force in agriculture: 54%[**]
[*] 1995.
[**] 1992.

Head of state (executive)
President Antonio Mascarenhas Monteiro, since 1991

Head of government
Prime Minister Carlos Alberto Wahnon de Carvalho Veiga, since 1991

Ethnic composition
About 60% of the population are mixed descendants of Portuguese settlers and African slaves and are called *mestiços* or creoles. The rest are mainly African. The European population is very small. The official language is Portuguese.

Religions
About 98% of the total population is Roman Catholic.

Political features
State type: emergent democratic
Date of state formation: 1975
Political structure: unitary
Executive: limited presidential

Assembly: one-chamber
Party structure: two-party
Human rights rating: N/A
International affiliations: ACP, CILSS, ECOWAS, IBRD, IMF, Lusophone, NAM, OAU, UN

Local and regional government

Cape Verde is divided into two districts (*distritos*), each of which is subdivided into seven councils (*concelhos*). The island of Santo Antão comprises three councils and the island of São Tiago four councils.

Political system

The 1990 multiparty constitution provides for an executive president, elected by universal adult suffrage, through an absolute majority system of voting, and a 72-member National Assembly (AN), elected by universal suffrage by simple plurality voting. Both serve five-year terms. The prime minister is nominated by the AN and appointed by the president. The formation of parties on a religious or geographical basis is prohibited.

Political parties

The two most significant parties are the Movement for Democracy (MPD) and the African Party for the Independence of Cape Verde (PAICV).

The MPD, which was formed in 1990, has a moderate centrist orientation and advocates administrative decentralization.

The PAICV was, until 1990, the only legal party and was originally formed in 1956, before independence from Portugal in 1975, as the African Party for the Independence of Portuguese Guinea and Cape Verde (PAIGC), in anticipation of the eventual union of the two countries, but when this was abandoned it adopted its present name. Its orientation is left-of-center African-Nationalist.

Political leaders since 1970

1975–91 Aristedes Pereira (PAICV), 1991–Antonio Mascarenhas Monteiro (MPD)

Latest elections

In the Decmeber 1995 assembly elections the MPD won an absolute majority, securing 50 of the 72 seats, with 61% of the vote. The PAICV, with 30% of the vote, won 21 seats. Turnout was 77%.

In the February 1991 presidential elections President Pereira (PAICV) was defeated by a former Supreme Court judge, Antonio Mascarenhas Monteiro (MPD), who was re-elected unopposed in February 1996.

Political history

The Cape Verde islands were colonized by the Portuguese in the 15th century and from the 1950s onwards a liberation movement developed. The mainland territory to which the Cape Verde archipelago is linked, Guinea, now Guinea-Bissau, was granted independence in 1974, and a process began for the eventual union of Cape Verde and Guinea-Bissau.

In 1975 Cape Verde secured its own independence from Portugal and a provisional government was set up, composed of Portuguese settlers and locally-born members of the PAIGC. In the same year the first National People's Assembly was elected and Aristides Pereira (b. 1923), the founder and secretary general of the PAIGC, became president of the new state.

A constitution was adopted in 1980 making provision for the coming together of Cape Verde and Guinea-Bissau, but by 1981 it had become clear that there was not enough support for the union so the idea was dropped and the PAIGC became the PAICV. Relations with Guinea-Bissau, which had cooled, gradually improved and under the guidance of Pereira, who was re-elected in 1981 and 1986, Cape Verde followed a careful policy of nonalignment and achieved considerable respect within the region. However, the decision in 1987 to decriminalize abortion offended many Catholics and unrest, from 1988, forced pluralist political reforms in 1990.

In the multiparty elections of 1991 the PAICV was heavily defeated by the recently formed Movement for Democracy (MPD) and the MPD's candidate, Antonio Mascarenhas Monteiro, won the presidency, on a low poll. Carlos Veiga was appointed prime minister and free market-orientated economic reforms, including privatization, were introduced.

In the 1995 Assembly elections, the MPD increased its majority and in the following year President Monteiro was re-elected.

CENTRAL AFRICAN REPUBLIC

La République Centrafricaine

Capital: Bangui

Social and economic data
Area: 622,984 sq km/240,535 sq miles
Population: 3,235,000[*]

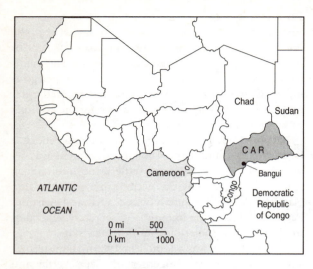

Pop. density per sq km/sq mi: 5/13[*]
Urban population: 48%[**]
Literacy rate: 27%[**]
GDP: $1,125 million[*]; per-capita GDP: $350[*]
Government defense spending (% of GDP): 1.8%[**]
Currency: franc CFA
Economy type: low income
Labor force in agriculture: 84%[**]
[*] 1995.
[**] 1992.

Head of state (executive)
President Ange-Félix Patassé, since 1993

Head of government
Prime Minister Anicet Georges Dologuele, since 1999

Ethnic composition
There are over 80 ethnic groups, but 66% of the population falls into one of three: the Banda, 30%, the Baya-Mandjia, 29%, and the Mbaka, 7%. There are clearly defined ethnic zones: the forest region, inhabited by Bantu groups, the Mbaka, Lissongo, Mbimu, and Babinga; the river banks, populated by the Sango, Yakoma, Baniri, and Buraka; and the savannah region, where the Banda, Zande, Sara, Ndle, and Bizao live. Europeans number less than 7,000, the majority being French. The official language is French and Sangho is the national language.

Religions
Figures for adherents to particular religions are not very reliable but it is estimated that a quarter of the population holds traditional, animist beliefs, about a third is Roman Catholic and another third Protestant, and about 5% is Muslim.

Political features
State type: emergent democratic
Date of state formation: 1960
Political structure: unitary
Executive: limited presidential
Assembly: two-chamber
Party structure: multiparty
Human rights rating: N/A
International affiliations: ACP, BDEAC, CEEAC, CEMAC, Francophone, FZ, G-77, IBRD, IMF, NAM, OAU, UN, WTO

Local and regional government
On the basis of French experience, the country is divided into 16 prefectures, further subdivided into 52 subprefectures, below which there are communes. Elected regional assemblies have existed since 1995.

Political system
The original constitution, adopted following independence in 1960, was annulled in 1972 and then a new version, which came into force in 1981, was suspended in a military coup within months of its adoption and legislative powers, which were to be held by an elected National Assembly, were placed in the hands of a Military Committee for National Recovery (CMRN). Four years later the CMRN was dissolved and a new 22-member Council of Ministers, containing both military and civilian members, was established. A new constitution was approved by referendum in 1986. In August 1992 a 'Grand National Debate' was held to discuss the country's political future and agreement was reached to hold future multiparty elections.

The new constitution, adopted in January 1995, provides for an executive president, who is head of state, directly elected for a six-year term, renewable once only. There is an 109-member National Assembly similarly elected for a five-year term, in three- and four-seat constituencies, and an advisory Economic and Regional Council, half elected by the Assembly and half appointed by the president, who also appoints a prime minister to lead a Council of Ministers. All elections are by the two-ballot majoritarian system. There is an appointed Constitutional Court.

Political parties
Of more than 20 active parties, the two most significant are the Central African People's Labor Party (MLPC) and the Central African Democratic Rally (RDC).

The MLPC was founded in 1979. It has a left-of-center authoritarian orientation. It is strongest in the north.

The RDC was founded in 1987 and until 1993 was

the only legal party. It was the organ of the former militarily controlled governing regime and has a right-of-center orientation. Much of its support comes from the south.

Political leaders since 1970

1965–79 Colonel Jean-Bédel Bokassa (military), 1979–81 David Dacko (MESAN), 1981–93 General André Kolingba (military), 1993–Ange-Félix Patassé (MLPC)

Latest elections

In the August–September 1993 presidential elections, the president of the MLPC, Ange-Felix Patasse, with 52.5% of the vote, defeated Abel Goumba, the candidate of the Group of Democratic Forces (CFD), representing 14 opposition groups, in the second ballot. The incumbent president, Kolingba, finished in fourth place in the first ballot.

In the Novmber-December 1998 Assembly elections, the MLPC won 47 of the 109 seats, the RDC, 20, and nine smaller parties and independents, 42. Turnout was 60% in the first round, when 46 deputies secured election, but was much lower in the second round.

Political history

The territory of Oubangi-Chari came under French influence in 1889 and was given self-government within what was then French Equatorial Africa in 1958. Two years later it achieved full independence. The leading political figure was Barthélémy Boganda who had founded the Movement for the Social Evolution of Black Africa (MESAN) and had been a leading figure in the campaign for independence. He became the country's first prime minister. A year before full independence he was killed in an air crash and succeeded by his nephew, David Dacko (b. 1930), who became president in the independent nation in 1960. In 1962 he established a one-party state, with MESAN as the only legal political organization. Dacko was overthrown in a military coup in December 1965 and the commander in chief of the army, Colonel Jean-Bédel Bokassa (b. 1921), assumed power.

Bokassa progressively increased his personal control of the political system and, in 1972, annulled the constitution and made himself life president. Two years later he awarded himself the title of Marshal of the Republic. In 1976 ex-president Dacko was persuaded to return as Bokassa's personal adviser and later that year the republic was restyled the Central African Empire (CAE). In 1977 Bokassa was crowned emperor at a lavish ceremony his country could ill afford. His rule became increasingly dictatorial and idiosyncratic, leading to revolts by students and, in April 1979, by school children, who objected to the compulsory wearing of school uniforms, manufactured by a company owned by the Bokassa family. Many of the children were imprisoned and it is estimated that at least 100 were killed, with the emperor, allegedly, being personally involved.

In September 1979, while Bokassa was in Libya, Dacko ousted him in a bloodless coup, backed by France. The country became a republic again, with Dacko as president. He initially retained a number of Bokassa's former ministers but, following student unrest, they were dropped and in February 1981 a new constitution was adopted, with an elected National Assembly. Dacko was elected president for a six-year term in March but opposition to him grew and in September 1981 he was deposed in another bloodless coup, led by the armed forces chief of staff, General André Kolingba. The constitution was suspended, as well as all political activity, and a military government installed. Undercover opposition to the Kolingba regime continued, with some French support, but relations with France improved following an unofficial visit by President François Mitterrand in October 1982.

By 1984 there was some evidence of an eventual return to constitutional government. The leaders of the banned political parties were granted an amnesty and at the end of the year the French president paid a state visit. In January 1985 proposals for a new constitution were announced and in September civilians were introduced for the first time into Kolingba's administration.

In 1986 former president and emperor, Bokassa, returned from exile and was tried for murder, illegal detentions, and embezzlement of state funds. Although he was found guilty and sentenced to death, President Kolingba announced in March 1988 that, on the recommendation of the country's senior judges, he had decided to commute the death sentence.

Demands for a more democratic political system grew, with pressure also being applied by France, an important donor of economic aid. In August 1992 there was a 'Grand National Debate' where it was agreed that a new multiparty constitution should be introduced. In its final form, it was adopted in January 1995.

Multiparty presidential elections, originally scheduled for 1992, were cancelled with Kolingba in last place. They were eventually held in August–September

1993 and resulted in Kolingba's defeat by Ange-Felix Patassé, leader of the Central African People's Labor Party (MLPC), who was a former prime minister. In the following month the MLPC secured the largest seat holding in the National Assembly and Patassé appointed Jean-Luc Mandaba, the MLPC vice president, as prime minister, heading a coalition government. In April 1995, anticipating a defeat in the National Assembly on a confidence motion, Mandaba resigned and was succeeded by Gabriel Koyambounou. Then, in February 1997, another 'government of national unity' was formed, headed by Michel Gbezera-Bria, the former foreign minister, who was an independent. The government included members of ten parties, but was dominated by the MLPC. Its formation followed several months of instability, in the wake of an army mutiny in November 1996. Meanwhile, a UN peacekeeping force was stationed to keep order and the country received IMF financial assistance to support its economic reforms.

In the Assembly elections, held in November and December 1998, the ruling MLPC remained the largest single party, but lacked an Assembly majority on its own. A coalition of opposition held, initially, 55 seats in the 109-member National Assembly, but lost its majority when, in January 1999, one coalition deputy defected to the ruling party's side. The opposition alleged that this deputy had been bribed by the MLPC and anti-government popular protests resulted. In January 1999 the independent Gbezera Bria was replaced as prime minister by Anicet Dologuele, of the MLPC, who also remained as finance minister. He formed a 25-member cabinet, which included four ministers from the opposition Movement for Democracy and Development (MDD), which had won eight seats in the election. However, three of the MDD ministers resigned after several days, as a result of pressure from party colleagues, who took part in an opposition boycott of parliament, which lasted until March 1999.

CHAD

The Republic of Chad
La République du Tchad

Capital: N'djamena

Social and economic data
Area: 1,204,000 sq km/495,755 sq miles

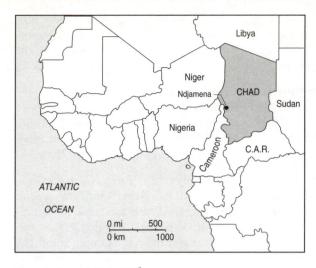

Population: 6,214,000[*]
Pop. density per sq km/sq mi: 5/13[*]
Urban population: 34%[**]
Literacy rate: 30%[**]
GDP: $1,145 million[*]; per-capita GDP: $185[*]
Government defense spending (% of GDP): 2.6 %[*]
Currency: franc CFA
Economy type: low income
Labor force in agriculture: 83%[**]
[*] 1995.
[**] 1992.

Head of state
President Idriss Déby, since 1990

Head of government
Prime Minister Nassour Ouaidou Guelendouksia, since 1997

Ethnic composition
Northern Chad is populated mainly by Arabs and the south by Pagan, or Kirdi, groups. There is no single dominant group in any region, the largest being the Sara, who comprise about a quarter of the total population. Europeans, mainly French, constitute a very small minority. The official languages are French and Arabic.

Religions
About 52% of the population is Sunni Muslim, living predominantly in the north, about 35%, predominantly in the south, follows traditional, animist religions, and about 5%, mainly the Sara, is Christian.

Political features
State type: emergent democratic
Date of state formation: 1960

Political structure: unitary
Executive: dual
Assembly: one-chamber
Party structure: multi-party
Human rights rating: N/A
International affiliations: ACP, BDEAC, CEEAC, CEMAC, CILSS, Francophone, FZ, IBRD, IMF, LCBC, NAM, OAU, OIC, UN, WTO

Local and regional government

Following French experience, the country is divided into 14 prefectures within which are 54 subprefectures, 27 administrative posts, and nine municipalities.

Political system

The 1996 constitution, which replaced an earlier 1992 version, provides for a shared executive, on the French model. It comprises a president who is directly elected for five years, with a restriction of two terms, who appoints a prime minister able to command a majority in the 125-member National Assembly. Assembly deputies are elected in 25 single-member and 34 multi-member constituencies and serve four-year terms. Elections are by the second-ballot majoritarian system. There is a Constitutional Court and plans to establish a second-chamber Senate, with members elected for six-year terms, with one-third being renewed each two years.

Political parties

Since 1991 some 60 parties have been authorized, the three most significant being the Patriotic Salvation Movement (MPS), the Union for Democratic Renewal (URD), and the National Union for Development and Renewal (UNDR). The MPS is a coalition of a number of groups which were instrumental in overthrowing Hissène Habré in 1990.

Political leaders since 1970

1960–75 François Tombalbaye (PPT), 1975–79 General Félix Malloum (military), 1979–82 General Goukouni Oueddi (military), 1982–90 Hissène Habré (UNIR), 1990– Idriss Déby (MPS)

Latest elections

Idriss Déby won the first multiparty presidential election in July 1996 and the MPS was successful in the January–February 1997 assembly elections. Déby won 69% of the second-round vote, defeating the URD leader, General Wadal Abdelkader Kamougue. In the Assembly elections, the MPS won 65 seats, the URD 29, and the UNDR 15. Other parties won 16 seats.

Political history

Chad, then called Kanem, was settled by Arabs from the 7th century onwards. From 1913 it was a province of French Equatorial Africa and then became an autonomous state within the French Community, in 1958, with François Tombalbaye as its prime minister. Full independence was achieved in 1960 and Tombalbaye was elected president. His party, the Sara-dominated Chadian Progressive Party (PPT), held 57 of the 85 National Assembly seats. He was soon faced with unrest, mainly because of disagreements between the nomadic Arabs of the north, who saw Libya as a natural ally, and the Sara Christians of the south, who felt more in sympathy with neighboring Nigeria.

A conflict began less on the basis of party divisions and more on the basis of loosely organized private armies, each loyal to a particular leader. By 1975 at least three groups claimed to be the true revolutionaries. In the north the Chadian National Liberation Front (Frolinat) led a revolt, the two leading figures in it being Goukouni Oueddi and the northerner, Hissène Habré.

Meanwhile Tombalbaye's attempts at 'Chadization' aroused opposition and in 1975 he was killed in a coup led by the former army Chief of Staff, Félix Malloum. Malloum made himself president of a Supreme Military Council but despite his appeals for national unity, Frolinat continued to oppose him, with support from Libya.

By 1978 Frolinat, now led by General Goukouni, had expanded its territorial control but was halted with the aid of French troops. Malloum tried to reach a political settlement by making the other former Frolinat leader, Hissène Habré, prime minister but in 1979 fighting broke out again and Malloum was forced to flee the country.

Conferences of rival groups in Nigeria eventually resulted in the formation of a provisional government (GUNT), with Goukouni as president. The Organization for African Unity (OAU) set up a peacekeeping force, composed of Nigerian, Senegalese, and Zairean troops, but this failed to prevent civil war breaking out between the armies of Goukouni and Habré.

By April 1981 Habré's Armed Forces of the North (FAN) were in control of half the country, forcing Goukouni to flee, eventually setting up a 'government in exile'. In 1983 a majority of OAU members agreed to recognize Habré's regime as the legitimate government but Goukouni, with Libyan support, fought on. After bombing raids by Libya, Habré appealed to France for help and 3,000 troops were sent as military instructors. Following a Franco-African summit, in August 1983, a ceasefire was agreed in December, the latitude line 16 degrees north eventually becoming the dividing line between the opposing forces. The Libyan president, Colonel Muammar Kadhafi, proposed a simultaneous withdrawal of French and Libyan troops and this was eventually accepted. Meanwhile Habré had dissolved the military arm of Frolinat and formed a new political party, the National Union for Independence (UNIR) but opposition to his regime grew.

In 1987 the Libyans intensified their military operations in northern Chad, producing an equal response from the Habré government, and renewed, if reluctant, support from France. It was announced in September 1987 that France, Chad, and Libya had agreed to observe a ceasefire proposed by the Organization of African Unity and in the same year Goukouni publicly backed Habré as the legitimate head of state. In May 1988 Colonel Kadhafi made a surprisingly generous offer to meet President Habré and resolve outstanding differences and in October 1988, with the civil war halted, full diplomatic relations between the two countries were restored.

A new constitution was approved in July 1990 but five months later the Patriotic Salvation Movement (MPS) rebel forces based in Sudan, led by Idriss Déby, the former Chadian army chief, and supported by Libya, defeated Habré's army and Deby was installed as president. The United States declined to recognize the new regime, because of its Libyan connections, but France agreed to send financial aid.

Despite attempted coups against it and the continuing activity of rebels, in 1991 and 1992, the Deby government retained control, promising the establishment of a democratic, multiparty political system in the near future. Following a National Conference in 1993, a transitional charter was adopted, prior to elections planned for 1994. The transition period was later extended to 1996.

Anti-government rebel forces remained active throughout 1998 and 1999, particularly the Movement for Democracy and Justice in Chad (MDJT), led by Youssouf Togoimi, a former interior minister. The rebel forces were drawn from the nomadic Toubou people, based in the mountainous northern region of Tibesti. In April 1999 the MDJT merged with two other rebel groups to form a more unified opposition to the government and this was soon reflected in military successes.

COMOROS

The Federal Islamic Republic of Comoros
La République fédérale islamique des Comores

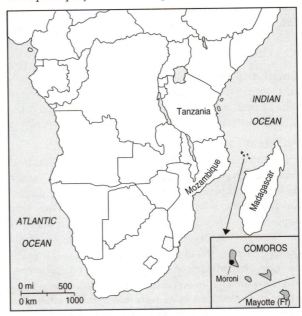

Capital: Moroni (on Njazidja)

Social and economic data
Area: 1,860 sq km/718 sq miles
Population: 630,000[*]
Pop. density per sq km/sq mi: 329/877[*]
Urban population: 29%[**]
Literacy rate: 48%[**]
GDP: $240 million[*]; per-capita GDP: $380[*]
Government defense spending (% of GDP): N/A
Currency: franc CFA
Economy type: low income
Labor force in agriculture: 83%[**]
[*] 1995.
[**] 1992.

Head of state (executive)
President Colonel Azali Assoumani, since 1999

Head of government
Colonel Azali Assoumani, since 1999

Ethnic composition
The population is of mixed origin, Africans, Arabs, and Malaysians predominating. The principal ethnic group is the Antalaotra. The languages are French and Arabic.

Religions

The majority of the population (98%) is Sunni Muslim and Islam is the state religion. There are about 2,000 Roman Catholics.

Political features

State type: military
Date of state formation: 1975
Political structure: federal
Executive: military
Assembly: one-chamber
Party structure: multiparty
Human rights rating: N/A
International affiliations: ACP, AL, Francophone, FZ, IBRD, IMF, IOC, NAM, OAU, OIC, UN

Local and regional government

The Comoros consists of three main islands, Njazidja (Grande Comore), with a population of 280,000, Nzwani (Anjouan), with 210,000, and Mwali (Moheli), with 35,000. Although each of the islands has a certain amount of autonomy, with its own governor and Council, it all constitutes a very limited form of federalism. The president appoints the governors and the federal government has responsibility for the islands' resources.

Political system

The October 1996 constitution provides for an executive president, directly elected for a six-year renewable term and a 43-member Federal Assembly elected for a four-year term. Elections are by the second-ballot majoritarian system. The president appoints a prime minister, as head of government, from the majority party in the Assembly. There is also an advisory Council of the Ulemas, or Muslim religious experts. Candidates for the presidency must be aged between 40 and 75 years.

Political parties

From 1979 Comoros was a one-party state, based on the Comoron Union for Progress (Udzima). Some 20 parties eventually emerged under the 1992 constitution, the two most significant being the National Rally for Development (RND) and the National Front for Justice (FNJ). The conservative RND was formed in 1996 by 24 parties supporting the government. The FNJ has an Islamic Fundamentalist orientation. Under the new 1996 constitution, the RND and FNJ became the only two legal organizations. There was a military coup in April 1999.

Political leaders since 1970

1975 Admed Abdallah Abderemane (Udzima), 1975–78 Ali Soilih (Front National Uni), 1978–90 Ahmed Abdallah Abderemane (Udzima), 1990–96 Said Mohammed Djohar (RDR), 1996–98 Mohammed Taki Abdoul Karim (RND), 1998–99 Majidine Ben Said Massonde (RND), 1999– Colonel Azali Assoumani (military)

Latest elections

The March 1996 presidential elections were won by Mohammed Taki Abdoul Karim (RND), who won 64% of the second-round vote, defeating Abbas Djoussouf of the pro-Western Forum for National Renewal (FRN).

The 1 and 8 December 1996 Federal Assembly elections were won by the RND, which secured 26 of the 43 seats. The FNJ won three seats, but the main opposition parties boycotted the poll and turnout fell to 20%.

Political history

The Comoros islands of Grande Comore, Anjouan, Moheli, and Mayotte became a French colony in 1912 and were attached to Madagascar in 1914. They separated from Madagascar and their status changed to that of a separate French Overseas Territory in 1947. Internal self-government was obtained in 1961 and in 1974 referenda on independence were held on the four islands. The first three islands voted in favor of independence. They ceded unilaterally from France in July 1975, but maintained ties via a defense pact and aid donations. As 'The Comoros', they were admitted into the United Nation in 1975, with Ahmed Abdallah Abderemane as the first president. However, the island of Mayotte, whose citizens had voted against independence, remained as a French dependency (see *Chapter 8*). In August 1975 a coup, led by Ali Soilih, deposed Abdallah and abolished the Assembly, resulting in a deterioration in relations with France. Ali Soilih was elected president and took on increased powers under a new constitution.

In 1978 Soilih was killed by French mercenaries, supposedly working for Abdallah. A federal Islamic republic was proclaimed, a new constitution adopted, establishing a single-party state, and Abdallah was elected president. With these changes, diplomatic relations with France were restored. In 1979 the Comoros became a one-party state and the powers of the federal government were increased. In the same year a plot by British mercenaries to overthrow Abdallah was foiled. In 1984 he was re-elected president and in the following year the constitution was amended, abolishing the post of prime minister and making Abdallah head of government as well as head of state, but in 1989 he was killed by rebel soldiers.

After months of uncertainty, with European mercenaries briefly ruling, in 1990 multiparty democracy was restored and Said Mohammed Djohar, a former president of the Supreme Court, was elected head of state. He sought to create a government of national unity, but was faced during 1991 and 1992 by several coup attempts. His administration was unstable, with the country's third transitional government being appointed in July 1992.

Multiparty assembly elections held in November 1992 resulted in no party winning a working majority, but in December 1993 the Rally for Democracy and Renewal (RDR) won control and its leader, Mohamed Abdou Madi, was appointed prime minister. In October 1994 he was replaced by Halifa Houmadi. Following criticisms of his administration, in April 1995 Houmadi resigned and was succeeded by Caabi El Yachroutu Mohamed. In September 1995 the increasingly unpopular president, Djohar, was briefly overthrown in a coup by mercenaries, led by Colonel Bob Denard, a former French marine. Denard had been behind the coups of 1975 and 1978 and the assassination of President Abdallah in 1989. After six days 80-year-old President Djohar was restored to power by French forces, but on the condition that he did not contest the March 1996 presidential election, which was won by Mohammed Taki Abdoul Karim, supported by the RND. A new government was formed in December 1997, led by Nourdine Bourhane, but this was dismissed in May 1998 following anti-government riots. Meanwhile, in August 1997, secessionist governments were formed on the islands of Anjouan and Moheli which had long sought independence.

Government attempts to retake Anjouan by military force failed. In November 1998 President Taki died of a heart attack, aged 62, and Majidine Ben Said Massonde, head of the constitutional court and a former prime minister, who came from Anjouan, took over as interim president, pending new elections. He appointed as prime minister, Abbass Djoussuf, leader of the Forum Party, the largest opposition party in the Federal Assembly. Djoussuf replaced Nourdine Bourhane, who had been dismissed in May 1998, and set about forming a national unity government, with the RND, and with two cabinet positions reserved for representatives of Anjouan and Moheli. In February 1999 an Organisation of African Unity (OAU) peace mission was sent to Anjouan to facilitate negotiations between rival militia factions who had recently clashed militarily. Two months later, on 25 April 1999, an OAU-brokered peace agreement was signed in Madagascar, resolving the crisis over Anjouan and Moheli. It provided for enhanced autonomy for the islands, the creation of new executive and legislative structures within a year and also a possible change in the federation's official title to the 'Union of Comoran Islands'. However, five days later, on 30 April 1999, there was a bloodless military coup – the country's 18th in 25 years. This followed three days of violent protests in opposition to the 25th May accord. The army's chief-of-staff, Colonel Azali Assoumani seized power, with the motive took of restoring public order, and combined the posts of president, prime minister and defence minister. He promised to honour the 25th April accord and to give up power within a year. His new cabinet included 11 civilian technocrats and a post reserved for a representative of Anjouan island. However, this coup was denounced by the leaders of Anjouan and Moheli and by the OAU. In June 1999 Assoumani was formerly sworn in as president.

CONGO, DEMOCRATIC REPUBLIC OF (FORMERLY ZAIRE)

The Democratic Republic of Congo (formerly Zaire)
(Congo–Kinshasa)
La République démocratique de Congo

Capital: Kinshasa

Social and economic data
Area: 2,345,000 sq km/905,409 sq miles
Population: 42,552,000[*]
Pop. density per sq km/sq mi: 18/47[*]
Urban population: 29%[**]
Literacy rate: 72%[**]
GDP: $5,315 million[*]; per-capita GDP: $125[*]
Government defense spending (% of GDP): 2.0%[**]
Currency: new zaïre
Economy type: low income
Labor force in agriculture: 72%[**]
[*] 1995.
[**] 1992.

Head of state and government
President Laurent-Désiré Kabila, since 1997

Ethnic composition
Almost the whole population is of African descent, distributed among over 200 tribes, the most numerous being the Kongo, the Luba, the Lunda, the Mongo, and the Zande. The official language is French and there are four national languages: Kiswahili, Tshiluba, Kikongo, and Lingala.

Religions
About half the population are Roman Catholics, 26% belong to Protestant churches and 17% to the Kimbanguist Protestant-African Church, while the remainder follow traditional, animist beliefs.

Political features
State type: military
Date of state formation: 1960
Political structure: unitary
Executive: military
Assembly: suspended
Party structure: suspended
Human rights rating: 40%
International affiliations: ACP, CEEAC, CEPGL, G-24, IAEA, IBRD, IMF, NAM, OAU, UN, WTO

Local and regional government
The country is divided into ten regions, including the capital territory, below which are subregions. Administration is by appointed commissioners.

Political system
On 28 May 1997, following the overthrow of the Mobuto regime by Laurent Kabila, Zaire was renamed the Democratic Republic of Congo and a 15-point constitutional decree was promulgated cancelling all previous constitutions. All power was vested in the head of state, pending a new constitution. The head of state rules by decree and all political parties are banned. In May 1998 it was announced that a 300-member Constituent Assembly would be appointed to hold interim legislative power and draft a new constitution.

Prior to 1997 there had been a 730-member transitional legislature (HCR-PT), comprising a 435-member High Council of the Republic (HCR) formed in 1992, and a 210-member National Legislative Council, which had been the elected assembly under the 1978 one-party constitution.

Political parties
In May 1997 all parties except Laurent Kabila's Alliance of Democratic Forces for the Liberation of Congo-Zaire (CAFOL estd. 1996), were banned. Prior to 1997, the dominant force was the Popular Movement of the Revolution (MPR). Formed in 1967 as Zaire's only political party, it was immediately fused into the state machinery, party officials being, at the same time, government officials. The party, led by President Mobuto, had an African socialist orientation.

The three most significant opposition groups formed after 1991 were the Sacred Union of Radical Opposition and Allies (Usoral), the Union for Democracy and Social Progress (UPDS), the Republican and Democratic Union (URD), and the Congolese National Movement- Lumumba (MNC).

The Usoral is an alliance of a number of small parties. Its overall orientation is left-of-center. The UPDS was formed in 1982 and also has a left-of-center orientation. The URD was a group that was expelled from Usoral in May 1994.

The MNC is a coalition of seven left-of-center parties formed in 1994 to support the former prime minister, Patrice Lumumba.

Political leaders since 1970
1965–97 Marshal Mobuto Sese Seko (MPR), 1997– Laurent-Désiré Kabila (military)

Latest elections
Elections are scheduled for 1999. Elections to the now-dissolved National Legislative Council were last held in 1987 and were won by the MPR.

Political history
Formerly ravaged by the slave trade, the region of what is now Zaire was, in the 1870s, claimed by King Leopold II (1835–1909) of Belgium as a personal colony, termed the

Belgian Free State. This claim received international recognition in 1885. It ceased to be a personal possession and was renamed the Belgian Congo in 1907, emerging as an important exporter of minerals. In the post-World War II period, an independence movement, spearheaded by the Congolese National Movement (MNC), gathered momentum and the Belgian government quickly acceded to the movement's demands, granting the country full independence in June 1960, as the Republic of the Congo. Many thought the Belgian government's decision too precipitate in that it produced a number of immediate problems which could have been anticipated and perhaps avoided.

The new state was intended to have a unitary structure and be governed centrally from Léopoldville (Kinshasa) by President Joseph Kasavubu and Prime Minister Patrice Lumumba (1925–61), the leader of the MNC, but Moise Tshombe, a wealthy business executive, argued for a federal solution and, becoming dissatisfied with the government's response to his requests, established his own political party and declared the rich mining province of Katanga, where he was based, an independent state, under his leadership.

Fighting broke out, which was not properly quelled by Belgian troops, and the United Nations Security Council agreed to send a force to restore order and protect lives. Meanwhile, there were disagreements between President Kasavubu and Prime Minister Lumumba on how the crisis should be tackled and this division between them prompted the Congolese army commander, Colonel Sese Seko Mobutu (1930–97), who was then known as Joseph-Désiré Mobotu and was a member of the MNC, to step in and temporarily take over the reins of government. Lumumba was imprisoned and later released and five months later power was handed back to Kasavubu.

Soon afterwards it was announced that Lumumba had been murdered and the white mercenaries employed by Tshombe were thought to be responsible. The outcry which followed this announcement resulted in a new government being formed, with Cyrille Adoula as prime minister. During the fighting between Tshombe's mercenaries and United Nations forces the UN secretary general, Dag Hammarskjöld (1905–61), flew to Katanga province to mediate and was killed in an air crash on the Congolese–Northern Rhodesian border. The attempted secession of Katanga was finally stopped in 1963 when Tshombe went into exile, taking many of his followers with him to form the Congolese National Liberation Front (FNLC). In July 1964

Tshombe returned from exile and President Kasavubu appointed him interim prime minister until elections for a new government could be held.

In August 1964 the country embarked upon what was hoped to be a new era of stability, as the Democratic Republic of the Congo, but a power struggle between Kasavubu and Tshombe soon developed and again the army, led by Mobutu, intervened. He established what he called a 'second republic', in November 1965. Two years later a new constitution was adopted and in 1970 Mobutu was elected president.

The following year the country changed its name from Congo (Kinshasa) to the Republic of Zaire and in 1972 the Popular Movement of the Revolution (MPR) was declared the only legal political party. In the same year the president adopted the name of Mobutu Sese Seko. Mobutu carried out a large number of political and constitutional reforms which brought stability to what had once seemed an ungovernable country, but the harshness of some of his policies brought international criticism as well as domestic opposition to his regime.

In 1990 he made some concessions to that opposition by agreeing moves towards multiparty politics and in 1991 new political parties were allowed to register. However, a promised constitutional conference was postponed and Mobutu tried to maintain his control by juggling with the post of prime minister among politicians likely to win popular support.

In August 1991 a national conference on the political future of Zaire began its deliberations and soon came into conflict with Mobutu. In its closing session, in December 1992, it dissolved the National Legislative Council and elected a 435-member transitional legislature, the High Council of the Republic (HCR). The HCR was dominated by opponents of Mobutu who, when it claimed the right to appoint a prime minister, retaliated by appointing a rival administration.

This confrontational situation persisted until June 1994 when it was agreed to merge the HCR with the National Legislative Council into a new transitional assembly, the High Council of the Republic-Parliament of Transition (HCR-PT). Léon Kengo Wa Dondo (URD) was elected prime minister by the HCR-PT and subsequently appointed by President Mobutu. Kengo immediately set about the task of ensuring domestic stability and restoring international confidence in the country, but he was soon faced with a currency crisis and was forced to close half of Zaire's foreign embassies because their upkeep could not be afforded. The country's problems were exacerbated when, in May 1995, news was given of an outbreak of the Ebola virus, for which there is no known vaccine or cure. There was also a continuing secessionist movement in mineral-rich Shaba province (formerly Katanga) and tribal clashes in Kivu province and in August 1995 thousands of refugees were forcibly repatriated to Burundi and Rwanda. Such was the breakdown in law and order that Zaire's continuation as a nation-state was precarious.

During 1996 the government was opposed by rebel forces and in November 1996 Laurent Kabila, a veteran Marxist revolutionary, emerged as their leader. President Mobutu, who had left the country, returned in December 1996, but in May 1997 government forces were overwhelmed by the rebels and Mobutu fled again. On the 28 May 1997 Zaire was renamed the Democratic Republic of Congo and Kabila took over the presidency. In September 1997 Mobutu died in Morocco, where he had been granted asylum. Kabila suspended the constitution and in May 1998 appointed a constituent assembly to draw up a new one.

From mid-1998 the Kabila regime faced mounting opposition from rebel forces based in the Tutsi-dominated east. Military assistance had to be secured from Angola, Chad, Namibia, Zimbabwe, and Sudan and there were fears that the conflict might escalate into a broader central African war, involving several states. Rwanda and Uganda provided backing for the rebels, who accused the Kabila regime of corruption and incompetence.

In June 1999 Rwanda stopped its assistance to the rebels in the civil war, while Chad withdrew its troops, which had assisted President Kabila. This was followed, in July 1999, by the governments involved in the war in Congo signing a ceasefire. President Kabila agreed to an amnesty for the rebels and their supporters, while South Africa promised to provide troops to help police any ceasefire. However, the rebels rejected a ceasefire and continued to fight on.

CONGO, REPUBLIC OF

The Republic of the Congo (Congo–Brazzaville)
La République du Congo

Capital: Brazzaville

Social and economic data
Area: 342,000 sq km/132,047 sq miles

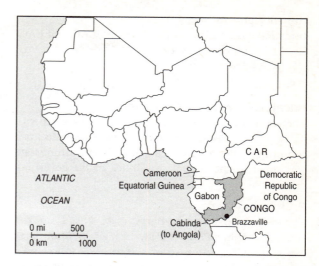

Population: 2,516,000[*]
Pop. density per sq km/sq mi: 7/19[*]
Urban population: 42%[**]
Literacy rate: 16%[**]
GDP: $1,785 million[*]; per-capita GDP: $710[*]
Government defense spending (% of GDP): 1.7%[**]
Currency: franc CFA
Economy type: low income
Labor force in agriculture: 62%[**]
[*] 1995.
[**] 1992.

Head of state and government
Denis Sassou-Nguesso, since 1997

Ethnic composition
The vast majority of Congolese are Bantus and comprise 15 main ethnic groups and 75 tribes. The Kongo, or Bakongo as they are sometimes called, account for about 45% of the population, then come the Bateke, or Teke, about 20%, and then the Mboshi, or Boubangui, about 16%. The official language is French.

Religions
More than a quarter of the population follows traditional, animist beliefs, nearly half is Roman Catholic, and a fifth is Protestant. There are also about 40,000 Muslims.

Political features
State type: in a state of transition
Date of state formation: 1960
Political structure: unitary
Executive: unlimited presidential
Assembly: two-chamber[**]
Party structure: multiparty[*]

Human rights rating: N/A
International affiliations: ACP, BDEAC, CEEAC, CEMAC, Francophone, FZ, IBRD, IMF, NAM, OAU, UN, WTO

** Suspended.

Local and regional government

The country is divided into nine provinces, each with its popularly elected regional council and executive committee. They act under the direction of commissars appointed by the central committee of the governing party.

Political system

The Congo was a one-party state based on the Congolese Labor Party (PCT), until a new multiparty constitution was adopted in March 1992, following a referendum. This provided for an executive president and a two-chamber assembly, comprising a 125-member National Assembly and a 60-member Senate. The president is directly elected by universal adult suffrage for a five-year term and the National Assembly is similarly elected for the same length of term. Members of the Senate serve a six-year term. The second ballot voting system is used. The president appoints a prime minister and cabinet.

In October 1997 the constitution was suspended when Denis Sassou-Nguesso seized power and a transitional government was established. With new elections pending, the legislature was replaced by a 75-member National Transitional Council. Work began during 1999 on framing a new constitution to be presented for approval by referendum.

Political parties

Until the adoption of the new multiparty constitution in 1992 the only legal party was the Congolese Labor Party (PCT). There are now more than 30 active parties. The four most significant are, the Pan-African Union for Social Democracy (UPADS); the Union for Democratic Renewal (URD), a seven-party alliance which includes the Congolese Movement for Democracy and Integral Development (MCDDI), led by Bernard Kolelas; the Rally for Democracy and Development (RDD) and the PCT.

UPADS, led by Pascal Lissouba, has a moderate, left-of-center orientation; the RDP is centrist; and the MCDDI center-right.

The PCT, led by Denis Sassou-Nguesso, was formed in 1969 to replace the National Revolutionary Movement (MNR). It is a Marxist–Leninist party, committed to the path of what it calls 'scientific socialism',

and is a member of the six-party United Democratic Forces (UDF) coalition formed in 1994.

Political leaders since 1970

1968–77 Marien Ngouabi (PCT), 1977–79 Colonel Jacques-Joachim Yhombi-Opango (military), 1979–92 Denis Sassou-Nguesso (PCT), 1992–97 Pascal Lissouba (UPADS), 1997– Denis Sassou-Nguesso (PCT)

Latest elections

In the August 1992 multiparty presidential elections there were 17 candidates, the front runners being Pascal Lissouba (UPADS), Bernard Kolelas (MCDDI), and Denis Sassou-Nguesso (PCT). The second ballot produced a straight fight between Lissouba and Kolelas, which Lissouba won, with 61% of the vote.

The results of the 1992 Senate elections were as follows:

Republic of Congo latest election results

Party	Seats
UPADS	23
MCDDI	13
PCT	3
Other parties	21

In the May–June 1993 National Assembly elections, UPADS won 69 of the 125 seats but the opposition parties contested the results and demanded fresh elections. Eventually, it was agreed to rerun elections in 11 disputed constituencies in October 1993. The final result still left UPADS with 47 seats. The MCDDI won 28 seats, the PCT, 15, the Rally for Democracy and Social Progress (RDPS), 10, and other parties, 25 seats. A 75-member National Transitional Council, comprising appointed members, replaced this assembly in January 1998.

Political history

After years of exploitation by Portuguese slave traders, the Congo became a colony within French Equatorial Africa in 1910. It was declared an autonomous republic within the French Community in 1958 and Abbé Youlou, a Roman Catholic priest who involved himself in politics and was suspended by the church, was elected prime minister and then president when full independence was achieved in 1960. Two years later plans were announced for the creation of a one-party state but in 1963, following industrial unrest, Youlou was forced to resign.

A new constitution was approved and Alphonse Mossamba-Débat, a former finance minister, became president, adopting a policy of what he described as 'scientific socialism'. He declared the National Revolutionary Movement (MNR) to be the only permitted political party. In 1968 a military coup, led by Captain Marien Ngouabi, overthrew Mossamba-Débat and the National Assembly was replaced by a National Council of the Revolution. Ngouabi proclaimed a Marxist state but kept close economic links with France.

In 1970 the PCT, as the MNR had become known, became the sole legal party and three years later a new constitution provided for an assembly chosen from a single party list. In 1977 Ngouabi was assassinated in a coup and eventually replaced by Colonel Joachim Yhombi-Opango. Two years later Yhombi-Opango, having discovered a plot to overthrow him, handed over the government to the Central Committee of the PCT and eventually Denis Sassou-Nguessou (b. 1943) became president.

Sassou-Nguessou steadily moved his country out of the Soviet sphere of influence and in 1982 the new regime received formal recognition by France In 1984 and 1989 Sassou-Nguessou was re-elected for further five-year terms but dissatisfaction with his administration grew and in a national conference on the country's political future, in February–June 1991, the president was severely criticized, his executive powers reduced, and an interim government, under a prime minister, appointed until a new constitution was in place and multiparty elections were held.

The constitution was overwhelmingly approved, by referendum, and in March 1992 Pascal Lissouba became the country's first democratically elected president and his party, the Pan-African Union for Social Democracy (UPADS), the largest party in both the National Assembly and the Senate. Sassou-Nguessou took his defeat gracefully.

President Lissouba appointed Stéphane Bongho-Nouarra prime minister to lead a minority 'war cabinet' to tackle the economic problems of a country crippled by a huge burden of external debt. In November 1992 Bongho-Nouarra lost a vote of confidence and the president dissolved the National Assembly and called for fresh elections. They were eventually won by UPADS and in January 1993 General Yhombi-Opango was appointed prime minister. Followers of the opposition parties disputed the May–June 1993 election results, resulting in strikes and violence and a month-long curfew, during which some 40 people were killed.

In January 1995, in an attempt to achieve political stability, the prime minister resigned to allow the president to bring parties other than UPADS into the government. General Yhombi-Opango was asked to form a new administration, which now included members of parties formerly in opposition. Market-centerd reforms, including privatization, were introduced under the encouragement of the IMF.

In October 1997 the government was ousted by former president Sassou-Nguesso, who set up a transitional government pending fresh administrative elections and proceeded to rule by decree. During 1998 and 1999 government forces became engaged in an increasingly serious military conflict with 'Ninja' rebels who were supporters of a former prime minister, Bernard Kolelas, and who were based in south-western Congo. The clashes led to the flight of thousands of refugees to Brazzaville and to Kinshasa, in the neighbouring Democratic Republic of Congo.

CÔTE D'IVOIRE

The Republic of the Ivory Coast
La République de la Côte d'Ivoire

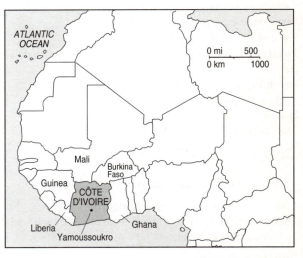

Capital: Abidjan (*de facto* and legislative); Yamoussoukro (*de jure* and administrative)

Social and economic data
Area: 322,460 sq km/124,470 sq miles
Population: 13,695,000[*]
Pop. density per sq km/sq mi: 110/42[*]
Urban population: 42%[**]

Literacy rate: 54%[**]
GDP: $9,250 million[*]; per-capita GDP: $675[*]
Government defense spending (% of GDP): 1.0%[**]
Currency: franc CFA
Economy type: low income
Labor force in agriculture: 65%[**]
[*] 1995.
[**] 1992.

Head of state (executive)
President Henri Konan Bédié, since 1993

Head of government
Prime Minister Daniel Kablan Duncan, since 1993

Ethnic composition
There is no single dominant ethnic group and the main tribes include the Agni, Baoule, Krou, Senoufou, and Mandingo. There are also about 2 million Africans who have settled from neighboring countries, particularly Burkina Faso. Europeans number about 70,000. The official language is French.

Religions
About 60% of the population follows traditional, animist beliefs, about 20% is Sunni Muslim, and 15% Roman Catholic.

Political features
State type: emergent democratic
Date of state formation: 1960
Political structure: unitary executive/limited presidential
Assembly: one-chamber
Party structure: multiparty[*]
Human rights rating: 75%
International affiliations: ACP, BOAD, ECOWAS, FZ, G-24, IAEA, IBRD, IMF, NAM, OAU, UEMOA, UN, WTO

[*] Though dominated by one party.

Local and regional government
The country is divided into 49 departments, each with its own elected council.

Political system
The constitution dates from independence in 1960 and was amended in 1971, 1975, 1980, 1985, 1986, 1990, and 1994. It provides for an executive president, who is head of state, elected by universal adult suffrage, through a majoritarian voting system of the second ballot, for a five-year term, and a single-chamber 175-member National Assembly, elected in the same way and also serving a five-year term. The president, who

since 1994 must be Ivoirian by birth or have Ivoirian parents, appoints a prime minister, as head of government. In 1997 President Konan Bédié proposed that a second chamber, termed the Senate, be established.

Political parties
A multi-party system has been operating since 1990 and there are now some 90 registered parties.

The ruling party is the Democratic Party of the Ivory Coast (PDCI), founded in 1946 by Félix Houphouët-Boigny, as a branch of the African Democratic Rally (RDA). It has a nationalistic free-enterprise orientation.

In October 1994 a split appeared in the PDCI and a breakaway party, the centrist Rally of Republicans (RDR), was formed. This is led by Djény Kobina and supported by the former prime minister, Alassane Ouattara.

Among the opposition groups, the most significant are the Ivoirian People's (or Popular) Front (FPI) and the Ivoirian Labor (or Workers') Party (PIT). Both have left-of-center orientations.

Political leaders since 1970
1960–93 Félix Houphouët-Boigny (PDCI), 1993– Henri Konan Bédié (PDCI)

Latest elections
In the October 1995 multiparty presidential election, the incumbent president, Henri Konan-Bédié, secured an overwhelming victory with 96% of the vote. Turnout was 45%, but the chief opposition parties boycotted the poll. There were several deaths during a violent campaign. The PDCI also secured a clear victory in the November–December 1995 assembly elections. It won 148 seats to the RDR's 14 and FPI's 12.

Political history
Formerly a province of French West Africa, which had been colonized in the 19th century, the Côte d'Ivoire was given self-government within the French Community in 1958 and then full independence in 1960, when a new constitution was adopted. Félix Houphouët-Boigny (1905–93), leader of the Democratic Party of the Ivory Coast (PDCI), was the country's first president. He maintained close links with France after independence and this support, combined with a good economic growth rate, gave his country a high degree of political stability. He was very much a pragmatist in politics and was criticized by some other African leaders for maintaining links with South Africa. He countered the criticism by arguing that a dialogue between blacks and whites was essential.

As a strong believer in independence for black African states, he denounced Soviet and other forms of intervention in African affairs and travelled extensively to improve relations with the Western powers.

In the president's advancing years opposition to him grew, particularly as the economy deteriorated, with per-capita incomes falling by 25% between 1987 and 1993 as an IMF-promoted austerity program was implemented. However, despite the appearance of rival parties, Houphouët-Boigny and the PDCI retained their control in multiparty elections in 1990. In December 1993 the veteran president died, at the age of 88, and, in accordance with the terms of the constitution, the president of the National Assembly, Henri Konan Bédié (b. 1934), became head of state for the remainder of the presidential term. This prompted the resignation of the disenchanted prime minister, Alassane Ouattara, who was replaced by Daniel Kablan Duncan. It was believed that new birth and residency restrictions for prospective presidential candidates, which were introduced in 1994, were designed to prevent the ambitious Ouattara from becoming a candidate. Between October and November 1995 President Konan Bédié and the PDCI won clear victories in multiparty elections that were boycotted by many opposition parties.

In May 1999 the government ordered the temporary closure of university campuses in response to a wave of student unrest which they suspected was being manipulated by the youth wing of the opposition Rally of Republicans (RDR) party, who were unhappy with arrangements for the 2000 presidential election.

DJIBOUTI

The Republic of Djibouti
Jumhuriya Djibouti

Capital: Djibouti

Social and economic data
Area: 23,220 sq km/8,958 sq miles
Population: 566,000[*]
Pop. density per sq km/sq mi: 24/63[*]
Urban population: 86%[**]
Literacy rate: 12%[**]
GDP: $565 million[*]; per-capita GDP: $995[*]
Government defense spending (% of GDP): 5.3%[*]
Currency: Djibouti franc
Economy type: low income

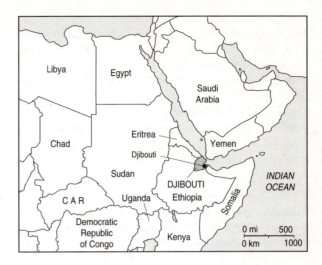

Labor force in agriculture: N/A
[*] 1995.
[**] 1992.

Head of state (executive)
President Ismael Omar Guelleh, since 1999

Head of government
Prime Minister Barkat Gourad Hamadou, since 1978

Ethnic composition
The population is divided chiefly into two Hamitic groups, the Issas (Somalis) in the south and the minority Afars (or Danakil) in the north and west. Ethnic rivalry between the two is intense, with an Afars' insurgency underway since 1991. There are also minorities of Europeans, mostly French, as well as Arabs, Sudanese, and Indians. The official language is French.

Religions
Virtually the whole population (95%) is Sunni Muslim.

Political features
State type: authoritarian nationalist
Date of state formation: 1977
Political structure: unitary
Executive: unlimited presidential
Assembly: one-chamber
Party structure: multiparty[*]
Human rights rating: N/A
International affiliations: ACP, AL, IBRD, IGADD, IMF, NAM, OAU, OIC, UN

[*] Though dominated by one party.

Local and regional government
For administrative purposes, the country is divided into five districts.

Political system

The September 1992 constitution, which was approved by a referendum, provides for an executive president, elected by universal adult suffrage and serving a six-year term, and for the operation of four political parties. There is a single-chamber assembly, the 65-member Chamber of Deputies, elected for a five-year term. It comprises 33 Issa and 32 Afar members, returned in multi-seat constituencies. The president, who is also commander in chief of the armed forces, appoints a prime minister and Council of Ministers (cabinet).

Political parties

Between 1981 and 1992 the only permitted party was the People's Progress (or Popular Rally for Progress) Party (RPP). Although three other parties are now allowed to operate, the only one that has made any impact is the Democratic Renewal Party (PRD).

The RPP was formed in 1979 to replace the African People's League for Independence (LPAI), the dominant party before and after independence. Its orientation is basically nationalist.

The PRD was formed in 1992. It has a left-of-center orientation.

A United Opposition Front (UOF) was formed in 1992 and included the Front for the Restoration of Unity and Democracy (FRUD), an Afars' guerrilla movement formed in 1991. In 1996 FRUD split, with one faction continuing military operations and another securing legal recognition. In 1998 there were four recognized political parties and 13 banned parties.

Political leaders since 1970

1977–99 Hassan Gouled Aptidon (RPP) 1999– Ismael Omar Guelleh (RPP)

Latest elections

In the December 1997 assembly elections all seats were won by the RPP-FRUD alliance, which secured 79% of the vote. The RPP won 54 of the seats and FRUD 11. The PRD won 19% of the vote, but no seats.

In the April 1999 presidential contest Ismael Omar Guelleh of the RPP was elected with 74% of the vote. His rival, Moussa Ahmed Idriss, the PRD candidate, obtained 26%. Turnout was around 60%.

Political history

Djibouti, with its excellent deep port, became a French colony in 1862, being part of French Somaliland, and in 1945 was declared an overseas territory. In 1967 it was renamed the French Territory of the Afars and the Issas.

There were frequent calls for independence, particularly from the Issas community, sometimes resulting in violence, and this goal was eventually achieved in 1977. Hassan Gouled Aptidon (b. 1916), who had been active in the independence movement, was elected the first president.

In 1979 all existing political parties were combined to form the People's Progress Party (RPP) and the government embarked on the task of bringing together the two main tribes, the Issas, who traditionally had strong links with Somalia, and the Afars, who had been linked with Ethiopia, through a policy of 'rapid detribalization'.

In 1981 a new constitution was adopted, making the RPP the only legal party and providing for the election of a president after nomination by the RPP. President Gouled was subsequently elected. The following year a Chamber of Deputies was elected from a list of RPP nominees. Under Gouled, Djibouti pursued a largely successful policy of amicable neutralism with its neighbors, concluding treaties of friendship with Ethiopia, Somalia, Kenya, and the Sudan, and tried to assist the peace process in East Africa. Although affected by the 1984–85 droughts, it managed to maintain stability with the help of famine relief aid from the European Community.

The septuagenarian Gouled was re-elected in 1987 and again in 1993, after constitutional changes which allowed a limited number of opposition parties to operate. Despite these changes, no party other than the RPP has made a significant impact on the political scene, so that Djibouti has remained a *de facto* one-party state. In 1991 an Afars-dominated movement, the Front for the Restoration of Unity and Democracy (FRUD), commenced guerrilla activities against the regime, in the northeast. However, in June 1994 a majority faction of FRUD signed a peace accord with the government. In December 1997, the RPP, in alliance with FRUD, won all assembly seats in new elections.

In February 1999 the 83-year-old President Gouled announced that he was retiring and would not contest the April 1999 presidential elections. The ruling RPP selected his chief-of-staff, Ismael Omar Guelleh, as its candidate. Guelleh easily defeated Moussa Ahmed Idriss, behind whom opposition parties had united. However, Idriss declared that Guelleh had won through 'massive fraud'. Guelleh was sworn in as president in May 1999 and immediately re-appointed as prime minister, Barkat Gourad Hamadou, who had been in office since 1978.

EQUATORIAL GUINEA

The Republic of Equatorial Guinea
La República de Guinea Ecuatorial

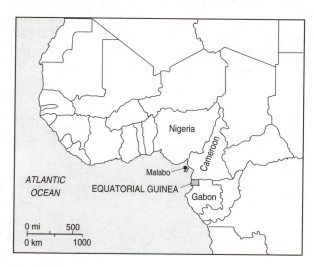

Capital: Malabo

Social and economic data
Area: 28,100 sq km/10,849 sq miles
Population: 389,000*
Pop. density per sq km/sq mi: 14/36*
Urban population: 29%**
Literacy rate: 50%**
GDP: $155 million*; per-capita GDP: $400*
Government defense spending (% of GDP): 1.3%*
Currency: franc CFA
Economy type: low income
Labor force in agriculture: 66%**
* 1995.
** 1992.

Head of state (executive)
President Brigadier General (retired) Teodoro Obiang Nguema Mbasogo, since 1979

Head of government
Prime Minister Angel Serafin Seriche Dougan, since 1996

Ethnic composition
Between 80% and 90% of the population is of the Fang ethnic group, of Bantu origin. Most of the other groups have been pushed to the coast by the Fang expansion. The official language is Spanish.

Religions
About 96% of the population is Roman Catholic. The rest follow traditional, animalist beliefs.

Political features
State type: authoritarian nationalist
Date of state formation: 1968
Political structure: unitary
Executive: unlimited presidential
Assembly: one-chamber
Party structure: multiparty*
Human rights rating: N/A
International affiliations: ACP, BDEAC, CEEAC, CEMAC, FZ, IBRD, IMF, NAM, OAU, UN

* Though dominated by one party.

Local and regional government
For administrative purposes, the country is divided into seven provinces.

Political system
The November 1991 constitution, which was approved by referendum and amended in 1995, provides for multiparty politics, with an executive president, who is head of state, elected by universal suffrage for a seven-year term. There is a single-chamber assembly, the 80-member House of Representatives, also popularly elected for a five-year term by proportional representation in multi-member constituencies. The president appoints a prime minister and Council of Ministers.

Political parties
Until 1992 only one party was allowed to operate, the Democratic Party of Equatorial Guinea (PDGE). Of the other groups that have since formed, the most significant are the opposition Popular Union (UP), People's Social Democratic Convention (CSDP) and the Social Democratic Union of Equatorial Guinea (UDSGE).

The PDGE was formed in 1987 as the government party. It has a strong nationalist and authoritarian orientation. The CSDP was formed in 1992 and has a left-of-center orientation. The UDSGE was founded in 1990 and also has a left-of-center orientation, but is supportive of the government.

Political leaders since 1970
1968–79 Francisco Macias Nguema (military), 1979–91 Brigadier General (retired) Teodoro Obiang Nguema Mbasogo (military/PDGE)

Latest elections

In February 1996 President Obiang was re-elected unopposed for another seven-year term, securing 99% of the vote; the opposition parties boycotted the vote.

In the second multiparty assembly elections, held on 6 March 1999, the PDGE, with 86% of the vote, won 75 of the 80 seats, the CSDP, 1, and the Popular Union (UP), 4. The contest was criticized for its lack of fairness by opposition and foreign observers. Turnout was officially put at 95%, although the main opposition parties boycotted the poll.

Political history

After 190 years of Spanish rule, during which period a harsh plantation system was established, Equatorial Guinea became fully independent in 1968, with Francisco Macias Nguema as the nation's first president, heading a coalition government. He soon assumed dictatorial powers, however, and in 1970 outlawed all existing political parties, replacing them with one, the United National Party (PUN). Two years later he declared himself president for life and established a tight control of the press and radio. Between 1976 and 1977 there were many arrests and executions. He also established close relations with the Soviet bloc.

In 1979 he was overthrown in a coup led by his nephew, Colonel Teodoro Obiang Nguema Mbasogo, with at least the tacit approval of Spain. Macias was later tried and executed. Obiang expelled the many Soviet technicians and advisers and renewed economic and political ties with Spain. He banned political parties and ruled through a Supreme Military Council and withstood four coup attempts between 1981 and 1988. In 1982, after pressure was exerted by the United Nations, a new constitution was adopted, promising an eventual return to civilian rule, but nothing resulted. In 1991, responding to public pressure, President Obiang allowed a referendum which gave overwhelming support for a change to multiparty politics.

In the first multiparty assembly elections, in November 1993, the PDGE won a clear majority, amid allegations of vote-rigging by opposition politicians and foreign observers.

The 1996 presidential elections were boycotted by the opposition. There were reports during 1998 of continued repression of political opponents, suggesting that there had not been a genuine move to pluralist politics.

The ruling PDGE achieved a crushing victory in the March 1999 legislature elections, but the opposition Popular Union (UP), led by Andres Moises Mba Ada, alleged that voting papers had been withheld from opposition supporters and that there had been arrests and harassment of UP activists. Outside observers from Spain supported some of these allegations. In protest, the UP boycotted the new legislature and Joaquin Elema, leader of the Co-ordinating Committtee of the Democratic Opposition of Equatorial Guinea (CODE) announced plans after the elections to set up a government-in-exile. Severo Moto leads the opposition in exile.

ERITREA

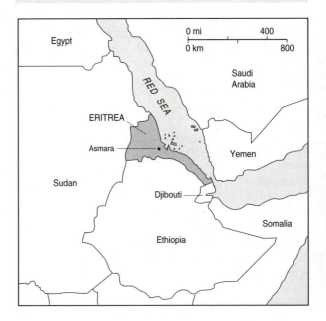

Capital: Asmara (Asmera)

Social and economic data

Area: 117,600 sq km/45,406 sq miles
Population: 3,437,000[*]
Pop. density per sq km/sq mi: 29/76[*]
Urban population: 17%[*]
Literacy rate: N/A
GDP: $580 million[*]; per-capita GDP: $170[*]
Government defense spending (% of GDP): 5.7%[*]
Currency: Ethiopian birr
Economy type: low income
Labor force in agriculture: N/A
[*] 1995.
[**] 1992.

Head of state and of government
President Issaias Afewerki, since 1993

Ethnic composition
There are several ethnic groups, including the Amhara and the Tigrais. The main language is Tigrinya.

Religions
About 50% of the population (chiefly lowlanders) follows Sunni Islam and the remainder (chiefly highlanders) adheres to Coptic Christianity.

Political features
State type: nationalistic socialist
Date of state formation: 1993
Political structure: unitary
Executive: unlimited presidential
Assembly: one-chamber
Party structure: one-party[*]
Human rights rating: N/A
International affiliations: ACP, COMESA, IBRD, IGADD, IMF, OAU, UN

[*] Effective.

Local and regional government
A regional system was inherited from Ethiopia but in May 1995 a new structure was approved, based on six administrative regions, further divided into subregions and villages.

Political system
In May 1997 a new constitution was adopted, providing for a president to be popularly elected for a maximum of two five-year terms and a National Assembly comprising the 75-member Central Committee of the People's Front for Democracy and Justice (PFDJ) and 75 other members to be nominated. The president appoints a prime minister, but this mandate can be revoked by a two-thirds Assembly vote.

Political parties
Although several parties function, the dominant one is the People's Front for Democracy and Justice (PFDJ). It changed its name in 1994 from the Eritrean People's Liberation Front (EPLF), in which guise it had been in the vanguard of the movement to secure independence from Ethiopia. It has a left-of-center orientation.

Since independence the PFDJ's dominance has been challenged by breakaway factions, some of which have combined to form the opposition Eritrean National Pact Alliance, and by the Eritrean Liberation Front (ELF).

Political leaders since 1970
1993– Issaias Afewerki (EPLF/PFDJ)

Latest elections
Provision was made for multiparty elections to take place during 1998. There were elections in the regions during 1997 and 1998.

Political history
Eritrea was occupied by Italy in 1882 and declared a colony in 1890. In 1935 it was used as a base for Italy's invasion of Ethiopia and designated part of Italian East Africa in 1936. In 1941, during World War II, Italian forces in Eritrea were defeated by the British and after the war the country was federated with Ethiopia in 1952 by the United Nations, and then made an Ethiopian province in 1962. This sparked a strong secessionist movement, which was to continue for 30 years as the Ethiopian military government fought hard to hold on to the province. In addition to the problems caused by the fighting between Ethiopian and Eritrean forces, there were severe famines caused by successive droughts.

The most durable secessionist force was the Eritrean People's Liberation Front (EPLF), founded in 1958. By 1977 it controlled much of the region, but then the new Ethiopian regime of Colonel Mengistu Haile Mariam, receiving military aid from the Soviet Union, turned back the tide until the late 1980s. In 1990 the EPLF's armed wing captured the strategic port of Massawa. This made the deployment of Ethiopian troops in the region untenable and in 1991 the Mengistu military regime was toppled in Ethiopia. After a referendum held in April 1993 showed overwhelming, 99.8%, support for independence, the EPLF declared the secession of Eritrea and in May 1993 this separate state was recognized by the new Ethiopian government. International recognition soon followed.

A transitional government was established by the EPLF, now renamed the People's Front for Democracy and Justice (PFDJ), with multiparty elections planned within the four-year period of transition, while a constitution was drafted. Issaias Afewerki was elected head of state and head of government by the PFDJ.

In May 1998 fighting broke out between Eritrean and Ethiopian forces over disputed borders.

This conflict continued at a low scale, before escalating into full-scale fighting from February 1999. There was particularly fierce fighting in late March and mid-June 1999, with claims by each side that they had killed, wounded or captured more than 8,000 of the opposing force. However, in July 1999 both states agreed, at an Organisation of African Unity (OAU) meeting, to a plan to end the war, with mediation by Algeria. In May 1999 a peace agreement was signed with Sudan, ending five years of inter-state tension.

ETHIOPIA

The Federal Democratic Republic of Ethiopia

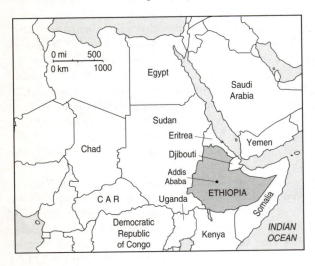

Capital: Addis Ababa

Social and economic data
Area: 1,106,200 sq km/427,106 sq miles
Population: 54,938,000*
Pop. density per sq km/sq mi: 50/129*
Urban population: 13%**
Literacy rate: 62%**
GDP: $5,725 million*; per-capita GDP: $105*
Government defense spending (% of GDP): 2.1%**
Currency: Ethiopian birr
Economy type: low income
Labor force in agriculture: 80%**
* 1995.
** 1992.

Head of state
President Negasso Gidada, since 1995

Head of government
Prime Minister Meles Zenawi, since 1995

Ethnic composition
The country contains over 70 different ethnic groups, the two main ones being the Galla, mainly in the east and south of the central plateau, who comprise about 40% of the population, and the Amhara and Tigrais, largely in the central plateau itself, who constitute about 35% of the population. The official language is Amharic.

Religions
About 35% of the population is Sunni Muslim and 45% belongs to the Ethiopian Orthodox Church (Tewahida). There are also significant numbers of animists and Christians.

Political features
State type: emergent democratic*
Date of state formation: 11th century
Political structure: federal
Executive: parliamentary
Assembly: two-chamber
Party structure: multiparty**
Human rights rating: 13%
International affiliations: ACP, COMESA, G-24, IAEA, IBRD, IGADD, IMF, NAM, OAU, UN

* In a state of transition.
** Though dominated by one party.

Local and regional government
Between 1952 and 1962 Ethiopia was a federation and then became a unitary state. In 1994 it returned to its federal status on the basis of nine states: Tigré, Afar, Amara, Oramia, Somali, Benshangui, Gambela, Harer, and Peoples of the South. Unusually, each state enjoys the right to secede.

Political system
A new constitution was ratified in December 1994. Under its terms, Ethiopia returned to federal status, based on nine states. Controversially, the constitution includes provision for any one of the nine states to secede from the federation. It also provides for a multi-party system, with a two-chamber federal assembly. The federal assembly comprises a 117-member upper house, the Council of the Federation, comprising members selected by state assemblies and the 22 minority nationalities, and a 548-member Council of People's Representatives, directly elected in single-member seats for a five-year term. The federal assembly elects the president for a four-year term. Formerly, the president was head of government, but under the 1994 constitution, the prime minister is the real holder of executive power.

Political parties

Until 1991 the only legal political party was the Marxist–Leninist Workers' Party of Ethiopia (WPE), which was established in 1984. Since then a number of parties in opposition to the WPE have been established, the most significant being the Ethiopian People's Revolutionary Democratic Front (EPRDF), which now dominates the political scene. Many of the other parties are regionally based.

The EPRDF was formed in 1989 through an amalgamation of smaller groupings, including the Tigré People's Liberation Front, the Ethiopian People's Democratic Movement, the Oromo People's Democratic Union (OPDU), and the Afar Democratic Movement. The Tigréan people are the dominant force in the EPRDF, which has a left-of-center orientation.

Political leaders since 1970

1916–74 Haile Selassie (emperor), 1974–77 General Tefere Bante (military), 1977–91 Colonel Mengistu Haile Mariam (WPE), 1991– Meles Zenawi (EPRDF)

Latest elections

In August 1995 Negasso Gidada (OPUD) was elected president by the federal assembly.

In the country's first multi-party elections, in May 1995, the EPRDF secured a landslide victory in the federal assembly. It won 483 out of the 548 seats in the lower house, while regional groups won 46 seats.

Political history

After a long period of subordination to Egypt, Ethiopia became independent in the 11th century as the Kingdom of Abyssinia. It survived the European scramble for Africa, defeating an attempted Italian invasion in 1896. In the 20th century, one man, Haile Selassie (1891–1975), came to dominate the country for more than 50 years. He became regent in 1916, king in 1928, and emperor in 1930, Westernizing the country. During the Italian occupation of Abyssinia between 1935 and 1936 he lived in exile in England, but was restored to power in 1941 after the country was liberated by British forces. In 1963 Emperor Haile Selassie promoted the foundation of the Organization of African Unity (OAU), which held its first conference in Addis Ababa. He was deposed by the armed forces in 1974, following a disastrous famine in 1973, high inflation, growing unemployment, and demands for a more democratic form of government. His palace and estates were nationalized, the parliament was dissolved, and the constitution suspended. He died in 1975 at the age of 83 in a small apartment in his former palace in Addis Ababa.

General Teferi Bante, who had led the uprising and had been made head of state, was killed in 1977 by fellow officers and Colonel Mengistu Haile Mariam (b. 1937) replaced him. A one-party Marxist–Leninist-influenced regime was established, with collective farming promoted, with adverse consequences. Throughout the period of Haile Selassie's reign, and that of his predecessor, Emperor Menelik II, there had always been attempts by various regions which had been annexed to secede, particularly from Tigré and from Eritrea, which was ceded to Ethiopia in 1952. The 1975 revolution encouraged these secessionist movements to increase their efforts and the military government had to fight to hold on to Eritrea and the southeast region of Ogaden, where Somalian troops were assisting local guerrillas. The communist Soviet Union, which had adopted Ethiopia as a new ally, threatened to cut off aid to Somalia, and Cuban troops assisted Mengistu in ending the fighting there. The struggle for independence by Eritrea and the adjoining province of Tigré continued. In the midst of this confusion there was acute famine in the northern provinces, including Eritrea, after the failure of the rains for three successive seasons. In addition to a massive emergency food aid program from many Western nations, the Ethiopian government tried to alleviate the problem by resettling people from the northern area to the more fertile south. By 1986 more than half a million had been resettled.

In September 1987 civilian rule was formally reintroduced under a new constitution, with Mengistu elected as the country's first president. He was the only candidate and retained his emergency powers. The civil war continued until the leading opposition alliance, the Ethiopian People's Revolutionary Democratic Front (EPRDF), offered a ceasefire in July 1990, leading to the ousting of Mengistu in May 1991. He fled the country and the EPRDF established an interim government prior to elections. In July 1991 the EPRDF leader, Meles Zenawi, was elected president by the National Assembly. Meanwhile, drought conditions exacerbated Ethiopia's problems and led to many deaths, despite massive food aid from Western nations. With the end of hostilities, the EPRDF showed itself to be remarkably calm and disciplined. This augured well for future democratic development and the economic situation also began to improve, with private farming and the market sector being encouraged. However, unrest continued in the Oromo region, where some groups were pressing for the creation of an independent state of Oromia.

As part of the peace process, it was agreed that a referendum on Eritrean independence should be held. This was held in April 1993 and there was an overwhelming vote in favor. In May 1993 Eritrea was formally recognized by Ethiopia as a fully independent state.

A constituent assembly was elected in Ethiopia by multiparty elections held in June 1994, with the EPRDF winning the vast majority of the seats, and in December a new constitution was adopted, making Ethiopia a federal parliamentary state. In the elections for a permanent assembly in May 1995, the EPRDF won a decisive majority and Zenawi became prime minister.

In May 1998 disputes over borders led to fighting between Ethiopian and Eritrean troops. This conflict continued, escalating from February 1999. However, in July 1999 both countries agreed, at an Organisation of African Unity (OAU) meeting, to a plan to end the war, with mediation by Algeria.

GABON

The Gabonese Republic
La République gabonaise

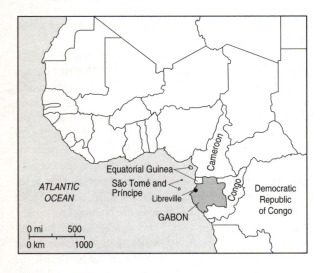

Capital: Libreville

Social and economic data
Area: 267,667 sq km/103,347 sq miles
Population: 1,283,000*
Pop. density per sq km/sq mi: 5/12*
Urban population: 47%**

Literacy rate: 12%**
GDP: $3,760 million*; per-capita GDP: $2,930*
Government defense spending (% of GDP): 1.7%**
Currency: franc CFA
Economy type: middle income
Labor force in agriculture: 76%**
* 1995.
** 1992.

Head of state (executive)
President Omar Bongo, since 1967

Head of government
Prime Minister Jean-François Ntoutoume-Emane, since 1999

Ethnic composition
There are 40 Bantu tribes in four main groupings: the Fang, the Eshira, the Mbede, and the Okande. There are also Pygmies and about 10% of the population is European, mostly French. The official language is French.

Religions
About 70% of the population is Christian, mainly Roman Catholic, and the rest mostly follows traditional, animist beliefs.

Political features
State type: emergent democratic
Date of state formation: 1960
Political structure: unitary
Executive: limited presidential
Assembly: two-chamber
Party structure: multiparty*
Human rights rating: N/A
International affiliations: ACP, BDEAC, CEEAC, CEMAC, FZ, G-24, IAEA, IBRD, IMF, NAM, OAU, OIC, OPEC, UN, WTO

* Though dominated by one party.

Local and regional government
For administrative purposes, the country is divided into nine provinces, ranging in population from about 50,000 to nearly 200,000. These are, in turn, subdivided into 37 departments. The provinces are administered by governors and the departments by prefects, all appointed by the president.

Political system
The 1991 constitution provides for an executive president, directly elected by universal adult suffrage for a five-year term, renewable once only, and a 120-member National Assembly, and a 91-member Senate. National

Assembly deputies are elected in single-seat constituencies for a five-year term, while senators are elected for six-year terms by local and departmental councillors. Elections are by the second-ballot majoritarian system. The president appoints a prime minister who, in turn, appoints a Council of Ministers (cabinet), in consultation with the president.

Political parties

Until 1990 the only legally permitted party was the Gabonese Democratic Party (PDG). There are now eight parties represented in the National Assembly, and 20 others functioning outside. The two most significant parties, other than the PDG, are the Gabonese Progress Party (PGP) and the National Rally of Woodcutters (RNB).

The PDG was formed in 1968 by Omar Bongo, who dissolved the former ruling party, the Gabonese Democratic Bloc (BDG), and created a one-party state. The party has a strongly nationalist orientation and is a political vehicle for the president, who is its secretary general.

The PGP is a left-center grouping formed in 1990. The RNB was also formed in 1990 and incorporates the Movement for National Regeneration (MORENA). It is center-left. In 1998 a new party was formed, the Gaullists' rally (RDG), commiting itself to Gabon becoming an integral part of France.

Political leaders since 1970

1967– Omar Bongo (PDG)

Latest elections

Omar Bongo was re-elected president in December 1993 with a 66.6% vote share. There were 7 other candidates. The two closest challengers were Pierre Mamboundou (16.5%) and Paul Mba Abessole (RNB; 13.4%).

In the December 1996 multiparty assembly elections, the PDG secured a clear majority, winning 84 seats out of 120. The RNB won eight seats. Senate elections, held January–February 1997, resulted in the PDG winning 53 of 91 seats, and the RNB 20.

Political history

Gabon was a province of French Equatorial Africa from 1889 until it achieved full independence in 1960. There were then two main political parties, the Gabonese Democratic Bloc (BDG), led by the pro-French Léon M'ba (1902–67), and the Gabonese Democratic and Social Union (UDSG), led by Jean-Hilaire Aubame.

Although the two parties were evenly matched in popular support, M'ba became president on independence and Aubame, foreign minister. In 1964 the BDG wanted the two parties to merge but this was resisted by the UDSG, whereupon M'ba called a general election. Before the elections took place M'ba was deposed in a military coup led by supporters of Aubame but, with the help of France, M'ba was restored to office. Aubame was later found guilty of treason and imprisoned. The UDSG was outlawed and most of its members joined the BDG.

In 1967 M'ba, although in failing health, was re-elected. He died later the same year and was succeeded by Albert-Bernard Bongo (b. 1935). In the following year he dissolved the BDG and established the Gabonese Democratic Party (PDG) as the only legal political party. Bongo was re-elected in 1973 and, announcing his conversion to Islam, changed his first name to Omar. He was re-elected in 1979, 1986, 1993, and 1999, pursuing a pro-Western policy course.

Gabon, with its great reserves of uranium, manganese, and iron, is the richest per-capita country in mainland black Africa, and Bongo and his predecessors have successfully exploited these resources. Although operating an authoritarian regime, he managed to dilute any serious opposition to him. However, he was eventually forced to concede to mounting popular demands, including strikes and antigovernment riots, for a more democratic form of government and in 1990 a multiparty system was introduced. The PDG achieved narrow victories in the 1990 and 1993 multiparty assembly and presidential elections, although the opposition alleged fraud. A government of national unity, including opposition representatives, was formed by Prime Minister Casimir Oye M'ba. He was replaced as prime minister by Paulin Obame-Nguema (PDG) in October 1994. The PDG won a clear majority in the 1996 assembly elections.

Omar Bongo's re-election as president in December 1998 was marred by allegations by a defeated opposition candidate, Pierre Mamboundou, of the High Council of the Resistance (HCR) party, that there had been voting fraud. However, an opposition call for a general strike to force fresh elections was largely ignored. In January 1999 Obame-Nguema resigned as prime minister and was replaced by Jean-Francois Ntoutoume-Emane (PDG), a housing minister who had recently served as Bongo's election campaign manager.

GAMBIA

The Republic of the Gambia

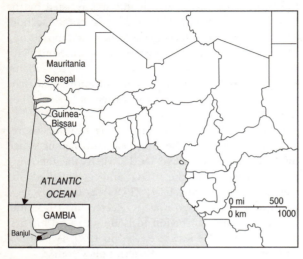

Capital: Banjul

Social and economic data
Area: 11,300 ksq km/4,363 sq miles
Population: 1,081,000 million[*]
Pop. density per sq km/sq mi: 96/248[*]
Urban population: 24%[**]
Literacy rate: 27%[**]
GDP: $355 million[*]; per-capita GDP: $330[*]
Government defense spending (% of GDP): 3.8%[**]
Currency: dalasi
Economy type: low income
Labor force in agriculture: 84%[**]
[*] 1995.
[**] 1992.

Head of state and head of government
Captain Yahya Jammeh, since 1994

Ethnic composition
There is a wide mix of ethnic groups, the largest being the Mandingo, comprising about 40% of the population. The other main groups are the Fula, the Wolof, the Jola, and the Serahuli. The official language is English.

Religions
Eighty-eight per cent of the population is Sunni Muslim. The rest is mainly Anglican Protestant (9%) or animist, following the beliefs of the Jola tribe.

Political features
State type: emergent democratic
Date of state formation: 1965

Political structure: unitary
Executive: limited presidential
Assembly: one-chamber
Party structure: multiparty
Human rights rating: N/A
International affiliations: ACP, CILSS, CW, ECOWAS, IBRD, IMF, NAM, OAU, OIC, OMVG, UN, WTO

Local and regional government
There is considerable variety in the forms of local government in Gambia. In the capital city there is an elected council and some areas have part-elected and part-appointed councils. In others authority rests with the tribal chiefs.

Political system
Gambia is an independent republic within the Commonwealth. The original constitution dates from independence in 1970 but was suspended following a coup d'etat in 1994. The new constitution came into effect in January 1997. It provides for an executive president popularly elected for a five-year renewable term and a National Assembly with 45 members directly elected by universal adult suffrage, through a simple majority voting system, plus four members nominated by the president. Government ministers are appointed by the president, but are responsible to both the president and the National Assembly.

Political parties
There are some nine political parties, the two most significant being the Alliance for Patriotic Reorientation and Construction (APRC) and the United Democratic Party (UDP). Both were formed in 1996, following the lifting of the ban on political parties. They both have left-of-centre orientations.

Between 1994 and 1996 political parties were banned, but prior to 1994 the People's Progressive Party (PPP) was the main party.

The PPP was formed in 1959 and in 1965 merged with the Democratic Congress Alliance and then, in 1968, with the Gambia Congress Party. In its various forms, it was the dominant party since the granting of independence. There were calls at one time to make Gambia a one-party state but these were resisted by Sir Dawda Jawara, who was the party's secretary general. The PPP had a moderate centrist orientation and was a strong supporter of the Commonwealth.

Political leaders since 1970
1970–94 Sir Dawda Karaba Jawara (PPP), 1994– Captain Yahya Jammeh (military/APRC)

Latest elections

In the September 1996 presidential election, Yahya Jammeh was elected with 55.8% of the popular vote. He defeated three rivals, including Ousainou Darboe (UDP), who won 35% of the vote.

In the January 1997 National Assembly elections, the APRC won 33 of the 45 elective seats, with 52% of the vote, and the UDP seven seats, with 34% of the vote. Two other parties also won seats.

Political history

Originally united with Sierra Leone, Gambia became a British Crown Colony in 1843 and an independent colony within the British Empire in 1888. Political parties were formed in the 1950s, internal self-government was granted in 1963, and full independence within the Commonwealth was achieved in 1965, with Dawda K Jawara (b. 1924), a British university-educated veterinary surgeon, as prime minister.

Gambia declared itself a republic in 1970, Jawara becoming president, thus replacing the British monarch as head of state. He was re-elected in 1972, 1977, 1982, and 1987, with Gambia standing out as one of Africa's few stable and functioning multiparty democracies during these decades. In 1981 an attempted coup against him was thwarted with the help of Senegalese troops and this strengthened the ties between the two countries to such an extent that plans were announced for their merger into a confederation of Senegambia. This was, however, abandoned in 1989.

In the April 1992 presidential and assembly elections Jawara won a fifth term and the People's Progressive Party (PPP) held its majority, but in July 1994, following a coup led by junior army officers, President Jawara fled the country and was given asylum in Senegal. Lieutenant Yahya Jammeh named himself president and established a Provisional Ruling Council of the Patriotic Armed Forces (PRCPF), promising to fight corruption and a return to real democracy. The international community condemned the coup and donor countries stopped their aid programs. The lucrative tourist industry was also badly damaged. Two attempted counter-coups, in November 1994 and January 1995, failed.

In 1996 a multiparty political system was established but (the now retired) Captain Jammeh was popularly elected president and his political party, the Alliance for Patriotic Reorientation and Construction (APRC) won the January 1997 parliamentary elections.

GHANA

The Republic of Ghana

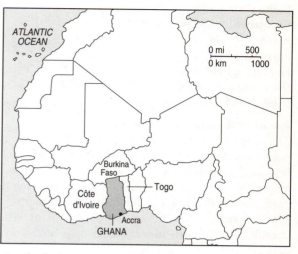

Capital: Accra

Social and economic data

Area: 238,540 sq km/92,101 sq miles
Population: 17,434,000[*]
Pop. density per sq km/sq mi: 73/189[*]
Urban population: 35%[**]
Literacy rate: 60%[**]
GDP: $6,720 million[*]; per-capita GDP: $385[*]
Government defense spending (% of GDP): 1.2%[**]
Currency: cedi
Economy type: low income
Labor force in agriculture: 59%[**]
[*] 1995.
[**] 1992.

Head of state and head of government

President Flight Lieutenant Jerry Rawlings, since 1981

Ethnic composition

There are over 75 ethnic groups in the country. The most significant are the Akan, in the south and west, comprising about 44% of the population. Then come the Mole-Dagbani, in the north, the Ewe, in the south, the Ga, in the region of the capital city, and the Fanti, in the coastal area. The official language is English.

Religions

About 30% of the population is Protestant, 25% Roman Catholic, 20% Sunni Muslim, and about 20% follow traditional, animist beliefs.

Political features

State type: emergent democratic
Date of state formation: 1957
Political structure: unitary
Executive: limited presidential
Assembly: one-chamber
Party structure: two-party
Human rights rating: *53%*
International affiliations: ACP, CW, ECOWAS, G-24, IAEA, IBRD, IMF, NAM, OAU, UN, WTO

Local and regional government

The country is divided into ten regions. They range in population from just over 1 million to just over 2 million and are each headed by a regional minister, answerable to the central government. They are subdivided into 58 districts, which, in turn, are further subdivided into 267 subdistricts. Tribal chiefs still wield considerable authority in some areas, however.

Political system

The April 1992 multiparty constitution for Ghana's Fourth Republic, which was approved in a referendum, provides for a president who is both head of state and head of government, elected by universal adult suffrage for a four-year term, renewable once only. There is a single-chamber 200-member House of Parliament, also elected by simple plurality for a four-year term. The president appoints a vice president and Council of Ministers (cabinet), with the approval of Parliament.

There is also a 25-member Council of State, consisting of presidential nominees and representatives of the regions, to advise the president and a 20-member National Security Council.

Political parties

The 1979 constitution was suspended in 1981 and all political parties were banned. When the ban was lifted in 1992, the National Democratic Congress (NDC) was formed by a coalition of pro-Rawlings groups. It has a centrist orientation. In June 1999 the National Reform Party (NRF) was formed as a breakaway from the NDC by members critical of President Rawlings.

Its main rival is the left-of-center New Patriotic Party (NPP), founded in 1992 by supporters of former prime minister, Kofi Busia. There are seven other parties.

Political leaders since 1970

1969–72 General Akwasi Afrifa (military-PP), 1972–78 Colonel Ignatius Acheampong (military), 1978–79 Frederick Akuffo (military), 1979 Flight Lieutenant Jerry Rawlings (military), 1979–81 Hilla Limann (PNP), 1981– Flight Lieutenant (retired) Jerry Rawlings (military/NDC)

Latest elections

Rawlings was re-elected in the December 1996 presidential elections, securing 57.2% of the popular vote and defeating two challengers. In the December 1996 parliamentary elections the NDC won 133 of the 200 seats, and the NPP, 60.

Political history

Ghana was formed by a merger of a British colony, the Gold Coast, which was established in 1874 after the Dutch were ousted, with a British administered United Nations Trust Territory, which was part of Togoland. The great interior kingdom of Ashanti was conquered in 1898 and a successful cocoa-based economy was established. The country achieved full independence in 1957, with Dr Kwame Nkrumah (1909–72), who had been prime minister of the Gold Coast since 1952, as president. Nkrumah embarked on a policy of what he called 'African socialism' and established an authoritarian regime. In 1964 he declared Ghana a one-party state, with the Convention People's Party (CPP), which he led, as the only legal political organization. He then dropped his original stance of international nonalignment and forged links with the Soviet Union and other communist countries.

His autocratic methods created many enemies and in 1966 he was deposed, while on a visit to China, and the leader of the coup, General Joseph Ankrah, established a National Liberation Council. It released many political prisoners and carried out a purge of CPP supporters. In 1969 Ankrah was replaced by General Akwasi Afrifa, who announced plans for a return to civilian government. A new constitution established an elected National Assembly and a nonexecutive presidency. A new grouping, the Progress Party (PP), won a big majority in the assembly and its leader, Kofi Busia, was appointed prime minister. The following year Edward Akufo-Addo became the civilian president.

However, the state of the economy worsened and, disenchanted with the civilian administration, the army seized power again in 1972. The constitution was suspended and all political institutions replaced by a National Redemption Council (NRC), under Colonel Ignatius Acheampong. In 1976 he, too, promised a return to civilian rule but critics doubted his sincerity and in 1978 he was replaced by his deputy, Frederick Akuffo, in a bloodless coup. Like his predecessors, Akuffo also announced a speedy return to civilian government but before elections could be held he, in turn, was deposed by junior officers, led by Flight Lieutenant Jerry Rawlings (b. 1947). Rawlings, a populist, stated his intentions to be to root out widespread corruption and promote 'moral reform'.

In 1979 civilian rule was restored again, but two years later Rawlings seized power again, complaining about the incompetence of the government. He established a Provisional National Defense Council (PNDC), with himself as chair, again suspending the constitution, dissolving Parliament, and banning political parties. Although the policies of the charismatic Rawlings were initially supported, his failure to revive the economy caused discontent and resulted in a number of popular demonstrations and attempted coups.

Calls for a return to multiparty politics grew and in April 1992 a constitution for a new Fourth Republic was approved by referendum. In September 1992 Rawlings resigned his airforce commission to contest the presidential elections as a civilian and in November he was re-elected, amid claims of fraud by his opponents. During 1994 more than 6,000 people were killed in ethnic clashes in the country's Northern Region, forcing the imposition, for six months, of a state of emergency. Rawlings was re-elected for a final term as president in December 1996 and his National Democratic Congress (NDC) won the concurrent legislative elections.

During 1999 the country received substantial loans from the IMF to support the government's economic reform programme.

GUINEA

The Republic of Guinea
La République de Guinée

Capital: Conakry

Social and economic data
Area: 245,860 sq km/94,927 sq miles
Population: 6,500,000[*]
Pop. density per sq km/sq mi: 26/68[*]
Urban population: 27%[**]
Literacy rate: 24%[**]
GDP: $3,595 million[*]; per-capita GDP: $555[*]
Government defense spending (% of GDP): 1.4%[**]
Currency: Guinea franc
Economy type: low income

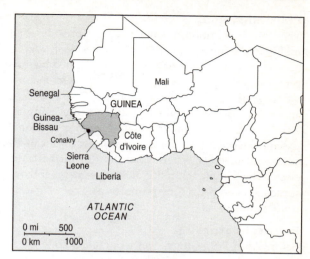

Labor force in agriculture: 78%[**]
[*] 1995.
[**] 1992.

Head of state (executive)
President General Lansana Conté, since 1984

Head of government
Prime Minister Lamine Sidime, since 1999

Ethnic composition
There are some 24 tribal ethnic groups, the main ones being the Malinke, the Peul, and the Soussou. Since independence the government has tried to unify the country by breaking down traditional ethnic barriers. The official language is French.

Religions
About 90% of the population is Sunni Muslim and there are animist and Roman Catholic minorities.

Political features
State type: emergent democratic
Date of state formation: 1958
Political structure: unitary
Executive: limited presidential
Assembly: one-chamber
Party structure: multiparty
Human rights rating: N/A
International affiliations: ACP, CEAO (observer), ECOWAS, IBRD, IMF, MRU, NAM, OAU, OIC, OMVG, UN

Local and regional government
The country is divided into eight provinces, each administered by an appointed governor. There are also elected provincial councils.

Political system

The 1991 constitution, amended in 1992, provides for a multiparty political system with a president who is head of state and head of government, elected by universal adult suffrage, through the second-ballot majoritarian system, for a five-year term. The president appoints a council of ministers and a prime minister. There is a 114-member single-chamber National Assembly elected for a four-year term by means of an additional member system. One third of the seats are elected by simple plurality in single-member constituencies and the rest by proportional representation from national lists.

Political parties

Before April 1992 Guinea was a one-party state. Since then more than 40 parties have been officially recognized and nine have secured parliamentary representation. The most significant are the Party of Unity and Progress (PUP), the Rally of the Guinean People (RPG), the Union of the New Republic (UNR), and the Party for Renewal and Progress (PRP).

The PUP is an authoritarian centrist grouping supporting President Conté. The opposition RPG, led by Alpha Condé, is centrist, while the UNR and PRP have left-of-center orientations.

Political leaders since 1970

1958–1984 Ahmed Sékou Touré (PDG), 1984– General Lansana Conté (military/PUP)

Latest elections

Lansana Conté was elected in the 14 December 1998 presidential elections with 54% of the popular vote, defeating four challengers. Mamadou Bah of the PRB was second, with 25% of the vote.

In the June 1995 National Assembly elections the results were as follows:

Guinea latest election results

Party	Seats
PUP	71
RPG	19
UNR	9
PRP	9
Other parties	6

Political history

Guinea was formerly the colony of French Guinea from 1890, and part of French West Africa. It became fully independent in 1958, after a referendum had rejected, unlike other parts of French West Africa, a proposal to remain a self-governing colony within the French Community. The first president was Ahmed Sékou Touré (1922–84), who made the Democratic Party of Guinea (PDG) the only legal political organization and embarked upon a policy of socialist revolution. There were unsuccessful attempts to overthrow him in 1961, 1965, 1967, and 1970 and, suspicious of conspiracies by foreign powers, he put his country for a time into virtual diplomatic isolation. By 1975, however, relations with most of his neighbors had returned to normal and in 1978 there was reconciliation with France.

Touré initially trod a path of rigid Marxism, ruthlessly crushing opposition to his policies, but gradually moved towards a mixed economy, private enterprise becoming legal in 1979. His domestic regime was, nevertheless, authoritarian and harsh. Externally, he positively sought closer relations with the Western powers, particularly France and the United States. He was re-elected unopposed in 1980 but in March 1984 died while undergoing heart surgery in the United States.

Before the normal machinery for electing his successor could be put into operation, the army staged a bloodless coup, suspending the constitution, outlawing the PDG, and setting up a Military Committee for National Recovery, with Major General Lansana Conté (b. 1945) at its head. He pledged to restore democracy and respect human rights, releasing hundreds of political prisoners and lifting restrictions on the press. Conté then implemented an IMF-approved economic reform program and made strenuous efforts to restore his country's international standing through a series of overseas visits. He was successful enough to persuade some 200,000 Guineans who had fled the country during the Touré regime to return. Nevertheless, he continued to head an unelected military regime.

Anti-government strikes and mass protests in 1991 persuaded the government to promise to allow at least one opposition party to function at some time in the future and in December 1991 a new constitution was announced. In April 1992 provision was made for multiparty politics, with a mixed military – civilian Transitional Committee for National Recovery being set up. A year later Conté won the open presidential election. The president's party, the Party of Unity and Progress (PUP), also won a convincing victory in the 1995 National Assembly elections. In June 1998 peace was agreed with dissident rebels.

Conté was re-elected in the December 1998 presidential election. However, the poll was marred by eve-of-poll riots, which claimed six lives and left a hundred injured. The government had banned street demonstrations, but had allowed Alpha Condé, leader of the opposition Rally of the Guinean People (RPG) to return from exile to participate in the election. Condé finished in third place, with 17% of the vote, and was arrested after the poll, whilst trying to cross the closed border to Cote d'Ivoire wearing a disguise. His detention provoked violent demonstrations on 21 December 1998 during which two people were killed. On 30 December 1998 Condé was charged with illegally employing mercenaries in an attempt to overthrow the government. In March 1999 Lamine Sidime, formerly the president of the Supreme Court, was appointed prime minister by President Conté, replacing Sidia Toure, who had occupied this post since its creation in July 1996.

GUINEA-BISSAU

Republic of Guinea-Bissau
República da Guiné-Bissau

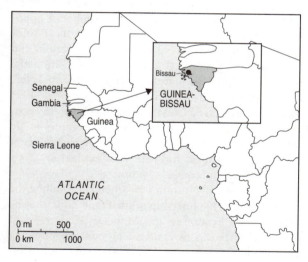

Capital: Bissau

Social and economic data
Area: 36,130 sq km/13,950 sq miles
Population: 1,050,000*
Pop. density per sq km/sq mi: 29/75*
Urban population: 20%**
Literacy rate: 37%**
GDP: $265 million*; per-capita GDP: $255*

Government defense spending (% of GDP): 3.0%*
Currency: Guinea peso
Economy type: low income
Labor force in agriculture: 82%**
* 1995.
** 1992.

Head of state (executive)
President (acting) Malan Bacai Sanhá, since 1999

Head of government
Prime Minister Francisca Fadul, since 1998

Ethnic composition
The majority of the population originate from Africa and comprise five main ethnic groups, the Balante, in the central region, the Fulani, in the north, the Malinke, in the north-central area, and the Mandyako and the Pepel near the coast. The official language is Portuguese.

Religions
About 60% of the population follows traditional, animist beliefs, about 35% is Sunni Muslim, and about 5% is Roman Catholic.

Political features
State type: military
Date of state formation: 1974
Political structure: unitary
Executive: military
Assembly: one-chamber
Party structure: multiparty*
Human rights rating: N/A
International affiliations: ACP, CILSS, ECOWAS, IBRD, IMF, NAM, OAU, OIC, OMVG, UN, WTO

* Though dominated by one party.

Local and regional government
The country is divided into eight regions and one autonomous section, based on the capital, Bissau. All have elected councils.

Political system
Until 1991 Guinea-Bissau was a one-party state, the 1984 constitution (amended in 1991 and 1996) describing the African Party for the Independence of Portuguese Guinea and Cape Verde (PAIGC) as 'the leading force in society and in the nation' and the state as an 'anti-colonialist and anti-imperialist republic'. Although Cape Verde chose not to be united with Guinea-Bissau, preferring independence, the title of the original party which served the two countries has been retained. The revised constitution provides for a National People's Assembly elected in multimember constituencies, by the limited

vote system, and a president, who is an executive head of state, directly elected by the second-ballot majoritarian system. The Assembly is elected for four years and the president for five years. The president, who is also commander in chief of the armed forces, appoints a prime minister and other ministers. There was a military coup in May 1999.

Political parties
The PAIGC was the only legally permitted party until 1991, when the Supreme Court ended 17 years of one-party rule by legalizing other groups. Now 13 other parties operate, the most significant being the Guinea-Bissau Resistance Party–Bafata Movement (RGB-MB) and the Party for Social Renovation (PRS).

The PAIGC was formed in 1956 and was originally the ruling party for both Guinea-Bissau and Cape Verde. It has a nationalistic-socialist orientation and has been organized on top-down Leninist lines.

The RGB-MB was founded in 1986 in Lisbon. It has a centrist orientation. The PRS was formed in 1992. It has a left-of-center orientation.

Political leaders since 1970
1973–80 Luiz Cabral (PAIGC), 1980–99 Brigadier General João Bernardo 'Niño (PAIGC) Vieira, 1999– Malan Bacai Sanhá (independent/military).

Latest elections
João Vieira narrowly won the July–August 1994 presidential election, in the second round, with 52% of the vote defeating Kumba Isla of the PRS in the run-off round.

In the July 1994 assembly elections, the PAIGC won a clear majority, with 62 of the 100 seats and 46% of the vote. The RGB-MB won 19% of the vote and 19 seats and the PRS, 10% and 12 seats.

Political history
Guinea-Bissau, as part of the Portuguese empire, was governed jointly with Cape Verde until 1879, when it became a separate colony, with the name Portuguese Guinea. Agitation for independence intensified after World War II and this resulted in the formation, in 1956, of the African Party for the Independence of Portuguese Guinea and Cape Verde (PAIGC). In the face of Portugal's refusal to grant independence, fighting broke out in 1961 and by 1972 the PAIGC claimed to be in control of two-thirds of the country. The following year the 'liberated areas' were declared independent and in 1973 a National People's Assembly was set up and Luiz Cabral appointed president of a State

Council. Some 40,000 Portuguese troops were used to try to put down the uprising, suffering heavy losses. However, before a clear outcome was reached, a sudden coup in mainland Portugal proved a sufficient distraction to bring the fighting to an end and the PAIGC negotiated independence with the new government in Lisbon. In 1974 Portugal formally acknowledged Guinea-Bissau as a sovereign nation.

The PAIGC set about laying the foundations for a socialist state which was intended to include Cape Verde, but in November 1980, four days before approval of the constitution, the inhabitants of Cape Verde, feeling that Guinea-Bissau was being given preferential treatment in the constitutional arrangements, decided to withdraw. Cabral was deposed in a coup and Colonel João Vieira (b. 1939) became chair of a Council of Revolution. At its 1981 Congress, the PAIGC decided to retain its name, despite Cape Verde's withdrawal, and its position was confirmed as the only legal party, with Vieira, a party member since 1960, as its secretary general. Normal relations between Guinea-Bissau and Cape Verde were restored in 1982. Constitutional changes in 1984 created an executive presidency.

In January 1991, in response to public pressure, the PAIGC formally approved the introduction of 'integral multi-partyism' and later that year a number of opposition parties were legalized. In July 1994 the PAIGC obtained a clear majority in the Assembly elections and in the following month Brigadier General Vieira had a narrow victory in the first multiparty presidential election, attracting 52% of the vote. In October 1994 Manuel Saturnino da Costa, the hardline secretary general of the PAIGC, was appointed prime minister. He inherited an economy which, crippled by high levels of external indebtedness and with inflation at 100%, was heavily reliant on foreign economic aid.

In 1996 the constitution was amended to allow the country to seek membership of the Franc Zone and the West African Economic and Monetary Union. From June 1998 there was civil and military unrest, following an attempt by General Ansumane Mane to topple president Vieira. The army rebellion was defeated, after President Vieira received military support from Senegal and Guinea. But thousands fled from the capital and there was renewed fighting in October 1998. Mane was supported by Muslim separatists, based in the north.

In all, half the country's population of one million was displaced by the fighting. In November 1998 a Portuguese-brokered peace agreement was signed, in Abuja, Nigeria, by the government and the rebel forces loyal to Mane to end the five-month-long conflict. It was agreed that troops from Guinea and Senegal would be withdrawn in January 1999, and replaced by 712 troops from the Economic Community of West African States (ECOWAS) Monitoring Group (ECOMOG), comprising troops from Togo, Benin, the Gambia, and Niger; there would be a ceasefire; and a government of national unity would be established, to prepare for elections in November 1999. It was agreed, in December 1999, by a joint commission established under the Abuja Accord, that Carlos Correia would be replaced as prime minister by Francisco Fadul, an adviser to General Mane, and, in February 1999, a government of national unity was formed. However, in May 1999 fighting resumed and troops loyal to Mane carried out a military coup, toppling Vieira. On 14 May 1999, Malan Bacai Sanhá, the moderate Speaker of the National Assembly, was appointed acting president. In June 1999 ECOWAS troops withdrew.

KENYA

Republic of Kenya
Jamhuri ya Kenya

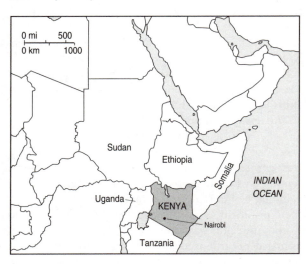

Capital: Nairobi

Social and economic data
Area: 580,646 sq km/223,027 sq miles
Population: 29,292,000[*]
Pop. density per sq km/sq mi: 50/131[*]
Urban population: 25%[**]

Literacy rate: 69%[**]
GDP: $7,585 million[*]; per-capita GDP: $260[*]
Government defense spending (% of GDP): 2.3%[*]
Currency: Kenya shilling
Economy type: low income
Labor force in agriculture: 81%[**]
[*] 1995.
[**] 1992.

Head of state and head of government
President Daniel arap Moi, since 1978

Ethnic composition
The main ethnic groups are the Kikuyu, about 21%, the Luhya, 14%, the Luo, 13%, the Kalenjin, 11%, the Kamba, 11%, the Kisii, 6%, and the Meru, 5%. The official language is Swahili.

Religions
The adherence to religions varies from tribe to tribe and area to area. About 25% of the population is Roman Catholic, 24% belong to Independent African Churches, 18% are Protestant, 6% are Sunni Muslim, chiefly near the coast and around Nairobi, and a fifth of the populace follows traditional, animist beliefs.

Political features
State type: emergent democratic
Date of state formation: 1963
Political structure: unitary
Executive: limited presidential
Assembly: one-chamber
Party structure: multiparty[*]
Human rights rating: 46%
International affiliations: ACP, COMESA, CW, IAEA, IBRD, IGADD, IMF, IWC, NAM, OAU, UN, WTO

[*] Though dominated by one party.

Local and regional government
Regional and local governments display features from the days of British colonial rule. The country is divided into eight provinces, including the city of Nairobi, which are further subdivided into 40 districts. The provinces are administered by provincial commissioners and the districts by district commissioners. Below the commissioner level there are municipal councils, town councils, county councils, urban councils, and area councils.

Political system
Kenya became a republic, within the Commonwealth, in 1964 and the constitution dates from independence in 1963. It was amended in 1964, 1969, 1982, 1988, 1991, 1992, and 1997. It provides for a president,

elected by universal adult suffrage for a five-year term, and a single-chamber National Assembly, serving a similar term.

A 1992 amendment requires a presidential candidate to win not only a majority of the national votes but to be endorsed by at least 25% of voters in at least five of the country's eight provinces. Critics of the amendment alleged that it was introduced to assist President Moi in the 1992 elections.

The Assembly has 224 members, 210 elected by universal adult suffrage, through a simple plurality voting system, 12 nominated by the president and the attorney general and speaker as *ex officio* members. From 1969 to 1982 Kenya was a one-party state in fact and then became one in law. In December 1991 a constitutional amendment, allowing multiparty politics, became effective. A further amendement, in September 1997, granted all political parties equal access to the media and ended detention without trial. The vice president and Cabinet of Ministers are appointed by the president, who must be at least 35 years of age.

Political parties

Until 1991 the only legitimate party was the Kenya African National Union (KANU). Since 1992 opposition parties have been formed, the most significant being the Forum for the Restoration of Democracy-Asili (FORD-Asili), the Forum for the Restoration of Democracy-Kenya (FORD-Kenya), the Democratic Party (DP), the National Development Party (NDP), and the Social Democratic Party (SDP).

The predecessor to KANU was the Kenya African Union (KAU), formed in 1944, mainly by members of the Kikuyu tribe. Jomo Kenyatta became its leader in 1947 and then KAU was proscribed in 1952, following the Mau Mau violence and Kenyatta's imprisonment. On his release, in 1961, he set about merging KAU with its rival, the Kenya African Democratic Union (KADU). KANU was subsequently formed, with Kenyatta as its leader. Its orientation is now nationalistic and centrist, and very much a political vehicle for the president.

FORD-Asili and FORD-Kenya were both formed in 1992 and have left-of-center Luo and Luhya orientations.

The DP was founded a year earlier in anticipation of the restoration of multiparty politics. It has a centrist orientation and is Kikuyu dominated. The NDP was formed in 1994 and the SPP in 1992. They both have left-of-center orientations.

In May 1995 a new center-left party, Safina, was formed by Richard Leakey (b. 1944), a renowned palaeoanthropologist. From November 1995 it formed the hub of an anti-KANU alliance, incorporating the DP, FORD-Asili, and FORD-Kenya.

Political leaders since 1970

1964–78 Jomo Kenyatta (KANU), 1978– Daniel arap Moi (KANU)

Latest elections

The presidential election of 29 December 1997 was won by Daniel arap Moi, who secured 40.6% of the vote to win a fifth and final term. His nearest rival, Mwai Kibaki (DP), won 31.5% of the vote. In the concurrent assembly elections KANU won 114 seats, the DP, 41, the NDP, 22, FORD-Kenya, 18, the SDP, 16, and Safina, 5. Again, there were accusations of pro-government intimidation during the poll.

Political history

An East African Protectorate was forcibly formed in 1895 by the British, which became the colony of Kenya in 1920. A white planting community settled in highland areas, displacing many Kikuyu, and during the 1920s a black protest movement developed. The country came close to civil war, as pronationalist groups carried out a campaign of violence. The Kenya African Union (KAU) was founded in 1944 and in 1947 Jomo Kenyatta (1894–1978), a member of Kenya's largest tribe, the Kikuyu, became its president. Three years later a secret society of young Kikuyu militants was formed, called Mau Mau, which had the same aims as KAU but sought to achieve them by violent means. Although Kenyatta disassociated himself from the Mau Mau risings of 1952–56, he was not trusted by the British authorities and was imprisoned in 1953.

The terrorist campaign had largely finished by 1956 and the state of emergency which had been imposed was lifted and Kenyatta released in 1961. The country was granted internal self-government in 1963 and Kenyatta, who had become leader of the Kenya African National Union (KANU), became prime minister and then president after full independence, within the Commonwealth, was obtained in 1964. He continued as president until his death in 1978, during which time his country achieved considerable stability and he became a widely respected world leader.

He was succeeded by the vice president, Daniel arap Moi (b. 1924), who built on the achievements of his predecessor, launching an impressive four-year procapitalist development plan. An attempted coup by junior airforce officers in 1982 was foiled and resulted, for a while, in political detentions and press censorship. The airforce and Nairobi University were also temporarily dissolved. In the same year the National Assembly declared Kenya a one-party state. President Moi was re-elected in 1983 and 1988 and his position seemed secure, but as his rule became increasingly autocratic, demands for multiparty politics grew. Moi resisted these calls until 1991, when, influenced by pressure exerted by foreign aid donors, a constitutional amendment allowed for this.

Nevertheless, his critics have also argued that he was not fully committed to pluralist politics. A constitutional amendment in 1992, which would seem to assist him in presidential elections, tended to support this view and there have been regular complaints about the fairness of the conduct of elections. President Moi and KANU were successful in the 1992 multiparty elections, soon after which FORD-Asili and FORD-Kenya agreed to form a united front to fight future elections. In 1993 a temporary suspension of parliament by the president provoked unrest in Nairobi and there were tribal clashes in the Rift Valley region. In 1994 the country was afflicted by a terrible drought, during which almost a fifth of the population was threatened by famine. In July 1995 it was claimed by the US-based Human Rights Watch Africa that more than 1,500 Kenyans had died as a result of political violence since 1991. The regime of President Moi has continually been criticized internally and internationally for its political and human rights abuses. In 1997 the president promised greater democracy but has so far failed to deliver. The results of the latest presidential and assembly elections in 1997 were again disputed by opposition parties and during 1998 there were fears of an outbreak of civil war following communal violence in central regions. Corruption and financial mismanagement led to a deteriorating economic situation.

LESOTHO

The Kingdom of Lesotho

Capital: Maseru

Social and economic data
Area: 30,350 sq km/11,718 sq miles
Population: 1,996,000[*]
Pop. density per sq km/sq mi: 66/170[*]
Urban population: 21%[**]
Literacy rate: 59%[**]
GDP: $1,520 million[*]; per-capita GDP: $765[*]

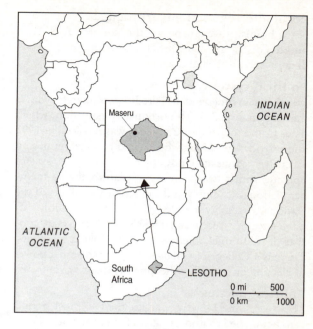

Government defense spending (% of GDP): 5.5%[**]
Currency: loti
Economy type: low income
Labor force in agriculture: 23%[**]
[*] 1995.
[**] 1992.

Head of state
King Letsie III, since 1996

Head of government
Prime Minister Bethuel Pakalitha Mosisili, since 1998

Ethnic composition
Almost the entire population are Bantus, of Southern Sotho, or Basotho, stock. The official language is English.

Religions
About 45% of the population is Roman Catholic and 48% Protestant (Anglican and Lesotho Evangelical).

Political features
State type: emergent democratic
Date of state formation: 1966
Political structure: unitary
Executive: parliamentary
Assembly: two-chamber
Party structure: multiparty[*]
Human rights rating: N/A
International affiliations: ACP, COMESA, CW, IBRD, IMF, NAM, OAU, SADC, UN, WTO

[*] Though dominated by one party.

Local and regional government

For administrative purposes, the country is divided into ten districts. Each district has an appointed coordinator and an elected council.

Political system

Lesotho is an independent hereditary monarchy within the Commonwealth. The original constitution, which dates from independence in 1966, was replaced in 1993 and provides for a king who is head of state but has no executive or legislative powers. A parliamentary system operates with a two-chamber legislature, the 80-member National Assembly and the Senate. Members of the National Assembly are elected by universal adult suffrage for a five-year term. The 33-member Senate consists of traditional chiefs and 11 nominated members. There is a College of Chiefs with the traditional power of electing or removing the king by majority vote.

Political parties

There are some 14 active parties, the two most significant being the Lesotho Congress for Democracy (LCD) and the Basotho National Party (BNP).

The LCD was formed in 1997 by members of the Basotho Congress Party (BCP) which had been the major force in the country's politics. It has a left-of-center orientation.

The BNP was formed in 1958 by Chief Leabua Jonathan and soon became his personal political machine. It has a right-of-center orientation. In 1999, Justin Lekhanya, the former military ruler, became the BNP's secretary-general.

Political leaders since 1970

1970–86 Chief Leabua Jonathan (BNP), 1986–90 General Justin Lekhanya (military), 1990–93 Colonel Elias Ramaema (military), 1993–98 Dr Ntsu Mokhehle (BCP), 1998– Bethuel Pakalitha Mosisili (LCD)

Latest elections

In the May 1998 general election the LCD, with 60% of the vote, secured a landslide victory, winning 78 of the 80 National Assembly seats. The BNP won 25% of the vote and one seat. However, there were allegations of electoral fraud, which led to popular protests and an army mutiny.

Political history

Lesotho, founded as a state entity in the 1820s by the Sotho leader, Moshoeshoe I (c. 1790–1870), was formerly called Basutoland. As such, it became a British dependency in 1868 and then a colony. It was given internal self-government in 1965, with the paramount chief of the Basotho people since 1960, the Oxford-educated Moshoeshoe II (b. 1938), as king. It achieved full independence, as Lesotho, in 1966. The Basotho National Party (BNP), a conservative group favoring limited cooperation with South Africa, remained in power from independence until 1986. Its leader, Chief Leabua Jonathan, became prime minister in 1966 and after 1970, when the powers of the king were severely curtailed and he was forced into an eight-month exile in the Netherlands, the country was effectively under the prime minister's control.

From 1975 an organization called the Lesotho Liberation Army (LLA) carried out a number of attacks on BNP members, with the support, it was alleged, of the South African government. The South Africans denied complicity but, at the same time, pointed out that Lesotho allowed the then banned South African nationalist movement, the African National Congress (ANC), to use it as a base. Economically, Lesotho was dependent on South Africa but openly rejected the policy of apartheid. It came under pressure from Pretoria to sign a nonaggression pact, similar to the Nkomati Accord between South Africa and Mozambique, but Jonathan's government consistently refused to do so.

In January 1986 South Africa imposed a border blockade, cutting off food and fuel supplies to Lesotho, and a few weeks later the government of Chief Jonathan was ousted and replaced in a coup led by General Justin Lekhanya. He announced that all executive and legislative powers would be placed in the hands of the king, ruling through a Military Council, chaired by General Lekhanya, and a Council of Ministers. A week after the coup about 60 ANC members were deported to Zambia and on the same day the South African blockade was lifted.

In February 1990 General Lekhanya was removed from office and replaced by Colonel Elias Ramaema. At the same time King Moshoeshoe II was deposed and replaced by his son, Letsie III (b. 1963). King Moshoeshoe went into exile. Soon after taking over the reins of government Ramaema announced that political parties would be allowed to operate again and King Moshoeshoe was allowed to return in July 1992, in the role of a tribal chief rather than monarch.

In early 1993 Colonel Ramaema kept his promise, relinquishing military control, and multiparty elections were held. The Basotho Congress Party (BCP) won all the assembly seats and its leader, Dr Ntsu Mokhehle, became prime minister. In January 1994 fighting broke out between rival army factions, a potential civil war being averted by prompt action by the Organization of African Unity (OAU).

In August 1994 King Letsie III dissolved the Assembly, dismissed the prime minister and said he would return the throne to his father, Moshoeshoe II. The leaders of South Africa, Zimbabwe, and Botswana intervened, giving King Letsie a deadline of 1 September for reinstating the elected government of Dr Ntsu Mokhehle and on 14 September 1994 this was done. In January 1995 King Letsie abdicated and King Moshoeshoe returned to the throne as a nonexecutive monarch. A year later, he was killed in a car crash and his son succeeded him as Letsie III.

In June 1997 there was a leadership dispute within the BCP and Dr Mokhehle announced the formation of a new party, the Lesotho Congress for Democracy (LCD), taking many of the BCP members with him. Mokhehle died in January 1999.

The May 1998 general election was convincingly won by the new LCD. However, there were charges of electoral fraud, fuelling widespread unrest. In September 1998 South African Development Community (SADC) troops entered the country, allegedly to prevent an antigovernment coup by mutinous elements within the Lesotho Defence Force, (LDF). The action was criticized by international observers.

In May 1999 the SADC forces withdrew from Lesotho, although a number of SADC advisers remained to assist with the training of the LDF.

LIBERIA

The Republic of Liberia

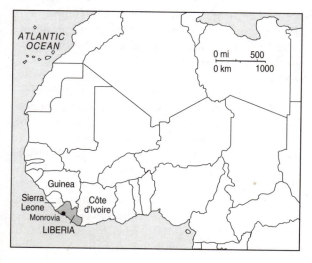

Capital: Monrovia

Social and economic data
Area: 111,370 sq km/43,000 sq miles
Population: 2,700 ,000[*]
Pop. density per sq km/sq mi: 24/63[*]
Urban population: 47%[**]
Literacy rate: 40%[**]
GDP: $1,800 million[*]; per-capita GDP: $670[*]
Government defense spending (% of GDP): 3.2%[*]
Currency: Liberian dollar
Economy type: low income
Labor force in agriculture: 74%[**]
[*] 1995.
[**] 1992.

Head of state and head of government
President Charles Ghankay Taylor, since 1997

Ethnic composition
Ninety-five per cent of the population are members of indigenous tribes, which include the Kpelle, the Bassa, the Gio, the Kru, the Grebo, the Mano, the Krahn, the Gola, the Gbandi, the Loma, the Kissi, the Vai, and the Bella. The other 5% are descended from slaves repatriated from the United States. The official language is English.

Religions
Liberia is officially a Christian state but all religions are tolerated and traditional, animist practices widely followed. The main Christian churches are Lutheran, Anglican, Roman Catholic, Baptist, and United Methodist, to which a quarter of the population belongs. A similar proportion, 24%, follows Sunni Islam.

Political features
State type: emergent democratic
Date of state formation: 1847
Political structure: unitary
Executive: limited presidential
Assembly: two-chamber
Party structure: multiparty
Human rights rating: N/A
International affiliations: ACP, ECOWAS, IAEA, IBRD, IMF, MRU, NAM, OAU, UN

Local and regional government
The country is divided into nine counties, each administered by an appointed superintendent. In addition, there are six territories and the capital district of Monrovia.

Political system

From 1980 to 1984 Liberia was under the military rule of a People's Redemption Council (PRC). In 1984 the PRC was dissolved and its functions taken over by an Interim National Assembly appointed by the president, pending a new constitution which came into effect in 1986. This provided for a two-chamber National Assembly, consisting of a Senate with 26 members elected for a nine-year term in two-seat constituencies, and a House of Representatives of 64, elected by universal adult suffrage, through a simple plurality voting system, for a six-year term. The president was to be elected in the same way for a similar term. A civil war began in 1990 which threw the country into chaos before an interim government was established in 1991. This was replaced by a series of transitional administrations until, after elections in July 1997, a settled government was established. The president appoints a cabinet, whose members require confirmation from the Senate.

Political parties

From the end of January 1997, the armed factions ceased to operate as military organizations and several of them were reconstructed as political parties. Thirteen of them contested the 1997 elections. The dominant force is the National Patriotic Party (NPP); the other two significant groupings are the Unity Party (UP) and the All Liberian Coalition Party (ALCOP). The NPP, led by Charles Taylor, was formed in 1997 by members of the armed faction, the National Patriotic Front of Liberia (NPFL), the UP was formed in 1984, and the ALCOP in 1997, again by a former armed group, the United Liberation Movement for Democracy. They all have left-of-center orientations.

Political leaders since 1970

1944–71 William Tubman (TWP), 1971–80 William Tolbert (TWP), 1980–90 Samuel Kenyon Doe (NDPL), 1990–94 Amos Sawyer (NPFL), 1994–95 David Kpormakor (IGNU), 1995–96 Wilton Sankawulo (transitional collective government), 1996–97 Ruth Perry (interim Council of State), 1997– Charles Ghankay Taylor (NPP)

Latest elections

In July 1997 Charles Taylor (NPP) was elected president with 75.3% of the vote. He defeated 12 challengers. In concurrent elections the NPP won clear majorities in both the House and the Senate. It won 49 of the 64 House seats and 21 of the 26 Senate seats. The UP won seven and three seats in the respective chambers and the ALCOP, three and two.

Political history

Liberia was founded in 1821 by the American Colonization Society as a settlement for black slaves from the southern United States. It became an independent republic in 1847 and between 1878 and 1980 politics were dominated by the True Whig Party, which provided all the country's presidents. William Tubman (1895–1971), a descendant of US slaves, was president from 1944 until his death in 1971 and was succeeded by the vice president, William R Tolbert, who was reelected in 1975.

In 1980 Tolbert was assassinated in a military coup led by Master Sergeant Samuel Doe (b. 1950), who suspended the constitution, banned all political parties, and ruled through an appointed People's Redemption Council (PRC). The first Liberian of local ancestry to rule the nation, he proceeded to stamp out corruption in the public service, encountering considerable opposition and making enemies who were later to threaten his position.

A new draft constitution, providing for an elected two-chamber National Assembly and an elected president, was approved by the PRC in 1983 and by national referendum the following year. Political parties were allowed to function again, provided they registered with a new body, the Special Electoral Commission (SECOM). In August 1984 Doe founded the National Democratic Party of Liberia (NDPL) and announced that he proposed to stand for the presidency.

By early 1985, 11 political parties had been formed but only five eventually registered in time for the elections. Doe's party won clear majorities in both chambers of the Assembly, although there were complaints of election fraud, and Doe himself was elected president.

By 1990 there was considerable opposition to Doe which developed into a civil war, the government being challenged by Charles Taylor, a former state employee who had been charged with theft, and Prince Yormie Johnson, a friend of Taylor who had broken away to form a splinter group. In the face of international efforts to find a solution, the war continued and in September 1990 Doe was captured and killed. Taylor's political wing, the National Patriotic Front of Liberia (NPFL), set up an interim government, headed by Amos Sawyer, an academic lawyer. Despite the installation of this government, and the signing of a peace agreement, in October 1991, rebel forces outside the mainstream groups continued to fight. A predominantly Nigerian West African military force, known as ECOMOG, was sent in to the country to attempt to impose some order in a war that had claimed 150,000 lives and rendered 2 million homeless.

In August 1993 a collective presidency was agreed but this soon collapsed and was replaced by a transitional government, which was later disputed by the military leaders. Another peace agreement, between the NPFL, Ulimo, and the Armed Forces of Liberia, led by Hezekiah Bowen, was signed in September 1994 but fighting continued. In January and February 1995 Ghanaian-backed peace moves also foundered but in August 1995 an agreement, brokered by the Ghanaian president, Flight Lieutenant Jerry Rawlings, was accepted by Charles Taylor and the leaders of the other main military factions, George Boli and Alhaji Kromah. In September 1995 a collective executive, consisting of the three warlords and chaired by the academic, Wilton Sankawulo, was established as an interim administration until elections in 1996. However, fighting between the factions continued until an ECONAS-brokered peace plan was agreed in August 1996. An interim Council of State was set up, chaired by the former senator, Ruth Perry, and in July 1997 presidential and assembly elections were held, Charles Taylor and his supporters being successful in both. On the eve of the poll, Taylor made a national apology for the war, but was elected as he was considered the most likely leader to unite the country.

In September 1998 a plot to overthrow the government was uncovered and thwarted. The former warlords, Roosevelt Johnson and Alhaji Kromah, were suspected as being behind the plot. In January 1999 the Nigerian-led ECOMOG monitoring force was withdrawn from Liberia in recognition of the improvement in the security situation.

MADAGASCAR

The Democratic Republic of Madagascar
Repoblika Demokratika n'i Madagaskar

Capital: Antananarivo (Tananarive)

Social and economic data
Area: 587,041 sq km/226,658 sq miles
Population: 14,303,000 [*]
Pop. density per sq km/sq mi: 24/63[*]
Urban population: 25%[**]

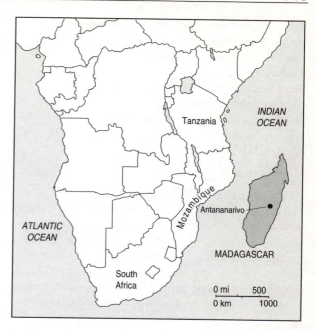

Literacy rate: 53%[**]
GDP: $3,180 million[*]; per-capita GDP: $225[*]
Government defense spending (% of GDP): 1.1%[*]
Currency: Malgasy franc
Economy type: low income
Labor force in agriculture: 81%[**]
[*] 1995.
[**] 1992.

Head of state (executive)
President Didier Ratsiraka, since 1996

Head of government
Prime Minister Tantely Andrianarivo, since 1998

Ethnic composition
There are 18 main Malagasy tribes of Malaysian-Polynesian origin. There are also minorities of French, Chinese, Indians, Pakistanis, and Comorans. Despite a common ethnic heritage, the inhabitants of the highlands, mainly the Merinas, have frequently found themselves in conflict with the coastal tribes, known as the *côtiers*. The official languages are Malagasy and French.

Religions
About 47% of the population follows traditional, animist beliefs and about 50% is Christian, of which about half is Roman Catholic and half Protestant. There is also a Muslim minority.

Political features
State type: emergent democratic

Date of state formation: 1960
Political structure: unitary*
Executive: limited presidential
Assembly: two-chamber
Party structure: multiparty
Human rights rating: N/A
International affiliations: ACP, COMESA, Francophone, IAEA, IBRD, ICC, ICFTU, IMF, IOC, NAM, OAU, UN, WTO

* In transition to federal.

Local and regional government

The country is divided into six provinces, with a three-tiered substructure, based on traditional village assemblies, or *fokonolona*. It is intended to set up a federal system, based around six autonomous provinces with their own legislative councils and executive governors. A constitutional amendment on these lines was approved in March 1998 by 51% of votes in a national referendum.

Political system

The 1992 constitution provides for an executive president, who is head of state, and a two-chamber assembly, a 150-member National Assembly and a Senate. Since 1995 the president has worked with a prime minister who is appointed by the president from candidates nominated by National Assembly parties. However, constitutional amendments approved in 1998 have enhanced presidential powers, including the right to dissolve the National Assembly and remove the latter's power of impeachment. The president and National Assembly are elected by universal adult suffrage for five- and four-year terms respectively. The president is elected by the two-ballot majoritarian system, while the National Assembly comprises 82 members elected in single-member constituencies and 68 in two-member constituencies.

One-third of the Senate is appointed by the president and two-thirds selected by an electoral college of local and regional representatives.

Political parties

Until 1990 the only permitted political movement was the National Front for the Defense of the Malagasy Socialist Revolution (FNDR). Its main opposition was the Comité des Forces Vives.

The FNDR was formed in 1976 around the Advance Guard of the Malagasy Revolution (AREMA) which Didier Ratsiraka established as the nucleus of a single national party with a left-of-center orientation.

The Comité des Forces Vives was also a coalition of left-of-center groups.

There are now more than 100 political groupings, the most significant being AREMA, the Movement for the Progress of Madagascar (MFM), Leader Fanilo (Torch), and Asa Vita/Fampitsara (AVI). The MFM was formed in 1972 and has a liberal, free-market orientation. Leader Fanilo was formed in 1993 as a party of 'non-politicians' opposed President Zafy. The AVI was formed in 1997 to promote human rights. It has a left-of-center orientation. AREMA adopted the name Association for Madagascar's Renaissance in 1997.

Political leaders since 1970

1960–72 Philibert Tsiranana (PSD), 1972–75 General Gabriel Ramanantsoa (military), 1975–93 Lieutenant Commander Didier Ratsiraka (AREMA), 1993–96 Albert Zafy (Comité des Forces Vives), 1997– Didier Ratsiraka (AREMA)

Latest elections

The November–December 1996 presidential election was won by the former president, Didier Ratsiraka, with 50% of the vote in the second ballot. He narrowly defeated the recently ousted Albert Zafy, who won 49.3% of the run-off vote. Turnout was 50%, but Zafy made accusations of poll-rigging.

The most recent National Assembly elections, held on 17 May 1998, were won by President Ratsiraka's AREMA, which secured 63 of the 150 seats. Leader Fanilo won 16 seats and the AVI 14 seats. Six other parties secured representation, while independents won 325 seats. Turnout was below 50%.

Political history

Formerly a French colony, forcibly annexed in 1896, Madagascar became an autonomous state within the French community in 1958. This followed a nationalist uprising in 1947–48 that was suppressed with heavy loss of life. It achieved full independence, as a republic, in 1960. The country's history since independence has been greatly influenced by the competing interests of Madagascar's two main ethnic groups, the coastal tribes, known as the *côtiers*, and the highland people, represented by the Merina.

The first president of the republic was Philibert Tsiranana, leader of the Social Democratic Party (PSD), which identified itself with the coastal-based *côtiers*. In 1972 the army, representing the Merina, took control of the government and pursued a more nationalistic line than Tsiranana. This caused resentment among the *côtiers* and, with rising unemployment, led to a government crisis in 1975 which resulted in the imposition of martial law under a National Military Directorate and the banning of all political parties.

Later that year a new, socialist constitution was approved and Lieutenant Commander Didier Ratsiraka (b. 1936), a *côtier*, was elected president of the Democratic Republic of Madagascar. Political parties were allowed to operate again and in 1976 the Front-Line Revolutionary Organization (AREMA) was formed by Ratsiraka, as the nucleus of a single party for the state. By 1977 all political activity was concentrated in the leftwing National Front for the Defense of the Malagasy Socialist Revolution (FNDR) and all the candidates for the National People's Assembly were FNDR nominees. In 1977 the National Movement for the Independence of Madagascar (MONIMA), a radical socialist party, withdrew from the FNDR and was declared illegal. MONIMA's leader, Monja Jaona, unsuccessfully challenged Ratsiraka for the presidency.

Despite social and political discontent, particularly among the Merinas, Ratsiraka was re-elected and AREMA marginally increased its Assembly seat total in the 1989 elections.

There were coup attempts against the government in 1990 and then in October 1991, after widespread civil unrest following the army's firing into a crowd during an August 1991 general strike, Ratsiraka was forced to surrender some of his powers and create a new unity government, which included opposition members. A referendum, in August 1992, gave clear support for a return to multiparty politics and a revised constitution was introduced, transferring some of the president's powers to a prime minister, as head of government. The coalition opposed to Ratsiraka, the Comité des Forces Vives, won both the February 1993 presidential and June 1993 Assembly elections, its leader Albert Zafy, becoming president. He appointed Francisque Ravony prime minister and this was confirmed by the National Assembly. In 1995 Zafy and Ravony, disagreed over the issue of who had the authority to appoint the prime minister, the president or the Assembly. In a referendum held in September 1995 voters decided in favor of the president and a month later Ravony was replaced by Emmanuel Rakotovahiny (UNOD), who was an ally of Rafy.

During 1996 there were repeated clashes between President Zafy and the National Assembly, resulting in his impeachment and removal from office In subsequent elections, in September 1996, the former president, Didier Ratsiraka, returned to office. His AREMA party polled strongly in parliamentary elections in May 1998, while a constitutional referendum, approved in

March 1998, increased the president's powers and proposed the creation of a federal state.

MALAWI

The Republic of Malawi
D Ziko La Malawi

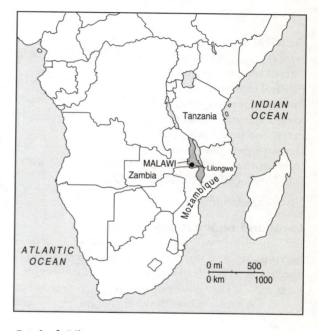

Capital: Lilongwe

Social and economic data
Area: 118,480 sq km/45,745 sq miles
Population: 9,461,000[*]
Pop. density per sq km/sq mi: 80/207[*]
Urban population: 42%[**]
Literacy rate: 48%[**]
GDP: $1,625 million[*]; per-capita GDP: $175[*]
Government defense spending (% of GDP): 1.2%[*]
Currency: Malawi kwacha
Economy type: low income
Labor force in agriculture: 82%[**]
[*] 1995.
[**] 1992.

Head of state and head of government
President Bakili Muluzi, since 1994

Ethnic composition
Almost all the people are indigenous Africans but divided ethnically into numerous tribes, the main ones

being the Chewa, the Nyanja, the Tumbuka, the Yao, the Lomwe, the Sena, the Tonga, and the Ngoni. There are also Asian and European minorities. The official languages are English and Chichewa.

Religions

About 30% of the population is Protestant and 25% Roman Catholic. The remainder is mostly Sunni Muslim (16%) or follows traditional, animist beliefs (20%).

Political features

State type: emergent democratic
Date of state formation: 1964
Political structure: unitary
Executive: limited presidential
Assembly: one-chamber[*]
Party structure: multiparty
Human rights rating: 33%
International affiliations: ACP, COMESA, CW, IBRD, IMF, NAM, OAU, SADC, UN, WTO

[*] Two-chamber from May 1999.

Local and regional government

For administrative purposes, the country is divided into three regions, which are further subdivided into 24 districts. Regions are the responsibility of cabinet ministers and districts are administered by appointed commissioners. At a lower level there are chiefs' and subchiefs' areas.

Political system

The May 1994 multiparty constitution, adopted after a referendum, provides for a president, who is head of state and head of government, and a single-chamber legislature, the National Assembly. The president is elected by universal adult suffrage for a five-year term. The National Assembly has 177 members, elected in single-member seats by proportional representation, for a five-year term. The president appoints and leads ministers who are responsible to him or her. In 1995 proposals for a second-chamber senate were approved, to be implemented by May 1999.

Political parties

Until 1993 the Malawi Congress Party (MCP) was the only party legally allowed to operate. Now there are some 13 other authorized parties, the most significant being the United Democratic Front (UDF) and the Alliance for Democracy (AFORD).

The MCP was founded in 1959 by Hastings Banda to lead the fight for independence. It became very much his personal political machine. Its orientation can best be described as rightwing multiracial.

The UDF was founded in 1992 and has a center-left orientation. AFORD was also formed in 1992 and in 1993 absorbed the Malawi Freedom Movement. It has a centrist orientation.

Political leaders since 1970

1966–94 Hastings Kamuzu Banda (MCP), 1994– Bakili Muluzi (UDF)

Latest elections

The leader of the UDF, Bakili Muluzi, was re-elected president on 15 June 1999 with 52.4% of the vote, his nearest rival, Gwanda Chakuamba (MCP/AFORD), obtaining 45.2%.

In the June 1999 National Assembly elections, the UDF won 93 seats, the MCP, 66, AFORD, 29, and independents 4 seats. The UDF attracted 47% of the vote, the MCP, 34%, and AFORD, 11%.

Political history

Malawi, which came under British rule in 1891, was formerly the protectorate of Nyasaland. White settlers moved into its fertile south, taking African land. This led to a violent uprising in 1915, led by the Reverend John Chilembwe. Between 1953 and 1964, the country formed part of the white-dominated Central Africa Federation of Rhodesia and Nyasaland, which comprised what are now Zimbabwe, Zambia, and Malawi. Dr Hastings Kamuzu Banda (c. 1903–97), through the Malawi Congress Party (MCP), led a campaign for independence, being imprisoned briefly in 1959, and in 1963 the Federation was dissolved. Nyasaland became independent, as Malawi, in 1964 and two years later a republic and a one-party state, with Dr Banda, who had been prime minister since 1963, as its first president.

Banda governed his country in a very personal way, brooking no opposition, and his foreign policies were, at times, rather idiosyncratic. He astonished his black African colleagues in 1967 by officially recognizing the white-only republic of South Africa and, in 1971, became the first African head of state to visit that country. In 1976, however, he also recognized the socialist government in Angola.

In 1977 he embarked upon a policy of what can best be described as cautious liberalism, releasing some political detainees and allowing greater press freedom, but these moves proved insufficient to satisfy his critics, including important foreign aid donors, and in 1992, in the wake of industrial riots, he promised a referendum on constitutional change.

The referendum, held in June 1993, showed a clear, 63%, majority in favor of a multiparty system and a new constitution was drafted and approved. This included, in November 1993, the repeal of the institution of life presidency that had been conferred on Banda in 1971. In the May 1994 presidential and assembly elections, the newly formed United Democratic Front (UDF) was victorious. Its leader, Bakili Muluzi (b. 1943), became president and a coalition government was formed, comprising the UDF and the Alliance for Democracy (AFORD). Foreign aid inflows were restored. Early in 1995 the veteran Dr Hastings Banda, who had undergone brain surgery in 1993, and his former aide, John Tembo, who had headed the police and the MCP's armed youth wing, the Malawi Young Pioneers, were formally charged with the murder of political opponents in 1983. Banda was acquitted in December 1995 and died in November 1997. In June 1996 AFORD withdrew from the coalition but President Muluzi continued with the support of opposition parties, although the MCP boycotted parliament until April 1997.

The re-election of Muluzi as president in June 1999, defeating the MCP-AFORD candidate Gwanda Chakuamba, was followed by violent protests. However, in the concurrent National Assembly elections the opposition parties won the largest number of seats.

MALI

The Republic of Mali
La République du Mali

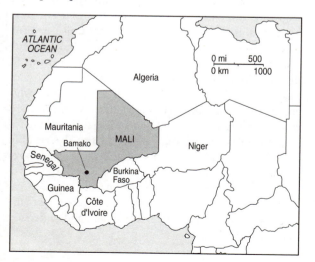

Capital: Bamako

Social and economic data
Area: 1,240,000 sq km/478,766 sq miles
Population: 10,462,000[*]
Pop. density per sq km/sq mi: 8/22[*]
Urban population: 25%[**]
Literacy rate: 32%[**]
GDP: $2,410 million[*]; per-capita GDP: $230[*]
Government defense spending (% of GDP): 2.4%[*]
Currency: franc CFA
Economy type: low income
Labor force in agriculture: 86%[**]
[*] 1995.
[**] 1992.

Head of state (executive)
President Alpha Oumar Konaré, since 1992

Head of government
Prime Minister Ibrahim Boubacar Keita, since 1994

Ethnic composition
About half the population belongs to the Mande group of tribes, which include the Bambara, the Malinke, and the Sarakole. Other significant tribes are the Fulani, the Minianka, the Senutu, the Songhai, and the nomadic Tuareg in the north. The official language is French.

Religions
About 80% of the population is Sunni Muslim, about 2% is Christian, and the rest mostly follows traditional, animist beliefs.

Political features
State type: emergent democratic
Date of state formation: 1960
Political structure: unitary
Executive: limited presidential
Assembly: one-chamber
Party structure: multiparty[*]
Human rights rating: N/A
International affiliations: ACP, BOAD, CEAO, CILSS, ECOWAS, FRANCOPHONE, FZ, IAEA, IBRD, IMF, NAM, OAU, OIC, OMVS, UEMOA, UN, WTO

[*] Though dominated by one party.

Local and regional government
The country is divided into six regions and 42 counties, or *cercles*, which are further subdivided into 279 *arrondissements*. All are administered by officials of the national government.

Political system

The January 1992 multiparty constitution, approved by referendum, provides for an executive president, who is head of state, and a single-chamber legislature, the National Assembly. The president and the Assembly are elected by the second-ballot majoritarian system for five-year terms. Of the 160 members of the National Assembly, 13 represent the interests of Malians abroad. The president appoints the prime minister, as head of government, and he or she in turn appoints other ministers, who may not be members of the assembly.

Political parties

Until 1991 the only legally permitted party was the nationalist-socialist Malian People's Democratic Union (UDPM), which was formed in 1976. Now more than 60 parties have been officially recognized, the most significant being the Alliance for Democracy in Mali (ADEMA), the Party for National Rebirth (PARENA), and the Democratic and Social Convention (CDS).

ADEMA was formed in 1990, PARENA in 1995, and the CDS in 1996. They have left-of-center orientations.

Political leaders since 1970

1968–91 Lieutenant Moussa Traoré (military/UDPM), 1991–92 Lieutenant Colonel Amadou Toumani Toure (military), 1992– Alpha Oumar Konaré (ADEMA)

Latest elections

The April 1997 National Assembly elections were annulled by the Constitutional Court because of 'serious irregularities'. In the July–August 1997 re-run elections, ADEMA won 129 of in the enlarged 147-member body seat; PARENA won seats, and the CDS four. Five other parties won representation, but leading opposition parties, such as the National Congress for Democratic Initiative (CNID) and the Rally for Democracy and Progress (RDP) boycotted the poll. Turnout was low and at least two were killed in poll-related violence.

In the May 1997 presidential elections the ADEMA leader, Alpha Oumar Konaré, was re-elected with 95.9% of the first-round vote. The main opposition parties boycotted the poll in protest against 'chaotic' assembly elections a month earlier. Consequently, turnout was only 28%.

Political history

Because of its comparatively isolated position, Mali escaped European contact until France conquered the region between 1880 and 1895 and established a colony. It then was called French Sudan and formed part of French West Africa. In 1959, with Senegal, it formed the Federation of Mali. Senegal soon left and Mali became a fully independent republic in 1960, with Modibo Keita as its first president.

Keita imposed an authoritarian socialist regime, but the failure of his economic policies led to his removal in an army coup in 1968. The constitution was suspended and all political activity banned, the government being placed in the hands of a Military Committee for National Liberation (CMLN) with Lieutenant Moussa Traoré as its president and head of state. The following year he became prime minister as well.

Traoré promised a return to civilian rule and in 1974 a new constitution was adopted, formally making Mali a one-party state. A new national party, the Malian People's Democratic Union (UDPM), was announced in 1976. Despite opposition from students to a one-party state and objections by the army to civilian rule, Traoré successfully made the transition so that by 1979 Mali had a constitutional form of government, but with ultimate power lying in the party and the military establishment.

In March 1991, following violent demonstrations against one-party rule, Traoré was ousted by troops led by Lieutenant Colonel Amadou Toumani Toure, who dissolved the UDPM and set up an interim government, pending a new multiparty constitution. This was adopted in January 1992 and in April 1992 the main opposition party, the Alliance for Democracy in Mali (ADEMA) won both the assembly and presidential elections. Alpha Oumar Konaré (b. 1946) became president and Younoussi Toure, prime minister. However, following student unrest the latter resigned and was succeeded, in April 1993, by a national unity government, headed by Abdoulaye Sekou Sow. Further student riots, in February 1994, led to the appointment of Ibrahim Boubacar Keita as prime minister. A peace pact was signed at Bamako in 1992 with Tuareg rebels, who had been fighting in northern Mali. President Konaré was re-elected in May 1997 and his party obtained a large majority in the August 1997 National Assembly elections, although elements of the opposition boycotted these polls.

In January 1999 the former military dictator General Traoré, already serving a life sentence for 'crimes of violence', was found guilty of embezzlement and sentenced to death.

MAURITANIA

Islamic Republic of Mauritania
Jumhuriyat Mauritaniya al-Islamiya

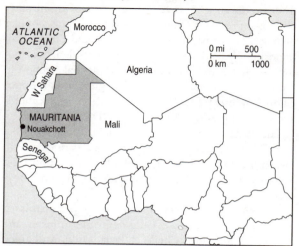

Capital: Nouakchott

Social and economic data
Area: 1,030,700 sq km/397,955 sq miles
Population: 2,211,000*
Pop. density per sq km/sq mi: 2/6*
Urban population: 50%**
Literacy rate: 34%**
GDP: $1,050 million*; per-capita GDP: $475*
Government defense spending (% of GDP): 1.9%*
Currency: ouguiya
Economy type: low income
Labor force in agriculture: 69%**
* 1995.
** 1992.

Head of state (executive)
President Maawiya Ould Sid'Ahmed Taya, since 1984

Head of government
Prime Minister Cheikh el Avia Ould Mohamed Khouna, since 1998

Ethnic composition
Over 80% of the population is of Moorish or Moorish-black origin. About 18% is black African, concentrated in the south, and there is a small European minority. The official language is Arabic, while Poular, Wolof, and Solinke are national languages.

Religions
Islam is the state religion and almost the entire population is Sunni Muslim of the Malekite rite.

Political features
State type: emergent democratic
Date of state formation: 1960
Political structure: unitary
Executive: limited presidential
Assembly: two-chamber
Party structure: multiparty*
Human rights rating: N/A
International affiliations: ACP, AL, AMF, AMU, CEAO, CILSS, ECOWAS, IBRD, IMF, NAM, OAU, OIC, OMVS, UN, WTO

* Though dominated by one party.

Local and regional government.
The country is divided into 12 regions plus the capital district of Nouakchott. Each region has its own governor and within it are departments, administered by prefects, and within the departments, *arrondissements*. There are appointed regional assemblies.

Political system
The July 1991 multiparty constitution provides for an executive president, who is head of state, and a two-chamber assembly, consisting of the Senate and the National Assembly. The president is elected by universal suffrage for a six-year term with no restrictions on re-election. The 56-member Senate is indirectly elected for a six-year term by municipal councillors, with one-third of seats being renewed every two years and three being elected by Mauritanians abroad. The 79-member National Assembly is directly elected for a five-year term in single-member constituencies by the second-ballot majoritarian system. There are three advisory bodies, the Constitutional Council, the Supreme Islamic Council, and the Economic and Social Council. The president appoints the prime minister, as head of government.

Political parties
Since the legalization of parties in 1991 some 21 have been recognized, the four most significant being the Social Democratic Republican Party (PRDS), the Mauritanian Party for Renewal (MPR), the Rally for Democracy and National Unity (RDNU), and the Union of Democratic Forces (UDF).

The PRDS was founded in 1991 as the political vehicle of President Taya. It has a left-of-center orientation.

The MPR and RDNU were also founded in 1991, with similar orientations.

Religious-political parties are outlawed by the constitution.

Political leaders since 1970

1960–78 Moktar Ould Daddah (PPM), 1978–79 General Moustapha Ould Mohamed Salek (military), 1979 Colonel Ahmed Ould Bouceif (military), 1979–84 Colonel Mohamed Khouni Ould Haidalla (military), 1984– Colonel Maawiya Ould Sid'Ahmed Taya (military/PRDS)

Latest elections

In December 1997 President Taya was re-elected with 90.2% of the popular vote, defeating four challengers. Turnout was 74%.

In the October 1996 National Assembly elections, the PRDS won 71 of the 79 seats. The UDF boycotted the polls. The PRDS also held 42 of the 56 Senate seats, after indirect elections in April 1998.

Political history

French influence was first apparent in Mauritania in the 17th century and, after a period of partial colonization in 1903, it became a full colony, and part of French West Africa, in 1920. It was given internal self-government, within the French Community, in 1958 and full independence in 1960. Moktar Ould Daddah, leader of the Mauritanian People's Party (PPM), was elected president in 1961.

In 1975 Spain ceded the western part of the Sahara to Mauritania and Morocco, leaving it to them to decide how to share it. Without consulting the Saharan people, Mauritania occupied the southern area, leaving the rest to Morocco. A resistance movement developed against this occupation, called the Popular Front for Liberation, or the Polisario Front, with the support of Algeria, and both Mauritania and Morocco found themselves engaged in a guerrilla war, forcing the two countries, who had formerly been rivals, into a mutual defense pact. Mauritania's economy was gravely weakened by the conflict and in 1978 President Daddah was deposed in a bloodless coup led by Colonel Mohamed Khouni Ould Haidalla. Single-party rule was imposed under the Military Committee for National Salvation.

Peace with the Polisario was eventually achieved in August 1978, when Mauritania renounced its claim to Western Sahara, allowing diplomatic relations with Algeria to be restored. Diplomatic relations with Morocco were broken in 1981 when Mauritania formally recognized the Polisario regime in Western Sahara (see *Chapter 8*). Normal relations were restored in 1985.

Meanwhile, in December 1984, while Colonel Haidalla was attending a Franco-African summit meet-ing in Burundi, Colonel Maawwiya Ould Sid'Ahmed Taya (b. 1943), the prime minister since 1981, led a bloodless coup to overthrow him. During 1991 calls for a more democratic political system grew and a referendum produced a massive vote in favor of multi-party elections. President Ould Taya acceded to this popular demand. The constitution was changed and a number of opposition parties formed, but the president was not universally trusted. He won the presidential election in January 1992, amid claims of poll-rigging, and the opposition boycotted the March 1992 assembly elections, allowing the president's party, the PRDS, a clear win.

The PRDS won an absolute majority in the 1996 assembly elections and President Taya was re-elected in December 1997. However, elements of the opposition accused the government of ballot-rigging and boycotted both polls.

In November 1998 President Taya dismissed Mohamed Lemine Ould Guig as prime minister and replaced him with Cheik el Avia Ould Mohamed Khouna (PRDS), who had earlier served in this position between 1996 and 1997.

MAURITIUS

The Republic of Mauritius

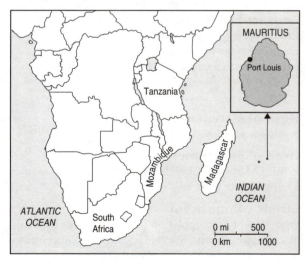

Capital: Port Louis

Social and economic data

Area: 2,040 sq km/788 sq miles
Population: 1,142,000*

Pop. density per sq km/sq mi: 612/1,449[*]
Urban population: 37%[**]
Literacy rate: 83%[**]
GDP: $3,815 million[*]; per-capita GDP: $3,340[*]
Government defense spending (% of GDP): 0.5%[*]
Currency: Mauritian rupee
Economy type: middle income
Labor force in agriculture: 19%[**]
[*] 1995.
[**] 1992.

Head of state

President Cassam Uteem, since 1992

Head of government

Prime Minister Dr Navin Ramgoolam, since 1995

Ethnic composition

There are five principal ethnic groups within the islands: French, black Africans, Indians, Chinese, and Mulattos, or Creoles. Indo-Mauritians predominate, constituting 67% of the population, followed by Creoles, 29%, Sino-Mauritians, 3.5%, and Europeans, 0.5%. The communities have sharply differing values and occupations so that inter-ethnic rivalries are intense. English is the official language but Creole is spoken by more than 50% of the population, Hindi by 22%, and Bhojpuri by 19%.

Religions

Fifty-one per cent of the population is Hindu, 17% Sunni Muslim, 30% Christian, mostly Roman Catholic, and less than 1% is Buddhist. Roman Catholicism is the oldest religion and on Rodrigues island, where 90% of the population is European or Creole, almost all are adherents to it.

Political features

State type: liberal democratic
Date of state formation: 1968
Political structure: unitary
Executive: parliamentary
Assembly: one-chamber
Party structure: multiparty
Human rights rating: N/A
International affiliations: ACP, COMESA, CW, IAEA, IBRD, IMF, IOC, NAM, OAU, SADC, UN, WTO

Local and regional government

The island of Mauritius is divided into nine districts, while the island of Rodrigues has one of its two representatives on the Legislative Assembly acting as 'Minister for Rodrigues'. Locally, there are elected urban and village councils.

Political system

Mauritius is an independent republic within the Commonwealth. The constitution dates from independence in 1968 and was amended in 1969 and 1991. It provides for a president, who is formal head of state, and a single-chamber National Assembly. There is a parliamentary-type executive, with a prime minister appointed by the president from the National Assembly on the basis of Assembly support. The president also appoints a Council of Ministers, on the advice of the prime minister, and all are collectively responsible to the Assembly. The president is elected by the Assembly for a five-year term. The Assembly has 66 members: 62 elected by universal adult suffrage, through a simple plurality (limited vote) voting system, in multimember constituencies, with four 'additional members' selected by the president, in consultation with the judiciary, from among the 'runners up' at the general election. This is done in an effort to ensure a balance in representation between the islands' different ethnic groups. The attorney general, if not an elected member, is the other Assembly member. The Assembly serves a five-year term. The island of Mauritius has 20 three-member constituencies and Rodrigues island has one two-member constituency. One of the elected members is designated Minister for Rodrigues.

Political parties

There are some 14 active political parties, the five most significant being the Mauritius Socialist Movement (MSM), the Mauritius Labor Party (MLP), the Mauritius Social Democratic Party (PMSD), the Mauritian Militant Movement (MMM), and the Organization of Rodriguan People (OPR).

The MSM was formed in 1983 as a successor to the Mauritius Socialist Party, which itself was an outgrowth from the Mauritian Militant Movement. It has a moderate socialist orientation, and campaigned to make Mauritius a republic within the Commonwealth.

The MLP describes itself as 'democratic socialist', but is really a centrist body, orientated towards Hindu Indians. It was originally formed in 1936 to campaign for the rights of cane-field workers and proceeded to dominate Mauritian politics up to 1982. It is led by Navin Ramgoolam.

The PMSD is also an old-established party, but of a more conservative hue. Drawing its support from

Franco-Mauritian landowners and the Creole middle classes, it is pro-Western, anti-communist, and determinedly Francophile in its policy outlook. It joined the MSM-led coalition government in February 1995.

The MMM was formed in 1970 as a workers' party, enjoying strong backing from the trade union movement and boasting broad cross-community membership. It has a left wing orientation and is led by Paul Bérenger. The party split in 1993 and the faction which remained within the government coalition adopted the designation Renouveau Militant Mauricien (RMM), under the leadership of Prem Nababsing.

The OPR is a small party representing the inhabitants of Rodrigues island.

Political leaders since 1970

1968–82 Sir Seewoosagur Ramgoolam (MLP), 1982–95 Sir Aneerood Jugnauth (MSM), 1995 Dr Navin Ramgoolam (MLP)

Latest elections

In the December 1995 general election, the MSM was defeated by the opposition MLP-MMM coalition, which won 60 of the 62 elected assembly seats. They attracted 65% of the vote, against 20% for the MSM-RMM. The OPR won the two elected Rodrigues Island seats. Within the successful coalition, the MLP won 35 seats and the MMM, 25.

Political history

The Republic of Mauritius is in the Indian Ocean east of Madagascar and consists of the island of Mauritius and the dependencies of Rodrigues island, Agalega island, and the Cargados Carajos, or St Brandon islands.

Mauritius island, then uninhabited, was discovered by the Dutch in 1598 and named after Prince Maurice of Nassau. It was colonized during the 17th century, but abandoned in 1710. The French reoccupied it, with Rodrigues, in 1715 and established sugar cane plantations to be worked by imported African slaves. During the Napoleonic War of 1803–15 the island group was captured by Britain and then formally ceded to it by France in 1814. From then until 1903 it was administered with the Seychelles as a single colony. As a separate colony, Mauritius developed rapidly to become a major sugar cane producer. With the abolition of slavery in 1834, a switch from imported African workers to indentured labor from India took place. Although originally brought in on short-term contracts, many Indian immigrants chose to stay, establishing the ethnic pattern which exists today.

Following several decades of campaigning for self-rule, spearheaded by the Mauritius Labor Party (MLP), the islands were granted internal self-government in July 1957 and full independence, within the Commonwealth, in March 1968. The MLP's leader, Dr Seewoosagur Ramgoolam, who had been chief minister since September 1961, became the country's first prime minister.

During the 1960s Mauritius enjoyed rapid economic growth on the basis of a strong market for sugar. This made possible a substantial rise in social spending and the successful implementation of an urgently needed population control program. However, in the early 1970s, as export markets declined and economic conditions generally deteriorated, opposition to the Ramgoolam government grew, led by the newly formed leftwing Mauritius Militant Movement (MMM), headed by Paul Bérenger. It played a leading role in organizing a wave of strikes in 1971, the government responding by imposing a state of emergency and postponing the Legislative Assembly elections which were due in August 1972.

The governing MLP and Mauritius Social Democratic Party (PMSD) coalition eventually broke up in December 1973, but Ramgoolam stayed in power by establishing a new alliance with the Muslim Committee of Action (CAM). In the December 1976 general election, the MMM emerged as the largest single party, but Ramgoolam succeeded in forming a new governing coalition of the MLP, CAM, and PMSD. Against a background of rising unemployment and industrial unrest, the ruling coalition was eventually defeated in the election of June 1982, the MMM, in alliance with the Mauritius Socialist Party (PSM), winning all 60 seats on Mauritius island. The PSM's leader, Aneerood Jugnauth (b. 1930), became the new prime minister, promising to pursue radical policies, based on nonalignment in foreign affairs, the extension of state control of the economy, and a proposal to make Mauritius a republic within the Commonwealth. Within a year, however, sharp differences emerged within the coalition, including Jugnauth's objection to a MMM campaign to make Creole the national language. He dissolved the coalition in March 1983 and formed a new MSM minority administration.

Lacking a working majority, Jugnauth had to call for fresh elections in August 1983. These resulted in the MSM forming an electoral alliance with the MLP and PMSD and Jugnauth becoming prime minister again, on the understanding that the MLP's leader, Sir

Seewoosagur Ramgoolam, as he now was, would be made president if Mauritius became a republic. When the government failed to secure legislative approval for this constitutional change, Ramgoolam was appointed governor general on the retirement of the existing holder of the post, in December 1983. He died two years later and was replaced as governor general by Sir Veerasamy Ringadoo, a former finance minister.

The new MSM, MLP, and PMSD coalition was weakened in February 1984, when the MLP withdrew, but it remained in office with the support of 11 dissident MLP members. Then, in December 1985, its reputation was tarnished when an attempt was made to 'cover up' a Mauritius–Netherlands drugs smuggling scandal involving MSM and PMSD members. Despite these difficulties, improvements in the economy enabled a new alliance of the three parties to secure another majority in the 1987 general election.

A coalition of the MSM, MMM, and OPR won the 1991 general election and in the following year republican status was achieved. In 1993 the MMM split. Those deputies remaining within the government coalition formed the Renouveau Militant Mauricien (RMM), while the remaining deputies, under the leadership of Paul Bérenger, formed an opposition pact with the MLP. In 1995 Mauritius joined the Southern African Development Community (SADC).

In December 1995 the MLP-MMM secured a landslide general election victory and Navin Ramgoolam became prime minister. The MMM withdrew from the coalition in June 1997, after the dismissal of its leader, Paul Bérenger, as foreign minister and deputy prime minister.

MOZAMBIQUE

The Republic of Mozambique
A República de Moçambique

Capital: Maputo

Social and economic data
Area: 799,380 sq km/308,642 sq miles
Population: 16,500,000[*]
Pop. density per sq km/sq mi: 21/53[*]
Urban population: 30%[**]
Literacy rate: 27%[**]
GDP: $1,355 million[*]; per-capita GDP: $85[*]
Government defense spending (% of GDP): 3.7%[*]

Currency: metical
Economy type: low income
Labor force in agriculture: 85%[**]
[*] 1995.
[**] 1992.

Head of state (executive)
President Joaquim Alberto Chissano, since 1986

Head of government
Prime Minister Pascoal Mocumbi, since 1994

Ethnic composition
The majority of people belong to local tribal groups, the largest being the Makua-Lomue, comprising about 38% of the population. The other significantly large group, of about 24%, is the Tsonga. The official language is Portuguese.

Religions
Most people, 60%, follow traditional, animist beliefs, while 15%, or 2 million people, are Sunni Muslims, and 14% are Roman Catholics.

Political features
State type: emergent democratic
Date of state formation: 1975
Political structure: unitary
Executive: limited presidential
Assembly: one-chamber
Party structure: two-party
Human rights rating: 53%

International affiliations: ACP, COMESA, CW, IBRD, IMF, Lusophone, NAM, OAU, SADC, UN, WTO

Local and regional government

The country is divided into 11 provinces, including Maputo city, within which are districts, cities, and localities. Each province has a governor and elected assembly.

Political system

The November 1990 multiparty constitution, as amended in 1996, provides for an executive president, directly elected for a five-year term, renewable twice only, and a single-chamber Assembly of the Republic with 250 members also directly elected by universal adult suffrage for a five-year term by proportional representation. The president, who is also commander in chief of the armed forces, appoints the prime minister and a Council of Ministers (cabinet).

Political parties

Until 1990 the National Front for the Liberation of Mozambique (Frelimo) was the only legally permitted party. It was formed in 1962 and reconstituted in 1977 as a 'Marxist–Leninist vanguard party'. From 1990 it became a 'free-market' party.

There are now more than 20 other parties, the most significant being the civilian arm of the Mozambique National Resistance (MNR or Renamo), which, with South African support, fought a civil war with Frelimo between 1980 and 1992. It has a right-of-center orientation.

Political leaders since 1970

1975–86 Samora Machel (Frelimo), 1986– Joaquim Alberto Chissano (Frelimo)

Latest elections

In the October 1994 presidential elections, Chissano won 53% of the vote, defeating the Renamo leader, Afonso Dhlakama, who obtained 33%.

The results of the October 1994 assembly elections were as follows:

Mozambique latest election results

Party	% votes	Seats
Frelimo	44.3	129
Renamo	37.9	112
Others	17.8	9

Political history

Mozambique became a Portuguese colony in 1505 and was subsequently exploited, with forced labor, for its gold and ivory, as well as being a source of slaves for export. Guerrilla groups had actively opposed Portuguese rule from the early 1960s, the various left wing factions combining to form Frelimo. As the government in Lisbon came under increasing strain, Frelimo's leader, Samora Machel (1933–86), demanded nothing short of complete independence and, in 1974, internal self-government was granted, with Joaquim Chissano (b. 1939), a member of Frelimo's Central Committee, as prime minister. A year later full independence was achieved and Machel became the country's first president.

He was immediately faced with the problem of hundreds of thousands of Portuguese settlers departing, leaving no trained replacements in key economic positions. Two activities had been the mainstay of the Mozambique economy, transit traffic from South Africa and Rhodesia and the export of labor to South African mines. Although Machel declared his support for the African National Congress (ANC) in South Africa, and the Patriotic Front in Rhodesia, he knew that he still had to coexist and trade with his two white-governed neighbors. He put heavy pressure on the Patriotic Front for a settlement of the guerrilla war and this eventually bore fruit in the Lancaster House Agreement of 1979 and the eventual electoral victory of Robert Mugabe of Zimbabwae, a reliable friend of Mozambique.

From 1980 onwards the country was confronted with the twin problems of widespread drought, which affected most of southern Africa, and attacks by dissidents, under the banner of the Mozambique National Resistance (Renamo), also known as the MNR, who were covertly, but strongly, backed by South Africa. These attacks were concentrated on Mozambique's vital and vulnerable transport system. Machel, showing considerable diplomatic skill, had, by 1983, repaired relations with the United States, undertaken a successful European tour, and established himself as a respected African leader. His sense of realism was shown in his relations with South Africa. In March 1984 he signed the Nkomati Accord, under which South Africa agreed to deny facilities to the MNR and Mozambique, in return, agreed not to provide bases for the banned ANC. Machel took steps to honour his side of the bargain but was doubtful about South Africa's good faith. On 19 October 1986 he died in an air crash near the South African border on a return flight from Zambia. Despite the suspicious circumstances of his death, a subsequent inquiry pronounced it an accident.

The following month Frelimo's Central Committee elected the foreign minister, and former prime minister, Joaquim Chissano, as his successor. In his acceptance speech, Chissano pledged himself to carry on with the policies of his predecessor. Chissano strengthened the ties Machel had already forged with Zimbabwe and Britain and in February 1987 took the unprecedented step of informally requesting permission to attend the Commonwealth Heads of Government summit in Vancouver in October. This was seen by some observers as a prelude to a request for Commonwealth membership, but the Commonwealth secretary general, Sir 'Sonny' Ramphal, described such speculation as misleading. Mozambique's economic problems were aggravated in the early months of 1987 by food shortages, following another year of drought.

Despite the Nkomati Accord, South Africa continued to train and arm the MNR. Mozambique's reply was to mount a Front Line States regional army with a combination of Zimbabwean, Tanzanian, and Mozambique troops. In May 1988 it was announced that Mozambique and South Africa had agreed to revive a joint security commission which had originally been set up under the Nkomati Accord and in September 1988 President P W Botha of South Africa paid a visit to Mozambique. In December 1988 the Tanzanian government announced the withdrawal of its troops, initiating a relaxation of tension and guerrilla activity, and in 1990 a partial ceasefire was agreed.

Meanwhile, Chissano abandoned one-party rule, to make his regime more acceptable, and peace talks with the MNR opened in 1991. In August 1992 a peace accord was agreed and a treaty signed by Chissano and the MNR leader, Afonso Dhlakama, in October. This provided for a permanent ceasefire, to be monitored by 6,000 United Nations troops, and the disarmament of Renamo.

After Frelimo's victories in the multiparty presidential and assembly elections, in November 1994, the MNR leadership said it would cooperate with the government in the post-election era. IMF-promoted economic reforms, aimed at reconstructing the devastated economy, provoked fuel price riots in Maputo in November 1993. In January 1995 the last UN peace-keeping troops were withdrawn. In November 1995 Mozambique, which is surrounded by six Commonwealth countries, was accepted into Commonwealth membership. The use of English had been increased and the country's laws and institutions adapted to fit Commonwealth practice.

NAMIBIA

The Republic of Namibia
Republiek van Namibie

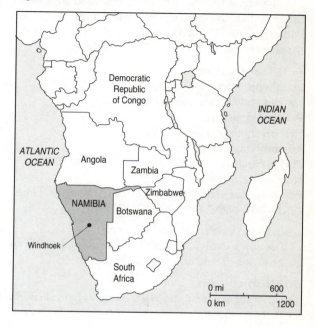

Capital: Windhoek

Social and economic data
Area: 824,292 sq km/318,261 sq miles
Population: 1,500,000[*]
Pop. density per sq km/sq mi: 2/5[*]
Urban population: 29%[**]
Literacy rate: 38%[**]
GDP: $3,100 million[*]; per-capita GDP: $2,070[*]
Government defense spending (% of GDP): 2.7%[*]
Currency: Namibian dollar
Economy type: middle income
Labor force in agriculture: 44%[**]
[*] 1995.
[**] 1992.

Head of state (executive)
President Sam Nujoma, since 1990

Head of government
Prime Minister Hage Geingob, since 1990

Ethnic composition
Eighty-five per cent of the population is black African, 51% of whom belong to the Ovambo tribe. The rest includes the pastoral Nama and Bushmen. There is a

6% white minority. The official languages are Afrikaans and English.

Religions

Christianity is the main religion, practised by 85% of the population. Among the Christians, 50% are Lutherans, 20% Roman Catholics, 6% members of the Dutch Reformed Church, and 6% Anglicans.

Political features

State type: emergent democratic
Date of state formation: 1990
Political structure: unitary
Executive: limited presidential
Assembly: two-chamber
Party structure: two-party
Human rights rating: N/A
International affiliations: ACP, COMESA, CW, IAEA, IBRD, IMF, NAM, OAU, SADC, UN, WTO

Local and regional government

The country is divided into 13 regions, each with an elected council, and administrative districts.

Political system

The multiparty constitution dates from independence in 1990. It provides for an executive president, who is head of state, elected by universal adult suffrage for a five-year term, renewable twice, through the second-ballot majoritarian system. There is also a National Assembly of 72 members elected by proportional representation for five years, plus up to six nonvoting members nominated by the president. The president appoints a prime minister as head of government and a cabinet.

There is also a 26-member advisory National Council, comprising two indirectly elected representatives from each of the 13 regional councils, serving a six-year term.

Political parties

Of some 15 active parties, the two most significant are the South-West Africa People's Organization (SWAPO) and the Democratic Turnhalle Alliance (DTA).

SWAPO was founded in 1958 and is led by Sam Nujoma. Campaigning for full and unconditional independence for the territory and the establishment of a classless socialist society, it was banned in 1960 and forced to operate from bases in neighboring Angola and Zambia. It has a left-of-center orientation.

The DTA was formed in 1977 and is a coalition of moderate centrist African, colored, and white parties.

Political leaders since 1970

1990– Sam Nujoma (SWAPO)

Latest elections

Sam Nujoma won the December 1994 presidential election, obtaining 76.34% of the vote against 24% for Mishake Muyongo of the DTA.

The results of the concurrent National Assembly elections were as follows:

Namibia latest election results

Party	% votes	Seats
SWAPO	73.9	53
DTA	20.8	15
Other parties	5.3	4

Political history

Deterred by the coastal Namib Desert, European penetration of Namibia was delayed until the 18th century. British and Dutch missionaries first moved into the area, before, in 1884, Britain incorporated a small enclave around Walvis Bay in Cape Colony, while the Germans forcibly annexed the remainder of the territory in the same year. In 1903–4 there were massacres of the Herero people and, in 1915, during World War I, South African forces seized control of the German colony.

Administration of the area, now designated South West Africa (SWA), was entrusted to the Union of South Africa under the terms of a League of Nations, mandate in 1920 and, in 1925, a limited measure of self-government was granted to the territory's European inhabitants. After World War II, South Africa applied, in 1946, to the newly established United Nations (UN) for the full incorporation of the mandated lands, rich in diamonds and uranium, within its Union. This demand was rejected and, instead, South Africa was called upon to prepare a trusteeship agreement for the area.

The South Africans, however, rejected this request and instead proceeded to integrate South West Africa more closely with Pretoria, granting the territory's white voters representation in the Union's parliament in 1949 and extending to it its own apartheid laws in October 1966. In response to these measures, the South West African People's Organization (SWAPO) was established in 1958 by an Ovambo, Sam Nujoma (b. 1929), to lead a campaign for an end to racial discrimination and for the granting of full independence from South Africa. The organization was harassed by the South African authorities and its more radical wing, led by Nujoma, was forced into exile in 1960. Later, from the mid-1960s, Nujoma's exiled party established a military wing, the People's Liberation Army of Namibia (PLAN), and, utilizing bases in Angola and Zambia, proceeded to wage a guerrilla war of attrition against the South African occupying army.

South Africa's continued occupation of Namibia, as South West Africa was redesignated by the UN in 1968, met with an increasing challenge by international bodies from the late 1960s and was declared illegal by the International Court of Justice in 1971. Three years later the UN Security Council passed a resolution requiring South Africa to begin a transfer of power to Namibians by the end of May 1975 or face UN action. South Africa's prime minister, B J Vorster, responded by expressing willingness to enter into negotiations on Namibian independence, but not with SWAPO, an organization which the UN had, in 1973, formally recognized as the 'authentic representative of the Namibian people'.

During the mid-1970s the military conflict in Namibia and the bordering region escalated as Pretoria attempted, unsuccessfully, to topple the new Marxist government which had come to power in neighboring Angola in 1975. Tentative moves towards a settlement were made in 1978, with the holding of tripartite talks between SWAPO, South Africa, and the five Western members of the UN Security Council, the 'Contact Group'. At the conclusion of these discussions, SWAPO and the Pretoria regime conditionally accepted proposals involving a reduction in the level of South African troops and the release of political prisoners as the prelude to the holding of UN-supervised elections. These proposals were incorporated in UN Security Council Resolution 435 of September 1978. However, South Africa subsequently retracted, holding instead in December 1978, under its own terms, elections which were boycotted by SWAPO and not recognized by the West. A long period of political and military stalemate followed during which South Africa continued its armed offensive against Angola and the PLAN, and, at the same time, attempted to establish in Namibia a stable pro-Pretoria regime, based on a conservative coalition termed the Democratic Turnhalle Alliance (DTA). This experiment came to an end, however, in January 1983 when the DTA's leader, Dirk Mudge, resigned following disagreements with Pretoria and direct rule was reimposed.

Negotiations between Pretoria, the Western powers, neighboring African states, and Namibian political forces continued during the succeeding years, but repeatedly foundered on South Africa's insistence that any withdrawal of its military forces from both Angola and Namibia should be linked to the departure of the 50,000 Cuban troops stationed in Angola. In June 1985 South Africa established a new 'puppet regime' in Namibia, termed the 'Transitional Government of National Unity' (TGNU). It was dominated by political representatives drawn from the white and black ethnic minority communities, and contained only one minister from the dominant Ovambo tribe. The TGNU, which failed to gain recognition from the UN or Western powers, attempted to reform the apartheid system in Namibia and adopt a new draft constitution, but was seriously divided between its conservative and moderate wings. In particular, more reformist, non-white elements within the TGNU sought to move away from a political structuring based on ethnic, rather than national or geographical, lines. This was firmly opposed, however, by the South African administrator general, Louis Pienaar, since it would destroy the safeguards, called 'minority rights', which had been established to protect white interests.

During 1987–88 major strides towards resolving the Namibian–Angolan issues began finally to be made. A path-finding agreement was signed by the South African and Angolan governments in August 1988, providing for an immediate cessation of military activities, followed by a rapid withdrawal of South African and Cuban forces from Angola and South Africa's troops from Namibia.

In April 1989 a strong UN peacekeeping force was stationed in Namibia, as a prelude to freely open internationally supervised elections later in the year. The elected assembly would then adopt and approve a new independence constitution. Sam Nujoma, the SWAPO president, returned in September and elections for a Constituent Assembly in November were won decisively by his party. The new constitution was adopted in February 1990 and Nujoma was sworn in as president of the independent mineral-rich republic of Namibia in March 1990. Namibia immediately entered the Commonwealth.

The Walvis Bay enclave, the only deep-water port on Namibia's coast, became a matter of dispute between the Namibian and South African governments but eventually, in August 1993, the government in Pretoria surrendered its sovereignty over it. The dramatic political changes in South Africa during 1993–94 were warmly welcomed in Namibia and close relations between the two countries were cemented. SWAPO won the December 1994 National Assembly elections and Nujoma was re-elected for another term. The parliamentary majority SWAPO secured was sufficiently large, at greater than two-thirds, to enable it to amend the constitution if it wished. This it did, in October 1998, to allow President Nujoma to stand for a third term in 1999.

NIGER

The Republic of Niger
La République du Niger

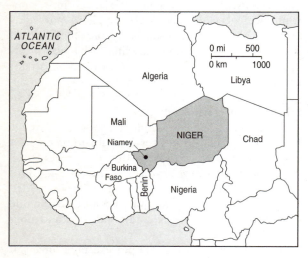

Capital: Niamey

Social and economic data
Area: 1,267,000 sq km/489,191 sq miles
Population: 8,846,000*
Pop. density per sq km/sq mi: 7/18*
Urban population: 19%**
Literacy rate: 28%**
GDP: $1,965 million*; per-capita GDP: $225*
Government defense spending (% of GDP): 0.9%*
Currency: franc CFA
Economy type: low income
Labor force in agriculture: 85%**
* 1995.
** 1992.

Head of state (executive)
Major Daouda Malam Wanke, Chairman of the National Council for Reconciliation, since 1999

Head of government
Prime Minister Ibrahim Assane Mayaki, since 1997

Ethnic composition
Three tribes make up over 75% of the population. They are the Hausa, mainly in the central and southern areas, the Djerma-Songhai, in the southwest, and the Beriberi-Manga, in the east. There is also a significant number of the Fulani tribe, mainly nomadic, and, in the north, the Tuareg. There has been a Tuareg and Toubou insurgency in recent years, but a ceasefire accord was signed in December 1997. The official language is French.

Religions
About 85% of the population is Sunni Muslim. Most of the rest follow traditional, animist beliefs.

Political features
State type: military
Date of state formation: 1960
Political structure: unitary
Executive: military
Assembly: one-chamber
Party structure: multiparty
Human rights rating: N/A
International affiliations: ACP, BOAD, CEAO, CILSS, ECOWAS, Francophone, FZ, IAEA, IBRD, IMF, IsDB, LCBC, NAM, OAU, OIC, UEMOA, UN, WTO

Local and regional government
The country is divided into seven departments, each headed by a prefect, assisted by a regional advisory council. Within the departments are 32 *arrondissements* and 150 communes.

Political system
The May 1996 multiparty constitution, which was approved by a referendum, provided for an executive president, who was head of state, and a single-chamber National Assembly. The president was elected by universal suffrage for a five-year term, renewable once only. The 83-member National Assembly was similarly elected for the same length of term. Seventy-five members were elected in multi-seat constituencies and eight in single-seat national minority constituencies. The president appointed a prime minister and a Council of Ministers (cabinet). The constitution was abrogated by the April 1999 military coup and the National Assembly dissolved. Power was transferred to a 13-member military junta, the National Council for reconciliation, (CRN), while a new constitution was being drafted by a Consultative Council.

Political parties

Of some 20 registered parties, the most significant are the National Union of Independents for the Revival of Democracy (UNIRD), the Union for Democratic and Social Progress-Amana (UDPS-Amana), the Front for Democracy and Progress (FDP), and the Niger Alliance for Democracy and Progress-Zaman Lahiya (ANDP-Zaman Lahiya).

Political leaders since 1970

1958–74 Hamani Diori (NPP), 1974–87 Lieutenant Colonel Seyni Kountché (military), 1987–93 Colonel Ali Seybou (military), 1993–96 Mahamane Ousmane (CDS), 1996–99 Ibrahim Barre Mainassara (military Independent) 1999– Major Daouda Malam Wanke (military)

Latest elections

In July 1996 Brigadier General Mainassara was controversially elected president winning 52.22% of the popular vote. He defeated four challengers, including the former president, Mahamane Ousmane, who attracted 20% support. The results of the November 1996 National Assembly elections were as follows:

Niger latest election results

Party	Seats
UNIRD	56
ANDP	8
UDPS	4
Others	15

* Two seats decided in by-elections.
** Four seats decided in by-elections.

Political history

Formerly part of French West Africa from 1901, Niger achieved full independence in 1960. Hamani Diori (1916–89), the prime minister since 1958, was elected president and re-elected in 1965 and 1970. Maintaining very close and cordial relations with France, Diori seemed to have established one of the most stable regimes in Africa, and the discovery of uranium deposits promised a sound economic future. However, his practice of suppressing opposition to his party, the Niger Progressive Party (NPP), coupled with a severe drought between 1968 and 1974, resulted in widespread civil disorder and, in April 1974, he was ousted in a coup led, reluctantly, by the French-trained army chief of staff, Lieutenant Colonel Seyni Kountché (1931–87).

Kountché suspended the constitution and established a military government with himself as president. He immediately set about trying to restore the economy and negotiating a more equal relationship with France, through a cooperation agreement signed in 1977. Threatened by possible droughts and consequential unrest, Kountché tried to widen his popular support by liberalizing his regime but died in November 1987, while undergoing surgery in a Paris hospital, and was succeeded by the army Chief of Staff, Colonel Ali Seybou.

Seybou was confirmed as president in December 1989 but calls for a multiparty political system developed and in August 1991 he was divested of most of his executive powers, which were transferred to a transitional 15-member High Council of the Republic (HCR).

In March 1992 the transitional government collapsed, amid economic problems and tribal unrest, spearheaded by the secessionist-minded nomadic Tuaregs in the north, and calls for multi-party politics were renewed. Following a referendum in December 1992, a new constitution was approved and two months later Mahamane Ousmane was elected president. In the concurrent assembly elections an alliance of left-of-center parties, the Alliance of the Forces for Change (AFC), won an absolute majority. In September 1994 the Niger Party for Democracy and Socialism (PNDS-Tarayya) withdrew its support from the governing coalition, forcing a general election. In the subsequent January 1995 elections the AFC was returned but with a reduced majority. In January 1996 President Ousmane was ousted by the military, led by Brigadier General Ibrahim Barre Mainassara and four months later the two men faced each other in elections, Mainassara winning the contest. Meanwhile, a civilian government had been installed, but with a military presence in the background. Amid a resumption of rebel activity in the north, and famine in parts of the country, Ibrahim Assane Mayaki was appointed, in November 1997, as the new prime minister. In January 1998 several opposition political leaders were arrested in connection with an alleged plot to assassinate President Mainassara. Two months later, there were violent anti-government protests.

On 9 April 1999 the increasingly unpopular President Mainassara was shot dead by his own military guard and was replaced by Major Daouda Malan Wanke, the head of the presidential guard. This coup came in the wake of opposition demands that Mainassara resign after, on 7 April 1999, the Supreme Court annulled the results of local elections, held in February 1999, which had brought victory for the opposition. After the coup, the National Assembly was dissolved and Wanke was declared head of a National Council for Reconciliation (CRN), comprising 14 military officers, which was charged with overseeing a return to civilian government after elections in November 1999. Ibrahim Mayake remained in post as prime minister and Wanke received some support from opposition parties. In May 1999, as a first step towards a return to constitutional rule, a Constitutional Council was formed, comprising senior political figures, including four former prime ministers, and representatives of important religious and ethnic groups. Its task was to draft a new constitution and regulate all areas of life. In June 1999 the Council recommended a semi-presidential form of government, with a balance of power between the president, prime minister and National Asembly. A referendum, held in July 1999, brought a vote in favour of power-sharing between the army and civilians. However, turnout was only 30%.

NIGERIA

The Federal Republic of Nigeria

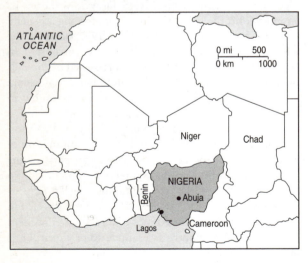

Capital: Abuja

Social and economic data
Area: 923,000 sq km/356,681 sq miles
Population: 108,467,000[*]
Pop. density per sq km/sq mi: 117/304[*]
Urban population: 37%[**]
Literacy rate: 51%[**]
GDP: $28,420 million[*]; per-capita GDP: $265[*]

Government defense spending (% of GDP): 2.9%[*]
Currency: naira
Economy type: low income
Labor force in agriculture: 45%[**]
[*] 1995.
[**] 1992.

Head of state and head of government
President General Olusegan Obasanjo, since 1999

Ethnic composition
There are more than 250 tribal groups in the country, the main ones being the Hausa and Fulani in the north, the Yoruba in the south, and the Ibos in the east. The non-African population is relatively small and numbers no more than about 30,000. The official language is English.

Religions
About half the population is Sunni Muslim, settled predominantly in the north, about 35% is Christian, divided between Roman Catholics and Protestants, found chiefly in the south, and the remainder mostly follow traditional, animist beliefs.

Political features
State type: energent democratic
Date of state formation: 1960
Political structure: federal
Executive: limited presidential
Assembly: two-chamber
Party structure: multiparty
Human rights rating: 49%
International affiliations: ACP, CW, ECOWAS, G-15, G-24, IAEA, IBRD, IMF, LCBC, NAM, OAU, OPEC, UN, WTO

Local and regional government
The country is divided into 36 states plus a federal capital. There are also some 774 local government councils.

Political system
Nigeria is a federal republic of 36 states and the Federal Capital Territory. The constitution is based on one of 1979 which was amended following a military coup in December 1983. Another coup in 1985 made further changes. The president was made head of state, commander in chief of the armed forces, and chair of the Armed Forces Ruling Council (AFRC).

The draft of a new constitution was published in 1988 and implemented in stages. It provides for an executive president and a two-chamber National Assembly, consisting of a 91-member Senate and a 593-member House of Representatives, all elected by universal suffrage. The constitution contains strong elements of the United States model, the directly elected president being given power to veto legislation and the assembly power to override that veto by a two-thirds majority vote.

This legislature was dissolved following a November 1993 coup. A new 26-member military-dominated Provisional Ruling Council (PRC) was established, along with a Federal Executive Council, or cabinet. A new federal constitution came into force for the 1999 general election, with the Senate increased to 109 members and the House of Representatives reduced to 360 members. The Senate comprises 36 three-member constituencies plus one single-member constituency (the Federal Capital). Both chambers are elected for four-year terms.

Political parties

The ban on political parties imposed in 1979 was lifted in 1989 and then gradually parties were approved under conditions stipulated by the Provisional Ruling Council. In November 1993 parties were banned again and the new ban was lifted in 1995.

The two most significant parties before the 1995 ban were the left-of-center Social Democratic Party (SDP) and the right-of-center National Republican Convention (NRC), both formed in 1989.

The military ruler General Sanni Abacha legalized only five, pro-regime political parties. True liberalization did not take place until August 1998, when Abacha's successor, Major General Abubakar set up an Independent National Electoral Commission (INEC) which invited parties to register. Only parties which received more than 5% of the vote in at least 24 of the country's 36 states in the December 1998 local elections were given formal registration to participate in the February 1999 national elections.

Only three of the more than thirty new parties which had been formed met this criterion: the centrist People's Democratic Party (PDP); the right-wing All People's Party (APP); and the left-of-centre Yoruba-based Alliance for Democracy (AFD). The PDP, formed in Lagos in August 1999, with Alex Ekwueme, the country's vice-president between 1979 and 1983 as its chairman, contained many leading politicians and is the most ethnically broad-based of Nigeria's political parties. It provided the country's new president, Olusegun Obasanjo. The APP contains many politicians who had supported the late military ruler, General Sani Abacha.

Political leaders since 1970

1966–1975 Colonel Yakubu Gowon (military), 1975–79 General Olusegun Obasanjo (military), 1979–83 Shehu Shagari (NPN-NPP coalition), 1983–85 Major General Muhammed Buhari (military), 1985–93 Major General Ibrahim Babangida (military), 1993 Ernest Shonekan (interim), 1993–98 General Sanni Abacha (military), 1998–99 Major General Abdusalam Abubakar (military) 1999– General Olusegun Obasanjo (PDP)

Latest elections

The results of the 20 February 1999 assembly elections were as indicated in the table below.

Party	Senate seats	% vote	House of Representatives seats	% vote
PDP	59	56.4	206	57.1
APP	24	31.2	74	30.6
AFD	20	12.4	68	12.4
Undeclared	6		12	

The most recent presidential election, held on 27 February 1999, was won by the PDP candidate, General Olusegun Obasanjo, with 62.8% of the national vote. He defeated the APP and AFD's joint candidate, Olu Falae, who won 37.2% of the vote. Falae claimed that there had been electoral irregularities in six states, but the Court of Appeal rejected these claims.

Political history

The British founded a colony at Lagos in 1861 and gradually extended it by absorbing surrounding areas until by 1914 it had become Britain's largest African colony. It achieved full independence, as a constitutional monarchy within the Commonwealth, in 1960 and became a republic in 1963. The republic was based on a federal structure, introduced in 1954, so as to accommodate the regional differences and the many tribes.

The ethnic differences, including the fact that groups of tribes were in different parts of the vast country, always contained the ingredients for a potential conflict. The discovery of oil in the southeast in 1958 made it very much richer than the north and this exaggerated the differences.

Nigeria's first president, in 1963, was Dr Nnamdi Azikiwe (b. 1904), who had been a banker, then established an influential newspaper group and played a leading part in the nationalist movement, pressing for independence. He came from the eastern Ibo tribe. His chief rival was Sir Abubakar Tafawa Balewa (1912–66), who was prime minister from 1957 until he was assassinated in a military coup in 1966. The coup had been led by mainly Ibo junior officers, from the eastern region. The offices of president and prime minister were suspended and it was announced that the state's federal structure would be abandoned.

Before this took place, the new military government was overturned in a counter-coup by a mostly Christian faction from the north, led by Colonel Yakubu Gowon (b. 1934). He re-established the federal system and appointed a military governor for each region. Soon afterwards thousands of Ibos in the north were slaughtered. In 1967 a conflict developed between Gowon and the military governor of the eastern region, Colonel Chukwuemeka Odumegwu-Ojukwu, about the distribution of oil revenues, which resulted in Ojukwu's declaration of an independent Ibo state of Biafra. Gowon, after failing to pacify the Ibos, ordered federal troops into the eastern region and a civil war began. It lasted until January 1970, when Biafra surrendered to the federal forces.

In 1975 Gowon was replaced in a bloodless coup led by Brigadier Murtala Mohammad, but he was killed within a month, in a coup led by General Olusegun Obasanjo, who announced a gradual return to civilian rule and in 1979 the leader of the National Party of Nigeria (NPN), Shehu Shagari, became president.

In December 1983, following a deterioration in the economy caused by falling oil prices, Shagari's government was deposed in another bloodless coup, led by Major General Muhammed Buhari, who established a military administration. In 1985 there was another peaceful coup which replaced Buhari with a new military government, led by Major General Ibrahim Babangida (b. 1941), the army chief of staff. He promised a return to a democratic civilian government in 1989, but in 1987 announced that the transition would not now take place until 1992. A draft constitution was debated in the assembly throughout 1988 but agreement on its final form was not reached. In 1989 the ban on political activity was lifted and parties were approved within strict criteria. Assembly elections were held in July 1992, the left-of-center Social Democratic Party (SDP) winning a majority of seats, but it was announced that the National Assembly would not be opened until after presidential elections had taken place. These were held in June 1993 and the SDP candidate, Chief Moshood Abiola, claimed victory. President Babangida refused to accept the result and declared the elections void.

After much manoeuvring, the two main parties, the SDP and the right-of-center National Republican Convention (NRC), agreed to form an interim government which excluded Abiola, who left the country. In August 1993 Babangida stepped down and handed over power to an interim, nonelected government, led by Chief Ernest Adegunle Shonekan. Meanwhile, Abiola had returned and in November 1993 the Nigerian High Court ruled that the military government was illegal. A week later Shonekan was removed in a bloodless coup and General Sanni Abacha seized power, banning all political parties, arresting Abiola and reinstating the 1979 constitution. On taking power, Abacha announced that he would establish a National Constitutional Conference (NCC) to determine the country's political future.

In October 1994 the High Court ruled that the detention of Abiola was illegal and in December 1994 the NCC recommended that military rule should continue until at least the end of 1995, despite the lifting of the ban on political parties in June of that year. In March 1995 the former ruler, General Olusegun Obasanjo, and Major General Shehu Musa Yar'Adua were accused of plotting a coup and were sentenced to 25 years' imprisonment, after a secret trial.

In October 1995 General Abacha attempted to ease international pressure on his regime by announcing that the death sentences on 14 other coup plotters would be commuted and that there would be a return to civilian rule in 1998. However, in November 1995 the Commonwealth suspended Nigeria's membership as punishment for the execution of nine human rights activists, including Ken Saro-Wiwa (1941–1995), who had led a campaign for self-determination for the minority Ogoni tribe and for environmental protection.

In April 1998 Abacha called assembly elections but they were boycotted by opposition parties. Then, two months later, he died and was replaced by General Abdusalam Abubakar, who promised a speedy return to civilian rule. In July 1998 Chief Moshood Abiola, who claimed to have won the 1993 presidential election, died, reportedly of a heart attack.

In August 1998 General Abubakar announced a timetable for the return to democratic civilian rule. This provided for the establishment of a 14-member Independent National Electoral Commission (INEC), the immediate registration of political parties, the holding of local elections in December 1998 and state and governorship elections in January 1999, federal legislature and presidential elections in February 1999, and the swearing in of a new civilian president in May 1999. The centrist People's Democratic Party (PDP) won sweeping victories in the local and state elections of December 1998 and January 1999, winning control of 20 of the 35 states where elections were held and over 50% of the national vote. This provided the platform for the PDP to win a clear victory in the federal legislature elections of February 1999 and for its candidate, General Olusegun Obasanjo, to be directly elected president later in the same month. Obasanjo, who came from the southern-based Yoruba community had been military ruler between 1976-79 and, along with Abubakar, had been the country's only military ruler to have voluntarily transferred back to a civilian ruler. He was sworn in as president on 29 May 1999 and pledged to make national reconciliation amongst the country's diverse ethnic groups his priority and also to launch a drive against corruption, restore the country's economic infrastructure, proceed with privatization, and eliminate unnecessary barriers to foreign investment. However, despite being a Yoruba, Obasanjo was viewed by the important southwest Yoruba region as being a representative of northern and military interests, so that there were fears that, after the PDP's victory, there might be renewed calls for secession in Yoruba areas. The suspension of Nigeria's membership of the Commonwealth was lifted in May 1999, after President Obasanjo took office. Nigeria also began to receive financial assistance from the IMF during 1999, ending a 10-year rift. On taking office, Obasanjo launched an immediate investigation into all contracts entered into by the Abubakar regime since 1 January 1999. This followed a sharp contraction in the country's foreign exchange reserves, from $7 billion to $4 billion, forcing the introduction of exchange controls in June 1999, amid claims that the outgoing military regime had engaged in the looting of state funds and assets. In June 1999 President Obasanjo carried out a purge of the military, removing all 150 senior military officers who had held political office between 1985-99, in a move designed to ensure that the military would remain subordinate to the elected civilian administration. He also established an 8-member human rights investigation panel, to investigate human rights abuses committed by the military between 1983 and 1999.

RWANDA

The Republic of Rwanda
Republika y'u Rwanda
La République rwandaise

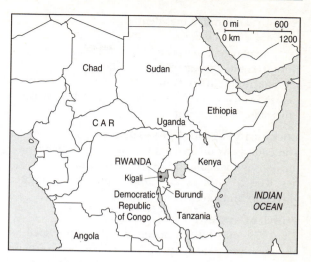

Capital: Kigali

Social and economic data
Area: 26,340 sq km/10,170 sq miles
Population: 7,750,000[*]
Pop. density per sq km/sq mi: 294/762[*]
Urban population: 6%[**]
Literacy rate: 50%[**]
GDP: $1,130 million[*]; per-capita GDP: $150[*]
Government defense spending (% of GDP): 4.4%[*]
Currency: Rwanda franc
Economy type: low income
Labor force in agriculture: 93%[**]
[*] 1995.
[**] 1992.

Head of state (executive)
President Pasteur Bizimungu, since 1994

Head of government
Prime Minister Pierre-Celestin Rwigyema, since 1995

Ethnic composition
About 84% of the population belongs to the Hutu tribe, most of the others being Tutsis. There are also Twa and Pygmy minorities. The official languages are Kinyarwanda and French.

Religions
About a quarter of the population follows traditional, animist beliefs, nearly half is Roman Catholic, 8% is Protestant, and 8% Sunni Muslim.

Political features
State type: authoritarian nationalist[*]
Date of state formation: 1962
Political structure: unitary

Executive: unlimited presidential[*]
Assembly: one-chamber
Party structure: multiparty[*]
Human rights rating: 48%
International affiliations: ACP, CEEAC, CEPGL, COMESA, IBRD, IMF, KBO, NAM, OAU, UN, WTO
[*] In a state of transition.

Local and regional government

The country is divided into 11 prefectures which are further subdivided into 145 communes, or municipalities. The communes are administered by appointed governors and have elected councils.

Political system

The 1978 constitution, amended in 1991, provided for an executive president and a single-chamber 70-member assembly, the National Development Council (CND). It has since been superseded by a May 1995 multiparty constitution. The president and the CND are elected by universal adult suffrage, through a simple plurality voting system, for a five-year term. The president, who may be re-elected up to the age of 60, appoints a prime minister and a Council of Ministers (cabinet). From July 1994 a Transitional National Assembly was formed, with multi-party elections scheduled for 1999.

Political parties

Until 1991 Rwanda was a one-party state, the sole legal party being the National Revolutionary Development Movement (MRND). When the constitution was amended other parties were accepted, among them the Rwanda Patriotic Front (FPR), the Republican Democratic Party (MDR), the Liberal Party (PL), the Social Democratic Party (PSD), and the Christian Democratic Party (PDC).

The MRND was formed in 1975. It has an extreme nationalist-socialist orientation and is Hutu dominated. It was implicated in the April–July 1994 genocide of thousands of Tutsis and was consequently excluded from the Transitional National Assembly.

The FPR represents the Tutsi minority community who were ousted from government in the 1960s. It is led by President Bizimungu, a Hutu.

The MDR evolved from groups formed in the 1960s and in the early 1990s it split into two factions, a mainly Hutu, progovernment group, and a multi-ethnic, anti-government group. Both have left-of-center orientations.

The PL was formed in 1991 and it, too, split into pro- and anti-government factions in the early 1990s. It has a moderate, Hutu centrist orientation.

The PSD was formed in 1991 as a breakaway from the MRND.

The PDC was formed in 1990. It has a Hutu Christian centrist orientation.

Political leaders since 1970

1962–73 Grégoire Kayibanda (Democratic Republican Movement-Parmehutu), 1973–94 Major General Juvénal Habyarimana (military/MRND), 1994 Theodore Sindikubgabo (interim), 1994– Pasteur Bizimungu (FPR)

Latest elections

In December 1994 70 members were appointed to the Transitional National Assembly, including 13 each from the FPR, MDR, PL, and PSD and six from the PDC. Pasteur Bizimungu was appointed president. Elections were last held in 1988, and were won by the MRND.

Political history

In the 16th century the Tutsi tribe moved into the country and took over from the indigenous majority Hutus, establishing a feudalistic kingdom. Then, at the end of the 19th century German colonizers arrived and forced the Tutsi king to allow the country to become a German protectorate. It was linked to the neighboring state of Burundi within the empire of German East Africa until after World War I, when it came under Belgian administration as a League of Nations, later United Nations, trust territory.

In 1961 the monarchy was abolished and Ruanda, as it was then called, became a republic. It achieved full independence in 1962 as Rwanda, with Grégoire Kayibanda as its first president. Fighting broke out in 1963 between the two main tribes, the Hutu and the Tutsi, resulting in the loss of, it is estimated, some 20,000 lives, before an uneasy peace was agreed in 1965. Kayibanda was re-elected president in 1969 but by the end of 1972 the tribal warfare had restarted and in July 1973 the head of the National Guard, Major General Juvénal Habyarimana (1937–94), led a bloodless coup, ousting Kayibanda and establishing a military government.

Meetings of the assembly were suspended and all political activity banned until a new ruling party was formed. It was the National Revolutionary Development Movement (MRND) and was the only legally permitted political organization. A referendum held at the end of 1978 approved a new constitution designed to fulfil Habyarimana's promise, in 1973, to return to normal constitutional government within five years, and cautious moves in this direction were started in 1990.

In the same year the Rwanda Patriotic Front (FPR), an army consisting mainly of Tutsi refugees, invaded the country from neighboring Uganda, with the object of overthrowing the Hutu-dominated Habyarimana government. Much of the north was occupied and guerrilla fighting continued until, in October 1992, a power-sharing agreement between the government and the FPR was concluded, resulting in the signing of an agreement in Arusha, Tanzania, in August 1993.

In April 1994 President Habyarimana was killed when the aircraft in which he was returning with the Burundi president, Cyprien Ntaryamira, was shot down on its approach to Kigali airport. His death unleashed violence on an unprecedented scale and destroyed the peace accord which had been signed the previous year. The speaker of the assembly, Theodore Sindikubgabo, became president with a transitional, Hutu-dominated, government headed by Prime Minister Jean Kambanda. The new government was rejected by the FPR, who resumed fighting, forcing the government to flee from Kigali. It was estimated that more than 500,000 people, mainly Tutsis, had been killed and 2 million displaced as refugees, many fleeing to Zaire, Burundi, and Tanzania as a result of the frenzied clashes between Hutu militias and the Tutsi-dominated FPR. A French humanitarian mission, Opération Turquoise, attempted to protect refugees and stem the spread of cholera and dysentry in the over-crowded refugee camps.

In July 1994 the FPR declared victory and established a coalition government led by Faustin Twagiramungu, a Hutu member of the Republican Democratic Party (MDR), as prime minister and Pasteur Bizimungu, of the FPR, as president, but excluding the MRND. Major General Paul Kagame, the FPR's military leader, became vice president and defense minister. Despite this seeming rapprochement, there were still reports of Hutus being killed by Tutsi soldiers.

As more evidence of rapes and genocide was revealed, steps were started to investigate allegations, the United Nations Security Council adopting a resolution to establish an International Criminal Tribunal in Arusha, Tanzania, instead of in Kigali, as the Rwandan government had planned.

In March 1995 there was another major outbreak of ethnic violence in neighboring Burundi and it was feared that it might spread to Rwanda. It failed to do so but presented the government in Kigali with another refugee problem, as thousands of Hutus fled from Burundi to avoid Tutsi attacks. It was reported that many Hutu refugees had died in the ensuing confusion, either by being trampled to death, or at the hands of Rwandan, mainly Tutsi, soldiers. In August 1995 President Bizimungu dismissed Prime Minister Twagiramungu following his open criticism of the domination of his government by the FPR. The new prime minister, Pierre-Celestin Rwigyema (MDR), was another Hutu.

Cases of genocide, mainly by Hutu rebels, were reported throughout 1996 and 1997 and in March 1998 the French National Assembly set up a commission to investigate. In May 1998 the UN secretary general paid a controversial visit to the country, following allegations that the UN had not done enough to halt the killings. Since 1996, the Rwanda Liberation Army (RLA), a Hutu-rebel group, has been behind a series of massacres of Tutsi refugees, while in 1998 there was growing conflict with the neighboring Democratic Republic of Congo.

Local elections were held in March 1999, the first vote since the 1994 genocide. However, in June 1999 the government decided to extend its mandate to rule for another four years, without holding elections. In June 1999, Rwanda ended its military support for rebel groups in the Democratic Republic of Congo.

SÃO TOMÉ E PRÍNCIPE

The Democratic Republic of São Tomé e Príncipe
A República Democrática de São Tomé e Príncipe

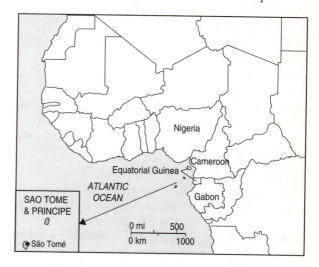

Capital: São Tomé

Social and economic data
Area: 944 sq km/372 sq miles
Population: 125,000*

Pop. density per sq km/sq mi: 130/336[*]
Urban population: 26%[**]
Literacy rate: 57%[**]
GDP: $45 million[*]; per-capita GDP: $360[**]
Government defense spending (% of GDP): N/A
Currency: dobra
Economy type: low income
Labor force in agriculture: 54%[**]
[*] 1995.
[**] 1992.

Head of state (executive)
President Miguel Trovoada, since 1991

Head of government
Prime Minister Guilherme Posser da Costa, since 1999

Ethnic composition
The population is predominantly African. The official language is Portuguese.

Religions
About 70% of the population is Christian, mostly Roman Catholic, but church and state are separated.

Political features
State type: emergent democratic
Date of state formation: 1975
Political structure: unitary
Executive: limited presidential
Assembly: one-chamber
Party structure: multiparty
Human rights rating: N/A
International affiliations: ACP, CEEAC, IBRD, IMF, NAM, OAU, UN

Local and regional government
For administrative purposes, the country is divided into seven counties. Six of them are on São Tomé. The smaller island of Príncipe forms one county in itself, with internal autonomy and its own seven-member regional assembly and five-member government, since 1994.

Political system
The August 1990 multiparty constitution, approved by a referendum, provides for an executive president, who is head of state, and a single-chamber 55-member National Assembly. The president is directly elected by the second-ballot majoritarian system, for a five-year term, and is limited to two successive terms. The National Assembly is elected for a four-year term by proportional representation, using 12 multimember constituencies. The president appoints the prime minister and ministers on the latter's advice.

Political parties
Until 1990 the only legal party was the Movement for the Liberation of São Tomé e Príncipe-Social Democratic Party (MLSTP-PSD). There are now some five other parties, the most significant being the Democratic Convergence Party-Reflection Group (PCD-GR) and the Independent Democratic Action (ADI).

The MLSTP-PSD was founded in 1972 by Manuel Pinto da Costa from an earlier nationalistic group. It has a nationalist and socialist orientation.

The PCD-GR was formed in 1987 by a breakaway faction of the MLSTP. It has a moderate left-of-center orientation and is led by Alda Bandeira. The ADI was founded in 1992 to support President Trovoada. It has a centrist orientation.

Political leaders since 1970
1975–91 Manuel Pinto da Costa (MLSTP), 1991– Miguel Trovoada (independent/ADI)

Latest elections
In July 1996 President Trovoada was re-elected for a second five-year term, securing 52% of the run-off vote to defeat Manuel Pinto da Costa (MLSTP), an ex-president.

The results of the 8 November 1998 National Assembly elections were as follows:

São Tomé e Príncipe latest election results

Party	Seats
MLSTP-PSD	31
PCD-GR	8
ADI	16

Political history
The two islands of São Tomé e Príncipe were first colonized by the Portuguese in the late 15th century. They became important trading posts for ships on their way to the East Indies, supplying sugar and later cocoa and coffee, which were produced using forced labor. They were declared an overseas province of Portugal in 1951 and were given internal self-government in 1973. An independence movement, the Movement for the Liberation of São Tomé e Príncipe (MLSTP), led by Dr Manuel Pinto da Costa (b. 1937) and formed in Gabon in 1972, took advantage of a military coup in Portugal, in 1974, and persuaded the new government in Lisbon to formally recognize it as the sole representative of the people of the islands. Full independence followed, in July 1975, with a one-

party socialist regime being established.

Dr Pinto da Costa became the first president and in December a National People's Assembly was elected. During the first few years of his presidency there were several unsuccessful attempts to depose him and, with a worsening economy, Pinto da Costa began to reassess his country's international links which had made it overdependent on the Eastern bloc and, in consequence, isolated from the West.

In 1984 he formally proclaimed that in future São Tomé e Príncipe would be a nonaligned state and gradually the country turned more towards nearby African states, as well as maintaining its links with Lisbon. However, an invasion and coup attempt in 1988 was only foiled with the help of Angolan and East European troops. In 1990, influenced by the collapse of communism in Eastern Europe, the MLSTP abandoned Marxism and, following a referendum in August 1990, a new, multiparty constitution was approved. Pinto da Costa retired in advance of assembly and presidential elections and in January 1991 his party, the MLSTP-PSD, was defeated by the Democratic Convergence Party (PCD-GR) in the National Assembly elections. With a parliamentary majority, the PCD's leader, Norberto José d'Alva Costa Alegre, became prime minister. The March 1991 presidential election was won by an independent candidate, Miguel Trovoada. In July 1994 the prime minister, in dispute with President Trovoada over control of the budget, was dismissed and replaced by Evaristo do Espirito Santo Carvalho, leader of the small People's Alliance (AP). In October 1994 the MLSTP-PSD, in early legislative elections, returned to power, although one seat short of an overall assembly majority. Its chairperson, Carlos da Graça, was appointed prime minister. With unemployment standing at 38% and the level of foreign indebtedness at $165 million, an attempted coup 'to recover the dignity of the country', was launched in August 1995 by junior army officers, led by Lieutenant Manual Quintas de Almeida. However, within days, power was handed back to the civilian government.

In September 1996 the government lost a vote of confidence in the National Assembly and a coalition administration was formed, headed by Raul Bragança Neto, of the MLSTP-PSD, as prime minister.

The November 1998 National Assembly elections brought victory once again for the MLSTP-PSD, running in alliance with the PCD-GR. Turnout was 65% and international observers described the poll as 'just, free and transparent'. In January 1999 the vice-president of the MLSTP-PSD, Guilherme Posser da Costa replaced his colleague Raul Braganca Neto as prime minister. However, like his predecessor he soon came into conflict with President Trovoada (ADI), who sought to block a number of his appointments. The continuance of this power struggle seemed set to hamper Posser da Costa in his drive to rescue the economy and improve living standards.

SENEGAL

The Republic of Senegal
La République du Sénégal

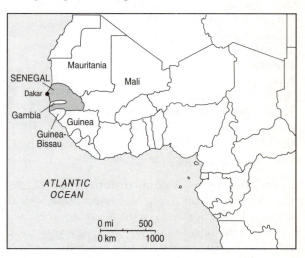

Capital: Dakar

Social and economic data
Area: 197,000 sq km/76,123 sq miles
Population: 8,102,000[*]
Pop. density per sq km/sq mi: 41/106[*]
Urban population: 41%[**]
Literacy rate: 38%[**]
GDP: $5,070 million[*]; per-capita GDP: $630[*]
Currency: franc CFA
Government defense spending (% of GDP): 1.9%[*]
Economy type: low income
Labor force in agriculture: 81%[**]
[*] 1995.
[**] 1992.

Head of state
President Abdou Diouf, since 1981

Head of government
Prime Minister Habib Thiam, since 1993

Ethnic composition
Senegal has a great ethnic diversity. The Wolof group are the most numerous tribes, comprising about 36% of the population. The Fulani comprise about 21%, the Serer 19%, the Diola 7%, and the Mandingo 6%. Within each main group are many individual tribes. The official language is French.

Religions
More than 90% of the population is Sunni Muslim, 5% Christian, chiefly Roman Catholic, and 5% follow traditional, animist traditional beliefs.

Political features
State type: nationalistic socialist
Date of state formation: 1960
Political structure: unitary
Executive: unlimited presidential
Assembly: one-chamber
Party structure: multiparty*
Human rights rating: 71%
International affiliations: ACP, BOAD, CEAO, CILSS, ECOWAS, FZ, G-15, IAEA, IBRD, IMF, IWC, NAM, OAU, OIC, OMVG, OMVS, UEMOA, UN, WTO

* Though dominated by one party.

Local and regional government
The country is divided into ten regions, each with an appointed governor and elected assembly. There is a further subdivision into departments, *arrondissements*, and villages. Departments are administered by prefects, *arrondissements*, by subprefects, and villages by chiefs.

Political system
The constitution dates from 1963 and has since been amended. It provides for a single-chamber, 140-member National Assembly and an executive president, who is head of state and commander in chief of the armed forces. The president is directly elected by universal adult suffrage for a seven-year term, limited (since 1993) to two terms. The Assembly is elected for a five-year term through the additional member majoritarian system of voting, with 70 deputies elected nationally by proportional representation and 70 representing single-member constituencies. The president appoints a prime minister as head of government. Constitutional amendments are adopted if carried by a three-fifths' majority vote of the National Assembly. There have been proposals to introduce a second chamber, the Senate.

Political parties
Between 1966 and 1974 Senegal was a one-party state, but now, although there are some 30 registered parties, and 11 with Assembly representation, three dominate the political scene. They are the Senegalese Socialist Party (PS), led by President Abdou Diouf, the Senegalese Democratic Party (PDS), and the Union for Democratic Renewal (URD).

The PS began in 1949 as the Senegalese Progressive Union (UPS). In 1976 it was reconstituted in its present form. It is a democratic socialist party.

The PDS was formed in 1976. It has a liberal centrist orientation. The URD was formed in 1998 by a former minister in Diouf's government.

Political leaders since 1970
1960–80 Léopold Sédar Senghor (UPS-PS), 1981– Abdou Diouf (PS)

Latest elections
In the February 1993 presidential election, Abdou Diouf was re-elected with 58.4% of the vote, while his PDS rival Abdoulaye Wade won 32%.

In the May 1998 National Assembly elections, which were contested by 18 parties, the PS won 93 seats, the PDS, 23, and the URD, 11.

Political history
After 300 years as a French colony, Senegal became an independent republic in September 1960, with the poet-politician Léopold Sédar Senghor (b. 1906), leader of the Senegalese Progressive Union (UPS), which had spearheaded the independence movement after World War II, as its first president. An attempted federation with Mali in 1959–60 proved to be unsuccessful. In 1962 Senghor took over the post of prime minister and four years later, in 1966, made the UPS the only legal party. In 1970 he relinquished the office of prime minister to a young protégé, Abdou Diouf (b. 1935), who, in 1976, was to be named his successor. In 1973 Senghor was re-elected and began to honour his promise to allow the return to multiparty politics. In December 1976 the UPS was reconstituted to become the Senegalese Socialist Party (PS) and two opposition parties were legally registered. In the 1978 elections the PS won over 80% of the Assembly seats and Senghor was decisively re-elected. He retired at the end of 1980 and was succeeded by Diouf, who immediately sought national unity by declaring an amnesty for political offenders and permitting more parties to register.

In 1980 Senegal sent troops to Gambia to protect it against a suspected Libyan invasion, and it intervened again in 1981 to thwart an attempted coup. As the two countries came closer together, agreement was reached on an eventual merger and the confederation of Senegambia came into being in February 1982, but this was abandoned in 1989. Senegal maintained close links with France, allowing it to retain military bases.

In the 1983 elections Diouf and his party were again clear winners and later that year he further tightened his control of his party and the government, abolishing the post of prime minister, but this was subsequently reinstated.

Despite open opposition, Diouf and the PS remained firmly in power and were decisively re-elected in 1988. The opening up of the party system, ironically, strengthened, rather than weakened, the one-party state. In April 1989 violent clashes over border grazing rights, in both Senegal and Mauritania, threatened to create a rift between the two countries but full diplomatic relations were restored in 1992.

In February 1993 Diouf was re-elected president and in the subsequent assembly elections, in May 1993, the PS was returned with a clear, though slightly reduced, majority. There were clashes between government forces and separatist rebels in the southern Casamance province during 1993. A ceasefire agreement was signed in July 1993, but it broke down in 1995. The PS claimed victory in the May 1998 assembly elections, despite allegations of fraud. A new upper chamber, the senate, was formed in January 1999.

SEYCHELLES

The Republic of the Seychelles

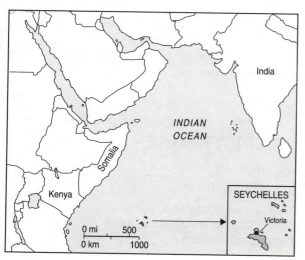

Capital: Victoria

Social and economic data
Area: 450 sq km/174 sq miles
Population: 74,000*
Pop. density per sq km/sq mi: 164/425*
Urban population: 50%**
Literacy rate: 58%**
GDP: $490 million*; per-capita GDP $6,625*
Government defense spending (% of GDP): 3.9%*
Currency: Seychelles rupee
Economy type: middle income
Labor force in agriculture: 10%**
* 1995.
** 1992.

Head of state and head of government
President France-Albert René, since 1977

Ethnic composition
The majority of the population is Creole, of mixed black and European parentage. There is a small European minority, mostly French and British. The official languages are English, French, and Creole.

Religions
About 90% of the population is Roman Catholic and Roman Catholicism is a quasi-state religion. About 7% is Anglican.

Political features
State type: emergent democratic
Date of state formation: 1976
Political structure: unitary
Executive: limited presidential
Assembly: one-chamber
Party structure: multiparty*
Human rights rating: N/A
International affiliations: ACP, CW, IBRD, IMF, IOC, IWC, NAM, OAU, UN

* Though dominated by one party.

Local and regional government
There is no local government as such, administration coming almost entirely from the center.

Political system
Seychelles is a republic within the Commonwealth. The June 1993 multiparty constitution, which was approved in a referendum, provides for a president, who is head of state and head of government, and a single-chamber 34-member National Assembly. The president, who is also commander in chief of the armed forces, is elected by universal adult suffrage for a five-year term, and is limited to a maximum of three successive terms.

Twenty-five members of the National Assembly are directly elected from single-member constituencies by universal adult suffrage and the remaining nine are elected from a national list on a proportional basis.

Political parties

Until 1991 the only legally permitted party was the Seychelles People's Progresssive Front (SPPF). Now several other parties operate, the most significant being the Democratic Party (DP) and the United Opposition (UO).

The SPPF was founded in 1964 as the Seychelles People's United Party (SPUP) and in 1978 adopted its present name. It has a nationalistic socialist stance and is led by President René.

The DP was formed in 1992 as the successor to the Seychelles Democratic Party (SDP), which, under James Mancham, was the governing party between 1970 and 1977. It has a left-of-center orientation.

The UO is a recently formed, left-of-center grouping.

Political leaders since 1970

1970–77 James Mancham (SDP), 1977– France-Albert René (SPUP/SPPF)

Latest elections

The incumbent president, France-Albert René (SPPF), won the March 1998 presidential elections, with a 66.7% vote share, defeating Wavel Ramkalawan (UO), with 19.5%, and Sir James Mancham (DP), with 13.8%.

The results of the concurrent National Assembly elections were as follows:

Seychelles latest election results

Party	% votes	Seats
SPPF	61.70	30
UO	26.1	3
DP	12.1	1
Others	0.1	0

Political history

Seychelles is a group of 115 islands, scattered over an area of more than a million square kilometres. They were colonized by the French in 1768, captured by the British in 1794, and formally ceded by France in 1814 to became a British Crown Colony in 1903.

In the 1960s several political parties were formed, campaigning for independence, the most significant being the Seychelles Democratic Party (SDP), led by James Mancham, and the Seychelles People's United Party (SPUP), led by France-Albert René (b. 1935). At a constitutional conference in London in 1970 René demanded complete independence while Mancham favored integration with the United Kingdom. Agreement was not reached and so a further conference was held in 1975 when internal self-government was agreed.

The two parties then formed a coalition government, with Mancham as prime minister. Eventually full independence was achieved in June 1976. Seychelles became a republic within the Commonwealth, with Mancham as president and René as prime minister. The following year René staged an armed coup, while Mancham was attending a Commonwealth conference in London, and declared himself president. Mancham went into exile.

After a brief suspension of the constitution, a new one was adopted, creating a one-party state, with the SPUP being renamed the Seychelles People's Progressive Front (SPPF). René, as the only candidate, was formally elected president in 1979 and then re-elected for another five-year term in 1984. There were several unsuccessful attempts to overthrow him, including one staged by South African mercenaries in 1981. René followed a policy of nonalignment but maintained close links with Tanzania, which provided defense support.

A successful tourism-based economy was developed, providing the highest per-capita living standards in Africa.

In 1991 René promised to return to pluralist politics. In July 1992 a 20-member commission was popularly elected to draft a new constitution. Its first draft was rejected in a referendum held in November 1992, but in June 1993 a multiparty constitution was approved and adopted. Sir James Mancham, the former deposed president, returned and in the July 1993 presidential elections was defeated by René. The ruling SPPF also won a majority in the National Assembly.

René was re-elected in March 1998 and the SPDF retained its assembly majority.

SIERRA LEONE

The Republic of Sierra Leone

Capital: Freetown

Social and economic data

Area: 71,740 sq km/27,712 sq miles
Population: 4,402,000[*]

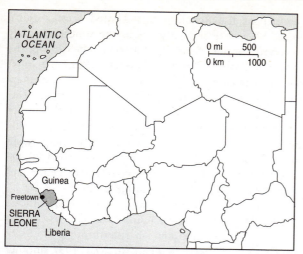

Pop. density per sq km/sq mi: 61/159*
Urban population: 31%**
Literacy rate: 21%**
GDP: $765 million*; per-capita GDP: $175*
Government defense spending (% of GDP): 5.7%*
Currency: leone

Economy type: low income
Labor force in agriculture: 70%**
* 1994.
** 1992.

Head of state and head of government
President Ahmed Tejan Kabbah, since 1998

Ethnic composition
There are some 18 tribal groups in the country, three of which comprise nearly 70% of the population. They are the Mende, the Tenne, and the Limbe. The official language is English.

Religions
Most people, 52%, follow traditional, animist beliefs. There are Sunni Muslim (38%) and Anglican Christian (6%) minorities.

Political features
State type: emergent democratic*
Date of state formation: 1961
Political structure: unitary
Executive: limited presidential
Assembly: one-chamber*
Party structure: multiparty*
Human rights rating: 67%
International affiliations: ACP, CW, ECOWAS, IAEA, IBRD, IMF, MRU, NAM, OAU, OIC, UN, WTO

* In a state of transition.

Local and regional government
The country is divided into three provinces, Northern, Southern, and Eastern, plus the Western area, which includes Freetown. Each province has a cabinet minister responsible for it. The provinces are divided into districts, within which are 148 chiefdoms, each controlled by a tribal chief.

Political system
The 1991 constitution provided for a multiparty political system after 13 years of one-party rule but in April 1992 President Momoh was ousted in a coup led by Captain Valentine Strasser, who set up a 25-member military National Provisional Ruling Council (NPRC), later known as the Supreme State Council. The 1991 constitution was reinstated with the return to civilian rule in 1996. It provides for an executive president, directly elected for up to two five-year terms, and an 80-member House of Representatives, elected for five years. It comprises 68 members elected by proportional representation, with a 5% cut-off limit, and 12 paramount chiefs from the districts.

Political parties
Between 1978 and 1991 the only permitted party was the All People's Congress (APC). Since then a number of parties have been formed, the most significant being the Sierra Leone People's Party (SLPP), the United People's Party (UNPP), and the People's Democratic Party (PDP).

The APC was founded by Sierra Leone's first president, Siaka Stevens, in 1960. It has a moderate socialist orientation.

The SLPP was formed in 1961 and has a left-of-center orientation. The UNPP and PDP are more recent creations with similar orientations.

Political leaders since 1970
1968–85 Siaka Stevens (APC), 1985–92 Major General Joseph Saidu Momoh (APC), 1992–96 Captain Valentine Strasser (military), 1996 Brigadier General Julius Maada Bio (military), 1996–97 Ahmed Tejan Kabbah (SLPP), 1997–98 Major Johnny Paul Koromah (military), 1998– Ahmed Tejan Kabbah (SLPP)

Latest elections
Ahmed Tejan Kabbah was elected president in March 1996, with 59.5% of the second-ballot vote. He defeated the UNPP leader, John Karefa-Smart. Kabbah's SLPP also won the February 1996 House of Representatives elections, securing 27 of the 68 elective seats, with 36% of the vote. The UNPP (22%),

won 17 seats, the PDP (15%), and other parties 12 seats.

Political history

In 1787 the area which is now Sierra Leone was bought by English philanthropists to provide a settlement, called Freetown, for freed slaves and in 1808 it became a British colony. The interior was conquered in 1896. It achieved full independence, as a constitutional monarchy within the Commonwealth, in 1961, with Sir Milton Margai, leader of the Sierra Leone People's Party (SLPP), as prime minister.

Margai died in 1964 and was succeeded by his half-brother, Dr Albert Margai. The 1967 general election was won by the All People's Congress (APC), led Dr Siaka Stevens (1905–88), but the result was disputed by the army, which assumed control and set up a National Reformation Council, forcing the governor general to temporarily leave the country. In the following year another army revolt brought back Stevens as prime minister and in 1971, after the 1961 constitution had been changed to make Sierra Leone a republic, he became president. He was re-elected in 1976 and the APC, having won the 1977 general election by a big margin, began to demand the creation of a one-party state. A new constitution, making the APC the sole legal party, was approved by referendum in 1978 and Stevens was sworn in as president for another seven-year term.

As the date for the next presidential election drew near, Stevens, who was now 80, announced that he would not stand for re-election and an APC conference in August 1985 endorsed the commander of the army, Major General Joseph Saidu Momoh (b. 1937), as the sole candidate for party leader and president. He was formally elected in October 1985. Momoh appointed a civilian cabinet and immediately disassociated himself from the policies of his predecessor, who had been criticized for failing to prevent corruption within his administration.

In March 1991 President Momoh said he welcomed a return to multiparty politics and this was endorsed with 60% support in a referendum. However, Momoh was deposed in April 1992 and the army, led by the young officer, Captain Valentine Strasser (b. 1965), resumed control. Strasser said he was still committed to pluralist politics at some future date. Meanwhile, the government found itself involved in a continuing struggle with rebel forces operating from neighboring Liberia, where a civil war was raging. The struggle had begun in 1991 when the rebels, fighting under the banner of the Revolutionary United Front (RUF), made several territorial gains in the southeast. They received support from the Liberian rebel group, the National Patriotic Front of Liberia (NPFL). The government responded by recruiting South African mercenaries and new conscripts to train and improve its small, ill-equipped army. An attempt, in November 1994, to negotiate a ceasefire failed and the guerrilla war continued, with foreign nationals being taken hostage by the RUF. The death toll exceeded 20,000 and there were 500,000 refugees in Sierra Leone and 250,000 in neighboring Guinea and Liberia.

In January 1996 Strasser was ousted by fellow officers led by Brigadier General Julius Maada Bio who two months later restored civilian rule through the SLPP leader, Ahmed Tejan Kabbah. In May 1997 another coup reinstated military rule in the person of Major Johnny Paul Koromah. Following an intervention by the Economic Community of West African States (ECOWAS), led by Nigeria, civilian rule was restored in March 1998. A 'final ceasefire' was agreed with the RUF in May 1996, but this far led to hold.

Peace talks aimed at resolving the 8-year-old civil war began in April 1999, in Togo. The rebels offered an immediate cease-fire, but President Kabbah initially rejected this, calling for their withdrawal first from diamond areas. However, after fighting flared up again, a cease-fire was agreed, starting on 24 May 1999. Although there were violations of this cease-fire, peace talks continued, culminating in an agreement, signed in Togo in July 1999. Under its terms, the rebels were given four ministerial posts, including that of vice-president for their leader, Foday Sankoh, who also became chair of the country's mineral resources commission.

SOMALIA

Somali Democratic Republic
Jamhuuriyadda Dimuqraadiga Soomaaliya

Capital: Mogadishu

Social and economic data

Area: 637,660 sq km/246,202 sq miles
Population: 9,077,000[*]
Pop. density per sq km/sq mi: 14/37[*]
Urban population: 35%[**]
Literacy rate: 24%[**]
GDP: $2,800 million[*]; per-capita GDP: $310[*]

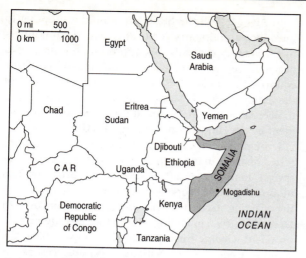

Government defense spending (% of GDP): 6.2%[**]
Currency: Somali shilling
Economy type: low income
Labor force in agriculture: 76%[**]
[*] 1995.
[**] 1992.

Head of state and head of government
President Ali Mahdi Mohammed, since 1991

Ethnic composition
Somalia is one of the most ethnically homogeneous countries in Africa. Ninety-eight per cent of the population is indigenous Somali, about 84% of Hamitic stock and 14% Bantu. However, the people are divided into some 100 clans, based on patrilineal ties that go back many generations, with intense clan rivalries. The official language is Arabic and the national language; Somali.

Religions
Islam is the state religion, most people being Sunni Muslims. There is also a Roman Catholic minority.

Political features
State type: military authoritarian[*]
Date of state formation: 1960
Political structure: federal[*]
Executive: military[*]
Assembly: none
Party structure: none
Human rights rating: N/A
International affiliations: ACP, AL, AMF (suspended), IBRD, IGADD, IMF, NAM, OAU, OIC, UN
[*] In a state of transition.

Local and regional government
In March 1993 proposals were agreed for a federal sys-
tem of government based on 18 regions, further subdivided into districts.

Political system
At a conference in March 1993, 15 representatives of the main political factions agreed to set up a 74-member Transitional National Council (TNC), with three representatives from the 18 administrative regions, five from the capital, Mogadishu, and one from each of the factions who had signed the agreement. It was also agreed that a federal system would be established, but in May 1994 the leaders of the self-proclaimed Republic of Somaliland, covering the territory of the former British Somaliland in the north, said they would never form a federal state with Somalia.

In 1998 Somalia was in a state of *de facto* anarchy, without any formal government structures and with rival clans disputing control, although there were hopes of holding elections to a 189-seat legislature.

Political parties
Political parties in Somalia are based more on clans than ideology and so tend to function in different areas of the country. This clan division contributed to the civil war and the near anarchy after 1989.

The most dominant current grouping is the United Somali Congress (USC-Hawiye clan), based in Mogadishu and central Somalia. Other groups include the Somali Patriotic Movement (SPM-Darod clan), the Somali Salvation Democratic Front (SSDF-Majertein clan), the Somali Democratic Alliance (SDA-Gadabursi clan), the United Somali Front (USF-Issa clan), and the Somali National Movement (SNM).

The SPM was formed in 1989 in southern Somalia. The SSDF was formed in 1981, in the center. The SDA is an alliance of various, mainly southern, groups and was formed in 1992. It opposes the SNM. The USF was formed in 1989 in the northwest.

The SNM is the ruling party in the self-declared independent 'Republic of Somaliland', situated in the northwest. It is led by Abdel-Rahman Ahmed Ali, who was the state's president between 1991 and 1993. It draws support from the nomadic Isaaq clan.

Political leaders since 1970
1969–91 Major General Muhammad Siad Barre (SRSP), 1991– Ali Mahdi Mohammed (USC), 1993 Mohammad Ibrahim Egal (SNM)[*]

[*] Republic of Somaliland.

Latest elections
Elections were promised in 1995 but could not be held

due to the civil war.

In the 1984 Assembly elections members were chosen from a single list of 171 Somali Revolutionary Socialist Party (SRSP) candidates.

Political history

European interest in this part of Africa was stimulated by the opening of the Suez Canal in 1869. Britain, in the north in 1886, and Italy, in the south, established colonies and Somalia became a fully independent republic in 1960 through the merger of British and Italian Somaliland.

After achieving independence Somalia was involved in disputes with its neighbors because of its insistence on the right of all Somalis to self-determination, wherever they had settled. This applied particularly to those living in the Ogaden region of Ethiopia and in northeast Kenya. A dispute over the border with Kenya resulted in a break in diplomatic relations with the United Kingdom for five years, between 1963 and 1968. A dispute with Ethiopia led to an eight-month war, in 1978, in which Somalia was defeated by Ethiopian troops assisted by Soviet and Cuban weapons and advisers. There was a rapprochement with Kenya in 1984 and, in 1986, the first meeting for ten years between the Somalian and Ethiopian leaders.

The first president of independent Somalia was Aden Abdullah Osman and he was succeeded, in 1967, by Dr Abdirashid Ali Shermarke, of the Somali Youth League (SYL), which had become the dominant political party. In October 1969 President Shermarke was assassinated, providing an opportunity for the army to seize power, under the leadership of the commander in chief, Major General Muhammad Siad Barre (1910–95). He suspended the 1960 constitution, dissolved the National Assembly, and banned all political parties. He then formed a military government, the Supreme Revolutionary Council (SRC), to rule by decree, and the following year declared Somalia a socialist state.

In 1976 the SRC transferred power to a newly created Somali Revolutionary Socialist Party (SRSP) and in 1979 a new constitution for a socialist one-party state was adopted. In 1977 Somali guerrillas drove the Ethiopians out of the predominantly Somali-inhabited Ogaden, but, with support from the Soviet Union, the Ethiopians later regained the territory. Barre was re-elected in January 1987, but opposition to his regime grew in the north, led by the Ethiopian-backed Somali National Movement (SNM), operating across the Ethiopian border.

In August 1989 the SRSP announced a proposal to introduce a multiparty political system, an announcement viewed cynically by opposition groups, who began to resort to violence in different parts of the country. In January 1991 rebel forces took control of the national capital, Mogadishu, and Barre was forced to flee. Ali Mahdi Mohammed was made interim president by the United Somali Congress (USC).

Drought and the political confusion, as rival groups seized districts in the north and south, resulted in widespread famine. An international aid program was mounted, but its work was constantly interrupted by the warring factions, who looted food convoys. In December 1992, following an initiative by outgoing US president, George Bush, 28,000 US troops entered the country, under United Nations (UN) auspices, as the United Task Force (UNITAF), ostensibly to protect aid supplies. Then, in an attempt to establish some sort of social and political order, they became involved in clan conflicts. Joined by other international forces, they became, in May 1993, the UN Operation in Somalia (UNOSOM-II). However, by the end of 1994 US, Canadian, French, South Korean, and Belgium contingents withdrew, reducing the strength of UNOSOM-II to 15,000 troops.

Fighting continued, particularly, from November 1991, between the forces of the Hawiye clan USC, led by Ali Mahdi Mohammed, and the Abgal subclan, which had broken with the USC, the Somali National Alliance (SNA), led by General Muhammad Farah Aidid. The situation became more confused until, in March 1994, a peace agreement between the two main rival warlords was concluded. The remit of UNOSOM-II was modified to give it a more peacekeeping and less interventionist role and plans were made for its progressive withdrawal. Even though there was still considerable instability, by March 1995 the last troops had, rather ignominiously, left the country, with the warlords General Aidid and Ali Mahdi Muhammed continuing to contest for power. It was revealed that the former president, Barre, had died in January 1995, in exile in Nigeria, at the age of 84.

In northwest Somalia an independent 'Republic of Somaliland', comprising much of the territory of former British Somaliland, was declared in 1991, with Abdel-Rahman Ahmed Ali, leader of the Somali National Movement (SNM), as its president. However, this failed to secure international recognition and by 1994 Ahmed Ali, who had been replaced as the republic's president by Muhammad Ibrahim Egal in May

1993, was advocating negotiations between north and south to sort out the country's problems. This proposal was rejected by President Ibrahim Egal. Fighting continued throughout 1996 and in July of that year Muhammad Farah Aidid died of gunshot wounds. His son, Hussein Mohamed Aidid, succeeded him as SNA leader. In January 1997 26 Somali factions met to form a 41-member National Salvation Council to 'create conditions for peace' and two months later, following a severe drought, famine conditions were reported in the southwest. In May 1997 the two main faction leaders were reported to have reached a peace agreement but fighting continued. Eventually, in December 1997, a peace accord was signed in Cairo. However, in March 1998 the validity of the Cairo agreement was questioned and there was renewed fighting in the south.

In June 1999 the Ethiopian army invaded Somalia in support of opponents of warlord Hussein Aidid.

SOUTH AFRICA

Republic of South Africa
Republiek van Suid-Afrika

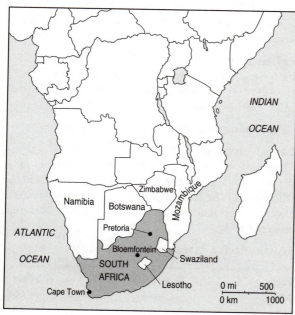

**Capital: Pretoria (administrative),
Bloemfontein (judicial), Cape Town**

(legislative)

Social and economic data
Area: 1,222,037 sq km/471,830 sq miles
Population: 40,436,000[*]
Pop. density per sq km/sq mi: 33/86[*]
Urban population: 50%[**]
Literacy rate: 80%[**]
GDP: $130,920 million[*]; per-capita GDP: $3,240[*]
Government defense spending (% of GDP): 2.99%[*]
Currency: rand
Economy type: middle income
Labor force in agriculture: 14%[**]
Unemployment rate: 45%[*]
[*] 1995.
[**] 1992.

Head of state and head of government
President Thabo Mbeki, since 1999

Ethnic composition
Seventy-five per cent of the population is black African, 13% white, of European stock, 9% previously known as colored, of mixed black and European parentage, and 3% Asian. There are 11 official languages, including Afrikaans, English, Xhosa (21%), Zulu (16%), Sesotho, Swazi, Ndebele, Venda, and Tsonga.

Religions
Most whites and African-Europeans and about 60% of the Africans are Christians. There are over 2 million Roman Catholics, about 2 million Anglicans, and about 1.5 million members of the Dutch Reformed Church. About 60% of the Asians are Hindus and 20% are Muslims. There are also about 120,000 Jews.

Political features
State type: emergent democratic
Date of state formation: 1910
Political structure: unitary
Executive: limited presidential
Assembly: two-chamber
Party structure: multiparty
Human rights rating: 50%
International affiliations: CW, IAEA, IBRD, IMF, IWC, NAM, OAU, SADC, UN, WTO

Local and regional government
Although it is not a federal state, South Africa has a strongly devolved system of government based on nine regions: Eastern Cape, Eastern Transvaal, Kwazulu/Natal, Northern Cape, Northern Province, North West, Free State, and Western Cape. Each region has its own

legislature of between 30 to 80 members, based on population size, elected by a proportional representation voting system. Parties with over 10% of legislature seats are entitled to a proportionate number of portfolios in the cabinet.

The organs of the central government are regionally dispersed, the administrative capital being at Pretoria, in PWV, the seat of the judiciary in Bloemfontein, in the Orange Free State, and the National Assembly at Cape Town, in Western Cape. Multiracial municipal councils have seats allocated on a 30% white, 30% non white, and 40% nonracial basis.

Political system

The November 1993 multiparty Interim Constitution provides for a president, who is head of state and head of government, supported by at least two deputy presidents, and a two-chamber parliament, comprising a 400-member National Assembly and a 90-member Senate, both with five-year terms.

Members of the National Assembly are elected by a system of proportional representation, 200 being taken from national party lists and 200 from regional party lists. Members of the Senate are indirectly elected on the basis of ten from each of the nine regional legislatures.

The president is elected by the National Assembly. Any party with at least 20% of the national vote is entitled to nominate a deputy president, to be appointed by the president. The first deputy president, who acts as prime minister, is nominated by the majority party and the second deputy president by the second largest party in the National Assembly. Any party with at least 5% of the national vote is entitled to a number of cabinet portfolios, proportionate to the number of seats it has in the National Assembly. The president allocates the portfolios. There is an 11-member Constitutional Court.

A new constitution was submitted to the Constitutional Court in September 1996 but was rejected. An amended version was approved in October 1996 and came into force in 1997. It contains most of the provisions of the interim constitution with a strengthening of individual rights, by including a Bill of Rights.

Political parties

Of over 40 political parties, the most significant are the African National Congress of South Africa (ANC), the New National Party (NNP), the Inkatha Freedom Party (IFP), the Freedom Front (FF), the Democratic Party (DP), the Pan-Africanist Congress (PAC), and the African Christian Democratic Party (ACDP).

The ANC was formed in 1912 and was banned from 1960 to 1990. In 1985 it opened its membership to all races. It has a moderate left-of-center orientation and is led by Thabo Mbeki.

The NNP was founded in 1912 as the National Party (NP) and was the all-white ruling party until 1994. It now has a moderate right-of-center orientation and is led by Marthinur Van Schalkwyk.

The IFP was originally founded as an African Liberation Movement, with mostly Zulu support. It was reconstructed in 1990 as a multiracial party. It has a centrist orientation and is led by Chief Mangosuthu Buthelezi and is in a governing coalition with the ANC.

The FF was formed in 1994. It has a white, rightwing orientation and is led by General (retired) Constand Viljoen.

The DP was formed in 1989 by a merger of the Independent Party, the National Democratic Movement, and the Progressive Federal Party. It has a multiracial, moderate, centrist orientation and is led by Tony Leon.

The PAC was formed in 1959 by ANC dissidents. It has a black, left-of-center, nationalist orientation and is led by Stanley Mogoba.

The ACDP was formed in 1993. It has a Christian right-of-center orientation and is led by the Reverend Kenneth Meshoe.

Political leaders since 1970[*]

1966–78 B J Vorster (NP), 1978–89 P W Botha (NP), 1989–94 F W de Klerk (NP), 1994–99 Nelson Mandela (ANC) 1999– Thabo Mbeki (ANC)

[*] Prime minister to 1984, president thereafter.

Latest elections

The results of the 2 June 1999 second nonracial multi-party National Assembly elections were as shown in the table below. The turnout was 89%. Thabo Mbeki, was elected president in June 1999 by the National Assembly.

South Africa latest election results

Party	% votes	Seats
ANC	66.4	266
DP	9.4	38
IFP	8.6	34
NNP	6.9	28
UDM	3.4	14

ACDP	1.4	6
FF	0.8	3
PAC	0.7	3
Other parties	2.2	2

Political history

1. 17th century to 1990

South Africa, where black African states had been long established, was first settled by Europeans in the 17th century. The Dutch were the first, establishing the colony of Cape Town in 1652, followed by the French and then the British. The descendants of the Dutch and French Huguenots were the farmers, or Boers, who established their first republic in Natal in 1839. The British, meanwhile, had annexed the Cape in 1814 and were moving in the same direction as the Boers (or Afrikaners). By the middle of the 19th century the British controlled the Cape and had acquired Natal in 1843 through helping the Boers defend themselves against the Zulus. The Boers then trekked northwards and westwards, in the Great Trek of 1835–37, and created republics in the Transvaal and Orange Free State, which were later recognized by the British. The discovery of diamonds in 1867 and gold in the Witwatersrand in south Transvaal in 1886 led to rivalry between the British and the Boers, and this, together with Boer resentment of the British policy of imperialism and the fear of their culture being destroyed, resulted in a series of wars in 1880–81 and 1899–1902. The Boer resistance to British attempts to annex their republics was led by Paul Kruger (1825–1904). After fortunes had wildly fluctuated, the Boers were eventually defeated and peace was agreed with the signing of the Treaty of Vereeniging in 1902.

The eventual outcome was the passing by the British Parliament, in 1909, of the South Africa Act, which established a new British dominion called the Union of South Africa, consisting of the former colonies of the Orange River, Transvaal, the Cape, and Natal. The Act guaranteed equal status for people of British or Boer descent. The Union came into being in 1910, with Louis Botha (1862–1919), the Boer leader and soldier, as the first prime minister of the new state. An Afrikaner insurrection, led by Christian de Wet (1854–1922), was suppressed and German Southwest Africa, now Namibia, was conquered during 1914–15. In 1919 Botha was succeeded by his protégé, General Jan Christian Smuts (1870–1950).

Smuts, who was prime minister from 1919 to 1924 and from 1939 to 1948, headed the South Africa Party, preaching toleration and conciliation, but the National Party (NP), which had been established in 1912 as an opposition movement, was much less liberal, particularly under its post-World War II leader, Daniel Malan (1874–1959). In 1912 the African National Congress (ANC) was also formed to campaign against white supremacy. It drew its support predominantly from the black and immigrant Asian communities and during the 1920s there was black industrial protest. During World War II, South Africa joined the Allied cause.

The NP came to power in 1948, under Malan, who introduced the policy of apartheid, or race segregation, attempting to justify it on the grounds of separate, but equal, development. Its effects, however, were to deny all but the white minority a voice in the nation's affairs and facilities and areas of residence were segregated into white, black, and colored zones (the Group Areas Act). In the 1950s the ANC led a campaign of civil disobedience until it, and other similar movements, were, in 1960, declared illegal. In 1964 its leader, Nelson Mandela (b. 1918), was given life imprisonment for alleged sabotage. He was to become a central symbol of black opposition to the white regime.

Malan was succeeded in 1958 by Hendrik Verwoerd (1901–66), who refused to change his policies, despite criticisms from within the Commonwealth. Following a decision to assume republican status, in 1961, South Africa withdrew from the Commonwealth. Verwoerd remained in office until his assassination in 1966 and his successor, B(althazar) J(ohannes) Vorster (1915–83), continued to follow the same line. 'Pass laws', restricting the movement of blacks within the country, were introduced, causing international outrage, and ten 'homelands' (*Bantustans*) were established to contain particular ethnic groups. By the 1980s many of the white regime's opponents had been imprisoned without trial and it was estimated that more than 3 million people had been forcibly resettled in black townships between 1960 and 1980. This provoked responses from the black community in the form of strikes and an uprising in Soweto in 1976. Complaints of police brutality brought international condemnation, particularly when news was given of the death in police detention of the black community leader, Steve Biko (1946–77), in September 1977.

Despite this, the NP continued to increase its majority at each election, with the white opposition parties failing to make any significant impact. In 1978 Vorster resigned and was succeeded by P(ieter) W(illem) Botha

(b. 1916), who seemed determined to resist the pressures from his party's extreme rightwing hardliners and give more scope to its liberal members. He embarked upon a policy of constitutional reform which would involve coloreds and Indians, but not blacks, in the governmental process. The inevitable clash occurred and in March 1982 Dr Andries Treurnicht (1921–93), leader of the hardline (*verkrampte*) wing, and 15 other extremists, were expelled from the NP. They later formed a new party, the Conservative Party of South Africa (CPSA), which advocated a new partitioning of the country, along racial lines.

Although there were considerable doubts about P W Botha's proposals within the colored and Indian communities, as well as among the whites, he went ahead and, in November 1983, they were approved by 66% of the voters in an all-white referendum. The new constitution came into effect in September 1984. In 1985 a number of apartheid laws were amended or repealed, including the ban on sexual relations or marriage between people of different races and the ban on mixed racial membership of political parties, but the underlying inequalities in the system remained and the dissatisfaction of the black community grew. Serious rioting broke out in the black townships, with Soweto, near Johannesburg, becoming a focal point, and, despite the efforts of black moderates such as Anglican Bishop of Johannesburg Desmond Tutu (b. 1931) to encourage peaceful resistance, violence grew.

Calls for economic sanctions against South Africa grew during 1985 and 1986 and at the Heads of Commonwealth conference in Nassau in October 1985, it was decided to investigate the likelihood of the South African government dismantling apartheid and thus avoiding the need to impose full sanctions. It was eventually concluded that there were no signs of genuine liberalization. Reluctantly, the British prime minister, Margaret Thatcher, agreed to limited measures, while some leading Commonwealth countries, notably Australia and Canada, took additional independent action. The US Congress eventually forced President Ronald Reagan to move in the same direction.

In the face of this international criticism, State President Botha announced that he would call elections in 1987 to seek a renewal of his mandate. The results were gains for the National and Conservative parties. Growing support for the Conservative Party was evidenced by wins in Assembly by-elections in March 1988. State President Botha's reaction, in April 1988, was to propose more 'constitutional reform', which

would give blacks more control over their own affairs. The proposals were criticized by both whites and blacks. By South African standards Botha's plans were revolutionary but, nevertheless, the whites would retain the main levers of power. Despite this, there were signs of clandestine movements. It was announced in May 1988 that a group of white South African politicians opposed to apartheid, including two members of the House of Assembly, had had secret discussions in Germany with representatives of the ANC, which was being led in exile by Nelson Mandela's colleague, Oliver Tambo (1917–93).

In January 1989 State President Botha suffered a stroke and early in February announced that he was giving up the NP leadership but would remain president until the end of his current term and would not seek re-election. In an unusually speedy election the party leadership passed to F(rederik) W(illem) de Klerk (b. 1936) by a very narrow majority in a third ballot.

In June 1989 F W de Klerk announced a five-year plan for 'constitutional reform'. It was widely criticized by his opponents as a continuation of apartheid in a disguised form. However, after a tentative start, the new state president moved quickly and further than his critics had expected. In 1989 he ordered the release from prison of Walter Sisulu and other leading ANC members and, in February 1990, in a dramatic speech at the opening of the House of Assembly, he announced sweeping reforms, including the unbanning of the ANC, the lifting of the state of emergency, a moratorium on capital punishment, and the repeal of the Separate Amenities Act, which had segregated blacks from whites. A week later Nelson Mandela was released. All restrictions on the movement of Mandela and his ANC colleagues were lifted and during the following months he travelled widely, attracting considerable international support. In December 1990 Oliver Tambo returned to South Africa. Namibia also achieved independence from South Africa in 1990.

2. 1991 to 1998

In June 1991 the remaining laws which had enshrined the apartheid system were repealed and in September 1991 President de Klerk announced that his proposals for constitutional change would be put to the white minority in a referendum. In March 1992 the referendum resulted in a 68.6% 'Yes' and a 31.4% 'No' vote for change.

The negotiations between the government and black representatives were impeded by friction between the ANC, whose supporters are chiefly Xhosas, and the Zulu

Inkatha movement, led by Chief Mangosuthu Gatsha Buthelezi (b. 1928), the prime minister of the Zulu homeland of KwaZulu since 1972, who was accused of instigating violence against ANC members. The national security forces were also suspected of clandestinely encouraging Inkatha and other ANC opponents. In June 1992, 42 ANC supporters were killed at a political rally in the black township of Boipatong, near Johannesburg, allegedly by Inkatha supporters. Mandela immediately called off the constitutional talks, but they were later resumed.

In February 1993 Mandela and President de Klerk agreed to the formation of a government of national unity, after free elections. This was initially opposed by Chief Buthelezi, because he had not been consulted, and by white rightwing extremists who, in April, shot and killed a prominent ANC member, Chris Hani. In the same month Oliver Tambo suffered a stroke and died. In September 1993 a multiracial Transitional Executive Council (TEC) was established while a new constitution was being agreed. The constitution was ratified in November and free nonracial elections were scheduled for April 1994. Meanwhile, in October 1993, in recognition of their efforts, Mandela and de Klerk were jointly awarded the Nobel Peace Prize.

The April 1994 elections resulted in a clear victory for the ANC and Nelson Mandela was elected president by the new National Assembly, with Thabo Mbeki being nominated first deputy president by the ANC and F W de Klerk nominated second deputy president by the NP.

In President Mandela's first administration the majority of portfolios went to the ANC but NP members were given, among others, the key posts of Provincial Affairs and Constitutional Development and Finance, while Chief Buthelezi was awarded Home Affairs.

The restoration of South Africa within the international community was confirmed in July 1994, when it returned to Commonwealth membership. It also joined the Organization of African Unity (OAU) in June 1994 and the Southern African Development Community (SADC). In November 1994 the Restitution of Lands Bill was passed, restoring land to dispossessed black people.

The dramatic changes in the country's political and social systems have aroused expectations among the black majority which the Mandela government will have difficulty in fulfilling in the time scale that some of its supporters expect. Nevertheless, it is certain that there will be no going back and that South Africa's future as

Africa's leading state is assured. During 1995 levels of crime and violence rose to alarmingly new levels and in local elections, in November 1995, although the ANC achieved a clear victory, voter apathy was such that turnout slumped to barely 30% in some areas.

In May 1996 a permanent constitution was agreed and approved, after amendment by the Constitutional Court in October. There followed significant political changes. In September 1997 F W de Klerk announced his retirement from active politics and in December the presidency of the ANC passed to Thabo Mbeki, Mandela's chosen successor. Since South Africa's reinstatement on the international stage, it has shown sound leadership within the continent, but its interference in Lesotho's internal affairs, in September 1998, caused some concern.

The June 1999 general election saw the ANC increase its share of the national vote by 4% to 66%, while support for the National Party slumped by 13% to 7%, as many white voters switched to the Liberal Democratic Party, which had played on white fears of crime and corruption to raise its share of the vote by 8% to nearly 10%. The mainly Zulu Inkatha Party defied opinion poll predictions that it faced a 'wipe out' at the election and, with 9% of the vote, remained the third largest party in the new Assembly. The ANC fell just one seat short of the two-thirds majority in the National Assembly, which it needed to amend the constitution. This majority was achieved after the election by the formation of a coalition with the Indian-led Minority Front (MF), which had one seat. The ANC also polled strongly in the concurrent elections to provincial assemblies, winning in seven of the nine provinces, the exceptions being the Inkatha stronghold of Kwazulu/Natal and the Western Cape, where a National Party and Democratic Party coalition was formed. After the election, the 81-year-old Nelson Mandela retired, as had been agreed in April 1999, and the former deputy president, Thabo Mbeki was elected unopposed by the National Assembly, on 14 June 1999, to become the country's new president. He declared his government's main challenge to be to ensure that prosperity came much faster to the millions who still lived in poverty and that fighting against corruption, crime, racism and the AIDS crisis were other key priorities. His new 30-member cabinet included eight women, while the Inkatha leader, Chief Buthelezi, remained as home affairs minister. The deputy leader of the ANC, Jacob Zuma, became deputy president after Buthelezi rejected an offer of this post.

SUDAN

The Republic of Sudan
Al Jamhuryat al-Sudan

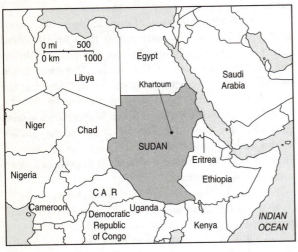

Capital: Khartoum

Social and economic data
Area: 2,505,800 sq km/967,494 sq miles
Population: 28,947,000[*]
Pop. density per sq km/sq mi: 12/30[*]
Urban population: 23%[**]
Literacy rate: 27%[**]
GDP: $12,000 million[*]; per-capita GDP: $415[*]
Government defense spending (% of GDP): 4.3%[**]
Currency: Sudanese pounds
Economy type: low income
Labor force in agriculture: 64%[**]
[*] 1995.
[**] 1992.

Head of state and government
President Lieutenant General Omar Hasan Ahmad al-Bashir, since 1989

Ethnic composition
There are over 50 ethnic groups and nearly 600 sub-groups in the country, but the population is broadly distributed between Arabs, in the north, and black Africans, in the south. The Arabs are numerically greater and dominate national affairs, and the official language is Arabic.

Religions
People of the north are mostly Sunni Muslims (70%) and Islam is the state religion. In the south they are mostly Christians (8%) or followers of traditional, animist beliefs (20%).

Political features
State type: military authoritarian[*]
Date of state formation: 1956
Political structure: federal
Executive: military[*]
Assembly: one-chamber
Party structure: multiparty (in suspension)[*]
Human rights rating: 18%
International affiliations: ACP, AL, AMF (suspended), COMESA, IAEA, IBRD, IGADD, IMF, NAM, OAU, OIC, UN

[*] In a state of transition.

Local and regional government
In February 1994 the country was divided into 26 states with governors, assisted by state ministers, appointed by the president. The states are (with the capitals in brackets): Bahr-al-Jabal (Juba), Upper Nile (Malakal), Red Sea (Port Sudan), Lakes (Rumbek), Gezira (Madani), Southern Darfur (Nyala), Jonglei (Bor), Southern Kordofan (Kaduqli), Khartoum (Khartoum), Sinnar (Sinjah), Eastern Equatoria (Kapoeta), Northern Bahr-al-Ghazal (Aweil), Northern Darfur (Fashir), Northern Kordofan (Ubayyid), Northern (Dunqulah), Gadaref (Gadaref), Western Kordofan (Fulah), Western Equatoria (Yambio), Western Bahr al-Ghazal (Wau), Western Darfur (Junaynah), Kassala (Kassala), Nahr-al-Nil (Damir), Warab (Warab), Unity (Bantu), White Nile (Radah), and Blue Nile (Damazin).

Political system
The 1973 constitution was suspended following a military coup in April 1985 and the country was placed under a 15-member Transitional Military Council (TMC). Another military coup in 1989 installed a Revolutionary Command Council (RCC) and an appointed 300-member Transitional National Assembly, prior to the reinstatement of democratic government. In May 1998 a new constitution was approved in a national referendum and the ban on political parties was lifted. There is a president, directly elected for a five-year term and a 400-member legislature, the National Assembly. The latter comprises 273 deputies, directly elected for four-year terms in single-seat constituencies and 125 indirectly elected by a national conference of Sudan's 'modern forces'. Executive power is now held by a Council of Ministers,

appointed by the president but responsible to the National Assembly, and led by a prime minister (currently also Omar al-Bashir). A constitutional court was introduced in January 1999.

Political parties
Political parties were officially banned in 1989, but the fundamentalist National Congress, which is led by Omar al-Bashir and Dr Hassan al-Turabi, has influence over the National Assembly. It is the successor party to the National Islamic Front (NIF).

The Sudan People's Liberation Army (SPLA) is a militarily controlled political group, which has conducted a secessionist war, mainly in the Christian south, against the government since 1984. Since then it has split into two competing factions, led by Torit leader, John Garang, and the other by Riek Machar.

There are also parties which existed before 1989 and then went into exile.

Political leaders since 1970
1969–85 Colonel Gaafar Muhammad al-Nimeri (military/SSU), 1985–86 General Swar al-Dahab (military), 1986–89 Sadiq al-Mahdi (NNUP-DUP coalition), 1989– Lieutenant General Omar Hasan Ahmad al-Bashir (military-influenced)

Latest elections
In March 1996 the first pluralist elections since 1989 were held. The incumbent President al-Bashir was elected with 75.7% of the vote, defeating 40 other candidates. Legislative elections were also held in March 1996, but parties were not formally allowed to participate. However, the NIF and other Islamic fundamentalists dominated.

Political history
In the early 19th century Egypt tried to gain control of the Sudan but was thwarted by the resistance of the many, fragmented tribes. In the 1880s, however, a fanatical religious leader, Abdullah al-Taashi, succeeded where Egypt could not. He launched a rebellion against Egypt, and its protector, Britain, leading to the fall of Khartoum. It was eventually recovered by a combined British–Egyptian force, led by Lord Kitchener (1850–1916), and an Anglo-Egyptian condominion was established in 1899. This lasted until Sudan achieved independence, as a republic, in 1956.

Two years later a coup ousted the civil administration and a military government was set up under a Supreme Council of the Armed Forces. In 1964 it, too, was overthrown and civilian rule reinstated, but, five years later, the army returned in a coup led by Colonel Gaafar Muhammad al-Nimeri (b. 1930). All political bodies were abolished, a Revolutionary Command Council (RCC) was set up, and the country's name was changed to the Democratic Republic of the Sudan. Close links were soon established with Egypt and in 1970 an agreement in principle was reached for eventual union. In 1972 this should have become, with the addition of Syria, the Federation of Arab Republics, but internal opposition blocked both developments.

In 1971 a new constitution was adopted, Nimeri confirmed as president, and the Sudanese Socialist Union (SSU) declared to be the only legally permitted party. Nimeri came to power in a left wing revolution but soon turned to the West, and particularly the United States, for support. The most serious problem initially confronting him was the near civil war between the Muslim north and the non-Muslim south, which had started as long ago as 1955. He tackled it by agreeing, at a conference in Addis Ababa in 1972, to the three southern provinces being given a considerable degree of autonomy, including the establishment of a High Executive Council (HEC) to cater specifically for their distinctive needs. Towards the end of 1973 elections took place for a Regional People's Assembly for southern Sudan and some months later a National People's Assembly, for the whole country, was established.

By 1974 Nimeri had broadened his political base but his position still relied on army support. Three years later, as he felt his position to be more secure, he embarked on a policy of reconciliation, bringing some of his former opponents into his administration and then, in 1980, creating a high degree of devolution by reorganizing the country into six regions, each with its own assembly and a degree of executive autonomy. The National People's Assembly was dissolved, as powers had been devolved to the regional assemblies, and the southern HEC was also disbanded. There was still dissatisfaction, however, about a proposed redivision of the southern region.

In 1983 Nimeri was re-elected for a third term but his regional problems persisted and he was forced to send more troops from the north to the south. In trying to pacify the south he alienated the north and then caused considerable resentment among the non-Muslim southerners by announcing the imposition of strict Islamic laws to replace the existing penal code. By 1984 he was faced with widespread unrest, demonstrated by strikes in the north in protest against his economic policies and disillusionment in the south. The situation there had deteriorated so much that a separatist movement had emerged, the Sudan People's Liberation Movement (SPLM), whose troops, the Sudan People's Liberation Army (SPLA) had taken control of large areas in the region of the Upper Nile.

In March 1985 a general strike was provoked by a sharp devaluation of the Sudanese pound and an increase in bread prices, but the underlying discontent was more deep-seated. While he was on a visit to the United States, Nimeri was deposed in a bloodless coup led by General Swar al-Dahab, a supporter of Nimeri who had been forced to take over because of the threat of an army mutiny. Swar al-Dahab set up a Transitional Military Council (TMC) and announced that he would hand over power to a civilian administration within a year. At the end of the year the country's name was changed to 'The Republic of Sudan'.

The SPLA's initial response to the 1985 coup was encouraging. It declared a ceasefire and then presented Swar al-Dahab with a series of demands. He tried to conciliate by suggesting the cancellation of the redivision of the southern region and the reinstatement of the HEC there, but these concessions were not enough and fighting broke out again. This continued throughout 1985 but, although the SPLA refused officially to recognize the TMC, secret informal discussions were taking place between representatives of both sides.

A provisional constitution was adopted in October 1985 and an election held for a Legislative Assembly in April 1986. The election was fought by more than 40 parties but no one emerged with a clear majority. A coalition government was formed, with Ahmed Ali El-Mirghani of the Democratic Unionist Party (DUP) as head of state and Oxford-educated Sadiq al-Mahdi, of the Islamic-nationalist New National Umma (People's) Party (NNUP), as prime minister, heading a coalition Council of Ministers. The assembly was charged with producing the draft of a permanent constitution. In another move towards reconciliation with the south, John Garang, the SPLA leader, was offered a seat on the Council of Ministers but declined it.

By 1987 the south had become even more unstable and was now in the throes of a civil war between the army and the SPLM. The situation there was aggravated by drought, famine, and an unprecedented influx of refugees from neighboring states, such as Ethiopia and Chad, which had been experiencing their own internal conflicts.

In April 1988 Dr al-Mahdi announced the second break-up of his coalition and the formation of a new government of national unity. He was re-elected prime minister for another term and in May 1988 a new coalition was formed, which included members of the NNUP, DUP, and the fundamentalist National Islamic Front (NIF). In December 1988 a peace accord with the SPLA was signed, but fighting continued.

In July 1989 Dr al-Mahdi was removed in a coup led by Brigadier General Omar Hasan Ahmad al-Bashir, who suspended all political activity and established a Revolutionary Command Council (RCC). Bashir made peace overtures to the SPLA leader, Colonel John Garang, but rumours of agreements between the government and the rebels were subsequently discounted. Throughout 1990 and 1991 the situation continued to be unpredictable, with reports of many lives lost, particularly in the southeast, where the Islamic fundamentalist military government waged a ruthless campaign against the largely Christian and animist population.

In 1991 there was a reported split within the SPLA and, although this was denied, when the Sudanese government reconvened peace talks in May 1992, under the auspices of the Nigerian government, two SPLA delegations attended, the Torit faction, led by John Garang, and SPLA-United, led by Riek Machar. Although the negotiations ended in June 1992 with a communiqué committing all parties to 'peaceful negotiations' at a future date, fighting continued and the death toll continued to mount.

In September 1993 the regional Inter-Governmental Authority on Drought and Development (IGADD), whose members include Djibouti, Ethiopia, Kenya, Somalia, and Uganda, as well as Sudan, launched another peace initiative and agreement was reached between the Sudanese government and the two SPLA factions for talks later in the year.

In October 1993 President Bashir revealed a constitutional reform package, dissolved the RCC, and appointed a civilian government and in January 1995 the rival SPLA leaders, Garang and Machar, were reported to have agreed a ceasefire to a war that had cost thousands of lives and left nearly 2 million as refugees. Fresh IGADD-sponsored talks between the government and the rebels began in May 1994 but ended in deadlock in September 1994. In September 1995 two days of student-led rioting in Khartoum claimed several lives.

In March 1996 pluralist elections were held for the first time since 1989. President al-Bashir was confirmed in office and in the following month a new government was appointed. Food and water shortages led to riots in Khartoum. By early 1997 the war in the south had intensified and in February the South African president, Nelson Mandela, attempted to mediate between the government and the southern rebels. Eventually in October 1997 peace talks began but made little progress and in November the United States imposed sanctions, accusing the government of supporting international terrorism and possessing an 'abysmal record' on human rights. In December 1997 US Secretary of State Madeleine Albright demonstrated her country's criticism of the Khartoum government by meeting leaders of the rebel forces.

In April 1998 aid agencies reported an impending famine in the south, although its severity was disputed by some observers. In June 1998 a new constitution was approved and the ban on political parties and trade unions was lifted, with effect from January 1999. After government successes in July 1998, the SPLA declared a three-month ceasefire.

In January 1999 the voting age was reduced from 18 years to 17 and a new Islamic dress code, including the wearing of a headscarf, was imposed on women. President al-Bashir stated, in February 1999, that the secession of the south might be considered if it would end the long-running civil war. However, such a development was unacceptable to the southern-based SPLA. In May 1999 the former president, Gaafar al-Nimeri, returned to Sudan after 14 years' exile in Egypt and immediately registered his political party, the Alliance of People's Working Forces. In June 1999, as internal shortages increased, the UN distributed food to more than 100,000 people.

SWAZILAND

The Kingdom of Swaziland
Umbuso Weswatini

Capital: Mbabane (administrative), Lobamba (legislative and royal)

Social and economic data
Area: 17,400 sq km/6,718 sq miles
Population: 832,000*
Pop. density per sq km/sq mi: 48/124*
Urban population: 28%**
Literacy rate: 55%**
GDP: $1,055 million**; per-capita GDP: $1,270*

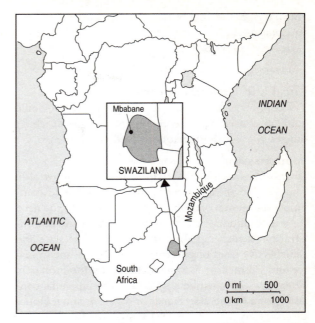

Government defense spending (% of GDP): N/A
Currency: lilangeni
Economy type: middle income
Labor force in agriculture: 74%**
* 1995.
** 1992.

Head of state (absolute)
King Mswati III, since 1986

Head of government
Prime Minister Sibusiso Barnabas Dlamini, since 1996

Ethnic composition
About 90% of the population is indigenous African, distributed among the Swazi, Zulu, Tonga, and Shangaan tribes. There are European and Afro-European, called Eurafrican, minorities numbering about 22,000. The official languages are English and siSwati.

Religions
About three-quarters of the people are Christians, chiefly Protestants (36%), Roman Catholics (11%), and members of Independent African Churches (28%), and about 20% follow traditional, animist beliefs.

Political features
State type: absolutist
Date of state formation: 1968
Political structure: unitary
Executive: absolute
Assembly: two-chamber
Party structure: one-party*

Human rights rating: N/A
International affiliations: ACP, COMESA, CW, IBRD, IMF, NAM, OAU, SADC, UN, WTO

[*] In transition to multiparty.

Local and regional government

The country is divided into four regions, with regional councils consisting of representatives of the 40 chieftancies into which the nation is further subdivided.

Political system

Swaziland is a monarchy within the Commonwealth. The 1978 constitution represents an attempt to combine a traditional pattern of government with the need for a more modern system of consultation and administration. It makes the monarch the head of state and the effective head of government, with a prime minister and Council of Ministers chosen by the monarch. There is a two-chamber legislature, the Libandla, consisting of a 30-member Senate and a 65-member House of Assembly. Twenty senators are appointed by the monarch and ten are elected by the House of Assembly from among its own members. Since 1993, 55 members of the House of Assembly have been directly elected from candidates nominated by traditional local councils (*Tinkhundlas*), and ten are appointed by the monarch. Elections are on the second-ballot majoritarian principle, with the second round being contested by the three leading first-round candidates.

In 1996 the king appointed a 15-member commission to draft a new constitution.

Political parties

Political activity by groups other than the Imbokodvo National Movement (INM) was banned in 1973 and this ban was formalized in the 1978 constitution. The INM was formed in 1964 and has a traditional nationalist orientation. It serves as a political instrument for the monarchy.

Since the announcement of constitutional reforms in 1993 a number of political groupings have re-emerged, and there were six active parties in 1998.

Political leaders since 1970

1968–82 King Sobhuza II, 1982–83 Queen Dzeliwe, 1983–86 Queen Ntombi, 1986– King Mswati III

Latest elections

Elections to the House of Assembly were held, on a nonparty basis, in September and October 1998.

Political history

Swaziland, which had formed a traditional kingdom for the Swazi peoples, was jointly ruled by the United Kingdom and the Transvaal republic, established by the Boers, from 1890 until the end of the South African war of 1899–1902. It then forcibly became a British protectorate in 1904 and, in 1907, a High Commision Territory. The United Kingdom Act of Parliament which established the Union of South Africa, in 1910, made provision for the possible inclusion of Swaziland, with other High Commission Territories, within the Union, but the British government said that this would never be done without the agreement of the people of the Territories. In the knowledge of this constitutional provision, the South African government repeatedly asked for Swaziland to be placed under its jurisdiction but this was resisted by the British government and by the people of Swaziland themselves. The requests ended when, in 1967, Swaziland was granted internal self-government and then achieved full independence, within the Commonwealth, in 1968.

The 1963 constitution, which the British government introduced before full independence, provided for a parliamentary system of government with King Sobhuza II as head of state. In 1973, with the agreement of the assembly, the king suspended the constitution and assumed absolute powers. Then, in 1978 a new constitution was announced, providing for a two-chamber assembly, whose members would be partly appointed by the king and partly elected by an electoral college representing the 40 chieftancies.

King Sobhuza died in 1982 and, in accordance with Swazi tradition, the role of head of state passed to the queen mother, Dzeliwe, until the king's heir, Prince Makhosetive, reached the age of 21, in 1989. In August 1983, however, Queen Dzeliwe was ousted by another of King Sobhuza's wives, Ntombi, who was formally invested as queen regent in October. A power struggle developed within the royal family and in November 1984 it was announced that the crown prince would succeed to the throne in April 1986, three years before he would attain his majority. In April 1986 he was formally invested as King Mswati III (b. 1968).

During 1991 a royal commission toured the country, listening to people's views on constitutional change. Direct assembly elections were introduced in 1993 and in 1994 the king announced that he was to set up a commission, representative of the government and outside interests, to recommend a new constitution. A member of the South African Customs Union, Swaziland has close economic ties with South Africa and uses the South African rand alongside its own currency.

In May 1996 the king unexpectedly dismissed Prime Minister Prince Jameson Mbilini Dlamini and replaced him with Barnabas Sibusiso Dlamini. The ban on political parties was not lifted, despite strikes and popular prodemocracy protests, during 1996 and 1997.

Dlamini was re-appointed prime minister following legislature elections in October 1998 and the king abolished the 21-member, advisory Swaziland National Council.

TANZANIA

The United Republic of Tanzania
Jamhuri ya Muungano wa Tanzania

Capital: Dodoma (legislative and official), Dar es Salaam (joint administrative)

Social and economic data
Area: 945,090 sq km/364,901 sq miles
Population: 28,846,000*
Pop. density per sq km/sq mi: 31/79*
Urban population: 22%**
Literacy rate: 46%**
GDP: $4,800 million*; per-capita GDP $165*
Government defense spending (% of GDP): 2.7%*
Currency: Tanzanian shilling
Economy type: low income

Labor force in agriculture: 79%**
* 1995.
** 1992.

Head of state (executive)
President Benjamin Mkapa, since 1995

Head of government
Prime Minister Frederick Sumaye, since 1995

Ethnic composition
Ninety-nine per cent of the population are Africans, and are ethnically classified as Bantus, but they are distributed among over 130 tribes. The main tribes are the Bantu, the Vilotic, the Nilo-Hamitic, the Khoisan, and the Iraqwi. English and Swahili are the official languages.

Religions
About a third of the people are Sunni Muslims and about 97% of these live on the island of Zanzibar. The rest of the population are mainly Christians, in the Anglican, Greek Orthodox, Lutheran, or Roman Catholic (12%) churches, or follow traditional, animist beliefs (35%).

Political features
State type: emergent democratic
Date of state formation: 1961
Political structure: unitary
Executive: limited presidential
Assembly: one-chamber
Party structure: multiparty*
Human rights rating: 41%
International affiliations: ACP, COMESA, CW, G-15, IAEA, IBRD, IMF, KBO, NAM, OAU, SADC, UN, WTO

* Though dominated by one party.

Local and regional government
Zanzibar has its own constitution, providing for a president, elected by universal adult suffrage, through a simple plurality voting system, for a five-year term, and a House of Representatives, comprising elected members and up to 25 appointees. The president also sits in the union cabinet.

The country is divided into 20 mainland regions and three regions on the island of Zanzibar, and two on Pemba, administered by appointed regional or divisional commissioners. On the mainland the regions are further subdivided into districts, and on Zanzibar the divisions are subdivided into areas. There are part-elected and part-appointed representative councils.

Political system

The 1977 constitution made Tanzania a one-party state, the party being the Revolutionary Party of Tanzania (CCM), but in 1992 legislation was passed allowing opposition parties to operate.

The constitution, as amended, provides for an executive president elected by universal suffrage for a five-year term, renewable once only. There is a single-chamber National Assembly of 275 members; 182 are elected from mainland constituencies and 50 from Zanzibar. Additionally, 37 seats are reserved for women, five are nominated by the Zanzibar government, and one is reserved for the attorney general. Elections are by a simple plurality voting system and the National Assembly has a life of five years.

The president appoints two vice presidents from members of the National Assembly, one of whom is termed prime minister. The president also appoints and presides over a cabinet. Presidential vetoes can be overridden by a two-thirds National Assembly vote.

Political parties

Until 1992 the only legal party was the Revolutionary Party of Tanzania (CCM). It was founded in 1977 by an amalgamation of the Tanganyika African National Union (TANU), covering the mainland, and the Afro-Shirazi Party, covering the islands of Zanzibar, and its constitution pledged it 'to establish a socialist democratic state by self-help'. The party has a left-of-center orientation.

After 1992 a number of other parties were formed to contest the 1995 multiparty elections. These included the Civic United Front (CUF), the Tanzania People's Party (TPP), the Democratic Party (DP), the centrist National Party for Construction and Reform-Mageuzi (NCCR-Mageuzi), the National League of Democrats (NLD), and the Movement for multiparty Democracy (MMD). All date from 1992 or 1993.

The CCW, TPP, DP, NCCR, NLD, and MMD have left-of-center orientations. The CUF is a centrist, Zanzibar-based grouping.

In May 1998 a new party was formed, the Justice and Development Party. It too has a left-of-center orientation.

Political leaders since 1970

1964–85 Julius Nyerere (CCM), 1985–95 Ali Hassan Mwinyi (CCM), 1995– Benjamin Mkapa (CCM)

Latest elections

In October 1995 the first multiparty elections to the National Assembly and the presidency were held. In November 1995 Benjamin Mkapa (CCM) was declared president, winning 62% of the vote, and the CCM captured 186 assembly seats to the opposition's 46. The CUF won 24 of the latter seats, while in the presidential election Augustine Mrema of the NCCR attracted 28% of the vote.

Political history

What is now Tanzania had strong links with Arab, Indian, and Persian traders long before Europeans arrived and there is still evidence of those links in the country's religions and customs. The Germans were the first Europeans to establish themselves on the mainland, and Tanganyika, as it was called, became part of German East Africa. Meanwhile, the British had declared Zanzibar a protectorate. Tanganyika was taken away from Germany after World War I and Britain was given a mandate to govern it. After World War II a movement for independence developed and in 1961 Tanganyika was given internal self-government and later the same year full independence, within the Commonwealth. Tanzania was founded by the merger of Tanganyika and Zanzibar in 1964.

Julius Nyerere (b. 1922) became the country's first prime minister, in 1961, but gave up the post some six weeks after independence to devote himself to the development of the Tanganyika African National Union (TANU), which he had formed in 1954. However, in December 1962, when Tanganyika became a republic, he returned to become the nation's first president. Zanzibar became an independent sultanate in 1963 and, following an uprising, a republic within weeks. The Act of Union with the mainland was signed in April 1964 and Nyerere became president of the new United Republic of Tanzania. Despite the union, the island of Zanzibar has retained its own constitution.

Nyerere dominated the nation's politics for the next 20 years, being re-elected in 1965, 1970, 1975, and 1980, and became one of Africa's most respected politicians. Known throughout Tanzania as 'Mwalimu' ('teacher'), he established himself as a genuine Christian-Socialist who attempted to put into practice a philosophy which he fervently believed would secure his country's future. He committed himself in the Arusha Declaration of 1967, the name coming from the northern Tanzanian town where he made his historic statement, to building a socialist state for the millions of poor peasants, through a series of village cooperatives (*ujamas*). In the final years of his presidency economic pressures forced him to compromise his ideals and accept a more capitalistic society than he would have wished, but his achievements have been many, including the best public health service on the African continent, according to United Nations officials, and a universal primary school system.

Relations between Tanzania and its neighbors have been variable. The East African Community (EAC) of Tanzania, Kenya, and Uganda, which was formed in 1967, broke up in 1977 and links with Kenya became uneasy, particularly as Kenya had embarked on a more capitalistic economic policy than Tanzania. In 1979 Nyerere sent troops into Uganda to support the Uganda National Liberation Front in its bid to overthrow President Idi Amin. This enhanced Nyerere's reputation but damaged his country's economy.

In March 1984 Nyerere announced his impending retirement and it was widely expected that he would be succeeded by the prime minister, Edward Sokoine, but he was killed in a road accident in the same year. The president of Zanzibar, Ali Hassan Mwinyi (b. 1925), was adopted as the sole presidential candidate by the CCM Congress in December 1985. In 1990 Nyerere retired as CCM chairperson and was succeeded by Mwinyi. President Mwinyi, encouraged by the IMF, instituted a program of economic liberalization.

In May 1992 legislation was passed permitting multi-party politics and soon afterwards a number of groups formed in anticipation of free elections in 1995. Ethnic unrest and violence in neighboring Burundi created the influx into northern Tanzania of huge numbers of refugees during 1994 and 1995. Benjamin Mkapa was elected president in November 1995 and the CCM won a strong assembly majority.

In August 1998 the US embassy in Dar es Salaam was bombed in a similar fashion to an explosion in Nairobi, Kenya.

TOGO

The Togolese Republic
La République togolaise

Capital: Lomé

Social and economic data
Area: 56,790 sq km/21,927 sq miles
Population: 3,930,000[*]
Pop. density per sq km/sq mi: 69/179[*]
Urban population: 29%[**]
Literacy rate: 43%[**]
GDP: $1,270 million[*]; per-capita GDP: $325[*]
Government defense spending (% of GDP): 2.5%[*]

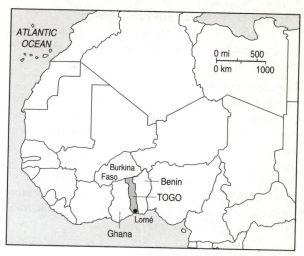

Currency: franc CFA
Economy type: low income
Labor force in agriculture: 64%[**]
[*] 1995.
[**] 1992.

Head of state (executive)
President General Etienne Gnassingbé Eyadéma, since 1967

Head of government
Prime Minister Eugen Koffi Adoboli, since 1999

Ethnic composition
Most of the people in the north are of Sudanese Hamitic origin, while those in the south are mostly black African. They are distributed among some 37 different tribes. There are also European, Syrian, and Lebanese minorities. The official languages are French, Ewe, and Kabre.

Religions
About 50% of the population follows traditional, animist beliefs, about 35% is Christian, chiefly Roman Catholic, and about 15% is Sunni Muslim.

Political features
State type: emergent democratic
Date of state formation: 1960
Political structure: unitary
Executive: limited presidential
Assembly: one-chamber
Party structure: multiparty[*]
Human rights rating: 48%
International affiliations: ACP, BOAD, CEAO (observer), ECOWAS, Francophone, FZ, IBRD, IFM, NAM, OAU, UEMOA, UN, WTO

Local and regional government

The country is divided into four regions, administered by appointed inspectors, who are advised by elected councils.

Political system

The September 1992 multiparty constitution, which was approved in a referendum, provides for an executive president, who is head of state, and a single-chamber National Assembly. The president is elected by universal suffrage for a five-year term. Elections are by the second-ballot majoritarian system. The 81-member National Assembly is similarly elected for the same length of term. The president appoints the prime minister on the basis of assembly support.

Political parties

Until 1991 the only legal party was the Assembly of the Togolese People (RPT). Since then more than 60 parties have officially registered, the most significant, in addition to the authoritarian RPT, being the Action Committee for Renewal (CAR) and the Togolese Union for Democracy (UTD).

The RPT was founded in 1969. It has a nationalist socialist orientation and is led by President Eyadéma. The CAR and the UTD were formed in 1991. They have centrist and center-right orientations.

For electoral purposes, the parties tend to form broad coalitions.

Political leaders since 1970

1967–91 General Etienne Gnassingbé Eyadéma (RPT), 1991–93 Joseph Kokou Koffigoh (transitional), 1993– General Etienne Gnassingbé Eyadéma (RPT)

Latest elections

President Etienne Gnassingbé Eyadéma was re-elected in June 1998, winning 52.1% of the vote. His closest challenger was Gilchrist Olympio of the Union of the Forces of Change (UFC), who secured 34% of the vote.

In the 21 March 1999 National Assembly elections the RPT won 79 seats, and independents the remaining two. Opposition parties boycotted the poll as they continued to contest the result of the June 1998 presidential election, during which, it was alleged, there was brutal intimidation of government opponents. Turnout was officially put at 66%, but the opposition claimed it was barely 10%.

Political history

Originally part of the Kingdom of Togoland, Togo was a German protectorate from 1884 to 1914, when the country was invaded by French and British forces. In 1922 it became a League of Nations mandated territory and responsibility for it was split between France and Britain. The French eastern part was administered separately, as French Togo, while the British part, called British Togoland, was included within the British Gold Coast. In 1957 the inhabitants of British Togoland chose to remain part of the Gold Coast, which was later to become Ghana, while French Togoland voted to become an autonomous republic within the French Union.

The new French Togolese republic was given internal self-government in 1956 and full independence in April 1960, and Sylvanus Olympio, leader of the United Togolese (UT) party, became the first president in an unopposed election in April 1961. In 1963 Olympio was overthrown and killed in a military coup and his brother-in-law, Nicolas Grunitzky, who had gone into exile, was recalled to become provisional president. A referendum approved a new constitution and Grunitzky's presidency was confirmed. In January 1967 he, in turn, was deposed in a bloodless military coup, led by Lieutenant General Etienne Gnassingbé Eyadéma (b. 1937). The constitution was suspended and Eyadéma assumed the presidency and banned all political activity. Six years later he founded a new party, the Assembly of the Togolese People (RPT), and declared it the only legal political organization.

There were several unsuccessful attempts to overthrow him and Eyadéma responded by promising a new constitution and multiparty elections. However, in August 1991, under pressure from foreign creditors and internal strikes, he was stripped of his powers by a national conference held to determine the country's political future. In addition, the RPT was dissolved and an appointed High Council of the Republic (HCR) replaced the National Assembly, with Joseph Kokou Koffigoh appointed as head of a transitional government. After some abortive attempts by loyal troops to restore Eyadéma's powers, there was some rapprochement between him and the HCR and it was agreed that a referendum on constitutional change would be held. This took place in September 1992 and showed an overwhelming desire for a return to full democracy. While the RPT in theory no longer existed, it was, in reality, still an active force. The other parties had coalesced into broad groupings, the main one being the Collective of Democratic Opposition-2 (COD-2), some 26 political organizations and trade unions, which included the Action Committee for Renewal (CAR) and the Togolese Union for Democracy (UTD). Early in

1993 unsuccessful talks were held in France between representatives of the main political groupings in an attempt to resolve the constitutional crisis and the situation became more complicated when Eyadéma and Koffigoh, having partly restored their relationship, in February 1993, agreed to form a new 'crisis government', headed by Koffigoh. This move was strongly opposed by COD-2 and the HCR.

In April 1993 Eyadéma and Koffigoh agreed a timetable for multiparty elections and as the situation improved in the following month, after direct talks between the president and representatives of COD-2, it was announced in June 1993 that Koffigoh had formed a new grouping of six parties, the Coordination of New Forces (CFN), in anticipation of the elections.

The presidential contest took place in August 1993 and Eyadéma was elected with more than 90% of the vote, amid allegations of ballot-rigging by his opponents. Assembly elections were eventually held in February 1994, in a tense atmosphere, after attempts had been made to assassinate Eyadéma. The CAR won 36 seats and its coalition partner, the UTD, 7, while Eyadéma's party, the RPT, obtained 35. Koffigoh's party, the Coordination of New Forces (CFN), secured only one seat. The result was later changed, after claims of irregularities, leaving the CAR with 34 seats, the UTD, 6, and the RPT, 35.

Koffigoh resigned and, after discussions, in April 1994 President Eyadéma appointed Edem Kodjo, the UTD leader, as prime minister. This was rejected by the opposition CAR which withdrew from its partnership with the UTD. Eventually Kodjo formed a government consisting of UTD and RPT members with others from minor parties. The CAR, still dissatisfied with the election results and Kodjo's appointment, boycotted the National Assembly until August 1995.

In August 1996, following a disagreement with President Eyadéma, Prime Minister Kadjo resigned and was replaced by Kwassi Klutse. In June 1998 President Eyadéma was re-elected.

The March 1999 National Assembly elections resulted in a landslide victory for the ruling RPT, as a result of an opposition boycott in protest against the result of the presidential election, which they continued to dispute. This prompted Prime Minister Klutse to resign and he was replaced, in May 1999, by Eugen Koffi Adoboli, who had previously worked for the UN Conference on Trade and Development (UNCTAD). In June 1999 the government agreed to hold talks with the opposition in July 1999. This met a key demand for the re-establishment of political dialogue which was set by the EU when it suspended co-operation with Togo in 1993.

UGANDA

The Republic of Uganda

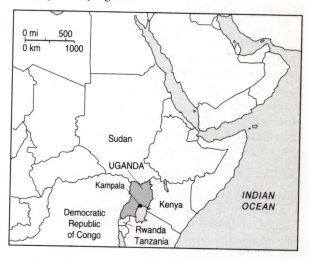

Capital: Kampala

Social and economic data
Area: 24,139 sq km/93,104 sq miles
Population: 20,620,000[*]
Pop. density per sq km/sq mi: 86/221[*]
Urban population: 12%[**]
Literacy rate: 48%[**]
GDP: $4,670 million[*]; per-capita GDP $225[*]
Government defense spending (% of GDP): 2.6%[*]
Currency: new Uganda shilling
Economy type: low income
Labor force in agriculture: 86%[**]
[*] 1995.
[**] 1992.

Head of state (executive)
President Yoweri Museveni, since 1986

Head of government
Prime Minister Apolo Nsimbabi, since 1999

Ethnic composition
There are about 40 different tribes concentrated into four main groups: the Bantu, who are the most numerous, the Eastern Nilotic, the Western Nilotic, and the

Central Sudanic. There are also Rwandan, Sudanese, Zairean, and Kenyan minorities. The official languages are English and Swahili.

Religions
Approximately 60% of the population is Christian, three-quarters Roman Catholic and the rest Protestant, about 6% is Sunni Muslim, and the remainder mostly follow traditional, animist beliefs.

Political features
State type: authoritarian nationalist
Date of state formation: 1962
Political structure: unitary
Executive: unlimited presidential
Assembly: one-chamber
Party structure: one-party*
Human rights rating: 46%
International affiliations: ACP, COMESA, CW, IAEA, IBRD, IGADD, IMF, KBO, NAM, OAU, OIC, UN, WTO

* In transition to multiparty.

Local and regional government
The country is divided into ten provinces which are further subdivided into 39 districts. The provinces are administered by governors, appointed by the president, and they, in turn, appoint commissioners to administer the districts. At the grassroots level, there is a network of 'resistance councils', which have responsibility for local administration.

Political system
In 1985 a military coup suspended the 1967 constitution and dissolved the 126-member National Assembly. A power-sharing agreement between the head of a Military Council, General Tito Okello, and Yoweri Museveni, leader of the National Resistance Army (NRA), which had been formed to overthrow the regime of Milton Obote, was concluded in December 1985 and this led to the dissolution of the Military Council and the establishment of a National Resistance Council (NRC), consisting of 210 elected and 68 presidentially appointed members, to act as a legislative body prior to the adoption of a new constitution. Its chairperson, President Museveni, acted as chief executive, appointing a prime minister. In September 1995 a Constituent Assembly, comprising 214 elected and 74 nominated members enacted a new constitution. Under the 1995 constitution, there is an executive president, who is directly elected for a five-year term and a 276-member National Parliament. This comprises 214 deputies elected in single-member constituencies, 39 seats reserved for women (indirectly elected in each district) and 23 other indirectly elected representatives of the military (10 seats), the disabled (5), youth (5), and trade unions (3).

Political parties
The activities of political parties were suspended in 1986, but they were not banned. This suspension has been extended until 2000, when a referendum on introducing a multiparty system is to be held. Of the 'dormant' parties, the most significant are the National Resistance Movement (NRM), the Democratic Party (DP), the Conservative Party (CP), the Uganda People's Congress (UPC), and the Uganda Freedom Movement (UFM).

The authoritarian NRM is the political wing of Yoweri Museveni's National Resistance Army (NRA). It was originally established in 1980 to oppose the regime of Milton Obote.

The DP was founded in 1953 and banned in 1969 when a one-party state was established. It has a centrist orientation. The CP dates from 1979. It has a center-right orientation. The UPC was formed in 1960 and was made the only legal party, by Milton Obote, between 1969 and 1971. It has a left-of-center orientation. The UFM was formed in 1987. It has a left-of-center stance.

Political leaders since 1970
1966–71 Milton Obote (UPC), 1971–79 Major General Idi Amin Dada (military), 1979 Yusuf Lule (UNLF), 1979–80 Godfrey Binaisa (UNLF), 1980–85 Milton Obote (UPC), 1985–86 General Tito Okello (military), 1986– Yoweri Museveni (NRA-NRM broad coalition)

Latest elections
President Museveni scored a landslide victory in the May 1996 presidential election and the NRM was also successful in concurrent assembly elections. In the presidential contest, Museveni secured 74% of the vote to 24% for the DP leader, Paul Kwanga Ssemogerere. The parliamentary election was officially contested on nonparty lines, but it was estimated that at least 156 of those returned were members of the NRM.

Political history
The British East Africa Company concluded treaties with local rulers to develop Uganda in the 1890s. In 1894 the territory was made a British protectorate and was divided into five regions, four of them governed directly by Britain, with the assistance of native chiefs, and one, Buganda, ruled by its traditional prince, the

Kabaka, under the British Crown. In the 1950s internal self-government was given, with four provinces controlled by local ministers and Buganda by the Kabaka.

Uganda achieved full independence, within the Commonwealth, in 1962 with Dr Milton Obote (b. 1924), leader of the Uganda People's Congress (UPC) which he had founded in 1960, as prime minister. Buganda and the other four regions continued to enjoy a fair degree of self-government so that in 1963, when republican status was assumed, it was on a federal basis and King Mutesa II (1924–69), the former Kabaka of Buganda, became president of the whole country, with Obote as his prime minister.

Obote wanted to establish a one-party state, to which the king objected. Having failed to win the argument by persuasion, Obote mounted a coup in 1966 and deposed King Mutesa. Obote took over as head of state as well as head of government, making himself executive president. One of his first acts was to end the federal status. After an attempt to assassinate him in 1969, Obote banned all opposition and established what was effectively a one-party state. In 1971 he was overthrown in an army coup led by Major General Idi Amin Dada (b. 1926), who suspended the constitution and all political activity and took legislative and executive powers into his own hands. Obote fled the country and took refuge in neighboring Tanzania.

Amin proceeded to wage what he called an 'economic war' against foreign domination, resulting in mass expulsions of the economically successful Asian community, many of whom settled in Britain. Then in 1976 he claimed that large tracts of Kenya historically belonged to Uganda and also accused Kenya of cooperating with the Israeli government in a raid on Entebbe airport to free Jewish hostages held in a hijacked aircraft. Relations with Kenya became strained and diplomatic links with Britain were severed. During the next two years the Amin regime carried out a widespread campaign against any likely opposition, resulting in thousands of deaths and imprisonments.

In 1978, when he annexed the Kagera area of Tanzania, near the Uganda border, the Tanzanian president, Julius Nyerere, sent troops to support the Uganda National Liberation Army (UNLA), which had been formed to fight Amin. Within five months Tanzanian troops had entered the Uganda capital, Kampala, forcing Amin to flee, at first to Libya and then to Saudi Arabia.

A provisional government, comprising a cross-section of exiled groups, the United Liberation Front (UNLF), was set up, with Dr Yusuf Lule as president. Two months later Lule was replaced by Godfrey Binaisa who, in turn, was overthrown by the army. A Military Commission made arrangements for national elections which were won by the UPC and Milton Obote came back to power. Obote's government was soon under pressure from a range of exiled groups operating outside the country and guerrilla forces inside and he was only kept in office because of the presence of Tanzanian troops. When they were withdrawn in June 1982 a major offensive was launched against the Obote government by the National Resistance Movement (NRM), led by Lule and Yoweri Museveni (b. 1944), and its military wing, the National Resistance Army (NRA). By 1985 Obote was unable to control the army, which had been involved in indiscriminate killings, and was ousted in July 1985 in a coup led by General Tito Okello. Obote fled to Kenya and then Zambia, where he was given political asylum.

Okello had little more success in controlling the army and, after a short-lived agreement of power-sharing with the NRA, in January 1986 he left the country and fled to Sudan. Yoweri Museveni was sworn in as president in the same month and immediately announced a policy of national reconciliation, promising a return to normal parliamentary government within three to five years. He formed a cabinet in which most of Uganda's political parties were represented. The political stability provided by the new regime enabled the economy to improve, with an IMF-backed recovery program being instituted, the promotion of foreign investment, and Ugandan Asians being encouraged to return and reclaim their businesses.

In 1989 the National Resistance Council (NRC), which had replaced the National Assembly as an interim legislative body, extended its term of office to allow time for a new constitution to be drafted. In March 1993 a draft constitution was published by the government and 12 months later a Constituent Assembly was elected to debate it. The new constitution of September 1995 extended the rule of the NRC for a further five years. In July 1993, in an effort to increase his popularity, President Museveni reinstated the country's four tribal monarchies, with Ronald Metebi being crowned as a ceremonial king of the Buganda people, 26 years after the monarchy was abolished.

President Museveni and his party were successful in the May 1996 elections.

During February 1999 Rwanda Hutu guerrillas crossed into Uganda from Congo and abducted and murdered eight foreign tourists. In retaliation, President Museveni sent troops into the Congo. In April 1999 Kintu Musoke retired after five years as prime minister and was replaced by Apolo Nsimbabi, the former eduucation minister. Meanwhile, peace talks began between the government and two rebel groups: the Uganda National Rescue Front; and the Lord's Resistance Army (LRA), which was active in the northwest. They were offered an amnesty, if they adopted democratic methods.

ZAMBIA

The Republic of Zambia

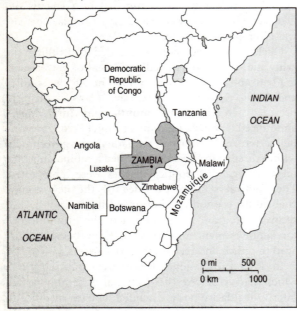

Capital: Lusaka

Social and economic data
Area: 752,620 sq km/290,588 sq miles
Population: 9,200,000[*]
Pop. density per sq km/sq mi: 12/32[*]
Urban population: 42%[*]
Literacy rate: 73%[**]
GDP: $3,605 million[*]; per-capita GDP: $395[*]
Government defense spending (% of GDP): 1.9%[**]
Currency: Zambian kwacha
Economy type: low income
Labor force in agriculture: 38%[**]

[*] 1995.
[**] 1992.

Head of state and head of government
President Frederick Chiluba, since 1991

Ethnic composition
Over 95% of the population are indigenous Africans, belonging to more than 70 different tribes, the most numerous being the Bantu-Botatwe and the Bemba. The official languages are English, Tonga (16%), Bemba, Lozi, Nyanja, Kaonda, Lunda, and Luvale.

Religions
About 70% of people are Christians, about a third of them Roman Catholics and the rest Protestants. There are also substantial Muslim, animist, and Hindu minorities.

Political features
State type: emergent democratic
Date of state formation: 1964
Political structure: unitary
Executive: limited presidential
Assembly: two-chamber
Party structure: multiparty[*]
Human rights rating: 57%
International affiliations: ACP, COMESA, CW, G-15, IAEA, IBRD, IMF, NAM, OAU, SADC, UN, WTO

[*] Though dominated by one party.

Local and regional government
The country is divided into eight provinces: Northern, Western, Southern, Eastern, Northwestern, Central, Luapula, and the Copperbelt, each with a responsible minister of state, working through civil servants. Below this level, local administration reflects some of the features of the unreformed English local government system.

Political system
Zambia is an independent republic within the Commonwealth. Its August 1991 multiparty constitution provides for a president, who is head of state and head of government, and a single-chamber 150-member National Assembly. The president is elected by universal adult suffrage for a five-year term, renewable once only. The National Assembly is similarly and concurrently elected using single-member constituencies. There is an advisory body, the 27-member House of Chiefs, consisting of four chiefs from each of the Northern, Western, Southern, and Eastern Provinces, three each from the Northwestern, Luapula, and Central Provinces, and two

from the Copperbelt Province. The House of Chiefs may submit resolutions to the National Assembly and advises the president on matters referred to it. In May 1996 the constitution was amended to require presidential candidates to be third-generation Zambians. This meant that former President Kuanda would be unable to contest the presidency.

Political parties

From 1972 to 1990 the United National Independence Party (UNIP) was the only legal political party. Now there are more than 17 active parties, the most significant, in addition to the UNIP, being the Movement for Multiparty Democracy (MMD), the Multiracial Party (MRP), the Zambia Democratic Congress (ZDC), and the National Party (NP).

The UNIP was formed in 1959 as a breakaway group from the African National Congress (ANC), which called itself the Zambian African National Congress (ZANC). It changed to its present name in 1964. It has an African socialist orientation and is led by Kebby Musokotwane.

The MMD was formed in 1990 by a combination of trade unionists and some former members and opponents of the UNIP. It has a center-left orientation and is led by President Chiluba. Subsequent splits in the MMD have resulted in the formation of two splinter parties: the National Party (NP) and the Caucus for National Unity (CNU).

The MRP is a moderate left-of-center and, as its name indicates, multiracial party. The ZDC was formed in 1995 and is centrist. In 1999 it became a key member of a new Movement for Multiparty Democracy (MMD), which embraced four other opposition parties. The NP was formed in 1993 by former members of the MMD.

Political leaders since 1970

1964–91 Kenneth David Kaunda (UNIP), 1991– Frederick Chiluba (MMD)

Latest elections

In November 1996 the MMD candidate president Frederick Chiluba, was re-elected with 69.5% of the vote. The nearest challenger was the ZDC leader, Dean Mung'ombo, with 13% of the vote.

The MMD also secured an overwhelming victory in the National Assembly, winning 131 of the 150 National Assembly seats.

Political history

As Northern Rhodesia, Zambia was administered by the British South Africa Company of Cecil Rhodes (1853–1902) between 1889 and 1924, when it became a British protectorate. In 1953 it became part of a federation which included Southern Rhodesia, now Zimbabwe, and Nyasaland, now Malawi, but the mainly black Northern Rhodesians objected to the white dominance of Southern Rhodesia and, despite opposition from white settlers, started an independence movement. The Federation of Rhodesia and Nyasaland was dissolved in 1963 and Northern Rhodesia was granted internal self-government. Within months it became the independent republic of Zambia, within the Commonwealth, with Dr Kenneth Kaunda (b. 1924), leader of the United National Independence Party (UNIP), as its first president. In 1972 it was declared a one-party state and this brought a period of greater internal stability.

Externally, Zambia was economically dependent on neighboring white-ruled Rhodesia and relations between the two countries deteriorated because of its support for the Patriotic Front, led by Robert Mugabe (b. 1924) and Joshua Nkomo (b. 1917). When Zimbabwe, as Rhodesia became, achieved independence in 1980 good relations were restored.

Despite his imposition of strict economic policies, Kaunda was convincingly re-elected in 1983 and 1988, but popular opposition to him grew. After a referendum held in 1990 on a return to multiparty democracy received strong support, President Kaunda agreed to end one-party rule. In October 1991, in the first multiparty elections for more than 20 years, Kaunda lost the presidency to the leader of the newly formed Movement for Multiparty Democracy (MMD), Frederick Chiluba (b. 1943), and his ruling party, the UNIP, was soundly defeated in the assembly elections. This was the first democratic change of government in English-speaking black Africa. President Chiluba immediately removed the six-year-old state of emergency, but reimposed it in March 1993, claiming the threat of a coup. This led to a split in the MMD, with the National Party (NP) being formed by disillusioned MMD members, led by Arthur Wina (d. 1995), and attracting the allegiance of 17 deputies. In 1992 Kaunda gave up the UNIP leadership. A privatization drive was launched by President Chiluba, reversing the statist policies of his predecessor, but the economy was faced with the problem of high inflation (200% in 1993) and rapidly diminishing reserves of its staple export, copper.

Chiluba was re-elected in November 1996 and the MMD was victorious in the assembly elections. In

October 1997 a state of emergency was declared following an abortive coup attempt. In February 1998 the former president, Kenneth Kaunda, was charged with involvement in an anti-government coup but the charges were subsequently dropped.

However, in March 1999 he was stripped of his Zambian citizenship by the High Court, on the grounds that his parents were from Malawi. During 1998 and 1999 relations deteriorated with neighbouring Angola, as a result of allegations that prominent Zambians were supplying the Angolan rebel movement, UNITA, with arms. However, in April 1999 an agreement was signed with Angola which was designed to reduce tensions and promote greater cooperation.

ZIMBABWE

The Republic of Zimbabwe

Capital: Harare (formerly Salisbury)

Social and economic data
Area: 390,759 sq km/150,873 sq miles
Population: 11,150,000[*]
Pop. density per sq km/sq mi: 29/74[*]
Urban population: 30%[**]
Literacy rate: 67%[**]

GDP: $6,300 million[*]; per-capita GDP: $565[*]
Government defense spending (% of GDP): 4.2%[*]
Currency: Zimbabwe dollar
Economy type: low income
Labor force in agriculture: 65%[**]
[*] 1995.
[**] 1992.

Head of state and head of government
Executive President Robert Gabriel Mugabe, since 1980

Ethnic composition
There are four distinct ethnic groups in the country: indigenous Africans, who account for about 95% of the population, Europeans, mainly British, who account for about 3.5%, and Afro-Europeans and Asians, who each comprise about 0.5%. The official language is English.

Religions
About 40% of the population follows traditional animist beliefs and about 30% is Anglican (Protestant) Christian, and 15% Roman Catholic.

Political features
State type: nationalistic socialist
Date of state formation: 1980
Political structure: unitary
Executive: unlimited presidential
Assembly: one-chamber
Party structure: one-party[*]
Human rights rating: 65%
International affiliations: ACP, CW, G-15, IAEA, IBRD, IMF, NAM, OAU, SADC, UN, WTO

[*] Effectively.

Local and regional government
The country is divided into eight provinces, administered by the central government. There are local authorities in cities and towns, with elected mayors and councils.

Political system
Zimbabwe is an independent republic within the Commonwealth. Its constitution dates from independence in 1980 and originally contained many features of the British parliamentary system. However, seven amendments have made significant changes so that what originally approximated to a parliamentary executive is now a presidential one, and what was formerly a multiparty system has become, in effect, a one-party system.

In its amended form, the constitution provides for a president who is both head of state and head of government, with the title executive president. The current president was elected by a simple plurality of members of the assembly but future elections will be by universal adult suffrage, and the holder of the office will serve a six-year term and be eligible for re-election. The president chooses and appoints a vice president and cabinet. He or she has power to veto a bill passed by the assembly but this veto can be overruled by a two-thirds assembly vote. In several respects the Zimbabwean presidency contains features of the limited executive of the United States.

The assembly consists of a single-chamber 150-member House of Assembly, with 120 members elected by universal adult suffrage, through a party list system of proportional representation, 12 nominated by the president, 10 traditional chiefs, and 8 provincial governors. Members serve a six-year term.

Political parties

The two main political parties, the Zimbabwe African National Union-Patriotic Front (ZANU-PF) and the Zimbabwe African People's Union (ZAPU), merged in 1987 to become ZANU-PF. Although ZANU-PF is not officially declared as the only legal party and 18 other groups continue to function, they have little electoral impact so that Zimbabwe is, effectively, a one-party state.

ZANU-PF began in 1963 as the Zimbabwe African Union (ZANU), led by Robert Mugabe, breaking away from ZAPU, founded by Joshua Nkomo two years earlier. During the years of opposition to the white-dominated regime the two groups operated together as the Patriotic Front (PF) and between 1974 and 1979 both were banned. The two leaders returned to take a leading part in the independence negotiations in 1979–80 and the parties merged in 1987. The new combined party has an African socialist orientation.

In October 1996 ZANU-PF formally dropped the use of Marxism–Leninism as its guiding principle.

Political leaders since 1970

1964–79 Ian Smith (RF), 1979–80 Bishop Abel Muzorewa (ANC), 1980– Dr Robert Gabriel Mugabe (ZANU-PF)

Latest elections

In the April 1995 general election, ZANU-PF won 118 of the 120 elective seats, being unopposed in 55 contests. The Reverend Ndabaningi Sithole was one of the two opposition deputies elected. Five leading opposition parties, led by Bishop Abel Muzorewa, head of the United Parties (UP), boycotted what they termed 'fraud-

ulent elections', with the state media vigorously promoting ZANU-PF and more than 100,000 being unable to vote as a result of chaotic registration.

In March 1996 President Mugabe was re-elected unopposed.

Political history

Cecil Rhodes (1853–1902), through the British South Africa Company, began the exploitation of the rich mineral resources of the region north of South Africa in the 1880s, the area north and south of the Zambezi River becoming known as Rhodesia. When the British South Africa Company's charter expired in 1923 the southern section, or Southern Rhodesia, became a self-governing British colony and 30 years later, in 1953, it joined Northern Rhodesia (Zambia) and Nyasaland (Malawi) to form a multiracial Central African Federation. The federation's economy was to be built on labor from Nyasaland, mineral resources from Northern Rhodesia and expertise from Southern Rhodesia. Within ten years, however, the federation was dissolved and Northern Rhodesia, and Nyasaland went their separate and independent ways as the new states of Zambia and Malawi.

The degree of self-government to be enjoyed by Southern Rhodesia after disengagement from the federation was limited by the British government's insistence on retaining the power to veto any legislation which discriminated against black Africans. This was accepted by some, but not all, white Rhodesians. Among those who objected to it were the members of the Rhodesian Front Party (RF), a grouping of white politicians committed to maintaining racial segregation. Their leader, Winston Field, became the country's first prime minister.

Meanwhile, African nationalists were campaigning for full racial democracy and the African National Congress (ANC), which had been formed in 1934, was, in 1957, reconvened under the leadership of Joshua Nkomo (1917–1999). It was banned in 1959 and Nkomo went into exile to become leader of the National Democratic Party (NDP), which had been formed by some Congress members. When the NDP was also banned in 1961, Nkomo created the Zimbabwe African People's Union (ZAPU) and this, too, was declared unlawful in 1962. In 1963 a split developed within ZAPU, one group, led by the Reverend Ndabaningi Sithole (b. 1920), forming the Zimbabwe African National Union (ZANU), with Robert Mugabe (b. 1924) as its secretary general.

In April 1964 Field resigned and was replaced by Ian Smith (b. 1919), who rejected terms for independence proposed by Britain which would require clear progress towards majority rule. Four months later ZAPU and ZANU were banned and Nkomo and Mugabe imprisoned. In November 1965, after further British attempts to negotiate a formula for independence, Smith annulled the 1961 constitution and unilaterally announced Rhodesia's independence. Britain broke off diplomatic and trading links and the United Nations initiated economic sanctions, which were bypassed by many multinational companies. The British prime minister, Harold Wilson, had talks with Smith in 1966 and 1968 but they were abortive on both occasions. In 1969 Rhodesia declared itself a republic and adopted a new constitution, with white majority representation in a two-chamber assembly.

ZAPU and ZANU had begun a guerrilla war against the Smith regime, which at times was supported by armed South African police. In 1971 the draft of another agreement for independence was produced which the British government said must be acceptable to the Rhodesian people 'as a whole'. A commission was sent from Britain in 1972 to test public opinion and it reported back that the proposals were unacceptable. Informal discussions continued and in 1975 a conference was convened in Geneva, attended by deputations from the British government, the Smith regime, and the African nationalists, represented by the moderate Bishop Abel Muzorewa (b. 1925), president of the ANC, which had been formed in 1971 to oppose the earlier independence arrangements, and Robert Mugabe and Joshua Nkomo, who had been released from detention and had formed a joint Patriotic Front. An independence date of 31 March 1978 was agreed, but not the composition of an interim government. Smith prevaricated and at the beginning of 1979 produced a new 'majority rule' constitution, which contained an inbuilt protection for the white minority, but which he had managed to get Muzorewa to accept. In June 1979 Bishop Muzorewa was pronounced prime minister of what was to be called Zimbabwe Rhodesia.

The new constitution was denounced by Mugabe and Nkomo as another attempt by Smith to perpetuate the white domination, and they continued to lead the Zimbabwe African National Liberation Army from bases in neighboring Mozambique. In August of that year the new British prime minister, Margaret Thatcher, attended her first Commonwealth Heads of Government conference in Lusaka. She was not expected to be sympathetic to the exiled black nationalists but, under the influence of the foreign secretary,

Lord Carrington, and the conference host, President Kenneth Kaunda of Zambia, she agreed to a constitutional conference in London at which all shades of political opinion in Rhodesia would be represented. The conference, in September 1979, at Lancaster House, resulted in what became known as the Lancaster House Agreement and paved the way for full independence. A member of the British Cabinet, Lord Soames (1920–87), was sent to Rhodesia as governor general, with full powers to arrange a timetable for independence.

Economic and trade sanctions were immediately lifted and a small Commonwealth Monitoring Force supervised the disarming of thousands of guerrilla fighters who brought their weapons and ammunition from all parts of the country. A new constitution was adopted and elections were held, under independent supervision, in February 1980. They resulted in a decisive win for Robert Mugabe's ZANU-PF party. The new state of Zimbabwe became fully independent in April 1980, with the Reverend Canaan Banana as president and Robert Mugabe as prime minister.

During the next few years a rift developed between Mugabe and Nkomo and between ZANU-PF and ZAPU supporters. Nkomo was accused of trying to undermine Mugabe's administration and was demoted and then dismissed from the cabinet. Fearing for his safety, he left the country, spending some months in Britain. ZAPU was also opposed to the proposal by ZANU-PF, in 1984, for the eventual creation of a one-party state.

Mugabe's party increased its majority in the 1985 and 1990 elections and, relations between the two leaders having improved, a complete merger took place in 1987. In the same year, as President Banana retired, Mugabe combined the roles of head of state and head of government and assumed the title of executive president, with Nkomo becoming vice president. In 1990 he proposed that the *de facto* one-party state should become one in law but this did not attract wide support.

Freak drought conditions in 1991 and 1992 placed great strains on the nation's economy and Mugabe's popularity. No substantial rival had yet emerged to challenge his position; however, the government has been forced, under the World Bank's auspices, to introduce some free-market reforms. In the April 1995 general election ZANU-PF, winning votes in rural areas as a result of its land distribution scheme, secured another crushing victory. In October 1995 Ndabaningi Sithole, leader of the opposition ZANU-Ndonga, was arrested and charged with plotting a coup against Mugabe, and was eventually convicted. In 1996 the government announced a controversial land-acquisition program which would redistribute farms owned by white citizens to resettle thousands of black farmers. In 1998 there were civil and student riots in protest against alleged government corruption, and calls for the removal of President Mugabe.

In November 1998, in response to increasing political and workers' unrest directed against rising fuel prices, the deteriorating economy, and involvement in the Congo war, President Mugabe issued a ban on trade union strikes and mass anti-government actions. In January 1999 the extent of the new land redistribution programme was scaled down from involving the seizure of 841 white-owned farms to only 118. However, this compromise failed to dissuade the IMF from withholding financial assistance payments to Zimbabwe and, in retaliation, it was announced, in April 1999, that the government had broken off relations with the IMF. Meanwhile, in June 1999 the human rights group, African Rights, produced a scathing report on Mugabe's government, accusing it of corruption, human rights abuse, and lack of respect for the rule of law. In July 1999 Joshua Nkomo, the vice-president, died, aged 82.

The Middle East and North Africa

This region extends from the Mediterranean Sea in the north to the Arabian Sea and the Tropic of Cancer in the south, and from the Atlantic Ocean in the west to the borders of Afghanistan and Pakistan in the east. It is mostly desert country, with the climatic conditions associated with this kind of terrain, and is traditionally the home of the nomad, forced into a life of wandering in search for vegetation. It is also, of course, with the notable exception of Israel, the land of the Arab. Indeed, the whole region is often referred to as the Arab world. The total population of the region is in excess of 270 million and is thinly dispersed over an area of more than 11 million square kilometres.

Islam is the dominant religion and is officially decreed as such in 14 of the 18 states. The kingdom of Saudi Arabia lies at the heart of this Islamic domain, housing the two cities most revered by Muslims, Mecca and Medina. In contrast, Israel is the home of Judaism, despite the presence of more than half a million Muslims. The other state in the region where a substantial number of its citizens do not follow Islamic codes is Lebanon, which has a Maronite Christian minority of nearly a million.

The Jewish question, of whether Israel can coexist with its Arab neighbors, has been at the heart of politics in this part of the world for more than 70 years, and for much of that time it was associated with the British and French presence in the Middle East.

After World War I, the League of Nations gave Britain control of Iraq, Palestine, and Transjordan, while France, as the other major European victor, acquired responsibility for Lebanon and Syria. The two European powers colluded in extending their control of the region, Britain taking Egypt under its protection and then, by a series of treaties with the ruling monarchs, most of the states in the Persian Gulf. Only Saudi Arabia retained its independence, under the skilful guidance of King Ibn Saud. France, in turn, took control of Morocco, Algeria, and Tunisia.

Meanwhile, Britain, while fulfilling its pledge to free the Arabs from Turkish rule, also promised, through the declaration by Foreign Secretary Arthur Balfour (1848–1930) in 1917, to establish in Palestine a 'National Home for the Jewish people'. This resulted in an increase in Jewish immigration during the 1920s and 1930s, in the face of growing Arab opposition. Even though the Balfour Declaration had been made,

Britain, largely out of self-interest, tended to side with the Arab states, but the holocaust in Nazi Germany created such worldwide sympathy for the Jewish cause the demands for an independent state of Israel that became irresistible. The rest of the account of the relations between Jews and Arabs is given in the political histories of the countries involved. It has been partly recounted at this stage because the current political situation in the region cannot be properly understood if this aspect of its history is overlooked.

In economic terms the Middle East and North Africa constitutes a relatively wealthy region, but that wealth is unevenly distributed. Bahrain, Israel, Kuwait, Qatar, Saudi Arabia, and the United Arab Emirates all enjoy high per-capita incomes, some comparable to, or better than, those of Northern and Western European states. The average citizen of Kuwait and the United Arab Emirates, for example, enjoys a higher living standard than his or her opposite number in the United Kingdom or the United States. At the other extreme, Egypt and Yemen have low-income economies, with Algeria, Iran, Iraq, Jordan, Lebanon, Libya, Morocco, Oman, Syria, and Tunisia all falling into the middle-income bracket. The wealth of most of the wealthiest countries has been derived from oil, while Israel has maintained its living standards through industry and enterprise, plus substantial subsidies from its friends in the West, particularly in the United States.

The comparatively high literacy rates in some of the richest states are a reflection of the generous, if paternalistic, way in which their rulers have invested their wealth in education and social services. On the other hand, there are other countries in the region, such as Egypt, Yemen, and Oman, where half or more of the population is illiterate. It is difficult to obtain an accurate picture of the degree of civil liberties enjoyed in some countries, particularly the absolutist states, but, with some few exceptions, human rights ratings over the region are not good.

The political systems of the 18 states, as shown in Table 56, fairly accurately reflect their respective cultures and histories. Seven have absolutist regimes and these can be mostly traced back to Islamic traditions and a long acceptance of monarchical rule. Four have been classified as nationalistic socialist systems, most of which were created as a reaction to domination by a European power and the need to establish a national, independent identity. One, Iran, with an Islamic nationalist regime, has not only embraced Islam as a faith but has incorporated it into its political system.

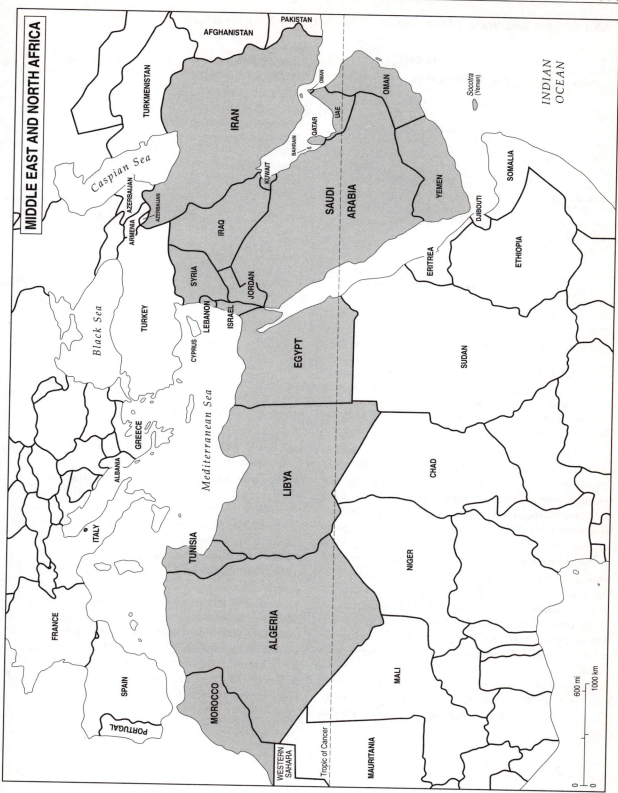

MIDDLE EAST AND NORTH AFRICA

AFGHANISTAN

PAKISTAN

TURKMENISTAN

IRAN

OMAN

OMAN

Socotra (Yemen)

INDIAN OCEAN

Caspian Sea

AZERBAIJAN

AZERBAIJAN

ARMENIA

QATAR

UAE

BAHRAIN

KUWAIT

SAUDI ARABIA

YEMEN

SOMALIA

Black Sea

TURKEY

IRAQ

SYRIA

JORDAN

LEBANON

ISRAEL

CYPRUS

DJIBOUTI

ERITREA

ETHIOPIA

GREECE

EGYPT

SUDAN

Mediterranean Sea

ALBANIA

ITALY

LIBYA

CHAD

FRANCE

TUNISIA

NIGER

SPAIN

PORTUGAL

ALGERIA

MOROCCO

MALI

MAURITANIA

WESTERN SAHARA

Tropic of Cancer

600 mi

1000 km

0

0

Middle East and North Africa: Social, Economic, and Political Data

Country	Area (sq km/sq miles)	c. 1995 Population (million)	c. 1995 Pop. density per sq km/sq mile	c. 1992 Adult literacy rate (%)	World ranking	Income type	c. 1991 Human rights rating (%)
Algeria	2,381,750/919,607	27.325	11/30	57	136	middle	66
Bahrain	691/267	0.549	795/2,056	70	118	high	N/A
Egypt	997,738/385,232	58.978	59/153	48	153	low	50
Iran	1,648,000/636,302	59.275	36/93	54	141	middle	22
Iraq	438,317/169,237	19.925	45/118	60	131	middle	17
Israel	20,700/7,992	5.383	260/674	96	52	high	76
Jordan	98,000/37,838	5.198	53/137	80	105	middle	65
Kuwait	17,818/6,880	1.576	89/229	73	115	high	33
Lebanon	10,452/4,036	2.915	277/722	80	105	middle	N/A
Libya	1,775,500/685,531	4.899	3/7	64	127	middle	24
Morocco	458,730/177,118	26.590	58/150	50	149	middle	56
Oman	212,457/82,031	2.077	10/25	38	163	middle	49
Qatar	11,440/4,417	0.540	47/122	51	147	high	N/A
Saudi Arabia	2,150,000/830,127	17.451	8/21	62	129	high	29
Syria	184,050/71,062	13.844	75/195	65	124	middle	30
Tunisia	164,150/63,379	8.733	53/138	65	124	middle	60
United Arab Emirates	83,600/32,278	2.388	29/74	54	141	high	N/A
Yemen	540,000/208,497	15.800	29/76	39	162	low	49
Total/average/range	*11,193,393/4,321,833*	*273.446*	*24/63*	*38–96*	*–*	*–*	*17–76*

* Though dominated by one party.

A = appointed, AMS = additional member system, E = elected, F = Federal, PL = party list, PR = proportional representation, SB = second ballot, SP = simple plurality, Lib-dem = liberal democratic, Em-dem = emergent democratic, Nat-soc = Nationalistic socialist, Lim-pres = limited presidential, Islam-nat = Islamic nationalist, U = unitary.)

Six states can be said to have democratic systems, that of Israel being now well established, but the other five, of more recent origin. Egypt has had a pluralist political system, though dominated by one party, since 1971 and Morocco since 1992. Algeria has had a pluralist system since 1995, but there has been an ongoing war with Islamic militants. Lebanon has struggled to maintain some semblance of democratic government since 1990, with internecine struggles always threatening to destroy it. The now united Yemen democracy is still in its infancy and its future remains precarious.

The continuing sense of insecurity in the region is evidenced by the high levels of government spending on defense in several countries. Defense expenditure in recent years has reached nearly 10% of the gross domestic product in Israel and Jordan and has well exceeded that figure in Iraq, Kuwait, Oman, and Saudi Arabia. These are considerably higher than the global average, with seven of the countries appearing in the world 'top 15' in terms of proportionate defense spending.

After the 1988 ceasefire in the Iran–Iraq war, there seemed a chance of peace returning to this troubled region but Iraq's invasion of Kuwait in 1990 again threw the Middle East into turmoil. Despite the prompt response by the Western powers, and the subsequent punitive measures taken, Iraq remains a threat to the region's stability as long as its leader, Saddam Hussein, controls its destiny.

Israel, and its relations with the Arab world, is the other key to long-lasting stability. The positive moves from the Arab side, mainly at the instigation of the United States, have changed the political climate and it is not inconceivable that during the next decade Israel's isolation may be finally ended and an independent Palestine state established.

Table 56

World ranking	Date of state formation	State structure	State type	Executive type	Number of assembly chambers	Party structure	Lower house electoral system
52	1962	U	Em-dem	Lim-pres	2	multi	PR-PL
–	1971	U	Absolutist	Absolutist	none	none	N/A
75	1922	U	Lib-dem	Lim-pres	1	multi*	mixed-E/A
100	1499	U	Islam-nat	Unlim-pres	1	none	SB
104	1932	U	Nat-soc	Unlim-pres	1	one	PR-PL
39	1958	U	Lib-dem	Parliamentary	1	multi	PR-PL
53	1946	U	Absolutist	Absolutist	2	multi	SP
90	1961	U	Absolutist	Absolutist	1	none	SP
–	1944	U	Em-dem	Dual	1	multi	PR-PL
99	1951	U	Nat-soc	Unlim-pres	1	one	I
66	1956	U	Em-dem	Dual	2	multi	PR-PL
77	1951	U	Absolutist	Absolutist	none	none	N/A
–	1971	U	Absolutist	Absolutist	none	none	N/A
95	1932	U	Absolutist	Absolutist	none	none	N/A
93	1946	U	Nat-soc	Unlim-pres	1	one	SP
60	1956	U	Nat-soc	Unlim-pres	1	one	PR-AMS
–	1971	F	Absolutist	Absolutist	none	none	N/A
77	1990	U	Em-dem	Lim-pres	1	multi	SP
–	–	–	–	–		–	–	–

Recommended reading

Ayubi, N *Political Islam: Religion and Politics in the Arab World*, Routledge, 1991

Cobban, H *The PLO*, Cambridge University Press, 1984

Luciani, G (ed.) *The Arab State*, Routledge, 1990

Ovendale, R *The Origins of the Arab–Israeli Wars*, 2nd edn., Longman, 1992

Ovendale, R *The Longman Companion to the Middle East since 1914*, Longman, 1992

Sluglett, P and M *The Times Guide to the Middle East*, 3rd edn., Times Books, 1996

Zubaida, S *Islam, the People and the State*, Tauris, 1993

ALGERIA

Democratic and Popular Republic of Algeria
El Djemhouria El Djazairia Demokratia Echaabia

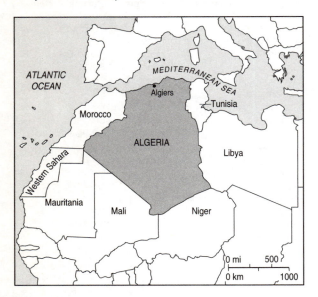

Capital: Algiers (al-Jazair)

Social and economic data
Area: 2,381,750 sq km/919,598 sq miles
Population: 27,325,000[*]
Pop. density per sq km/sq mi: 11/20[*]
Urban population: 53%[**]
Literacy rate: 57%[**]
GDP: $44,600 million[*]; per-capita GDP: $1,630[*]
Government defense spending (% of GDP): 2.5%[*]
Currency: Algerian dinar
Economy type: middle income
Labor force in agriculture: 26%[**]
Unemployment rate: 23.8%[*]
[*] 1995.
[**] 1992.

Head of state (executive)
President Abdel-Aziz Bouterflika, since 1999

Head of government
Prime Minister Ismail Hamdani, since 1998

Ethnic composition
Ninety-nine per cent of the population is of Arab Berber origin, the rest being of European extraction, mainly French. Arabic is the official language but French is widely used.

Religions
Islam is the state religion and 99% of the population is Sunni Muslim.

Political features
State type: emergent democratic
Date of state formation: 1962
Political structure: unitary
Executive: unlimited presidential
Assembly: two-chamber
Party structure: multiparty
Human rights rating: 66%
International affiliations: AL, AMF, AMU, G-24, IAEA, IBRD, IMF, NAM, OAPEC, OAU, OIC, OPEC, UN

Local and regional government
Revealing a combination of French and Arab influence, the country is divided into 48 departments or provinces (*wilayat*), ranging in population from 2 million to less than 65,000, which are further subdivided into communes (*daira*). Each department and commune has an elected assembly. These assemblies are under the direct supervision of the minister of the interior, who appoints administrative governors (*wali*).

Political system
The current constitution was adopted in 1976 and amended in 1989 and 1996. It created a socialist Islamic republic with, originally, the National Liberation Front (FLN) as the only legally permitted political party. The FLN nominated the president, who was then elected by popular vote for a five-year term. There is a National People's Assembly of 380 deputies, elected for a five-year term by proportional representation, and a 144-member Council of the Nation, two-thirds of whose members are elected from regional and municipal authorities, the other third being appointed by the president. The Council's term is six years, one half of the members being replaced every three years.

In 1989 a new constitution allowed parties other than the FLN to operate and multiparty elections to take place. However, in 1992 the constitution was suspended and elections cancelled when it appeared likely that Islamic fundamentalists would be voted into office. A five-member High State Council, with strong military representation, was appointed and its chair became state president. In 1995 efforts were made to persuade non-fundamentalist opposition parties to participate in a multiparty direct presidential election to be held under the majoritarian two-ballot system. The president must be a Muslim over 40 years of age, and may hold office for a maximum of two terms.

Political parties

From a number of radical Muslim organizations which were started from the 1920s onwards, calling for the expulsion of the French from Algeria, there developed a young socialist group who in 1954 formed the National Liberation Front (FLN), with a military wing, the National Army of Liberation (ALN). When full independence from France was obtained in 1962 the FLN became the only legal party.

From 1989 other parties were allowed to operate with certain restrictions, which precluded those based on religion, language, race, gender, or region. There are now some 39 active parties, the most significant, in addition to the FLN, being: the National Democratic Rally (RND); the Social Movement for Peace (MSP); Nahdah; the Front of Socialist Forces (FFS); and the Rally for Culture and Democracy (RCD). The RND is a centrist party formed in 1997 that supports President Zeroual and the military; the NSP is a moderate Islamic party formed in 1997; Nahdah is a fundamentalist Islamic group; the FFS is a left-of-center party originally formed in 1963, and revived in 1990; and the RCD is a moderate, secular party formed in 1989.

Political leaders since 1970

1965–79 Houari Boumédienne (military), 1979–92 Benjedid Chadli (FLN), 1992 Mohammed Boudiaf (emergency government), 1992–94 Ali Kafi (emergency government), 1994–99 Lamine Zeroual (transitional government), 1999– Abdel-Aziz Bouteflika (FLN)

Latest elections

The most recent direct presidential election was held on 15 April 1999 and resulted in the election of Abdel-Aziz Bouteflika, a former foreign minister (1963–65 and 1965–79) and the military-backed candidate of the FLN, who secured 74% of the votes cast. However, his victory was disputed since the six other candidates competing withdrew several days before voting took place since they contended that the military was intervening to rig the result in Bouteflika's favour. The victor rejected these claims and the government claimed that turnout exceeded 60%. However, outside observers disputed this figure, with opposition-leaked information from the interior ministry suggesting the true turnout figure was as low as 23%. In the assembly elections of June 1997, the RND secured 156 seats; the MSP, 69; the FLN, 62; Nahdah, 34; the FFS, 20; and the RCD,

19. The RND, captured 36% of the vote against 16% apiece for the MSP and FLN. Turnout was 64%. The opposition claimed votes had been 'massively rigged', but international observers judged the elections to be generally fair, although there had been some intimidation by the 300,000-strong security forces deployed. The week before polling saw 40 killings in the continuing civil war. Indirect elections to the upper house, the Council of the Nation, resulted in the pro-Zeroual RND's securing in December 1997, 80 of the 96 elected seats, against ten for the FLN, four for the FFS, and two for the MSP.

Political history

Algeria was conquered by the French in the 1830s and soon became one of France's major colonies. French nationals were encouraged to settle in Algeria and become permanent residents, enjoying greater economic and political power than the local Muslim inhabitants. Unlike most of France's other overseas possessions, however, Algeria was regarded as an extension and part of mainland France. The disparity between the rights of the European minority and the Arab majority led to a bitter war for independence, led by the FLN, in 1954. Under considerable international pressure, the French president, Charles de Gaulle, in 1959 accepted the principle of national self-determination for Algeria and full independence was eventually achieved in 1962. The following year a one-party republic was created, with Ahmed Ben Bella (b. 1916) as its first president.

In 1965 a military group, led by Colonel Houari Boumédienne (1925–78), deposed Ben Bella, suspended the constitution and ruled through a Revolutionary Council. In 1976 a new constitution, confirming Algeria as an Islamic socialist one-party state, was approved. Boumédienne died in 1978 after a long illness and there was a smooth transfer of power to Benjedid Chadli (b. 1929), secretary general of the FLN, who, in 1979, felt sufficiently confident of his position to release Ben Bella from the house arrest which had been imposed following the 1965 coup. In the same year the FLN adopted a new structure, with a Central Committee nominating the party leader who would automatically become president. Under this revised system, Chadli was re-elected in 1983.

During Chadli's terms as president significant steps were made in improving relations with France and the United States and in 1981 Algeria enhanced its international reputation by acting as an intermediary in securing the release of the American hostages in Iran. In

1988 diplomatic relations with Morocco were restored after a 12-year break and a similar restoration with Egypt was sought.

Despite Algeria's considerable wealth of natural resources, President Chadli was forced to introduce austerity measures which proved highly unpopular with consumers. This unpopularity was heightened by the feeling that he was moving away from the socialist principles of his predecessor, Boumédienne, and favoring an elite few at the expense of the majority. Acts of violence erupted in 1988, to which the army reacted promptly and harshly, but Chadli managed to moderate the uprisings by promising constitutional changes which would make the government more responsive to popular opinion.

In 1989 the constitution was amended, allowing political parties other than the FLN to function, and in December 1991 the first multiparty assembly elections were held. A decisive win in the first round for the fundamentalist Islamic Salvation Front (FIS), led by Dr Abbasi Madani, resulted in the cancellation of the second round and Chadli's resignation.

He was replaced by an army-dominated five-member High State Council (HSC), chaired by Mohammed Boudiaf, and in February 1992, a state of emergency was imposed. Five months later, in June 1992, President Boudiaf was assassinated, probably by fundamentalists, and Ali Kafi (b. 1928) became the new head of the HSC. Algeria's future as a democratic state seemed to be hanging in the balance.

The emergency government continued in the face of increased violence by Islamic extremists, spearheaded by the Armed Islamic Group (GIA), whose stronghold was Boufarik. In June 1993 proposals for a return to democratic government were unveiled and in August 1993 Redha Malik was appointed prime minister. However, the violence continued, claiming the death, among others, of a former prime minister, Kasdi Merbah. By October 1994 Islamic extremists were targeting foreigners, causing many of them to leave the country. The government's reaction became more determined and the army's dominant position was increased in January 1994 when the defense minister General Liamine Zeroual (b. 1941) was appointed president by the HSC.

In March 1994 a dialogue with the banned FIS was opened and in April 1994 a new government, under Prime Minister Mokdad Sifi, was formed. However, the violence continued and by mid-1995 the three-year war between the security forces and Islamic militants had claimed more than 40,000 lives. The economy was consequently damaged, with the level of unemployment exceeding 20%. In a further effort to secure peace, President Zeroual initiated a national dialogue with representatives of all of the main political groups.

The leaders of the FIS, who had been denied power and imprisoned, were released in July 1994, but as the violence escalated, were reimprisoned in November 1994. The extremists continued their campaign of terror, hijacking a French airliner in December 1994. A multiparty presidential election was held in November 1995. However, the FIS remained banned and the main left wing opposition parties, the FLN and FSS, refused to participate, arguing that there needed to be national reconciliation before any election was held. Zeroual won the election and the National Democratic Rally (RND), which supported his regime, polled strongly in legislative elections in 1997, although there were opposition claims of ballot-rigging. In July 1997 Dr Abbasi Madani, the leader of the outlawed FIS, was freed on parole. Nevertheless, the civil war, which had claimed 80,000 lives between 1992–97, continued. In September 1998 President Zeroual announced his intention to step down before the end of his term of office, throwing the country into a state of uncertainty.

The presidential election of April 1999 was won by the FLN's and military's candidate, Abdel-Aziz Bouteflika, an experienced former foreign minister. However, the new president lacked a firm popular mandate since the election had been boycotted at the last minute by opposition candidates, who claimed that the military intended to rig the outcome. After his victory, Bouteflika declared that the new government, while seeking to bring an end to the continuing civil war through dialogue, would not re-legalize the FIS and would continue with the military crackdown against terrorist activity. He also, however, gave priority to the promotion of economic development so as to reduce the unemployment and poverty which, he believed, lay at the heart of the country's unrest. In June 1999 Abassi Madani, leader of the FIS, announced an end to the FIS fighting and called on other rebel groups to follow his lead. Concurrently, President Bouteflika promised an amnesty for groups which gave up violence.

BAHRAIN

State of Bahrain
Daulat al-Bahrain

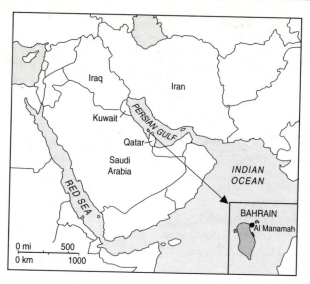

Capital: Manama (Al Manamah)

Social and economic data
Area: 691 sq km/267 sq miles
Population: 549,000*
Pop. density per sq km/sq mi: 795/3056*
Urban population: 83%**
Literacy rate: 70%**
GDP: $4,525 million*; per-capita GDP: $8,240*
Government defense spending (% of GDP): 5.2%*
Currency: Bahrain dinar
Economy type: high income
Labor force in agriculture: 3%**
* 1995.
** 1992.

Head of state (executive)
Emir Sheikh Hamad bin-Isa al-Khaliga, since 1999

Head of government
Prime Minister Sheikh Khalifa bin-Sulman al-Khalifa, since 1970

Ethnic composition
About 73% of the population is Arabic and about 9% Iranian. There are Pakistani and Indian minorities. Arabic is the official language but English is widely spoken.

Religions
Islam is the state religion and of the 475,000 Muslims, about 60% are Shi'ite and 40% are Sunni. There are about 25,000 Christians.

Political features
State type: absolutist

Date of state formation: 1971
Political structure: unitary
Executive: absolute
Assembly: there has been no elected assembly since 1975
Party structure: none
Human rights rating: N/A
International affiliations: AL, AMF, DDS, GCC, IBRD, IMF, NAM, OAPEC, OIC, UN, WTO

Local and regional government
There is no recognizable local government system.

Political system
The 1973 constitution provided for an elected National Assembly of 30 members, but it was dissolved in 1975 after the prime minister said he could not work with it. Bahrain is now governed by the emir, by decree, through a cabinet chosen by him and consisting mainly of his close relatives. Those who are not related are drawn from the wealthiest merchant families in the state. In 1992 the emir appointed a 30-member Consultative Council for a four-year term. The Council was increased in size to 40 members in 1996.

Political parties
There are no recognizable political parties.

Political leaders since 1970
1961–99 Sheik Isa bin-Sulman al-Khalifa (emir), 1999– Sheikh Hamad bin-Isa al-Khaliga

Latest elections
There have been no elections since the dissolution of the assembly in 1975.

Political history
Bahrain is a traditional Arab monarchy and became a British Protected State in the 19th century, with government shared between the ruling sheikh and a British adviser. In 1928 Iran, then called Persia, claimed sovereignty but in 1970 accepted a United Nations' report showing that the inhabitants of Bahrain preferred independence.

In 1968 Britain, as part of a policy of reducing its overseas commitments, announced its intention to withdraw its forces and Bahrain joined two other territories which were also under British protection, Qatar and the Trucial States, now called the United Arab Emirates, to form a Federation of Arab Emirates. In 1971 both Qatar and the Trucial States left the Federation and Bahrain became an independent nation, signing a new treaty of friendship with Britain.

In 1973 a constitution was introduced providing for an elected National Assembly but two years later the prime minister, Sheikh Khalifa, complained of obstruction by the assembly which was then dissolved. Since then the emir and his family have ruled with virtually absolute power. Following the Iranian revolution of 1979, relations between the two countries became uncertain, with fears of Iranian attempts to disturb Bahrain's stability. Bahrain became a focal point in the Gulf region, its international airport the center of Gulf aviation and the new Gulf University sited in the country. A causeway linking it to Saudi Arabia has also been constructed. Oil was discovered in Bahrain in the 1930s, providing the backbone for the country's wealth. Oil reserves are likely to be depleted early in the 21st century, but gas reserves will last a further 50 years and the economy has diversified to include a significant financial services sector.

In the 1990–91 Gulf War, Bahrain supported the UN-sponsored action against Iraq and in October 1991 signed a defense cooperation agreement with the United States. In recent years Bahrain has been in dispute with Qatar over the sovereignty of the oil-rich Hawar islands, with respective claims being submitted to the International Court of Justice in The Hague. Since 1994 there has been a bombing campaign against the regime and protests by Shi'ite groups demanding the re-establishment of an elected National Assembly. In March 1996 a consultative assembly was appointed.

In March 1999 the emir, Sheikh Isa, who had ruled Bahrain since the death of his father, Sheikh Sulman bin-Hamed al-Khalifa in November 1961, died at the age of 65, after suffering a heart attack. He was succeeded as emir by his eldest son, Crown Prince Sheikh Hamad, who had previously been commander-in-chief of the Bahrain Defence Force. The new ruler pledged to maintain close political and military ties with the West, but there were also hopes that he might be more accommodating to opposition demands for democratic reforms.

EGYPT

Arab Republic of Egypt
Jumhuriyat Misr al-Arabiya

Capital: Cairo

Social and economic data
Area: 997,738 sq km/385,229 sq miles

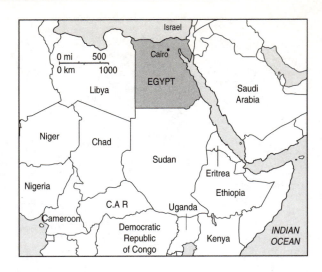

Population: 58,978,000[*]
Pop. density per sq km/sq mi: 59/153[*]
Urban population: 44%[**]
Literacy rate: 48%[**]
GDP: $45,500 million[*]; per-capita GDP: $770[*]
Government defense spending (% of GDP): 4.3%[*]
Currency: Egyptian pound
Economy type: low income
Labor force in agriculture: 34%[**]
Unemployment rate: 11.0%[*]
[*] 1995.
[**] 1992.

Head of state (executive)
President Hosni Mubarak, since 1981

Head of government
Prime minister Kamel Ganzuri, since 1996

Ethnic composition
Native Egyptians comprise over 93% of the population, mainly of Hamitic stock. Arabic is the official language but English and French are also used.

Religions
Islam is the state religion and 90% of the population is Muslim, nearly all Sunni. Since 1992 there has been an insurgency by militant Islamic fundamentalists, who have carried out terrorist attacks on Coptic Christians, tourists, and members of the governing class.

Political features
State type: liberal democratic[*]
Date of state formation: 1922
Political structure: unitary
Executive: limited presidential

Assembly: one-chamber
Party structure: multiparty*
Human rights rating: 50%
International affiliations: AG (observer), AL, AMF, DDS, G-15, G-24, IAEA, IBRD, IMF, NAM, OAPEC, OAU, OIC, UN, WTO

* Though dominated by one party.

Local and regional government

For administrative purposes, the country is divided into 25 governorates, ranging in population from about 10,000 to over 5 million. Each has an appointed governor and elected council.

Political system

The 1971 constitution, amended in 1977 and 1980, provides for a single-chamber People's Assembly (Majlis ash-Shaab) of 454 members, ten nominated by the president and 444 elected from 222 constituencies. Four hundred of the candidates for election are chosen from lists prepared by the parties and the remaining 44 are independents. The second-ballot majoritarian system of voting is used. The Assembly serves a five-year term. The president is nominated by the Assembly and then elected by popular referendum for a six-year term. The president appoints one or more vice presidents and a Council of Ministers, headed by a prime minister, and is eligible for re-election. Kamel Ganzuri has been the prime minister since 1996.

There is also a 258-member Advisory Council (Majlis ash-Shura), partly elected and partly appointed.

Political parties

There are some 16 political parties, the four most significant being the National Democratic Party (NDP), the Socialist Labor Party (SLP), the Liberal Socialist Party, and the New Wafd Party.

The NDP was formed in 1978 as the official government party, absorbing the older Arab Socialist Party. It has a moderate center-left orientation.

The SLP was also founded in 1978 and is the official opposition party. It has its origins in the Egyptian Youth party and has a centrist orientation.

The Liberal Socialist Party dates from 1978. It has a strong free-enterprise outlook, favoring an 'open-door' economic policy.

The New Wafd Party is Egypt's oldest political grouping, dating back to 1919. After being banned, it was reconstituted in 1978 under its current name, then disbanded and reformed in 1983. It is a strongly nationalist right-of-center body.

Political leaders since 1970

1970–81 Anwar Sadat (ASU), 1981– Hosni Mubarak (NDP)

Latest elections

The elections in November–December 1995 were again dominated by the NDP, which won 310 of the 444 elected seats. President Mubarak was re-elected by national referendum in October 1993.

Political history

Egypt has existed as a unified state for more than 50 centuries, during which time it has come under Persian, Roman, and Byzantine rule. From the 16th century until 1882, when it was occupied by Britain, Egypt was part of the Turkish Ottoman Empire. In 1914 it was made a British protectorate and given nominal independence in 1922, under King Fuad I (1868–1936). He was succeeded in 1936 by King Farouk I (1920–65) and Britain agreed to recognize Egypt's full independence, announcing a phased withdrawal of its forces, except from the Suez Canal, Alexandria, and Port Said, where there were important naval bases. The departure of the British was delayed by the start of World War II and the consequent campaign in Libya, which ended in the defeat of the German and Italian forces which had threatened the security of the Canal Zone. British troops were eventually withdrawn in 1946, except for the Suez Canal garrison.

In the immediate postwar years a radical movement developed, calling for an end to the British presence and opposition to Farouk for his extravagant lifestyle and his failure to prevent the growth of the new state of Israel. This led, in 1952, to a bloodless coup by a group of young army officers, led by General Mohammed Neguib (b. 1901) and Colonel Gamal Abdel Nasser (1918–70), who overthrew Farouk and replaced him with a military junta. The 1923 constitution was suspended and all political parties were banned. The following year Egypt declared itself a republic, with General Neguib as president and prime minister. In 1954 Nasser assumed the post of prime minister and an agreement was signed for the withdrawal of British troops from the Canal Zone by 1956. Then, following a dispute with Neguib, Nasser took over as head of state.

At home he embarked on a large-scale program of social reform and abroad became a major force for the creation of Arab unity. In 1956 a new constitution was adopted, strengthening the presidency, to which Nasser was elected unopposed. Later that year British forces were withdrawn in accordance with the 1954 agreement. When the United States and Britain cancelled their offers of financial help to build the ambitious Aswan High Dam, Nasser responded by announcing the nationalization of the Suez Canal. In a contrived operation, Britain, France, and Israel invaded the Sinai Peninsula and two days later Egypt was attacked. Strong pressure from the United States brought a ceasefire and an Anglo-French withdrawal. The effect of the abortive Anglo-French operation was to push Egypt towards the USSR and enhance Nasser's reputation in the Arab world.

In 1958 Egypt and Syria merged to become the United Arab Republic (UAR), with Nasser as president, but three years later Syria withdrew, although Egypt retained the title of UAR until 1971. The 1960s saw several short-lived attempts to federate Egypt, Syria, and Iraq. Despite these failures Nasser enjoyed increasing prestige among his neighbors while at home, in 1962, he founded the Arab Socialist Union (ASU) as Egypt's only recognized political organization.

In 1967 Egypt, as the acknowledged champion of the Arab world, led an attack on Israel which developed into the Six-Day War. It ended ignominiously, with Israel defeating all its opponents, including Egypt. One result of the conflict was the blocking of the Suez Canal which was not opened again to traffic until 1975. Following Egypt's defeat, Nasser offered his resignation but was persuaded to stay on. In 1969, at the age of 52, he suffered a fatal heart attack and was succeeded by the vice president, Colonel Anwar Sadat (1918–81).

In 1971 a new constitution was approved and the title 'Arab Republic of Egypt' was adopted. Sadat continued Nasser's policy of promoting Arab unity but proposals to create a federation of Egypt, Libya, and Syria again failed. In 1973 an attempt was made to regain territory lost to Israel. After 18 days' fighting US Secretary of State Henry Kissinger (b. 1923) arranged a ceasefire, resulting in Israel's evacuation of parts of Sinai, with a UN buffer zone separating the rival armies. This US intervention strengthened the ties between the two countries, while relations with the USSR cooled.

In 1977 Sadat, surprisingly, travelled to Israel, to address the Israeli parliament and make a dramatic plea for peace. Other Arab states were dismayed by this move and diplomatic relations with Syria, Libya, Algeria, and the Yemen, as well as the Palestine Liberation Organization (PLO), were severed. Despite this opposition, Sadat pursued his peace initiative and at the Camp David talks in the United States he and the Israeli prime minister, Menachem Begin, signed two agreements. The first laid a framework for peace in the Middle East and the second a framework for a peace treaty between the two countries. In 1979 a treaty was signed and Israel began a phased withdrawal from the Sinai Peninsula. Egypt was, in consequence, expelled from the Arab League.

Soon after his accession to the presidency, Sadat began a program of liberalizing his regime, but met opposition from Muslim fundamentalists and in 1981 was assassinated by a group of them. He was succeeded by Lieutenant General Hosni Mubarak (b. 1928), who had been vice president since 1975. The line of succession from Nasser had thus been maintained and, just as Sadat had continued the policies of his predecessor, so did Mubarak. In the 1984 elections the National Democratic Party (NDP), which Sadat had formed in 1978, won an overwhelming victory in the Assembly, strengthening Mubarak's position.

Egypt's relations with other Arab nations improved and in 1987 it was readmitted into membership of the Arab League. Domestically, Mubarak had increasing problems with Muslim fundamentalists, making him increasingly dependent on the support of the army.

In 1988 full diplomatic relations with Morocco were restored and full relations with Libya and Syria followed.

Egypt played a full part as one of the allies in the 1990–91 Gulf War against Iraq and has done much to reinstate itself as leader of the Arab world. The arrival of a more flexible Labor administration in Israel, in 1992, allowed Mubarak to play a pivotal role in Middle East peace negotiations, bridging the gap between the Arab and Western worlds. In October 1993, despite a deteriorating economy, with the rate of unemployment exceeding 20%, Mubarak was re-elected, unopposed, for a third term as president. In June 1995 he survived an assassination attempt, allegedly by fundamentalist militants, while attending an OAU meeting in Ethiopia. In November 1997 a number of visitors were killed or injured in an attack in the tourist area of Luxor, prompting fears of further Algerian-style attacks by Islamic extremists.

IRAN

Islamic Republic of Iran
Jomhori-e-Islami-e-Irân

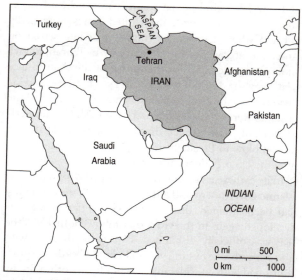

Capital: Tehran

Social and economic data
Area: 1,648,000 sq km/636,296 sq miles
Population: 59,275,000[*]
Pop. density per sq km/sq mi: 36/93[*]
Urban population: 58%[**]
Literacy rate: 54%[**]
GDP: $82,000 million[*]; per-capita GDP: $1,380[*]
Government defense spending (% of GDP): 3.9%[**]
Economy type: middle income
Labor force in agriculture: 37%[**]
[*] 1995.
[**] 1992.

Head of state and head of government
President Dr Seyyed Muhammad Khatami, since 1997

Ethnic composition
About 63% of the population is of Persian origin, 18% Turkic, 13% other Iranian, 3% Kurdish, and 3% Arabic. Farsi (Persian) is spoken by about half the population.

Religions
Islam is the state religion and most (97%) of the population is Shi'ite Muslim. There is a minority of Sunni Muslims, and about 300,000 Christians and 80,000 Jews.

Religious leader
Ayatollah Seyed Ali Khamenei ('Guide to the Revolution'), since 1989

Political features
State type: Islamic authoritarian nationalist
Date of state formation: 1499
Political structure: unitary
Executive: unlimited presidential
Assembly: one-chamber
Party structure: one-party
Human rights rating: 22%
International affiliations: CP, ECO, G-24, IAEA, IBRD, IMF, NAM, OIC, OPEC, UN

Local and regional government
Iran has a long tradition of strong local government and the country is divided into 24 provinces, 472 counties, and 499 municipalities. The provinces are administered by governor generals, the counties by governors, and the municipalities by lieutenant governors or sherifs.

Political system
The constitution, which came into effect on the overthrow of the shah in 1979, provides for a president elected by universal adult suffrage and a single-chamber legislature, called the Islamic Consultative Assembly (Majlis ash-Shura), of 270 members, elected by the majoritarian voting system of the second ballot. The president and the assembly serve a term of four years. Laws passed by the Majlis must be approved by a 12-member Guardian Council of appointed Muslim jurists. The president is the executive head of government. There is also a 83-member Council of Experts, composed entirely of clerics, which appoints a religious leader (*wali faqih*) who exercises supreme authority as a quasi-head of state and ensures that decisions taken by the government comply with Islamic precepts. The Council is popularly elected every eight years.

Political parties
Although around 15 political parties exist, only one is officially recognized: Nehzat-Azadi (Liberation Movement of Iran). This party was formed in 1961, and emphasizes human rights, as defined by Islam.

Political leaders since 1970[*]
1953–79 Shah Mohammad Reza Pahlavi, 1979–80 Mehdi Bazargan (IRP), 1980–81 Abolhasan Bani-Sadr (IRP), 1981–89 Seyyed Ali Khomeini (IRP), 1989–97 Ali Akbar Hashemi Rafsanjani (independent), 1997– Muhammad Khatami (independent).

[*] Seyed Ali Khamenei has been religious leader, since 1989.

Latest elections
Elections to the Majlis ash-Shura were held in

March–April 1996; 110 of the deputies elected belonged to the extreme Islamic Combatant Clergy Association, and 80 to the moderate Servants of Iran's Construction. Turnout was 77%. In May 1997 Sayed Muhammad Khatami, an Islamic moderate, was elected president, securing 69% of the vote and defeating three rivals. Council of Experts elections were last held in October 1998, but were boycotted by the opposition Iran Freedom Movement because of the exclusion of many moderate candidates.

Political history

Persia, as Iran was known before 1935, has been a sovereign state since the end of the 15th century. It adopted its first democratic constitution in 1906 after revolutionaries had rebelled against the despotism of the shahs of the Qajar dynasty, who had ruled Persia since the 18th century. In the early part of the 20th century the country became the subject of British, Russian, and Turkish exploitation until a coup, in 1925, by Colonel Reza Khan, a Cossack officer, deposed the existing shah and resulted in his election as shah, with the title Reza Shah Pahlavi. In 1941 he abdicated in favor of his son, Mohammad Reza Pahlavi (1919–80), who embarked on a massive program of modernization to bring the country into the 20th century.

During World War II, Iran, as it had become, was occupied by British, American, and Russian troops until the spring of 1946. Anti-British and anti-American feeling grew and in 1951 the newly elected prime minister, Dr Mohammed Mussadeq, obtained legislative approval for the nationalization of Iran's largely foreign-owned petroleum industry. With American collusion, Mussadeq was deposed in a 1953 coup and the dispute over nationalization was settled the following year when oil drilling concessions were granted to a consortium of eight companies. The shah assumed complete control of the government and between 1965 and 1977 Iran enjoyed a period of political stability and economic growth, based on oil revenue.

In 1975 the shah had introduced a one-party political system, based on the Iran National Resurgence Party (Rastakhis), but opposition to his regime was becoming increasingly evident. The most effective challenge came from the exiled religious leader, Ayatollah Ruhollah Khomeini (1900–89), who carried on his campaign from France, founding the Islamic Republican Party (IRP) in 1978. He demanded a return to the principles of Islam and pressure on the shah became so great that in 1979 he left the country, leaving the way open for Khomeini's return.

Khomeini proceeded to appoint a provisional government but power was placed essentially in the hands of the 15-member Islamic Revolutionary Council, controlled by himself. Iran was declared an Islamic Republic and a new constitution, based on Islamic principles, was adopted. Relations with the United States were badly affected when a group of Iranian students seized 66 American hostages at the US embassy in Tehran, to give support to a demand for the return of the shah to face trial. Even the death of the shah, in Egypt in 1980, did little to resolve the crisis, which was not ended until all the hostages were released in January 1981. The hostage crisis not only damaged US-Iranian relations, but dealt a mortal blow to President Jimmy Carter's hopes of winning the US presidency for a second term.

In its early years several rifts developed within the new Islamic government and although by 1982 some stability had been attained, disputes between different factions developed again in the years that followed. In 1987, the IRP was officially disbanded. Externally, the war with Iraq which broke out in 1980, following a border dispute, continued with considerable loss of life on both sides. By 1987 both sides in the war had increased the scale of their operations, each apparently believing that outright victory was possible. Then, in 1988, the leaders of the two countries, somewhat surprisingly, agreed to a ceasefire and the start of talks about a permanent solution to the dispute.

Not only was the end of the war seen in 1988 but also the beginnings of a rapprochement between Iran and the Western powers. The burden of the fighting, and the enormous loss of life, had obviously affected the attitude of the ruling regime, allowing more moderate elements, such as the speaker of the Assembly, to exercise greater influence. The restoration of diplomatic relations with Britain at the end of 1988 was reversed, however, because of Islamic opposition to the publication of *The Satanic Verses* by the British-based author, Salman Rushdie. Ayatollah Khomeini issued a fatwa, or public order, for his assassination and Iran seemed to have reverted to its extremist, unpredictable character. Then, in July 1989, Ayatollah Khomeini died. He was succeeded as religious leader by Ayatollah Ali Khamenei (b. 1940), while the pragmatic speaker of the Assembly, Hashemi Rafsanjani (b. 1934), became executive president. Apart from occasional setbacks and expressed suspicions about Iran's military intentions and its maltreatment of the Kurdish people of northern Iran, relations with the Western powers progressively improved. In June 1993 Rafsanjani was re-elected, but his efforts to promote free-market reforms to stimulate an ailing economy, with unemployment at 25%, have been repeatedly thwarted by the opposition of clerics. Supporters of President Rafsanjani won a clear victory in the March 1996 Assembly elections, and in May 1997 the widely respected Dr Seyyed Muhammad Khatami was elected president. In May 1998 there were signs that the new leadership was seeking a rapprochement with the West, indicated by the effective lifting of the fatwa on Salman Rushdie in October 1998.

In local council elections, held in February 1999, liberal and centrist candidates, supportive of the reformist Khatami, outpolled conservative Islamists. A month later, during a state visit to Italy, the first by an Iranian leader to Western Europe since the 1979 revolution, President Khatami spoke of a new era of détente and pledged that the government would oppose terrorism and the spread of nuclear arms. This he followed, in May 1999, with a groundbreaking visit to traditionally hostile Saudi Arabia and exchanging ambassadors with the United Kingdom. Conservative legislators attempted to fight back, in May 1999, by launching an impeachment motion against the moderate culture minister, Ayatollah Mohajerani, who had relaxed censorship and who was accused of spurning Islam in favour of 'Western decadence'. However, it narrowly failed and in July 1999 the country was rocked by large, six-day-long pro-democracy demonstrations and riots in Tehran, by students who were protesting against the recent banning of a liberal newspaper. Khatami denounced the rioters, but these demonstrations suggested that the Islamic Revolution may have now run its course and that the direction of Iranian politics lay in the direction of greater political pluralism.

IRAQ

Republic of Iraq
al-Jumhuriya al-'Iraqiya

Capital: Baghdad

Social and economic data
Area: 438,317 sq km/169,235 sq miles
Population: 19,925,000[*]
Pop. density per sq km/sq mi: 45/118[*]
Urban population: 73%[**]
Literacy rate: 60%[**]
GDP: $23,000 million[*]; per-capita GDP: $1,150[*]
Government defense spending (% of GDP): 14.8%[*]
Currency: Iraqi dinar

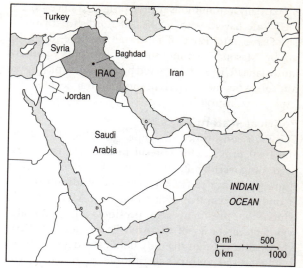

Economy type: middle income
Labor force in agriculture: 13%[**]
[*] 1995.
[**] 1992.

Head of state and head of government
President Saddam Hussein, since 1979

Ethnic composition
About 79% of the population is Arab, 16% Kurdish, mainly in the northeast, 3% Persian, and 2% Turkish. The Kurds have, for a long time, pressed for greater autonomy which has been promised and then often replaced by harsh repressive measures. The official language is Arabic, spoken by about 80% of the population.

Religions
Islam is the state religion and about 51% of the population is Shi'ite Muslim and 43% is Sunni Muslim. The Sunni Muslims are mainly in the north of the country and the Shi'ites in the south.

Political features
State type: nationalistic socialist
Date of state formation: 1932
Political structure: unitary
Executive: unlimited presidential
Assembly: one-chamber
Party structure: one-party
Human rights rating: 17%
International affiliations: AL, AMF (suspended), IAEA, IBRD, IMF, NAM, OAPEC, OIC, OPEC, UN

Local and regional government
The country is divided into 18 governorates, administered by appointed governors. In the Kurdish north there

is a partially autonomous region, protected since 1992 as a US 'safe haven', with a 105-seat Kurdish parliament. The Democratic Party of Kurdistan (DPK; estd. 1946), led by Masoud Barzani, and the Patriotic Union of Kurdistan (PUK; estd. 1975) led by Jalal Talabani, dispute control. In the marsh lands in southern Iraq there is low-level Shi'ite insurgency.

Political system

The 1970 constitution, amended in 1973, 1974, 1980, and 1990, provides for a president who is head of state, head of government, and chair of a Revolutionary Command Council (RCC). Day-to-day administration is under the control of a Council of Ministers over which the president also presides. They are also regional secretaries of the Arab Ba'ath Socialist Party which, although not the only political party in Iraq, so dominates the country's institutions as to make it virtually a one-party state. In effect, therefore, Iraq is ruled by the Arab Ba'ath Socialist Party through its regional secretary and other leading members. There is a 250-member National Assembly, elected for a four-year term by universal suffrage through a proportional representation voting system, but it has little real power. Thirty of the Assembly's seats are reserved for representatives of the autonomous regions of Arbil, D'hok and As-Sulaimaniya.

Political parties

Although there are, in theory, a number of parties, in reality there is only one which has real political power, the Arab Ba'ath Socialist Party. It was originally founded in Damascus in 1947 and came to prominence in Iraq in 1968 and since then has dominated the country's politics. Its orientation is socialist and strongly nationalistic.

Political leaders since 1970

1968–79 Ahmed Hassan al-Bakr (Arab Ba'ath Socialist Party), 1979– Saddam Hussein (Arab Ba'ath Socialist Party)

Latest elections

In the March 1996 elections for the National Assembly, the Arab Ba'ath Socialist Party, as part of the National Progressive Front coalition, won a majority of the 250 seats, which were contested by 689 candidates. Turnout was 93.5%.

In September 1995 the National Assembly unanimously approved Saddam Hussein as the sole candidate, for a further seven-year term, in a national presidential plebiscite. This was held in October and there was officially a 99.96% vote in favor of Saddam Hussein, with turnout put at 99.47%.

Political history

Formerly part of the Turkish Ottoman Empire, Iraq was placed under British administration by the League of Nations in 1920. This was the start of a long, and generally amicable, relationship. In 1932 Iraq became a fully independent kingdom and the following year the reigning king, Faisal I (1885–1933), who had ruled since 1921, died, to be succeeded by his son, Ghazi. The leading figure behind the throne was the strongly pro-Western General Nuri el-Said (1888–1958), who held the post of prime minister from 1930 until 1958. In 1939 King Ghazi was killed in a motor accident and Faisal II (1935–58) became king at the age of three, his uncle Prince Abdul Ilah acting as regent until 1953 when the king assumed full powers.

In 1955 Iraq signed the Baghdad Pact, a regional collective security agreement, with the USSR seen as the main potential threat, and in 1958 joined with Jordan to form an Arab Federation, with King Faisal II as head of state. In July of that year, however, a revolution overthrew the monarchy and King Faisal, Prince Abdul Ilah, and General Nuri were all assassinated. The constitution was suspended and Iraq was declared a republic, with Brigadier Abdul Karim Kassem (1914–63) as head of a leftwing military regime. He withdrew from the Baghdad Pact in 1959 and, after tenuously holding on to power for five years, was killed in another coup in 1963.

The leader of this coup was Colonel Salem Aref. He established a new constitutional government, ended martial law and within two years had introduced a civilian administration. He died, however, in an air crash in 1966. His brother, who succeeded him, was, in turn, ousted in a revolution led by the Arab Ba'ath Socialist Party in 1968 and replaced by Major General Ahmed al-Bakr who concentrated power in the hands of a Revolutionary Command Council (RCC), taking for himself the posts of head of state, head of government, and chair of the RCC.

In 1979, Saddam Hussein (b. 1937), who for several years had been the real power behind the scenes, replaced al-Bakr as chair of the RCC and state president. Saddam Hussein, who had joined the Arab Ba'ath Socialist Party in 1957, had been forced to flee Iraq in 1959 after attempting to assassinate General Kassem, was imprisoned in 1964 for plotting to overthrow the succeeding regime, and had played a leading role in the 1968 revolution. In 1980 he introduced a 'National Charter', reaffirming a policy of nonalignment and a constitution which provided for an elected National

Assembly. The first elections took place that year.

Externally, Iraq had, since 1970, enjoyed a fluctuating relationship with Syria, sometimes distant and sometimes close enough to contemplate a complete political and economic union. By 1980, however, the atmosphere was cool. Relations between Iraq and Iran had been tense for some years, with disagreement about the border between them, which runs down the Shatt-al-Arab waterway. The 1979 Iranian revolution made Iraq more suspicious of Iran's future intentions and in 1980 a full-scale war broke out.

Despite Iraq's potentially weaker military strength, Iran made little territorial progress and by 1986 it seemed as if a stalemate might have been reached. The fighting intensified however in late 1986 and early 1987, with heavy human and material losses on both sides. By 1988 Iraq was enjoying greater military success, then, somewhat unexpectedly, the Iranian government responded to an initiative by the United Nations secretary general and agreed to a ceasefire.

The end of hostilities freed Iraq's well disciplined army to deal with the Kurdish rebels who, in their quest for greater autonomy, had taken advantage of the government's preoccupation with the Iran–Iraq War. Many Kurds were reported to have fled the country into neighboring Turkey or Iran.

In the early months of 1990 Iraq initiated a 'war of words' against neighboring Kuwait, claiming that it held territory and oil reserves belonging to Iraq. In August 1990 the words turned into deeds and Iraq invaded and speedily occupied Kuwait. Following initiatives by the United States, Britain, and France, the UN Security Council agreed to impose sanctions on Iraq and then, in February 1991, military attacks.

The ground war, following a massive use of air power, was short and effective, lasting just 100 hours, and Kuwait was freed. The UN ceasefire resolution imposed on Iraq, and enforced by economic sanctions and a special commission, required that it destroyed its chemical and biological weapons and ceased attempts to develop nuclear weapons. However, Saddam Hussein remained in power and, although much of his offensive capability was reduced, he was still able to persecute the Kurdish and Shi'ite minorities in northern Iraq and the southern marshlands. This persuaded the West to declare 'safe haven' no-fly zones to protect these minority communities. Hopes in the West that internal opposition would weaken his position and eventually displace him were not fulfilled and in late 1994 there were even signs of military activity near the border with Kuwait. A show of strength by the United States dissipated that threat. In August 1995 Saddam Hussein's position seemed less secure as, with the economy in a state of collapse, a number of his key associates defected. These included two of Saddam Hussein's sons-in-law and their wives who fled to Jordan, whose ruler, King Hussein, was the cousin of Iraq's former king, Faisal II. Saddam Hussein increasingly fell back on the support of his sons, Udai and Qusai, heads of the intelligence services, both of whom were given vice presidential authority in May 1995.

In September 1996 troops were moved into Kurdish areas in the north, prompting a US response of aerial attacks on military targets in the south. In December 1997 there was a major confrontation with the UN, following Iraqi objections to US members of the team given the task of inspecting sites suspected as being used by Iraq for the production of weapons of mass destruction. Eventually, in March 1998, the UN secretary general was successful in securing an agreement to allow the inspections of proceed. However, further confrontation followed in November 1998, which was only resolved at the last possible moment.

In December 1998 Iraq again barred UN inspectors from visiting sites at Ba'ath party headquarters, provoking fresh airstrikes by American and British planes. In March 1999 official UN reports expressed continuing concerns, arising from the monitoring work of the UN Special Commission (UNSCOM) on Iraq, about Iraq's weapons programme and about widespread hardship amongst its population as a result of international sanctions. There continued to be reports of sporadic Iraqi violations of the US- and UK-aircraft patrolled 'no-fly zones' northern and southern Iraq and unrest increased in the south after the assassination, in February 1999, of Grand Ayatollah Mohammed Sadeq al-Sadr, a senior Shi'ite Muslim cleric, in the southern holy city of Najaf.

ISRAEL

State of Israel
Medinat Israel

Capital: Jerusalem (not recognized by the United Nations)

Social and economic data
Area: 20,700 sq km/7,992 sq miles

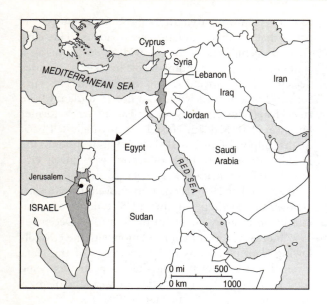

Population: 5,383,000[*]
Pop. density per sq km/sq mi: 260/674[*]
Urban population: 92%[**]
Literacy rate: 96%[**]
GDP: $87,875 million[*]; per-capita GDP: $16,320[*]
Government defense spending (% of GDP): 9.2%[*]
Currency: new shekel
Economy type: high income
Labor force in agriculture: 2%[**]
Unemployment rate: 6.9%
[*] 1995.
[**] 1992.

Head of state
President Ezer Weizmann, since 1993

Head of government
Prime Minister Ehud Barak, since 1999

Ethnic composition
About 85% of the population is Jewish. Most of the rest of the population is Arab. The official language is Hebrew, spoken by the majority of the population; Arabic is the second language and English is also used.

Religions
Judaism is the state religion and about 85% of the population professes to adhere to it. There are also about 527,000 Muslims and about 94,000 Christians. Ninety per cent of Palestinians are Muslim (chiefly Sunni).

Political features
State type: liberal democratic
Date of state formation: 1948

Political structure: unitary
Executive: parliamentary
Assembly: one-chamber
Party structure: multiparty
Human rights rating: 76%
International affiliations: AG (observer), CERN (observer), IAEA, IBRD, IMF, UN, WTO

Local and regional government
The country is divided into six administrative districts, each controlled by a district commissioner. Within the districts there are 31 municipalities and 115 local councils. There are also 48 regional councils, containing representatives from 700 villages. Elections for regional and local councils coincide with those for the Knesset (assembly) and also operate through a proportional representation voting system. Since 1994 Palestinians in the occupied territories of the Gaza strip (325 sq km/125 sq miles, population 1.7 million), the Jericho enclave (60 sq km/23 sq miles, population 40,000), and the West Bank of the Jordan (5,819 sq km/2,247 sq miles, population 0.9 million) have had a measure of autonomy. The Israeli military withdrew from the Gaza Strip and Jericho in mid-1996, and a five-year period of interim self-government under a Palestinian National Authority (PNA) began. Legislative elections in January 1996 were won by the mainstream al-Fatah faction of the Palestine Liberation Organization (PLO), whose leader, Yasser Arafat, was elected to become head of the PNA. An 88-member Palestinian Council was also elected.

Political system
Israel does not have a written constitution. In 1950 the single-chamber assembly, the Knesset, voted to adopt a state constitution by evolution over an unspecified period of time. As in the other few states without written constitutions, such as the United Kingdom and New Zealand, a number of laws have been passed which are considered to have particular constitutional significance and they could, at some time, be codified into a single written document.

Supreme authority rests with the Knesset, whose 120 members are elected by universal adult suffrage, through a party list system of proportional representation, for a four-year term. It is, however, subject to dissolution within that period. The president is a constitutional head of state and is elected by the Knesset for a maximum of two five-year terms, renewable once only. The prime minister and cabinet are mostly drawn from, and collectively responsible to, the

Knesset, but occasionally a cabinet member may be chosen from outside. Since 1996 the prime minister has been directly elected for a four-year term.

Political parties

There are currently some 33 political parties, several of the small ones being rather like religious pressure groups. The two most significant of the main parties are the Israel Labor Party (or One Israel) and the Consolidation Party (Likud). The proportional representation voting system not only encourages the growth of small, specifically orientated, parties but also frequently results in broad-based coalition governments.

The Israel Labor Party was formed in 1968 by a merger of three existing Labor groups, Mapai, Rafi, and Achdut Ha'avoda. Mapai was the Israel Workers' Party and started life in 1930 but its origins go back to the turn of the century in Europe, and particularly in Russia. In its present form, the Labor Party has a generally moderate left-of-center orientation.

Likud was founded in 1973 as an alliance of several right-of-center groupings. Under its present leadership by Binyamin Netanyahu (b. 1949) it has adopted a much harder line than the Labor Party towards its Arab neighbors and Israeli–Palestinian relations generally.

Political leaders since 1970

1969–74 Golda Meir (Labor Party), 1974–77 Yitzhak Rabin (Labor Alignment coalition), 1977–83 Menachem Begin (Likud coalition), 1983–84 Yitzhak Shamir (Likud coalition), 1984–86 Shimon Peres (Labor-Likud National Unity coalition), 1986–88 Yitzhak Shamir (Likud-Labor National Unity coalition), 1988–90 Yitzhak Shamir (Likud-Labor Party coalition), 1990–92 Yitzhak Shamir (Likud), 1992–95 Yitzhak Rabin (Labor-led coalition), 1995–96 Shimon Peres (Labor-led coalition), 1996–99 Binyamin Netanyahu (Likud), 1999– Ehud Barak (One Israel/Labor led coalotion)

Latest elections

The results of the 17 May 1999 Knesset general election were as follows:

Israel latest election results

Party	% of the vote	Seats
Labor (One Israel)	20.1	26
Likud	14.1	19
Others	65.7	75

Labour fought the election as part of a One Israel alliance, which had been formed by Ehud Barak in March 1999 to incorporate other leftwing and centrist groups, notably David Levi's Gesher and Meimad, a liberal religious party. However, its share of the national vote fell by more than 6% compared to May 1996. Likud's vote share fell even further, by 11%, as 13 minor parties, securing individually between 1.9% and 13% of the vote, secured representation. The best performance by minor parties were Shas (Sephardic Jews Guardians), an ultra-orthodox Jewish party that won 17 seats, with 13% of the vote; the Meretz-Democratic Israel, a leftist alliance which supports Palestinian self-determination, which won 10 seats and 8% of the vote. In all, 31 parties contested an election which was notable for the success of the first Arab woman candidate, Hosniya Jabara of the Meretz party.

The second direct popular election of the prime minister was also held on 17 May 1999 and resulted in a clear victory for Ehud Barak, the candidate of Labor (One Israel), who secured 56.1% of the vote, defeating the incumbent prime minister, Binyamin Netanyahu of Likud, who secured 43.9% of the vote. Ezer Weizmann of the Labor Party was re-elected president of the Knesset in March 1998, defeating Shaul Amor of Likud.

Political history

The Zionist movement, calling for an independent community for Jews in Palestine, started in the 19th century, and in 1917 Britain declared its support for the idea. In 1920 Palestine was placed under British administration by the League of Nations and the British government was immediately faced with the rival claims of Jews who wished to settle there and the indigenous Arabs who were opposed to them. In 1937 Britain proposed two separate communities, Arab and Jewish, an idea which was accepted by the Jews but not by the Arabs, and fighting broke out between them. In 1947, after the murder of 6 million Jews in European concentration camps by Germany's Nazi regime, this plan for a partition was supported by the United Nations (UN). In 1948, when Britain ended its Palestinian mandate, Jewish leaders immediately proclaimed a new, independent State of Israel, with David Ben-Gurion (1886–1973) as prime minister.

Although it had no specific frontiers, the new state won wide recognition in the non-Arab world. Neighboring Arab states reacted by sending forces into Palestine to crush the new nation but with no success. Indeed, when a ceasefire agreement had been reached, in 1949, Israel was left in control of more land than had originally been allocated under the UN partition plan. The non-Jewish occupied remainder of Palestine, known as the West Bank, was incorporated into Jordan. The creation of this *de facto* state encouraged Jewish immigration on a large scale, about 2 million having arrived from all over the world by 1962. Meanwhile, hundreds of thousands of Arab and indigenous Palestinian residents had fled from Israel to neighboring countries, such as Jordan and Lebanon. In 1964 a number of exiled Palestinian Arabs founded the Palestine Liberation Organization (PLO), with the declared ultimate aim of overthrowing the State of Israel.

Throughout the 1960s there was considerable tension between Israel and Egypt, which, under President Gamal Abdel Nasser, had become an important leader in the Arab world. His nationalization of the Suez Canal in 1956 provided an opportunity for Israel, in collusion with Britain and France, to attack Egypt and occupy a part of Palestine which Egypt had controlled since 1949, the Gaza Strip. The British–French–Israeli attack on Egypt was soon called off under US and UN pressure and Israel was forced to withdraw from the Strip in 1957. Ten years later, the Six-Day War, as it was called, between Egypt and Israel, eventually left the Israelis with large territorial gains, including the whole of Jerusalem, the West Bank area of Jordan, the Sinai Peninsula in Egypt, and the Golan Heights in Syria. These were all immediately incorporated into the State of Israel.

Ben-Gurion resigned in 1963 and was succeeded by Levi Eshkol, leading a coalition government, and then in 1968 three of the coalition parties combined to form the Israel Labor Party. In 1969 Golda Meir (1898–1978), the Labor Party leader, became prime minister, continuing in office until 1974. In 1973, during the final months of her last administration, another Arab–Israeli war broke out, coinciding with Yom Kippur, the holiest day of the Jewish year. Israel was attacked simultaneously by Egypt and Syria and after nearly three weeks of bitter fighting, resulting in heavy losses, ceasefire agreements were reached.

Golda Meir resigned in June 1974 and was succeeded by General Yitzhak Rabin (1922–95), heading a Labor-led coalition. In the 1977 elections the Consolidation (Likud) bloc, led by Menachem Begin (1913–92), won an unexpected victory and Begin became prime minister. Within five months relations between Egypt and Israel underwent a dramatic change, mainly because of initiatives by President Anwar Sadat of Egypt, encour-

aged by the US administration of President Jimmy Carter. Sadat made an unprecedented visit to Israel to address the Knesset and the following year the Egyptian and Israeli leaders met at Camp David, in the United States, to sign agreements for peace in the Middle East. A peace treaty was signed in Washington in March 1979 and the following year Egypt and Israel exchanged ambassadors, to the dismay of most of the Arab world. Israel withdrew completely from Sinai by 1982 but continued to occupy the Golan Heights. In the same year a major crisis was created when Israel, without consulting Egypt, advanced through Lebanon and surrounded West Beirut, in pursuit of 6,000 PLO fighters who were trapped there. A complete split between Egypt and Israel was narrowly avoided by the efforts of the US special negotiator, Philip Habib, who secured the evacuation from Beirut to various Arab countries of about 15,000 PLO and Syrian fighters in August 1982. Israel's alleged complicity in the massacre of hundreds of people in two Palestinian refugee camps increased Arab hostility.

Prolonged talks between Israel and Lebanon, between December 1982 and May 1983, resulted in an agreement, drawn up by US secretary of state, George Shultz (b. 1920), calling for the withdrawal of all foreign forces from Lebanon within three months. Syria refused to acknowledge the agreement and left some 40,000 troops, with about 7,000 PLO members, in the northeast, and Israel retaliated by refusing to withdraw its forces from the south. During this time Begin was faced with increasingly difficult domestic problems, including rapidly rising inflation. There was also growing opposition to his foreign policies and, in his private life, he had become depressed by the death of his wife. In September 1983 he resigned and Yitzhak Shamir (b. 1915) formed a shaky coalition. Elections in July 1984 failed to produce a conclusive result, with the Labor Alignment, led by Shimon Peres (b. 1923), winning 44 Knesset seats and Likud, led by Shamir, 41. Neither leader was able to form a viable coalition so eventually, after weeks of negotiation, it was agreed that a Government of National Unity would be formed, with Peres as prime minister for the first 25 months and Shamir as his deputy, and then a reversal of the positions. Peres was, therefore, in charge of the government until October 1986, when Shamir took over.

Meanwhile, the problems in Lebanon continued. In March 1984, under pressure from Syria, President Amin Gemayel of Lebanon rejected the 1983 treaty with Israel, but the Government of National Unity in

Tel Aviv continued with its plans for the withdrawal of its forces, even though it might lead to outright civil war in southern Lebanon. Guerrilla groups of the Shi'ite community of southern Lebanon took advantage of the situation by attacking and inflicting losses on the departing Israeli troops. Israel replied with ruthless attacks on Shi'ite villages. Most of the withdrawal was completed by June 1985.

Several peace initiatives by King Hussein of Jordan failed, largely because of Israeli and US suspicions about the role and motives of the PLO, some of whose supporters were alleged to have been involved in hijacking and other terrorist incidents in and around the Mediterranean area. There were, however, signs of improvements in 1985. Prime Minister Peres met King Hussein secretly in the south of France and later, in a speech to the United Nations, Peres said he would not rule out the possibility of an international conference on the Middle East, with wide representation. PLO leader Yasser Arafat (b. 1929) also had talks with King Hussein and later, in Cairo, publicly denounced the use of terrorism by the PLO outside territories occupied by Israel.

Domestically, the Government of National Unity was having some success with its economic policies, inflation falling in 1986 to manageable levels, but differences developed between Peres and Shamir over the concept of an international peace conference. Towards the end of 1987 international criticism of Prime Minister Shamir's handling of an intifada (Palestinian uprising) in the occupied territories grew and this widened the gulf between him and Peres. Despite Foreign Minister Peres' support for a conference proposed by US secretary of state, George Shultz, Prime Minister Shamir resolutely opposed the idea.

Meanwhile, Palestinian deaths continued. In April 1988 the military commander of the PLO, and Yasser Arafat's closest colleague, Abu Jihad, was assassinated at his home in Tunis, allegedly by the Israeli secret service. His death triggered off an increase in violence in the occupied territories.

King Hussein's unexpected announcement in July 1988 that Jordan was shedding its responsibility for the West Bank and transferring it to the PLO seemed likely to have an impact on Israel's general election in November of that year. Prime Minister Shamir said he would abide by the Camp David Agreement and not try to annex the West Bank after Jordan's withdrawal, but would resist any attempt by the PLO to set up a Palestinian government there. Shimon Peres' reaction was more conciliatory.

The 1988 general election failed to produce a clear victory for either of the two main parties and, after months of discussion, Labor agreed to join another coalition with Likud, but this collapsed in 1990 and Shamir continued in power, with the help of religious groups.

In 1990 US secretary of state, James Baker (b. 1930), proposed a Middle East peace conference which Shamir at first opposed. Later he agreed to participate, providing the PLO was not directly represented. The conference began in 1991 but progress was slow because of Shamir's intransigence and the continuing policy of establishing Jewish settlements in the Palestine occupied territories. The success of Labor in the June 1992 general election, with Yitzak Rabin coming to power as prime minister, brought a new sense of immediacy to the negotiations.

At the beginning of 1993 the ban on contacts with the PLO was lifted and later in the year Prime Minister Rabin and PLO leader, Yasser Arafat, signed an agreement which led to the withdrawal of Israeli forces from Jericho and the Gaza Strip in March 1994. Despite attempts by extremists on both sides to wreck it, the peace process continued with strong US encouragement. An agreement with Jordan was signed in October 1994 and in the same month, in recognition of their efforts, Rabin and Arafat were jointly awarded the Nobel Peace Prize. In September 1995, further Israeli–PLO talks produced an accord, signed in Washington, on the extension of Palestinian self-rule from Gaza and Jericho to most of the rest of the West Bank. Israeli troops were to be withdrawn over a six-month period, an elected 88-member Palestinian Council set up, to hold power for three years, many Palestinian prisoners to be released, and the PLO to revoke certain clauses in its 'covenant' calling for the destruction of Israel. However, there remained the threat that the deal might be wrecked by militants on either side, notably the extremist Palestinian Hamas group and 140,000 armed Jewish settlers living in the West Bank among 1.2 million Palestinians. These fears deepened in November 1995 when Prime Minister Rabin was assassinated by a Jewish rightwing extremist, when leaving a peace rally in Tel Aviv. The foreign minister, Shimon Peres, took over as prime minister, but lacking Rabin's military background seemed less likely to ensure that the peace process would continue to attract support from a wide range of Israeli opinion.

In the May 1996 general election, Labor lost control

of the Knesset, and the Likud leader, Binyamin Netanyahu, was also elected prime minister by a narrow margin, supported by an eight-party coalition of rightwing minority parties. At first Netanyahu seemed likely to be more pragmatic about relations with the Palestinians than had been feared, but delays in Israel's agreed withdrawals from the occupied territories and the establishment of new Jewish settlements in Palestinian areas raised concern about the possible collapse of the peace process. During 1997 and 1998 the United States put strong diplomatic pressure on Netanyahu, but the future of the process remained uncertain. At the same time the PLO leader, Yasser Arafat, was faced with growing militancy among extremists in the Palestinian ranks. In October 1998 a peace accord was signed between Israel and the PLO, at a conference held ay Wye, Maryland, in the United States. It provided for Israel to return a further 14% of the West Bank to full Palestinian control (making 40% in total), and for the PLO to crack down against terrorism and remove all references to the destruction of Israel from its national charter.

Implementation of the Wye agreement began in November 1998, involving a redeployment of Israeli forces in the West Bank, the return of 13% of the West Bank to the Palestinians over a three-month period, the release of a number of Palestinian prisoners, and the signing of a protocol for the opening of a Palestinian airport. As a goodwill gesture, the PLO announced that it would not declare an independent Palestinian state in May 1999, as it had previously threatened. However, Israel grew increasingly intransigent during the spring of 1999 as divisions within the Knesset over the handling and direction of the Middle East peace process prompted a vote in favour of holding an early general election, in May 1999. This election failed to produce a conclusive outcome, with 15 parties winning Knesset seats and support for the two main parties, Likud, most sharply, and Labour falling. However, the Labour party leader, Ehud Barak, decisively defeated the incumbent Binyamin Netanyahu in the concurrent direct election of the prime minister. In July 1999 Barak formed a new broad-based, seven-party coalition government, which embraced Meretz, on the left, and the orthodox-Jewish Shas party. David Levy remained as foreign minister, while Avraham Shohat, a former Labour finance minister, returned to that post. Barak, who pledged that he would seek to give fresh impetus to the Middle East peace process and halt further Jewish settlements in the West Bank, secured unexpected praise from Syria's President Assad as a 'strong and honest man'. Later, in July 1999, Prime Minister Barak met US President Clinton and announced a 15-month time-frame to decide whether there could be a breakthrough on a final settlement with Syria, Lebanon and the Palestinians.

JORDAN

Hashemite Kingdom of Jordan
al-Mamlaka al-Urduniya al-Hashemiyah

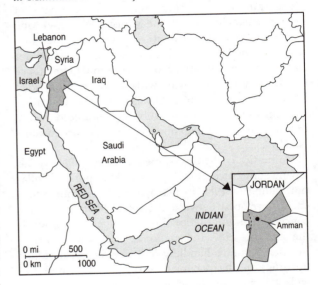

Capital: Amman

Social and economic data
Area: 98,000 sq km/37,838 sq miles
Population: 5,198,000[*]
Pop. density per sq km/sq mi: 53/137[*]
Urban population: 69%[**]
Literacy rate: 6%[**]
GDP: $6,354 million[*]; per-capita GDP: $1,220[*]
Government defense spending (% of GDP): 6.7%[*]
Currency: Jordanian dinar
Economy type: middle income
Labor force in agriculture: 10%[**]
[*] 1995.
[**] 1992.

Head of state (executive)
King Abdullah bin Hussein, since 1999

Head of state (executive)

Prime minister Abdul-Raouf Rawabdeh, since 1999

Ethnic composition

The majority of the people are of Arab descent and there are minorities of Circassians, Armenians, and Kurds. The official and most widely used language is Arabic.

Religions

Eighty per cent of the population is Sunni Muslim. The king can trace his unbroken ancestry back to the prophet Muhammad. There is also a Christian minority.

Political features

State type: absolutist
Date of state formation: 1946
Political structure: unitary
Executive: semi-absolute
Assembly: two-chamber
Party structure: multiparty
Human rights rating: 65%
International affiliations: AL, AMF, IAEA, IBRD, IMF, NAM, OIC, UN

Local and regional government

The country is divided into eight governorates. Three of them are known collectively as the West Bank and responsibility for them was relinquished by Jordan in 1988.

Political system

Jordan is not a typical constitutional monarchy on the Western model, since the king is effectively both head of state and head of government. The current constitution dates from 1952 but has been amended in 1974, 1976, and 1984. It provides for a two-chamber National Assembly of a Senate of 40, appointed by the king for an eight-year term, with half retiring every four years, and a House of Representatives of 80, elected by universal adult suffrage, through a simple plurality voting system, for a four-year term. The House is subject to dissolution within that period. The king governs with the help of a Council of Ministers (cabinet), whom he appoints and who are responsible to the Assembly. The cabinet is headed by a prime minister. Despite the existence of an elected assembly, Jordan has more absolutist than democratic characteristics, but there is evidence of gradual change, with gradual democratization being promoted from 1989.

Political parties

Political parties were banned in 1963, partially restored in 1971, banned again in 1976, and then allowed to operate in 1992.

By 1997, 15 parties had registered but independent groups, loyal to the king, still predominate. The most significant party is the Islamic Action Front (IAF), a fundamentalist party backed by the Muslim Brotherhood.

Political leaders since 1970

1952–1999 King Hussein ibn Talal, 1999– King Abdullah bin Hussein

Latest elections

In the November 1997 House of Representatives elections progovernment supporters polled strongly. Most of the 524 candidates were independents, and only five members of political parties won seats. Pro government candidates won 62 seats, nationalist and leftwing candidates ten seats, and independent Islamists, 8 seats. The main opposition party, the IAF, boycotted the poll in protest at the 1994 Jordan–Israel peace treaty. No women were elected. Turnout was 55%. A new Senate was appointed in November 1997.

Political history

Palestine, which included the West Bank of present-day Jordan and Transjordan, which is the present-day East Bank, were part of the Turkish Ottoman Empire until it was dissolved after World War I. They were then both placed under British administration by the League of Nations. Transjordan acquired increasing control over its own affairs, separating from Palestine in 1923 and achieving complete independence when the British mandate expired in 1946. The mandate for Palestine ran out two years later, in 1948, whereupon Jewish leaders claimed it for a new state of Israel. Fighting broke out between Jews and Arabs until a ceasefire was agreed in 1949. By then Transjordan forces had occupied part of Palestine to add to what they called the new state of Jordan. The following year they annexed the West Bank.

In 1953 Hussein ibn Talal (b. 1935) came to the Jordanian throne at the age of 17, because of his father's mental illness, and ruled the country until his death in 1999. In February 1958 Jordan and Iraq formed an Arab Federation which came to an end five months later when the Iraqi monarchy was overthrown. During his reign, King Hussein I survived many upheavals in his own country and neighboring states, including attacks on his life, and maintained his personal control of Jordan's affairs as well as playing an important role in Middle East affairs. His relations with his neighbors fluctuated but was on the whole his was a moderating influence. The loss of the West Bank territories to Israel during the Six-Day War of 1967 severely damaged the Jordanian economy.

After the Israeli invasion of Lebanon in 1982, King Hussein found himself playing a key role in attempts to bring peace to that part of the world, establishing an acceptable working relationship with the Palestine Liberation Organization (PLO) leader, Yasser Arafat. By 1984 the Arab world was clearly split into two camps, with the moderates represented by Jordan, Egypt, and Arafat's PLO, and the militant radicals by Syria, Libya, and the rebel wing of the PLO. In 1985 King Hussein and Arafat put together a framework for a Middle East peace settlement. It would involve bringing together all the interested parties, including the PLO, but Israel objected to the PLO representation. Further progress was hampered by the alleged complicity of the PLO in a number of terrorist operations in that year and King Hussein's attempts to revive the search for peace were unsuccessful. In July 1988 King Hussein dramatically announced that he would cease to regard the West Bank as part of Jordan and would no longer have responsibility for its administration. His main motive seemed to be to provoke the PLO into taking over Jordan's previous role and accelerating the movement towards the creation of a Palestinian state.

The king's image as a peace broker was severely damaged by his support for Saddam Hussein during the 1991 Gulf War, but success in the US-inspired Middle East peace talks helped his rehabilitation, and in 1994 a peace treaty with Israel was signed, under United States', auspices. Since 1992, with the re-establishment of a multiparty system, a greater measure of political pluralism was tolerated by King Hussein. The November 1997 Assembly elections were boycotted by the opposition parties, and the majority of the successful independent candidates supported the king. During 1998 King Hussein spent several months in the United States undergoing treatment for lymph cancer. In January 1999 he appointed his eldest son, Abdullah, crown prince, replacing his brother Hamzch, who had been crown prince for 33 years. Abdullah succeeded his father as King on his death later in the month.

In February 1999 King Abdullah II appointed an ally of his father, Abdul-Raouf Rawabdeh, as prime minister and in May 1999 he held talks with the Palestinian leader, Yassar Arafat, to forge a united Arab position before the renewal of Middle East peace negotiations with Israel.

KUWAIT

State of Kuwait
Dowlat al-Kuwait

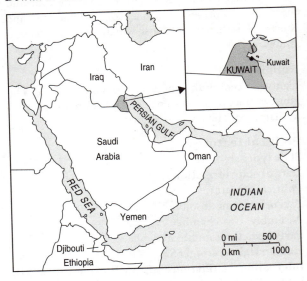

Capital: Kuwait

Social and economic data
Area: 17,819 sq km/6,880 sq miles
Population: 1,576,000*
Pop. density per sq km/sq mi: 89/229*
Urban population: 96%**
Literacy rate: 73%**
GDP: $28,940 million*; per-capita GDP: $18,360*
Government defense spending (% of GDP): 11.8%*
Currency: Kuwaiti dinar
Economy type: high income
Labor force in agriculture: 2%**
* 1995.
** 1992.

Head of state (executive)
Emir Sheikh Jabir al-Ahmad al-Jabir as-Sabah, since 1977

Head of government
Crown Prince Sheikh Saad al-Abdullah as-Salim as-Sabah, since 1978

Ethnic composition
About 42% of the population is Kuwaiti, 40% non-Kuwaiti Arab, 5% Indian and Pakistani, and 4% Iranian. The official language is Arabic but English is also used in commercial transactions.

Religions

Islam is the state religion and most of the population is Muslim, about 70% Sunni and 30% Shi'ite.

Political features

State type: absolutist
Date of state formation: 1961
Political structure: unitary
Executive: absolute
Assembly: one-chamber
Party structure: none
Human rights rating: 33%
International affiliations: AL, AMF, BDEAC, DDS, GCC, IAEA, IBRD, IMF, NAM, OAPEC, OIC, OPEC, UN, WTO

Local and regional government

The country is divided, for administrative purposes, into four districts, each with an appointed governor.

Political system

The 1962 constitution was partly suspended by the emir in 1976 and reinstated in 1980. It vests executive power in the hands of the emir, who governs through an appointed prime minister and Council of Ministers. The current prime minister is the emir's eldest son, the crown prince. There is a single-chamber National Assembly (Majlis al-Umma) of 50 members, elected on a restricted suffrage for a four-year term by native-born adult Kuwaiti males (over the age of 21) fulfilling strict residence requirements. In July 1986 however it was dissolved, Sheikh Jabir III preferring to govern with an unelected consultative council. It was reconstituted and elections were held in 1992. Despite some semblance of constitutional government, Kuwait is, in effect, a personal monarchy and an absolutist state.

Political parties

No parties are allowed, but there are unofficial groups within the Assembly.

Political leaders since 1970

1965–77 Sheikh Sabah al-Salim as-Sabah, 1977– Sheikh Jabir al-Ahmad al-Jabir as-Sabah

Latest elections

The most recent National Assembly elections were held on 3 July 1999, using double seat constituencies. Only non-partisans were allowed to stand, but subsequent analysis suggested that around 14 of those elected were liberal reformists (an increase of 10 on October 1996), while the remainder were split evenly between pro-government candidates and more extreme Islamists. Turnout was 80%.

Political history

Part of the Turkish Ottoman Empire from the 16th century, Kuwait made a treaty with Britain in 1899 enabling it to become a self-governing protectorate until it achieved full independence in 1961. Oil was first discovered in 1938 and its large-scale exploitation began after 1945, transforming Kuwait City from a small fishing port into a thriving commercial center. The oil revenues have enabled ambitious public works and education programs to be undertaken.

Sheikh Abdullah al-Salim as-Sabah took the title of emir in 1961 when he assumed full executive powers. He died in 1965 and was succeeded by his brother, Sheikh Sabah al-Salim al-Sabah. He, in turn, died in 1977 and was succeeded by Crown Prince Jabir (b. 1928), who appointed Sheikh Saad al-Abdullah as-Salim as-Sabah as his heir apparent.

Kuwait has used its considerable wealth not only to improve its infrastructure and social services but, also to enable it to serve as a strong supporter of the Arab cause generally.

Its association with Iraq has long been precarious and in August 1990, after making territorial demands, Saddam Hussein invaded the country and occupied it. The emir fled to Saudi Arabia, while US-led United Nations military coalition successfully defeated Iraq in the 'Operation Desert Storm' Gulf War of February 1991. Considerable material damage was sustained but it was hoped that, with the Sabah dynasty restored, Kuwait would live up to the democratic hopes of its liberators. However, although there have been some cautious moves towards more democratic institutions, it remains basically an absolutist state. With Saddam Hussein still in power, normal stable relations with Iraq have yet to be restored.

In June 1998 a dispute arose between the government and the National Assembly over their respective powers.

In May 1999 the emir dissolved the National Assembly, more than a year ahead of schedule, and called fresh elections. This followed a dispute among legislators, who had accused the Islamic Affairs minister of distributing copies of the Koran with missing verses. The elections, held in July 1999, saw reformist candidates poll strongly. Meanwhile, the emir issued a decree, in May 1999, that Kuwaiti women would be allowed to vote and stand for public office from 2003. It was believed that the dynamic deputy prime minister, Sheikh Sabah al-Sabah, who was the cousin of the Crown Prince and prime minister, Sheikh Saad, was behind this initiative and that, in future, he would play a more prominent role in assisting at the helm of the government.

LEBANON

Republic of Lebanon/The Lebanon
al-Jumhouria al-Lubnaniya/al-Lubnan

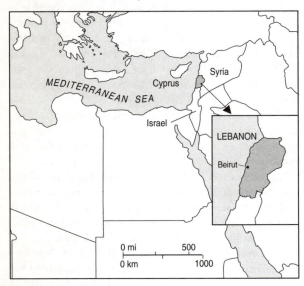

Capital: Beirut (Bayrouth)

Social and economic data
Area: 10,452 sq km/4,036 sq miles
Population: 2,915,000[*]
Pop. density per sq km/sq mi: 277/722[*]
Urban population: 85%[**]
Literacy rate: 80%[**]
GDP: $10,670 million[*]; per-capita GDP: $3,360[*]
Government defense spending (% of GDP): 5.3%[*]
Currency: Lebanese pound
Economy type: middle income
Labor force in agriculture: 14%[**]
[*] 1995.
[**] 1992.

Head of state (executive)
President General Emile Lahoud, since 1998

Head of government
Prime Minister Selim al-Hoss, since 1998

Ethnic composition
About 90% of the population is Arab. There are Armenian, Assyrian, Jewish, Turkish, and Greek minorities. The official language is Arabic but French is also used.

Religions
There are about 1 million Shi'ite Muslims, 900,000 Maronite Christians, associated with the Roman Catholic Church, 500,000 Sunni Muslims, 150,000 members of the Greek Orthodox Church, 200,000 Druzes, and 100,000 members of the Armenian Church.

Political features
State type: emergent democratic
Date of state formation: 1944
Political structure: unitary
Executive: dual
Assembly: one-chamber
Party structure: multiparty
Human rights rating: N/A
International affiliations: AL, AMF, G-24, IAEA, IBRD, IMF, NAM, OIC, UN

Local and regional government
The country is divided into five regional units (*maofazats*), each administered by an appointed prefect.

Political system
Under the 1926 constitution, which was amended in 1927, 1929, 1943, 1947, and 1990, legislative power is held by the National Assembly (Majlis al-Nwab), whose 128 members, divided equally between Christians and Muslims, are elected by universal adult suffrage, through a party list system of proportional representation. The assembly serves a four-year term. The president is elected by the assembly for a six-year term, although Elias Hrawi was allowed to serve a nine-year term, 1989–98. Presidents appoint a prime minister and cabinet who are collectively responsible to the assembly. The 1990 amendment to the constitution reduced the powers of the president and increased those of the prime minister (and the Assembly speaker) so as to achieve a better balance between them. The sharing of power between the two executives has some similarity with that provided for in the French constitution. In an attempt to preserve religious harmony, the constitution ensures that the president is always a Maronite Christian, while the prime minister is a Sunni Muslim and the speaker of the National Assembly is a Shi'ite Muslim. The cabinet includes six Christians and five Muslims.

Political parties

There are currently around 30 political parties but membership of the National Assembly is more easily recognized in terms of religious groupings. The seven most significant parties are the Phalangist Party, the Progressive Socialist Party (PSP), the National Liberal Party (NLP), the National Bloc, the Lebanese Communist Party (PCL), the Amal group, and Hizbollah.

The Phalangist Party was established in 1936 by a group of young rightwing nationalists who were impressed by the growth of fascism in Nazi Germany. Their main aim was to secure independence from France. In its present form the party has moved nearer to the center and can best be described as having a nationalistic Maronite Christian and radical orientation. The party is led by Georges Saadé, and has 100,000 members.

The PSP was founded in 1949 by Kamal Jumblat, the Druze leader. It is now led by his son, Walid. It has a moderate socialist orientation.

The NLP dates from 1958 and was formed by Camille Chamoun at the end of his presidential term. It has a center-left orientation.

The National Bloc is a moderate, Maronite grouping in the center of the political spectrum.

The PCL was originally established in 1924 but did not become politically active until 1936. It is a nationalist communist party and was once closely allied with its Syrian counterpart, but this link seems now to have been broken.

Amal ('Hope') is a Shi'ite Islamic party led by Nabi Berri, while Hizbollah (Party of God) is an Islamic fundamentalist Shi'ite body.

Political leaders since 1970

1970–76 Sulaiman Franjiya (military-led coalition), 1976–82 Elias Sarkis (Lebanese Front), 1982 Bachir Gemayel (assassinated before he assumed office), 1982–88 Amin Gemayel (Phalangist Party), 1988–89 Michel Aoun (military), 1989 René Mouawad (Maronite), 1989–98 Elias Hrawi (Maronite), 1998– General Emile Lahoud (Maronite)

Latest elections

Presidential elections were held in October 1998, and resulted in the Syrian-backed army chief, General Emile Lahoud, being unanimously elected to parliament as the country's tenth post-independence president.

The general election, held in five stages in August–September 1996, resulted in 34 Maronite Catholics, 27 Sunni Muslims, 27 Shi'ite Muslims, 14 Greek Orthodox, 8 Druze and 18 other deputies being elected.

Political history

Originally part of the Turkish Ottoman Empire, Lebanon was administered by France, under a League of Nations mandate, from 1920 to 1941. Independence was declared in 1941, it became a republic in 1943, with a constitution that provided for power-sharing between the main religious groups, and achieved full autonomy in 1944. Historically, it has had strong links with Syria, but Lebanon has had a much richer mix of religions and cultures, including a large Christian community and Arabs of many sects. Christians and Muslims lived peacefully together for many years and this social stability enabled Lebanon, until the mid-1970s, to become a major commercial and financial center.

The thriving business district of Beirut was largely destroyed in 1975–76 and Lebanon's role as an international trader has been greatly reduced. After the establishment of the state of Israel in 1948, Lebanon was a natural haven for thousands of Palestinian refugees. The Palestine Liberation Organization (PLO) was founded in Beirut in 1964, with a large and destabilizing influx of Palestinians to Lebanon occurring after the 1967 Arab–Israeli war. It moved its headquarters to Tunis in 1982. The presence of PLO forces in Lebanon was the main reason for Israel's invasion and much of the subsequent civil strife. This internal fighting has been largely between leftwing Muslims and conservative Christian groups, mainly members of the Phalangist Party. There have also been differences between traditional Muslims, with pro-Iranian attitudes, such as the Shi'ite, and the deviationist Muslims, such as the Druze, backed by Syria. In 1975 the fighting developed into a full-scale civil war.

A ceasefire was agreed in 1976 but fighting broke out again in 1978 when Israeli forces invaded south Lebanon in search of PLO guerrillas. The United Nations secured Israel's agreement to a withdrawal and set up an international peacekeeping force, but to little avail. In 1979 Major Saad Haddad, a rightwing Lebanese army officer, with Israeli encouragement, declared an area of about 2,000 square kilometres in southern Lebanon an 'independent free Lebanon' and the following year Christian Phalangist soldiers took over an area north of Beirut. Throughout this turmoil the Lebanese government found itself virtually impotent. In 1982 the presidency was won by Bachir Gemayel (1947–82), the youngest son of the founder of the Phalangist Party, but, before he could assume office, he was assassinated and his brother, Amin (b. 1942), took his place.

Following exhaustive talks between Lebanon and Israel, under United States auspices, an agreement was signed in May 1983, declaring an end to hostilities and calling for the withdrawal of all foreign forces from the country within three months. Syria refused to recognize the agreement and left about 40,000 troops, with about 7,000 PLO fighters, in northern Lebanon. Israel responded by refusing to take its forces from the south. Meanwhile, a full-scale war blew up between the Christian Phalangists and the Muslim Druze soldiers in the Chouf Mountains, resulting in the defeat of the Christians and the creation of another mini-state, controlled by the Druze. The multinational force was drawn gradually, but unwillingly, into the conflict until it was eventually withdrawn in the spring of 1984.

Unsuccessful attempts were made in 1985 and 1986 to bring the civil war to an end as Lebanon, and particularly Beirut, saw its infrastructure and earlier commercial prosperity virtually destroyed in a battlefield for the Iranian-backed Shi'ite Hizbollah ('Children of God') and the Syrian-backed Shi'ite Amal. In May 1988 President Hafez al-Assad of Syria, after several previous abortive attempts, sent his troops into southern Beirut, with the agreement of Lebanon and Iran, to attempt to restore order and secure the release of hostages believed to be held there.

The end of Amin Gemayel's presidency in 1988 threatened to add a fresh dimension to Lebanon's troubles. Attempts to agree a suitable Maronite Christian successor in August of that year initially failed and the presidential election was postponed. When his term came to an end, in September 1988, Gemayel felt it necessary to establish at least a caretaker administration and appointed General Michel Aoun to head a military government. This decision was opposed by Prime Minister Selim El-Hoss, who set up his own rival administration.

In May 1989 the Arab League succeeded in arranging a truce and, despite Aoun's opposition, in November René Mouawad, a Maronite Christian, was made president. Within 17 days he was assassinated. Another Maronite, Elias Hrawi (b. 1930), was elected as his successor. Aoun continued to defy the elected president for another year but eventually surrendered. Gradually, a sense of normality returned to the country, and particularly Beirut, with the continuing presence of Syrian troops helping to preserve order. Progressively, Western hostages held there were released and the appointment

as prime minister in October 1992 of the moderate business executive, Rafiq al-Hariri, offered promise of a lasting peace. However, Hizbollah guerrillas continued to control the Beka'a Valley and were active in the south of the country, provoking intermittent raids by Israeli forces which continued to occupy a buffer security zone.

In October 1995 the president's six-year term was extended by three years by the National Assembly, and in the September 1996 elections, Prime Minister Rafiq al-Hariri secured a solid block of support. Controversial Israeli attacks on alleged Hizbollah targets in southern Lebanon continued to be carried out. In November 1998 the Syrian-backed General Emile Lahoud became president. Lahoud was head of the Lebanese army. His selection indicated the effective control exerted over the state of Syria, whose army occupied much of Lebanon.

In November 1998 Rafiq al-Hariri resigned as prime minister since he considered that President Lahoud was seeking to exert too much influence over the composition of the new government. He was replaced, in December 1998, by Selim al-Hoss, a Western-trained economist who had twice previously served as prime minister during the Lebanese civil war. He pledged to push ahead with his predecessor's reconstruction initiatives and support the president's drive against corruption, while also pursuing a programme of fiscal austerity to reduce a budget deficit which had reached 15% of GDP. In southern Lebanon there was continuing violence during early 1999 as Hezbollah Islamic guerrillas clashed with Israel's troubled and mutinous proxy militia, the South Lebanese Army (SLA). In June 1999 the SLA was forced to withdraw from the Jezzine area, which it had occupied, and the election is Israel of a new coalition government, headed by Ehud Barak, who promised full withdrawal of Israel's soldiers from Lebanon, was welcomed by the Lebanese leadership. The Israeli withdrawal from south Lebanon began in June 1999.

LIBYA

The Great Socialist People's Libyan Arab State of the Masses
Daulat Libiya al-'Arabiya al-Elshtrakiya al-Jumhuriya

Capital: Tripoli (Tarabulus)

Social and economic data
Area: 1,775,500 sq km/685,524 sq miles

Population: 4,899,000*
Pop. density per sq km/sq mi: 3/7*
Urban population: 84%**
Literacy rate: 64%**
GDP: $32,900 million*; per-capita GDP: $6,751*
Government defense spending (% of GDP): 5.5%*
Currency: Libyan dinar
Economy type: middle income
Labor force in agriculture: 18%**
* 1995.
** 1992.

Head of state and head of government
Revolutionary Leader Colonel Muammar al-Kadhafi, since 1969

Ethnic composition
The great majority of people are of Berber and Arab origin, with a small number of Tebou and Touareg nomads and semi-nomads, mainly in the south. The official language is Arabic but English and Italian are used, particularly in commercial transactions.

Religions
Most of the population, over 96%, are Sunni Muslims but Islam is not the state religion. There are also about 38,000 Roman Catholics.

Political features
State type: nationalistic socialist
Date of state formation: 1951
Political structure: unitary
Executive: unlimited presidential
Assembly: one-chamber

Party structure: one-party
Human rights rating: 24%
International affiliations: AL, AMF, AMU, IAEA, IBRD, IMF, NAM, OAPEC, OAU, OIC, OPEC, UN

Local and regional government
For administrative purposes, the country is divided into 13 provinces (*baladiyat*). Below this level are municipalities. A feature of Libya's approach to government is the spread of people's committees, to encourage popular involvement, at all levels.

Political system
The 1977 constitution created an Islamic socialist state and the machinery of government is designed to allow the greatest possible popular involvement, through a large congress and smaller secretariats and committees. There is a General People's Congress (GPC) of 1,112 members, which elects a secretary general who was intended to be the head of state. In 1979, however, Colonel Kadhafi, although still head of state, gave up the post of secretary general. The GPC meets for about a week each year, and is serviced by a General Secretariat, which is the nearest equivalent to an assembly in the Libyan system. The executive organ of the state is the 24-member General People's Committee, which is the equivalent of a Council of Ministers or cabinet and replaces the structure of ministries which operated before the 1969 revolution. Its secretary since 1997, Mohammed Ahmed al-Mangoush, is broadly equivalent to a prime minister.

Political parties
The Arab Socialist Union (ASU) is the only political party, although it has no official existence. Despite the elaborately democratic structure that has been created, ultimate political power rests with the party and the revolutionary leader, Colonel Kadhafi.

The ASU was formed by Colonel Kadhafi in 1971 as a mass party equivalent of the Arab Socialist Union of Egypt. Since its establishment he has tried to increase popular involvement almost to the extent of making its active membership too diffused. It has a radical left-wing orientation, accurately reflecting the predisposition of its leader.

Political leaders since 1970
1969– Muammar al-Kadhafi (ASU)

Latest elections
It is difficult to identify elections in the conventional sense. GPC delegates are drawn from 1,500 directly elected Basic and 14 Municipal People's Congresses,

trade unions, 'popular committees', and professional organizations, with voting often being by a show of hands or a division into yes and no camps.

Political history

Formerly an Italian colony, Libya was occupied and then governed by Britain from 1942 until it achieved independence, as the United Kingdom of Libya, in 1951, Muhammad Idris-as-Sanusi becoming King Idris. Formerly a poor country, the development of oil reserves since the 1960s has transformed the Libyan economy. The country enjoyed internal and external stability until a bloodless revolution in 1969, led by young nationalist officers, deposed the king and proclaimed a Libyan Arab Republic. Power was placed in the hands of a Revolution Command Council (RCC), with Colonel Muammar al-Kadhafi (b. 1942) as chairperson and the Arab Socialist Union (ASU) as the only legally permitted political party.

The charismatic but unpredictable Kadhafi, who had been born into a nomadic family, was soon active in the Arab world, proposing a number of schemes for unity, none of which was permanently adopted. In 1972 it was for a federation of Libya, Syria, and Egypt and then, later in the same year, a merger between Libya and Egypt. In 1980 the proposal was for a union with just Syria and in 1981 with Chad. Domestically, Kadhafi tried to run the country on a socialist-Islamic basis, with people's committees pledged to socialism and the teachings of the Holy Koran. A constitution adopted in 1977 made him secretary general of the General Secretariat of a large General People's Congress (GPC), with over 1,000 members, but in 1979 he resigned the post so that he could devote more time to 'preserving the revolution'.

Kadhafi's attempts to establish himself as a leader of the Arab world have brought him into conflict with the Western powers, and particularly the United States. He became, in the eyes of US president Ronald Reagan, a threat to world peace similar to Fidel Castro, the communist leader of Cuba. In particular, the US administration objected to Libya's presence in Chad and its attempts to unseat the French–US-sponsored government of President Habré. The United States has linked Kadhafi to terrorist activities throughout the world, despite his denials of complicity, and the killing of a member of the US military in a bomb attack in Berlin in April 1986 prompted a raid by US aircraft, some of them based in Britain, on Tripoli and Benghazi, including Kadhafi's personal headquarters.

Within the Arab world, Kadhafi is seen as something of a maverick. In the spring of 1988, encouraged by a marked improvement in the state of the Libyan economy, he embarked on a dramatic program of liberalization, freeing political prisoners and encouraging private businesses to operate.

He also made a surprisingly conciliatory offer to recognize the independence of Chad and give material help for the reconstruction of the country. In September 1988 Kadhafi, again surprisingly, won praise from Amnesty International by his announcement of the ending of a formal army and its replacement by a 'people's army', the Jamahariya Guard.

Early in 1989 the United States government accused Libya of building a chemical weapons factory. Soon afterwards, but in a supposedly unrelated incident, two Libyan fighter planes were shot down by aircraft operating with the US navy off the North African coast. Libyan extremists were allegedly involved in the destruction of a Pan-Am airliner over Lockerbie in Scotland in 1988 and, when Kadhafi refused to release two suspects for trial, the UN imposed trade sanctions in 1992.

His country's association with terrorist activities, always denied, have tended to make Kadhafi an international outcast, but there is increasing evidence of his desire to be rehabilitated. In February 1998, the International Court of Justice ruled that it had jurisdiction over the long-running dispute between Libya, the United Kingdom, and the United States concerning the Lockerbie incident of 1988. Two Libyans suspected of the crime arrived in April 1999, in a neutral country, the Netherlands, to be tried under Scottish law and before Scottish judges. This development led to UN sanctions, imposed in 1992, to be lifted, and in July 1999, to the UK resuming diplomatic relations with Libya. In June 1998 there was a reported assassination attempt on President Kadhafi.

MOROCCO

The Kingdom of Morocco
al-Mamlaka al-Maghribiya

Capital: Rabat

Social and economic data

Area: 458,730 sq km/177,117 sq miles
Population: 26,590,000*

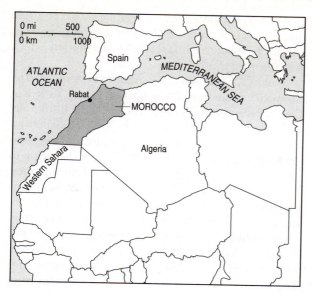

Pop. density per sq km/sq mi: 58/150*
Urban population: 47%**
Literacy rate: 50%**
GDP: $29,545 million*; per-capita GDP: $1,110*
Government defense spending (% of GDP): 4.3%*
Currency: dirham
Economy type: middle income
Labor force in agriculture: 46%**
Unemployment rate: 16.0%*
* 1995.
** 1992.

Head of state (executive)
King Sayyid; Muhammad VI ibn-Hassan, since 1999

Head of government
Prime Minister Abderrahmanen el-Yousifi, since 1998

Ethnic composition
Most of the population consists of indigenous Berbers. Pure Berbers are, however, gradually becoming less numerous than Arab-Berbers, although the distinction now has little social or political significance. There is a sizeable Jewish minority. The official language is Berber; French and Spanish are also spoken in certain regions.

Religions
Islam is the state religion and about 98% of the population is Muslim. There are also about 60,000 Christians, mostly Roman Catholics, and about 30,000 Jews.

Political features
State type: emergent democratic
Date of state formation: 1956
Political structure: unitary

Executive: dual
Assembly: two-chamber
Party structure: multiparty
Human rights rating: 56%
International affiliations: AL, AMF, AMU, IAEA, IBRD, IMF, NAM, OIC, UN, WTO

Local and regional government
The country is divided into seven provinces and 41 prefectures. The four provinces of Spanish Sahara are also administered by Morocco; see *Chapter 8*. The provinces and prefectures have appointed governors and prefects and there are indirectly elected councils.

Political system
Morocco is not a normal constitutional monarchy in that the king, in addition to being the formal head of state, also presides over his appointed cabinet and has powers, under the 1972 constitution, to dismiss the prime minister and other cabinet ministers, as well as to dissolve the assembly. The executive thus displays aspects of the French model, particularly since a 1992 constitutional amendment, passed after a national referendum, gave greater powers to the assembly and prime minister.

The constitution was amended following a referendum in September 1996, to provide for a two-chamber assembly, with the lower house, the 325-member House of Representatives, now being directly elected by proportional representation. (Formerly a third of its members were indirectly elected by interest groups.) The House of Representatives has a five-year term. The new upper house, the 270-member Chamber of Councillors, serves a six-year term. It is directly elected to represent local authorities and the professions. One third of its membership is renewed every three years. The new parliament was elected in November 1997.

Political parties
There are currently some political parties, the most significant being the Constitutional Union (UC); the National Rally of Independents (RNI); the Popular Movement (MP); the National Democratic Party (PND); the National Popular Movement (MNP); Istiqlal; the Socialist Union of Popular Forces (USFP); and the Social Democratic Movement (MDS).

The UC was formed in 1982 and has a rightwing orientation. The RNI was founded in 1978 by an independent group of progovernment politicians. It has an essentially royalist orientation.

The MP was created in 1957 and legalized in 1959. It draws much of its support from the rural communities and has a moderate centrist orientation.

The PND was founded in 1981 as a result of a split within the RNI; it has a moderate nationalistic stance. The PND, UC, and MP are part of a broader, center-right progovernment Wifaq grouping. The MNP is a center-right grouping.

Istiqlal was formed in 1943 as the independence party. It has a nationalistic centrist orientation.

The USFP started in 1959 as part of the National Union of Popular Forces (UNFP). Dissidents broke away in 1974 to found the USFP. It has a progressive socialist orientation and is allied with Istiqlal in the left-nationalist Koutla grouping. The MDS has a left-of-center orientation.

No Islamic parties are permitted.

Political leaders since 1970
1961–99 King Hassan II; 1999–   King Muhammad VI

Latest elections
In the November 1997 House of Representatives elections, the USFP won 57 seats; the UC, 50; the RNI, 46; the MP, 40; Istiqlal, 32; the MDS, 32; the MNP, 19; and the PND, 10. Seven other parties, each of which secured between 1–4% of the vote, won 39 seats. The election result proved inconclusive, with no individual party securing more than 13% of the vote. Turnout was 58%.

In the December 1997 indirect elections to the Chamber of Councillors the RNI, won 42 seats; the MDS, 33; the UC, 28; the MP, 27; the PND, 21; Istiqlal 21; USFP, 16; and the MNP, 15.

Political history
After hundreds of years of being part of a series of vast Muslim empires, European influence came to Morocco in the 16th century, in the shape of the Portuguese. It was then the turn of the Spanish and French in the 19th century. In 1912 Morocco was split into Spanish and French protectorates and in 1925 the Rif rebellion stirred nationalist sentiment. The country became fully independent as the sultanate of Morocco in 1956, with Mohammed V, who had been reigning since 1927, as head of state. The two former protectorates were soon joined by Tangier, which until then had been designated an international zone. The Sultan was restyled King Mohammed of Morocco in 1957 and died three years later, in 1960.

He was succeeded by the crown prince, who became King Hassan II (1929–1999). During his reign King Hassan has appointed numerous prime ministers and, despite several attempts to depose or kill him, retained his personal position. Between 1960 and 1972 a number of constitutions were formulated in an attempt to find a successful marriage between personal royal rule and demands for a more democratic form of government. The most recent is the 1972 constitution, which was amended in 1992.

Most of King Hassan's reign came to be dominated by Morocco's claims to what was Spanish Sahara, an area to the southwest of Morocco, considered to be historically Moroccan. Under pressure from King Hassan, who encouraged a 'Green March' of unarmed peasants into the territory, Spain agreed, in 1975, to cede the region to Morocco and Mauritania, leaving the eventual division to them. The local inhabitants, who had not been consulted, reacted violently through an independence movement, the Polisario Front, which won the support of Algeria. Within a year of Spain's departure, Morocco and Mauritania found themselves involved in a guerrilla war. Algeria's support for Polisario, which included permitting the establishment of a government in exile in Algiers, the Sahrawi Arab Democratic Republic (SADR), prompted King Hassan in 1976 to sever diplomatic relations. In 1979 Mauritania agreed a peace treaty with the Polisario forces, whereupon King Hassan immediately annexed that part of Western Sahara which Mauritania had vacated. Polisario reacted by raising the scale of its operations. In 1983 a summit meeting of the Organization of African Unity (OAU) proposed an immediate ceasefire, direct negotiations between Morocco and Polisario, and the holding of a referendum in Western Sahara on the issue of self-determination.

Morocco agreed in principle to the proposals but refused to deal directly with Polisario. Although the war was costly, it allowed King Hassan to capitalize on the patriotic fervour it generated among Moroccans. Then, in 1984, he surprised the world by signing an agreement with Colonel Kadhafi of Libya, who, until then, had been helping Polisario. At the same time, Morocco was becoming increasingly isolated, with more countries recognizing the SADR, which had embarked upon a new military and diplomatic offensive. The isolation showed signs of ending with the announcement in May 1987 that better relations with Algeria had been achieved. In November 1987 Polisario guerrillas agreed to a ceasefire in Western Sahara and South Morocco and in May 1988 Morocco and Algeria announced that they were resuming full diplomatic relations. Although a peace plan with the Polisario Front had been agreed, fighting continued until a ceasefire in 1991. Early in 1989 it was announced that diplomatic relations with Syria had been restored. Morocco was the only Maghreb (northwest African) state to send troops as part of the US-led coalition in the 1991 Gulf War.

In the 1993 general election, the first held since 1984, the center-left parties improved their position in the direct elections, but the center-right won more seats overall. After the results had been finally digested, the king appointed a new nonparty government, led by one of his most trusted ministers, Karim Lamrani, who continued in office. The king said the center-left, the Kutlah, had refused to form a government with his allies and the center-right, the Wifaq, said they needed a spell out of office to allow them to reconstruct. In May 1994 Lamrani was dismissed and replaced by another royal ally, Abdellatif Filali.

In 1996 the constitution was amended to create a two-chamber assembly, but elections to the lower house, the House of Representatives, in November 1997, proved inconclusive. Eventually, the king appointed Abderrahmanen and former political prisoner, el-Yousifi (b. 1924) as prime minister in February 1998. It was the first time in King Hassan's reign that a leader of the opposition had headed the government. A veteran socialist, el-Yousifi led the Socialist Union of Popular Forces (USFP). He formed a coalition which included other members of the left-nationalist Koutla bloc, as well as the centrist National Rally of Independents (RNI), led by the king's brother-in-law, Ahmed Osman.

However, de facto power continued to be wielded by Driss Basri, who had served as interior minister for more than 20 years. In July 1999 King Hassan died and was succeeded by his son, Muhammad VI, a 35-year-old with strong humanitarian instincts. He inherited a country in which 12 million people lived below the poverty line, unemployment exceeded 20%, and a third of the budget was used to service national debt. Reformers hoped that Muhammad's accession would lead to the sidelining of Basri and to el-Yousifi, who was recovering from an operation on a brain tumour, being given greater authority. An early positive move was the agreement to re-open, in August 1999, the country's border with Algeria.

OMAN

Sultanate of Oman
Sultanat 'Uman

Capital: Muscat

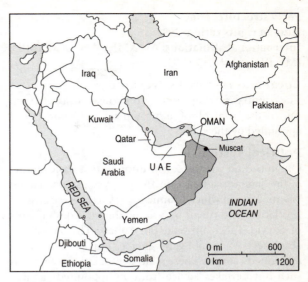

Social and economic data
Area: 212,457 sq km/82,030 sq miles
Population: 2,077,000*
Pop. density per sq km/sq mi: 10/25*
Urban population: 11%**
Literacy rate: 38%**
GDP: $10,580 million*; per-capita GDP:$5,090*
Government defense spending (% of GDP): 15.1%*
Currency: Omani rial
Economy type: middle income
Labor force in agriculture: 50%**
* 1995.
** 1992.

Head of state and head of government
Sultan Qaboos bin Said, since 1970

Ethnic composition
The great majority of the population is Arab but there are also substantial Iranian, Baluchi, Indo-Pakistan, and East African minorities. The official language is Arabic but English is generally used in commercial transactions.

Religions
Islam is the state religion and about 75% of the population is Ibadi Muslim and the rest Sunni Muslim.

Political features
State type: absolutist
Date of state formation: 1951
Political structure: unitary
Executive: absolute
Assembly: there is no elected assembly

Party structure: none
Human rights rating: 49%
International affiliations: AL, AMF, DDS, GCC, IBRD, IMF, IWC, NAM, OIC, UN

Local and regional government

The country is divided into 41 provinces (*wilayat*), each under the control of a provincial governor (*wali*) appointed by the sultan.

Political system

Oman had no written constitution until a Basic Statute of the State was adopted in 1996. It defines Oman as an Islamic state in which Islamic law (*sharia*) is the basis of legislation, and rule is by Sultani, the male descendents of Sayyid Turki bin Said bin Sultan. The sultan has absolute power, ruling by decree, but assisted by an appointed cabinet. There is no democratic assembly as such but he takes advice from an appointed cabinet. There is an advisory Consultative Council (Majlis) of 59 appointed members, taken from a list of candidates chosen by notables, provincial governors, and sheikhs. It can review legislation, question ministers, and make policy proposals. It meets twice a year. An appointed 41-member Council of State was also set up in December 1997, comprising former ministers, business men, academics, and four women. In June 1998 the life of the council was extended to 30 June 2002.

Political parties

There are no political parties.

Political leaders since 1970

1970– Sultan Qaboos bin Said

Latest elections

No free elections are held.

Political history

As Muscat and Oman, the country had a very close relationship with Britain, being under its protection from the 19th century. When its complete independence was recognized in 1951, as the Sultanate of Oman, the two countries signed a Treaty of Friendship. Said bin Taimur, who had been sultan since 1932 and whose dynasty went back to the 18th century, was overthrown by his son, Qaboos bin Said (b. 1940), in a bloodless coup in 1970. With the economy boosted by exploitation of vast oil reserves from the late 1960s, Qaboos bin Said embarked on a much more liberal and expansionist policy than that of his conservative father. Oman benefits from its natural wealth but conflicts in neighboring countries, such as Yemen, Iran, Iraq, and Afghanistan, have not only emphasized the country's strategic importance but put its own security at risk. The sultan has tried to follow a path of nonalignment, maintaining close ties with the United States and other NATO countries. Like most Middle East states in recent years, Oman has had to deal with militant Islamic extremists, seeking to destabilize the regime.

QATAR

State of Qatar
Dawlat Qatar

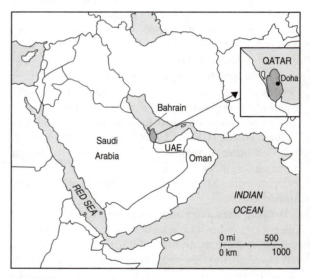

Capital: Doha

Social and economic data

Area: 11,440 sq km/4,417 sq miles
Population: 540,000*
Pop. density per sq km/sq mi: 47/122*
Urban population: 79%**
Literacy rate: 51%**
GDP: $7,450 million*; per-capita GDP: $13,800*
Government defense spending (% of GDP): 4.4%**
Currency: Qatar rial
Economy type: high income
Labor force in agriculture: 3%**
* 1995.
** 1992.

Head of state (executive)

Emir Sheikh Hamad bin Khalifa al-Thani, since 1995

Head of government
Prime minister Sheil Abdallah bin Khalifa al-Thani, since 1996

Ethnic composition
Only about 25% of the population are indigenous Qataris, 40% being Arabs, and the others Pakistanis, Indians, and Iranians. The official language is Arabic but English is generally used in commercial transactions.

Religions
Islam is the state religion. Most people (98%) are Sunni Muslims of the strict Wahhabi persuasion.

Political features
State type: absolutist
Date of state formation: 1971
Political structure: unitary
Executive: absolute
Assembly: there is no assembly
Party structure: none
Human rights rating: N/A
International affiliations: AL, AMF, DDS, GCC, IAEA, IBRD, IMF, NAM, OAPEC, OIC, OPEC, UN

Local and regional government
Local government is the overall responsibility of the Minister of Municipal Affairs. Each of the largest towns has a partly elected and partly appointed municipal council.

Political system
A provisional constitution adopted in 1970 confirmed Qatar as an absolute monarchy, with the emir holding all executive and legislative powers. The emir appoints a Council of Ministers and effectively leads the body. There is a 35-member Advisory Council, with limited powers to question ministers. In June 1998 the life of the Council was extended to 30 June 2002.

Political parties
There are no political parties. However, in March 1999 an opposition political grouping, the Higher National Council for the Defence of Political Detainees in Qatar, was formed in Paris, France, to campaign for political liberalization.

Political leaders since 1970
1949–72 Sheikh Ahmad al-Thani, 1972–95 Sheikh Khalifa bin Hamad al-Thani, 1995– Sheikh Hamad bin Khalifa al-Thani

Latest elections
There are no national legislature elections, but in March 1999 there were nationwide elections to a new central municipal council, which has advisory powers over issues such as public health. The 29 seats were contested by 220 candidates, including six women, who were allowed to contest seats and vote for the first time in the country's history. Turnout was below 50%.

Political history
Formerly part of the Turkish Ottoman Empire, Qatar was evacuated by the Turks in 1914 and the British government gave formal recognition in 1916 to Sheikh Abdullah al-Thani as its ruler, guaranteeing protection in return for an influence over the country's external affairs.

In 1968 Britain announced its intention of withdrawing its forces from the Persian Gulf area by 1981 and Qatar decided to try to form an association with other Gulf states. Terms could not be agreed, however, and on 1 September 1971 the country became fully independent. A new Treaty of Friendship with Britain was signed to replace the former arrangements.

In the meantime the ruler, Sheikh Ahmad, had announced a provisional constitution which would provide for a partially elected consultative assembly, while retaining ultimate power in the emir's hands. However, in 1972, while Sheikh Ahmad was out of the country, his cousin, the crown prince Sheikh Khalifa, who held the post of prime minister, led a bloodless coup and declared himself emir. He embarked upon an ambitious program of social and economic reform, curbing the extravagances of the royal family. An Advisory Council was appointed, in accordance with the 1970 constitution, and its membership was expanded in 1975.

Mineral-rich Qatar has had good relations with most of its neighbors and is regarded as one of the more stable and moderate Arab states, although there have been recent territorial disputes with Bahrain and Saudi Arabia. In 1990–91 it joined the United Nations' coalition forces against Iraq in the Gulf War.

In June 1995, in another bloodless coup, Sheikh Khalifa bin Hamad al-Thani was ousted by his son, the crown prince and defense minister Sheikh Hamad bin Khalifa al-Thani. In March 1996 Sheikh Khalifa survived an assassination and coup attempt.

SAUDI ARABIA

*The Kingdom of Saudi Arabia
al-Mamlaka al-'Arabiya as-Sa'udiya*

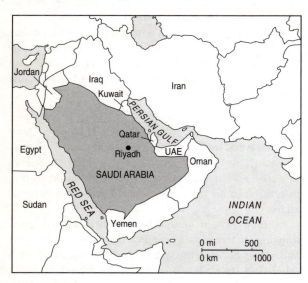

Capital: Riyadh

Social and economic data
Area: 2,150,000 sq km/830,119 sq miles
Population: 17,451,000*
Pop. density per sq km/sq mi: 8/21
Urban population: 74%**
Literacy rate: 62%**
GDP: $133,540 million*; per-capita GDP: $7,650*
Government defense spending (% of GDP): 10.6%*
Currency: rial
Economy type: high income
Labor force in agriculture: 48%**
* 1995.
** 1992.

Head of state and head of government
King Fahd Ibn Abdul Aziz al-Saud, since 1982

Ethnic composition
About 90% of the population is Arab and 10% Afro-Asian. Arabic is the official language and is widely spoken.

Religions
Islam is the state religion. The great majority of the population, 92%, is Sunni Muslim, chiefly of the Wahhabi sect, and the rest is Shi'ite Muslim. Saudi Arabia is the center of Islam, containing the two holiest places, Mecca and Medina.

Political features
State type: absolutist
Date of state formation: 1932
Political structure: unitary
Executive: absolute
Assembly: there is no elected assembly
Party structure: none
Human rights rating: 29%
International affiliations: AL, AMF, DDS, GCC, IAEA, IBRD, IMF, NAM, OAPEC, OIC, OPEC, UN

Local and regional government
The country is divided into 13 provinces which are sub-divided into districts and subdistricts. Each province is administered by a governor general, each district by a governor, and each subdistrict by a headman. There are provincial councils whose members are elected by tribal chiefs.

Political system
Saudi Arabia is an absolute monarchy, with no assembly and no political parties. A constitution, the Basic Law of Government, was adopted in 1992. The king rules, in accordance with Islamic law (Sharia), by decree. He appoints and heads a Council of Ministers (cabinet) whose decisions are the result of a majority vote, but always subject to the ultimate sanction of the king. The crown prince is first deputy prime minister. The formation of a 60-member Consultative Council (Majlis al-Shura) in 1992, to be appointed every four years in accordance with the Islamic principle of 'consultation' (which excludes members of the Al-Saud family), suggested that tentative steps were being taken towards a more democratic form of government. In addition, in 1992 a law was passed limiting ministers to four years in office. The line of royal succession passes from brother to brother according to age, although some sons of King Ibn Saud have renounced their succession rights. All sons and grandsons of the king must be consulted before a new king is installed.

Political parties
There are no political parties.

Political leaders since 1970
1964–75 King Faisal, 1975–82 King Khalid, 1982– King Fahd

Latest elections
There is no provision for free elections.

Political history
Originally part of the Turkish Ottoman Empire, mod-

ern Saudi Arabia is almost entirely the creation of King Ibn Saud (1880–1953), a Wahhabi who, after the dissolution of the Ottoman Empire in 1918, fought rival Arab rulers until in 1926 he had established himself as the undisputed king of the Hejaz and sultan of Nejd (central Arabia). Six years later this area became the United Kingdom of Saudi Arabia. Oil was discovered in the late 1930s and commercially exploited from the 1940s, providing the basis of the country's great prosperity. Today, it provides one-eighth of the world's oil.

King Ibn Saud died in 1953 and was succeeded by his eldest son, Saud Ibn Abdul Aziz (1902–69). During King Saud's reign relations between Saudi Arabia and Egypt became strained and criticisms of the king within the royal family grew to such an extent that in November 1964 he was forced to abdicate in favor of his brother, Crown Prince Faisal Ibn Abdul Aziz (1904–75). Under King Faisal, Saudi Arabia became an influential leader among Arab oil producers.

In 1975 King Faisal was assassinated by one of his nephews and his half-brother, Khalid Ibn Abdul Aziz (1913–82), who had been made crown prince, succeeded him. Khalid was in failing health and found it increasingly necessary to rely on his other brother, Crown Prince Fahd (b. 1923), to perform the duties of government, so that he became the country's effective ruler. Saudi Arabia had by now become the most influential country in the Arab world, giving financial support to Iraq in its war with Iran and drawing up proposals for a permanent settlement of the Arab–Israeli dispute.

King Khalid died suddenly of a heart attack in 1982 and was succeeded by Fahd, his half-brother Abdullah becoming crown prince and his full brother, Prince Sultan, defense minister.

Saudi Arabia made an enormous financial contribution to the 1991 Gulf War against Iraq, as well as providing a base for allied operations. The war cost the country at least $60 billion.

In October 1994 the king announced the appointment of a Higher Council for Islamic Affairs, as an 'ombudsman of Islamic activity in educational, economic and foreign policy', and in August 1995 a major cabinet reshuffle was effected, bringing in 15 new faces. The latter were chiefly technocrats and included six members of the consultative Majlis al-Shura. However, the key defense, foreign affairs, and interior ministries remained firmly in the hands of royal princes. King Fahd has also instituted a gradually evolving policy of privatization. However, with falling oil prices leading to a slowdown in economic growth, there has been an increase in the level of Islamic militant opposition to the Al-Saud regime. In June 1996 a terrorist bomb killed 19 people at a US Air Force base.

SYRIA

Syrian Arab Republic
al-Jumhuriya al-'Arabiya as-Suriya

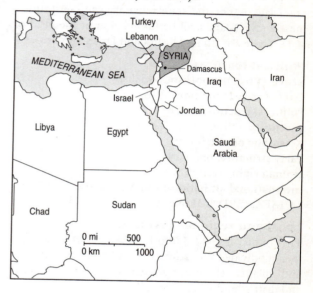

Capital: Damascus (Dimashq)

Social and economic data
Area: 184,050 sq km/71,062 sq miles
Population: 13,844,000[*]
Pop. density per sq km/sq mi: 75/195[*]
Urban population: 51%[**]
Literacy rate: 65%[**]
GDP: $15,780 million[*]; per-capita GDP: $1,140[*]
Government defense spending (% of GDP): 6.8%[*]
Currency: Syrian pound
Economy type: middle income
Labor force in agriculture: 30%[**]
Unemployment rate: 6.8%[**]
[*] 1995.
[**] 1992.

Head of state and (executive)
President Hafez al-Assad, since 1971

Head of government
Prime minister Mahmoid Zuabi, since 1987

Ethnic composition
More than 90% of the population are Arabs, but there are enormous differences between them in language and regional affiliations and, to a lesser extent, religion. There are also differences between the settled and nomadic people. The official language is Arabic, with Kurdish as a minority tongue.

Religions
The great majority of people (90%) are Sunni Muslims, but Islam is not the state religion. The constitution merely says 'Islam shall be the religion of the head of state'. There are Shi'ite Muslim and Druze minorities.

Political features
State type: nationalistic socialist
Date of state formation: 1946
Political structure: unitary
Executive: unlimited presidential
Assembly: one-chamber
Party structure: one-party
Human rights rating: 30%
International affiliations: AL, AMF, BADEA, DDS, G-24, IAEA, IBRD, IMF, NAM, OAPEC, OIC, UN

Local and regional government
The country is divided into 13 provinces which are further subdivided into administrative districts, localities, and villages. There are elected provincial assemblies and district and village councils.

Political system
The 1973 constitution provides for a president elected by universal adult suffrage, through a simple plurality voting system, for a seven-year term. The president is head of state, head of government, secretary general of the Ba'ath Arab Socialist Party, and president of the National Progressive Front, the umbrella organization for five socialist parties which dominate the country's politics. Syria is therefore, in reality, if not in a strictly legal sense, a one-party state. There is a single-chamber 250-member assembly, the National People's Assembly (Majlis al-Sha'ab), also elected by universal adult suffrage, by simple plurality voting in 15 multi-seat constituencies, for a four-year term, with 83 seats reserved for independent candidates. The president appoints vice presidents and governs with a prime minister and Council of Ministers whom he or she also appoints.

Political parties
Since 1972 political groups have operated as a single party under the name of the National Progressive Front.

Syria has a long history of leftwing politics and the National Progressive Front includes the Communist Party of Syria, a pro-Soviet party established in 1924, the Arab Socialist Party, the Arab Socialist Unionist Party, the Syrian Arab Socialist Union Party, and the 800,000-member Ba'ath Arab Socialist Party, which is the hub of the organization. It dates from 1947 and is the result of a merger of the Arab Revival Movement and the Arab Ba'ath Party, both of which were founded in 1940. The National Progressive Front has a pro-Arab socialist orientation.

Political leaders since 1970
1970– Hafez al-Assad (Ba'ath Arab Socialist Party)

Latest elections
The results of the December 1998 elections for the Majlis al-Sha'ab were as follows:

Syria latest election results

Party	Seats
National Progressive Front	167
Independents	83

The most recent presidential election was in February 1998, when President Assad was re-elected unopposed in a national referendum.

Political history
Syria was part of the Turkish Ottoman Empire until 1918 and came under French control in 1920 as a result of a secret treaty, the Sykes–Picot Agreement, concluded by two British and French diplomats, Sir Mark Sykes and Georges Picot. They agreed the partitioning of the Turkish Empire, identifying the respective spheres of influence of Britain and France in the Middle East and North Africa. As part of the deal, France was given a free hand in Syria.

The Syrians resented the French occupation and there were several revolts in the 1920s and 1930s. As World War II loomed, the government in Paris changed its policy, against the wishes of the French army in Syria, and promised independence. This was proclaimed in 1944 but, because of the reluctance of French officers to relinquish power, full independence did not come until 1946. There followed a period of military dictatorship and a series of coups. In 1958

Syria merged with Egypt, to become the United Arab Republic (UAR), but in 1961, following another army coup, it seceded and an independent Syrian Arab Republic was established.

In 1963 a government was formed mainly from members of the Arab Socialist Renaissance (Ba'ath) Party but three years later it was removed in another coup by the army. In 1970 the moderate wing of the Ba'ath Party, led by Lieutenant General Hafez al-Assad (b. 1928), seized power in yet another bloodless coup and in the following year Assad was elected president. Soon afterwards he formed the five main political parties into one broad group, under his leadership, as the National Progressive Front.

Since then President Assad has remained in office without any serious challenges to his leadership. In 1983 he was reported to have suffered a heart attack but recovered in an apparently weakened condition. This event aroused speculation about his possible successor but no specific name emerged.

Externally Syria has, under President Assad, played a leading role in Middle East affairs. In the Arab–Israeli Six-Day War of 1967 it lost territory to Israel and after the Yom Kippur War of 1973 Israel formally annexed the Golan Heights, which had previously been part of Syria. During 1976 Assad progressively intervened in the civil war in Lebanon, eventually committing some 50,000 troops to the operations. Relations between Syria and Egypt cooled after President Sadat's Israel peace initiative in 1977 and the subsequent Camp David agreement, but were restored in 1989.

Assad's authority was made evident in 1985 when he secured the release of 39 US hostages from an aircraft hijacked by the extremist Shi'ite, group Hizbollah ('Party of God'), and he played a significant part in securing the release of Western hostages in Lebanon. The return of Lebanon to a degree of normality was very much the product of the actions of Assad, who sent in Syrian forces in 1990 to defeat the Lebanese Christian militia of Michel Aoun. His contribution to the defeat of his old rival, Saddam Hussein, when Syria supported the US-led United Nations military coalition against Iraq in the 1991 Gulf War, was also significant.

Formerly an international pariah as a result of its alleged sponsorship of terrorism, Syria's relations with the Western world, and particularly the United States, progressed positively during 1993 and 1994, into 1995. Prospects for an Israeli withdrawal from the Golan Heights were also improved after US-sponsored talks and a summit meeting in Alexandria between the pres-

idents of Egypt and Syria and King Fahd of Saudi Arabia. Assad was re-elected for a fifth term as president in 1998 and, since the collapse of the Soviet Union, which used to be Syria's most important trading partner, has introduced a number of economic reforms to encourage investment and stimulate growth.

President Assad is working closely with his Egyptian counterpart, President Mubarak, in trying to keep the Middle East peace process alive. However, with the election in May 1996 of the hardline Binyamin Netanyahu as Israeli prime minister, relations deteriorated. In June 1997 the border with Iraq, which had been closed in 1980 as a result of Syria's support for Iran in the Iran-Iraq conflict, was re-opened, indicating a warming in relations between the Ba'athist rivals.

TUNISIA

Republic of Tunisia
al-Jumhuriya at-Tunisiya

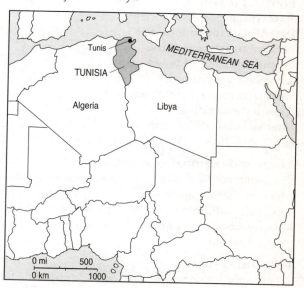

Capital: Tunis

Social and economic data
Area: 164,150 sq km/63,679 sq miles
Population: 8,733,000[*]
Pop. density per sq km/sq mi: 53/138[*]
Urban population: 57%[**]
Literacy rate: 65%[**]
GDP: $16,370 million[*]; per-capita GDP: $1,870[*]

Government defense spending (% of GDP): 2.0%[*]
Currency: Tunisian dinar
Economy type: middle income
Labor force in agriculture: 22%[**]

[*] 1995.
[**] 1992.

Head of state (executive)

President Zine el-Abidine Ben Ali, since 1987

Head of government

Prime minister Hamed Karoui, since 1989

Ethnic composition

About 10% of the population is pure Arab, the remainder being of Berber-Arab stock. There are small Jewish and French communities. The official language is Arabic but French is also widely spoken.

Religions

Islam is the state religion and about 99% of the population is Sunni Muslim. There are also Jewish and Christian (Roman Catholic) minorities.

Political features

State type: nationalistic socialist
Date of state formation: 1956
Political structure: unitary
Executive: unlimited presidential
Assembly: one-chamber
Party structure: effectively one-party
Human rights rating: 60%
International affiliations: AL, AMF, AMU, IAEA, IBRD, IMF, NAM, OAU, OIC, UN, WTO

Local and regional government

The country is divided into 23 regions, or governorates, which are further subdivided into delegations and sectors, all administered by appointed officials. Municipalities are more democratically governed by elected councils.

Political system

A new constitution was adopted in 1959, providing for a president who is both head of state and head of government, elected by universal adult suffrage through a simple plurality voting system for a five-year term and eligible for re-election. In 1985 Habib Bourguiba was made President for Life by the National Assembly, but in 1988 his successor announced a number of important constitutional changes. They included the abolition of the post of President for Life; a limitation on the presidency to a maximum of three five-year terms; the maximum age for presidential candidates to be set at

70; and the minimum age for assembly candidates to be reduced from 28 to 25. There is a single-chamber National Assembly of 163 members, serving a five-year term. One hundred and forty-four are elected by simple plurality voting and 19 seats are reserved for opposition parties; this procedure was introduced in 1993. The president governs through an appointed Council of Ministers, led by a prime minister. The minimum voting age is 20 years.

Political parties

In 1963 Tunisia became a one-party state, the party being the Destourien Socialist Party (PSD), led by President Habib Bourguiba. Since 1981, however, additional parties have been officially recognized.

The PSD was formed in 1934 as a splinter group from the old Destour (Constitution) Party. It was renamed the Constitutional Democratic Rally (RDC) in 1988 and has a moderate, nationalistic socialist orientation. It continues to dominate the political scene but President Ben Ali has warned his followers to prepare themselves to operate in a more pluralistic system.

There are now some 11 active political parties. The Movement of Democratic Socialists (MDS), the ex-communist Renovation Movement (MR), and the banned radical Islamic Renaissance Party (al-Nahda) are the chief opposition parties.

Political leaders since 1970

1956–87 Habib Bourguiba (PSD), 1987– Zine el-Abidine Ben Ali (PSD)

Latest elections

In the March 1994 presidential election, Zine el-Abidine Ben Ali was re-elected, as the only candidate, with more than 99% of the votes cast.

In the March 1994 National Assembly elections, the RCD, with 98% of the vote, won all 144 of the seats contested on the usual simple-majority list basis. The other 19 seats were distributed between six smaller parties and independents who came second in the national poll.

Political history

After being subjected to rule by Phoenicians, Carthaginians, Romans, Byzantines, Arabs, Spaniards, and Turks, Tunisia came under French control in 1883. After World War I an independence movement began to grow and in 1934 the Destourien Socialist Party (PSD) was founded by Habib Bourguiba (b. 1903) to lead the campaign. Tunisia was granted internal self-government in 1955 and full independence in 1956, with Bourguiba as prime minister. A year later the monarchy was abolished and Tunisia became a republic, with Bourguiba as president.

A new constitution was adopted in 1959 and the first National Assembly was elected. Between 1963 and 1981 the Destourien Socialist Party (PSD) was the only legally recognized party but since that date others have been allowed to operate. President Bourguiba followed a distinctive line in foreign policy, establishing close links with the Western powers, including the United States, but joining other Arab states in condemning the US-inspired Egypt–Israeli treaty. He also allowed the Palestine Liberation Organization (PLO) to use Tunis for its headquarters from 1982. This led to an Israeli attack in 1985 which strained relations with the United States. Relations with Libya also deteriorated to such an extent that diplomatic links were severed in 1985.

Bourguiba ruled his country firmly and paternalistically and his long period in Tunisian politics made him a national legend, evidenced by the elaborate mausoleum which has been built in anticipation of his eventual departure. In November 1987, however, his younger colleagues became impatient and staged an internal coup, declaring him 'mentally and physically unfit for office' and forcing him to retire at the age of 84. The former prime minister, Zine el-Abidine Ben Ali (b. 1936), replaced him as president and chair of the ruling PSD and Hedi Baccouche was appointed prime minister. After taking up supreme office Ben Ali moved quickly to establish his own distinctive policy line and style. His new government showed itself to be more tolerant of opposition than Bourguiba's and in December 1987 over 2,000 political prisoners were granted an amnesty. They included 608 members of the fundamentalist Islamic Tendency Movement (MTI). As a further indication of greater liberalization, the unpopular State Security Court, established during Bourguiba's regime, was disbanded and there have been some moves towards privatization in the economy. In 1988 Ben Ali changed the PSD's name to the Constitutional Democratic Rally (RDC) and tightened his personal control of it by appointing two-thirds of the membership of its Central Committee. Despite competition from opposition parties, the RDC won virtually all the National Assembly seats in the 1994 elections.

The greater liberality in Tunisia in recent years has given encouragement to fundamentalists to flex their muscles, although their political vehicle, the Renaissance Party, is banned. Like other Middle East states, Tunisia has had to deal with the sometimes violent activities of Islamic militants.

UNITED ARAB EMIRATES

al-Imarat al-'Arabiya al-Muttahida

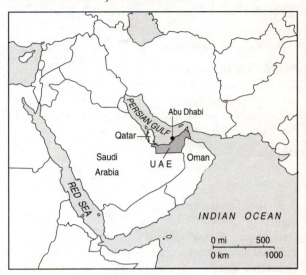

Capital: Abu Dhabi

Social and economic data
Area: 83,600 sq km/32,278 sq miles
Population: 2,388,000[*]
Pop. density per sq km/sq mi: 29/74[*]
Urban population: 82%[**]
Literacy rate: 54%[**]
GDP: $42,800 million[*]; per-capita GDP: $17,900[*]
Government defense spending (% of GDP): 4.8%[*]
Currency: UAE dirham
Economy type: high income
Labor force in agriculture: 5%[**]
[*] 1995.
[**] 1992.

Head of state and head of government
President Sheikh Zayed Bin Sultan al-Nahayan, since 1971

Supreme council of rulers
Abu Dhabi:[**] Sheikh Zayed Bin Sultan al-Nahayan, since 1966

Dubai:[*] Sheikh Maktoum Bin Rashid al-Maktoum, since 1990

Sharjah: Sheikh Sultan Bin Muhammad al-Quasimi, since 1972

Ras al-Khaimah: Sheikh Saqr Bin Muhammad al-Quasimi, since 1948

Umm al-Qaiwain: Sheikh Rashid Bin Ahmad al-Mu'alla, since 1981

Ajman: Sheikh Humaid Bin Rashid al-Nuami, since 1981

Fujairah: Sheikh Hamad Bin Muhammad al-Sharqi, since 1974

* Prime minister.
** Deputy prime minister.

Ethnic composition
The Emirates have a very mixed population, including many immigrants. About 75% are Iranians, Indians, or Pakistanis and only about 25% are Arabs. Arabic is the main language.

Religions
Sunni Islam is the state religion and it is almost universally followed.

Political features
State type: absolutist
Date of state formation: 1971
Political structure: federal
Executive: absolute
Assembly: there is no elected assembly
Party structure: none
Human rights rating: N/A
International affiliations: AL, AMF, DDS, GCC, IAEA, IBRD, IMF, NAM, OAPEC, OIC, OPEC, UN, WTO

Local and regional government
The country is a federation of seven self-governing emirates, each with its own absolute ruler.

Political system
A provisional constitution for the United Arab Emirates was put into effect in December 1971. It provided for the union of seven sheikhdoms, formerly known as the Trucial States, in a federal structure. These provisional arrangements have subsequently been extended, until a permanent constitution is produced.

In accordance with the provisional constitution, the highest authority is the Supreme Council of Rulers which includes the sheikhs of all the emirates. The Council elects two of its members to be president and vice president of the federal state. The president then appoints a prime minister and Council of Ministers. There is a federal National Council of 40 members appointed by the emirates for a two-year term and this operates as a consultative assembly. Each of the rulers is a hereditary emir and an absolute monarch in their own country.

Political parties
There are no political parties.

Political leaders since 1970
1971– Sheikh Zayed Bin Sultan al-Nahayan

Latest elections
There are no popularly elected bodies.

Political history
The British government signed treaties with the sultans and sheikhs of seven emirates on the southern shores of the Persian Gulf and the Gulf of Oman during the 19th century and, from 1892, became responsible for their defense. Collectively, they were called the Trucial States. In 1952, on British advice, they set up a Trucial Council, consisting of all seven rulers, with a view to eventually establishing a federation.

In the 1960s they became very wealthy through the exploitation of oil deposits and, believing that they were now strong enough to stand alone, and as part of a policy of disengagement from overseas commitments, in 1968 the British government announced that it was withdrawing its forces within three years.

The seven Trucial States, with Bahrain and Qatar, formed a Federation of Arab Emirates, which was intended to become a federal state, but in 1971 Bahrain and Qatar decided to secede and become independent nations. Six of the Trucial States then agreed to combine to form the United Arab Emirates, which came into being in December 1971. The remaining sheikhdom, Ras al-Khaimah, joined in February 1972. Sheikh Zayed, the ruler of Abu Dhabi, became the first president.

In 1976 Sheikh Zayed, disappointed with the slow progress towards centralization, announced that he would not accept another five-year term as president. He was persuaded to continue, however, with assurances that the federal government would be given more control over such activities as defense and internal security. In recent years the United Arab Emirates have played an increasingly important role in Middle East affairs and during the liberation of Kuwait in the 1991 Gulf War, losing 17 UAE nationals in the process. In 1987 diplomatic relations with Egypt were resumed and Sheikh Zayed paid an official visit to Cairo during which he signed a trade treaty between the two countries.

The collapse of the Bank of Credit and Commerce International (BCCI) in 1991 was estimated to have cost the UAE $10 billion. The government was highly critical of the Bank of England's role in the affair. In May 1998 following a meeting with US vice-president Al Gore, it was announced that Sheikh Khalifa had placed an order for 80 US F-16 fighter aircraft, to replace his country's ageing fleet of French Mirage fighters.

YEMEN

Republic of Yemen

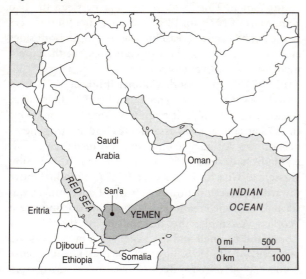

al-Jamhuriya al-Yamaniya

Capital: San'a (political), Aden (economic and commercial)

Social and economic data
Area: 540,000 sq km/208,495 sq miles
Population: 15,800,000*
Pop. density per sq km/sq mi: 29/76*
Urban population: 31%**
Literacy rate: 39%**
GDP: $4,040 million*; per-capita GDP: $260*
Government defense spending (% of GDP): 3.9%*
Currency: rial (north), dinar (south); both are legal currency throughout the country
Economy type: low income
Labor force in agriculture: 63%**
* 1995.
** 1992.

Head of state (executive)
President Ali Abdullah Saleh, since 1990

Head of government
Prime minister Abdal Karim al-Iryani, since 1998

Ethnic composition
Until the departure of Yemenite Jews for Israel in 1948, they were the predominant ethnic group in the country. Now most of the population are Arabs. Arabic is the main language.

Religions
Most of the population are Muslims, divided roughly equally between the Sunni (54%) and Zaidist Shi'ite (46%) orders. Islam is the state religion.

Political features
State type: emergent democratic
Date of state formation: 1990
Political structure: unitary
Executive: limited presidential
Assembly: one-chamber
Party structure: multiparty
Human rights rating: 49%
International affiliations: AL, AMF, IAEA, IBRD, IMF, NAM, OIC, UN

Local and regional government
The country is divided into 38 provinces and then further subdivided into districts and villages. There are appointed governors at the higher levels and traditional village headmen.

Political system
The Republic of Yemen was founded on 22 May 1990, when North and South Yemen were united. A constitution was approved in May 1991, providing for a 301-member assembly, the House of Representatives, and a five-member Presidential Council. The constitution underwent major revision in September 1994, when the Presidential Council was abolished and a president, directly elected by universal adult suffrage, was instituted. The amended constitution defines the state as a multiparty democracy, with a market-based economy and Islamic sharia law as the source of all legislation. The assembly is elected for a four-year term, and the president serves a five-year term, renewable once only. The president appoints a Council of Ministers, headed by a prime minister.

Political parties
Over 30 political parties were legalized after the publication of the draft constitution in December 1989, and out of these there emerged two main regionally based groupings: the General People's Congress (GPC) and the Yemen Reform Group (al-Islah).

The GPC is the power base of President Saleh and, with its main following in the north of the country, it has a left-of-center orientation.

The southern-based YSP is the power base of Ali Salim al-Bid, who was the president of South Yemen before unification. It has a leftwing traditionally Marxist orientation.

Al-Islah was formed in 1990 as a coalition of the Muslim Brotherhood and the pro-Saudi tribal confederation of the north. It has a right-of-center Islamist orientation, and is a coalition ally of the GPC.

Political leaders since 1970

North Yemen: 1967–74 Abdur Rahman al-Iriani (Republican), 1974–77 Ibrahim al-Hamadi (military), 1977–78 Ahmed ibn Hussein al-Ghashmi (military), 1978–90 Ali Abdullah Saleh (GPC)

South Yemen: 1969–78 Salim Rubayi Ali (NF), 1978–80 Abdul Fattah Ismail (YSP), 1980–86 Ali Nasser Muhammad (YSP), 1986–90 Haider Abu Bakr al-Attas (YSP)

United Yemen: 1990– Ali Abdullah Saleh (GPC)

Latest elections

The results of the April 1997 general election are set out below. The YSP, which has been weakened by the 1994 civil war in southern Yemen, boycotted the polls.

President Ali Abdullah Saleh was confirmed for a five-year term by the House of Representatives in October 1994. However, in future the president will be elected directly.

Yemen latest election results

Party	Seats
GPC	187
al-Islah	53
Independents	54
Other parties	7

Political history

The Yemen Arab Republic, or North Yemen, was under Turkish rule from 1517 to 1918, when it secured its independence. Imam Yahya became king and remained monarch until he was assassinated in 1948. His son, Imam Ahmad, succeeded him and ruled in what can best be described as a sadistic fashion, keeping the country isolated and backward, until he was deposed in a military coup in 1962.

The kingdom of Yemen was then renamed the Yemen Arab Republic (YAR), provoking a civil war between royalist forces, assisted by Saudi Arabia, and republicans, supported by Egypt. By 1967 the republicans, under Marshal Abdullah al-Sallal, had won. Later that year Sallal was deposed while on a foreign visit and a Republican Council took over.

Meanwhile, Britain had withdrawn from South Yemen and, with the installation of a repressive regime

there, hundreds of thousands of South Yemenis fled to the YAR, many of them forming guerrilla groups with the aim of overthrowing the communist regime in South Yemen. This resulted in a war between the two Yemens from 1971 until 1972, when, under the auspices of the Arab League, a ceasefire was arranged. Both sides agreed to a union of the two countries but the agreement was not implemented.

In 1974 the pro-Saudi Colonel Ibrahim al-Hamadi seized power in North Yemen and by 1975 there were rumours of a possible attempt to restore the monarchy. In 1977 al-Hamadi was assassinated and another member of the Military Command Council, which al-Hamadi had set up in 1974, Colonel Ahmed ibn Hussein al-Ghashmi, took over. In 1978 a gradual move towards a more constitutional form of government was started, with the creation of an appointed Constituent People's Assembly, the dissolution of the Military Command Council and the installation of al-Ghashmi as president. In 1978, however, he was killed when a bomb exploded in a suitcase carried by an envoy from South Yemen.

This incident worsened relations between the two Yemens and war broke out once more. The Arab League again intervened to arrange a ceasefire and for the second time the two countries agreed to unite. This time, however, definite progress was made so that by 1983 a joint Yemen Council was meeting at six-monthly intervals.

In 1983 President Ali Abdullah Saleh (b. 1942) of North Yemen submitted his resignation to the Assembly, as his term of office neared its end. His resignation was refused and he was re-elected for a further five years. In 1988 his presidency was extended to a third term.

In the aftermath of the 1978 killing of al-Ghashmi, the president of South Yemen, Rubayi Ali, was deposed and executed. Two days later the three political parties in South Yemen agreed to merge to form a 'Marxist–Leninist vanguard party', the Yemen Socialist Party (YSP), and Abdul Fattah Ismail became its secretary general. In December Ismail was appointed head of state but four months later resigned, on the grounds of ill health. He subsequently went into exile and was succeeded by Ali Nasser Muhammad.

Meanwhile, in 1985 Ali Nasser Muhammad was re-elected secretary general of the YSP and its political bureau for another five years. He soon began taking steps to remove his opponents, his personal guard shooting and killing three bureau members. This act of violence led to a short civil war and the eventual dismissal of Ali Nasser from all of his posts in the party and the government. A new administration was formed, with Haidar Abu Bakr al-Attas as president, chair of the Presidium of the Supreme People's Council, and secretary general of the YSP Political Bureau.

A more conciliatory climate had been created in the South and the new government, influenced by the loss of economic aid from the fast disintegrating Soviet Union, immediately committed itself to continuing the process of eventual union with the economically more prosperous YAR. In November 1987 the presidents of the two Yemens met for talks and in March 1988 a joint committee on foreign policy sat for the first time in Aden. A draft constitution for the two Yemens was published in December 1989, providing for a multiparty system of government, and in January 1990 the border between the two states was opened to allow free movement from both sides.

In May 1990 the new Republic of Yemen was established and the General People's Congress (GPC), of the north, led by Ali Abdullah Saleh, and the Yemen Socialist Party (YSP), of the south, led by Ali Salim al-Bid, formed an alliance. In the light of the history of disputes between the two formerly separate states, the unification process had been remarkably smooth, but Yemen's economy was fragile, particularly the south which had suffered from central planning, and its stability was severely threatened during the 1991 Gulf War, when its leaders opposed the US-led operations against Iraq. The first free elections in April 1993

resulted in the GPC winning most assembly seats, but not an overall majority. As a result, a three-party coalition government was established, with Saleh as president, al-Bid, vice president, and the former president of South Yemen, Haider Abu Bakr al-Attas, prime minister.

The general election was soon overshadowed by differences between the former north and south leaders, neither apparently willing to make concessions to the other. Soon after the elections al-Bid visited the United States, to consult with his opposite number, Al Gore, without discussing the matter with President Saleh. On his return al-Bid retired to his southern stronghold, refusing even to attend elections for the Presidential Council.

These incidents were symptomatic of a deeper-seated distrust which became so acute that by April 1994 civil war had broken out, with a new southern state, the Democratic Republic of Yemen (DRY), being proclaimed in May 1994. However, within two months the northern forces of President Saleh had inflicted a crushing defeat on those of the south. Saleh was magnanimous in victory and al-Bid fled into exile, where he headed a National Opposition Front.

In September 1994 Saleh introduced major constitutional changes, consolidating his own party's position, and in October formed a new two-party coalition with al-Islah. The cabinet was chaired by Prime Minister Abdel Aziz Abdel Ghani (GPC), with three other GPC members and one al-Islah member as his deputies. Having firmly secured his place, Saleh himself was re-elected president in October 1994, and the GPC won a majority in the April 1997 assembly elections.

North America

North America encompasses a vast region of over 19 million square kilometres/7.3 million square miles, more than five times the size of Northern and Western Europe, or almost 15% of the world's surface. Despite this areal size, its inhabitants constitute only about 5% of the world population in two nation-states, Canada and the United States of America.

Geographically and climatically, it is a region of great contrasts and extremes. Parts of northern Canada and Alaska are well within the Arctic Circle, while southern Florida is only a few degrees north of the Tropic of Cancer. The two countries share an enormous coastline, which includes the Arctic, Atlantic, and Pacific oceans, within which are the Bering Sea, the Beaufort Sea, Hudson Bay, and the Gulf of Mexico.

Although the overall population density of the region is low, there are areas of considerable concentration, for example, 25 United States cities have populations of 0.5 million or more, eight have in excess of 1 million, and New York contains more than 7 million people. Canada, with a much smaller population than its neighbor, does not display equivalent concentrations, but its two largest cities, Toronto and Vancouver, have populations of more than 3 million and 1.8 million respectively.

North America is a markedly 'high-income' region; in fact the two countries which occupy it enjoy, between them, 29% of the world's annually created wealth. It follows naturally from this that Canadian and United States citizens experience very high living standards compared with most other people in the world.

Although the region was originally peopled by Native Americans and Inuit, the majority of today's inhabitants trace their histories back to European beginnings. Both Canada and the United States were once British colonies, Canada remaining a dependency, in one form or another, for over 280 years, while some of the states on the US eastern seaboard experienced colonial rule for about 200 years before violently winning their independence. Britain, however, was not the only European power to place its imprint on the region. France, the Netherlands, and Spain also vied for control, usually to secure a commercial advantage. Reminders of this early European exploitation are found in the French-speaking parts of Canada, in the southern states of the United States, particularly Louisiana, and in the Spanish-speaking communities of states such as California and New Mexico.

This colonial experience has affected the political cultures and structures of the two countries, but in different ways. Canada has retained its allegiance to the British Crown and has adhered to parliamentary institutions, even to the extent of calling one chamber of its assembly the House of Commons. The United States, on the other hand, has less kind memories of the past and has resolutely sought to ensure that individual political and social liberties can never be usurped by an autocratic executive again. Both countries rank high in human rights ratings but these have been achieved through different political routes.

Both, however, have federal structures of government, a fact that reflects the size of each country and its ethnic and cultural diversity. Within these federal systems can be seen the strong sense of independence still felt by individual provinces and states, each jealous of its right to retain a unique identity within the overall national picture. Both countries can be proud of a long history of political stability. For example, neither has been troubled by a serious threat to its established democratic system for more than 100 years.

Relations between the two states generally have been civilized and correct, rather than warm. Canada has always been conscious of being close to 'big brother' and has been suspicious of moves to 'Americanize' the Canadian way of life, culturally as well as economically. Realistically, however, Canadian political leaders have recognized the existence of common needs and goals and have been happy to join the United States in mutually beneficial endeavours, such as the North Atlantic Treaty Organization (NATO). At the same time, they have recognized that, as a 'superpower', indeed, with the demise of the Soviet Union, the world's sole remaining superpower, the United States' interests are far wider than Canada's could ever be, or they would want them to be. In recent years this recognition of the need to share the region in a constructive way has resurfaced in the shape of the 1989 free trade agreement between Canada and the United States. In 1992 it was expanded to include Mexico, and given the title the North American Free Trade Agreement (NAFTA). Its aim is to progressively create, over a 10–15 year period, a common market of some 375 million people and give the two northern states opportunities to invest in Mexico's low-wage economy.

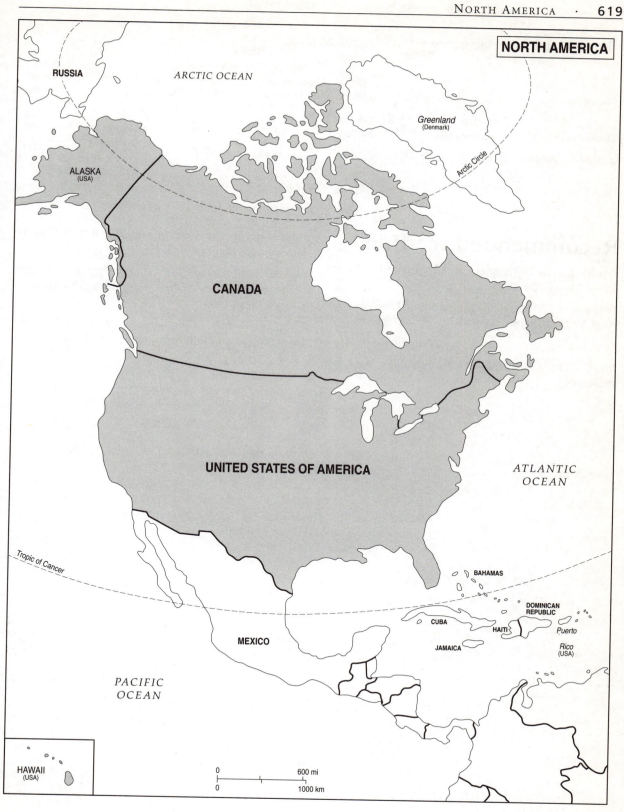

NORTH AMERICA

RUSSIA

ARCTIC OCEAN

Greenland
(Denmark)

ALASKA
(USA)

Arctic Circle

CANADA

UNITED STATES OF AMERICA

ATLANTIC
OCEAN

Tropic of Cancer

BAHAMAS

DOMINICAN
REPUBLIC

CUBA

HAITI

Puerto
Rico
(USA)

JAMAICA

MEXICO

PACIFIC
OCEAN

HAWAII
(USA)

0   600 mi
0   1000 km

North America: social, economic, and political data

Country	Area (sq km/sq miles)	c. 1995 Population (million)	c. 1995 Pop. density per sq km/sq mile	c. 1992 Adult literacy rate (%)	World ranking	Income type	c. 1991 Human rights rating (%)
Canada	9,970,610/3,849,672	29.248	3/8	96	52	high	94
United States	9,372,614/3,618,785	265.300	28/73	98	34	high	90
Total/average/range	*19,343,224/7,468,457*	*294.548*	*15/39*	*96–98*	–	–	*90–94*

F = Federal, SP = simple plurality, Lib-dem = liberal democratic, Lim-pres = limited presidential.

Recommended reading

Bowles, N *The Government and Politics of the United States*, Macmillan, 1993

Derbyshire, I *Politics in the United States: From Carter to Bush*, W & R Chambers, 1990

Esler, G *The United States of Anger*, Penguin Books, 1997

Jones, B D (ed.), *The New American Politics*, Westview Press, 1995

Landes, R G *The Canadian Polity: A Comparative Introduction*, Prentice Hall, 1995

McKenna, M C (ed.) *The American and Canadian Constitutions: A Comparative Perspective*, University of Calgary Press, 1993

Thomas, D (ed.) *Canada and the United States: Differences that Count*, Broadview Press, 1993

| | | | | | Number of | | Lower |
World ranking	Date of state formation	State structure	State type	Executive type	assembly chambers	Party structure	house electoral system
15	1867	F	Lib-dem	Parliamentary	2	multi	SP
21	1776	F	Lib-dem	Lim-pres	2	two	SP
–	–	–	–	–	–	–	–

Table 57

CANADA

Dominion of Canada

Capital: Ottawa

Social and economic data
Area: 9,970,010 sq km/3,849,672 sq miles
Population: 29,248,000·
Pop. density per sq km/sq mi: 3/8*
Urban population: 78%**
Literacy rate: 96%**
GDP: $574,000 million*; per-capita GDP: $19,600*
Government defense spending (% of GDP): 1.6%*
Currency: Canadian dollar
Economy type: high income

Labor force in agriculture: 5%*
Unemployment rate: 9.5%*
* 1995.
** 1992.

Head of state
Queen Elizabeth II, represented by Governor General Romeo A LeBlanc since 1995

Head of government
Prime Minister Jean Chrétien, since 1993

Ethnic composition
About 45% of the population is of British origin, 29% French, 23% of other European stock, and about 3% indigenous Indians or Eskimos/Inuits, who, known now as the 'first nations', have pressed recently for a measure of self-government. The official languages are English and French.

Religions
There are about 11.2 million Roman Catholics, 900,000 Anglicans, 316,000 members of the Greek Orthodox Church, and 150,000 members of the Ukrainian Greek Orthodox Church.

Political features
State type: liberal democratic
Date of state formation: 1867
Political structure: federal
Executive: parliamentary
Assembly: two-chamber
Party structure: multiparty
Human rights rating: 94%
International affiliations: AG (observer), APEC, CSCE, CW, ESA (cooperating), G-7, G-10, IAEA, IBRD, IMF, NACC, NAFTA, NAM (guest), NATO, OAS, OECD, UN, WTO

Local and regional government
Canada is a federation of ten provinces: Alberta, British

Columbia, Manitoba, New Brunswick, Newfoundland, Nova Scotia, Ontario, Prince Edward Island, Québec, and Saskatchewan; and three territories: the Yukon, Northwest Territories and Nunavut (formerly part of the Northwest Territories). The provinces range in territorial size from Prince Edward Island, with 5,660 sq km/2185 sq miles, to Québec, with 3,246,389 sq km/1,253,437 sq miles. Their populations vary from 122,506 for Prince Edward Island to 8,625,107 for Ontario. The size and populations of the territories are equally diverse. Yukon is the smaller, with 22,135 people within 531,844 sq km/205,346 sq miles, compared with Northwest Territories, with 45,471 people spread over an area of 3,246,389 sq km/1,253,437 sq miles.

Each province has a single-chamber assembly, popularly elected for a five-year term, and a premier who is appointed by the lieutenant governor on the basis of support in the provincial assembly. Each premier heads an executive council.

There is considerable decentralization from the federal government to the provincial governments, the respective powers being set out in the constitution, the former being essentially concerned with matters affecting the whole nation, and the latter purely provincial affairs.

Political system

The constitution is based on five Acts of the British Parliament, the Quebec Act, 1774, the Constitutional Act, 1791, the Act of Union, 1840, the British North America Act, 1867, and the Constitution Act, 1982. The British North America Act stated that the constitution should be similar in principle to that in Britain and the Canada Act gave Canada power to amend its constitution and added a Charter of Rights and Freedoms, to recognize the nation's multicultural background. Paradoxically, although Britain had always avoided adopting a written constitution for itself, it gave itself powers to prescribe for another sovereign state. The Canada Act therefore represented the formal ending of these powers and the guarantee of Canada's complete independence. Canada has, nevertheless, voluntarily retained the British monarch as a symbolic head of state and maintained its membership of the Commonwealth.

The federal parliament consists of two chambers, the Senate and the House of Commons. The 104 members of the Senate are appointed for life, or until the age of 75, by the governor general. They must be resident in the provinces they represent and, as persons of standing, are the equivalent of life peers in the British House of Lords.

The House of Commons has 301 members, elected by universal adult suffrage, through a simple plurality voting system. The federal prime minister is chosen by the governor general from the party which can command support in the House of Commons and, as in the British system, is accountable, with the cabinet, to the House of Commons. Parliament has a maximum life of five years but may be dissolved within that period. Again as in Britain, legislation must be passed by both chambers and then signed by the governor general.

Political parties

Of some 17 political parties, the most significant are the Liberal Party, the Bloc Québécois, and the Reform Party.

The Liberal Party of Canada developed in the late 19th century as the Canadian counterpart of the Liberal Party in Britain. It strongly supports the autonomy of Canada, the maintenance of universal welfare policies, and freedom of trade, particularly within the continent of North America.

The Bloc Québécois was formed in 1990 as a Francophone separatist party, committed to independence for the French-speaking province of Québec. It is led in Quebec by Lucien Bouchard, as provincial prime minister from January 1996.

The Reform Party is a populist rightwing grouping, based largely in the western provinces.

Political leaders since 1970

1968–79 Pierre Trudeau (Liberal), 1979–80 Joe Clark (Progressive Conservative), 1980–84 Pierre Trudeau (Liberal), 1984 John Turner (Liberal), 1984–93 Brian Mulroney (Progressive Conservative), 1993 Kim Campbell (Progressive Conservative), 1993– Jean Chrétien (Liberal)

Latest elections

The 2 June 1997 House of Commons general election results are shown below.

Canada latest election results

Party	% votes	Seats
Liberals	38.4	155
Reform Party	19.4	60
NDP	18.9	21
PCP	11.0	20
Bloc Québécois	10.7	44
Others	1.6	1

Political history

Canada was discovered in 1497 by John Cabot

(1425–1500), who thought he had found the route to China. In 1534 Jacques Cartier (1491–1557) landed and claimed the country for France and in 1583 Sir Humphrey Gilbert (1537–83) visited Newfoundland and claimed it for England. During the next two centuries both countries expanded their trading activities and colonization schemes, the rivalry inevitably leading to war. The former French colonists resented the British victory over France in 1759 and, in an effort to pacify them, in 1791 the country was divided into English-speaking Upper and French-speaking Lower Canada. The two parts were united in 1841 and in 1867 the self-governing dominion of Canada, within the British Empire, was founded.

From 1896 to 1911 the Liberal Party was in power under a French Canadian, Wilfred Laurier (1841–1919). His government fell because of dissatisfaction with his attempts to strengthen trade links with the United States and he was succeeded by Robert Borden (1854–1937), heading a Conservative administration. He successfully organized Canada for war in 1914 and was the first Dominion prime minister to attend an Imperial War Cabinet meeting. In 1921 the Liberals returned to office, under W L Mackenzie King (1874–1950), and they were to dominate Canadian politics for the next three decades, with Mackenzie King until 1948 and then with Louis St Laurent (1882–1973) until 1957.

The Progressive Conservatives returned to power in 1957, after 36 years in the wilderness. The Liberals, under Lester Pearson (1897–1972), returned to office in 1963 and Pearson remained prime minister until he was succeeded by former law professor, Pierre Trudeau (b. 1919), in 1968. Trudeau maintained Canada's defensive alliance with the United States but sought to widen its influence on the world stage. At home he was faced with the problem of dealing with the separatist movement in Québec and set about creating what he called the 'just society'. Although a French Canadian himself, Trudeau was totally opposed to the idea of separatism for any part of the country. His success in achieving his objectives may be judged by his ability to win two elections in a row, in 1972 and 1974.

Then, in 1979, with no party having an overall majority in the Commons, the Progressive Conservatives, led by Joe Clark (b. 1939), formed a government. Later that year Trudeau announced his retirement from politics but when, in 1980, Clark was defeated on his government's budget proposals, Trudeau reconsidered his decision and, with the disso-

lution of parliament, won the general election with a large majority. Trudeau's third administration was concerned with the question of 'patriation', or the extent to which the Parliament in Westminster had power to determine the constitution of Canada. Eventually the position was resolved with the passing of the Canada Act of 1982, which was the last piece of legislation of the United Kingdom Parliament to have force in Canada.

In 1983 Clark was replaced as leader of the Progressive Conservatives by Brian Mulroney (b. 1939), a business executive with no previous political experience, and in 1984 Trudeau retired to be replaced as Liberal leader and prime minister by John Turner (b. 1929), a former minister of finance. Within nine days of taking office, Turner called a general election and the Progressive Conservatives, under Mulroney, won the largest majority in Canadian history. Soon after forming his administration, Mulroney began an international realignment, placing less emphasis on links Trudeau had established with Asia, Africa, and Latin America, and more on cooperation with Europe and a closer 'special relationship' with the United States. One aspect of this closer cooperation was discussion about the possibility of greater freedom of trade between the two countries, culminating in a free-trade agreement which was signed in 1988.

The relationship between the federal government and the provinces was still a live political issue. In April 1987 Prime Minister Mulroney reached agreement with the ten provincial premiers in the Meech Lake Accord. This was intended to give all the provinces considerable powers in appointments to the Senate and Supreme Court, a veto over many possible constitutional amendments, and financial compensation to any province which opted out of any new national shared-cost program in favor of its own program. The Accord was strongly criticized by former prime minister Trudeau as likely to destroy the equilibrium between Ottawa and the provinces which he had created and which Mulroney had inherited. The 1988 general election was fought mainly on the issue of the free-trade agreement negotiated with the United States, the Conservatives winning with a clear, but reduced, majority.

In August 1992 a constitutional reform package, replacing the Meech Lake Accord, and called the Pearson Agreement, was put together. This gave greater autonomy to the provinces, and a particular recognition to Québec, but, when put before the electorate in a referendum in October 1992, it was rejected. By this time Prime Minister Mulroney's popular standing had sunk to an unprecedented low and in February 1993 he resigned. In June he was succeeded by Canada's first woman prime minister, Kim Campbell (b. 1947).

In the general election, four months later, the PCP suffered a resounding defeat, its seat-holding in the House of Commons falling from 157 to two, and the separatist Bloc Québécois became the official opposition party. The Liberals increased their seat tally by nearly 100 and their leader, Jean Chrétien (b. 1934), became prime minister. Within two months Kim Campbell had resigned the PCP leadership and four months later another leading female politician, Audrey McLaughlin (b. 1936), gave up the NDP leadership. In Québec, where the Parti Québécois was in power under the leadership of Jacques Parizeau, a referendum on separation was held in October 1995. The separatists, drawing strong support from the province's French-speaking majority, attracted 49.4% of the vote, just short of a majority, with a 94% turnout. Another referendum is expected at a later date.

The Chrétien government pursued a policy of fiscal retrenchment and privatization which, helped by export-led economic growth, substantially reduced the budget deficit. This provided the platform for its re-election in June 1997, albeit with a reduced majority. Support for the Liberals was strongest in Ontario, including Toronto, while the Reform Party polled strongly in the western provinces. In Quebec, the Bloc Québécois captured 39% of the vote and was strongly challenged by the PCP, whose leader was Jean Charest. Charest advocated enhanced autonomy within Canada, and in April 1998 changed parties to become leader of the Liberal Party in Quebec.

By January 1999 the rate of unemployment had fallen to 7.8%, its lowest level since 1980, and the rate of inflation to 0.6%, the lowest rate since 1962.

UNITED STATES OF AMERICA (USA)

Capital: Washington DC

Social and economic data
Area: 9,372,614 sq km/3,618,785 sq miles
Population: 265,300,000[*]
Pop. density per sq km/sq mi: 28/73[*]
Urban population: 76%[**]

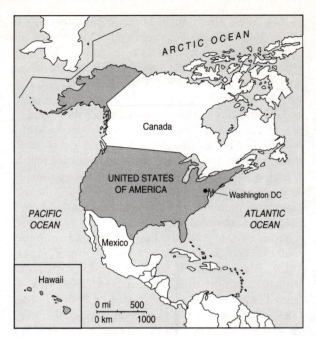

Literacy rate: 98%[**]
GDP: $7,100,00 million[*]; per-capita GDP: $26,800[*]
Government defense spending (% of GDP): 3.8%[*]
Currency: US dollar
Economy type: high income
Labor force in agriculture: 3%[**]
Unemployment rate: 5.6%[*]
[*] 1995.
[**] 1992.

Head of state and of government
President William (Bill) J Clinton, since 1993

Ethnic composition
Approximately three-quarters of the population are of European origin, including 29% who trace their descent from British and Irish stock, 8% from German, 5% from Italian, and 3% each from Scandinavian and Polish. Twelve per cent are black, or African-Americans, 8% Hispanic, and 3% Asian and Pacific Islander. Blacks form 30% of the population of the states of the 'Deep South', namely Alabama, Georgia, Louisiana, Mississippi, and South Carolina. Asians are most thickly concentrated in California. Although the main language is English, there are significant Spanish-speaking minorities, especially in southern California, Texas, Arizona, and New Mexico, where Hispanics form 37% of the population.

Religions
More than 30% of the population, or 79 million, are

Protestants, chiefly belonging to the Baptist (31 million), Methodist (12 million), Lutheran (8 million), Presbyterian (4.2 million), Anglican (2.4 million), Assemblies of God (2.2 million), United Church of Christ (1.7 million), Disciples of Christ (1.0 million), and Seventh Day Adventist (0.8 million) churches. Twenty-two per cent, or 59 million, are Roman Catholics, 2% (5.9 million) Jewish, 2% (4.2 million) Eastern, including Greek, Orthodox, 2% (4.3 million) Mormons, and 2% (4 million) Muslims, of whom 1.3 million are African-American 'Black Muslims'. The rest of the population professes no religion or belongs to small, distinctive sects or creeds. Church and state are strictly separated.

Political features

State type: liberal democracy
Date of state formation: 1776
Political structure: federal
Executive: limited presidential
Assembly: two-chamber
Party structure: two-party
Human rights rating: 90%
International affiliations: AfDB, AG (observer), ANZUS, APEC, AsDB, BIS, CP, EBRD, ECE, ECLAC, ESCAP, G-5, G-7, G-10, IAEA, IBRD, ICC, ICFTU, IDB, IEA, IMF, IWC, LORCS, NACC, NAFTA, NATO, NEA, OAS, OECD, OSCE, PC, UN Security Council (permanent member), WTO

Local and regional government

Below the state level there are 2,994 counties, over 18,000 municipalities, and almost 17,000 townships, with wards and precincts below them. Office holders are elected to fill political and administrative and judicial posts at all these levels.

Political system

The United States is a federal republic comprising 50 states and the District of Columbia. Under its 1787 constitution, which became effective in March 1789 and has since been subject to 27 amendments, the constituent states are reserved considerable powers of self-government. The federal, or central, government concentrated originally on defense, foreign affairs, and the coordination of 'interstate' concerns, leaving legislation in other spheres to the states, each with its own constitution, elected assembly (bicameral in all states except Nebraska), governor, Supreme Court, and local taxation powers. Since Roosevelt's 1930s 'New Deal', however, the federal government has increasingly impinged upon state affairs and become the principal revenue raising and spending agency.

The US federal government is characterized by a deliberate separation of the executive from the legislative and judicial functions. At the head of the executive branch of government is a president, elected every four years, on a fixed date in November, in a national contest by universal adult suffrage. Votes are counted at the state level on a first-past-the-post, winner-takes-all basis, with each state being assigned a slate of seats, equivalent to the sum of its congressional representatives, in a national 538-member Electoral College. This College later, in mid-December, formally elects the president. The victor is thus the candidate who secures the highest number of Electoral College votes, not necessarily the highest number of popular votes across the country. Once elected, the president, who must be at least 35 years of age, and born in the United States, serves as head of state, commander in chief of the armed forces, and head of the civil service. He or she is restricted, under the provisions of Amendment 22, which was adopted in 1951, to a maximum of two terms and, once elected, cannot be removed except through impeachment by Congress. Following Amendment 20, the presidential term begins on 20 January after elections in the previous November. (Congress convenes on 3 January.)

The president works with a personally selected cabinet team, subject to the Senate's approval, whose members are debarred from serving in the legislature. For this reason, the cabinet is composed of specialists who concentrate on the work of their own departments and who are frequently drawn from business or academic, rather than party political, backgrounds. To coordinate policy-making and draw up strategic plans, the president is served by an ever-growing White House Office of personal political aides and trouble-shooting assistants. This team is headed by a chief of staff, and includes the National Security Council (NSC), the Domestic Council, the Office of Management and Budget (OMB), and the Council of Economic Advisers (CEA) as functionalist support units.

The second branch of government, Congress, the federal legislature, consists of two equally powerful chambers, the 100-member Senate and the 435-member House of Representatives. Senators, who must be at least 30 years of age, serve fixed six-year terms, two being elected from each state in a state-wide race, regardless of size or population. A third are elected at a time, biennially, with no restrictions being placed on re-election.

Representatives, who must be at least 25 years of age, are elected from single-member constituencies of roughly equal demographic size, of 450,000 to 700,000, to serve for fixed two-year terms, again with no restrictions on re-election. By custom, representatives are expected to live in the districts for which they are elected.

Congress has sole powers of legislation and operates through a system of specialized standing, select, and investigative committees, which are composed of members drawn from parties in accordance with their relative strength in each chamber. They have the authority to call an array of witnesses from the executive branch and outside. These powerful committees, whose work is televised on C-SPAN, independent cable TV station, are chaired by senior members of the party controlling the chamber and are liberally staffed by advisory assistants.

The Senate is the more powerful chamber of Congress, its approval being required for key federal appointments and for the ratification of foreign treaties. In addition, it is the Senate which hears cases of impeachment brought against federal officials, following a vote in favor of proceeding by the House of Representatives. A two-thirds majority in support of a guilty verdict is needed for impeachment to succeed. Before President Clinton in 1998 only one president, Andrew Johnson in 1868, had undergone the full impeachment process, and he survived by one vote.

The House of Representatives is of greatest importance in the fiscal sphere, all spending bills being required, under the terms of Section 7 of Article 1 of the constitution, to originate in this chamber. This makes the House's budget and finance committees particularly important.

The president needs to work with Congress to persuade it to adopt his or her policy program, addressing it in January for an annual 'State of the Union' speech and sending periodic 'messages' and 'recommendations'. The president's success depends on the office holder's level of party support in Congress, bargaining skills, and current public standing. To become law, legislation, which is initially proposed by individual senators and representatives and worked upon in committee, requires the approval of both chambers of Congress. If differences arise, a special 'Joint Congressional Committee', composed of senior members drawn from both chambers, is convened to produce a compromise agreement. The president retains, however, the option of imposing vetoes, which can only be overridden by two-thirds majorities in both congressional houses.

Constitutional amendments require two-thirds majorities from both chambers of Congress and subsequent ratification by at least three-quarters, or 38, of the nation's 50 state legislatures, within a seven-year time span. Alternatively, it is possible for a constitutional amendment to be initiated by two-thirds of state legislatures, calling for the convening of a special National Constitutional Convention. Measures adopted at this convention then require the subsequent approval by constitutional conventions in 38 states to become law.

The third branch of government, the judiciary, headed by the Supreme Court, interprets the written US Constitution to ensure that a correct balance is maintained between federal and state institutions, and the executive and legislature, and that the civil rights enshrined in Amendments 1–10, 'The Bill of Rights', adopted in 1791, are upheld.

The Supreme Court consists of nine judges appointed by the president, subject to the Senate's approval, who serve life terms and are removable only through impeachment. Headed since 1986 by Chief Justice William H Rehnquist (b. 1924), and with a conservative majority, it is an unusually influential and potentially 'activist' body, enjoying the power to effectively veto legislation and overturn executive actions which it rules to be unconstitutional. For example, in June 1998 the Supreme Court ruled that the new power of 'line-item veto' extended to the president by Congress in 1996 was unconstitutional. The power, which was used by President Clinton in 1997, enabled the president to strike out particular parts of legislation, rather than the whole bill. The Supreme Court viewed it as an excessive delegation of the legislative role to the executive.

The United States is, in addition, responsible for the administration of a number of Pacific Island territories, including American Samoa and the US Virgin Islands, which are governed by local legislatures and a governor. They are described more fully in Chapter 8. Each of these territories, as well as the 'self-governing territories' of Puerto Rico and Guam, sends a nonvoting delegate to the US House of Representatives.

Political parties

Two broad 'catch-all' party coalitions, divided regionally and ideologically, dominate American politics: the Democrats and the Republicans. The first-past-the-post electoral system, the presidential nature of American politics, and the ability of the existing parties to embrace broad ranges of opinion have been key factors in fostering this party polarization and working against the emergence of additional third or fourth parties. The two parties are surprisingly evenly matched: each captured 49% of the vote in the 1996 congressional elections, and in 1998, control of the executive and legislative branches was split between the two parties in 31 state contests.

The Democratic Party (D) was originally founded in 1792 by Thomas Jefferson, one of the drafters of the Declaration of Independence of 1776, to defend the rights of individual states against the centralizing moves of the Federalists. First, under the designation Democratic Republicans, and then, from 1828, Democratic Party, it held power almost continuously between 1800 and 1860. During the Civil War, 1861–65, it became identified with the defeated rural Confederate States of the South, a region which became a stronghold for the party, electing senators and representatives of a conservative and illiberal hue.

In the northeastern seaboard states, a substantially different Democratic Party emerged during the years between 1865 and 1920 in terms of ideological outlook. It sought out and won over the majority of the new immigrant minority communities, the Irish, Poles, Italians, Catholics, and Jews, who flooded into the industrializing coastal cities during this period.

During the 1930s Great Depression, this new urban power base was strengthened when, under the leadership of Franklin D Roosevelt, the party pressed ahead with a 'New Deal' program of social reform and state interventionism. This attracted to the Democrats a broad coalition of support, establishing the party, which had been overshadowed by the Republicans between 1861 and 1932, as the new majority party at both the local and congressional level. This is shown in Table 58.

Between 1933 and 1968 the Democratic Party secured the presidency for its candidate during 28 of the 36 years and control of both chambers of Congress during all but four of these years. The party's northeastern wing, founded on a network of strong, worker-orientated, urban, organizational 'machines', was dominant during these years, espousing a philosophy of liberalism which favored an extended role for the federal government. During the 1960s, however, as this northeastern wing pressed for civil rights reform, desegregation, equal opportunity, and voting rights for the black community, the party's southern conservative 'Dixiecrat', or 'Boll Weevil', wing became increasingly alienated.

In presidential elections, southern electors began to vote regularly for Republican nominees, and, within Congress, 'historical', or 'yellow-dog', Democrat Dixiecrats voted against the Democratic presidents Kennedy and Johnson on social issues. Intra-party divisions widened during the later 1960s, as northern liberal opposition to the Vietnam War mounted, setting in

Party control of the presidency and Congress since 1859 — Table 58

The presidency		Senate		House of Representatives	
Republican	1861–1865	Democrats	1859–1860	Republicans	1859–1874
Democrat	1865–1868	Republicans	1861–1878	Democrats	1875–1880
Republican	1869–1884	Democrats	1879–1880	Republicans	1881–1882
Democrat	1885–1888	Republicans	1881–1892	Democrats	1883–1888
Republican	1889–1892	Democrats	1893–1894	Republicans	1889–1890
Democrat	1893–1896	Republicans	1895–1912	Democrats	1891–1894
Republican	1897–1912	Democrats	1913–1918	Republicans	1895–1910
Democrat	1913–1920	Republicans	1919–1932	Democrats	1911–1916
Republican	1921–1932	Democrats	1933–1946	Republicans	1917–1932
Democrat	1933–1952	Republicans	1947–1948	Democrats	1933–1946
Republican	1953–1960	Democrats	1949–1952	Republicans	1947–1948
Democrat	1961–1968	Republicans	1953–1954	Democrats	1949–1952
Republican	1969–1976	Democrats	1955–1980	Republicans	1953–1954
Democrat	1977–1980	Republicans	1981–1986	Democrats	1955–1994
Republican	1981–1992	Democrats	1986–1994	Republicans	1995–
Democrat	1993–	Republicans	1995–		

train a drive to democratize the party's organizational structure and candidate selection procedures, with the use of primary contests open to all voters identifying themselves as party supporters. Election procedures replaced the caucus, or closed-door party meeting, and state convention, or open-door party meeting, systems.

The Democratic Party today is composed of at least five significant wings or tendencies. The first is a still sizeable, though now reduced, southern conservative, or neo-liberal, faction, sometimes referred to as the party's 'congressional wing'. The second is a larger, traditionally dominant grouping of northern 'New Deal' liberals, known as the 'presidential wing'. The third group consists of the radical prairie-populist liberals of the midwestern agricultural-industrial states, most notably Minnesota. The fourth, smaller, faction consists of the Trumanite 'Defense Democrats'. The fifth party faction, which is strongest outside Congress at the city government level, is the ultra-liberal 'Rainbow Coalition' movement.

The southern 'congressional wing', comprising around a dozen senators and 40 representatives, is organized in the Conservative Democratic Forum (CDF). This forms a 'swing' grouping within Congress, sometimes aligning with Republican congressmen in votes on economic, social, and defense issues. Southern conservatives and moderate liberals also work together in the influential Democratic Leadership Council (DLC). Founded in 1985, and incorporating state governors, the fiscally conservative but socially liberal DLC is the section of the party most closely associated with President Bill Clinton and Vice President Al Gore.

The northern 'presidential wing' is interventionist in both the economic and social spheres, and moderate on defense. It adheres to many of the tenets of the Americans for Democratic Action (ADA) organization, which was established in 1947. Its leading representatives include Massachusetts senator Edward Kennedy (b. 1932), and New York State governor until 1994, Mario Cuomo.

The roots of the midwestern populists can be traced back to the People's Party, founded during the 1890s, and the Progressive Party, which operated during the interwar years to represent the interests of small farmers against those of big business.

The Trumanite 'Defense Democrats' have been represented since the 1970s by New York senator Daniel Patrick Moynihan. While liberal in the economic and social sphere, they have favored a firm, traditionally anti-communist, foreign policy.

The 'Rainbow Coalition' is a movement embracing black, Hispanic, feminist, student, homosexual, and anti-nuclear minority groupings, and has been led by the charismatic African-American civil rights leader, the Reverend Jesse Jackson (b. 1941).

All of these minority communities support the Democratic Party by overwhelming margins in elections. Catholics, Jews, unionized workers, and families on lower incomes constitute other important broadband Democrats support blocks.

The Republican Party (R), also popularly known as the Grand Old Party (GOP), was formed in Michigan in 1854 by a coalition opposed to slavery. It secured the election of its candidate, Abraham Lincoln, to the presidency in 1860, and became identified with the wealthy and industrializing victorious North during the Civil War. The party also won the support of people in the rural and small-town areas of the midwest. These included the long-settled Protestant majority community and the new frontier states of the Pacific coast. All this support was put together in an electoral coalition which dominated at the federal level until the early 1930s.

The Republicans were outflanked by Roosevelt during the 1930s and 1940s; then, under the leadership of Dwight D Eisenhower during the 1950s, came to accept the popular social and economic reforms of the 'New Deal' era and its aftermath, and, in the process, extended their support base. In ideological outlook, however, the Republicans continued to be positioned to the right of the Democrats in both the economic and social spheres. In terms of voter identification, they also lagged behind their center-left rivals, registering a national identification level of 35% compared to 45% for the Democrats.

During recent decades, the Republicans have dominated at the presidential level, having won five of the eight electoral contests held since November 1964. They enjoy a firm regional support base in the center and west of the country and poll strongly among the white Protestant community and those having higher incomes. The party has made significant inroads into the traditionally Democrat-dominated South. It has attracted many elected Democratic defectors since the start of the Clinton presidency, including five representatives and senators and more than 100 state and local-level politicians since the November 1992 presidential election. After the November 1994 midterm congressional elections, the GOP held a majority of the South's

House and Senate seats for the first time since the Civil War.

Ideologically, until the election of Richard Nixon as president in 1968, the GOP was dominated by a big business-orientated, and relatively liberal, northeastern 'Wall Street' wing, one of whose most prominent members was the influential former New York state governor, and vice president, Nelson A Rockefeller (1908–79). This northern liberal grouping has, however, contracted significantly since the 1970s. It is now reduced to a minority rump, although Rudolph Giuliani (b. 1944), the mayor of New York since 1994, and a former Democrat, is a populist heir to this tradition.

Instead, the Republicans have become dominated by a western and midwestern small-town majority grouping, described as the 'Main Street' wing, and epitomized by the figures of Barry Goldwater (1909–98), who fought for the presidency unsuccessfully in 1964, Ronald Reagan, Kansas senator Bob Dole, Texas senator Phil Gramm (the last two of whom contested the party's presidential nomination in 1996), and Newt Gingrich, House speaker from 1995 until the 1998 election. This wing adheres to a conservative and individualist 'small government' philosophy of reduced taxation, a balanced budget, and a Christian moral code. The Conservative Caucus, which is an organization established in 1974 by Howard Phillips, and the Heritage Foundation, established by Paul Weyrich, have served as lobbyists and think-tanks for this faction, which includes Empower America, an organization formed by Jack Kemp (b. 1935), a former senator from New York, and Steve Forbes Jr, a billionaire publisher.

To the right of the new party mainstream stands an increasingly vocal Christian fundamentalist activist grouping, led by the Reverend Pat Robertson (b. 1930), who had established the Christian Broadcasting Network in 1960 and later formed the Freedom Council as a political pressure group, before challenging George Bush for the party's presidential nomination in 1988. By 1995 the Christian Coalition, directed by Ralph Reed (b. 1961), claimed 1.6 million members and dominated 18 state Republican parties and partly controlled 13 more.

Also standing on the far right of the GOP is Patrick Buchanan (b. 1938), a conservative columnist who served in the Reagan administration and contested for the party's presidential nomination in 1996, advocating extreme social conservatism and populist economic nationalism.

Each of the major parties has only a rudimentary national organization, with no official membership, and, although party politicians in Congress group together for committee assignment purposes, they seldom vote en bloc.

A four-day National Convention is convened every four years for each of the two parties, during the summer immediately preceding a presidential contest, to elect a presidential candidate and adopt a party 'platform', which is a nonbinding manifesto. Delegates to these large, 2,200–4,200-member, bodies are elected through state-level primaries, caucuses, or conventions, and are pledged to vote for particular candidates.

Between Conventions, party business is carried on by a National Committee, elected by state parties. The Committee's primary functions are to set the rules for the presidential primaries and National Conventions and coordinate fund-raising activities. The Republican National Committee is the better organized, having made considerable progress in the use of modern direct-mail fund-raising techniques since the early 1970s and thus established itself as an important source of finance for Senate, as well as presidential, campaigns.

Despite this progress, party organization remains concentrated at the state level. Here the true, localized 'party systems' of American politics are to be found. In comparison with Western European political parties, however, state parties are informally organized, the choice of party candidates being unusually open because of the primary system of selection and because aspirants for office are heavily reliant on generating their own funding resources. They do this by drawing on donations from interest groups via Political Action Committees (PACs), to contest expensive, media-dominated elections. This pattern has fed through to Congress, where the legislative process is unusually atomized and individualistic.

Numerous minor parties also operate in the United States. The ultra-individualist and free-market Libertarian Party, which was established in 1971, has secured less than 1% of the vote in presidential contests. It did, however, win a seat in the Alaska state legislature in 1978. Of greater importance have been the independent presidential challenges by breakaway members from the major parties. For example, George Wallace, a renegade southern Democrat, secured 13% of the national vote and 46 Electoral College seats in November 1968, and John Anderson, a liberal-Republican, 7% of the popular vote, though no Electoral College seats, in November 1984. Then on November 1992, the maverick populist billionaire businessman, H Ross Perot, captured 19% of the national vote. This was the best third-candidate performance since 1912. He formally formed the Reform Party in 1995 to contest the presidential election, but won only 8% of the vote. The 1998 Reform Party candidate Jesse Ventura was elected governor of Minnestota.

Political leaders since 1970·

1969–74 Richard M Nixon (R), 1974–77 Gerald R Ford (R), 1977–81 Jimmy E Carter (D), 1981–89 Ronald W Reagan (R), 1989–93 George H W Bush (R), 1993–William J Clinton (D)

Latest elections

In the most recent presidential elections, held on 5 November 1996, President Bill Clinton secured a clear victory over his Republican challenger, Bob Dole, to become the first elected Democratic incumbent to secure re-election since FD Roosevelt did so in 1944. Clinton captured 49% of the popular vote and 379 Electoral College seats to Dole's 41% and 159 seats. Clinton raised his share of the national vote by six points over 1992 and won in 31 of the 50 states, situated principally in the west, northeast, and east-center. His vote tally, at 47.4 million, was a Democrat record and he attracted particular support from women (55% of whom voted for Clinton), voters under the age of 30, blacks (84%), and Hispanics (72%), who turned out in record numbers in opposition to recent Republican-sponsored measures that cut benefits for legal immigrants. The Kansas-born Dole polled most strongly in the thinly populated farming states of the center and in the south (excluding Florida, Louisiana, Arkansas, and Tennessee). Ross Perot, the maverick 'third party' populist candidate, attracted 8% of the vote (down 11% on 1992). Other candidates, who included Ralph Nader, a consumer-advocate who ran as the Green Party candidate, attracted under 2% of the vote. Turnout, at 49%, was its lowest since 1924, reflecting widespread apathy. A record $2 billion was spent on the 1996 presidential and concurrent congressional elections.

As usual, the presidential election contest in November 1996 was preceded by a prolonged 'primary campaign' among an assortment of candidates seeking main party nomination by securing a majority of delegate votes at the August 1996 National Conventions. Unusually, President Clinton secured his party's nomination without challenge, enabling him to conserve campaign funds for television 'attack ads' directed against his eventual Republican opponent. The Republican contest was characterized by an unwilling-ness of substantial figures from Washington or the state leadership to enter the race. In particular, Pete Wilson, governor of the large western state of California, after initially hinting that he might run, declared his non-participation in October 1995. This left only one significant contender: Bob Dole, the 73-year-old Senate majority leader (until May 1996), who had previously launched two unsuccessful bids for the party's nomination and, in 1976, had been the vice presidential running-mate of the defeated president, Gerald Ford. Despite his acerbic campaigning style and the lack of a clear political vision, Dole used his party connections and financial backing to 'lock up' the party nomination by mid-March 1996. He was helped in this by a front-loading of primaries, with a 'Super Tuesday' of primaries, mainly in the southern states, in early March. His most serious intra-party challengers had been Pat Buchanan, a rightwing 'America-first' populist-nationalist who advocated protectionism and surprisingly won the opening New Hampshire primary in February 1998; Steve Forbes, a billionaire publishing tycoon who spent more than $15 million of his own funds promoting the idea of a 17% 'flat tax' and won an early primary in Arizona; and Lamar Alexander, a moderate former governor of Tennessee.

The most recent congressional and state elections were held on 3 November 1998. In the House of Representatives, where elections were held in all 435 constituencies, the Republicans won 223 seats (down five on November 1996), the Democrats 211 (up five) and an independent Socialist, Bernie Sanders, held on (for a fifth successive term) to one seat in Vermont. In the Senate, where elections were held for 34 seats, the position remained unchanged after this election, with the Republicans holding 55 seats to the Democrats' 45. The Democrats' performance in the House elections was the strongest of any party of a sitting president during a mid-term election year since 1934. However, turnout, at 36%, was the lowest since 1942, although turnout among black and Hispanic voters improved compared to the mid-term elections of 1994. The Democrats and Republicans spent over $162 million in 'soft' money (money raised from donations and spent on the party's general campaign, rather than to support a specific candidate) during these elections: double the amount spent for the November 1994 elections.

There were concurrent governorship (gubernatorial) elections at the state level, in 36 of the 50 states. The Democrats achieved an important victory in the populous state of California, winning its governorship for the first time in 16 years, and made a recovery in the South by winning in Alabama and South Carolina. For the Republicans, the most important victories were by the two sons of former president George HW Bush: by George W Bush, who secured re-election in Texas with a massive 69% of the vote to emerge as the frontrunner for the party's presidential nomination for November 2000; and Jeb Bush, who won (at his second attempt) in Florida. After these elections the Republicans held 31 state governorships (down one on the position before the elections), the Democrats 17 (unchanged), an independent (Angus King in Maine), one, while the Reform Party held its first governorship, after Jesse Ventura, a former wrestler, unexpectedly won in Minnesota. State elections were also accompanied by voting on an unprecedented number (235) of voter propositions (referenda). These included approval by voters in Washington state (following the earlier example set by California's voters in November 1996) of an 'Initiative 200' to end 'affirmative action' racial quotas in state contracting and employment. Voters in Alaska, Arizona, and Washington state also approved controversial propositions to approve the medical use of marijuana.

Political history

1. Early settlings to Vietnam War

The land area covered by the contemporary United States of America (USA) was first settled by the American Indians, groups who migrated from Asia across the Bering land bridge over 25,000 years ago. Today, a million of their descendants survive, more than half living on reservations. European exploration of the continent commenced with the Norse in the 9th century. Later, during the 16th century, Florida and Mexico were colonized by the Spanish, and, during the 17th century, portions of the east coast, in New England and Pennsylvania, were occupied by the British, the Great Lakes and Louisiana by the French, New Jersey by the Dutch, and Delaware by the Swedes. The Swedish and Dutch settlements were subsequently acquired by the British, who controlled the territory between New England and the Carolinas. Following the Anglo-French Seven Years' War, between 1756 and 1763, Canada, Florida, and East Louisiana were also brought under British sovereignty by the terms of the Treaty of Paris of 1763.

In 1775 the 13 English-speaking colonies of Connecticut, Delaware, Georgia, Maryland, Massachusetts, New Hampshire, New Jersey, New York, North Carolina, Pennsylvania, Rhode Island, South Carolina, and Virginia revolted against British colonial tax impositions, proclaiming their independence in July 1776. A provisional constitution, the Articles of Confederation, was adopted in 1777. Led by George Washington (1732–99) and with French aid, the confederated states succeeded in defeating the armies of George III in the War of American Independence, 1775–83.

A new constitution was drawn up for the independent federal republic in 1787, at the Philadelphia Convention, and came into force in 1789. A 'Bill of Rights' was added in 1791. This constitution provided for a directly elected House of Representatives, but, until the ratification of the 17th Amendment in 1913, only an indirectly elected Senate, whose members were chosen by state legislators. The president was selected by an Electoral College, with Washington, of the Federalist Party, being the first to occupy the position.

Initially, the United States extended west only to the Mississippi River and north to the Great Lakes. Louisiana, which was purchased from France, was added in 1803 and Florida, which was acquired from Spain, in 1819. Further former Spanish posses, including California and Texas, joined the Union between 1821 and 1853, following a war with Mexico between 1846 and 1848.

In 1861 the American Civil War broke out between the cotton-growing southern Confederate states of Alabama, Arkansas, Florida, Georgia, Louisiana, Mississippi, North Carolina, South Carolina, Tennessee, Texas, and Virginia and the more industrialized and urbanized northeastern Federal states, over the issue of 'states' rights' and the maintenance of slavery in the South. More than 600,000 died in the conflict, the North triumphing after the surrender of General Robert E Lee (1807–70) to General Ulysses S Grant (1822–85) at Appomattox on 9 April 1865.

Northern troops subsequently occupied the South, between 1865 and 1877, during a 'Reconstruction Period', and constitutional Amendments 13–15, which abolished slavery and guaranteed blacks civil rights, were adopted. Five days after the South's surrender, however, the North's Republican president, Abraham Lincoln (1809–65), who had been re-elected for a second term in November 1864, was assassinated by John Wilkes Booth (1838–65).

During the half century following the Civil War, the northeastern seaboard states underwent rapid industrialization, more than 30 million immigrants, predominantly European, being attracted to their cities. With the spread of railways, the agricultural frontier extended westwards towards the Rockies and the Pacific, while the new territories of Alaska, which was purchased from Russia in 1867, and Hawaii, which was acquired in 1898, were added. Externally, the United States adhered to an isolationist policy, not entering World War I until 1917.

After the war, the franchise was extended to women in 1920 by Amendment 19, and economic growth continued until the Wall Street stock market crash of October 1929. Thereafter, the country was plunged into a severe industrial and agricultural depression, bringing mass unemployment. Franklin D Roosevelt (1882–1945), the Democratic former governor of New York, who was elected president in November 1932, responded to this crisis by abandoning the *laissez-faire* policies of his Republican predecessor, Herbert C Hoover (1874–1964), and launching, under the slogan 'New Deal', a radical program of state intervention. 'Soft loans' (including very low interest rates) were provided to agriculturists and local authorities, employment-generating public works projects were launched, farm prices raised, and old-age and unemployment insurance schemes introduced. These measures helped to alleviate the depression, although it was not until World War II that full employment was re-established.

Politically, this 'New Deal' program drew to the Democratic Party new blocs of support, establishing it as the new, dominant, national party. Because of this, Roosevelt was re-elected president in 1936, 1940, and 1944, thus becoming the country's longest-serving leader.

The United States, after initially adhering to its isolationist stance, entered World War II in December 1941, following Japan's attack on Pearl Harbor in Hawaii. Its navy subsequently defeated the Japanese fleet at the Battle of Midway in June 1942, and its army divisions helped turn the tide against Germany in Europe between 1943 and 1945. However, it was not until August 1945 and the dropping of atom bombs on Hiroshima and Nagasaki that Japan formally ceased hostilities and surrendered.

Having established itself as a global 'superpower', through its decisive actions between 1941 and 1945, the United States remained internationalist during the postwar era. Under the presidency of the Democrat, Harry S Truman (1884–1972), who served between 1945 and 1952, a 'doctrine' of intervention in support of endangered 'free peoples', and of containing the spread of communism, was devised by Secretary of State (foreign

minister) Dean Acheson (1893–1971). This led to America's safeguarding of Nationalist Taiwan in 1949 and its participation, under United Nations', auspices, in the Korean War of 1950–53.

The United States, in addition, took the lead in creating new global and regional organizations designed to maintain peace: the United Nations (UN) in 1945, the Organization of American States (OAS) in 1948, the North Atlantic Treaty Organization (NATO) in 1949, and the South East Asia Treaty Organization (SEATO) in 1954. It also launched the Marshall Plan, between 1947 and 1952, to strengthen the economies of its European allies.

Domestically, President Truman sought to introduce liberal reforms, with the aim of extending civil and welfare rights, under the slogan a 'Fair Deal'. These measures were blocked, however, by a combination of southern Democrats and Republicans, in Congress.

Truman's foreign policy was criticized as being 'soft on communism' between 1950 and 1952, as a wave of anti-Soviet hysteria, spearheaded by the work of Senator Joseph McCarthy (1908–57), swept the nation. This rightward shift in the public mood provided the basis for Republican victories in the congressional and presidential elections of November 1952. The popular military commander, General Dwight ('Ike') Eisenhower (1890–1969), became president and was re-elected by an increased margin in November 1956.

Working with Secretary of State John Foster Dulles (1888–1959), Eisenhower adhered to the Truman–Acheson doctrine of 'containment', while at home he pursued a policy of 'progressive conservatism', designed to encourage business enterprise.

The Eisenhower era was one of growth, prosperity, and social change, involving the migration of southern blacks to the northern industrial cities and a rapid expansion in the educational sector. In the southern states racial tensions emerged, as a new black rights movement developed under the leadership of Dr Martin Luther King (1929–68). Responding to these new demands and developments, the youthful Massachusetts Democrat, John F Kennedy (1917–63), on the promise of a 'New Frontier' program of social reform, gained victory in the presidential election of November 1960. However, the new president, having emerged as a firm opponent of communism abroad, as evidenced by the Bay of Pigs Affair of 1961 and the Cuban Missile Crisis of 1962, and having proposed a sweeping domestic Civil Rights Bill, was assassinated in November 1963. It was left to his vice president and successor, the Texan Lyndon B Johnson

(1908–73), to oversee the passage of the 'Great Society' reforms.

These measures, which included the Equal Opportunities, Voting Rights, Housing, and Medicare Acts, guaranteed blacks new civil rights, including the effective right to vote in southern states, and significantly extended the reach of the federal government. They were buttressed by the judicial rulings of the Supreme Court chaired by Chief Justice Earl Warren (1891–1974), who occupied the post between 1953 and 1969.

Abroad, however, President Johnson became embroiled in the Vietnam War, 1964–75, which, with casualty numbers mounting, polarized American public opinion and created deep divisions within the Democratic Party.

2. Nixon to Reagan

Johnson decided not to run for re-election in November 1968 and the Democrat candidate, Vice President Hubert H Humphrey (1911–78), was defeated by the experienced Republican, Richard M Nixon (1913–94). Nixon, a staunch conservative, encountered worsening student and racial conflicts at home but enjoyed greater success abroad. Working with National Security Advisor Henry Kissinger (b. 1923), he began a gradual disengagement from Vietnam and launched a new policy of *détente* which brought about improvements in relations with the Soviet Union, a Strategic Arms Limitation Treaty (SALT 1) being signed in 1972, and with communist China.

Faced by a divided opposition led by the liberal George McGovern (b. 1922), Nixon gained re-election by an overwhelming margin in November 1972. During the campaign, however, Nixon's staff illegally broke into the Democratic Party's headquarters, in the Watergate building, in Washington DC. The resulting 'cover-up' created a damaging scandal which, with a congressional impeachment impending, forced the resignation of the president in August 1974.

Watergate shocked the American public, eroding confidence in the presidency, Republicans, and the Washington establishment. The more moderate Republican, Gerald R Ford (b. 1913), who had only been vice president since December 1973, succeeded Nixon as president. Maintaining the services of Kissinger, Ford adhered to his predecessor's policy of *détente*. He faced, however, a resurgent and hostile Democrat-dominated Congress which introduced legislation curbing the powers of the presidency, by means of the War Powers Resolution of 1973, which prohibits the president from keeping US forces in hostile situa-

tions for more than 90 days without congressional authorization, and forcing isolationism abroad. The new president also had to deal with an economic recession and fuel shortages. These had resulted from the 1973 Arab–Israeli War and the emergence of the Organization of Petroleum Exporting Countries (OPEC) who proceeded to force up world oil prices.

Ford ran in the presidential election of November 1976, but was defeated by the 'born again' southern Christian and anti-Washington outsider, James ('Jimmy') E Carter (b. 1924), who promised a new era of open and honest government.

Carter, the former governor of Georgia, was a fiscal conservative, but a social liberal, who sought to make welfare more cost effective through greater administrative efficiency. In addition, he pledged to end the fuel crisis by enforced conservation. This he substantially achieved through the Energy Acts of 1978 and 1980.

Overseas, President Carter pursued a 'new foreign policy' which emphasized human rights in America's foreign relations. In the Middle East, Carter came close to a peace settlement in 1978–79, effecting the Camp David Agreements of September 1978 between Egypt and Israel, followed by a peace treaty in March 1979. Also, in January 1979 America's diplomatic relations with communist China were fully normalized.

The Carter presidency was brought down, however, by a twin set of foreign policy and economic crises in 1979–80: the fall of the Shah of Iran in January 1979 and the consequent Iranian Islamic Revolution. The president's vacillating leadership style, defense economies, and moralistic foreign policy were blamed for weakening America's influence abroad. As a consequence, there was a resurgence in anti-communist feeling and mounting support for a new policy of rearmament and selective interventionism.

Carter responded to this new mood by enunciating the hawkish Carter Doctrine of 1980. This asserted that the United States had a vital interest in the Gulf region, which it would defend by force. It also supported a major new arms development program. The president's popularity plunged, however, during 1980 as, mainly because of a new round of OPEC-induced oil price rises, inflation gripped the country. During the same period American embassy staff were held hostage by Shi'ite fundamentalists in Tehran.

The arch conservative Republican Ronald W Reagan (b. 1911) benefited from Carter's difficulties and was swept to victory in the November 1984 presidential election, the Democrats also losing control of the

Senate for the first time in 26 years.

The new president, like his predecessor, was an 'outsider politician' who, from being a former screen actor and governor of California, had risen to prominence as an effective television-skilled campaigner. Reagan, drawing support from the 'Moral Majority' movement and 'New Right', called for a return to traditional Christian religious and family values and propounded a supply-side economic strategy, founded on reduced taxation, deregulation, and political decentralization, to get 'government off people's backs'.

In his approach to foreign affairs, Reagan rejected *détente* and spoke of the communist-controlled Soviet Union as an 'evil empire' which needed to be checked by a military build-up. He launched the space-based Strategic Defense Initiative (SDI) in 1983, and spoke of a readiness to employ force when necessary.

The early years of the Reagan presidency witnessed substantial reductions in taxation and sweeping cutbacks in federal welfare programs. This created serious hardship, as economic recession gripped the nation between 1981 and 1983. The official unemployment rate rose from a level of 7.8% in May 1980 to a postwar high of 10.8% in November 1982. Abroad, the president's new foreign policy led to a sharp deterioration in Soviet–American relations, ushering in a new 'cold war' era during the Polish 'Solidarity' crisis of 1981.

By the autumn of 1983, however, the US economy began a strong neo-Keynesian recovery, the unemployment level falling to 7% in June 1984, and, helped by the successful invasion of Grenada by US marines in October 1983 to foil an alleged Marxist coup, President Reagan recovered his popularity and was swept to a landslide victory on a wave of optimistic patriotism in the presidential election of November 1984. He defeated the Democratic ticket of Walter Mondale (b. 1928) and Geraldine Ferraro (b. 1935) by a record margin.

During 1985 and 1986 public support for President Reagan was maintained, as a radical tax-cutting bill was successfully pushed through Congress. In 1986, however, clouds began to gather on the economic horizon as a huge budget and trade deficit developed, while overseas the president faced mounting public opposition to his policies in Central America. He also encountered a formidable new superpower adversary in the form of the new reformist Soviet leader, Mikhail Gorbachev. Gorbachev pressed for arms reductions during superpower summits held in Geneva in November 1985 and Reykjavik in October 1986.

The Reagan presidency was rocked in November 1986 by the Republican Party's loss of control of the Senate, following midterm elections, and the disclosure of a damaging 'Iran–Contra' scandal, concerning American arms sales to Iran in return for the release of hostages, and the 'laundering' of profits to help the Nicaraguan Contra anti-communist guerrillas. This scandal dented public confidence in the administration and forced the resignation and dismissal of key cabinet members, including National Security Adviser Rear Admiral John Poindexter (b. 1936) in November 1986 and Chief of Staff Donald Regan (b. 1918) in February 1987.

Having reasserted presidential authority between 1981 and 1986, the ailing President Reagan began to forfeit power to a resurgent Congress during 1987. However, under the skilled leadership of his new chief of staff, Howard Baker (b. 1925), the president began to recover his standing in the national polls through emerging as a 'born again' convert to *détente*. This was evidenced by his signing in Washington in December 1987 a historic agreement with the Soviet Union to scrap intermediate-range nuclear forces (INF).

Reagan's popularity transferred itself to Vice President George Bush (b. 1924) who, despite selecting the inexperienced Dan Quayle (b. 1947), a two-term senator from Indiana, as his running-mate, and despite opposition charges that he had been indirectly involved in the Iran Contra proceedings, defeated the Democrats' candidate, Michael S Dukakis (b. 1933), the governor of Massachusetts, in the presidential election of November 1988. Bush captured 53% of the national vote to Dukakis's 46%, finishing ahead in 40 states. He thus became the first sitting vice president since the Democrat Martin Van Buren (1782–1862) in 1836 to secure the presidency through the ballot box.

3. 1989–1996

Bush came to power, after six years of economic growth, at a time of uncertainty. Reagan's tax-cutting policy, while stimulating the economy and reducing the level of unemployment to just 5%, had led to mounting federal trade and budget deficits, which had served to turn the United States into a debtor nation for the first time in its history and had helped trigger a Wall Street market stock market crash in October 1987.

Bush promised, on his inauguration, to 'make kinder the face of the nation and gentler the face of the world' and, despite his campaign rhetoric, sought to steer a more moderate and consensual course, both domestically and overseas, than his predecessor. There were minor domestic initiatives in the areas of education, drug control, and the environment, where problems had surfaced during the Reagan years. However, in general the first three years of the Bush presidency were dominated by events overseas, in particular the collapse of communism which occurred across Central and Eastern Europe from 1989. This made possible substantial defense savings and left America as the one remaining global superpower, with a long-awaited START (Strategic Arms Reduction Talks) treaty being signed with the Soviet Union in July 1991. Responding to the changed circumstances, President Bush spoke of building a 'new world order' in which the UN would play a more positive and interventionist role in supporting the spread and defense of liberal democracy. The Bush presidency was also characterized by greater US military assertiveness overseas, starting in December 1989 when 23,000 troops were sent to Panama to overthrow the corrupt Panamanian dictator, General Manuel Noriega. A year later, following Iraq's invasion and annexation of neighboring Kuwait on 2 August 1990, President Bush played the leading role in constructing and dominating a UN coalition with the purpose of forcing Iraq's withdrawal. After economic sanctions and diplomatic negotiations had failed, this multinational coalition, which included 430,000 US ground troops, 1,300 fighter and support aircraft, 2,000 tanks, and 55 warships and was led by the American general, H Norman Schwarzkopf, embarked, from 17 January 1991, on 'Operation Desert Storm'. This involved massive air attacks on Iraqi positions and, from 23 February 1991, a ground offensive. It succeeded in its objectives, with Iraq accepting ceasefire and withdrawal terms on 3 March 1991.

As US commander in chief during 'Operation Desert Storm', President Bush's public approval rating climbed to 90% in the spring of 1991 and his re-election in 1992 appeared inevitable. However, the president had much less success on the domestic front. The economy was marred both by recession and a crippling budget deficit, which forced Bush during 1990 to recant on his 1988 campaign promise not to raise taxes. There were also mounting social tensions, linked to unemployment, as witnessed most dramatically by violent riots on 29 April 1992 among the 'underclass' of Los Angeles.

As 1992 progressed and the economy entered a 'second-dip' phase of the recession, the president's popularity slumped dramatically, with his position being worsened by new revelations suggesting his possible involvement in the 'Iran-Contra' affair. Bush was criticized for his 'do-nothing' approach towards the domestic scene, both by his Democrat challenger for the

presidency, the neo-liberal Arkansas governor, Bill Clinton (b. 1946), and by the Texan billionaire, H Ross Perot (b. 1930), who entered the race as a well-funded conservative-populist independent, preaching the need for tough economic reform. The Bush campaign team attempted to attack perceived flaws in Clinton's character and to depict him as a 'tax and spend liberal'. However, these were resisted resolutely by a candidate who was drawn from the Democrat's more conservative southern wing. Running a skillful campaign, concentrating on a message of generational change and greater domestic intervention, Clinton secured a clear victory over the incumbent Bush in the November 1992 presidential election. Perot also polled surprisingly strongly, attracting 19% of the national vote, the highest share achieved by a third candidate since the 'Bull Moose' challenge of Theodore Roosevelt (1858–1919) in 1912. Drawing support from a wide range of social groups and geographical areas, Clinton had before him the prospect of consolidating this support so as to establish a neo-liberal 'New Democratic" electoral coalition which would replace the 'new Republican' coalition which had been constructed by Ronald Reagan.

During 1993 President Clinton faced repeated criticisms of his uncertain leadership and apparent lack of clear principles and strategy, especially overseas, where US intervention in Somalia in October 1993 resulted in the deaths of 18 members of the US military. His personal standing was also undermined by a series of allegations concerning sexual and financial misconduct, the latter, the 'Whitewater affair', concerning the Clintons' financial dealings, while he was governor of Arkansas, with the Whitewater Development Corporation. Nevertheless, President Clinton's record of success in Congress, in terms of votes won, was the best of any president since 1953. The two most important measures passed were the deficit reduction budget package, approved in August 1993, and the North Atlantic Free-Trade Agreement (NAFTA), ratified in November 1993. The former provided for a reduction in the federal deficit, which stood in 1993 at $255 billion, or 4% of GDP, by $496 billion over five years through a combination of spending cuts and tax increases, targeted at high earners. The latter, a measure first proposed by President Bush, provided for the formation of a North American free trade zone, embracing Canada, Mexico, and the United States, with trade barriers being phased out over a 15-year period.

During 1994, with a special counsel being appointed

to investigate the 'Whitewater affair' in January and congressional hearings commencing in July, and with a former Arkansas state clerical worker, Paula Jones, filing sexual harassment charges against Clinton in May, President Clinton continued to be dogged by scandals. These were eagerly seized upon by the president's Republican opponents, whose congressional leadership was now directed by Newt Gingrich (b. 1943), an aggressive radical-right Reaganite whose vigorous campaigns against alleged 'Democrat sleaze' had already resulted in the toppling of key Democratic members of Congress. President Clinton's key domestic reform measure, the overhaul of the country's health care system so as to provide, via a combination of market forces and federal regulations, health insurance for every US citizen, was entrusted to a task force overseen by Hillary Rodham Clinton, the president's wife, who is an accomplished lawyer. The proposed package was unveiled in September 1992 and gained broad public support. However, the measure was effectively killed by the powerful private health care lobby and was rejected by Congress in September 1994.

This came as a crushing blow to the Clinton presidency and, despite a background of buoyant economic growth, the Democrats were heavily defeated in the congressional and state elections of November 1994. The midterm reverse was so great that the Republicans secured control of both chambers of Congress for the first time since 1954 and held 60% of state governorships. Newt Gingrich, orchestrator of the Republican campaign, became the new House speaker and effective leader of the opposition. During 1995 he sought to secure implementation of a radical ten-point conservative-populist manifesto, 'Contract with America'. This included pledges to secure a balanced budget by 2002, tackle rising crime levels, limit congressional terms, reform welfare, drastically reduce the powers of the federal administration, and transfer responsibilities to state governments. With President Clinton being forced to share authority during 1995, Gingrich became a serious force for the conservative agenda.

By mid-April 1995, the lower chamber had approved all but one of the elements of 'Contract with America', the congressional term limits bill being rejected. However, the Senate, led by majority leader, Bob Dole (b. 1923), a candidate for the Republican Party's presidential nomination in 1996, had passed only two measures. In June 1995 President Clinton issued the first veto of his administration, rejecting a package of cuts in education and training. However, he also indicated a

determination to shift rightwards, responding to the changed public mood. Under the title the 'New Covenant', he unveiled his own proposals for the achievement of a balanced budget by 2005, through major reductions in Medicare (free healthcare for the old and disabled) and other welfare cuts, acknowledging that 'the era of big government is over'. Drawing upon the polling advice of Dick Morris, a renowned Republican-leaning political consultant, he responded to the concerns of middle-class suburbanites, the so-called 'soccer moms', about 'moral decline', by supporting curfews for teenagers, parental leave, school uniforms, V-chips to give parents control over television programs watched by their children, and bans on tobacco advertising. He thus positioned himself as the leader of the broad, sensible 'vital American center', defending the status quo against reckless 'Republican extremists', whose intransigence in budget negotiations had led to an eight-day shutdown in the non-essential operations of the federal government in November 1995. This strategy enabled Clinton's public approval rating to climb to a respectable 47% in August 1995.

From the autumn of 1995, after promoting peace initiatives in Bosnia, the Middle East, Haiti, and Northern Ireland, and with the US economy continuing to grow strongly, President Clinton's job approval ratings rose to above 50%, where they remained throughout 1996. This was despite the continuation of the Whitewater and Paula Jones enquiries. In January 1996 Hillary Clinton became the first-ever first lady to receive a grand jury summons, to testify in the Whitewater investigation; in May 1996 a jury in Little Rock, Arkansas, returned verdicts of guilty of conspiracy and fraud against two former business associates of Bill Clinton, in a connected case; and, in September 1996, Susan McDougal, a former business partner, went to prison rather than testify about the president's role in the failed Whitewater scheme. Nevertheless, the June 1996 report by the Senate Whitewater committee concluded that Hillary Clinton had probably played a role in limiting the investigation into the mysterious suicide, in July 1993, of Vince Foster, a White House aide, and that, when governor of Arkansas, Bill Clinton had given 'inappropriate assistance' to an Arkansas bond dealer. However, it did not find any substantial misdemeanours.

From the spring of 1996 attention focused on the race for the presidency. Bill Clinton secured renomination as the Democrat's candidate without challenge, while Bob Dole had effectively secured the Republican nomination by late March 1996. The US economy now entered its sixth year of growth (averaging 2.5% per year), with the unemployment rate down to 5% (more than 12 million new jobs having been created since 1992) and the federal budget deficit down to around 1% of GDP (against 5% in 1992), while a substantial nationwide drop in serious crime was recorded in 1995. Against this background in May 1996 a Harris poll showed President Clinton leading Dole in approval polls by 25%. In an effort to counter his image as a 'Washington insider' and concentrate fully on the campaign ahead, Dole stepped down as Senate majority leader in May 1996 and was replaced by Trent Lott, a staunch conservative Republican senator from Mississippi.

4. 1996–1999

In June 1996 the Democratic Party published a moderate policy program, 'Families First', and in August 1996, in an historic move, President Bill Clinton signed into law a Republican bill which abolished automatic federal welfare entitlements to poor families, a key tenet of liberalism that has existed since 1935. Instead, in an attack on the 'culture of dependency', federal aid became restricted to limited periods (of up to two years for welfare benefits), after which recipients would be expected to work, and the design of welfare programs was devolved to the states. This change was criticized by traditional Democrats, who feared it might push 2.6 million people into poverty, but President Clinton balanced it by securing a multi-phased increase in the minimum wage and an extension of health insurance coverage. At the Republicans' National Convention, held in San Diego, 12–15 August 1996, Jack Kemp (b. 1935), a Reaganite advocate of tax cuts and a former housing secretary, was selected as Bob Dole's running-mate. The Christian right ensured that the Republican platform (manifesto) included a proposal for a constitutional amendment to prohibit abortion, while Dole also pledged to cut income tax by 15%. In September 1996 US cruise missile attacks were launched against military targets in southern Iraq in retaliation for Saddam Hussein's earlier attacks on Kurdish safe havens within Iraq.

The November 1996 presidential election saw Bill Clinton, despite character attacks and 'sleaze allegations' from Republican opponents, comfortably securing re-election, with, at 49%, an increased share of the popular vote. The buoyant economy and the failure of the 73-year-old Dole to develop any effective positive campaigning themes explained Clinton's success. However,

in the concurrent congressional elections, the Republicans retained control of both the Senate and the House of Representatives. After the election, Clinton put together a new cabinet. The secretaries of state and defense, Warren Christopher and William Perry, retired and were replaced in early 1997 by Madeleine Albright (b. 1937), the former US representative at the UN, and William Cohen, a former Republican senator. This was indicative of an intention to fashion a bipartisan international policy. The White House chief of staff, Leon Panetta, who resigned, was replaced by Erskine Bowles, a North Carolina banker. However, Janet Reno and Robert Rubin were retained in the key posts of attorney general and treasury secretary. In his January 1997 re-inauguration address, President Clinton announced that the main priorities of his second term would be balancing the federal budget, improving education via tax credit incentives, making a success of welfare reform, and extending health insurance. He spoke of a need for a 'new kind of government' which works through empowerment rather than through bureaucracy and 'lives within its means and does more with less'.

President Clinton was faced with a hostile Republican-controlled Congress, and the special prosecutor, Kenneth Starr, continued to probe deeply into possible scandals which would damage the Democrats. Soon after the election, there were allegations that the Democrats' 1996 election campaign and President Clinton's legal defense costs had been funded partly by Asian nationals, from South Korea, Taiwan, and Indonesia, and possibly also indirectly by the Chinese government. An FBI inquiry and congressional investigations were approved and Clinton announced that the Democrats would no longer accept donations from foreign citizens and corporations and there would be an annual limit of $100,000 on contributions from individuals. The Democratic National Committee now returned $1.6 million of the $3 million which had been raised in 1996 by the American Chinese fund-raiser John Huang. In October 1997 Attorney General Reno ordered an expanded investigation into Democrat fund-raising for the 1996 election campaign, concentrating on the issue of telephone calls from the White House.

In July 1997 the president and Congress agreed a deal to balance the federal budget by 2002, through reducing federal spending by $270 million over five years (including $115 million savings from Medicare and further defense cuts: reducing defense spending to 16% of the federal budget, as against 27% in 1989) while increasing educational tax credits. However, such was the continuing buoyancy of the US economy, with GDP growth of 4% (the fastest rate for a decade) and unemployment at its lowest level for 23 years, that, in January 1998, President Clinton was able to announce that in 1998–99 the federal budget would be balanced, for the first time in 30 years. It also appeared that the August 1996 welfare reforms were having a significant impact, since, within a year, the number of welfare recipients had dropped by a quarter, to 10.7 million. There were also foreign policy triumphs during 1997–98, with America's successful promotion of an eastward expansion of NATO's membership, its support of the continuing peace initiatives in Bosnia, Northern Ireland, and the Middle East, and its adoption of a hard line against Iraq, in January 1998, which persuaded Iraq to allow UN weapons inspectors access to secret weapons and military sites.

However, President Clinton continued to be dogged by personal scandals. In May 1997 the Supreme Court ruled that Clinton could not claim presidential immunity from the charges raised in the Paula Jones civil case, and on 17 January 1998 he was forced to testify in his defense, in his lawyer's office, becoming the first serving president to be interrogated as a defendant in a court case. The case was dismissed in April 1998 by the district judge, who ruled that Miss Jones had suffered nothing worthy of redress, and it did not affect President Clinton's public approval ratings, which remained around 60%. However, from January 1998 a new, more damaging scandal unexpectedly broke, with media allegations that between 1995 and 1997 President Clinton had had consensual 'sexual relations' with a young White House intern, Monica Lewinsky (b. 1974); had lied, in denying it under oath during the Jones testimony; and had encouraged Miss Lewinsky to perjure herself. The president refuted these allegations and received strong support from the first lady. However, Kenneth Starr, the conservative Republican special prosecutor (independent counsel) who had been investigating the Whitewater affair with little success since August 1994, extended his inquiries to include the 'Lewinsky affair' ('Monicagate'). He subpoenaed witnesses to appear before a Washington grand jury in February 1998, including White House aides.

With further details emerging in the media and through the Internet, 'Monicagate' gripped media attention throughout 1998, distracting from the president's diplomatic and domestic initiatives. On 28 July 1998 Starr persuaded Lewinsky to testify, in return for immunity from prosecution, and she stated that there had been a relationship with the president, which had involved specific sexual contact, but declared that she had not been encouraged to lie by the president. On 17 August 1998 President Clinton testified for four hours to a grand jury, and admitted in a subsequent television broadcast that his relationship with Miss Lewinsky had been 'inappropriate' and that he had 'misled people' about it publicly for seven months. A snap opinion poll suggested that most Americans wished the president had spoken sooner, but now wanted the matter to be dropped. However, pressure within Congress and the media for the president to resign or be impeached, for perjury, increased in September 1998 when Starr presented the findings of his four-year-long $40-million inquiry to Congress. Starr's prurient 445-page report was published, with prosecutors claiming that it contained 'substantial and credible information' that might support impeachment, while Clinton's confidential videotaped testimony to the grand jury was released on national television on 21 September. The House of Representatives voted in October 1998 to impeach President Clinton on the grounds of perjury and obstruction of justice; the Senate trial began in January 1999 and President Clinton was aquitted of the charges the following month. Ten Republican Senators voted with the Democrats to acquit Clinton by a margin of 55 votes to 45 on the charge of perjury. Throughout the trial the president's national approval rating remained high, exceeding 70% in January 1999. After the trial verdict, President Clinton declared himself to be 'humbled and very grateful' to be acquitted and stated that he was 'profoundly sorry' for 'what I said and did to trigger these events'.

However, the Democrats polled unexpectedly strongly in the mid-term congressional and state elections of November 1998, as voters reacted to Republican attempts to exploit the 'Lewinsky affair'. The First Lady, Hillary Clinton, and Vice President Al Gore played a prominent role in the Democrats' campaign. The Democrats reduced the Republicans' majority in the House of Representatives by five seats, while there was no net change in the Senate, leaving the Republicans with a ten seat majority. Accepting responsibility for his party's poor performance, Newt Gingrich resigned as House speaker and was later replaced, in January 1999, by Dennis Hastert. In his January 1999 annual 'State of the Union' address President Clinton gave emphasis to his domestic policy agenda, in the areas of education, social security, and healthcare. He noted that, with economic growth continuing, unemployment, at 4.5%, was at its lowest peacetime level since 1957, and that projected federal budget surpluses would total $4,400 billion over the next 15 years. During 1999 a strong political debate developed between Democrats and Republicans over how best to make use of these surpluses. Democrats favoured emphasis to be given in investing in education and social welfare (Medicare and the social security, or pensions, programme), while Republicans preferred greater tax cuts, suggesting, in July 1999, $800 billion in tax cuts over ten years against the President's suggested tax breaks of $250 billion. In May 1999 the highly regarded Robert Rubin, who had been treasury (economics and finance) secretary since 1995, resigned and was replaced by his deputy, Lawrence Summers.

America remained active overseas, leading the 'Operation Allied Force' NATO campaign of air-strikes against Yugoslavia between March and June 1999, in response to the crisis in Kosovo, and continuing to promote peace initiatives in Northern Ireland and Israel-Palestine. However, increasingly attention began to shift towards the next presidential and congressional elections of November 2000. By June 1999 Dan Quayle, the vice-president between 1989 and 1993, Pat Buchanan and Steve Forbes, challengers in 1996, and George W Bush, the popular governor of Texas and son of the former president, had declared their intentions to contest for the Republican nomination, while Elizabeth Dole, the wife of the 1996 Republican contender, was another potential candidate. On the Democratic side, vice-president Gore remained the clear front runner, challenged only by the former New Jersey senator, Bill Bradley, while the First Lady, Hillary Clinton, had emerged as a possible candidate to contest, in New York state, for a seat in the US Senate.

Northern and Western Europe

The region Northern and Western Europe, as we have defined it, stretches from the Arctic Ocean in the north to the Mediterranean Sea in the south, and from the Atlantic Ocean in the west to the Adriatic in the east. It includes 23 nation-states, whose total populations amount to over 370 million, or 80 million more than the total number of people inhabiting the whole of the North American continent. However, the land area occupied by these 23 countries is less than a fifth of that within the boundaries of the United States and Canada and accounts for only 2.7% of the world's total land area. We are, therefore, looking at a comparatively large region, fairly densely populated, but with this density greatest near the geographical center and discernibly thinning out at the peripheries.

Climatically there are substantial variations, ranging from the tundra of northern Scandinavia to the warm temperate conditions enjoyed by those countries bordering the Mediterranean. Ethnically the differences are not as great and, with a few exceptions, most of the countries in this region have a common cultural heritage, a common Christian foundation, with a north-south Protestant–Catholic denominational division, and a shared history. There are distinct language differences, however, from country to country, the dominant tongues being English, French, German, and the Latin languages of Italy, Spain, and Portugal.

Paradoxically, although 15 of these 23 states are now members of the European Union, the history of the region has been one of division and war rather than cooperation and unity. Most of the major states have been rivals at one time or another and most have

Northern and Western Europe: social, economic, and political data

Country	Area (sq km/sq miles)	c. 1995 Population (million)	c. 1995 Pop. density per sq km/sq mile	c. 1992 Adult literacy rate (%)	World ranking	Income type	c. 1991 Human rights rating (%)
Andorra	468/181	0.064	137/354	100	1	high	99
Austria	83,850/32,375	8.047	96/249	100	1	high	95
Belgium	30,528/11,787	10.080	330/855	100	1	high	96
Denmark	43,080/16,633	5.251	122/316	99	8	high	98
Finland	338,139/130,556	5.095	15/39	99	8	high	99
France	543,965/210,026	57.747	106/275	99	8	high	94
Germany	357,000/137,838	81,410	228/591	99	8	high	98
Iceland	102,850/39,711	0.270	3/7	99	8	high	N/A
Ireland	70,283/27,136	3.626	52/134	99	8	high	94
Italy	301,225/116,304	57.193	190/492	97	44	high	90
Liechtenstein	160/62	0.031	194/500	99	8	high	N/A
Luxembourg	2,590/1,000	0.413	159/413	100	1	high	N/A
Malta	316/122	0.376	1,190/3,082	81	102	high	N/A
Monaco	1/0.4	0.031	31,000/77,500	100	1	high	99
Netherlands	40,844/15,770	15.500	380/983	99	8	high	98
Norway	324,219/125,182	4.370	13/35	99	8	high	97
Portugal	92,080/35,552	9.830	107/276	85	94	high	92
San Marino	61/24	0.025	410/1042	96	52	high	N/A
Spain	504,880/194,935	39.482	78/203	95	59	high	87
Sweden	449,700/173,630	8.780	20/51	99	8	high	98
Switzerland	41,290/15,942	6.995	169/439	99	8	high	96
United Kingdom	244,100/94,247	58.606	240/622	99	8	high	93
Vatican City State	0.4/0.15	0.001	2,500/6,667	100	1	high	N/A
Total/average/range	*3,571,629/1,379,013*	*373.222*	*104/271*	*81–100*	*–*	*–*	*87–99*

* Two-party blocs.

AMS = additional member system, E = elected, F = federal, I = indirect, LV = limited vote, PL = party list, PR = proportional representation, SB = second ballot, SP = simple plurality, STV = single transferable vote, U = unitary, Abs= absolutist, Lib-dem = liberal democratic, Em-dem = emergent democratic, Lim-pres = limited presidential, Theo = theocratic.

clashed militarily. England has been at war with Spain and France. France has clashed with most of Europe and, more recently, Germany has attempted to subjugate the entire continent. A desire to prevent a recurrence of war in Europe was the genesis of the European Community and that wish has been largely fulfilled, since the region has enjoyed peace and stability since World War II, even though countries on its periphery have fared less well. Today, the 15 states within the European Union have open frontiers for the movement of goods, capital, and people.

Despite containing less than 7% of the global population, Northern and Western Europe is a key region, containing most of the major political and economic powers. It was in this region where, during the post-Renaissance era, the world's first modern nation-states were formed and from this base the colonization of Africa, the Americas, and Asia was conducted. Indeed, as Chapter 8 shows, the United Kingdom, France, and the Netherlands remain significant colonial powers.

Economically, the 23 states of Northern and Western Europe now have much in common. All operate some form of mixed economy, based partly on market forces and state intervention, although within this mixture sharp policy differences are evident. Whereas there has been a tendency in recent years for a majority of governing regimes to have a centrist or left-of-center orientation, a minority has shifted to the right. All 23 countries in the region have high-income economies. Indeed, 16 of the world's 20 wealthiest states are situated within Northern and Western Europe, with Liechtenstein, Switzerland, Luxembourg, and Norway occupying positions in the world 'top five'. In 1995 average per-capita GDP in Northern and Western Europe

Table 59

World ranking	Date of state formation	State structure	State type	Executive type	Number of assembly chambers	Party structure	Lower house electoral system
1	1278	U	Em-dem	Parliamentary	1	multi	PR-AMS
14	1918	F	Lib-dem	Parliamentary	2	multi	PR-PL
12	1830	F	Lib-dem	Parliamentary	2	multi	PR-PL
4	940/1849	U	Lib-dem	Parliamentary	1	multi	PR-PL
1	1917	U	Lib-dem	Dual	1	multi	PR-PL
15	741	U	Lib-dem	Dual	2	two*	SB
4	1871/1949/1990	F	Lib-dem	Parliamentary	2	multi	PR-AMS
–	1944	U	Lib-dem	Parliamentary	1	multi	PR-PL
15	1937	U	Lib-dem	Parliamentary	2	multi	PR-STV
21	1861	U	Lib-dem	Parliamentary	2	multi	PR-AMS
–	1342	U	Lib-dem	Parliamentary	1	multi	PR-LV
–	1848	U	Lib-dem	Parliamentary	1	multi	PR-PL
–	1964	U	Lib-dem	Parliamentary	1	two	PR-STV
1	1297	U	Lib-dem	Parliamentary	1	none	SB
4	1648	U	Lib-dem	Parliamentary	2	multi	PR-PL
9	1905	U	Lib-dem	Parliamentary	2	multi	PR-PL
19	1128	U	Lib-dem	Dual	1	multi	PR-PL
–	301	U	Lib-dem	Parliamentary	1	multi	PR-LV
26	1492	U	Lib-dem	Parliamentary	2	multi	PR-PL
4	1523	U	Lib-dem	Parliamentary	1	multi	PR-PL
12	1648	F	Lib-dem	Lim-pres	2	multi	PR-PL
18	1707	U	Lib-dem	Parliamentary	2	two	SP
–	1377/1929	U	Abs/Theo	Abs	N/A	none	N/A
–	–	–	–	–	–	–	–

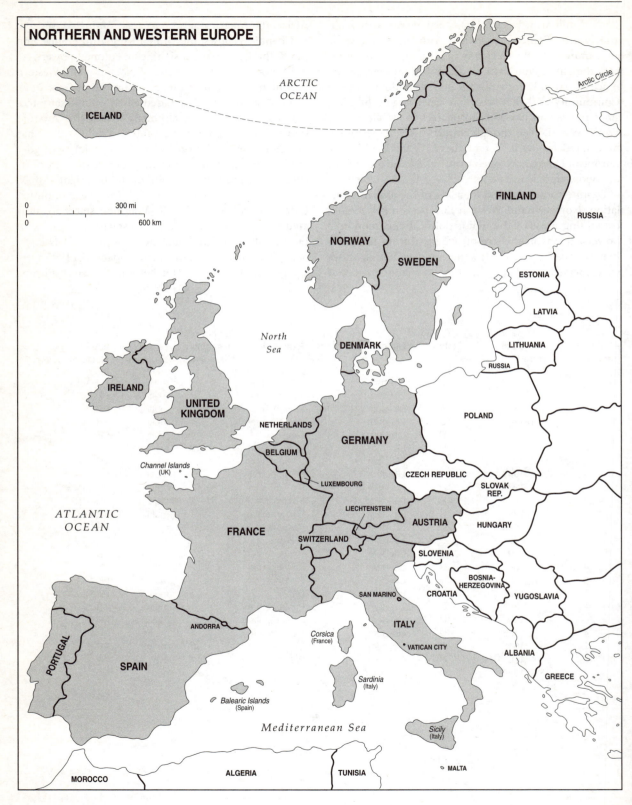

NORTHERN AND WESTERN EUROPE

exceeded $22,000 and the region generated almost a third of global GDP.

All the 23 states within Northern and Western Europe have comparatively high literacy rates, most being, in fact, in the 90% and over category. Urbanization levels are also high and human rights ratings, ranging from 87% in Spain to 99% in Finland, are the best in the world outside North America.

Some of the 23 states have significant regional problems within their national boundaries, based on linguistic, religious, or cultural differences. The most notable examples are to be found in Belgium, Spain, Italy, and the United Kingdom.

In Belgium differences between the Flemish-speaking north and the French-speaking south have resulted in a multiplicity of political parties, based on language distinctions as well as economic and social priorities. In reality, disagreements between the north and the south, and dissatisfaction with the peculiar position of Brussels, which is linguistically out of step with the rest of the country, owe as much to economic as to cultural disparities. However, in the 1991 general election more than a million Belgians voted for extremist and anti-political parties and in 1993 it was decided to establish a federation of three states: Flanders, Wallonia, and Brussels.

In Finland demands for greater recognition of the Swedish-speaking minority are growing progressively weaker. In Norway language differences are based more on dialects and these are being gradually assimilated into a common rural–urban approach. The passion generated by linguistic minorities on the Danish-German and Austrian–Italian borders has diminished markedly in recent years.

Switzerland provides a good example of how language and cultural variations can be successfully accommodated without disrupting social and political harmony. The fact that a federal approach was taken is less important than the willingness, over a long period of time, to show a tolerant respect for cultural and social differences. The strength of the Swiss economy, and the high living standards enjoyed by its citizens, have also helped to create these harmonious relationships.

While Spain was under a virtual military dictatorship until the death of General Franco in 1975 the demands of Basque separatists could be kept in check by force. However, since the return to pluralist politics a different approach has been necessary. A substantial devolution of powers, short of full federalism, seems to have gone a long way towards meeting regional aspirations.

In Italy strong regional divisions have also promoted political decentralization. The chief divide exists between the economically backward south, the 'Mezzogiorno', and the industrially highly developed north. The federalist Northern League has established itself as the dominant force in the northern region of Lombardy.

The Northern Ireland problem has been on the agenda of United Kingdom governments for more than half a century with no permanent answer. For more than two decades the approach was to match violence with violence and an attempt to find a political solution eluded successive governments. However, the 1998 'Good Friday' power-sharing agreement between the main political parties has produced real prospects of a lasting peace. The nationalist movements in Wales and Scotland have been substantially accommodated by the devolution measures adopted by the Blair government in 1998.

Putting aside regional disputes, politically the 23 nations now show great similarities. Twenty-one have been classified as liberal democracies and one, Andorra, is an emergent democracy. The Vatican City State, as the center of the Roman Catholic faith, is an absolutist theocratic regime.

A close examination of Table 59 reveals the extent of the political similarities. Four, Austria, Belgium, Germany, and Switzerland, are federal states and the remaining 19 are unitary. Twelve have two-chamber assemblies and ten have only one. Eighteen have parliamentary executives; one, Switzerland, has a limited presidential executive; one, the Vatican City State, has an absolute executive; and in three, France, Finland, and Portugal, the executive is 'dual', with responsibility shared between a president and a prime minister. Finally, the voting systems in 19 states are based on proportional representation, while a majoritarian system is used in three countries: France, Monaco, and the United Kingdom.

It is in the areas of party politics and electoral systems that a clear majority–minority situation arises. Eighteen of the 23 states have multiparty politics operating whereas three, France, Malta, and the United Kingdom, have more polarized two-party systems.

It would be dangerous to draw too firm conclusions about the effects of voting systems on party structures from this small sample, but it can be said that multiparty politics and some form of proportional representation seem to go hand in hand in most countries in Northern and Western Europe. It can also be said that the fact that many have had coalition governments for most of the postwar period does not seem to have, in any way, diminished the degree of democracy they have enjoyed, or their economic performances. Indeed, it can be cogently argued that the reverse is true.

In summary, although there are clear differences in approach to the political, economic, and social challenges facing them, the 23 states of Northern and Western Europe have more shared values than disagreements. Above all else, most have mature political systems which have survived many changes in the environments in which they function, and this maturity has created a keen sense of reality and tolerance in their dealings with the rest of the world. Probably the most encouraging sign is that the nations of Northern and Western Europe, whether or not they are European Union members, are increasingly coming together, rather than drifting apart.

Recommended reading

Aguero, F *Soldiers, Civilians and Democracy: Post-Franco Spain in Comparative Perspective*, Johns Hopkins University Press, 1995

Allum, O *State and Society in Western Europe*, Polity Press, 1995

Colomer, J (ed.) *Political Institutions in Europe*, Routledge, 1996

Derbyshire, I *Politics in France: From Giscard to Mitterrand*, W & R Chambers, 1990

Derbyshire, I *Politics in Germany: From Division to Unification*, W & R Chambers, 1991

Derbyshire, I and Derbyshire, J D *Politics in Britain: From Callaghan to Thatcher*, W & R Chambers, 1990

Fernández-Armesto, F *The Times Guide to the Peoples of Europe*, Times Books, 1994

Kavanagh, D *The Reordering of British Politics*, Oxford University Press, 1997

Lane, J E and Ersson, S O *Politics and Society in Western Europe*, 3rd edn., Sage, 1994

Meny, Y and Knapp, A *Government and Politics in Western Europe: Britain, France, Italy and Germany*, 2nd edn., Oxford University Press, 1993

Nicholson, F (ed.) *Political and Economic Encyclopaedia of Western Europe*, Longman, 1990

Rasmussen, J S and Moses, J C *Major European Governments*, 9th edn., Wordsworth, 1995

Rhodes, M, Heywood, P, and Wright, V (eds.) *Developments in West European Politics*, Macmillan, 1997

Roberts, G K and Hogwood, P *European Politics Today*, Manchester University Press, 1997

Smith, G *Politics in Western Europe*, 5th edn., Gower, 1989

Smith, G, Patterson, W E, and Padgett, S (eds.) *Developments in German Politics*, Macmillan, 1996

ANDORRA

Co-Principality of Andorra
Principat d'Andorra

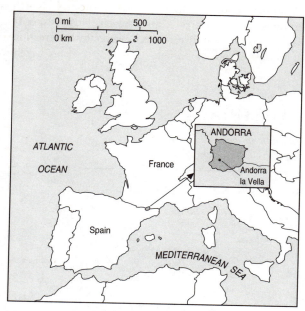

Capital: Andorra-la-Vella

Social and economic data
Area: 468 sq km/181 sq miles
Population: 64,000[*]
Pop. density per sq km/sq mi: 137/354[*]
Urban population: 94%[**]
Literacy rate: 100%[**]
GDP: $1,200 million[*]; per-capita GDP:$18,750[*]
Government defense spending (% of GDP): 0%
Currency: French franc and Spanish peseta
Economy type: high income
Labor force in agriculture: N/A
[*] 1995.
[**] 1992.

Head of government
Cap de Govern: Marc Forné Molne, since 1994

Ethnic composition
Twenty-five per cent of the population are Andorrans and 75% immigrant Spanish workers. Catalan is the local language.

Religions
Roman Catholicism is the chief religion.

Political features
State type: emergent democratic

Date of state formation: 1278
Political structure: unitary
Executive: parliamentary
Assembly: one-chamber
Party structure: multiparty
Human rights rating: 99%
International affiliations: CE, UN

Local and regional government
Andorra is divided into seven parishes (valleys), each administered by a communal council (*commun*). Councillors are elected by universal adult suffrage for four-year terms.

Co-heads of state
Episcopal Co-Prince: Monsignor Joan Martí Alanis, bishop of Seo de Urgel, Spain
French Co-Prince: Jacques Chirac, president of France, since 1995

Political system
Andorra had no formal constitution and was governed on semifeudal lines until 1993 when a constitution was approved by referendum. It describes the country as an independent, democratic co-principality and places sovereignty in the hands of the people, yet retains elements of its feudal origins through joint heads of state, the bishop of Urgel, in Spain, and the president of the French Republic. They are represented by permanent delegates, the vicar general of the Urgel diocese and the prefect of the French département of Pyrénées-Orientales. Although administratively independent, it had no individual international status until 1993, when it became a full member of the United Nations and in the following year was admitted into the Council of Europe. The 1993 constitution provides for a 28-member assembly, the General Council of the Valleys, serving a four-year term. Fourteen are elected on a national basis and 14 in dual constituencies in each of the seven valleys. The Council submits motions and proposals to the permanent delegates for approval, but the 1993 constitution has reduced the powers of the co-princes and their permanent delegates and increased those of the Andorran government, the Govern, which, for the first time, has power to raise revenue by income taxes and other fiscal means. The 12-member Govern is headed by a prime minister, who is called Cap ('head') de Govern. There is a Constitutional Court, and constitutional amendments require two-thirds approval by the General Council, followed by a referendum.

Political parties
Technically illegal until 1993, several groupings have

emerged. They include the centrist National Democratic Grouping (AND), New Democracy (ND), and the National Andorran Coalition (CNA); the center-right Liberal Union (UL); and the left-of-center National Democratic Initiative (IDN).

Political leaders since 1982

1982–84 Oscar Ribas Reig (Independent), 1984–90 Josep Pintat Solens (Independent), 1990–94 Oscar Ribas Reig (AND), 1994– Marc Forné Molne (UL)

Latest elections

In the 16 February 1997 elections under the new constitution the UL won 18 General Council seats; the AND, 6; the ND, 2; and the IDN, 2. Turnout was 82%.

Political history

Andorra's independence is viewed as dating from 1278, when an agreement (*pareage*) was entered into between France and the bishop of Seo de Urgel in Spain for the state's co-rule. Since then, possessing only an unpaid ceremonial militia, it remained dependent upon its larger neighbors for its security and continued existence.

Until 1970 only third-generation Andorran males had the vote. Now the franchise extends to all first-generation Andorrans of foreign parentage aged 28 or over. The electorate is still small, however, in relation to the total population, up to 75% of whom are foreign residents, who are constantly demanding political and nationality rights. Immigration, controlled by a quota system, is restricted to French and Spanish nationals intending to work in Andorra. Since the 1980s democracy, at first fragile, has gradually grown and in 1993 a national referendum overwhelmingly supported proposals for a democratic constitution. In December 1993, in the country's first elections under the new constitution, Oscar Ribas Reig of the National Democratic Grouping (AND), who had been head of government under the pre-constitution system, was elected president of the Govern, heading a broad coalition. Within less than a year he resigned the presidency, after losing the support of New Democracy (ND) members of his coalition, and was succeeded by the Liberal Union (UL) leader, Marc Forné Molne. He headed a minority government until the UL secured a parliamentary majority after elections in February 1997.

While maintaining its political and economic links with France and Spain, in 1993 Andorra became a full member of the United Nations and in the following year joined the Council of Europe.

Economically, the Co-Principality has progressed significantly during recent decades, utilizing its exemption, under the terms of an 1867 Franco-Spanish agreement, from the payment of import duties, to develop a growing tourist industry. About 10 million visitors currently pass through the state annually, purchasing low-priced consumer goods, while several thousand North Europeans use Andorra as a tax haven. This prosperity has been somewhat threatened, however, by the creation of a single European market.

AUSTRIA

Republic of Austria
Republik Österreich

Capital: Vienna

Social and economic data

Area: 83,850 sq km/32,375 sq miles
Population: 8,047,000[*]
Pop. density per sq km/sq mi: 98/249[*]
Urban population: 59%[**]
Literacy rate: 100%[**]
GDP: $216,547 million[*]; per-capita GDP: $26,900[*]
Government defense spending (% of GDP): 1.0%[*]
Currency: schilling
Economy type: high income
Labor force in agriculture: 8%[**]
Unemployment rate: 4.5%[*]
[*] 1995.
[**] 1992.

Head of state
President Thomas Klestil, since 1992

Head of government
Federal Chancellor Viktor Klima, since 1997

Ethnic composition
Ninety-eight per cent of the population is German, 0.7% Croatian, and 0.3% Slovene. German is the national language.

Religions
About 89% of the population is Roman Catholic, about 6% belongs to other Christian religions, and there are some 7,000 Jews.

Political features
State type: liberal democratic
Date of state formation: 1918
Political structure: federal
Executive: parliamentary
Assembly: two-chamber
Party structure: multiparty
Human rights rating: 95%
International affiliations: AG (observer), CE, CERN, EEA, ESA, EU, IAEA, IBRD, IMF, NAM (guest), OECD, OSCE, UN, WTO

Local and regional government
Austria is a federal republic divided into nine provinces or states (Länder), each with its own assembly and government. The states, with their populations, are: Wien (1.5 million), Niederösterreich (1.4 million), Oberösterreich (1.3 million), Steirmark (1.2 million), Tirol (0.6 million), Kärnten (0.5 million), Salzburg (0.4 million), Vorarberg (0.3 million), and Burgenland (0.27 million). The assemblies (*Landtag*) are very similar to the lower house of the federal assembly. Executive power is exercized by governors elected by the provincial assemblies.

Although, constitutionally, Austria is a federal state, there is a high degree of centralization, the federal government being responsible for education, the police, the postal service, the railways, social policies, and taxation.

Political system
The 1920 constitution was amended in 1929, suspended during the Hitler years, and reinstated in 1945. It provides for a two-chamber federal assembly, consisting of a National Council (Nationalrat) and a Federal Council (Bundesrat). The National Council has 183 members elected by universal adult suffrage, through a party list system of proportional representation, for a four-year term. It is subject to dissolution during this period. The Federal Council has 64 members elected by the provincial assemblies for varying terms, depending upon the life of each individual assembly. Each province provides a chair for the Federal Council for a six-month term of office. The federal president is the formal head of state and is elected by popular vote for a six-year term. The federal chancellor is head of government and chosen by the president on the basis of support in the National Council. He or she governs with a cabinet of their own choosing.

Political parties
There are currently around 17 active political parties, the most significant being the Social Democratic Party of Austria (SPÖ), the Austrian People's Party (ÖVP), Freedom (FPÖ), the Green Alternative Party (ALV), and the Liberal Forum (LF).

The SPÖ was founded in 1889 as the Social Democratic Party. It advocates democratic socialism and the maintenance of Austria's neutrality.

The ÖVP was founded in 1945 as the Christian Democratic Party. It describes itself as a 'progressive center party'.

The FPÖ dates from 1955, and afterwards took over from the League of Independents, which was wound up in 1956. It has a rightwing but populist orientation and advocates social reform, immigration control, and withdrawal from the EU. It changed its name from the Freedom Party of Austria to Freedom in 1995.

The ALV is an ecological party resulting from the union, in 1987, between the Austrian Alternative List (ALO) and another Green party, the BIP.

Political leaders since 1970
1970–83 Bruno Kreiksky (SPÖ), 1983–86 Fred Sinowatz (SPÖ-FPÖ coalition), 1986–97 Franz Vranitzky (SPÖ-ÖVP coalition), 1997– Viktor Klima (SPÖ-ÖVP coalition)

Latest elections
On 19 April 1998 Thomas Klestil (ÖVP) was re-elected for another six-year term, securing 63% of the popular vote. Turnout was 74%.

The results of the 17 December 1995 Nationalrat elections (turnout 82.7%) were:

Austria latest election results

Party	% votes	Seats
SPÖ	38.1	71
ÖVP	28.3	53
FPÖ	21.9	40
Liberal Forum	5.5	10
ALU	4.8	9

The results of the 1993 Bundesrat elections were: ÖVP, 33 seats, SPÖ, 27 seats, and FPÖ, 9 seats.

Political history

The first Austrian Republic was proclaimed in November 1918 after the break-up of the Dual Monarchy of Austria -Hungary. A constituent assembly, which had been formed, voted to make Austria an integral part of Germany but the peace treaties ruled out any Austria–Germany union. With the rise of Nazism in Germany in the 1930s there was considerable pressure on Austria, culminating, in 1938, in the Anschluss, or union, making Austria a province of Greater Germany until the end of the war in 1945.

Austria returned to its 1920 constitution in 1945, with a provisional government led by Karl Renner (1870–1950). The Allies had divided the country into four zones, occupied by the USSR, the United States, Britain, and France. The first postwar elections were held while the country was still occupied and resulted in an SPÖ-ÖVP coalition government. Austria's full independence was formally recognized in October 1955.

The first postwar noncoalition government was formed in 1966 when the ÖVP came to power with Josef Klaus as chancellor. In 1970 the SPÖ formed a minority government underr Bruno Kreisky (b. 1911) and increased its majority in the 1971 and 1975 general elections. In 1978 opposition to the government's proposals to install the first nuclear power plant nearly resulted in its defeat but it survived and, although the idea of a nuclear plant was abandoned, nuclear energy continued to be a controversial issue. In 1983 the SPÖ regime came to an end when it lost its overall majority and Kreisky resigned, refusing to join a coalition. The SPÖ decline was partly attributed to the emergence of new environmentalist groups, the VGÖ and the ALO. Fred Sinowatz, the new Chair of the SPÖ, formed an SPÖ-FPÖ coalition government.

In April 1985 international controversy was aroused with the announcement that Kurt Waldheim (b. 1918), former United Nations secretary general, was to be a presidential candidate. Despite allegations of his complicity in the Nazi regime, as a wartime officer in Yugoslavia, Waldheim was eventually elected president in January 1986. In June of that year Sinowatz resigned the chancellorship, for what he described as personal reasons, and was succeeded by Franz Vranitzky (b. 1937) but the SPÖ-FPÖ coalition broke up when an extreme rightwinger, Jorg Haider (b. 1950), became FPÖ leader.

In the November 1986 elections the SPÖ tally of National Council seats fell from 90 to 80 and the ÖVP's from 81 to 77, while the FPÖ increased its seats from 12 to 18. For the first time the Green lobby was represented and the VGÖ won eight seats. Vranitzky offered his resignation but was persuaded by the president to try to form a 'grand coalition', between the SPÖ and the ÖVP, on the lines of Austria's first postwar government. Agreement was eventually reached and Vranitzky remained as chancellor with the ÖVP leader, Alois Mock, as vice chancellor. Sinowatz denounced the coalition as a betrayal of socialist principles and resigned as chair of the SPÖ.

In the October 1990 Nationalrat elections the SPÖ held its position as the largest single party but its ÖVP partner lost a quarter of its votes and seats, the FPÖ taking up most of the ÖVP's losses. Vranitzky continued as chancellor with the ÖVP president as his deputy.

In July 1991, in a speech to the Nationalrat, Chancellor Vranitsky acknowledged that many Austrians, including some in prominent positions, had collaborated with the repressive measures and persecutions of Hitler's Third Reich. In August of the same year the European Community formally endorsed Austria's 1989 application for entry and full membership of the European Union (EU) was achieved in January 1995.

In the October 1994 general election rightwing parties made significant gains, the FPÖ increasing its Nationalrat seat tally from 33 to 42, while the SPÖ registered a net loss of 15 seats. The SPÖ-ÖVP, socialist-conservative 'grand coalition', collapsed in October 1995, following budget disagreements and disillusionment with the reality of EU membership, and its strict convergence criteria for monetary union. A general election was held in December 1995, which resulted in little real change.

In 1996 the SPÖ-ÖVP coalition government was reconstructed, under Vranitzky's continuing leadership. In January 1997, after more than ten years as prime minister, Vranitzky stepped down and was replaced as prime minister by Viktor Klima (SPÖ), the finance minister. This followed a poor performance by the SPÖ in elections to the European Parliament in October 1996, in which the FPÖ secured 28% of the vote, the SPÖ 29%, and the ÖVP 30%. The SPÖ polled strongly in regional elections held in March 1999, winning 42% of the vote, to become, for the first time, the dominant party, in Carinthia, the home state of Jorge Haider.

BELGIUM

Kingdom of Belgium
Royaume de Belgique
Koninkrijk België

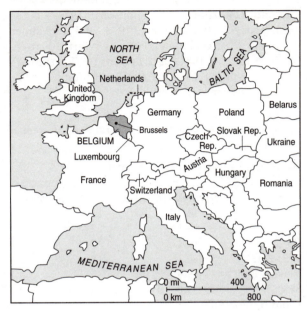

Capital: Brussels

Social and economic data
Area: 30,520 sq km/11,787 sq miles
Population: 10,080,000[*]
Pop. density per sq km/sq mi: 330/916[*]
Urban population: 97%[**]
Literacy rate: 100%[**]
GDP: $250,710 million[*]; per-capita GDP: $24,900[*]
Government defense spending (% of GDP): 1.7%[**]
Currency: Belgian franc
Economy type: high income
Labor force in agriculture: 3%[**]
Unemployment rate: 9.3%[*]
[*] 1995.
[**] 1992.

Head of state
King Albert II, since 1993

Head of government
Prime Minister Guy Verkofstadt, since 1999

Ethnic composition
The northern part of the country, Flanders, consists mainly of Flemings, of Teutonic stock, who speak Flemish (a language almost identical in form to Dutch), while in the south the majority of people are Walloons, of Latin stock, who speak French.

Religions
About 88% of the population is Roman Catholic. There are also about 35,000 Jews and substantial minorities of a number of Protestant denominations, including the Lutheran Church, the Church of England, the United Belgian Protestant Church, the Belgian Evangelical Mission, and the Union of Evangelical Baptist Churches.

Political features
State type: liberal democratic
Date of state formation: 1830
Political structure: federal
Executive: parliamentary
Assembly: two-chamber
Party structure: multiparty
Human rights rating: 96%
International affiliations: AG (observer), BENELUX, BLEU, BOAD, CE, CERN, CSCE, EEA, ESA, EU, G-10, IAEA, IBRD, IMF, NACC, NATO, OECD, UN, WEU, WTO

Local and regional government
Since 1980 Flanders and Wallonia had regional 'sub-governments', each with an elected regional assembly, with certain cultural and economic powers. There was also a separate Walloon Cultural Council. In 1993 the constitution was amended to provide for a federation of three mainly autonomous regions, Brussels, Flanders, and Wallonia, so as to reflect the country's linguistic and cultural diversity. The new constitution moved powers from the Senate to the elected regional assemblies, each of which has a life of five years. In addition, Belgium's four linguistic communities – Flemish, Francophone, Germanophone, and Brussels – have elected community assemblies.

For administrative purposes, the nation is divided into ten provinces which are further subdivided into 589 communes. Local government is conducted by a partnership of officials, appointed by the central government, and elected councillors, representing the views of the localities.

Political system
The constitution dates from 1831 and was subsequently amended a number of times, rewritten in 1971, and further revised in 1993 to create a federation. The parliamentary system contains features found in both

Britain and the United States. For example, the prime minister and cabinet are drawn from and responsible to the assembly, which, in turn, through a powerful committee system, exercises considerable control over the executive.

The assembly consists of two chambers, the Senate, with 71 members, and the Chamber of Representatives, with 150. Forty members of the Senate, whose powers were greatly reduced by the 1993 constitution, are nationally elected, through a party list system of proportional representation, 21 are indirectly elected, and ten coopted by the Flemish and Francophone communities. The Senate has a life of four years. The members of the Chamber of Representatives are elected by universal adult suffrage, through a party list system of proportional representation, also for a four-year term.

The prime minister is appointed by the king on the basis of assembly support. The king then appoints a cabinet on the advice of the prime minister.

Political parties

There are currently more than 20 active political parties, most of them reflecting the linguistic and social divisions within the country. The most significant parties are the Dutch-speaking Social Christian Party (CVP), the French-speaking Social Christian Party (PSC), the Dutch-speaking Socialist Party (SP), the French-speaking Socialist Party (PS), the Flemish Liberals and Democrats (VLD), the French-speaking Liberal Reform Party (PRL), the People's Union (Volksunie), the French-speaking Democratic Front (FDF), and the Flemish Vlaams Blok.

The CVP was founded in 1945. It has a center-left orientation. The PSC was formed at the same time and is the CVP's French-speaking equivalent. Collectively, the two parties now have over 180,000 members.

The SP is the Flemish wing of the Socialist Party and was founded in 1885. The PS is the French-speaking wing, which broke away in 1979. Both wings have left-of-center orientations.

The VLD is the successor to the PVV which was the Flemish wing of the Liberal Party and was formed in 1961, to replace the former Liberal Party. The PRL is the French-speaking wing and dates from 1979. Before that it was known as the Walloon Freedom and Reform Party. Both wings have a moderate centrist orientation.

The Volksunie was founded in 1954 and argues for allowing full scope for the promotion of a Flemish identity.

The Vlaams Blok is a rightwing Flemish nationalist grouping, more extreme than the other Flemish parties Ecolo and Agalev are two ecologist parties.

Political leaders since 1970

1968–72 Gaston Eyskens (CVP coalitions), 1972–74 Edmond Leburton (PSC coalition), 1974–78 Leo Tindemans (CVP coalitions), 1978–79 Paul Vanden Boeynants (PSC coalitions), 1979–81 Wilfried Martens (CVP coalitions), 1981 Mark Eyskens (CVP coalition), 1981–92 Wilfried Martens (CVP coalitions), 1992– Jean-Luc Dehaene (CVP coalition)

Latest elections

The results of the 13 June 1999 general election were as follows:

Belgium latest election results

Party	% votes	Chamber seats	Senate seats
VLD	14.3	23	6
CVP	14.1	22	6
PS	10.1	19	4
PRL-FDF	10.1	18	5
Vlaams Blok	9.9	15	4
SP	9.6	14	4
Ecolo (ecological)	7.3	11	3
Agalov (ecological)	7.0	9	3
Volksunie	5.6	8	2
PSC	5.9	10	3
Others	6.1	1	0

Political history

What is now the modern Kingdom of Belgium has experienced many changes of rule under many different political regimes, from the Romans of pre-Christian times, to the French, then the Spanish, then the Austrians, and then the French again. It formed part of the French Empire between 1794 and 1815, after which it was united with the Netherlands. Linguistic, religious, and historical differences made the marriage an unhappy one and in 1830 the Belgians rebelled. The great powers intervened and Belgium was given international recognition as an independent kingdom, under Leopold I of Saxe-Coburg (1790–1865). From that date the country developed rapidly to become a significant industrial and commercial force.

The experience of two world wars fought on its territory has made Belgium acutely aware of the dangers of the pursuit of purely national ends and since 1945 it has played a major part in international cooperation in Europe, being a founder member of the Benelux

Economic Union, the Council of Europe, and the European Community.

Its main internal political problems have stemmed from the division between French- and Dutch-speaking members of the population, aggravated by the polarization between Flanders in the north, which is predominantly Conservative, and French-speaking Wallonia in the south, which tends to be mainly Socialist. About 55% of the population is Dutch-speaking, 44% French-speaking, and the remainder speaks German. It has been a hereditary monarchy since 1830 and King Leopold III (1901–83), who had reigned since 1934, abdicated in 1951 in favor of his son, Baudouin I (1930–93).

Between 1971 and 1973, in an attempt to close the language and social divisions, amendments to the constitution were made. These involved the transfer of greater power to the regions, the inclusion of German-speaking members in the cabinet and linguistic parity in the government overall. Then, in 1974, separate Regional Councils and Ministerial Committees were established. In 1977 a coalition government, headed by Leo Tindemans (CVP), proposed the creation of a federal Belgium, based on Flanders, Wallonia, and Brussels, but the proposals were not adopted and in 1978 Tindemans resigned. He was followed by another coalition government headed by Wilfried Martens (b. 1936). In 1980 the language conflict developed into open violence and it was eventually agreed that Flanders and Wallonia should have separate regional assemblies with powers to spend up to 10% of the national budget on cultural facilities, public health, roads, and urban projects. Brussels was to be governed by a three-member executive. In 1993 the constitution was amended to provide for this threefold federation, with a reduction in the legislative powers of the Senate and an increase in those of the elected regional assemblies.

Such was the political instability that by 1980 Martens had formed no fewer than four coalition governments. In 1981 a new coalition, led by Mark Eyskens (CVP), lasted less than a year and Martens again returned to power. Between 1981 and 1982 economic difficulties resulted in a series of damaging public sector strikes and in 1983 linguistic divisions again threatened the government.

Martens formed yet another coalition government after the 1985 general election but this broke up in 1987 and the prime minister was asked by the king to continue until after further elections. These were held in December 1987 but failed to produce a conclusive result and, after a series of exploratory talks between political leaders, Martens formed a CVP-PS-SP-PSC-Volksunie coalition in May 1988. After the November 1991 general election, in which 1 million people voted for extremist and anti-political parties, he found it increasingly difficult to hold his coalition together and resigned. He was persuaded to carry on as a caretaker prime minister until, in March 1992, his CVP colleague, Jean-Luc Dehaene (b. 1940), was able to form a viable government.

In 1993 Dehaene, faced with deadlock in the coalition over a decision to reduce the budget deficit, offered his resignation but the king refused to accept it and eventually the dispute was resolved. King Baudouin, who had been a calming figure in the political process, died in July 1993 and was succeeded by his brother, Prince Albert (b. 1934).

A new federal constitution was approved in 1993, and in the general election of May 1995 Dehaene's CVP-PSC-SP-PS coalition held on to power, polling strongly in Flanders. The far-right Vlaams Blok attracted 12% support in Flanders. During 1996–97 the government faced periodic popular protests against its strategy of cutting expenditure in order to qualify for adoption of the European Single Currency in 1999.

In the general election held in June 1999 the parties of the governing coalition were punished by voters for the government's mishandling of a scandal over animal-feed poisoned with dioxins, which led to an EU ban on certain products. With the coalition having lost its majority, Prime Minister Dehaene resigned. In July 1999 Guy Verhofstadt, a Flemish Liberal (VLD), became prime minister, forming a coalition government with the Socialists and, for the first time in Belgium, the Greens, who had polled strongly in the June elections.

DENMARK

Kingdom of Denmark
Kongeriget Danmark

Capital: Copenhagen

Social and economic data
Area: 43,080 sq km/16,633 sq miles
Population: 5,251,000[*]
Pop. density per sq km/sq mi: 122/316[*]
Urban population: 85%[**]

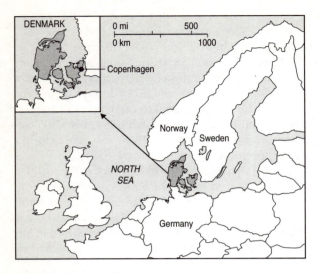

Literacy rate: 99%**

GDP: $156,000 million*; per-capita GDP: $29,700*

Government defense spending (% of GDP): 1.8%*

Currency: Danish krone

Economy type: high income

Labor force in agriculture: 6%**

Unemployment rate: 7.0%

* 1995.

** 1992.

Head of state

Queen Margarethe II, since 1972

Head of government

Prime Minister Poul Nyrup Rasmussen, since 1993

Ethnic composition

The Danes are a branch of the Scandinavian race which embraces the whole peninsula, including Sweden, Norway, and Finland as well as Denmark. Danish is the national language.

Religions

The Danish Lutheran Church is the established church and about 91% of the population belongs to it.

Political features

State type: liberal democratic

Date of state formation: c. 940/1849

Political structure: unitary

Executive: parliamentary

Assembly: one-chamber

Party structure: multiparty

Human rights rating: 98%

International affiliations: AG (observer), CBSS, CE, CERN, EEA, ESA, EU, IAEA, IBRD, IMF, IWC, NACC, NATO, NC, OECD, OSCE, UN, WEU (observer), WTO

Local and regional government

Denmark is divided into 14 counties (*amstkommuner*), varying in population from about 47,000 to nearly 620,000, plus one city and one borough. All have elected councils. At a lower level there are 277 districts, each with an elected council and mayor.

The two autonomous dependencies, the Faroe Islands and Greenland, enjoy home rule, with elected assemblies and executives, as described in Chapter 8. They also elect representatives to the national assembly, the Folketing.

Political system

The 1849 constitution has been revised on several occasions, the last being in 1953. It provides for a hereditary monarch, with no personal political power, and a single-chamber assembly, the Folketing. The prime minister and cabinet are drawn from and collectively responsible to the Folketing, which has 179 members, elected by adult franchise, 175 of the members representing metropolitan Denmark; two, the Faroe Islands and two, Greenland. Voting is by a party list system of proportional representation, with a 2% threshold for parliamentary representation. The Folketing has a life of four years, but may be dissolved within this period if the government is defeated on a vote of confidence. The government, however, need only resign on what it itself defines as a 'vital element' of policy.

Political parties

The proportional representation voting system favors the growth of political parties with distinctively different attitudes and policies. There are currently more than 20, the nine most significant being the Social Democrats (SD), the Conservative People's Party (KF), the Liberal Party (V), the Socialist People's Party (SF), the Radical Liberals (RV), the Center Democrats (CD), the Progress Party (FP), the Christian People's Party (KrF), and the Danish People's Party (DF).

The SD was founded in 1871 on Marxist principles but now has a moderate left-of-center orientation. Its members are drawn mainly from blue-collar workers and public service employees. It supports further European integration.

The KF was formed in 1916 by a mixture of landowners, intellectuals, and academics. It is a moderate, free enterprise party which accepts the need for state intervention to preserve the nation's social and economic balance.

The Venstre or V party is the Liberal Party of

Denmark and was established in 1870. It is a center-right grouping which supports free trade, a well-funded welfare system, but a minimum of state interference in other respects.

The SF was formed in 1959 by Aksel Larsen who had been the leader of the Danish Communist Party but was expelled because he refused to toe the Soviet line. As now constituted, it is a moderate, leftwing party which seeks to apply socialism in a distinctively Danish way.

The RV split from the Liberals in 1905 to pursue more radical policies. It is a strongly internationalist party which favors domestic policies of social reform, worker participation in industrial management, the control of monopolies, and the strengthening of private enterprise.

The CD is a moderate centrist party which was formed in 1973. It opposes extremes in politics and is a strong supporter of EU and NATO membership.

The FP began in 1972 as a strongly anti-bureacratic movement, promoting such radical ideas as the abolition of income tax, the disbanding of the civil service, and a drastic reduction in legislation.

The KrF was founded in 1970 as an interdenominational grouping which places emphasis on family values. It is a strong opponent of abortion and pornography.

The DF is a far-right party formed in 1995 by a breakaway group from the FP. It is strongly opposed to European Union membership and immigration.

Political leaders since 1970

1973–75 Poul Hartling (Liberal), 1975–82 Anker Jörgensen (Social Democrat and coalition), 1982–1993 Poul Schlüter (Conservative coalition), 1993– Poul Nyrup Rasmussen (Social Democrat-led coalition)

Latest elections

The results of the 11 March 1998 Folketing election are set out in the table below. Turnout was 86%.

Denmark latest election results

Party	% votes	Seats
SD*	36.0	63
V	24.0	42
KF	8.9	16
SF*	7.5	13
DF	7.4	13
CD	4.3	8
RV*	3.9	7
FP	2.4	4
KrF	2.4	4
Others	3.2	9

* Members of ruling coalition.

Political history

Part of a United Scandinavian Kingdom until the 15th century and then remaining linked with Norway until 1815, Denmark became an independent state in 1849. The constitution which was then adopted reaffirmed its status as a constitutional monarchy. Neutral in World War I, Denmark tried to preserve its neutrality in 1939 by signing a pact with Adolf Hitler, but was invaded by the Germans in 1940 and occupied until liberated by British forces in 1945.

Although traditionally a neutralist country, Denmark joined NATO in 1949 and the European Free Trade Association (EFTA) in 1960, resigning to join the European Community in 1973. Iceland was part of the Danish kingdom until 1945 and the other parts of non-metropolitan Denmark, the Faroe Islands and Greenland, were given special recognition by a constitution which has been successfully adapted to meet changing circumstances. The last rewriting occurred in 1953 when, among other things, provision was made for a daughter to succeed to the throne in the absence of a male heir, and a system of voting by proportional representation was introduced.

Moderate leftwing policies have tended to dominate Danish politics, and the voting system, often resulting in minority or coalition governments, has, on the whole, encouraged this moderate approach. In 1985 Denmark's tradition of neutrality was exemplified by evidence of a growing non-nuclear movement.

In the 1987 general election the center-right coalition, led by Poul Schlüter (b. 1929), lost seven seats, but Schlüter decided to continue with a minority government, holding 70 of the 179 Folketing seats. A government defeat over Denmark's non-nuclear defense policy prompted him to call a snap general election in May 1988. This resulted in slight gains for his center-right coalition but overall an inconclusive result. The queen asked Schlüter to form a new government, which he did in June 1988, on the basis of Conservative, Liberal, and Radical Liberal support, and the term of his coalition was renewed in the 1990 general election.

In June 1992 the Danish electorate sent shock waves through the European Community when, in a referendum, they declined to ratify the Maastricht Treaty on closer economic and political union by a narrow 49%:51% margin. Following a new referendum in May 1993, when 56.8% voted 'Yes', it was ratified.

In 1993 Prime Minister Schlüter resigned after a judicial inquiry had accused him of failing to reveal the truth about the prevention of Tamil refugees from Sri Lanka entering Denmark and he was replaced by Poul Nyrup Rasmussen (b. 1944), heading an SD-led coalition. Despite losses in the general election in the following year he narrowly retained his position by forming a minority SD-CD-RV coalition government, dependent on the support of leftwing parties. Helped by a buoyant economy, the left-of-center coalition narrowly maintained power after the March 1998 general elections, in which the far-right Danish People's Party (DF) attracted 7% of the vote on an anti-immigration platform. In May 1998 Denmark's voters approved, with a 55% 'Yes' vote, the June 1997 Amsterdam Treaty on increased integration within the European Union (EU).

FINLAND

Republic of Finland
Suomen Tasavalta

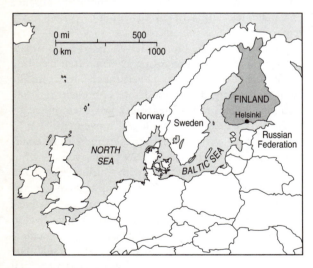

Capital: Helsinki

Social and economic data
Area: 338,139 sq km/130,556 sq miles
Population: 5,095,000[*]
Pop. density per sq km/sq mi: 15/39[*]
Urban population: 60%[**]
Literacy rate: 99%[**]
GDP: $105,200 million[*]; per-capita GDP: $20,650[*]
Government defense spending (% of GDP): 2%[*]
Currency: markka

Economy type: high income
Labor force in agriculture: 9%[**]
Unemployment rate: 17.4%[*]
[*] 1995.
[**] 1992.

Head of state (formal and executive)
President Martti Ahtisaari, since 1994

Head of government
Prime Minister Paavo Lipponen, since 1995

Ethnic composition
The great majority of Finns are descended from the inhabitants of Russia who were pushed northwards by Slav migrations. The majority speak Finnish, with a 6% minority speaking Swedish.

Religions
Ninety per cent of the population belongs to the Evangelical Lutheran Church.

Political features
State type: liberal democratic
Date of state formation: 1917
Political structure: unitary
Executive: dual
Assembly: one-chamber
Party structure: multiparty
Human rights rating: 99%
International affiliations: AG (observer), CBSS, CE, CERN, EEA, ESA (associate), EU, IAEA, IBRD, IMF, IWC, NAM (guest), NC, OECD, OSCE, PFP, UN, WTO

Local and regional government
The country is divided into 12 provinces (*laani*), each administered by an appointed governor. One of the provinces, Ahvenanmaa, which comprises the self-governing Åland Islands (pop. 24,000), also has an elected assembly (*landsting*) and local powers of legislation.

Political system
Under its constitution of 1919, as amended in 1987, Finland is a republic which combines a parliamentary system with a strong presidency. The single-chamber assembly, the Eduskunta, has 200 members, elected by universal adult suffrage, through a party list system of proportional representation, for a four-year term. The president is elected for six years by popular vote, in the first ballot if there is a clear majority, or in a run-off second ballot. The president appoints a prime minister and a cabinet, called a Council of State, all members of which are collectively responsible to the Eduskunta.

The relationship between the president and the prime minister and the Council of State is unusual, the nearest equivalent being in France. The president is entrusted with supreme executive power, and can ignore even a unanimous decision reached in the Council of State, but the prime minister is concerned with the day-to-day operation of the government so that to some extent they can, at times, both act as heads of government. Both the president and the Eduskunta can initiate legislation and the president has a right of veto, but that veto can be overruled by a newly appointed assembly. Because of the system of proportional representation, there is a multiplicity of parties, and the prime minister invariably heads a coalition Council of State.

Political parties

Of some 13 political parties, which contested the last general elections, the most significant are the Finnish Social Democratic Party (SSDP), the National Coalition Party (KOK), The Finnish Center Party (KESK), the Finnish Christian Union (SKL), the Swedish People's Party (SFP), the Finnish Rural Party (SMP), and the Left-Wing Alliance (VL).

The SSDP was founded in 1899 as a product of the growing working class movement. It has a moderate left-of-center orientation. The KOK was formed in 1918. It has a moderate right-of-center stance. The KESK dates from 1906 and is a radical center party, promoting the interests of rural areas and favoring decentralized government.

The SFP was founded in 1906 to represent the numerous Swedes who had become resident in Finland and established themselves as something of an elite group.

The SMP dates from 1956 and seeks to defend the interests of small farmers, industrial workers, and those with small businesses. The Left-Wing Alliance was formed in 1980 by a merger of a number of leftwing parties, including the communists.

Political leaders since 1970

1970 Teuve Aura (cabinet of experts), 1970–71 Ahti Karjalainen (KP-led coalition), 1971–72 Teuve Aura (caretaker cabinet), 1972 Rafael Paasio (SSDP), 1972–75 Kalevi Sorsa (SSDP-led coalition), 1975 Keijo Liinamaa (caretaker cabinet), 1975–77 Martti Miettunen (KP-led coalitions), 1977–79 Kalevi Sorsa (SSDP-led coalition), 1979–82 Mauno Koivisto (SSDP-led coalition), 1982–87 Kalevi Sorsa (SSDP-led coalitions), 1987–91 Harri Holkeri (KOK-led coalition),

1991–95 Esko Aho (KESK-led coalition), 1995– Paavo Lipponen (SSDP-led coalition)

Latest elections

In the 2 March 1999 Eduskunta elections, with a turnout of 68%, the results were as follows:

Finland latest election results

Party	% vote	Seats
SSDP*	22.9	51
KESK*	22.4	48
KOK*	21.0	46
VL*	10.9	20
Greens*	7.3	11
SFP*	5.1	11
Others	10.4	13

* Members of ruling coalition

In the February 1994 presidential elections Martti Ahtisaari (SSDP) won 53.9% of the votes, his rival, Elisabeth Rehn (SFP), obtaining 46.1%.

Political history

Finland was formerly an autonomous part of the Russian Empire and during the 1917 Russian revolution it proclaimed its independence. The new Soviet regime initially tried to regain control but acknowledged its independence in 1920. In 1939 the Soviet Union's request for military bases in Finland was rejected and the two countries were involved in the 'Winter War', which lasted for 15 weeks. Finland was defeated and forced to cede territory. In the hope of getting it back, it joined Nazi Germany in attacking the Soviet Union in 1941 but agreed a separate armistice in 1944. It was again forced to cede territory and in 1948 signed the Finno-Soviet Pact of Friendship, Cooperation and Mutual Assistance (the YYA Treaty). This was extended in 1955, 1970, and 1983.

Although the Treaty requires it to repel any attack on the USSR through Finnish territory by Germany or its allies, Finland has adopted and maintained a policy of strict neutrality. It signed a trade treaty with the EEC in 1973 and a 15-year trade agreement with the USSR in 1977.

Finnish politics have been characterized by instability in governments, more than 60 having been formed since independence, including many minority coalitions. The presidency, on the other hand, has been very stable, with only two presidents in over 30 years. The unusual device of a dual executive has, therefore, countered the instability and provided a consistency which might otherwise have been lacking. The Social Democratic and Center parties have dominated Finland's coalition politics for many years but the 1987 general election resulted in the Social Democrats (SSDP) entering government with their arch enemies, the Conservatives, and the Center Party being forced into opposition. The Center Party returned to power, however, in 1991 at the head of the country's first wholly nonsocialist coalition. It held power during a particularly severe economic recession, between 1990 and 1993, which sent unemployment up to 20%. In 1994 the political balance was restored when the SSDP won the presidency through their candidate, Martti Ahtisaari (b. 1937) and in the following year the party returned to power under its leader, Paavo Lipponen, after the general election of March 1995. He headed a five-party coalition which included all the main parties except the Center Party.

In recent years Finland has gradually relaxed its policy of strict neutrality, being admitted to the Council of Europe in 1989 and entering EU membership in 1995. The Lipponen government has pursued an austerity policy with the aim of securing entry into the European Single Currency in 1999. The markka joined the European Exchange Rate Mechanism (ERM) in August 1996.

In the March 1999 general election support for the SSDP fell back by 5% compared to 1995. However, it remained the largest single party, enabling Prime Minister Lipponen to narrowly survive in power, heading a five-party centre-left coalition. The new government agreed not to increase public spending in real terms over the four-year life span of the new legislature.

FRANCE

The French Republic
La République Française

Capital: Paris

Social and economic data
Area: 543,965 sq km/210,026 sq miles
Population: 57,747,000*
Pop. density per sq km/sq mi: 100/275*
Urban population: 74%**
Literacy rate: 99%**
GDP: $1,451,000 million*; per-capita GDP:$25,100*

Government defense spending (% of GDP): 3.1%**
Currency: French franc
Economy type: high income
Labor force in agriculture: 6%**
Unemployment rate: 11.6%
* 1995.
** 1992.

Head of state
President Jacques Chirac, since 1995

Head of government
Prime Minister Lionel Jospin, since 1997

Ethnic composition
The population is overwhelmingly drawn from French ethnic stock, of Celtic and Latin origins, with a Basque minority residing in the southwest. There are, in addition, more than 4 million immigrants, constituting 7% of the population. A third of these are drawn from Algeria and Morocco in Muslim North Africa and reside mainly in the Marseilles Midi region and in northern cities. A further fifth originate from Portugal and a tenth each from Italy and Spain. French is the principal language, although small minorities speak Breton, Basque, and Occitan (the ancient language of Languedoc, in the south).

Religions
More than 80% of the population describe themselves as Roman Catholics, although barely 15% are regular church attenders. There are substantial Muslim (2.5

million; 30% residing in Marseilles), Protestant (850,000), and Jewish minorities.

Political features

State type: liberal democratic
Date of state formation: AD 741
Political structure: unitary
Executive: dual
Assembly: two-chamber
Party structure: two-party[*]
Human rights rating: 94%
International affiliations: AG (observer), BDEAC, BOAD, CERN, CE, EEA, ESA, EU, Francophone, FZ, G-5, G-7, G-10, IAEA, IBRD, IMF, IOC, IWC, NACC, NATO, OECD, OSCE, PC, UN Security Council (permanent member), WEU, WTO

[*] Two party blocs.

Local and regional government

There are 22 regional councils (*conseils régionaux*), concerned primarily with economic planning, which were originally set up in 1973 as indirectly elected advisory bodies and have since 1986 been directly elected. Below these are 96 metropolitan department (large county) councils (*conseils généraux*) and 36,673 village and town councils, or communes, to which two ballot-council and mayoral elections are held every six years. Benefiting from recent decentralization initiatives, local mayors now control housing, transport, sport, schools, culture, welfare, and some aspects of law enforcement, and have some tax-raising powers. Many national-level French politicians are members of regional councils or mayors in their home areas, for example Prime Minister Alain Juppé is mayor of Bordeaux and former prime minister, Raymond Barre, is mayor of Lyon. However, since 1985, parliamentarians have been restricted to holding a maximum of two elected offices. Corsica, which was designated a *collectivité territoriale* in 1982, has its own directly elected legislative assembly, which has the authority to scrutinize National Assembly bills and to propose amendments applicable to the island. This is described in more detail in Chapter 8.

Political system

Under the October 1958 Fifth Republic constitution, the nation's 17th since 1789, France has a two-chamber parliament (parlement) and a 'dual' or shared executive. The parliament comprises the National Assembly (Assemblée Nationale) and the Senate (Sénat). The 577 members of the National Assembly are elected for a five-year term, subject to dissolution during this period, from single-member constituencies on the basis of a two-ballot 'run-off' absolute majority voting system. The 321 members of the Senate are indirectly elected, a third at a time, triennially, for nine-year terms by an electoral college composed of local National Assembly members, mayors, department council members, and delegates from municipal councils. Twenty-two National Assembly and 13 Senate seats are elected by overseas departments and territories, and 12 Senate seats by French nationals abroad.

For the March 1986 National Assembly elections, a party list system of proportional representation was employed, based on department level multimember constituencies. Within months of this contest, however, the new Chirac administration restored the traditional two-ballot 'run-off' system employed since 1958. Under this system, it is possible for candidates to be elected on the first ballot if they secure an absolute majority of the votes cast and at least one-quarter of the registered votes. Otherwise, a second poll is held a week later in which all the candidates who secured at least 12.5% of the total first ballot 'primary' vote are entitled to participate, and which is decided on a relative majority or simple plurality basis. In practice, left- and right-coalition party pacts are invariably entered into locally for this second ballot, with low polling first-ballot candidates agreeing to stand down, turning the follow-up ballot into a head-to-head duel between two contestants. Three-quarters of National Assembly seats are, in general, decided on the second ballot.

The National Assembly, whose work is conducted through six large, 61- and 121-member, functional standing committees, is the more dominant of the two chambers. It examines the annual budget first; the prime minister is drawn from its ranks; while, most importantly, its members are in a position to overthrow the government on a censure or confidence motion.

The Senate, whose membership, as a consequence of its electoral base, is skewed towards centrist- and independent-minded rural and small town representatives, acts as a partial, and sometimes salutary, check. It has the authority to temporarily veto legislation passed by the National Assembly and force amendments in specially convened 'joint conciliation conferences'. Senate vetoes can, however, be overridden by a 'definitive vote' in the National Assembly.

In comparative terms, the most striking feature of the French parliament is its restricted powers vis-à-vis the political executive. Under the terms of Article 34 of the 1958 constitution, it may only pass laws in a 'restricted domain', incorporating areas such as taxation, civic rights, electoral laws, nationalization, and penal matters, and may only lay down general guidelines or 'principles' in the areas of education, labor law, national defense organization, local government, and social security. In other policy spheres, the government, is empowered to legislate by executive decree. Even within areas inside its own domain, parliament may occasionally, for a specified period, delegate authority to the executive branch to rule by ordinances, countersigned by the president.

In addition, the French parliament is given, by Article 47, only 70 days to debate and vote on the annual budget. Once this period has elapsed, the government is permitted to impose the measure by ordinance. For other bills, the executive can employ 'guillotine' procedures, pledging its 'responsibility'. The bill then automatically proceeds if no opposition vote of censure is called and successfully passed within 24 hours. The executive can also insist on a single vote on the full text (*vote bloqué*) without accepting any floor amendments.

Finally, the parliamentary year was traditionally restricted, under the terms of Article 28, to a maximum length of only 170 days, distributed in two sessions between October–December and April–June. Outside this period the government was empowered to rule by decree. However, in August 1995 the constitution was amended to provide for an unbroken nine-month parliamentary session between October and June, with ministers being required to answer parliamentary questions once a week.

These restrictions on parliamentary authority were deliberately imposed by the framers of the 1958 constitution in an effort to strengthen the executive branch which had been notoriously weak during the Assembly-dominated Third (1870–1940) and Fourth (1946–58) Republics. In this purpose they have succeeded, though, in the process, the balance has, arguably, been shifted too greatly in the executive's favor. The newly elected President Chirac has redressed the balance somewhat, by extending the parliamentary session.

The authority of France's powerful executive is shared between the two figures of president and prime minister. The president is directly elected for a seven-year term by universal adult suffrage, candidates being required to gain an absolute poll majority either in a first ballot, open to a range of challengers, or in a second 'run-off' contest held a fortnight later between the two top-placed candidates who wish to participate again.

Once elected, the president combines the formal posts of head of state and commander in chief of the armed forces and assumes, by virtue of Article 5, the role of umpire, or 'guardian', of the constitution. The formal powers of the president are extensive, embracing the right to select the prime minister; preside over meetings of the Council of Ministers, or cabinet; countersign government bills; negotiate foreign treaties; initiate referenda; and dissolve the National Assembly and call fresh elections, subject to the qualification that only one dissolution is permitted per year.

According to the terms of Articles 20 and 21 of the 1958 constitution, ultimate control over policy-making, at least in the domestic field, seemed to have been assigned to the prime minister and Council of Ministers. The constitutional amendment of October 1962, which provided for the direct election of the president, to replace the previous arrangement of indirect election by a 'college' of members of parliament and department and municipal councillors, radically changed the executive power balance, enhancing the president's authority, since he or she was the sole nationally elected figure in the Republic. As a consequence, between 1958 and 1986 the president was seen as the 'legitimate' leader of the incumbent governing coalition. He or she was served by an extensive and influential 'Elysée office' and was able to assert dominance over the broad outlines of both domestic and external policy, the prime minister being assigned to the lowlier role of 'parliamentary manager', government organizer, and detailed policy implementer.

In March 1986, when the opposition coalition managed to secure a National Assembly majority and force President Mitterrand to appoint its leader, Jacques Chirac, as prime minister, this power balance was temporarily reordered. The new prime minister proceeded, between 1986 and 1988, to establish himself, in the domestic sphere at least, as the dominant executive force, leaving to the president a narrower figurehead, or symbolic, role. Fresh presidential and assembly elections in May and June 1988 brought to an end this party political executive split, but there was a new period of 'cohabitation' between March 1993 and May 1995, with Edouard Balladur as prime minister after the 'right coalition' secured a crushing victory in National Assembly elections. Since June 1997 there has been cohabitation between a socialist-party (PS) prime minister and a right-coalition president.

The cabinet ministers serving the president and prime minister are unusual in that they are drawn from both political and technocratic backgrounds and, as a consequence of the 'incompatibility' clause (Article 23) built into the 1958 constitution, are unable to hold parliamentary seats during their period in government. For this reason, National Assembly candidates are required to designate a running mate (*suppléant*) to assume their positions as deputies if they are appointed as government ministers or Constitutional Council members, or if they are elected to the Senate or Constitutional Council, or if they die. These *suppléants* are expected to stand down if a minister later resigns or is dismissed.

In some respects, the French ministerial cabinet is thus closer to the American 'specialist presidential' than the British parliamentary 'collective executive' model. French ministers do, however, participate in and lead National Assembly debates in their relevant areas, appear before standing committees, and are subject to written and oral questioning by Assembly members. Cabinet ministers also work closely with an unusually skilled and influential civil service, being served, themselves, by small, high-powered advisory 'cabinets'.

The 1958 constitution can be amended by parliament by means of a 60% majority vote in both chambers. Alternatively, under the terms of Article 11, the president is allowed, theoretically at the request of the government or parliament, to call a national referendum on constitutional change, as well as in connection with treaty ratification. Since 1961 there have been eight such referenda. The most recent, which concerned ratification of the Maastricht Treaty on European Union, was held on 20 September 1992. Turnout was 70%, with 51% of voters approving ratification of the Treaty. In August 1995 Article 11 was amended to enable the president to call referenda on a wider range of subjects, including economic and social policy and the public services. As a safeguard, when a referendum is called by the president, parliament is entitled to debate the issue.

Functioning as a judicial 'watchdog', there is a nine-member Constitutional Council (CC), whose task is to ensure that decrees and legislation proposed by the government and parliament conform to the precepts of the constitution and that a correct 'balance' is maintained between the executive and the legislature. Its members, who serve nonrenewable nine-year terms, are chosen, three at a time, at triennial intervals, a third by the president of the Republic, another third by the president of the Senate and a final third by the president of the National Assembly. Roland Dumas, for-

merly a PS foreign minister between 1984 and 1986 and between 1988 and 1993, became president of the Council in March 1995.

The Conseil d'Etat (CE), staffed by senior civil servants, is an additional, and older, judicial review body, which gives nonbinding advice on the constitutionality of bills introduced and serves as a final court of appeal in disputes between the citizen and the administration. Compared with the American Supreme Court or the German Federal Constitutional Court, both the CC and CE are bodies of restricted authority. Since 1974, however, when it was made possible for groups of 60 senators or Assembly members to send bills direct to the Constitutional Council for binding constitutional vetting, its influence has increased significantly. For example, in January 1994 the CC annulled the Balladur administration's attempted reform of the 1850 Loi Falloux, concerned with state and private education funding.

The constitution may be amended in two ways: by the National Assembly and Senate meeting in joint session as a Congress, with the proposed change receiving at least 60% support; or by the amendment bill being passed in identical form separately by the National Assembly and Senate and then approved by the public in a referendum. The constitutional reforms of August 1995 were secured by the former route, attracting 79% support within the constitutional Congress.

The French Republic also comprises four constituent 'overseas departments', French Guiana, Guadeloupe, Martinique, and Réunion, each of which has its own elected general and regional council; two overseas 'collective territories', Mayotte and St Pierre and Miquelon, which are administered by appointed commissioners assisted by elected general councils; and four 'overseas territories', French Polynesia, the French Southern and Antarctic Territories, New Caledonia, and the Wallis and Futuna Islands, which are governed by appointed high commissioners working with elected territorial assemblies. These territories, whose political structures are described more fully in Chapter 8, send members, as has already been noted, to the Republic's parliament.

Political parties

Contemporary French politics are dominated by three major and two minor political parties. On occasions, impelled by the country's pact-inducing two-ballot electoral process, these parties informally group themselves into two broader-based 'left' and 'right' coalitions, which are based around an ideological divide whose roots can be traced back to the French Revolution.

The dominant force on the left is the Socialist Party (Parti Socialiste: PS). The PS, though dating back ideologically to the Radical Republicans of the 19th century, was originally formed as a unified force in 1905 by Jean Jaurès (1859–1914). Later, at the December 1920 Tours congress, it split, the leftwing majority breaking away to form the French Communist Party (Parti Communiste Français: PCF), and leaving behind a moderate socialist rump under the banner Section Française de l'Internationale Ouvrière (SFIO) and led by Léon Blum (1872–1950).

The Socialists remained dwarfed by the PCF until the 1970s, but participated in a number of Third and Fourth Republic coalition governments and built up a solid local government base. The party's fortunes rapidly advanced from 1969, when the SFIO was radically remodelled. It adopted the designation PS and absorbed several smaller left and center-left groupings, while accepting a new electoral strategy based upon a tactical alliance with the PCF, the 'Union of the Left', which was established in 1972. The motive force behind these changes was François Mitterrand, a shrewd former wartime Resistance leader and postwar center-left National Assembly member, who eventually brought the PS into power in 1981, establishing in the process the party's clear ascendancy over the outmanoeuvred, fading PCF.

Currently, the PS, led since June 1995 by Lionel Jospin, has a membership of 109,000 and a national support rating of around 20–25%. Much of this support is drawn from blue- and white-collar workers, particularly those in the public sector. For example, a high proportion of its National Assembly members are ex-teachers or lecturers. Regionally, it polls strongest in the industrialized Central-Nord and Paris outer suburbs, as well as in the poor, small farmer areas of the southeast and southwest. The PS also enjoys the backing of the influential 700,000-member Confédération Française Démocratique du Travail (CFDT) labor union, which is led by Nicole Notat.

Within the party there are a number of ideological- and personality-based factions. These include groupings led by Lionel Jospin, on the center-left, and by former prime ministers, Laurent Fabius and Michel Rocard, on the social democratic rightwing. The left-wing former defense minister, Jean-Pierre Chevènement, also headed the 'Socialism and Realism' faction, until his resignation from the PS in April 1993 to set up the Citizens' Movement (SMPL), which opposes greater European integration. When President Mitterrand was in power, a dominant 'Mitterrandiste current' received support from both Jospin and Fabius, thus bridging the divide. Each faction enjoys representation on the party's ruling Executive Committee and National Secretariat through an internal system of proportional representation.

Closely allied to the PS is the Radical Socialist Party (PRS), known before 1996 as the Left Radical Movement (Mouvement des Radicaux de Gauche. MRG), a party which was founded in 1973 as a breakaway from the center-left Radical Party.

Further to the left is the PCF, a party which participated in a government coalition with the PS between 1981 and 1984. The PCF, although secure in the support of the powerful 640,000-member Confédération Générale du Travail (CGT) labor union and with local government bases in the 'red belt' inner suburbs around Paris, has been a declining electoral force since the mid-1970s, its share of the national vote having been more than halved to around 10%. The party's traditionally close ties with Moscow and fossilized ideological outlook have been prime alienating factors. Led between 1972 and 1994 by Georges Marchais (1920–97) and since January 1994 by National Secretary Robert Hue (b. 1946), a protégé of Marchais, the PCF's membership has fallen greatly from its late 1980s level of 450,000. The party was organized, until the early 1990s, on hierarchical 'democratic-centralist' lines and controlled from above by a 15–20-member Politburo. In 1987–88 the PCF was weakened by its expulsion of a small modernizing 'renovator' faction led by Pierre Juquin, who subsequently stood as an Independent Communist candidate in the April 1988 presidential election. Another leading reformer, Charles Fiterman, lost his National Assembly seat in the March 1993 general election.

On the right of the political spectrum, French party politics have become unusually fractionalized during recent years. The coalition which monopolized central power between 1958 and 1981 showed increasing signs of strain between 1988 and 1991, yet dominated national and local elections until 1997. The most influential party in the 'right coalition' is the Rally for the Republic (Rassemblement pour la République: RPR), which was formed in December 1976 by Jacques Chirac as a successor to the Union of Democrats for the Republic (UDR). The UDR, which was founded in 1968, is itself a successor to the Union for a New Republic (UNR), established by Charles de Gaulle in 1958. Neo-Gaullist in general policy outlook, the RPR, though showing signs of mellowing, favors a nationalistic approach in foreign policy matters and, domestically, a firm law and order program. In the economic sphere, however, the contemporary RPR has flirted with a 'new conservative' freer market and deregulationary strategy which differs substantially from the state interventionist and protectionist program favored by its UNR and UDR precursors. The RPR claims a membership of 150,000 and currently is supported by 15–20% of the electorate. Middle-class business and small shopkeeping groups, Catholic churchgoers, the elderly, and the rural areas of northern, western, and central France constitute core categories and bases of party support. Its president, until April 1999, was Philippe Séguin, a 'social Gaullist' who favors government intervention and who originally opposed the 1990 Maastricht Treaty. The deputy leader, Charles Pasqua, the former interior minister, heads an anti-European and anti-immigration rightwing faction, while Alain Juppé, the party's leader until June 1997, promoted moderate, pro-European center-right Gaullism. On Séguin's sudden resignation as party leader, in April 1999, Nicolas Sakorzy became interim president, but resigned within two months.

Challenging the RPR as the principal political force on the right is the Union for French Democracy (Union pour la Démocratie Française: UDF), an organization which was formed by President Valéry Giscard d'Estaing, Prime Minister Raymond Barre, and Jean Lecanuet in February 1978 to bring together the smaller parties of the center-right into an effective electoral alliance. Today, the UDF still remains an umbrella coalition rather than a formal political party, embracing an extensive range of opinions. In general, however, the policy outlook of UDF members is more liberal in the domestic and social policy spheres and more internationalist and pro-European in the external policy sphere than the RPR.

Within the UDF, which has been chaired by François Bayrou since September 1998, there are four main leader-orientated parties: the Democratic Force (FD), known before 1995 as the Center of Social Democrats (CDS; estd. 1976) and led by Bayrou; the Social Democratic Party (Parti Social-Démocrate: PSD), which was formed in 1973 and is led by Max Lejeune; the Radical Party (Parti Radical), which dates back to 1901 and was a dominant force during the Third and Fourth Republics and is now led by Thierry Cornillet; and the Popular Party for French Democracy (PPDF), formed in 1965 and led by Hervé de Charette, a former foreign minister. The Republican Party (RP), which was

founded under the designation 'Independent Republicans' in 1962 by Giscard d'Estaing, used to be part of the UDF. It changed its name to the RP in 1977 and to Liberal Democracy in June 1997, when Alain Madelin became leader. In May 1998 it withdrew from the UDF, but agreed to continue to work informally with the RPR and UDF in an electoral pact called 'The Alliance'. It is a strongly free-market and pro-European integration body. A few Liberal Democrats, led by Alain Lamassoure, decided to remain within the UDF, as the 'Republican Independent and Liberal Group'.

In April 1998 Charles Millon, a former defense minister, was expelled from the UDF for defying a leadership diktat that local parties should not accept FN support to secure regional government presidencies. He set up a new breakaway right-of-center party, known as 'The Right' which, although officially pro-European, attracts many anti-Maastrict and anti-immigrant voters. On the far right of the political spectrum, the National Front (Front National: FN), which was established in 1972 by the demagogic former paratrooper Jean-Marie Le Pen, has risen to national prominence since the early 1980s through its promotion of a crude racist and extremist program, founded on the twin planks of immigrant repatriation and the restoration of capital punishment. The FN has been excluded, with partial local exceptions, from electoral coalitions with the parties of the 'conventional right'. Despite this, it has managed to secure around 10–15% of the popular vote in national contests since the mid-1990s, polling particularly strongly in the Marseilles region. In 1998 Le Pen was banned from holding public office for one year, after assaulting a PS candidate during the 1997 general election. The party split in January 1999 when a breakaway National Front Notional Movement was formed by Bruno Megret, the former FN deputy leader Megret, who wanted to modernise the FN and who opposed Le Pens inflammatory leadership style, had been expelled from the FN in December 1998.

There are more than 30 other minor national and regional parties currently operating. These include the anti-Maastricht Treaty rightwing Movement for France, formed in November 1994 by the former UDF member, Philippe de Villiers; the state interventionist 'orthodox Gaullist' Movement of Democrats, which was established in 1974 by Michel Jobert; the far-left Revolutionary Communist League (LCR), which was formed in 1974 and is led by Alain Krivine; the Workers' Struggle Party (Lutte Ouvrière: LO), a Trotskyist party dating from 1968 and led by Arlette

Laguiller; the leftist Alternative Red and Green (AREV), formed in 1993 to replace the Unified Socialist Party (PSU; estd. 1960); the fundamentalist-ecologist Greens (Les Verts), which was established in 1984 and is led by Dominique Voynet; and the more pragmatic Génération Ecologie (estd. 1990), led by Brice Lalonde.

Since 1988 the financing of French political parties has been subject to regulation, with state subventions being introduced and upper spending limits imposed on parliamentary and presidential campaigns.

Political leaders since 1970
Presidents: 1969–74 Georges Pompidou (UDR), 1974–81 Valéry Giscard d'Estaing (RP/UDF), 1981–95 François Mitterrand (PS), 1995– Jacques Chirac (RPR)
Prime ministers: 1969–72 Jacques Chaban-Delmas (UDR), 1972–74 Pierre Messmer (UDR), 1974–76 Jacques Chirac (UDR), 1976–1981 Raymond Barre (UDF), 1981–84 Pierre Mauroy (PS), 1984–86 Laurent Fabius (PS), 1986–88 Jacques Chirac (RPR)*, 1988–91 Michel Rocard (PS), 1991–92 Edith Cresson (PS), 1992–93 Pierre Bérégovoy (PS), 1993–95 Edouard Balladur (RPR)*, 1995–97 Alain Juppé (RPR), 1997– Lionel Jospin (PS)**

* Shared power with the socialist President Mitterrand in a 'cohabitation' dual-executive administration.
** Shared power with President Chirac.

Latest elections
In the most recent presidential election, which was held in April–May 1995, Jacques Chirac (RPR) was elected on the second ballot, held on 7 May 1995, securing 52.6% of the popular vote compared to Lionel Jospin's (PS) 47.4%. In the first round of voting, held on 23 April, nine candidates participated. The results were: Jospin (PS), with a 23% vote share; Chirac (RPR), 21%; Edouard Balladur (RPR), 19%; Jean-Marie Le Pen (FN), 15%; Robert Hue (PCF), 9%; Arlette Laguiller (Trotskyist), 5%; Philippe de Villiers (Movement for France), 5%; Dominique Voynet (Greens), 3%; and Jacques Cheminade (New Solidarity Federation), 0.3%. Turnout was 78% in the first round and 80% in the second. Chirac's first-round vote share was the lowest achieved by any successful candidate since direct presidential elections began in 1965. In the second round a record 6% of ballot papers were left blank, so, in fact, Chirac won only 49.5% of the votes cast, making him the first president ever to be elected with less than half the total poll.

National Assembly elections were last held, in two rounds, on 25 May and 1 June 1997. The vote shares and seats won by each of the parties are set out below.

France latest election results

Party	% of first ballot vote	% of second ballot vote	Seats
PS	23.5	38.0	241
RPR	15.7	22.8	134
FN	14.9	5.6	1
UDF	14.2	20.8	108
PCF	10.0	3.8	38
PRS	1.5	2.2	12
Ecologist candidates	6.8	1.6	7
Other rightwing candidates	6.7	2.5	14
Other leftwing candidates	5.3	2.6	21
Others	1.4	0.1	1
Total	100.0	100.0	577

The PS, along with its PRS and other leftwing candidate allies, polled strongly. They attracted 43% of the second-round vote (up 12% on March 1993) and won 274 of the 577 seats. In contrast, the RPR and UDF, along with rightwing candidate allies, secured 46% of the second-round vote (down 12%) and 256 seats. The PCF, which won 10% of the first-round vote (up 1% on 1993), ended up with 38 seats (up 15), whereas the 'pariah party', the FN, despite securing 15% of the first-round vote (up 3%), its best ever result, won only one seat (up one). Support for ecologist candidates, at 7% of the vote, was slightly down on 1993. Turnout was 68% in the first-round and 71% in the second-round.

In mid-1995 the RPR-UDF 'right coalition' also controlled two-thirds of the seats in the Senate, 20 of the country's 22 regional councils, and four-fifths of departmental councils. A complex system of weighted proportional election is used in municipal elections, with half the seats automatically going to the party that secures an absolute majority in the first round of voting or tops the poll in the second-round run-off contest. The remaining seats are then divided proportionately among parties which secure at least 10% of the vote.

Political history

1. 741–1981
A united French state was first constituted in AD 741 by King Pepin (c. 715–768), founder of the Frankish Carolingian dynasty, whose successor, Charlemagne (747–814), established a pan-European empire. Authority was thereafter decentralized until the founding of the Paris-centerd Capetian dynasty (987–1328),

whose branches, the Valois (1328–1589) and Bourbon (1589–1792), ruled France for eight centuries. Under the Bourbon, King Louis XIV (1638–1715), who reigned from 1643 to 1715, a centralized absolutist state was established, served by a well organized bureaucracy. This monarchical ancient régime was overthrown during the early stages of the French Revolution (1789–99), with a Republic being declared in 1792 and parliamentary democracy established.

Later, following a coup in 1799, this system gave way to the military dictatorship of Napoléon Bonaparte (1769–1821), who was proclaimed Emperor of the French in 1804, inaugurating the 'First Empire' (1804–14). A new pan-European empire was temporarily carved out, before military defeats between 1812 and 1814 forced Napoléon's abdication and the restoration, under Louis XVIII (ruled 1814–24), Charles X (ruled 1824–30), and the 'citizen king' Louis-Philippe (ruled 1830–48), of the Bourbon dynasty.

Attempts to increase the monarch's powers were checked by revolutions in 1830 and 1848, the latter resulting in the Crown's overthrow and the establishment of the Second Republic in 1848. This was brought to an end in 1852 when the Republic's president, Louis Napoléon (1808–73), the nephew of Napoléon Bonaparte, re-established an expansionary system of plebiscitary autocracy, designated the Second Empire. Following his defeat in the Franco-Prussian War (1870–71), Louis Napoléon was ousted and a liberal parliamentary democracy, based on universal manhood suffrage, the Third Republic (1870–1940), was established. This Republic, riven by conflicts between the clerical and militarist right and the radical and socialist left, was characterized by government instability, with more than 100 different administrations during its life. Despite these strains and inner tensions, the Third Republic's political structure survived, remaining intact until the invasion, defeat, and occupation by German forces during the early stages of World War II.

During the war a collaborationist puppet government, the 'Vichy regime', headed by the veteran military leader, Marshal Henri Pétain (1856–1951), was established, with Nazi German backing, but was opposed by the underground maquis and UK-based Free French resistance organization, led by General Charles de Gaulle (1890–1970). With Allied support, France was liberated in August 1944 and a 'united front' provisional government, headed by de Gaulle, and including communists, was installed, while a new constitution was being framed. This interim administration was successful in restoring a sense of national unity. It also introduced a far-reaching series of pragmatic social and economic reforms, including the nationalization of strategic enterprises, the extension of the franchise to women, and the creation of a comprehensive social security system.

In January 1946 a new constitution was adopted, proclaiming the establishment of a Fourth Republic and providing for a weak political executive and powerful parliament, the National Assembly, which was to be elected under a generous system of proportional representation. De Gaulle, who had favored a strong presidentialist system, immediately resigned as interim president and set up, in 1947, a populist political movement of his own, the Rally for French People (RPF), which briefly rose to prominence before fading and being disbanded in 1953.

With numerous small party groupings achieving Assembly representation, political activity in the new Fourth Republic was characterized by intense factional bargaining and renewed executive instability: 26 different governments held power between 1946 and 1958. In these circumstances, effective executive authority passed into the hands of the French civil service, which, by introducing a new system of 'indicative economic planning', engineered rapid economic reconstruction. Decolonization in French Indochina in 1954 and Morocco and Tunisia in 1956, and entry into the European Economic Community (EEC) in 1957, were also achieved.

The Fourth Republic eventually collapsed in 1958 as a result of a political and military crisis over Algerian independence, which threatened to lead to a French army revolt. De Gaulle was called back from retirement in May 1958 to head a government of national unity. He proceeded to oversee the framing of a constitution for the new Fifth Republic which considerably strengthened the executive, in the shape of a president and prime minister. De Gaulle, who became president in January 1959, restored domestic stability and presided over the decolonization of Francophone Africa, including the granting of independence to Algeria in April 1962. Close economic links were maintained, however, with France's former colonies. He also initiated a new independent foreign policy, withdrawing France from the integrated military command structure of the North Atlantic Treaty Organization (NATO) in 1966 and developing an autonomous nuclear deterrent force, the *force de frappe*.

The de Gaulle era was one of rapid economic

growth, per-capita GDP almost doubling between 1960 and 1970, and socio-economic change, involving large-scale rural–urban migration and occupational transformation. Politically, however, it was a period characterized by a strong centralization of power and tight media censorship. In March 1967 the public reacted against this paternalism by voting the 'right coalition' a reduced National Assembly majority. A year later, in May 1968, major student and workers' demonstrations, termed the 'May Events', in Paris, which spread to the provinces, paralysed the nation and briefly threatened the government's continued existence. De Gaulle, responded by calling fresh National Assembly elections in June 1968 in which, fighting on a law and order platform, his Union of Democrats for the Republic (UDR) secured a landslide victory. Ten months later, however, in April 1969, de Gaulle was defeated in a referendum over proposals for Senate and local government reform. He resigned the presidency and retired from political affairs at the age of 79.

The man who had been de Gaulle's prime minister between 1962 and 1968, Georges Pompidou (1911–74), was elected as the new president in June 1969 and continued to pursue Gaullist policies until his death in April 1974.

Pompidou's successor as president was Valéry Giscard d'Estaing (b. 1926), leader of the center-right Independent Republicans. He attempted to set the country on a new, modernist course, introducing liberalizing reforms in the social sphere and establishing a more cooperative and activist role within the European Community (EC). His policies were undermined, however, by the internal wranglings of his ambitious 'right coalition' partner, Jacques Chirac (b. 1932), who served as prime minister between 1974 and 1976, before leaving to set up a new neo-Gaullist party, the Rally for the Republic (RPR). The government was also operating in the context of deteriorating external economic conditions.

Nevertheless, France performed better than many of its European competitors between 1974 and 1981, with the president launching a major nuclear power program to save on energy imports and a new prime minister, in the person of the former Sorbonne monetarist professor, Raymond Barre (b. 1924), following a new liberal 'freer market' economic strategy. However, with unemployment standing at 1.7 million on polling day, Giscard was defeated in the presidential election of May 1981 by the experienced Socialist Party (PS) leader, François Mitterrand (1916–1996), a former network commander in the French Resistance and an unsuccessful challenger for the presidency in 1965 and 1974.

2. 1981–1993

Mitterrand's victory, which constituted the first presidential success for the 'left coalition' during the Fifth Republic, was immediately succeeded by a landslide victory for the PS and its Communist Party (PCF) and Left Radical Movement (MRG) allies in the elections to the National Assembly which were held in June 1981. The new government, which was headed by the socialist-traditionalist former mayor of Lille, Pierre Mauroy (b. 1928), as prime minister, and included in its ranks four PCF ministers, set about implementing a radical and ambitious policy of social reform and political decentralization, with the aim of fundamentally transforming the character of French society. In the economic sphere, a program of industrial and financial nationalization and enhanced state investment and formal planning was instituted, while a series of reflationary budgets attempted to curb unemployment. In March 1983, however, financial constraints, during a period of deepening world recession, forced a switch towards a more conservative fiscal strategy of austerity, *le rigueur*. This U-turn in economic policy was completed in July 1984 when Mauroy was replaced as prime minister by the young social democratic technocrat, Laurent Fabius (b. 1946), a move which prompted the resignation from the government of the PCF's four cabinet ministers.

During 1985 and 1986, with a tightening of the fiscal screw, unemployment rose sharply to more than 2.5 million and, as a consequence, racial tensions and workers' unrest increased in urban areas. The extreme rightwing National Front (FN), led by Jean-Marie Le Pen (b. 1928), a former paratrooper and rightwing Poujadist deputy, campaigning for immigrant repatriation and a tougher penal policy, benefited from these conflicts, capturing 10% of the popular vote in the National Assembly elections of March 1986 and, helped by the recent adoption of a new proportional representation system, 35 assembly seats. In this election, the 'left coalition', now in tatters, lost its assembly majority, compelling President Mitterrand to appoint the leader of the 'right coalition' and mayor of Paris, Jacques Chirac, as his new prime minister in what was to be a unique experiment in power-sharing, or 'cohabitation'.

Chirac quickly succeeded in establishing himself as the dominant force in this 'shared executive' and proceeded to set about introducing a radical 'new conservative' program of denationalization, deregulation, and 'desocialization'. In this strategy, utilizing 'guillotine' and decree powers to steamroller measures through, he had initial success. However, during the autumn and winter months of 1986–87, Chirac's educational and economic reforms encountered serious opposition from students and workers, necessitating policy concessions which, combined with growing acrimony within the ranks of the 'right coalition', served fatally to undermine the prime minister's national standing.

As a consequence, Chirac was comfortably defeated by the incumbent Mitterrand in the presidential election of April–May 1988, by a margin of 54% of the national vote against 46%. In National Assembly elections, which were held in June 1988, the PS, despite disarray in the ranks of the 'right coalition', also emerged as the largest single party, capturing 260 of the 577 seats after securing 45% of the second-ballot vote, but failed to secure an overall parliamentary majority.

Interpreting the result as a reflection of the public's desire for government from the 'center', President Mitterrand appointed Michel Rocard (b. 1930), a popular moderate social democrat, as prime minister at the head of a minority PS government, which included several prominent center party representatives. The new prime minister pledged himself to implement a progressive program, aimed at protecting the underprivileged and improving the quality of life, and called upon the opposition parties to work with the PS for 'tolerance, justice, progress and solidarity'. Terming their strategy the 'opening to the center', the aim of the president and prime minister appeared to be to encourage defections from the ranks of the center-right Union for French Democracy (UDF) to a new left-of-center PS-led alliance. This would redress the imbalance between the 'conventional left' vis-à-vis the RPR-led 'conventional right', thus creating an effective social democratic and conservative based two-party system, leaving the extremist PCF and FN isolated and marginalized on the political fringes.

In June 1988 Prime Minister Rocard negotiated the Matignon Accord, designed to resolve a dispute over autonomy between indigenous Kanaks and French settlers in the strife-torn French overseas territory of New Caledonia. This agreement was approved in a referendum held in France in November 1988. Between 1988 and 1990, against the backcloth of a strong economic upturn, attention focused increasingly on the 'quality of life', with the Green Party gaining 11% of the national vote in the European Parliament elections of June 1989. However, the extreme-right National Front continued

to do well in municipal elections and, in December 1989, secured a National Assembly by-election victory in Dreux, west of Paris. This persuaded the government to adopt a harsher line against illegal immigration and to announce new programs for the integration of Muslim immigrants, from Algeria, Tunisia, and other areas with French colonial ties, into mainstream French society.

The Rocard government narrowly survived a censure vote in the National Assembly in November 1990. This followed an outbreak of serious student violence in Paris and earlier anti-police race riot in the Lyon suburbs. A commission set up to look at the problems of immigrant integration reported in 1991 that France's foreign population was 3.7 million (6.8% of the population), the same as in 1982. However, 10 million citizens were of 'recent foreign origin'.

The 1990–91 Gulf crisis, caused by the invasion and annexation in August 1990 of Kuwait by Iraq, which formerly had close ties with France, caused divisions within the PS. Following Iraqi violation of the French ambassador's residence in Kuwait in September 1990, the French government dispatched 5,000 troops to Saudi Arabia to participate in the US-led anti-Iraqi UN coalition. This prompted the resignation, in February 1991, of the leftwing defense minister, Jean-Pierre Chevènement. In an effort to provide 'new impetus' to his administration, in May 1991 President Mitterrand replaced Rocard with Edith Cresson (b. 1934), the former minister for European affairs, who became France's first woman prime minister. However, with the economy in recession since 1990 and unemployment climbing (to more than 10%), racial disturbances increasing, farmers protesting against a recently introduced agricultural restructuring program, and the reputation of the PS being damaged by a succession of financial scandals, opinion polls showed the acerbic Cresson to have become the most unpopular prime minister of the Fifth Republic. The public approval rating of Mitterrand, by now the Fifth Republic's longest-serving president, also slumped, standing at 35% in January 1992.

Not unexpectedly, the PS polled disastrously in regional council elections held in March 1992, capturing a humiliating 18% share of the national vote, finishing only narrowly ahead of the National Front and the ecologist parties, Les Verts and Génération Ecologie. President Mitterrand responded by dismissing Cresson and, in April 1992, appointed his close ally, Pierre Bérégovoy (1922–93), as the new prime minister.

As finance minister, Bérégovoy had been blamed by Cresson for the nation's economic troubles, having raised interest rates to match German levels in pursuit, a 'strong franc' policy, but he was respected by the country's financial community.

The new Bérégovoy administration pledged to cut taxes to stimulate economic recovery and set up new training schemes to help the unemployed. In addition, in an attempt to woo environmentalist voters, a moratorium on nuclear testing was announced. In September 1992 a national referendum was held on approval of the Maastricht Treaty on EC economic and political union. A 'Yes' vote of 51.1% was narrowly secured. In the 21 and 28 March 1993 National Assembly elections, the PS faced a united 'right coalition' opposition, with the RPR and UDF having signed a formal election pact as early as April 1991. As a consequence, and with the economy still mired in recession, which had been exacerbated by a slowdown in Germany, the PS was heavily defeated. Along with its allies, it attracted 32% of the national vote but captured just 70 of the 577 National Assembly seats, while the RPR, UDF, and other 'conventional right' allies won, with 58% of the vote, 484 seats, and thus a clear majority.

In the aftermath of this electoral debacle, Pierre Bérégovoy, who was greatly affected by media allegations of impropriety over a FFr1 million interest-free loan, committed suicide by gunshot in May 1993. Jacques Chirac, the recognized leader of the victorious 'right coalition', was unwilling to become prime minister, following his experience of 'cohabitation' between 1986 and 1988. Instead, his patrician RPR colleague, Edouard Balladur (b. 1929), who had been economy and finance minister between 1986 and 1988, was appointed prime minister on 29 March 1993, on the tacit understanding that he would not challenge Chirac for the RPR's presidential nomination in 1995.

3. 1993–1999

From March 1993 President Mitterrand, afflicted by prostate cancer and visibly ailing, became an increasingly remote head of state, concentrating on foreign affairs and his ceremonial functions, leaving Balladur's RPR-UDF administration to dominate the domestic scene. With the forceful Charles Pasqua as interior minister, this new government introduced a strict new anti-immigration program. However, its chief priorities were the reduction of the budget deficit, securing currency stability, and the creation of a more dynamic economy through measures such as further privatization, including the partial sale of state-owned Renault

motor vehicles, and a reduction in the level of the minimum wage paid to young workers. Although during 1993 French GDP contracted by 0.9%, the unemployment level edged up, beyond the 3 million mark, to 11.7%, and in July 1993 the EC's Exchange Rate Mechanism (ERM), in which the franc was bound, effectively collapsed, Balladur remained popular and respected as prime minister. During 1994 economic growth resumed. However, following student protests, the government was obliged to shelve its plans to introduce the lower minimum wage and three cabinet ministers resigned after judicial investigations into fraud charges. Still the RPR-UDF polled strongly in local cantonal elections in March 1994, capturing 45% of the first-round vote, but in the June 1994 elections to the European Parliament the two parties, which fielded separate candidate lists, won just 26% of the national vote. The PS polled even more disappointingly, attracting just 14% of the vote. This prompted the resignation of Michel Rocard, who had been PS leader since April 1993. Instead, in this Euro-election, voters turned to two new contrasting parties, 'The Other Europe', an anti-Maastricht party led by a UDF dissident, Philippe de Villiers, and 'Energie Radicale', a pro-European grouping led by Bernard Tapie, a flamboyant business executive and former PS-aligned populist minister who had been charged with fraud in December 1993 and was to be found guilty in 1995. Each of these parties attracted 12% of the popular vote.

On 18 January 1995 Prime Minister Balladur announced publicly his candidacy for the French presidential elections to be held in April–May 1995, to the chagrin of Jacques Chirac, who had declared himself a candidate on 4 November 1994. Balladur presented himself as an 'above-party' candidate 'for all the French people, without distinction, without exclusion' and appeared clear favorite to top the first ballot. The PS had hoped to persuade Jacques Delors (b. 1925), who was set to retire as president of the European Commission, to become its candidate. However, although it seemed likely that Delors might be elected French president, he believed that the PS would be unable to win a parliamentary majority and was unwilling to work with the 'right coalition' in a 'cohabitation' administration. The PS thus chose, on 2 February 1995, Lionel Jospin (b. 1937), a moderate former PS leader and education minister, as its candidate.

As campaigning moved underway, the aloof Balladur, whose reputation for integrity was besmirched by his implication in a telephone-tapping affair and his admission that he had profited from stock market dealings, rapidly lost ground to the experienced Chirac. Presenting himself in this, his third, presidential challenge as a more populist 'man of the people', under the slogan 'La France pour tous', Chirac pledged to raise public sector wages, boost pensions, help farmers, encourage job creation, but also to cut taxes and the budget deficit, and heal social rifts. In the first ballot, held on 23 April 1995, Chirac finished ahead of Balladur, attracting 21% of the vote to the latter's 19%, but, unexpectedly, Jospin, noted for his personal integrity and straightforward approach, finished in first position, with 23% of the vote. The extremist Jean-Marie Le Pen won 15% national support, as a record 37% of the vote went to fringe candidates. The second ballot head-to-head contest between Jospin and Chirac, held on 7 May 1995, resulted in the expected victory for the 'right coalition', but the margin was narrower than anticipated, with Chirac securing 52.6% of the vote.

Chirac was sworn in as president on 17 May 1995, being driven to his inauguration in an old Citroën CX to symbolically mark what he promised would be a 'simple presidency'. He appointed as prime minister the moderate pro-European, Alain Juppé (b. 1945), who had been foreign minister since 1993, and included a record 12 women ministers in the 42-member cabinet. A close RPR lieutenant of the new president, Juppé faced the problem of implementing the contradictory economic program which emerged from Chirac's electoral pledges. However, the new administration had a dynamic, but mixed, start. In June 1995, the new government unveiled an ambitious FFr 60-billion package to promote jobs – the French unemployment rate, at 12.2%, was well above the OECD average of 7.4% – and boost house construction, and help the poor and elderly through increasing the minimum wage and pensions, but also announced that nuclear tests would be resumed in the Pacific. The former measures were well received, but the last drew international condemnation. In the same month, the parties of the conventional right polled less strongly than expected in municipal elections and the extremist National Front captured the mayorships of three important southern towns, Toulon, Marignane, and Orange, and trebled its number of local councillors to 1,075. In August 1995 the constitution was amended significantly to widen the range of issues on which the president could call referenda and to extend parliamentary oversight of the executive through providing for a nine-month annual National Assembly session. In the same month, Alain Madelin, the rightwing finance minister who pressed for rapid cuts in welfare spending and reduction in taxes, was fired and replaced by the more moderate Jean Arthuis, as Prime Minister Juppé stressed the need for gradual reform 'without haste'. Dogged by accusations that he had used his influence when Paris's financial director to secure housing at a reduced cost for his son, the prime minister reshuffled his cabinet in November 1995, eliminating nine of its 42 posts, in an effort to recover lost momentum. This followed a wave of public sector strikes in protest against the government's controversial welfare reform proposals.

In January 1996, following the completion of six tests during 1995 in French Polynesia, President Chirac announced an end to French nuclear testing and called for a worldwide ban on testing. Two months later, in March 1996, France, along with the United Kingdom and the USA, signed a treaty which made the South Pacific a nuclear-free zone. Proposals were also made, in May 1996, to end conscription by 2002 and for a 30% reduction in armed personnel. This formed part of a broader package of austerity measures which were taken in order to ensure the French budget deficit was reduced to below 3% of GDP, the 'convergence criteria' (for 1998) stipulated in the Maastricht Treaty for participation in the European Single Currency (ESC) in 1999.

Throughout 1996 the Chirac–Juppé administration, which had broken electoral promises and seen unemployment rise to a postwar peak of 3.1 million (12.7% of the workforce) in January 1997, remained deeply unpopular. Labor unrest, which was the worst seen in France since 1968, escalated in November 1996, with protracted public-sector strikes. However, from the spring of 1997 the economy began to grow more rapidly and the public approval rating of Prime Minister Juppé rose to 30%, the same level as enjoyed by the PS leader, Lionel Jospin. President Chirac used this 'window of opportunity' to call a snap general election, intended to give the center-right government a *nouvel élan*.

The ruling coalition contested the May–June 1997 National Assembly elections on a program of tax and public spending cuts, while the opposition PS issued a joint declaration with the PCF which included pledges to create 700,000 jobs and reduce the working week from 39 to 35 hours. The PS, who were more 'Eurosceptical' than the center-right, also formed an electoral pact with environmentalist parties. Unexpectedly, the left-of-center PS-led red-green alliance secured victory, with 48% of the second-round vote, gaining 319 of the 577 National Assembly seats, including 38 for the PCF and seven for environmentalist parties. The 'mainstream right' RPR-UDF's share of the first-round vote, at 30%, was a Fifth Republic low and was 10% below the 1993 result. President Chirac's gamble of calling an early election had backfired disastrously and he was now faced with a five-year period of cohabitation with a PS-led government. The reasons for the RPR-UDF defeat included the personal unpopularity of Prime Minister Juppé and his cabinet (eight of 25 ministers standing for re-election were defeated), recent corruption scandals, the high levels of unemployment and taxation, and the strong polling of the far-right FN. Running on an anti-immigration and anti-European currency platform, the FN attracted a record 15% of the first-ballot vote. This enabled 133 FN candidates, who had surmounted the 12.5% support first-ballot hurdle, to contest the second round in which their candidacies helped split the rightwing vote. In contrast, the PS, PCF, and Greens put up a 'united front', in which candidates stood down in the second ballot in favor of the best-placed candidate of the left.

Alain Juppé resigned as prime minister in June 1997, and was replaced as RPR leader by Philippe Séguin (b. 1943), a 'social Gaullist' positioned on the leftwing of the party. The new prime minister, Lionel Jospin, put together a PS-dominated 15-member cabinet which included five women, two members of the PCF (which held the balance of power in the National Assembly), and representatives of Les Verts ('The Greens') for the first time ever, the Radical Socialist Party (PRS), and Jean-Pierre Chevènement of the 'Euro-sceptic' Citizens' Movement (MDC). The government's priorities were to create, over a five-year period, 700,000 jobs for the young unemployed; reduce the working week from 39 to 35 hours, without loss of pay; promote house construction; increase research and education spending; create a fairer taxation system; suspend privatization; and review previous immigration legislation.

In July 1997 it was announced that the drive to reduce the budget deficit, which stood at 3.7% of GDP, to the Maastrict convergence level would continue, but would be achieved through increasing business taxes and, in a policy U-turn, continued privatization. The new government granted residency permits to 54,000 immigrants who were unsure of their legal status (the 'sans papiers'), but broke its broader promise to abolish the tough immigration and citizenship laws ('Lois Pasqua') which had been introduced by the preceding Juppé govern-

ment. In September 1997 the government unveiled its plans to create 350,000 new jobs in the public sector (including schools and hospitals) by 2000, for 18 to 25 year olds on partly state-supported five-year contracts, while in February 1998 legislation was passed to reduce the working week to 35 hours by 2000 for companies with more than ten employees.

In January 1998 unemployed workers protested in Paris and occupied government buildings as part of a campaign for higher benefits for the jobless. However, Prime Minister Jospin responded by announcing the creation of a billion franc ($164 million) fund to help the unemployed through retraining and other measures. This, coupled with accelerating economic growth, helped maintain the government's approval ratings at remarkably high levels and in regional elections, held in March 1998, the ruling 'red-green' coalition performed well. It won 37% of the vote, against 36% for the RPR-UDF 'mainstream right' while the FN, with 15% of the vote again, held the balance of power in 19 of the 22 regions. This created a dilemma for the 'conventional right': whether or not to accept FN support to take control of certain regions. The RPR-UDF leadership outlawed such cooperation; however, four UDF members, including the former defense minister, Charles Millon, defied the party's leadership and retained their regional presidencies with FN support. As a consequence, they were expelled from the party. In response, in April 1998, Millon, who was president of Rhône-Alpes region, formed a new breakaway party, called 'The Right'.

By the spring of 1998 France had narrowly passed the Maastricht Treaty tests for the next stage of EMU and, in April 1998, the National Assembly approved French participation in the ESC. President Chirac, who enjoyed good relations with Prime Minister Jospin, had his highest ever public approval ratings by the autumn of 1998. However, he presided over a French right which remained in disarray.

The extreme right FN split in January 1999, with a breakaway National Movement being formed by the FN's 'modernist' former deputy leader, Bruno Maigret, who opposed Jean-Marie Le Pen's forceful leadership style. More seriously for President Chirac, in April 1999 Philippe Séguin resigned as president of the RPR on the grounds that he felt undermined by the manoeuvrings of Chirac and his aides. Consequently, the 'mainstream right' fought the June 1999 European Parliament elections as a divided force, with separate RPR and UDF lists being presented to voters. Its share of the national vote fell from 38% in the June 1994 Euro-elections to 35%, divided between three bodies: the centrist, Euro-federalist UDF, led by Francois Bayrou, with 9% support; the neo-Gaullist, pro-European, free market RPR, with 13% support; and a newly formed Eurosceptic Rally for Fvrance (RPF), led by Charles Pasqua, in association with Phillipe de Villiers, with 13% support. In the wake of this result, Nicolas Sarkozy resigned as the RPR's interim president.

In March 1999 Roland Dumas, the head of the Constitutional Court, took 'leave of absence' to enable him to fight allegations of corruption involving the oil company Elf Aquitaine. In May 1999 Prime Minister Jospin survived a vote of censure in the National Assembly, which followed criticism of his government's handling of a scandal on Corsica related to a police arson attack on an illegally built restaurant, allegedly on the orders of the prefect (head of the local administration).

Since October 1995 France and Germany have operated a 50,000-member 'Eurocorps' joint defense force, which has links to NATO and the Western European Union (WEU). In December 1995 France announced that it intended to partially rejoin the military structure of NATO although it would retain independent control of its nuclear forces.

GERMANY

Federal Republic of Germany (FRG)
Bundesrepublik Deutschland

Capital: Berlin*

* Berlin was chosen as the new official capital of the expanded FRG in 1991, but Bonn remained the administrative capital, and the site of the federal parliament, until mid-1999.

Social and economic data
Area: 357,000 sq km/137,838 sq miles
Population: 81,410,000*
Pop. density per sq km/sq mi: 228/590*
Urban population: 86%**
Literacy rate: 99%**
GDP: $2,252,000 million*; per-capita GDP: $27,600*
Government defense spending (% of GDP): 2.0%*
Currency: Deutschmark (DM)
Economy type: high income
Labor force in agriculture: 8%**
Unemployment rate: 12.9%*
* 1995.
** 1992.

Head of state
Federal President Johannes Rau, since 1999

Head of government
Chancellor Gerhard Schröder, since 1998

Ethnic composition
The population is overwhelmingly, 93%, of Germanic stock, but in the far north there are notable Danish and Slavonic ethnic minorities. Also, in 1997, 7.5 million foreigners, including 1.9 million officially recognized *Gastarbeiter* ('guest workers') were residing in the country, predominantly Turks and South Europeans (Greeks, Italians, and Yugoslavs), constituting 9% of the total population. By 1996 the FRG had received more than 320,000 refugees fleeing the Yugoslav civil war, but many began to be deported from 1997. German is the main language, but there is a small Serbian-speaking minority in eastern Germany. The law on citizenship, which dates back to 1913, makes ancestry the chief determinant of who is German. This has enabled around 200,000 people from Romania, Poland, and the former Soviet Union to settle in Germany each year during the 1990s, while fewer than 40,000 of the large ethnic Turkish community (which exceeds 2 million) are naturalized each year. However, the new Schröder government has pledged to change this law so as to allow 'non-blood Germans' to acquire citizenship more easily.

Religions
Forty-three per cent of the population is Protestant, belonging to the Lutheran Church, United Evangelical

The Länder (states) of the Federal Republic of Germany — Table 60

Länder	Area (sq km/sq miles)	1995 population ('000)	Capital	Länder government	Bundesrat seats
Eastern Germany					
Berlin	883/341	3,500	Berlin	CDU-SPD	4
Brandenburg	29,059/11,220	2,500	Potsdam	SPD	4
Mecklenburg-Western Pomerania	23,838/9,204	1,800	Schwerin	CDU-SPD	3
Saxony	18,337/7,080	4,800	Dresden	CDU	5
Saxony-Anhalt	20,445/7,894	2,800	Magdeburg	SPD-CDU	4
Thuringia	16,251/6,275	2,500	Erfurt	CDU-SPD	4
Total	*(108,813)/(42,013)*	*(17,900)*			*(23)*
Western Germany					
Baden-Württemberg	35,751/13,804	10,300	Stuttgart	CDU	6
Bavaria	70,553/27,241	11,800	Munich	CSU	6
Bremen	404/156	680	Bremen	SPD-FDP-Greens	3
Hamburg	755/292	1,650	Hamburg	SPD-Greens	3
Hesse	21,144/8,164	6,000	Wiesbaden	SPD-Greens	4
Lower Saxony	47,439/18,316	7,700	Hanover	SPD	6
North-Rhine-Westphalia	34,068/13,154	17,600	Düsseldorf	SPD	6
Rhineland-Palatinate	19,848/7,663	4,000	Mainz	SPD-FDP	4
Saarland	2,569/992	1,070	Saarbrucken	SPD	3
Schleswig-Holstein	15,728/6,072	2,650	Kiel	SPD-Greens	4
Total	*(248,259)/(95,853)*	*(63,510)*			*(45)*
All Germany	357,072/137,866	81,410	Berlin	CDU-CSU-FDP	69

* In September 1998.

Church, and churches of the Lutheran tradition; 36% is Roman Catholic, the faith being strongest in the south and west; 2%, drawn chiefly from the Turkish community, adheres to Sunni Islam; and 18% is nonreligious. The Protestant community predominates in the eastern *Länder* (states)and during the communist era was identified with the peace, ecological, and dissident movements.

Political features

State type: liberal democratic
Date of state formation: 1871/1949/1990*
Political structure: federal
Executive: parliamentary
Assembly: two-chamber
Party structure: multiparty
Human rights rating: 98%
International affiliations: AG (observer), BDEAC, BOAD, CE, CERN, CSS, EEA, ESA, EU, G-5, G-7, G-10, IAEA, IBRD, IMF, IWC, NACC, NAM (guest), NATO, OECD, OSCE, UN, WEU, WTO

* Germany was first united in 1871. The FRG was established in 1949 to which the *Länder* of eastern Germany acceded in 1990.

Local and regional government

Below the *Land* (state) administrations, which are described under *Political system*, there are elected town and district councils, empowered to levy and collect property taxes.

Political system

With memories of the destructive 1933–45 Nazi autocracy fresh in their minds, the Allied military governors and German provincial leaders in 1948–49 drafted the FRG's constitution with the clear goal of creating a stable parliamentary form of government, diffusing authority, and safeguarding liberties. The document, termed the 'Basic Law', borrowed eclectically from British, American, and neighboring European constitutional models, while drawing specific lessons from Germany's own flawed constitutional history.

To prevent an excessive centralization of power, a federal system of government was established, built around originally ten *Länder* (states), and 16 since unification in 1990, as shown in Table 60 above, each with its own constitution and elected single-chamber assembly (*Landtag* or *Bürgerschaft*), from which a government is drawn, headed by a minister-president. Bavaria is the exception, having two chambers. These *Länder* have original powers in the spheres of education, police, local government, culture, and environmental protection and are responsible for the administration of federal legislation through their own civil services. They have substantial local taxation authority and are assigned shares of federal income tax and value-added tax (VAT) revenues, being responsible for half of total government spending in the FRG. Plans to merge the Länder of Berlin and Brandenburg, from 1999, into one state, were rejected by Brandenburg's votes in a referendum in May 1996.

At the center, the May 1949 constitution, amended for unification in October 1990, established, through a deliberate system of checks and balances, a firmly rooted parliamentary democracy, built around a two-chamber legislature comprising a directly elected lower house, the *Bundestag* (Federal Diet or Assembly) of at least 656 members (currently 669), and an indirectly elected 69-member upper house, the *Bundesrat* (Federal Council).

Bundestag members are elected by universal adult suffrage for a four-year term, through a complicated form of 'personalized proportional representation', termed the additional member system (AMS). Under this system electors are given two votes, one, the *Erststimme*, for a local single-member district constituency seat, the result being decided by a simple plurality, and the other vote, the *Zweitstimme*, for a *Land* (state) party list. Half the assembly is filled by 'constituency members' and half by 'list members'. The *Zweitstimme* votes are decisive in determining proportionate party representation. They are totalled so as to establish percentage levels of party support at the state level and to work out proportionate seat allocations. To achieve such proportionality, list seats are added, where necessary, to those already gained by the parties locally from the *Erststimme* constituency contests. In this allot-

ment process, 'balancing' *Zweitstimme* seats are drawn in rank order from the topmost names appearing on the relevant party's state list. To qualify for shares of these state list seats, political parties must, however, have won at least 5% of the national vote or, alternatively, three direct *Erststimme* seats. In the special case of the December 1990 first all-German general election, the '5% rule' was applied separately to eastern and western Germany. Occasionally, as a result of unusual, regionally concentrated, *Erststimme* support, a party may secure more district Erststimme seats than it appears 'entitled' to on a state-wide percentage basis. It is allowed to retain these 'excess' (*Überhangmandate*) seats, the size of the Bundestag being increased accordingly. For example, the September 1998 general election resulted in 13 'excess mandate' seats.

Members of the Bundesrat are not directly elected. Instead, individual *Land* governments send nominated party delegations, consisting of between three to six members, dependent upon population size. For this reason, the Bundesrat is never dissolved, its composition only changing as *Land* governments rise and fall. The delegations sent to the current administrative capital, Bonn, which comprise senior *Land* ministers, automatically led by the minister-president, are required to cast their votes *en bloc*.

The Bundestag is the more dominant of the two chambers in the federal assembly, electing, from the ranks of the majority party or coalition, a chancellor (*Bundeskanzler*: prime minister) and a 16–20-member cabinet to constitute the executive government of the Federal Republic. Once elected, a chancellor can only be removed by Bundestag members through a 'constructive vote of no confidence', in which a majority of members vote positively in favor of an alternative executive leader. This constitutional device has been employed successfully on only one occasion, in September 1982, and brought into office the present chancellor.

The chancellor, who is served by a large, 400-member, private office, is a potentially powerful leader. However, the coalition character of postwar FRG politics, with the consequent apportionment of cabinet posts on a negotiated party basis, has meant that a number of leading ministers, for example foreign affairs minister Hans-Dietrich Genscher, who continuously held his post between 1974 and 1992, have been able to establish a significant degree of independence. More generally, German cabinet ministers, who are not required to be Bundestag deputies, although most are, are frequently technocrats who specialize in their department's affairs, serving lengthy terms, in contrast to the generalist ministers of most other West European states.

Work in both the Bundestag and Bundesrat is effected through a vigorous system of all-party functional committees. The Bundestag takes the lead in this legislative process. However, although the Bundesrat has few initiating rights, it enjoys considerable veto powers. Thus, all legislation relating to *Länder* responsibilities must receive its approval, more than 60% of Bundestag laws falling into this category. In addition, constitutional amendments, of which there have been more than 30 since 1949, require a two-thirds Bundesrat, and Bundestag, majority. Finally, on other matters, the Bundesrat is allowed to suggest amendments to Bundestag legislation, send disputed items to a joint Bundestag–Bundesrat 'conciliation committee' and can temporarily block items of which it disapproves until a countervailing 50% or 66% Bundestag vote is passed. For example, in the legislative period running up to the October 1994 general election, the Bundesrat, which was dominated by the opposition Social Democratic Party (SPD) and Greens, initially rejected 16% of the 504 laws approved by the Bundestag. Three of these laws were subsequently rejected, following mediation.

For the purpose of electing a federal president (*Bundespräsident*) as head of state, members of the Bundestag join together every five years with an equal number of representatives elected by *Land* parliaments in a special Federal Convention (*Bundesversammlung*). The president is, however, primarily a titular and ceremonial figure, possessing few effective powers.

Adherence to the 1949/1990 constitution is ensured by a special independent Federal Constitutional Court, based at Karlsruhe, which is staffed by 16 judges. They are selected half by the Bundestag and half by the Bundesrat, following nominations by balanced all-party committees, and serve terms of up to 12 years. The Court functions as a guarantor of civil liberties and adjudicator in federal–*Land* disputes. Similar constitutional courts function at the *Land* level.

Political parties

FRG politics have been dominated since 1949 by two major parties, the Christian Democratic Union (CDU: Christlich Demokratische Union Deutschlands) and Social Democratic Party (SPD: Sozialdemokratische Partei Deutschlands), and one minor party, the Free Democratic Party (Freie Demokratische Partei: FDP). A fourth party, the Greens (die Grünen), has emerged as a notable challenging force since the early 1980s, while the Bavarian-based Christian Social Union (CSU: Christlich Soziale Union) has worked in close, though sometimes uneasy, partnership with the CDU at the federal level. In the eastern *Länder*, the Party of Democratic Socialism (PDS: Partei des Demokratischen Sozialismus) is a significant force, being the reform-socialist heir to the formerly dominant communist Socialist Unity Party of Germany (Sozialistische Einheitspartei Deutschlands: SED).

With the exception of the November 1972 and September 1998 Bundestag elections, the conservative CDU has consistently gained most support at national level, forming the principal party of government between 1949 and 1969 and from 1982 to 1998. However, the SPD has been the dominant force during recent years at the *Länder* level, controlling the majority of state assemblies, either on its own or in partnership with the Greens and even, on occasions, with the FDP and, in a 'grand coalition', with the CDU. As a consequence, the SPD currently controls the federal Bundesrat and won the September 1998 federal elections.

The CDU was originally established at the state level in the autumn of 1945 as a loose amalgamation of independent Catholic and Protestant zonal parties who had resisted National Socialism (Nazism) during the interwar years and whose members shared a commitment to private enterprise, state welfare provision, and an antipathy to communism. During the 1950s, the CDU's support base, which had traditionally been concentrated in the rural, Catholic *Länder* of southern and western Germany and in rural, Protestant Schleswig-Holstein and Lower Saxony, broadened, as it absorbed further minor regional, centrist, and conservative parties. Ideologically, it became identified with the 'social market economy' approach to economic management, which became a key element behind the postwar West German 'economic miracle'. The success of this strategy drew to the party new blue-collar support, establishing it as a broadly based, 'catch-all', center-right force. In its approach to external relations, the CDU gave firm and early support to membership of the European Community (EC) and the North Atlantic Treaty Organization (NATO).

The CDU, led since 1998 by Wolfgang Schäuble, has a membership of 640,000. Since unification it has received an infusion of more than 100,000 members from the eastern *Länder*, predominantly Protestant, of a Calvinist disposition. Its sister party in Bavaria, the CSU, which was established in 1946, has a membership of 181,000. The CSU is a noticeably more conservative body and was led between 1961 and 1988 by the forthright Dr Franz-Josef Strauss. It was headed 1988–98 by Theo Waigel (b. 1939), the federal finance minister, and since 1998 by the premier of Bavaria, Dr Edmund Stoiber (b. 1943)

The CDU, constituting, as its name suggests, a 'Union' of *Land* groupings, is notoriously decentralized in structure. Financially, it draws an unusually high proportion, almost 30%, of its annual income in the form of donations, chiefly from business.

The dominant party on the left of the political spectrum is the SPD. Formed in 1875, during the Bismarckian era, it began as a Marxist body, drawing initial support from urban industrial workers. With a membership in excess of 1 million, it became the major political party in Germany during the liberal Weimar Republic (1919–33), forming governments between 1919 and 1920 and between 1928 and 1930. Following the defection of ultra-leftist groupings, its policy stance moderated but it was forced into exile during the Nazi era and was subsequently electorally weakened by the country's partition in 1945.

During the 1950s the SPD, with a national support rating of only 30%, found itself in perpetual opposition at the federal level, but held power at the state level in the industrialized western *Länder* of Bremen, Hamburg, Hesse, and North Rhine-Westphalia. However, at its 1959 Bad Godesberg conference, a fundamental revision of policy strategy was effected, bringing to an end the party's earlier opposition to membership of the EEC/EC and NATO, disavowing its traditional Marxist connections, class orientation, and anticlericalism and proclaiming its acceptance of the country's postwar 'social market economy' strategy. The adoption of this moderate, new, left-of-center Godesberg Program of Principles, coupled with the party's innovative espousal of East–West *détente* (*Ostpolitik*), and the dynamic new generation leadership provided by Willy Brandt and Helmut Schmidt, proved successful in significantly broadening the SPD's support base. This enabled it, in alliance with the FDP, to become the party of federal government between 1969 and 1982.

Between 1982 and 1998, as a result of mounting internal divisions over domestic and foreign policy which shifted its center of gravity leftwards and encouraged the FDP to switch allegiance to the CDU, the SPD was forced back into opposition at the federal level. The party remained, however, a significant force, having, in

1997, a membership of 780,000 and enjoying informal labor union support. Unification in 1990 brought to the party an additional 30,000 members from the eastern *Länder*. Its organizational structure is the most effective in the FRG, being unusually centralized, with control from above being effected by an elected National Executive Committee and inner 13-member Presidium, chaired since April 1999 by the leftwing Gerhard Schröder. Its organization is also among the most progressive, with, following rules passed at the SPD congress of August 1988, at least 40% of the party's posts, and a similar proportion of its Bundestag seats, being required to be filled by women by 1998.

The FDP, a centrist liberal grouping, although very small compared to the CDU and SPD in terms of national support, averaging 7% of the national vote in elections since 1949, has functioned as a critical 'hinge party'. Helped by the AMS electoral system, with the 'ticket-splitting' which this makes possible, the FDP has been in a position to regularly hold the balance of power in the Bundestag and has formed the junior partner in federal coalition governments in all but seven years, 1957–61 and 1966–69, between 1949 and 1998. As a reward for its assembly support, the FDP has received 20% of cabinet portfolios in these administrations, including such key ministries as foreign affairs, economic affairs, and justice. In addition, it secured the election of two of its leaders, Dr Theodor Heuss (1884–1963), between 1949 and 1959, and Walter Scheel (b. 1919), between 1974 and 1979, to the prestigious post of federal president and another, Martin Bangemann (b. 1934), to the EC Commission in 1988.

The FDP, although its antecedents go back to previous Second Reich (1871–1918) and Weimar Republic centrist groupings, was originally formed by Heuss in December 1948, by absorbing smaller liberal parties. During the 1950s its support came chiefly from marginal farming communities, the self-employed, and small-town conservatives. However, after Scheel became party chair in 1968, it became more progressive in its outlook, winning new support from white-collar groups. Today, there is still tension between its conservative-liberal wing, of which its leader until 1993, Count Otto Graf Lambsdorff (b. 1927), was a prominent member and which espouses a free market economic approach, and a more socially and environmentally conscious progressivist faction with a strong regional base in Baden-Württemberg, in the southwest and the northern city states of Hamburg and Bremen. In 1991 party membership stood at 200,000, two-thirds of whom were new recruits from the eastern Länder, after the eastern League of Free Democrats (BFD) was absorbed in 1990. However, between 1992 and 1995 the FDP polled disastrously in a series of state elections, falling below the 5% qualification level in all but one contest, Hesse in February 1995, and only secured representation in the Bundestag in the October 1994 federal election as a result of CDU supporters casting *Zweitstimme* votes for this coalition partner. This led former leader Lambsdorff, who retired from parliament in 1998 (along with Hans-Dietrich Genscher), to describe the party as being in 'existential danger'. In June 1995, with membership down to just 84,000, Wolfgang Gerhardt, from Hesse, replaced Klaus Kinkel as the FDP's chair, and by 1997 membership was down to 70,000. The party's future appeared to lie with the espousal of a mixture of social liberalism and free-market economics, as promoted by Guido Westerwelle (b. 1962), the young secretary general since 1994.

The FRG's fourth significant party, the Greens, originated as a loose coalition of locally-based environmental action groups which began operations during the later 1970s and had growing successes in a number of Land constituency contests. In January 1980 they were established as an umbrella organization which embraced these groupings and began to develop a unique 'postindustrial' or 'new politics' policy program, which included opposition to nuclear weapons and the NATO alliance, environmentalism, feminism, and utopian eco-socialism. Having secured representation in a number of *Landtage* and *Bürgerschäfte* between 1980 and 1983, the Greens succeeded in surmounting the 5% national support hurdle and captured seats in the Bundestag at both the 1983 and 1987 general elections.

Outside the assembly chambers, they played an even more prominent role at the head of a burgeoning 'peace movement' during the early and mid-1980s. By 1987 they claimed a national membership of 42,000. However, the party had become progressively divided into antagonistic radical ('Fundi'), moderate ('Realo'), and neutral ('Neutralo') factions, fomenting a series of anarchic feuds. The party has a highly decentralized organizational structure which has exacerbated such infighting. More impressively, the Greens, since their inception, have pioneered and operated a unique collective form of national and parliamentary leadership, with, until 1991, personnel being regularly rotated. Women are assured of equal representation at all executive levels. In 1998 the party had two national 'spokespersons', Jürgen Trittin and Gunda Röstel. The

Greens suffered a dip in support during 1989–91 as attention focused on the prospect of, and economic and social consequences of, reunification. As a result, their national support fell to below 4% in the October 1990 general election. However, in the 1994 general election, having merged with the eastern Germany-based Alliance '90, the Greens attracted, at 7.3%, a higher level of national support than the FDP and polled even more strongly in *Land* elections in 1995, notably in industrialized North Rhine-Westphalia, where they attracted 10% support. Led in the Bundestag by the pragmatic 'Realo' Joschka Fischer (b. 1948), the Greens in 1998 shared power in coalition governments with the SPD in four Länder, and supplanted the FDP as the 'third force' 'swing party' in the 1998 federal election. It held seats in 11 *Länder* assemblies, compared to only four for the FDP.

In the depressed eastern *Länder*, the PDS, the reformed and liberalized successor of the communist SED, which dominated East German politics between 1945 and 1989, has established itself as a significant force, thriving on local, eastern patriotism. The SED itself originated as the German Communist Party (KPD), which was formed in 1918, but was merged, in 1946, under Soviet pressure, with East Germany's SPD to form the SED. Currently, the reform-socialist PDS is led in parliament by the engaging Gregor Gysi (b. 1948), a Jewish lawyer from Berlin, with Lothar Bisky as party chair, and had a membership of 99,000 in 1997. It attracts nearly 20% support in the eastern *Länder*, but barely 1% of the vote in the western *Länder*. Sixty per cent of its members and 30% of its supporters are aged over 60.

Numerous minor parties also operate both nationally and regionally in the FRG. At the national level are the far-right German National Party (NPD: Nationaldemokratische Partei Deutschlands), which dates from 1964; the rightwing nationalist Republicans (die Republikaner); and the neo-Nazi German People's Union (DVU). The NDP rose briefly to prominence between 1966 and 1968 and, led by Martin Mussgnug, now claims a membership of 15,000. The 25,000-member Republicans, an anti-immigrant extremist party formed in 1983 by a former Nazi Waffen-SS officer, Franz Schönhuber, has polled strongly in local elections since the late 1980s, as has the DVU, a body set up in Munich in 1987 by Gerhard Frey, the wealthy publisher of the neo-Nazi *National Zeitung* newspaper. In 1993 the Republicans gained temporary representation in the Bundestag when Rudolf Krause, a rightwing

CDU deputy, defected to the party. In April 1998 the DVU attracted 13% of the vote in the Saxony-Anbalt state election. Schönhuber was ousted as leader of the Republicans and replaced by Rolf Schlierer (b. 1955) in December 1994, after the former had attempted to negotiate an alliance with the DVU. Other smaller neo-fascist groups have sprung up in the eastern *Länder*.

At the *Land* level, small regionalist parties, such as the South Schleswig Electoral Union (SSW: Sudschleswigscher Wahlerverband), established in 1948 to represent the Danish-speaking minority of northern Schleswig-Holstein, the Statt-Partei ('Instead of a Party'), established in Hamburg in September 1993, and the Work for Bremen (AFB) party, established in May 1995 as a breakaway from the PD, have secured Landtag representation.

Under the terms of Article 21 of the 'Basic Law', political parties have been assigned a special role, described as 'forming the political will of the people'. As a result, under the terms of the Party Law of 1967, which was amended in 1981, public financial support has been provided to assist their operations. Currently, parties which secure in excess of 0.5% of the federal vote are given an official subsidy of DM5 per vote received. Similar, though lower, subsidies are paid by *Land* governments for state contests and by the central government for European Parliament elections. These subsidies constitute a third of annual party revenues.

In return for this support, the parties are subject to regulation concerning internal financial and electoral matters, and the Federal Constitutional Court reserves the right to ban groupings which are deemed to be anti-democratic, and thus unconstitutional. This sanction was employed in 1952 and 1956, when the quasi-fascist Socialist Reich Party and ultra-leftist Communist Party of Germany (KPD: Kommunistische Partei Deutschlands) were outlawed. Since 1989 ten out of some 70 neo-Nazi groups have been banned, including the National Gathering (Nationale Sammlung) and Free German Workers' Party.

Political leaders since 1970

GDR: 1950–71 Walter Ulbricht (SED)[*], 1971–89 Erich Honecker (SED)[*], 1989 Egon Krenz (SED)[*], 1989–90 Hans Modrow (PDS)[**], 1990 Lothar de Maizière (CDU)[**]

FRG chancellors: 1969–74 Willy Brandt (SPD), 1974–82 Helmut Schmidt (SPD), 1982–98 Dr Helmut Kohl (CDU), 1998– Gerhard Schröder (SPD)

[*] Communist Party leader.
[**] Prime minister.

Latest elections

The most recent Bundestag elections, held on 27 September 1998, resulted in defeat for Chancellor Kohl's CDU-CSU-FDP governing coalition, which had held power since 1982, and victory for the left-of-center SPD, led by the charismatic Gerhard Schröder. As usual, the CDU did not contest Bavaria, while its sister party, the CSU, fought only Bavarian seats.

Combined support for the CDU-CSU fell by 6% on October to 35%, it lowest level since 1949, and the CDU-CSU won 245 of the 669 Bundestag seats. In contrast, the SPD vote rose by 4.5% to 41%, the party's best performance since 1980, and the SPD won 298 seats. Support for the CDU fell most dramatically in the eastern Länder, where it won just 28% of the vote (down 10%), finishing behind the SPD, with 35% of the vote, for the first time since re-unification. The FDP, helped by *Zweitstimme* votes cast by CDU supporters, managed to surmount the 5% vote-representation threshold and, with 6.2% of the vote, captured 44 seats. The Greens/Alliance '90 attracted 6.7% of the vote, a slightly lower share than in 1994, and won 47 seats, while the PDS, which secured a fifth of the vote in the eastern *Länder,* surmounted the 5% hurdle, winning 5.1% of the all-German vote and 35 Bundestag seats. The far-right Republicans won 1.8% of the vote and the DVU 1.2%, and thus no seats; There were 13 *Überhangmandaten* ('overhang' or 'excess seats') caused by a party having directly elected in a given *Land* more deputies than it was, on a proportional representation basis, entitled to. The size of the Bundestag was thus increased from 656 deputies to 669.

Political history

1. From 1871 to World War II

Formerly a confederation of 39 principalities within the Holy Roman Empire (First Reich), a united German Empire was forged in 1871, after two failed liberal democratic revolutions in 1830 and 1848, by Prussia's astute prime minister, the 'Iron Chancellor' Otto von Bismarck (1815–98), with the Hohenzollern King Wilhelm I (1797–1888) as German emperor (*kaiser*). A democracy of types did emerge after 1871, with a bicameral parliament (*Reichstag*) and universal male suffrage, but it was the kaiser and chancellor, as head of the traditional landed and military elite and buttressed by a nationalist and statist ideology, who wielded real power. During this imperial Second Reich (1871–1919), Germany advanced economically, emerging as an important industrial power, and carved out an extensive overseas empire. Military defeat in World War I brought the abdication of the kaiser and the creation of the parliamentary Weimar Republic in 1919. However, this experiment in liberal democracy lasted only 14 years, being overthrown by the fascist Nazi Third Reich dictatorship which was established from 1933 by Adolf Hitler (1889–1945), a believer in the notion of the existence of an Aryan German 'master race'. The Weimar Republic was encumbered by tremendous economic problems – brought on by post-war territorial losses, crippling reparation charges, and the onset of a world economic depression – and a flawed constitution, which created a confused 'dual executive,' with power shared by an elected president and a chancellor (prime minister) dependent for support on a lower house which was elected by a generous form of proportional representation which promoted party fission. Between 1919 and 1933, 15 different chancellors held office and in the final years of the Weimar era power shifted increasingly towards the conservative president, Paul von Hindenburg (1847–1934).

In the Reichstag election of November 1932 Hitler's National Socialist German Workers' (Nazi) Party secured 33% of the popular vote and in January 1933 von Hindenburg appointed Hitler as chancellor. An Enabling Act was passed in March 1933, granting Hitler dictatorial powers and, on the death of von Hindenburg in August 1934, the posts of president and chancellor were fused under Hitler's new designation Führer ('leader'). Freedom of speech and assembly was abolished; the 1919 Treaty of Versailles and reparations agreements were repudiated; the Rhineland was remilitarized in 1936 and Austria and the Czech Sudetenland annexed in 1938–39; and a long series of persecutions began, climaxing in the murder of millions of Jews, Gypsies, and political opponents. Although Hitler's interventionist and autarchic economic policies enjoyed a substantial measure of success at home, his decision to declare war on Poland on 1 September 1939, resulting in World War II, proved to be self-destructive. From the winter of 1942 German forces, which had controlled much of continental Europe, met with increasing external resistance, as the Soviet Red Army turned the tide at Volgograd (Stalingrad).

2. From 1945 to 1973

The Third Reich finally collapsed in May 1945, following the suicide of Hitler, as the allies advanced upon Berlin, and the large German Empire was thereafter dismembered. The eastern, Prussian, half was divided between Poland, the USSR, and the newly created Soviet satellite state, the German Democratic Republic (GDR). Out of the larger western portion, comprising the British, American, and French occupation zones, a new Federal Republic of Germany (FRG) was formed in May 1949. During the period of allied military control, 1945–49, a policy of demilitarization, decentralization, and democratization was instituted and a new, intended to be provisional, constitution framed. This constitution included the goal of eventual German reunification. Between 1948 and 1949, West Berlin was subjected to blockade by the Soviet Union, but survived to form a constituent *Land* in the FRG, following an airlift operation by the Allied powers.

Politics in the FRG during its first decade were dominated by the Christian Democratic Union (CDU), led by the popular Konrad Adenauer (1876–1967), a former lord mayor of Cologne who had been imprisoned by the Nazis between 1934 and 1944 for opposition to the regime and served as chancellor between 1949 and 1963. Adenauer and his economics minister, Ludwig Erhard (1897–1977), who was later chancellor between 1963 and 1966, established a successful new approach to economic management termed the 'social market economy' (*soziale Marktwirtschaft*), which involved the state's encouragement of free-market productive forces, combined with strategic interventions so as to reconcile interest-group differences, guide the market in a socially responsible direction, and secure adequate welfare provision.

This new 'liberal-corporatist' managerial approach, combined with the injection of aid under the Marshall Plan and the enterprise of the nation's labor force, more than 2 million of whom were refugees from the partitioned East (GDR), contributed towards a phase of rapid economic reconstruction and growth during the 1950s and 1960s, an era now termed the 'miracle years'. During this period, West Germany, as the FRG was then popularly known, was also reintegrated into the international community. It regained its full sovereignty in 1954, entered the North Atlantic Treaty Organization (NATO) in 1955, emerging as a loyal supporter of the United States, and, under Adenauer's committed lead, joined the new European Economic Community (EEC) in 1957. Close relations were also developed with France, enabling the Saarland to be amicably returned to Germany in January 1957.

In August 1961, East Germany's construction of a fortified wall around West Berlin, to prevent refugees from leaving the GDR, created a political crisis which vaulted West Berlin's mayor, Willy Brandt (1913–92), to international prominence. Domestically, Brandt played a pivotal role in shifting the Social Democratic Party (SPD) away from its traditional Marxist affiliation towards a more moderate position, following the party's 1959 Bad Godesberg conference. Support for the SPD steadily increased after this policy switch and the party joined the CDU in a 'grand coalition' led by the CDU's Kurt Kiesinger (1904–88), between 1966 and 1969, and then secured power itself, with the support of the Free Democratic Party (FDP), under the leadership of Brandt in 1969.

As chancellor, Brandt, working closely with the SPD's defense expert, Egon Bahr, introduced the new foreign policy of *Ostpolitik*, which sought reconciliation with Eastern Europe as a means of improving social contacts between the two Germanies. Treaties in 1970 normalized relations with the Soviet Union and Poland and recognized the Oder-Neisse border line, while, in September 1972, a 'Basic Treaty' was effected with East Germany, which acknowledged the GDR's borders and separate existence, enabling both countries to join the United Nations in 1973.

3. From 1974 to the opening of the Berlin Wall

Willy Brandt resigned as chancellor in May 1974, following a revelation that his personal assistant, Günther Guillaume, had been an East German spy. Brandt's replacement as chancellor, the former finance minister, Helmut Schmidt (b. 1918), adhered to *Ostpolitik* and emerged as a leading advocate of European cooperation, while at home he introduced a series of important social reforms.

In the federal election of October 1976, the SPD-FDP coalition only narrowly defeated the CDU-CSU. Four years later, however, it secured a comfortable victory after the controversial Franz-Josef Strauss (1915–88) had forced his way to the head of the CDU-CSU ticket. Soon after this election triumph, divisions emerged between the leftwing of the SPD and the liberal-conservative wing of the FDP on defense policy, particularly over the proposed stationing by the end of 1983 of new short- and medium-range Cruise and Pershing-II American nuclear missiles in West Germany. There were also differences on economic strategy, during a period of gathering world recession. Chancellor Schmidt fought to maintain a moderate centrist course and to hold together his party's factions, but the FDP eventually withdrew from the federal coalition in September 1982 and joined forces with the CDU, led by Dr Helmut Kohl (b. 1930), to unseat the chancellor in a 'constructive vote of no confidence'.

Helmut Schmidt immediately retired from politics and the SPD, led by the efficient but colorless Hans-Jöchen Vogel (b. 1926), was heavily defeated in the Bundestag elections of March 1983. In this contest, the SPD significantly lost votes on the left to the ascendant environmentalist Green party, which, capturing 5.6% of the national vote, became the first new party since 1957 to gain representation in the Bundestag.

The new Kohl administration, with the FDP's Hans-Dietrich Genscher (b. 1927) remaining as foreign affairs minister, adhered closely to the external policy of the previous chancellorship. At home, however, a freer market economy approach was pursued. With unemployment rising to a level of 2.5 million in 1984, problems of social unrest emerged, while violent demonstrations greeted the stationing of American nuclear missiles on German soil during 1983–84. Internally, the Kohl administration was also rocked by scandals over illegal party funding by business donors, the 'Flick Affair', which briefly touched the chancellor himself. However, a strong recovery in the German economy from 1985 enabled the CDU-CSU-FDP coalition to secure re-election in the federal election of January 1987.

In this contest, both the minority parties, the FDP and the Greens, polled strongly. In contrast, the opposition SPD, led this time by Johannes Rau (b. 1931), the popular Schmidtite minister-president of the large state of North Rhine-Westphalia, secured its lowest share of the national vote since 1961. This defeat opened divisions within the party over future tactical strategies, with a number of influential figures advocating an alliance with the Greens. By the summer of 1989, however, with the fortunes of the Greens in decline, as a result of internal conflicts and changing global strategic conditions, and with popular support for the SPD showing signs of returning, the party, now led once again by Hans-Jöchen Vogel, recommitted itself to a center-left course. At the *Land* level, the SPD, helped by local factors, secured a string of electoral victories. However, a disturbing feature of many of the elections held during 1989 was the rising level of support for far-right fascist parties, notably the Republicans and the German People's Union (DVU). This was a result of a sudden influx of both ethnic and non-ethnic German immigrants and asylum seekers, totalling 1.2 million during 1988–89, drawn predominantly from Eastern Europe, where previously firmly entrenched communist regimes were fast collapsing.

One such regime was the neighboring GDR. Formed

out of the Soviet zone of occupation, during the years immediately after 1945, a socialist regime on the Soviet Stalinist model had been established rapidly, involving the creation of a *de facto* one-party political system, the nationalization of industries and financial institutions, and agricultural collectivization. Popular opposition to this 'Sovietization' surfaced in mass demonstrations and a general strike in June 1953, at a time of food shortages. These were forcibly suppressed by Soviet troops and the ruling communist party (SED) was purged. In March 1954 the GDR secured full sovereignty from the USSR. Eight years later, in August 1961, the Berlin Wall was constructed to stem the growing movement of refugees to the FRG. During the 1960s economic reforms, known as the 'New Economic Mechanism', gave a boost to the East German growth rate, improving living conditions and easing social tensions. Minor reforms continued under the pragmatic Erich Honecker (1912–94), who replaced the Stalinist Walter Ulbricht (1893–1973) as SED leader in 1971 and supported the East–West *détente* process. However, as the 1980s progressed the SED regime became increasingly set in its ways and resisted the calls for more radical structural reform that began to be made by Mikhail Gorbachev, who became Communist Party leader in the Soviet Union in 1985.

Between May and November 1989, within the space of six months, the SED regime suddenly and unexpectedly collapsed. During much of this period, Honecker was personally incapacitated by serious illness and in his absence there was policy drift. The trigger for the regime's downfall was the decision by the reform-communist government in Hungary to open its borders to the West. This led to an exodus of tens of thousands of 'Ossis' (East Germans) to the FRG from August 1989, destabilizing the faltering GDR economy. At the same time, a grass-roots Protestant church-led prodemocracy movement began to gather strength. Centerd originally in Leipzig and around the intelligentsia-dominated Neue Forum (New Forum) dissident grouping, it became a mass movement, spreading to East Berlin and Dresden, with the visit to the GDR of Gorbachev on 6–7 October 1989.

Initially, these large demonstrations were broken up firmly by the GDR's security forces. However, from 9 October 1989 the will of the authorities faltered and, on 18 October 1989, Honecker and other 'old guard' colleagues resigned from their leadership positions. Egon Krenz (b. 1937), the former chief of the security forces (Stasi), took over as the new SED leader and head of

state, but proved unable to stabilize a fast deteriorating situation. He legalized the formation of opposition parties and on 9 November 1989 opened the Berlin Wall, allowing free movement to the FRG. However, revelations of long-standing corruption within the SED's ruling elite discredited both Krenz and the Communist Party. On 6 December 1989 Krenz resigned as head of state and two days later, at an extraordinary congress, the SED was thoroughly purged and relaunched as a new reform-socialist force, the Party of Democratic Socialism (PDS). Meanwhile Honecker was placed under house arrest awaiting trial on charges of treason, corruption, and abuse of power and in January 1990 the Stasi headquarters in East Berlin were stormed by a seething crowd. (Egon Krenz was convicted of manslaughter in 1997 in connection with sanctioning the killing of refugees fleeing across the Berlin Wall to the West in the 1980s.)

4. From 1990 to 1993

Hans Modrow (b. 1928), the respected reform-communist mayor of Dresden, directed the GDR's affairs as prime minister, heading an all-party coalition 'government of national responsibility' until a multiparty general election was held in March 1990. However, the East German economy continued to deteriorate, with 1,500 people leaving each day for the western *Länder*, following the 1989 exodus of 344,000, and countrywide work stoppages increasing. Surprisingly, the March 1990 GDR general election was won by the East German CDU-dominated three-party Alliance for Germany, which secured a 48% share of the vote, to the East German SPD's 22% and the PDS's 16%. The Alliance, led by Lothar de Maizière (b. 1940), a Protestant lay official and lawyer, was committed to securing rapid reunification with the FRG and immediately entered into negotiations with the Bonn government. With the crucial backing of the USSR and United States, whose agreement as wartime occupying powers in Berlin was required, this goal was achieved on 3 October 1990, with the official capital being designated as Berlin. The new FRG remained within NATO and, in return for the German promise of substantial payments, the USSR/Russia agreed to withdraw all Warsaw Pact troops from the eastern Länder by the end of 1994. This agreement was honoured, the last Russian troops leaving Berlin in August 1994. Political unification was preceded, from 1 July 1990, by German Economic and Monetary Union (GEMU), at a generous Ostmark-Deutschmark currency conversion rate of 1:1, and the establishment, in March 1990, of a trust body, the

Treuhandanstalt, to oversee the privatization of 8,000 state-owned industrial enterprises. Reunification was achieved by the GDR acceding to the FRG and its existing political institutions, although new *Land* constitutions were subsequently framed and approved in referenda by the eastern states between 1990–94. This resulted in the addition of six *Länder*, with a combined population of 17 million. State elections were held on 14 October 1990 in these new *Länder*, which had replaced 14 regions (*Bezirke*), and right-of-center parties polled strongly. Two months later, on 2 December 1990, the first all-German general election since 1932 was held. Popularly acclaimed as the 'Unification Chancellor', having set out a ten-point program for reunification as early as December 1989, Helmut Kohl and his CDU-CSU-FDP governing coalition secured a clear victory, winning 55% of the all-German vote. However, the new coalition government was to contain just three east German politicians. The SPD, led by the charismatic Saarland minister-president Oskar Lafontaine (b. 1943) and stressing the likely high future economic costs of the unification process, lost support in this general election, as did the Greens, who polled below the 5% electoral hurdle in the western *Länder*.

As predicted by the SPD, Chancellor Kohl's 'honeymoon period' was to be short-lived. As 1991–92 progressed tremendous problems arose in securing the smooth economic and social integration of the relatively backward eastern *Länder*, whose average income per head was less than half that enjoyed in western Germany and many of whose industries were over-manned, technologically outdated, and had been rendered 'market-less' as a result of the collapse of the Comecon trading bloc. Hundreds of thousands of 'Ossis' became unemployed as economic restructuring caused consecutive 15% and 20% declines in eastern German GDP in 1991 and 1992, with a third of the workforce either unemployed or on short-time, and more than 90% of 'Ossis' said they now felt like second-class citizens. This fuelled anti-Kohl demonstrations in Leipzig and Dresden in March 1991 and, later, neo-Nazi-directed racist violence. Foreign asylum seekers' hostels were specifically targetted, notably in Rostock in August 1992. The popular standing of Chancellor Kohl also plummetted in the western Länder during 1991–92. This was the consequence of the chancellor's backtracking on a campaign pledge not to raise taxes to pay for eastern Germany's integration and of successive hikes in German interest rates, as inflation began to climb to around 4% and the budget deficit increased,

and as the western German economy moved itself from boom conditions into recession, with the unemployment rate rising to more than 7%. The gathering international recession, itself partly caused by rising German interest rates, which badly damaged the European Exchange Rate Mechanism (ERM), exacerbated the situation. Defeat in Kohl's home *Land* of Rhineland-Palatinate in April 1991 meant that the CDU lost, to the SPD, the majority it had held in the Bundesrat upper house since October 1990.

Support for the CDU also slumped in the Hesse communal elections of March 1993, in which the extremist Republicans attracted 8% of the vote. Pressure mounted for the government to impose tighter restrictions on asylum-seeking immigrants. However, in general, despite the eastern German economy at last beginning to grow by 6%, against a 2% decline in the western *Länder*, 1993 was a year of *Verdrossenheit* ('disillusionment and dissatisfaction') with politics. Nevertheless, the 'solidarity pact' on the future funding of unification negotiated in March 1993 by Kohl with the SPD's leader since May 1991, Bjorn Enghölm (b. 1939), and state minister-presidents helped stabilize the situation, providing for a higher share of VAT receipts to go directly to *Länder*, thus reducing the extent of financial transfers required from western to eastern *Länder* after 1995, and imposing a 7.5% income tax surcharge to meet the resulting shortfall in federal revenue.

5. From 1994 to 1998

During 1994 there were a succession of state, European Parliament, and presidential elections, culminating in the holding of a general election on 16 October 1994 at a time when the all-German economy was beginning to revive. The SPD polled strongly in the Saxony-Anhalt state election in eastern Germany, held in June 1994, but lost ground, along with the FDP, in the Euro-elections of the same month. Roman Herzog (b. 1934), a former president of the Federal Constitutional Court and the CDU nominee of Chancellor Kohl, was elected in May 1994 by the two chambers of parliament to become the new state president, replacing the widely respected Richard von Weizsäcker (b. 1920), who had served a maximum two terms. However, the October 1994 general election saw the Bundestag majority of the ruling CDU-CSU-FDP coalition reduced substantially from 134 seats to just ten seats. The coalition's share of the all-German vote fell to 48%. The FDP polled particularly weakly, attracting less than 7% of the vote, while the CDU-CSU's combined vote share, at 41%, was their lowest ever in a federal election. The opposition SPD, led since June 1993 by Rudolf Scharping (b. 1948) and pledging to reduce unemployment and housing shortages and to impose a 10% 'solidarity surcharge' on high-income earners, captured 36% of the vote, up 3% on 1990; while the Greens re-entered parliament after winning 7% national support.

A largely unchanged new cabinet, headed by Chancellor Kohl, was sworn in on 17 November 1994. It pledged to implement a right-of-center program of continued privatization, tight control over public spending, fighting increasing levels of crime, and encouraging both a deepening and an expansion eastwards of the European Union (EU). However, the political future of an important stabilizing element within the coalition, the liberal FDP, appeared in doubt from 1995 after it failed to surmount the 5% representation hurdle in a succession of state elections, prompting its leader, Klaus Kinkel (b. 1936), the foreign minister, to resign in May 1995. The FDP seemed set to be supplanted as the crucial 'third force' and federal 'swing party' by the unpredictable Greens, whose support in state elections now averaged 10%. In June 1995 Germany broke with a 50-year-old taboo when the Bundestag approved the deployment of 1,500 soldiers and medical staff and fighter bombers in the Balkans war zone. Made possible by a 1994 Constitutional Court ruling allowing such armed missions outside the NATO region provided that they were for humanitarian reasons, this decision marked Germany's first tentative move towards a global military role.

Support for the SPD slumped to a postwar low of 23% in state elections in Berlin, a former stronghold, in October 1995. A month later, Scharping was replaced as party chair by Oskar Lafontaine. Meanwhile, the Kohl coalition was confronted with the dilemma of how to stimulate a faltering economy while ensuring that the public sector deficit did not overshoot the Maastrict Treaty criterion (of below 3% of GDP in 1997–98), which would have prevented entry into the European Single Currency (ESC) in 1999. By December 1995 German unemployment had reached a postwar high of 3.8 million and, in the following month, Chancellor Kohl unveiled a 50-point economic reflation plan involving major tax and welfare reforms, which was intended to halve unemployment by 2000. However, in April 1996 the government was unable to reach agreement with trade unions and employers over the related plans to reduce sick and unemployment pay and job protection, raise the retirement age for men and

women to 65, and freeze public sector pay for two years. There were 'warning strikes' by public sector workers in May 1996 and wider industrial unrest in the autumn, after the Bundestag passed an austerity budget in July 1996. In May 1996 the 16 *Länder* rejected the government's tax reform proposals, while in August 1996 government plans to cut the top rate of income tax from 53% to 40% divided the ruling coalition.

By January 1997, after several quarters of negative GDP growth, the unemployment level peaked at around 4.8 million, equivalent to 12.5% of the work force. It remained around this level throughout 1997–98, although there was real annual GDP growth of 2%. However, while the jobless rate was 10% in the western *Länder* it exceeded 20% in eastern Germany, fuelling frustration in a region where per-capita GDP was less than 60% of the western German level. This was reflected by a sharp increase in the level of racist and extreme-right criminal violence, which rose by a quarter in 1997, to 12,000 reported incidents. In the April 1998 elections in Saxony-Anhalt the xenophobic German People's Union (DVU) won an unprecedented 13% of the vote.

By September 1997 the opposition SPD led narrowly in national polls, but in elections in Hamburg secured its worst postwar result. However, the SPD used its majority in the federal Bundesrat to block the Kohl government's plans to reduce business taxes sharply. In March 1998 the charismatic Gerhard Schröder (b. 1944) was re-elected minister-president of Lower Saxony, with an increased share of the vote. This persuaded the SPD's national executive to select him, rather than Lafontaine, as the party's chancellor-candidate for the forthcoming general election. A charismatic, telegenic, colorful politician and former Marxist chairperson of the SPD's Young Socialists (*Jusos*), Schröder was now a centrist who enjoyed backing from industrialists and was dubbed 'Germany's Tony Blair'. The German economy grew strongly, by 3%, during 1998, enabling it to meet the Maastrict Treaty convergence criteria for the ESC, and Helmut Kohl, although now 68 years old, decided to seek an unprecedented fifth term as chancellor.

However, Kohl proved unable to close the gap in the national opinion polls which had opened during 1998, and, in the September 1998 general election, the CDU, which had pledged tax cuts and further market-centerd reforms, was defeated. The SPD, which had promised to reverse the recent government labor and welfare reforms, ran an unusually slick campaign. Kohl, who became the first postwar German chancellor to be removed at a general election, resigned as CDU chairperson and was replaced by Wolfgang Schäuble, the CDU's parliamentary leader; while Edmund Stoiber, Bavaria's recently re-elected premier, replaced Theo Waigel as CSU leader. Meanwhile, Gerhard Schröder negotiated a coalition with the Greens. This 'red-green' federal coalition faced the risk of being unstable, given the Greens erratic record in state governments, and their recent advocacy of measures such as tripling the price of petrol (over a ten-year period), ending Germany's reliance on nuclear fuel and restricting Germans to holidays in Majorca only one time in five years. The Greens' 'Realo' leader in the Bundestag, Joschka Fischer, became the new foreign minister and there was a commitment for a phasing out of Germany's 19 nuclear power stations. There remained open the possibility of the SPD forging, at a future date, an alternative coalition with either the FDP or the CDU, while Chancellor Schröder seemed likely to be constrained by differences within the SPD. The left-leaning and 'green-enthusiast' Oskar Lafontaine, who became the new finance minister, controlled the party machine and seemed likely to block any significant rightward shift in the SPD's ideological approach, despite Schröder's espousal of a 'new center' in which there would be less state regulation and greater rewards for self-reliance.

In March 1999 Hans Eichel, a former premier of the state of Hesse, became finance minister following the resignation of Oskar Lafontaine, who had been at odds with the more pro-business Chancellor Schröder over tax policy. Lafontaine also resigned as SPD chairman, being replaced by Schröder, and as a deputy. In April 1999 the Bundestag (lower house) held its opening session in its new home, the Reichstag building in Berlin. A month later, Johannes Rau, the former SPD minister-president of North-Rhine-Westphalia, was indirectly elected German president. In June 1999 Chancellor Schröder announced a package of measures to cut taxes and reduce the budget deficit through DM 30 billion of spending cuts in 2000.

ICELAND

Republic of Iceland
Island

Capital: Reykjavik

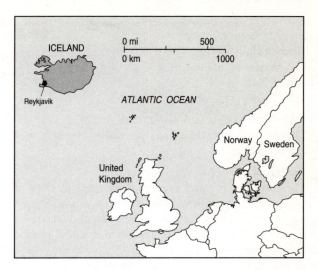

Social and economic data
Area: 102,850 sq km/39,711 sq miles
Population: 274,000[*]
Pop. density per sq km/sq mi: 2.7/7[*]
Urban population: 91%[**]
Literacy rate: 99%[**]
GDP: $6,686 million[*]; per-capita GDP: $24,500[*]
Government defense spending (% of GDP): 0.0%[**]
Currency: krona
Economy type: high income
Labor force in agriculture: 10%[**]
Unemployment rate: 4.9%[*]
[*] 1995.
[**] 1992.

Head of state
President Olafur Ragnar Grimsson, since 1996

Head of government
Prime Minister Davíd Oddsson, since 1991

Ethnic composition
Most of the population is descended from Norwegians and Celts. Icelandic is the official language.

Religions
The Evangelical Lutheran Church of Iceland is the national church, to which about 93% of the population adheres, but there is complete religious freedom. There are also about 1,800 Roman Catholics.

Political features
State type: liberal democratic
Date of state formation: 1944
Political structure: unitary
Executive: parliamentary

Assembly: one-chamber
Party structure: multiparty
Human rights rating: N/A
International affiliations: CE, EEA, EFTA, IAEA, IBRD, IMF, NACC, NATO, NC, OECD, OSCE, UN, WEU (associate), WTO

Local and regional government

The country is divided into provinces, districts, and municipalities.

Political system

The constitution dates from independence in 1944. It provides for a president, as head of state, who is elected for four years by universal adult suffrage, and an assembly, called the Althing. It has 63 members, also elected by universal adult suffrage, through a party list system of proportional representation, for a four-year term.

The president appoints the prime minister and cabinet on the basis of parliamentary support and they are collectively responsible to the Althing.

Political parties

There are some seven parties and the electoral system tends to encourage a spread of assembly representation and, hence, coalitions of parties. The main parties are the Independence Party (IP), the Progressive Party (PP), the People's Alliance (PA), the Social Democratic Party (SDP), the Awakening of the Nations (AN) party, and the Women's Alliance (WA).

The IP was formed in 1929 by an amalgamation of the Conservative and Liberal parties. It has a right-of-center orientation. The PP dates from 1916 and is a rural-based centrist party.

The PA was founded in 1956 by a union of SDP dissidents and the Socialist Unity Party. It has a socialist orientation and has, in the past, opposed Iceland's membership of NATO. In 1996 the Left–Green Alliance was formed as a breakaway group.

The SDP was formed in 1916 as the political arm of Iceland's labor movement. It has a moderate center-left orientation and favors entering the European Union.

The AN was formed in January 1995 as a leftwing breakaway from the SDP. The WA is also a comparatively new party, having been formed in 1983. It is an all-female party, concerned with the promotion of women's and children's interests.

In 1999 the SDP, PA, and WA fought the general election together, as the United Left.

Political leaders since 1970

1970–71 Johann Hafstein (IP-SDP coalition), 1971–74 Olafur Johannesson (PP-PA coalition), 1974–78 Geir Hallgrimsson (IP-PP coalition), 1978–79 Olafur Johannesson (PP-PA-SDP coalition), 1979–80 Benedikt Grondal (SDP), 1980–83 Gunnar Thoroddsen (IP-PA-PP coalition), 1983–87 Steingrímur Hermannsson (PP-IP coalition), 1987–91 Thorsteinn Pálsson (IP-PP-SDP coalition), 1991– Davíd Oddsson (IP-SDP coalition)

Latest elections

The results of the 8 May 1999 general election were as illustrated in the following table. Turnout was 84%.

Iceland latest election results

Party	% votes	Seats
IP	40.8	26
Left-Green Alliance	26.8	17
PPP	18.4	12
United Left (SDP/PA/WA)	9.1	6
Other parties	4.9	2

The June 1996 presidential election was won by the leftwing Olafur Ragnar Grimsson (PA), who attracted more than 40% of the vote, defeating three rival candidates.

Political history

Iceland became independent in 1944, when the convention which linked it to Denmark was terminated. In 1949 it joined the North Atlantic Treaty Organization (NATO) and the Council of Europe and in 1953 the Nordic Council. Since independence it has always been governed by coalitions of the leading parties, sometimes rightwing and sometimes leftwing groupings, but mostly moderate.

Externally, most of Iceland's problems have been connected with the excessive exploitation of the fishing grounds around its coasts, while domestically governments have been faced with the recurring problem of inflation. It became a member of the European Free Trade Association (EFTA) in 1970, but remains opposed to membership of the European Union (EU) since it perceives the EU's fishing quota policy as inimical to the nation's interest.

In May 1985 the Althing unanimously declared the country a 'nuclear free zone', banning the entry of all nuclear weapons. The 1987 elections ended control of the Althing by the coalition of the Independence and Progressive parties, giving more influence to the minor parties, including the Women's Alliance which doubled its seat tally. In the 1991 general election the Independence Party (IP) strengthened its position, in votes and seats, and a center-right coalition was formed with the Social Democratic Party (SDP), led by Davíd Oddsson (b. 1948) of the IP. A new coalition was formed with the PP after another general election in April 1995.

After a period of strong economic growth, with low inflation, the IP–PP centre-right coalition government, led by Oddsson, won a further term in office, after the general election of May 1999. This election saw an increase in the number of women deputies from 16 to 22.

IRELAND

Republic of Ireland
Eire
Poblacht Na hEireann

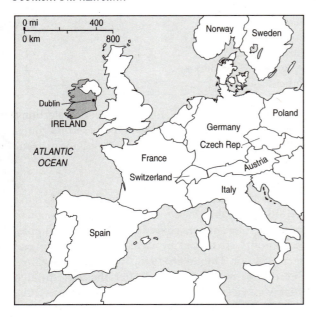

Capital: Dublin

Social and economic data
Area: 70,283 sq km/27,136 sq miles
Population: 3,626,000[*]
Pop. density per sq km/sq mi: 52/134[*]
Urban population: 58%[**]
Literacy rate: 99%[**]
GDP: $52,765 million[*]; per-capita GDP: $14,600[*]
Government defense spending (% of GDP): 1.2%[*]
Currency: punt
Economy type: high income

Labor force in agriculture: 14%[**]
Unemployment rate: 12.2.%[*]
[*] 1995.
[**] 1992.

Head of state
President Mary McAleese, since 1997

Head of government
Prime Minister Bertie Ahern, since 1997

Ethnic composition
Most of the population has Celtic origins. Although Irish (*Gaeltacht*) is the official language, English is most widely used and Irish is spoken only in restricted areas, mainly in the west. Official documents are printed in both languages.

Religions
Almost all the population is Christian, about 95% Roman Catholic.

Political features
State type: liberal democratic
Date of state formation: 1937
Political structure: unitary
Executive: parliamentary
Assembly: two-chamber
Party structure: multiparty
Human rights rating: 94%
International affiliations: CE, EEA, ESA, EU, IAEA, IBRD, IMF, IWC, OECD, OSCE, UN, WEU (observer), WTO

Local and regional government
The country is divided into four provinces containing 26 counties. The counties and towns have elected councils.

Political system
The 1937 constitution provides for a president, elected by universal adult suffrage, for a seven-year term, and a two-chamber National Parliament, consisting of a Senate (*Seanad éireann*) and a House of Representatives (*Dáil éireann*), serving a five-year term. The Senate has 60 members, 11 nominated by the prime minister, six are elected by the universities, and 43 by panels representative of most aspects of Irish life. The Dáil consists of 166 members elected by universal adult suffrage, through the single transferable vote system of proportional representation. The president appoints a prime minister (*Taoiseach*), who is nominated by the Dáil. He or she chooses the cabinet and all are collectively responsible to the Dáil, which is subject to dissolution

by the president if the government loses its confidence within the five-year term.

Political parties

The system of proportional representation encourages the formation of several parties, of which there are some 14, the five most significant being Fianna Fáil, Fine Gael, the Labor Party, the Progressive Democrats, and the Democratic Left.

The term Fianna Fáil literally means Soldiers of Destiny. The party was formed in 1926 by the charismatic leader, Éamon de Valera, and was originally a wing of Sinn Féin (The Workers' Party). It was always a party of radical republicanism, calling for the complete independence of Ireland. It now has a moderate center-right orientation and favors the peaceful reunification of the island.

Fine Gael means Irish Tribe, or United Ireland Party, and is descended from the Society of the Irish. It was originally founded in 1922 to support the first government established within the new Irish Free State, and was reformed in 1933. It has a moderate center-left orientation.

The Labor Party dates from 1912, when it was part of Ireland's Trade Union Congress. In 1930 it was decided to separate the industrial and political functions of the movement and the Labor Party became a separate organization. It has a moderate left-of-center orientation.

The Progressive Democrats party was formed as recently as 1985 and represents a new departure in Irish politics, being more radical than the other established parties. It seeks a peaceful solution to the problems in Northern Ireland, the encouragement of private enterprise, the abolition of the Seanad, and a clear distinction between church and state.

The Democratic Left is a left-of-center group formed in 1992.

Political leaders since 1970

1966–73 Jack Lynch (Fianna Fáil), 1973–77 Liam Cosgrave (Fine Gael-Labor coalition), 1977–79 Jack Lynch (Fianna Fáil), 1979–81 Charles Haughey (Fianna Fáil), 1981–82 Garret FitzGerald (Fine Gael-Labor coalition), 1982 Charles Haughey (Fianna Fáil), 1982–87 Garret FitzGerald (Fine Gael-Labor coalition), 1987–89 Charles Haughey (Fianna Fáil), 1989–92 Charles Haughey (Fianna Fáil-Progressive Democrats coalition), 1992 Albert Reynolds (Fianna Fáil-Progressive Democrats coalition), 1993–94 Albert Reynolds (Fianna Fáil-Labor coalition), 1994–97 John

Bruton (Fine Gael-Labor coalition), 1997– Bertie Ahern (Fianna Fáil-Progressive Democrats coalition)

Latest elections

The results of the June 1997 Dáil elections were as follows:

Ireland latest election results

Party	% votes	Seats
Fianna Fáil	39.3	77
Fine Gael	27.9	54
Labor Party	10.4	17
Progressive Democrats	4.7	4
Other parties	17.7	14

The results of the August 1997 Seanad elections were as follows:

Party	Seats
Fianna Fáil	29
Fine Gael	16
Labor Party	4
Progressive Democrats	4
Others	7

In the 30 November 1997 presidential elections, Mary McAleese (Fianna Fáil) won in the second round with 59% of the votes, defeating Mary Banotti (Fine Gael).

Political history

Ireland was joined to Great Britain by the Act of Union of 1801 but by the 1880s there was a strong movement for home rule. This was conceded in 1914 but its implementation was delayed by World War I, resulting in fierce riots in Dublin in 1916, the Easter Rebellion. Guerrilla activities continued after the war, through what was called the Irish Republican Army (IRA), which was formed by Michael Collins (1890–1922) in 1919. In 1921 a treaty gave southern Ireland dominion status within the British Commonwealth, while the six northern counties of Ulster remained part of the United Kingdom, but with limited self-government.

The Irish Free State, as southern Ireland was formally called in 1922, was accepted by IRA leader, Michael Collins, but not by many of his colleagues, who transferred their allegiance to Éamon de Valera (1882–1975), leader of the Fianna Fáil party. He, too, eventually acknowledged the partition in 1937, when a new constitution was proclaimed in Dublin, giving the country the name of Eire and establishing it as a sovereign state.

The IRA continued its fight for an independent, unified Ireland through a campaign of violence, mainly in Northern Ireland but also on the British mainland and, to a lesser extent, in the Irish republic. Eire remained part of the Commonwealth until 1949, when it left, declaring itself the Republic of Ireland, while Northern Ireland remained a constituent part of the United Kingdom.

Despite the sympathy of governments in Dublin for reunification, all have condemned the violence of the IRA and have dealt strongly with it within Ireland itself. In 1973 Ireland's traditional party, Fianna Fáil, which had held office for more than 40 years, was defeated and Liam Cosgrave (b. 1920) formed a coalition of the Fine Gael and Labor parties. In 1977 Fianna Fáil returned to power, with Jack Lynch (b. 1917) as prime minister. Meanwhile, the IRA violence intensified, with the murder of Earl Mountbatten of Burma in Ireland, in 1979, and the massacre of 18 British soldiers in Northern Ireland.

Lynch resigned later the same year and was succeeded by Charles Haughey (b. 1925), now leader of Fianna Fáil. His aim was a united Ireland, with a large measure of independence for the six northern counties. He called an early general election, in 1981, but failed to win a majority, allowing Dr Garret FitzGerald (b. 1926), leader of the Fine Gael party, to form another coalition with Labor. The following year, however, he was defeated on his budget proposals and resigned. Charles Haughey returned to office, with a minority government, but he too was forced to resign later the same year, resulting in the return of FitzGerald.

Various ideas were then explored in an effort to resolve the Irish problem, culminating in the signing of the Anglo-Irish Agreement in 1985, providing for regular consultation and the exchange of information on political, legal, security, and cross-border matters. The Agreement also said that no change in the status of Northern Ireland would be made without the consent of a majority of the people. The Agreement was strongly criticized by the leaders of Ulster's two main Protestant Unionist parties.

At the start of 1987 Garret FitzGerald's coalition came to the end of its life and a general election was called. It was won by Fianna Fáil and Charles Haughey returned to power. His relations with the British government proved to be more successful than many people had predicted and the Anglo-Irish Agreement continued to be honoured by the new administration.

Meanwhile, the young former finance and justice minister, Alan Dukes, had succeeded FitzGerald as leader of Fine Gael.

In 1989 Haughey, in an attempt to secure an overall majority in the Dáil, called a general election. Again he failed and was forced to form a coalition with the Progressive Democrats. His standing in the country, and within his own party, deteriorated and in February 1992 he lost the leadership to his former finance minister, Albert Reynolds (b. 1935). It was hoped that Reynolds' calm but firm approach would strengthen Ireland domestically and internationally.

At first these hopes seemed to have been realized and in June 1992 the Irish people voted emphatically to ratify the Maastricht Treaty on closer European union. However, as the year progressed, Reynolds' touch seemed to have deserted him and in November, after losing a confidence vote, he sought a personal mandate through a successful general election result. He did not, however, obtain his clear victory and was obliged to enter a coalition with the Labor Party, with its leader, Dick Spring (b. 1950), as his deputy.

Growing in confidence, in October 1993 Reynolds unveiled a six-year national development plan to achieve 'the transformation of Ireland' and in the following month furthered the Northern Ireland peace process by agreeing a 'joint declaration' with the United Kingdom's prime minister, John Major, aimed at securing a just and lasting settlement.

1994 started on a high note but fell away when, in November, after a deep disagreement with Dick Spring over a judicial appointment, Prime Minister Reynolds lost Labor's support and was forced to resign. After some manoeuvring, the Fine Gael leader, John Bruton (b. 1947), who had replaced Alan Dukes in November 1990, agreed a new 'rainbow coalition' with Labor and the Democratic Left. Reynolds relinquished the Fianna Fáil leadership and was succeeded by his former finance minister, Bertie Ahern.

The general election of June 1997 produced an inconclusive outcome, and Bruton resigned as prime minister. He was replaced by Ahern, who formed a Fianna Fáil-Progressive Democrats minority coalition. Ahern established a rapport with his British counterpart, Tony Blair, and together they set out to accelerate the Northern Ireland peace process, which led to an agreement by all political parties approved by referenda on both sides of the border in May 1998.

ITALY

Republic of Italy
Repubblica Italiana

Capital: Rome

Social and economic data
Area: 301,225 sq km/116,304 sq miles
Population: 57,193,000[*]
Pop. density per sq km/sq mi: 190/492[*]
Urban population: 69%[**]
Literacy rate: 97%[**]
GDP: $1,088,000 million[*]; per-capita GDP: $19,030[*]
Government defense spending (% of GDP): 1.8%[*]
Currency: lira
Economy type: high income
Labor force in agriculture: 10%[**]
Unemployment rate: 12.0%
[*] 1995.
[**] 1992.

Head of state
President Carlo Azeglio Ciampi, since 1999

Head of government
Prime Minister Massimo D'Alema, since 1998

Ethnic composition
The population is mostly Italian but there are minorities of German origin in the Dolomites and Slovenes around Trieste. Italian is the national language.

Religions
About 90% of the population is Roman Catholic. This was the state religion between 1929 and 1984.

Political features
State type: liberal democratic
Date of state formation: 1861
Political structure: unitary
Executive: parliamentary
Assembly: two-chamber
Party structure: multiparty
Human rights rating: 90%
International affiliations: AG (observer), ALADI (observer), CE, CERN, CSCE, EEA, ESA, EU, G-7, G-10, IAEA, IBRD, IMF, NACC, NATO, OECD, UN, WEU, WTO

Local and regional government
The country is divided into 20 regions, five of which, Sicily, Sardinia, Trentino-Alto Adige, Friuli-Venezia Giulia, and Valle d'Aosta, have a special status and enjoy a greater measure of autonomy, because of their geographical, cultural, or linguistic differences. Each region has a popularly elected council. Since the mid-1970s increasing powers have been devolved from the center to the regions and today more than 30% of the national budget is under regional control.

Political system
The 1948 constitution provides for a two-chamber assembly, consisting of a 315-member Senate and a 630-member Chamber of Deputies, both serving five-year terms. The 315 elected members of the Senate are regionally representative and there are also seven life senators. The voting age is set at 25 years for Senate elections, but at 18 years for the lower house. All members of the Chamber were formerly elected through a party list system of proportional representation, but in 1993 the electoral system underwent major reform. Now three-quarters of the members are elected by simple majority voting, the remaining quarter by the party list system. Candidates need at least 4% of the national vote to be successful. Polling is now confined to a single day, instead of being spread over two rounds. The two chambers have equal powers.

The president is a constitutional head of state and is elected for a seven-year term by an electoral college consisting of both assembly chambers and 58 regional representatives. The president appoints the prime minister and cabinet, which is called the Council of Ministers, and they are all collectively responsible to the assembly. Parliament may not be dissolved during the six-month period preceding the presidential election.

In June 1997 a parliamentary commission recommended establishing a federal system and a directly elected president with responsibility for foreign and defense policy; a reduction in the number of members of the Chamber of Deputies from 630 to 400; and a reduction in the number of senators from 315 to 200. The recommendations required approval by both assemblies and then popular endorsement by a national referendum.

Political parties

In the run-up to the 1996 general election two major blocs emerged: the center-left Olive Tree alliance and the rightwing Freedom Alliance.

The Olive Tree alliance comprised the Democratic Party of the Left (PDS), the Italian People's Party (PPI), the South Tyrol's People's Party (SUP), the Democratic Union (UD), Italian Renewal, and the Green Party (estd. 1997).

The Freedom Alliance included the Christian Democratic Center (CCD), Forza Italia (Go Italy!), the National Alliance (AN), the Panella List, and the Union of the Democratic Center (UDC).

The CCD is the rightwing of the Christian Democratic Party (DC) which was formed in 1943 as the successor to the pre-Fascist Popular Party. It is a Christian centrist party and strongly anti-communist.

Forza Italia was created in 1994 as a political vehicle for the media magnate, Silvio Berlusconi, owner of three television channels, several newspapers, and the AC Milan football team. He took the slogan of the AC Milan's supporters, 'Come on Italy!' as the party's name.

The AN was formerly part of the Italian Social Movement (MSI), a neo-Fascist party founded in 1946. It has a membership of 400,000 and is led by Gianfranco Fini.

The Panella List is a radical grouping consisting of the followers of the libertarian politician Marco Pannella.

The UDC developed from the Italian Liberal Party (PLI) which was founded in 1848 by Count Camilio di Cavour, who played such a key role in the unification of Italy. The PLI dominated the nation's politics in its early years but it moved steadily to the right.

The PPI is a revival of the pre-Fascist Popular Party, founded in 1919, which in 1943 was replaced by the Christian Democratic Party (DC). It has a Catholic centrist orientation.

The SUP is a regional party. The UD was formed in 1996, as was the other centrist party, Italian Renewal.

There is also the LN, or Lombard League, formed in 1979 and named after the 12th-century federation of northern cities that rebelled against the emperor, Frederick Barbarossa. It opposes the granting of subsidies by the economically rich north to the underdeveloped south and promotes the cause of federalism and regionalism. A conservative-populist body, it is led by Umberto Bossi (b. 1941).

The PDS was originally the Italian Communist Party, formed in 1921. It changed its name to the Democratic Party of the Left (PDS) in 1991. It has a moderate left-wing orientation. Led by Massimo D'Alema, it has a membership of 1.4 million.

Political leaders since 1970

1970 Mariano Rumor (DC-led coalition), 1970–72 Emilio Colombo (DC-led coalition), 1972–73 Giulio Andreotti (DC-led coalition), 1973–74 Mariano Rumor (DC-led coalition), 1974–76 Aldo Moro (DC-led coalition), 1976 Aldo Moro (DC), 1976–79 Giulio Andreotti (DC), 1979–80 Francesco Cossiga (DC-led coalition), 1980–81 Arnaldo Forlani (DC-led coalition), 1981–83 Giovanni Spadolini (PRI-led coalition), 1983 Amitore Fanfani (DC-led coalition), 1983–87 Bettino Craxi (PSI-led coalition), 1987 Amitore Fanfani (DC-led coalition), 1987–88 Giovanni Goria (DC-led coalition), 1988–89 Ciriaco De Mita (DC-led coalition), 1989–92 Giulio Andreotti (DC-led coalition), 1992–93 Giuliano Amato (PSI-led coalition), 1993–94 Carlo Azeglio Ciampi (DC-led coalition), 1994–95 Silvio Berlusconi (Freedom Alliance), 1995–96 Lamberto Dini (technocrat administration), 1996–98 Romano Prodi (PPI-led coalition), 1998– Massimo D'Alema (PDS-led coalition)

Latest elections

The April 1996 general election results were as follows:

Italy latest election results
Senate

Party	% votes	Seats
Olive Tree	41.2	157
Freedom Alliance	37.3	116
Northern League	10.4	27
Others	11.1	15

Chamber of Deputies

Party	% votes	Seats
Olive Tree	34.8	284
Freedom Alliance	44.0	246
Northern League	10.1	59
Others	11.1	41

Political history

Italy became a unified kingdom in 1861 and soon afterwards set about acquiring a colonial empire by a mixture of purchase and seizure. The Fascist period, between 1922 and 1943, was notable for an extensive program of public works but the liaison with Nazi Germany drew it into World War II and eventual defeat. In 1946, after a referendum, the monarchy was abolished and Italy became a republic, adopting a new constitution in 1948.

The postwar period has seen rapid changes of government and the striking of many deals between the political parties. Until 1963 the Christian Democrats were dominant but this was followed by a succession of coalition governments, most with Christian Democratic involvement. In 1976 the Communists became a significant force, winning more than a third of the votes for the Chamber of Deputies. With this show of support, they pressed for what they called the 'historic compromise', a broad-based government with representatives from the Christian Democratic, Socialist, and Communist parties, which would, in effect, be an alliance between communism and Roman Catholicism. This was rejected, however, by the Christian Democrats.

Apart from a brief period in 1977–78, the other parties successfully excluded the Communists from power-sharing, forcing them to become part of the opposition. In 1980 the Socialists returned to share power with the Christian Democrats and Republicans and they continued in a number of subsequent coalitions of mixed composition. Then, in 1983, the leader of the Socialist Party, Bettino Craxi (b. 1934), became the first Socialist prime minister in the republic's history, leading a coalition of Christian Democrats, Socialists, Republicans, Social Democrats, and Liberals. Despite criticisms of Craxi's strong-willed style of leadership, the coalition parties could find no acceptable alternative so continued to give him support. The Craxi government saw an improvement in the state of the Italian economy, although the north–south divide in productivity and prosperity persisted.

In August 1986 an agreement was reached that Craxi would hand over power to the DC leader, Ciriaco De Mita (b. 1928), in March 1987, allowing the coalition to stay in office until the general election in June 1988. However, when Craxi did resign the Socialists withdrew their support from the Christian Democrats, precipitating a constitutional crisis. Amitore Fanfani, of the Christian Democrats, headed a caretaker government

for a time, then Giovanni Goria (b. 1943) formed another unstable coalition, leaving Italian politics in a state of continuing uncertainty. Goria held office for eight months, twice threatening to resign, then in March 1988 he submitted his resignation on a nuclear power issue and it was accepted by the president. Ciriaco De Mita, leader of the Christian Democrats, then took up the challenge, forming a five-party coalition, including the Socialists, led by Craxi.

In February 1989 De Mita was replaced as DC leader by Arnaldo Forlani, but continued as prime minister. In May 1989, however, he resigned and, after much manoeuvring, the veteran politician, Giulio Andreotti, was recalled to form yet another coalition. In 1991 Andreotti formed another government, the 50th since the end of World War II, and remained in office until the April 1992 general election.

The result was inconclusive and threw the political system into disarray. President Cossiga resigned and it was a month before a permanent replacement could be found, in the shape of the veteran politician, Oscar Luigi Scalfaro (b. 1918). After weeks of bargaining, Giuliano Amato of the Socialist Party managed to form Italy's 51st postwar government, a broad coalition of parties. The uncertainty of the political situation had its effect on the economy and in September 1992 the lira was devalued and Italy withdrew from the European Exchange Rate Mechanism (ERM).

Amid allegations of corruption, Bettino Craxi resigned as Socialist Party leader and was replaced by Giorgio Benvenuto. Under the leadership of the brave, crusading Milan magistrate, Antonio Di Pietro, a wide-ranging Tangentopoli ('kickback city') probe was instigated from 1992. It revealed the long-suspected depth and systematic nature of political corruption. Clearly implicated in bribes-for-contracts deals and payoffs from the Mafia, leading politicians and business executives were arrested almost daily during 1993, with even Giulio Andreotti implicated. This led to the formation of a 'government of technocrats' headed by Carlo Azeglio Ciampi, a governor of the Bank of Italy. Meanwhile Craxi had been absolved from prosecution for corruption and Benvenuto had resigned the Socialist Party leadership and had been succeeded by Ottaviano del Turro.

Disillusionment with the instability in Italian politics stimulated a demand for the reform of the voting system and in a referendum in April 1993 there was an overwhelming vote for change. There were also votes to end the state financing of parties and abolish a number of state ministries.

In January 1994 Prime Minister Ciampi resigned to make way for a general election and, in anticipation of this, there was a fundamental realignment of the political parties, resulting in the formation of three main groupings, to the right, in the center, and to the left of the political spectrum. A new political force emerged in the shape of the media tycoon, Silvio Berlusconi (b. 1936), who launched Forza Italia as the spearhead of the rightwing Freedom Alliance. Berlusconi used his television channels and newspapers, and his own popularity as owner of the AC Milan football team, to promote his political ambitions and in the March 1994 elections the Freedom Alliance, led by Forza Italia, secured a surprise landslide victory. The formerly dominant Christian Democrats, who had disbanded and reformed themselves as the Popular Party within the centrist Pact for Italy, were so badly tarnished by the corruption scandals that they finished in a distant third position. After considerable manoeuvring, Berlusconi formed a rightwing coalition with Forza Italia, the profederalist Northern League (LN) and the neofascist National Alliance (AN) as the main partners.

Berlusconi's honeymoon as the nation's leader was short-lived. In July 1994 he was accused of fraud, through his many business interests, and his younger brother, Paolo ,was placed under house arrest. Opposition to his free-market economic policies provoked industrial resistance, including a one-day strike. In December 1994, rather than risk losing a confidence vote in parliament, Berlusconi resigned and was replaced by ex-banker Lamberto Dini, who had been an independent member of the Freedom Alliance government.

Dini led a cabinet of nonelected technocrats, receiving support from the Democratic Party of the Left (PDS), the Popular Party (the successor to the DC), and the LN, with fierce opposition being provided by Forza Italia and the AN.

The Dini administration sought to reform the state pensions system to reduce the budget deficit. With the support of the Reconstructed Communists, in October 1995, it survived a no-confidence vote called by Forza Italia, whose leader Berlusconi was set to stand trial in January 1996 on company tax evasion and bribery charges. In December 1997 he was convicted and given a ten-month suspended sentence, allowing him to avoid prison. In February 1996 Dini's government fell, after losing the backing of the PDS and LN, who opposed further fiscal austerity. After attempts to form a new government failed, a general election was called.

This brought victory for the center-left Olive Tree alliance, and Romano Prodi, of the People's Party (PPI), became prime minister. He introduced a 'tax for Europe' to ensure that Italy met the financial conditions set for participation in the European Single Currency (ESC) in 1999. Prodi resigned in October 1998 after losing, by a single vote, a no-confidence vote in parliament, after the PDS had withdrawn its support. The PDS leader, Massimo D'Alema, was invited to construct the country's 56th postwar government. His cabinet retained Lamberto Dini as foreign minister and Carlo Ciampi as finance minister, and his coalition was supported by Francesco Cossiga, leader of the centrist United Democrats.

A referendum, held in April 1999, saw overwhelming (more than 90%) support for ending the use of proportional representation to elect deputies. However, the measure failed as turnout was below the 50% level required to make the referendum binding. In May 1999 Carlo Azeglio Ciampi, a 78-year-old treasury minister and former prime minister, was elected president by the 1,010-member electoral college on the first ballot.

LIECHTENSTEIN

Principality of Liechtenstein
Fürstentum Liechtenstein

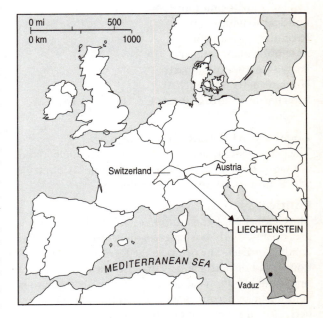

Capital: Vaduz

Social and economic data
Area: 160 sq km/62 sq miles
Population: 31,000*
Pop. density per sq km/sq mi: 104/500*
Urban population: 87%**
Literacy rate: 99%**
GDP: $1,430 million*; per-capita GDP: $46,200*
Government defense spending (% of GDP): 0%**
Currency: Swiss franc
Economy type: high income
Labor force in agriculture: 3%**
* 1995.
** 1992.

Head of state
Prince Hans Adam von und zu Liechtenstein II, since 1984

Head of government
Prime Minister Mario Frick, since 1993

Ethnic composition
The indigenous population is of German-speaking Alemannic origin, while a third are foreign-born resident workers.

Religions
Roman Catholicism is the main religion.

Political features
State type: liberal democratic
Date of state formation: 1342
Political structure: unitary
Executive: parliamentary
Assembly: one-chamber
Party structure: multiparty
Human rights rating: N/A
International affiliations: CE, EEA, EFTA, IAEA, OSCE, UN, WTO

Local and regional government
The principality is divided into two districts, Oberland (Upper Country) and Unterland (Lower Country), which, in turn, comprise 11 communes.

Political system
The October 1921 constitution established a hereditary principality, with a single-chamber parliament, the Landtag or Diet. The prince is the formal and constitutional head of state. He may dissolve parliament at any time and his approval is required for all legislation before it may become law. The Landtag has 25 members, elected for a four-year term, through a system of proportional representation, based on the use of two district-level constituencies and the rule that parties which secure less than 8% of the votes cast fail to qualify for the distribution of seats.

Until 1984 only men were entitled to vote. Women, who constitute 67% of the electorate, were then given suffrage, which now extends to all adults aged 20 and over.

A group of five people, a prime minister and four councillors, are elected by the Landtag to form the principality's government (Collegial Board) for the duration of parliament.

Political parties
There are four political parties, the two most dominant being the Patriotic Union (VU) and the Progressive Citizens' Party (FBP). The VU was founded in 1918 and remodelled in 1938. It has a firm support base in the mountainous south of the principality.

The FBP is a northern-based party. Both parties share a similar conservative ideological outlook.

Political leaders since 1978
1978–93 Hans Brunhart (VU), 1993 Markus Büchel (FBP), 1993– Mario Frick (VU)

Latest elections
In the 2 February 1997 Landtag elections the VU won 13 seats, the FBP, 10, and the Free List, 2 seats.

Political history
Liechtenstein was founded as a sovereign state in 1342 and has remained within its present boundaries since 1432. It did not, however, adopt its current name until 1719, when it was purchased by the present ruling family, and formed part of the Holy Roman Empire until 1806. Between 1815 and 1866 the state was a member of the German Confederation, before leaving to become a fully independent principality.

However, because of its small size and the decision to abolish its armed forces in 1868, Liechtenstein has found it convenient, while remaining neutral in external disputes, to associate itself with larger neighboring nations in international matters. For example, from 1923 it shared a customs union with Switzerland, which also represented it internationally. Previously Austria undertook its diplomatic representation. In 1991 it became a full member of the European Free Trade Area (EFTA) and in 1992 a member of the United Nations. It has been a member of the Council of Europe since 1978. It joined the European Economic Area (EEA) in May 1995, after two referenda had approved entry.

Liechtenstein is one of the world's richest countries, with an income per head comparable to that of Switzerland and Japan and twice as great as that of the United Kingdom. High technology precision engineering, international banking, aided by its favorable tax structure and legal system, and tourism constitute the three pillars of this successful economy. Around 80,000 foreign corporations have nominated offices in the principality.

After 42 years as the main government party, the FBP was defeated by the VU in 1970 but returned to power four years later. After a close election result in 1978 the VU returned to government and remained in office until 1993. There were two general elections in that year. In the first, in February, the FBP won most seats but not an overall majority and the leading FBP candidate, Markus Büchel, formed an FBP-VU coalition. Büchel was defeated on a vote of confidence moved by his own party in September, and another election was called. This time the VU secured a narrow majority and its leading candidate, Mario Frick, formed a new administration. He again narrowly retained power at the February 1997 general election. In April 1997 the FBP withdrew from the governing coalition, leaving the VU alone in power.

Prince Franz Josef II, who succeeded to the throne in 1938, and was *de facto* ruler for four and a half decades, handed over executive powers to his son and heir, Prince Hans Adam (b. 1945), in August 1984. He later died in 1989.

LUXEMBOURG

Grand Duchy of Luxembourg
Grand-Duché de Luxembourg

Capital: Luxembourg

Social and economic data
Area: 2,590 sq km/1,000 sq miles
Population: 413,000[*]
Pop. density per sq km/sq mi: 159/413/[*]
Urban population: 85%[**]
Literacy rate: 100%[**]
GDP: $16,880 million[*]; per-capita GDP: $40,870[*]
Government defense spending (% of GDP): 0.9%[*]
Currency: Luxembourg franc
Economy type: high income
Labor force in agriculture: 3%[**]

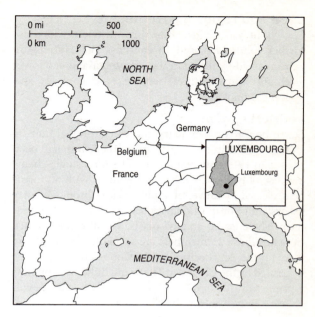

Unemployment rate: 2.5%[*]
[*] 1995.
[**] 1992.

Head of state
Grand Duke Jean I, since 1964

Head of government
Prime Minister Jean-Claude Junker, since 1995

Ethnic composition
Most of the population are descended from the Moselle Franks. Letzeburgish, a German-Moselle-Frankish dialect is the official language. French is used in government communications and German is the language of commerce and the media.

Religions
Ninety-five per cent of the population is Roman Catholic. There are also about 4,000 Evangelicals.

Political features
State type: liberal democratic
Date of state formation: 1848
Political structure: unitary
Executive: parliamentary
Assembly: one-chamber
Party structure: multiparty
Human rights rating: N/A
International affiliations: BENELUX, BLEU, CE, EEA, EU, IAEA, IBRD, IMF, NACC, NATO, OECD, OSCE, UN, WEU, WTO

Local and regional government

The country is divided into three districts, which are further subdivided into 13 cantons. The cantons are administered by the central government and at a lower level are municipalities, with elected councils and appointed mayors.

Political system

Luxembourg is a hereditary and constitutional monarchy. The constitution dates from 1868, but has been revised in 1919 and 1956. It provides for a single-chamber assembly, the Chamber of Deputies, with 60 members, elected by universal adult suffrage through a party list system of proportional representation, for a five-year term. There is also an advisory body called the Council of State whose 21 members are appointed by the grand duke for life. Any decision of the Council of State can be overruled by the Chamber. The grand duke also appoints a prime minister and Council of Ministers who are collectively responsible to the Chamber.

Political parties

There are some seven political parties, the most significant being the Christian Social Party (PCS), the Luxembourg Socialist Workers' Party (POSL), and the Democratic Party 'Liberals' (PD) and the Action Committee for Democracy and Pensions Justice (ADR).

The PCS was founded in 1914 as the Party of the Right. It took its present name in 1944. It has often been seen as the 'natural' party of government, having been a member of most coalitions. It stands for political stability and planned economic expansion, and is a strong European Union supporter. It has a moderate center-right orientation.

The POSL was formed in 1902 as the working class party, with strong links with the union movement. It has a moderate socialist orientation.

The PD dates from 1945 and was partly based on the anti-German resistance movement. Its predecessor was the prewar Liberal Party and PD members are now popularly described as the 'Liberals'. The party has a centrist orientation.

The ADR is a party orientated towards pensioners' rights.

Political leaders since 1970

1969–74 Pierre Werner (PCS-PD coalition), 1974–79 Gaston Thorn (POSL-PD coalition), 1979–84 Pierre Werner (PCS- PD coalition), 1984–95 Jacques Santer (PCS-POSL coalition), 1995– Jean-Claude Junker (PCS-POSL coalition)

Latest elections

The results in the 13 June 1999 general election were as follows:

Luxembourg latest election results

Party	% votes	Seats
PCS	30.2	19
POSL	24.2	13
PD	18.9	15
ADR	10.5	7
Greens	7.5	5
Others	5.6	1

Political history

Originally part of the Holy Roman Empire, Luxembourg became a duchy in 1354. It was made a Grand Duchy in 1815 but, like Belgium, under Netherlands rule. Belgium secured its independence in 1839, taking part of Luxembourg with it. The grand duchy achieved full independence in 1848.

Although a small country, Luxembourg occupies an important pivotal position in Western Europe, being a founder member of many international organizations, including the European Coal and Steel Community (ECSC), the European Atomic Energy Commission (EURATOM), and the European Community (EC) itself. It formed an economic union with Belgium and the Netherlands in 1948 (Benelux), which was the forerunner of wider European cooperation. Today, Luxembourg constitutes one of the European Union's three centers of administration.

Grand Duchess Charlotte, who had been the country's ruler, since 1919, abdicated in 1964 and was succeeded by her son Prince Jean (b. 1925). She died, aged 89, in 1985.

The proportional representation voting system has resulted in a series of coalition governments. The Christian Social Party headed most coalitions between 1945 and 1974 when its dominance was challenged by the Socialists. It regained pre-eminence in 1979 and is a leading member of the current administration.

In January 1995 Jacques Santer (b. 1937), who had been prime minister since 1984, was appointed president of the Commission of the European Union. He was succeeded by Jean-Claude Junker, leading a reformed PCS-POSL coalition government; after the POSL polled well in the June 1999 general election, it was expected that the PCS would form a centre-right coalition with the Democratic Party.

MALTA

Republic of Malta
Repubblika Ta'Malta

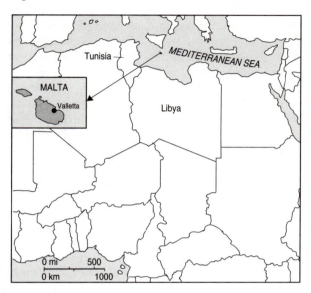

Capital: Valletta

Social and economic data
Area: 316 sq km/122 sq miles
Population: 376,000[*]
Pop. density per sq km/sq mi: 1,190/3,082[*]
Urban population: 88%[**]
Literacy rate: 81%[**]
GDP: $2,800 million[*]; per-capita GDP: $7,900[*]
Government defense spending (% of GDP): 1.1%[*]
Currency: Maltese lira
Economy type: high income
Labor force in agriculture: 5%[**]
Unemployment rate: 4.5%[*]
[*] 1995.
[**] 1992.

Head of state
President Guido de Marco, since 1999

Head of government
Prime Minister Dr Edward Fenech-Adami, since 1998

Ethnic composition
The population is essentially European, supposedly originating from Carthage. Both Maltese, which is a Semitic language, and English are spoken.

Religions
Roman Catholicism is the state religion and it is practised by about 98% of the population.

Political features
State type: liberal democratic
Date of state formation: 1964
Political structure: unitary
Executive: parliamentary
Assembly: one-chamber
Party structure: two-party
Human rights rating: N/A
International affiliations: ACP (observer), CE, CSCE, CW, IBRD, IMF, NAM, UN, WTO

Local and regional government
There is no local government as such, the whole country being administered as a single unit from the capital, Valletta.

Political system
The 1974 constitution provides for a single-chamber assembly, the House of Representatives, with 65 members elected by universal adult suffrage, through a system of proportional representation, using the single transferable vote, for a five-year term. There are 13 two- to four-member constituencies. The president is the formal head of state and is elected by the House, again for a five-year term. He or she appoints a prime minister and cabinet, drawn from and collectively responsible to the House, which is subject to dissolution within its five-year term.

The constitution was amended in 1987 providing for a change in assembly representation. Under the amendment any party which wins more than 50% of the total vote in a general election will automatically be given a majority in the House of Representatives, regardless of the number of seats it actually wins.

Political parties
There are five political parties but two have dominated Malta's politics since independence. They are the Malta Labor Party (MLP) and the Nationalist Party (PN).

The MLP was officially founded in 1921 and first came to power in 1955. It has a moderate left-of-center orientation and argues strongly for Malta's neutrality and nonalignment and opposes membership of the European Union. Led by Alfred Sant, it has 39,000 members.

The origins of the PN go back to 1880 but it became a recognizable party in the 1920s. It has a Christian right-of-center orientation and believes in European cooperation. It has 31,000 members.

Political leaders since 1970

1962–71 Giorgio Borg Olivier (PN), 1971–84 Dom Mintoff (MLP), 1984–87 Karmenu Mifsud Bonnici (MLP), 1987–96 Edward Fenech-Adami (PN), 1996–98 Alfred Sant (MLP), 1998– Edward Fenech-Adami (PN)

Latest elections

In the September 1998 general election, the PN was returned to power, winning 52% of the popular vote and 35 seats. The MLP won 30 seats with 47% of the vote. Turnout was 95%.

Political history

Malta became a British Crown Colony in 1815 and, subsequently, a vital naval base. Its importance was recognized by the unique distinction of the award of the George Cross decoration by the British monarch in 1942. From 1945 onwards the island enjoyed growing self-government and in 1955 Dom Mintoff (b. 1916), leader of the Malta Labor Party (MLP), became prime minister.

A referendum held in 1956 approved a proposal by the MLP for integration with the United Kingdom but this was strongly opposed by the conservative Nationalist Party (PN), led by Dr Giorgio Borg Olivier. Eventually, in 1958, the British proposals were rejected by Mintoff, who resigned, causing a constitutional crisis. By 1961 both parties were in favor of independence and, after Borg Olivier became prime minister in 1962, independence talks began. Malta became a fully independent state within the Commonwealth, and under the British Crown, in 1964, having signed a ten-year defense and economic aid treaty.

In 1971 Mintoff and the MLP were returned to power with a policy of international neutrality and nonalignment. He declared the 1964 treaty invalid and began to negotiate a new arrangement for leasing the Maltese NATO base and obtaining the maximum economic benefit from it for his country. Eventually, in 1972, a seven-year agreement was signed and Malta became a republic in 1974. In 1979 the British closed its naval base, necessitating diversification of the island's economy.

In the 1976 general, election the MLP was returned with a reduced majority. It also won a narrow majority in the House of Representatives in 1981, even though the Nationalists had a bigger share of the popular vote. As a result, Nationalist MPs refused to take up their seats for over a year. Relations between the two parties were also damaged by allegations of progovernment bias in the broadcasting service. At the end of 1984 Mintoff announced his retirement and Karmenu Mifsud Bonnici succeeded him as MLP leader and prime minister.

In the 1987 general election, the PN won a narrow votes victory and, as a result of the constitutional change, a narrow assembly majority. Its leader since 1977, Fenech-Adami (b. 1934), became prime minister. In 1992 the PN marginally increased its majority and retained power. Karmenu Mifsud Bonnici stepped down as MLP leader and was succeeded by Alfred Sant. In 1994 Victor Tabone completed his five-year term as president and was succeeded by Ugo Mifsud Bonnici, a former PN leader.

Since taking office, Prime Minister Fenech-Adami has taken a more pro-European and pro-American stance than some of his predecessors and in 1993 Malta received a positive response to its 1990 application for EU membership, being advised that only aspects of the island's economy and legal system might create difficulties.

In the October 1996 general election, the MLP secured a one-seat parliamentary majority, with 50.7% of the vote, and Alfred Sant became prime minister. Sant pursued a policy of neutrality and nonalignment, seeking to make Malta the 'Switzerland of the Mediterranean'. He froze Malta's EU application and withdrew from NATO's 'Partnership for Peace' program. However, facing intraparty opposition from the veteran Dom Mintoff, he called a snap general election in September 1998 and was narrowly defeated by the PN. Fenech-Adami became prime minister again and reactivated the country's EU application. In April 1999 Guido de Marco (PN) became president.

MONACO

Principality of Monaco
Principauté de Monaco

Capital: Monaco-Ville

Social and economic data

Area: 1 sq km/0.386 sq miles
Population: 31,000[*]
Pop. density per sq km/sq mi: 31,000/80,311[*]
Urban population: 100%[**]
Literacy rate: 100%[**]
GDP: $682 million[*]; per-capita GDP: $22,000[*]
Government defense spending (% of GDP): 0%[*]
Currency: French franc
Economy type: high income
Labor force in agriculture: 0%[**]
[*] 1995.
[**] 1992.

Head of state
Prince Rainier III, since 1949

Head of government
Minister of State Michel Lévêque, since 1997

Ethnic composition
Nineteen per cent of the population is Monegasque and 58% French. French is the official language but Monegasque (a mixture of French Provençal and Italian Ligurian), Italian, and English are also spoken.

Religions
The chief religion is Roman Catholicism.

Political features
State type: liberal democratic
Date of state formation: 1297
Political structure: unitary
Executive: parliamentary
Assembly: one-chamber
Party structure: non-party
Human rights rating: 99%
International affiliations: IAEA, IWC, OSCE, UN

Local and regional government
There is no local or regional government.

Political system
The 1911 constitution was modified in 1917 and then largely rewritten in 1962. It preserves Monaco as a hereditary principality, but an earlier concept of attributing the prince with a divine right to rule has been deleted. Legislative power is shared between the prince and a single-chamber National Council (*Conseil National*), with 18 members elected by universal adult suffrage for a five-year term. Voting is restricted to Monegasque citizens aged 21 and over, and a two-ballot majoritarian system is employed. Executive power is formally vested in the prince, Rainier III (b. 1923) since 1949, but, in practice, exercised by a four-member Council of Government, headed by a minister of state, who is a French civil servant chosen by the prince from a list of three candidates presented by the French government.

Political parties
There are no political parties as such but in recent years National Council elections have been contested by lists of candidates. In 1993 the centrist Liste Campora, led by Jean-Louis Campora, and the Liste Medecin, led by Jean-Louis Medecin, won 17 of the 18 seats. The dominant grouping since the 1960s has been the pro-Rainier Union Nationale et Démocratique (UND).

Political leaders since 1970
1986–94 Jean Aussell, 1994–97 Paul Dijoud, 1997– Michel Lévêque

Latest elections
In the National Council elections of the 1 and 8 February 1998, all 18 seats were won by the UND, with ten incumbents being re-elected. The National Union for the Future of Monaco (UNAM) and the Rally for the Monegasque Family (RFM) contested, but did not win any seats.

Political history
Once part of the Holy Roman Empire, Monaco became a Genoese possession during the 12th century, later coming under the rule of the Grimaldi dynasty in 1297. The principality, after alternate periods under Spanish, French, and Sardinian control, became an independent state, under the protection of France, in 1861 and that close relationship has continued. Agreements between the two countries, made in 1918–19, state that Monaco will be incorporated into France if the reigning prince dies without leaving a male heir. France is closely involved in the government of Monaco, providing a civil servant, of the prince's choosing, to head its Council of Government, as well as providing its interior minister. During World War II, the principality was occupied by the Italians (1941–43) and Germans (1943–45). The small state has developed into a prosperous center for tourism, which attracts four million visitors a year. Banking is also an important business and there are light industries, most notably cosmetics

and micro-electronics. Monaco is also attractive as a 'shelter' for tax exiles. It became a full member of the United Nations in 1993. Since the 1960s, the pro-Rainier Union Nationale et Démocratique (UND) has dominated, winning all the National Council seats in all the elections, with the exceptions of 1973 and 1993.

NETHERLANDS

Kingdom of the Netherlands
Koninkrijk der Nederlanden

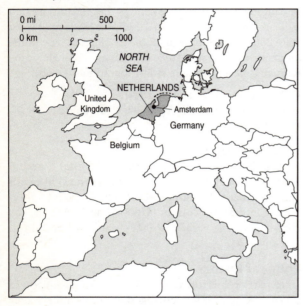

Capital: Amsterdam (seat of government: The Hague)

Social and economic data
Area: 40,044 sq km/15,770 sq miles
Population: 15,500,000*
Pop. density per sq km/sq mi: 380/983*
Urban population: 89%**
Literacy rate: 99%**
GDP: $371,040 million*; per-capita GDP: $23,940*
Government defense spending (% of GDP): 2.2%*
Currency: guilder
Economy type: high income
Labor force in agriculture: 5%**
Unemployment rate: 7.1%*
* 1995.
** 1992.

Head of state
Queen Beatrix Wilhemina Armgard, since 1980

Head of government
Prime Minister Wim Kok, since 1994

Ethnic composition
Most of the population is primarily of Germanic stock, with some Gallo-Celtic mixtures. There is also a sizeable minority of Indonesians and Surinamese, from the former East Indies colonies. The official and widely used language is Dutch.

Religions
About 38% of the population is Roman Catholic, about 30% is Protestant, distributed among 11 different denominations, and there are also other Christian and Jewish religious communities.

Political features
State type: liberal democratic
Date of state formation: 1648
Political structure: unitary
Executive: parliamentary
Assembly: two-chamber
Party structure: multiparty
Human rights rating: 98%
International affiliations: AG (observer), BENELUX, CE, CERN, EEA, ESA, EU, G-10, IBRD, IMF, IWC, NACC, NAM (guest), NATO, OECD, OSCE, UN, WEU, WTO

Local and regional government
The Netherlands has a well developed system of regional and local government. The country is divided into 12 provinces, each with an appointed sovereign's commissioner, who presides over a Provincial Council, elected in a similar fashion to the Second Chamber of the national assembly, and a Provincial Executive. There are also about 770 municipalities, with elected councils and executives, presided over by appointed burgomasters.

Political system
The Netherlands is a constitutional and hereditary monarchy. Its first constitution dates back to 1814 and, after many revisions, a new version, preserving much of what had preceded it, came into force in February 1983. It provides for a two-chamber assembly, called the States-General, consisting of a First Chamber of 75 and a Second Chamber of 150. Members of the First Chamber are indirectly elected by representatives of 12 Provincial Councils, for a six-year term, half retiring

every three years, and members of the Second Chamber are elected by universal adult suffrage, through a party list system of proportional representation, for a four-year term.

The queen appoints a prime minister as head of government, and a cabinet, or Council of Ministers, chosen by the prime minister. Although they are not permitted to be members of the assembly, they may attend its meetings and take part in debates and they are all collectively responsible to it.

Legislation is introduced in the Second Chamber but must be approved by both before it becomes law. The Second Chamber has the right to amend bills but the First Chamber can only approve or reject. There is also a Council of State, which is the government's oldest advisory body and acts like a collective elder statesperson. Its members are intended to represent a broad cross-section of the country's life, and include former politicians, scholars, judges, and business executives, all appointed for life. The queen is its formal president but its day-today operation is in the hands of an appointed vice president.

Political parties

The proportional representation system of elections to the Second Chamber encourages a multiplicity of political parties. Religion, as well as politics, often plays a large part in the formation of the various groups. The parties currently number more than 20, the most significant being the Christian Democratic Appeal (CDA), the Labor Party (PvdA), the People's Party for Freedom and Democracy (VVD), the Democrats '66 (D'66), the Political Reformed Party (SGP), the Evangelical Political Federation (RPF), the Reformed Political Association (GPV), the Green Left, and the General League of the Elderly (AOV).

The CDA was formed in 1980 by federating the Anti-Revolutionary Party (ARP), the Christian Historical Union (CHU), and the Catholic People's Party (CDA). It has a Christian right-of-center orientation.

The PvdA was created in 1946 by the union of the Socialist Democratic Workers' Party with other left-wing progressive groups. It is now a moderate left-of-center party.

The VVD dates from 1948 and is largely the present-day equivalent of the prewar Liberal State Party and the Liberal Democratic Party. It is a free-enterprise centrist party which strongly supports state welfare policies and industrial democracy. It has 68,000 members.

D'66, as its name implies, was founded in 1966 on a platform calling for constitutional reform. It is now a centrist party with strong advocacy for environmental issues.

The SGP is a Calvinist party dating from 1918, when the Anti-Revolutionary Party split. It has a centrist orientation. The RPF is another Calvinist party which was formed in 1975. It has a more radical stance than the SGP. The GPV is a third Calvinist party, dating from 1948. It is largely supported by the more fundamentalist members of the Church.

The Green Left is a left-of-center ecological grouping. The AOV is one of two newly formed parties promoting the needs and aspirations of pensioners.

Political leaders since 1970

1967–71 Petrus J S de Jong (VVD-led coalition), 1971–73 Barend Biesheuvel (ARP-led coalition), 1973–77 Joop den Uyl (PvdA-led coalition), 1977–83 Andries van Agt (CDA-led coalition), 1983–94 Ruud (Rudolph) Lubbers (CDA-led coalition), 1994– Wim Kok (PvdA-led coalition)

Latest elections

The results of the May 1998 Second Chamber elections were as follows:

Netherlands latest election results

Party	% votes	Seats
PvdA	29.8	45
VVD	24.7	38
CDA	18.4	29
D'66	9.0	14
Other parties	18.9	24

Political history

Holland, Belgium, and Flanders, then known as the Low Countries, were ruled by the Dukes of Burgundy in the 15th century and then by Spain from the 16th century. The Dutch rebelled against the tyranny of Philip II (1527–98) of Spain, and particularly his attempts to stamp out Protestantism. They temporarily won their freedom in 1579, only to have it taken away again, until eventually, in 1648, the independence of the Dutch Republic was recognized. Between 1795 and 1813 the country was overrun by the French, and then the Congress of Vienna joined the north as the Kingdom of the United Netherlands, under William I, in 1814. The southern part broke away, in 1830, to form the separate kingdom of Belgium.

Until 1945 the Netherlands had always followed a path of strict neutrality but its occupation by the

Germans between 1940 and 1945 persuaded it to adopt a policy of mutual cooperation with its neighbors. It became a member of the Western European Union (WEU), the North Atlantic Treaty Organization (NATO), the Benelux Customs Union, the European Coal and Steel Community (ECSC), the European Atomic Energy Community (EURATOM), and the European Community (EC) itself and, as a 'good European', it has been in the forefront of subsequent EC developments. For example, it was during its presidency in 1991 that the Maastricht Treaty, which converted the Community into a Union, was formulated. It was ratified by a clear parliamentary majority in 1992.

Meanwhile, in 1980 Queen Juliana (b. 1909), who had reigned since 1948, abdicated in favor of her eldest daughter, Beatrix (b. 1938).

All governments since 1945 have been coalitions of one kind or another, differences between the parties being concerned mainly with economic policies, apart from a major debate in 1981 about the siting of US cruise missiles on Dutch soil. The 1988 general election resulted in yet another coalition, with the CDA and the PvdA sharing 106 of the 150 seats in the Second Chamber. In May 1989 Prime Minister Ruud Lubbers (b. 1939) resigned following opposition to his proposals for tighter pollution laws, but, after the September general election, he was persuaded to return to lead yet another coalition.

The May 1994 general election was again inconclusive and, after months of negotiation, the Labor Party leader Wim Kok (b. 1938) formed the country's first 'left-right' coalition of the PvdA, VVD, and D'66. The PvdA strengthened its position in the May 1998 Second Chamber elections.

The ruling PvdA polled poorly in local elections held in February 1999, finishing in third place in terms of votes received. Three months later, the ruling 'rainbow' coalition fell apart after the D'66 pulled out when a bill which would allow for voter-led referenda to overturn certain government decisions was narrowly rejected by the Senate. However, Wim Kok remained in office as a caretaker prime minister and succeeded, in June 1999, to persuade the D'66 to rejoin the governing coalition.

NORWAY

Kingdom of Norway
Kongeriket Norge

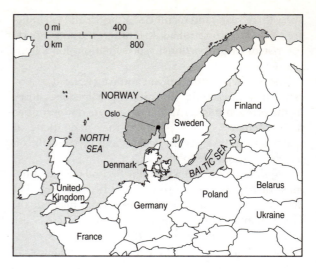

Capital: Oslo

Social and economic data
Area: 324,219 sq km/125,182 sq miles
Population: 4,370,000*
Pop. density per sq km/sq mi: 13/35*
Urban population: 76%**
Literacy rate: 99%**
GDP: $136,100 million*; per-capita GDP: $31,140*
Government defense spending (% of GDP): 2.6%*
Currency: Norwegian krone
Economy type: high income
Labor force in agriculture: 7%**
Unemployment rate: 4.9%*
* 1995.
** 1992.

Head of state
King Harald V, since 1991

Head of government
Kjell Magne Bondevik, since 1997

Ethnic composition
The majority of the population is of Nordic descent and there is a Lapp minority of about 20,000 in the far north of the country.

Religions
About 92% of the population belongs to the Church of Norway which is the established Evangelical Lutheran Church. There are also about 21,000 Roman Catholics.

Political features
State type: liberal democratic
Date of state formation: 1905
Political structure: unitary

Executive: parliamentary
Assembly: one-chamber
Party structure: multiparty
Human rights rating: 97%
International affiliations: CBSS, CE, CERN, EEA, EFTA, ESA, IAEA, IBRD, IMF, IWC, NACC, NAM (guest), NATO, NC, OECD, OSCE, UN, WEU (associate), WTO

Local and regional government

The country is divided into 19 counties (*fylker*), ranging in population from under 80,000 to nearly 450,000. The administrative head of each county is appointed by the central government and below the county level are municipalities. There are elected county and municipal councils. The political system in the Norwegian dependency of Svalbard is described in Chapter 8.

Political system

Norway is a constitutional hereditary monarchy and its constitution dates from 1814. The king is the formal head of state and the assembly consists of a single-chamber parliament, the Storting. The Storting has 165 members, elected for a four-year term by universal adult suffrage through a party list system of proportional representation. Once elected, it divides itself into two parts, a quarter of the members being chosen to form an upper house, the Lagting, and the remainder a lower house, the Odelsting.

All legislation must be first introduced in the Odelsting and then passed to the Lagting for approval, amendment, or rejection. A bill must be passed by both houses before it can become law, unless it has been passed twice by the Odelsting and rejected twice by the Lagting. In this case it will be considered by the combined Storting, who may then pass it by a two-thirds majority. Once a bill has had parliamentary approval it must receive the royal assent.

The king appoints a prime minister and State Council on the basis of support in the Storting, to which they are all responsible.

Political parties

There are currently some 14 political parties, the six most significant being the Norwegian Labor Party (DNA), the Conservative Party (the 'Right'), the Christian People's Party (KrF), the Center Party (Sp), the Progress Party (FrP), and the Socialist Left Party (SV).

The DNA was founded in 1887 as a democratic socialist party. It has a moderate left-of-center orientation and has favored membership of the European Union. It has 115,000 members.

The Conservative Party was founded in 1884 to oppose the Liberal Party, which at the time was pressing for a transfer of more power from the monarchy to parliament. Its orientation is now progressive right-of-center. Led by Jan Petersen, it has 68,000 members.

The KrF was formed in 1933 by a group of religious temperance Liberal Party dissidents. Since that time it has grown and widened its appeal. It has a center-left orientation.

The Sp originally started in 1920 as the Agrarian League. It soon changed its name to the Farmers' Party and adopted its present title in 1959. It now has a left-of-center nonsocialist orientation, with particular concern for rural interests.

The FrP is a rightwing populist grouping.

Political leaders since 1970

1965–71 Per Borten (Sp coalition), 1971–72 Trygve Bratteli (DNA), 1972–73 Lars Korvald (KrF coalition), 1973–76 Trygve Bratteli (DNA), 1976–81 Odvar Nordli (DNA coalition), 1981 Gro Harlem Brundtland (DNA coalition), 1981–83 Kare Willoch (Conservative Party), 1983–86 Kare Willoch (Conservative coalition), 1986–89 Gro Harlem Brundtland (DNA coalition), 1989–90 Jan Syse (Conservative coalition), 1990–96 Gro Harlem Brundtland (DNA coalition), 1996–97 Thorbjoern Jagland (DNA coalition), 1997– Kjell Magne Bondebik (KrF coalition)

Latest elections

The results of the September 1997 general election are set out below. Turnout was 74%.

Norway latest election results

Party	% votes	Seats
DNA	35.1	65
FrP	15.3	25
Conservatives	14.3	23
KrF	13.9	25
Sp	7.9	11
SV	6.0	9
Others	7.7	7

Political history

Norway was linked to Sweden until 1905 when it chose its own monarch, Prince Charles of Denmark, who took the title of King Haakon VII (1872–1957). He ruled for 52 years until his death. He was succeeded by his son, Olav V (1903–91) and his grandson, Harald V (b. 1937), who is the reigning monarch.

The experience of German occupation between 1940 and 1945 persuaded the Norwegians to abandon their traditional neutral stance and join the North Atlantic Treaty Organization (NATO) in 1949, the Nordic Council in 1952, and the European Free Trade Area (EFTA) in 1960. Norway was accepted into membership of the European Community in 1972 but a referendum held that year rejected the proposal and the application was withdrawn.

The country has enjoyed a generally stable political history, with the proportional representation system of voting often producing coalition governments. Its exploitation of the oil and gas resources of the North Sea have given it a per-capita income higher than most of its European neighbors, including France, Germany, and the United Kingdom. In 1988 Prime Minister Gro Harlem Brundtland (b. 1939), leader of the dominant Labor Party since 1981, was awarded the Third World Foundation annual prize for leadership in environmental and development issues.

In October 1989 Brundtland lost a vote of confidence and resigned. Her successor, Jan Syse, leading a Conservative-Liberal coalition, found himself in similar difficulties and a year later Brundtland returned, heading a minority Labor government.

In November 1992 it was announced that Norway would apply for readmission to the European Community, but this was eventually abandoned after a referendum held in November 1994 came out against membership.

Norwegian politicians have been diplomatically active in recent years, co-chairing peace negotiations in former Yugoslavia and playing a significant role in the Middle East peace process.

In October 1996 Gro Harlem Brundtland, who had earlier surrendered the DNA leadership, was succeeded as prime minister by the new DNA leader, Thorbjoern Jagland. The outcome of the September 1997 general election was Norway's first centrist government in 25 years. The coalition comprised the KrH, Sp and Liberal Party, and was led by Kjell Magne Bondevik of the KrF. It controlled less than a third of the Storting seats.

PORTUGAL

Republic of Portugal
República Portuguesa

Capital: Lisbon

Social and economic data
Area: 92,080 sq km/32,552 sq miles
Population: 9,830,000[*]
Pop. density per sq km/sq mi: 107/302[*]
Urban population: 36%[**]
Literacy rate: 85%[**]
GDP: $96,700 million[*]; per-capita GDP:$9,840[*]
Government defense spending (% of GDP): 2.9%[*]
Currency: escudo
Economy type: high income
Labor force in agriculture: 19%[**]
Unemployment rate: 5.5%[*]
[*] 1995.
[**] 1992.

Head of state
President Jorge Sampaio, since 1996

Head of government
Prime Minister Antonio Guterres, since 1995

Ethnic composition
Carthage and Rome were early influences on the ethnic composition of Portugal which is one of the oldest European countries. Most of the present-day population is descended from the Caucasoid peoples who inhabited the whole of the Iberian peninsula in classical and pre-classical times. There are a number of minorities from Portugal's overseas possessions and former possessions. Portuguese is the national language.

Religions
About 90% of the population is Roman Catholic but there is freedom of worship for all faiths.

Political features

State type: liberal democratic
Date of state formation: 1128
Political structure: unitary
Executive: dual
Assembly: one-chamber
Party structure: multiparty
Human rights rating: 92%
International affiliations: ALADI (observer), CE, CERN, EEA, EU, IAEA, IBRD, IMF, Lusophone, NACC, NAM (GUEST), NATO, OECD, OSCE, UN, WEU, WTO

Local and regional government

There are two Autonomous Regions, in the Azores and Madeira, to which significant powers have been devolved. Each has a minister responsible for it in the mainland government and a chairperson of a regional government, appointed by the minister. Local government on the mainland and in the Autonomous Regions is based on municipalities and parishes with elected councils. The overseas dependency of Macau (see Chapter 8) reverted to Chinese rule in 1999.

Political system

The 1976 constitution, revised in 1982, provides for a president, elected by universal adult suffrage, for a five-year term, and a single-chamber 230-member Assembly, elected through a party list system of proportional representation, and serving a four-year term. The president is limited to two successive terms. Four of the Assembly members represent Portuguese overseas territory.

The president appoints a prime minister and the latter's chosen Council of Ministers (cabinet), who are all responsible to the Assembly, which is subject to dissolution during its four-year term. There is also a Council of State, chaired by the president, which acts as a supreme national advisory body.

The relationship between the president and prime minister has been rather different from that of a constitutional head of state to a political head of government and, at times, has displayed aspects of the dual executive of the Fifth Republic of France. The president has often been an active politician rather than a formal symbol, and this has sometimes led to clashes between the two. Presidents have also been largely drawn from the armed forces and have had to work with civilian prime ministers. The current president is not only the first civilian to hold the post since the 1920s, but also a former prime minister himself.

Political parties

There are currently some 19 political parties, the four most significant being the Social Democratic Party (PSD), the Socialist Party (PS), the Popular Party (PP), and the Portuguese Communist Party (PCP). An electoral alliance, the United Democratic Coalition (UDC), of leftwing and ecological parties, was formed specifically to fight the 1986, 1991 and 1995 elections.

The PSD was quickly organized immediately after the coup of 1974 by former liberal members of the old National Assembly. It has a moderate center-right orientation and 130,000 members.

Originally the PS was founded in 1875 as Portugal's first socialist party. In its present form it dates from 1973. It is an internationalist party which takes a progressive, socialist stance and is led byAntónio Guterres. It had 100,000 members.

The PP was formed in 1974 as the Democratic Social Center Party (CDS) by officials of the Caetano government soon after it had been removed from office. It is now a rightwing force which opposes European integration.

The 140,000-member PCP is a leftwing socialist force which is a member of the Democratic Unity Coalition (CDU).

Political leaders since 1970

1968–74 Marcello Caetano (military), 1974–75 António Ribeiro de Spínola (military), 1975–76 Francisco da Costa Gomes, 1976–78 Mário Lopez Soares (PS), 1978–79 Carlos Mota Pinto (PS-CDS coalition), 1979–80 Francisco Sa Carneiro (AD coalition), 1980–83 Francisco Pinto Balsemão (PSD coalition), 1983–85 Mário Lopez Soares (PSD coalition), 1985–95 Aníbal Cavaco Silva (PSD), 1995– Antonio Guterres (PS)

Latest elections

In the January 1996 presidential election, Jorge Sampaio (PS) was elected with 53.8% of the vote. His closest rival, Anibale Cavaco Silva (PSD), obtained 46%.

The results of the October 1995 Assembly elections, with a turnout of 67%, were as follows:

Portugal latest election results

Party	% votes	Seats
PS	43.9	112
PSD	34.0	88
PP	9.1	15
CDU	8.6	15
Other parties	4.4	0

Political history

After being a monarchy for nearly 800 years, Portugal became a republic in 1910. The country remained economically backward and riddled with corruption until the start of the virtual dictatorship of António de Oliveira Salazar (1889–1970) in 1928. Social conditions were greatly improved at the cost of a loss of personal liberties.

Salazar was succeeded as prime minister in 1968 by Dr Marcello Caetano, who was unsuccessful at liberalizing the political system or dealing with the costly wars in Portugal's colonies of Angola and Mozambique. Criticisms of his administration led to a military coup in April 1974 to 'save the nation from government'. A Junta of National Salvation was set up, headed by General António Ribeiro de Spinola. He became president a month later, with a military colleague replacing the civilian prime minister. The new president promised liberal reforms, but, after disagreements within the Junta, Spínola resigned in September and was replaced by General Francisco da Costa Gomes. In 1975 there was a swing to the left among the military and President Gomes narrowly avoided a communist coup by collaborating with the leader of the moderate Socialist Party, Mário Soares (b. 1924).

In April 1976 a new constitution, designed to return the country gradually to civilian rule, was adopted, and the Supreme Revolutionary Council, which had been set up to head the new military regime, was renamed the Council of the Revolution and demoted to the role of a consultative body, under the chair of the president. Then Portugal's first free Assembly elections in 50 years were held. The Socialist Party won 36% of the vote and Soares formed a minority government. In June the army chief, General Ant too Ramalho Eanes (b. 1935), won the presidency, with the support of center and left-of-center parties. After surviving precariously for over two years, Soares resigned in July 1978.

A period of political instability followed, with five prime ministers in two and a half years until, in December 1980, President Eanes invited Francisco Balsemão, a cofounder of the Social Democratic Party (PSD), to form a center-party coalition. Balsemão survived many challenges to his leadership, which included his temporary resignation following a vote of no confidence, and then, in August 1982, he won a major victory when the Assembly approved his draft of a new constitution which would reduce the powers of the president, abolish the Council of the Revolution, and move the country to a fully civilian government. In December 1982, however, Balsemão resigned, but was recalled as a caretaker prime minister until a successor as PSD leader could be agreed.

In the April 1983 general election the Socialist Party (PS) won 101 of the Assembly's 230 seats and, after lengthy negotiations, Soares entered a coalition with the PSD, whose leader was now former finance minister, Professor Aníbal Cavaco Silva (b. 1939). In June 1985 the PS-PSD coalition broke up and a premature general election was called. The result was, again, inconclusive and the new PSD leader eventually managed to form a minority government. In the 1986 presidential election Mário Soares, the PS leader, won a surprising victory to become Portugal's first civilian president for 60 years. He promised a more open style of presidency which would work more cooperatively with the prime minister.

After a three-week political crisis, in which the left-wing opposition to Cavaco Silva's coalition forced a vote of confidence, President Soares dissolved the Assembly and called a general election, Cavaco Silva being asked to continue as caretaker prime minister. The result was an overwhelming victory for the PSD, strengthening Cavaco Silva's position at the expense of the left-of-center Democratic Renewal Party (PRD) and communists, and enabling Portugal's first majority government to be formed.

Portugal entered the European Community in 1986 and in the 1991 elections President Soares was re-elected and the PSD continued in office, with a slightly reduced majority.

Cavaco Silva stepped down as PSD leader for the October 1995 general election and was succeeded by the former defense minister, Fernando Nogueira. The election was won by the center-left António Guterres. The new PS minority administration pledged itself to continue the PSD's drive for closer integration of the European Union, including monetary union, and to increase spending on education. In March 1996 President Soares retired and was succeeded by his fellow socialist Jorge Sampaio.

In November 1998 a referendum was held on the government's plan to divide the country into eight mainland administrative regions, with local assemblies and regional presidents. Voters rejected the plan, with turnout at 52%. In March 1999 Marcelo Rebelo da Sousa resigned as leader of the opposition centre-right PSD after an anti-government alliance formed recently with the right-wing Popular Party (PP) collapsed.

SAN MARINO

Most Serene Republic of San Marino
Serenissima Repubblica di San Marino

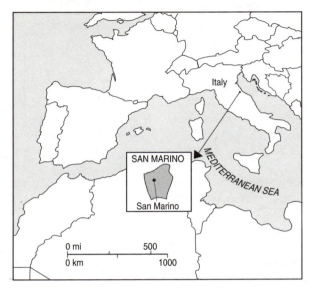

Capital: San Marino

Social and economic data
Area: 61 sq km/24 sq miles
Population: 25,500*
Pop. density per sq km/sq mi:410/1,0630*
Urban population: 90%**
Literacy rate: 96%**
GDP: $476 million*; per-capita GDP: $18,670*
Government defense spending (% of GDP): 0%**
Currency: Italian lira
Economy type: high income
Labor force in agriculture: 3%**
Unemployment rate: 3.9%*
* 1995.
** 1992.

Heads of state and heads of government
Two captains regent, elected for a six-month period

Ethnic composition
The population is predominantly Italian.

Religions
The chief religion is Roman Catholicism.

Political features
State type: liberal democratic
Date of state formation: *c.* AD 301

Political structure: unitary
Executive: parliamentary
Assembly: one-chamber
Party structure: multiparty
Human rights rating: N/A
International affiliations: CE, NAM (guest), OSCE, UN

Local and regional government
The country is divided into nine 'Castles', or districts, which correspond to the original nine parishes of the republic. Each 'Castle' is governed by a castle captain and an Auxiliary Council, who serve, respectively, two- and five-year terms.

Political system
Because of its small size, San Marino is able to operate a uniquely intimate form of direct democracy, echoing some of the features of the ancient Greek city states. It does not have a formal constitution, though a basic set of 'governing principles' was framed in 1600, and the system of government is derived from its early origins. For the whole country there is a single-chamber Great and General Council (*Consiglio Grande e Generale*) composed of 60 members, elected by universal adult suffrage for a five-year term, through a system of pro-portional representation. The Council elects two of its members, one representing the capital and one the country, to serve a six-month term as captains regent and together they share the duties of head of state and head of government. They preside over a cabinet of ten, elected by the Council for a five-year term, called the Congress of State.

To encourage expatriate voting, the state pays 75% of the return fare of any Sammarinese living abroad to return home to vote.

Political parties
There are six political parties, the four most significant being the San Marino Christian Democrat Party (PDCS), the Socialist Party (PS), the Progressive Democratic Party (PDP), and the Popular Alliance of San Marino Democrats (APDS).

The PDCS was formed in 1948 and has a Christian right-of-center orientation. The PS is an amalgamation of two left-of-center parties, the Socialist Party (PSS), formed in 1975, and the Socialist Unity Party (PSU).

The PDP is the reformed Communist Party, which was founded in 1941. It has a moderate leftwing orien-tation and has close links with its Italian counterpart, but has been losing support.

The APDS is a centrist force for institutional reform and the adoption of a constitution.

Latest elections

The results of the 31 May 1998 general election were as follows:

San Marino latest election results

Party	% votes	Seats
PDCS	40.9	25
PS	23.2	14
PDP	18.6	11
APDS	9.8	6
Others	7.5	4

Political history

San Marino was founded by a Christian saint, St Marinus, at the start of the 4th century AD as a refuge against religious persecution. It survived as a city-state after the unification of Italy in the late 19th century, thus being able to claim the distinction of being the world's oldest republic. It has a treaty of friendship with Italy, dating originally from 1862, but which was renewed in 1939 and 1971, and its multiparty system mirrors that of the larger country that surrounds it. A Communist-Socialist administration was in power between 1945 and 1957, when it was ousted in a bloodless 'revolution'. For the past 40 years it has been governed by a series of leftwing and center-left coalitions. The current one comprising and Christian Democrats and Socialists dates from March 1992. The state relies heavily on earnings derived from tourism, more than 3 million visitors passing through its borders annually, but also, in recent decades, it has developed a number of light industries, most notably cement, leather, and textile production, and a thriving banking sector.

San Marino became a full member of the United Nations in 1992.

In May 1998 the ruling Christian Democratic Party (PDCS) and Socialist Party (PS) coalition government remained in power after the general election.

SPAIN

Kingdom of Spain
Reino de Espania

Capital: Madrid

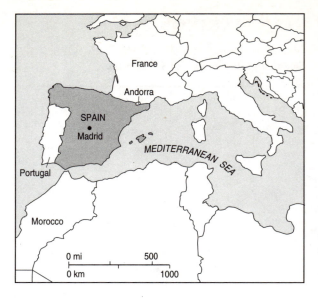

Social and economic data

Area: 504,880 sq km/194,935 sq miles
Population: 39,482,000[*]
Pop. density per sq km/sq mi: 78/203[*]
Urban population: 79%[**]
Literacy rate: 95%[**]
GDP: $532,350 million[*]; per-capita GDP:$13,480[*]
Government defense spending (% of GDP): 1.5%[*]
Currency: peseta
Economy type: high income
Labor force in agriculture: 13%[**]
Unemployment rate: 22.9%[*]
[*] 1995.
[**] 1992.

Head of state

King Juan Carlos I, since 1975

Head of government

Prime Minister José Maria Aznar López, since 1996

Ethnic composition

The present-day population can mostly trace its origins back to Moorish, Roman, and Carthaginian ancestry. The main language is Castilian Spanish. Catalan is spoken in the northeast, Basque in the north, and Galician in the northwest.

Religions

The majority of people are Roman Catholics. There are also about 300,000 Muslims and about 12,000 Jews.

Political features

State type: liberal democratic

Date of state formation: 1492
Political structure: unitary
Executive: parliamentary
Assembly: two-chamber
Party structure: multiparty
Human rights rating: 87%
International affiliations: AG (observer), ALADI (observer), CE, CERN, CSCE, EEA, ESA, EU, IAEA, IBRD, IMF, IWC, NACC, NAM (guest), NATO, OECD, UN, WEU, WTO

Local and regional government
The country is divided into 50 provinces and although not a federal state, Spain has developed a system of regional self-government, whereby each of the provinces has its own Council (*Diputaciuntry is divi*) and civil governor. The devolution process was extended in 1979 when 17 Autonomous Communities, or regions, were approved, each with an assembly, elected through a party list system of proportional representation for a four-year term, and a president of government, elected by the assembly. The powers of the autonomous Communities are specified in the constitution. The 17 Communities are Andalucía, Aragón, Asturias, the Balearic Islands, the Basque country, the Canary Isles, Cantabria, Castilla y León, Castilla-La Mancha, Cataluña, Extremadura, Galicia, Madrid, Murcia, Navarra, La Rioja, and Valencia. Since 1996, income tax receipts have been split between the national government and the regions.

Political system
The 1978 constitution creates a constitutional monarchy, with a hereditary king as formal head of state. He appoints a prime minister, called a president of government, and a Council of Ministers, all of whom are responsible to the National Assembly (Las Cortes Generales). The Cortes consists of two chambers, the Congress of Deputies, with 350 members, and the Senate, with 252. Deputies are elected by universal adult suffrage through a party list system of proportional representation, and 208 of the senators are directly elected to represent the whole country and 44 appointed by the assembly of the autonomous regions. All serve a term of four years.

Political parties
Until 1975 only one political party was permitted, the Falange, later to be known as the National Movement, but now some 21 national parties currently operate, the two most significant being the Socialist Workers' Party (PSOE) and the Popular Party (PP). There are also some 35 regionally-based parties.

The PSOE can be traced back to 1879 and the Socialist Workers' Party, which merged with the Popular Socialist Party in 1978 and adopted its present name. It now has about 360,000 members and a democratic socialist orientation. Felipe González was replaced as party leader in June 1997 by Joaquín Almunia.

The PP was formed in 1976 as the Popular Alliance (AP), shortly after General Franco's death. It has a right-of-center orientation and is led by José Maria Aznar (b. 1953). It has 570,000 members.

Also significant, with seats in the Cortes, are the United Left (IU), a leftwing coalition which includes the Communist Party, the (Catalan) Convergence and Union (CIU), and the Basque Nationalist Party (PNV).

Political leaders since 1970
1939–1974 Francisco Franco y Bahamonde (National Movement), 1974–76 Carlos Arias Navarro (National Movement), 1976–81 Adolfo Suárez González (UCD), 1981–82 Leopoldo Calvo Sotelo (UCD), 1982–96 Felipe González Márquez (PSOE), 1996–   José Aznar López (PP)

Latest elections
The results of the March 1996 Congress of Deputies elections were as follows:

Spain latest election results

Party	% votes	Seats
PP	38.8	156
PSOE	37.5	141
Other parties	33.7	53[*]

[*] Including 16 seats for the CIU.

Political history
Prior to the declaration of a republic in 1931, Spain had been a kingdom since the 1570s. It was a major international power in the 17th and 18th centuries but was weakened by political disunity in the 19th century. The creation of a republic did little to heal the regional rifts, particularly in Catalonia and the Basque area. At the same time, a political swing to the left by the republican government, coupled with criticisms and physical attacks on the church, antagonized the military. In 1936 a group of army commanders in Spanish Morocco revolted and the Spanish Civil War began. Spain soon became a battleground for virtually every ideology in Europe, as well as a test-bed for the weaponry of the ris-

ing Fascist and Nazi dictatorships. With their help, the insurgents, led by General Francisco Franco (1892–1975), won and in 1939 established a neofascist regime of strong, personal rule.

During World War II Spain remained neutral, though sympathetic towards Nazi Germany. In 1947 Franco, known as the *Caudillo* ('ruler'), allowed the revival of an assembly with limited powers, but which was not directly elected. He also announced that after his death the monarchy would be restored and named the grandson of the last monarch, Prince Juan Carlos de Bourbon (b. 1938), as his successor. Franco died in 1975 and King Juan Carlos succeeded him as head of state. There followed a slow but steady progress to democratic government, with a new liberal constitution being endorsed by referendum in December 1978. It confirmed Spain as a constitutional monarchy, allowed political parties to operate freely and guaranteed self-government to the provinces and regions. Adolfo Suárez, leader of the Democratic Center Party (UCD), became the first prime minister under the new constitution.

As Spain adjusted itself to constitutional government after 36 years of military rule, it faced two main internal problems – the demands for independence by extremists in the northern, Basque region and the possibility of rightwing elements in the army seizing power and reverting to a Franco-style government. It therefore embarked upon policies which were aimed to satisfy the calls for regional recognition and to firmly establish Spain within the international community. They included a devolution of power to the regions, entry into the North Atlantic Treaty Organization (NATO), and, later, membership of the European Community (EC).

By 1981, however, the government was showing signs of strain and Suárez suddenly resigned, to be succeeded by his deputy, Calvo Sotelo, who was immediately confronted with an attempted army coup in Madrid led by Lieutenant Colonel Antonio Tejero. At the same time the military commander of Valencia, Lieutenant General Milans del Bosch, declared a state of emergency there and sent tanks on to the streets. Both uprisings failed and the two officers were tried and imprisoned. Sotelo's decision to take Spain into NATO in 1982 was widely criticized and, after defections from the party, he was forced to call a general election in October 1982.

The result was a sweeping victory for the Socialist Workers' Party (PSOE), led by Felipe González (b. 1942). With the Basque separatist organization, ETA, stepping up its campaign for independence by widespread terror-ist activity, the government committed itself to strong anti-terrorist measures while, at the same time, promising a greater degree of devolution for the Basques. ETA's activities increased in intensity, however, spreading in 1985 to the Mediterranean holiday resorts and threatening Spain's lucrative tourist industry. Eventually a truce was agreed but this collapsed in 1989. The truce was revived in 1992 but was again short-lived. The threat of new violence remained but there were signs that ETA was losing support within the Basque community.

The PSOE had fought the election on a policy of taking Spain out of NATO and carrying out an extensive program of nationalization. Once in office, however, González showed himself to be a supreme pragmatist. His nationalization program was much more selective than had been expected and he left the decision whether or not to remain in NATO to a referendum to be held in the spring of 1986. In January 1986 Spain became a full member of the European Community and in March the referendum showed popular support for remaining in NATO. The PSOE won a clear majority in the July general election of that year, despite being faced with an electoral alliance by some of the main opposition parties. González was therefore returned for another term as prime minister. Tough policies to tackle the country's economic problems resulted in a wave of industrial strikes in 1987 and other expressions of dissatisfaction with the government. By 1988, however, there were clear signs that the government's prescriptions were working and the economy had become one of the fastest growing in Europe.

In November 1992 the Maastricht Treaty on greater European unity was formally ratified, but events were moving against the government. In April 1993, amid allegations of fraud within the PSOE, González said he would seek a general election to renew his mandate. Despite gains by the PP in the June 1993 election, the PSOE survived for a fourth term in office. In July 1993 González was able to form a minority government, which received support from the minor Catalan and Basque parties. Meanwhile the economy had moved into recession and unemployment had risen to over 20%, the highest in the European Union. The González administration responded by launching a major program of privatization. In September 1995 the CIU Catalan nationalist coalition, led by Jordi Pujol, the CIU Catalan regional president, announced that it was withdrawing its crucial support from the minority government. This resulted in the rejection of the draft budget in October 1995.

The PSOE was tarnished by corruption and telephone-tapping scandals, the high level of unemployment, and charges of the government's involvement in the killing of ETA suspects in the 1980s. Consequently, in the general election of March 1996, the right-of-center Popular Party won most of the Congress of Deputies seats. In May 1996, after weeks of negotiations, José Maria Aznar formed a minority government, which was dependent on the support of the regional parties, notably Pujol's CIU. In November 1996 Spain agreed to full integration within NATO, and in September 1998 ETA, following the example set in Northern Ireland, announced an end to its campaign of violence, although the prime minister expressed his scepticism.

However, in November 1998 the government announced that it would begin exploratory contacts with ETA. In May 1999, Josep Borrell, who, in 1998, had won the PSOE's first-ever primary contest to select the party's prime ministerial candidate for the next general election, resigned, as a result of the controversy surrounding alleged financial wrong-doings of two close former colleagues.

SWEDEN

Kingdom of Sweden
Konungariket Sverige

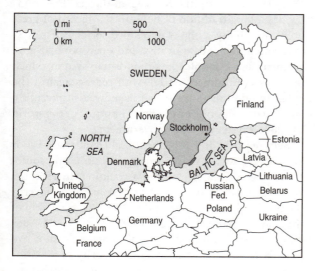

Capital: Stockholm

Social and economic data
Area: 449,700 sq km/173,630 sq miles
Population: 8,780,000*

Pop. density per sq km/sq mi: 20/51*
Urban population: 84%**
Literacy rate: 99%**
GDP: $209,700 million*; per-capita GDP: $23,900*
Government defense spending (% of GDP): 2.9%*
Currency: Swedish krona
Economy type: high income
Labor force in agriculture: 4%**
Unemployment rate: 7.7%*
* 1995.
** 1992.

Head of state
King Carl XVI Gustav, since 1973

Head of government
Prime Minister Goran Persson, since 1996

Ethnic composition
The population consists almost entirely of Teutonic stock, with small minorities of Lapps, Finns, and Germans. Swedish is the official language but minorities speak Finnish and Lapp.

Religions
The Evangelical Lutheran Church (Church of Sweden) is the established church and about 92% of the population belongs to it. There are other Protestant denominations, about 120,000 Roman Catholics, and about 16,000 Jews.

Political features
State type: liberal democratic
Date of state formation: 1523
Political structure: unitary
Executive: parliamentary
Assembly: one-chamber
Party structure: multiparty
Human rights rating: 98%
International affiliations: AG (observer), CBSS, CE, CERN, EEA, ESA, EU, G-10, IAEA, IBRD, IMF, IWC, NAM (guest), NC, OECD, OSCE, PFP, UN, WTO

Local and regional government
There is a strongly devolved system of local government, with 24 counties (*lan*) and 279 municipalities, all with representative institutions. It is estimated that at least 40% of public administration is conducted at a subnational level.

Political system
Sweden is a constitutional hereditary monarchy with the king as formal head of state and a popularly elected government. The constitution dates from 1809 and has

since been amended several times. It is based on four fundamental laws, the Instrument of Government Act, the Act of Succession, the Freedom of the Press Act, and the *Riksdag* (Parliament) Act. It provides for a single-chamber assembly, the Riksdag, of 349 members, elected by universal adult suffrage through a party list system of proportional representation, for a three-year term. The prime minister is nominated by the speaker of the Riksdag and then confirmed by a vote of the whole House. The prime minister chooses a cabinet and all are then responsible to the Riksdag. The king now has a purely formal role, the normal duties of a constitutional monarch, such as dissolving the Riksdag and deciding who should be asked to form an administration, being undertaken by the speaker of the Riksdag.

Political parties

There are currently around 15 active political parties, the most significant being the Social Democratic Labor Party (SAP), the Moderate Party (M), the Liberal Party (Fp), the Center Party (C), the Christian Democratic Community Party (KdS), the Left Party (Vp), and the Ecology Party (MpG).

The SAP was founded in 1889 and is Sweden's largest political party, with over 1 million members. It has a moderate center-left orientation and is led by Goran Persson. It has 203,000 members.

The Moderate Party was formed in 1904 as the Conservative Party. It changed its name in 1969. It has a right-of-center stance and is led by Carl Bildt. It has 100,000 members. The Liberal Party dates from 1902 and used to be the main opposition to the Conservatives. It has a center-left orientation.

The Center Party was founded in 1910 as the Agrarian Party, mainly to represent farming interests. It changed its name in 1958 in an attempt to widen the basis of its support. As its name implies, it has a centrist orientation. It is led by Lennart Daleus and has 140,000 members.

The KdS was formed in 1964 to promote Christian values in political life. It takes a Christian, centrist stance. The Vp dates originally from 1917 when it was the Left Social Democratic Party of Sweden. In 1921 it was renamed the Communist Party and later, in 1967, it adopted its present name. It has a reform socialist orientation and is opposed to the European Union. It is led by Gudrun Schyman.

The MpG is part of the European Green movement.

Political leaders since 1970

1969–75 Olof Palme (SAP), 1975–78 Thorbjörn Fälldin (Center Party coalition), 1978–79 Ola Ullsten (Liberal coalition), 1979–81 Thorbjörn Fälldin (Center-Moderate-Liberal coalition), 1981–82 Thorbjörn Fälldin (Center Party), 1982–86 Olof Palme (SAP), 1986–91 Ingvar Carlsson (SAP), 1991–94 Carl Bildt (Moderate), 1994–96 Ingvar Carlsson (SAP), 1996–Goran Persson (SAP)

Latest elections

The results of the September 1998 Riksdag elections are set out below. Turnout was 80%.

Sweden latest election results

Party	% votes	Seats
SAP	36.6	131
M	22.7	82
Vp	12.0	43
KdS	11.8	42
C	5.1	18
Fp	4.7	17
MpG	4.5	16
Others	2.6	0

Political history

Sweden has been a constitutional monarchy since the beginning of the 19th century. It was united with Norway until 1905, when King Oscar II (reigned 1872–1907) gave up the Norwegian throne. The country has a long tradition of neutrality, a record of great political stability, a highly developed social welfare system, and a flair for innovative and open popular government. For example, the ombudsman system, which provides the ordinary citizen with redress against the abuse of administrative power, is a Swedish invention and Sweden was one of the first countries in the world to adopt a system of open government.

Between 1951 and 1968 the Social Democratic Labor Party (SAP) was in power, sometimes alone and sometimes as the senior partner in a coalition. In 1968 the Social Democrats formed their first majority government since the mid-1940s and in 1969 the leadership of the party changed hands, Olof Palme (1927–86) becoming prime minister. In the general election two years later, Palme lost his overall majority but continued at the head of a minority government. During the next six years he carried out two major reforms of the constitution, reducing the chambers in the assembly from two to one in 1971, and in 1975 removing the last vestiges of the monarch's constitutional powers.

The 1976 general election was fought on the issue of the level of taxation needed to fund the welfare system and Palme was defeated, Thorbjörn Fälldin, leader of the Center Party, forming a center-right coalition government. The Fälldin administration fell in 1978 on the issue of its wish to follow a non-nuclear energy policy and was replaced by a minority Liberal government, led by Ola Ullsten. Fälldin returned in 1979, heading another coalition, and in a referendum held in the following year there was a narrow majority in favor of continuing with a limited nuclear energy program. Fälldin remained in power, with some cabinet reshuffling, until 1982, when the Social Democrats, with Palme, returned with a minority government.

Palme was faced with deteriorating relations with the USSR, arising from suspected violations of Swedish territorial waters, but the situation had improved substantially by 1985. After the general election in that year, Palme was able to continue with Communist support and then, in February 1986, Sweden and the world were shocked by the news of his murder by an unknown assailant in the center of Stockholm, as he and his wife were returning home on foot from a visit to a cinema. The deputy prime minister, Ingvar Carlsson (b. 1934), took over as prime minister and leader of the SAP, continuing the broad policy line of his predecessor. In the 1988 general election the SAP government of Carlsson was re-elected but in the September 1991 general election he was defeated and the Moderate Party leader, Carl Bildt (b. 1949), formed a 'bourgeois coalition' comprising the Moderate Party, Liberal Party, Center Party, and KdS. This set out to dismantle some aspects of Sweden's vaunted 'social democratic' welfare system. As the economy deteriorated during 1992, with the unemployment rate climbing to 14%, Bildt's conservative coalition, in an unprecedented fashion, agreed to work with the Social Democrats to solve the country's problems.

In the 1994 general election, the SAP increased its vote share and seat holding and returned to power, Ingvar Carlsson preferring to lead a minority government and rejecting the offer of a center-left coalition. In November 1994 the Swedish people, in a referendum, voted in favor of European Union membership. This was achieved in January 1995. In August 1995 it was announced that Carlsson would step down as prime minister in 1996 once his party had chosen a replacement. The favorite to succeed him was the deputy prime minister, Mona Sahlin, until in November 1995 Sahlin faced a criminal investigation into an alleged misuse of a government credit card.

In the country's first ever elections to the European Parliament in September 1995 the turnout at 40% was well below half the normal level for assembly elections. The Social Democrats attracted only 29% support, while nearly a third of the electorate voted for anti-EU Green and Left party candidates. Goran Persson succeeded Carlsson as prime minister in March 1996 and pursued a tight fiscal strategy to reduce inflation to below 1%. Consequently, unemployment rose and the SAP polled badly in the September 1998 Riksdag elections, losing 9% of its support, and the future of the government depended on the Vp and MpG parties, both of which campaigned for a referendum on whether Sweden should join the European Single Currency.

SWITZERLAND

The Swiss Confederation
Schweizerische Eidgenossenschaft
Confédération Suisse
Confederazione Svizzera

Capital: Bern

Social and economic data
Area: 41,290 sq km/15,942 sq miles
Population: 6,995,000[*]

Pop. density per sq km/sq mi: 169/439[*]
Urban population: 63%[**]
Literacy rate: 99%[**]
GDP: $286,000 million[*]; per-capita GDP: $40,900[*]
Government defense spending (% of GDP): 1.9%[**]
Currency: Swiss franc
Economy type: high income
Labor force in agriculture: 6%[**]
Unemployment rate: 3.3%[*]
[*] 1995.
[**] 1992.

Head of state and head of government

Ruth Dreifuss, since 1999

Ethnic composition

The great majority of people are of Alpine stock. There is also a strong Nordic element. There are three official languages: German, spoken by about 70%, French by 20%, and Italian by 10%. Romansch is also spoken in some areas.

Religions

About 47% of the population is Roman Catholic and about 44% is Protestant.

Political features

State type: liberal democratic
Date of state formation: 1648
Political structure: federal
Executive: limited presidential
Assembly: two-chamber
Party structure: multiparty
Human rights rating: 96%
International affiliations: AG (observer), CE, CERN, EFTA, ESA, G-10, IMF, IWC, NAM (guest), OECD, OSCE

Local and regional government

Switzerland is a federation of 20 cantons and six half-cantons, a canton (derived from Old French) being the name for a political division. The federal government is allocated specific powers by the constitution and the residue is left with the cantons, each having its own constitution, assembly, and government. At a level below the cantons are more than 3,000 communes, whose populations range from fewer than 20 to 350,000, in the case of Zürich. Direct democracy is encouraged through communal assemblies and referenda.

Political system

The constitution dates from 1874 and provides for a two-chamber Federal Assembly, consisting of a National Council (Nationalrat) and a Council of States (Standerat). The National Council has 200 members, elected by universal adult suffrage, through a party list system of proportional representation, for a four-year term. The Council of States has 46 members, each canton electing two representatives and each half-canton one. Members of the Council of States are elected for three or four years, depending on the constitutions of the individual cantons. The federal government is in the hands of a Federal Council (Bundesrat), consisting of seven members elected for a four-year term by the Assembly, and each heading a particular federal department. The Federal Assembly also appoints one member to act as federal head of state and head of government for a year, the term of office beginning on 1 January. As related in *Chapter 6*, Switzerland is noted for its frequent resort to referenda and citizens' initiatives.

Political parties

There are currently more than 20 nationally-based political parties, the most significant being the Radical Democratic Party of Switzerland (FDP/PRD), the Swiss Social Democratic Party (SP/PS), the Christian Democratic Party of Switzerland (CVP/PDC), the Swiss People's Party (SVP/UDC), the Swiss Liberal Party (LPS/PLS), and the Green Party (GPS/PES). The alternative acronyms in brackets are derived from the German or French spelling of each name.

The FDP/PRD led the movement which resulted in the creation of the Federative State and constitution of 1848 and has been an important force in Swiss politics ever since. It has a radical center-left orientation.

The SP/PS was founded in 1888 as a Marxist party. Since then its outlook has been modified so that it now has a moderate left-of-center stance.

The CVP/PDC was formed in 1912 as the Conservative People's Party. It changed its name in 1957. It is a Christian moderate centrist party.

The SVP/UDC dates from 1919 when it began more as a broad-based interest group than a political party. At one time it had the name of the Farmers', Artisans' and Bourgeois Party. It now has a centrist orientation.

The LPS/PLS began in the early 19th century as the Swiss Liberal-Democratic Union. It changed its name in 1977. It is a federalist center-left party.

The GPS/PES is a product of the growth of ecological interest groups and parties which has been evident throughout Europe during recent decades.

Political leaders since 1970

The federal president is appointed by the Federal

Assembly to serve a one-year term, from January to December.

Latest elections

The results of the October 1995 National Council elections were as follows:

Switzerland latest election results

Party	% votes	Seats
FDP/PRD*	20.2	45
SP/PS*	21.8	54
CVP/PDC*	17.0	34
SVP/UDC*	14.9	29
GPS/PES	5.0	9
LPS/PLS	2.7	7
Other parties	18.4	2

*Members of the ruling coalition.

The October 1995 National Council elections proved to be no challenge to the four-party center-right coalition, which includes the pro-European, urban-based Social Democrats, and the anti-EU, rural based Swiss People's Party, which has governed the country since 1959.

Political history

Switzerland has for centuries been recognized as the leading neutral country of the world and, as such, has been the base for many international organizations and the host of many international peace conferences. Although it was once the home of the League of Nations, it has not, as yet, itself become a member of the United Nations. A referendum held in 1986 rejected the advice of the government and came out overwhelmingly against membership. Entry into the European Union (EU) and European Economic Area has also been opposed. Its domestic politics have been characterized by coalition governments and a stability which has enabled it to become one of the richest per-capita countries in the world.

Switzerland has tended to be a male-orientated nation and women were not allowed to vote in federal elections until 1971. The first female cabinet minister was not appointed until 1984. She resigned in 1988 and another woman was not appointed until 1993. Since 1959 a broad-based coalition, comprising the Social Democrats, the Swiss People's Party, the Radical Democratic Party, and the Christian Democrats, has held power.

In December 1999 the Federal Assembly elected the interior minister, Ruth Dreifuss, as the country's first female president. During the same month, a bilateral trade agreement was signed with the EU which was expected to boost annual GDP by 0.5%. In a referendum, held in April 1999, voters approved a number of changes to the constitution, including enshrining the right to strike and abolishing the country's gold standard status. In referenda held in June 1999, the Swiss voted to tighten immigration. This came after 1,700 Kosovar Albanians had been given refuge in Switzerland during the spring of 1999.

UNITED KINGDOM (UK)

United Kingdom of Great Britain and Northern Ireland

Capital: London

Social and economic data
Area: 244,100 sq km/94,247 sq miles
Population: 58,606,000*
Pop. density per sq km/sq mi: 240/622*
Urban population: 89%**
Literacy rate: 99%**
GDP: $1,150,000 million*; per-capita GDP: $19,650*
Government defense spending (% of GDP): 3.4%*
Currency: pound sterling
Economy type: high income
Labor force in agriculture: 2%**
Unemployment rate: 8.4%*

* 1995.
** 1992.

Head of state
Queen Elizabeth II, since 1952

Head of government
Prime Minister Tony Blair, since 1997

Ethnic composition
The people of the United Kingdom consist of 81.5% English, 9.6% Scots, 2.4% Irish, 1.9% Welsh, and 2% West Indians, Asians, and Africans. English is the predominant language, with Welsh spoken by about a fifth of the Welsh population. Gaelic is a smaller minority tongue.

Religions
There are two established religions, the (Anglican) Church of England and the (Presbyterian) Church of Scotland. Nominally 55% of the population is Anglican, but only 5% is practising and regularly attends church. There are also substantial numbers of Roman Catholics (9%), Jews, Muslims (2%), and Hindus, many of whom are devout adherents to their sects.

Political features
State type: liberal democratic
Date of state formation: 1707/1921*
Political structure: unitary
Executive: parliamentary
Assembly: two-chamber
Party structure: two-party
Human rights rating: 93%
International affiliations: AG (observer), CE, CERN, CW, EEA, ESA, EU, G-5, G-7, G-10, IAEA, IBRD, IMF, IWC, NACC, NATO, OECD, OSCE, PC, UN, WEU, WTO

* Great Britain 1707; United Kingdom 1921.

Local and regional government
The United Kingdom consists of four countries within a unitary system: England, with about 83% of the total population, Scotland, with about 9%, Wales, with about 5%, and Northern Ireland, with about 3%.

The government minister responsible for the internal affairs of England is the home secretary, who is based in London. The minister for Scotland's internal affairs is the secretary of state for Scotland, who is based partly in London and partly in Edinburgh. There are more than 5,000 civil servants working in the Scottish Office in Edinburgh. The minister responsible for the internal affairs of Wales is the secretary of state for Wales, who is based partly in London and partly in Cardiff, where the Welsh Office employs about 2,000 civil servants. Since elections in May 1999, Scotland has had its own 129-member elected assembly based in Edinburgh, with restricted tax-raising powers, and Wales an elected 60-seat assembly in Cardiff, but with no powers to levy taxes.

The minister responsible for Northern Ireland's internal affairs is the secretary of state for Northern Ireland, who is based partly in London and partly in Belfast. From 1922 until 1972 Northern Ireland had its own elected parliament, but the violence and discord there persuaded the United Kingdom government in London to dissolve it in 1972 and to govern the province directly through the secretary of state. Following the historic 'Good Friday' peace agreement, Northern Ireland has had its own 108-member elected assembly in Stormont since June 1998; the agreement also provided for cross-border bodies with Ireland. The Assembly has devolved authority in areas such as health, social security, and education, and there are special provisions to ensure participation of all sections of the community. After elections in June 1998, David Trimble, the Ulster Unionist Party leader, became 'First Minister', or Northern Ireland's equivalent of a prime minister. The home secretary and the secretaries of state for Scotland, Wales, and Northern Ireland are all members of the United Kingdom cabinet.

Geographically within the British Isles, and enjoying the protection of the United Kingdom government, but politically not strictly a part of the United Kingdom, are the Channel Islands of Jersey, Guernsey, Sark and their dependencies, and the Isle of Man; see Chapter 8. The Channel Islands have their own assembly and government and are not bound by legislation of the UK Parliament. The Isle of Man enjoys a broadly similar independence.

Following a major review in 1995, England is divided into 45 all-purpose unitary authorities and 36 counties, within which are district authorities and, within them, parish councils. Northern Ireland has 26 single-tier district councils.

Political system
The United Kingdom is a classic example of a constitutional monarchy based on a system of parliamentary government. There is no written constitution, the main features being contained in individual pieces of legislation and certain practices followed by successive governments which are regarded as constitutional conventions. Cabinet government, which is at the heart

of the system, is founded on convention, and the relationship between the monarch, as head of state, and the prime minister, as head of government, is similarly based. In theory this makes the unwritten constitution extremely flexible. In practice, however, it is as rigid as if it were written, and more rigid than many that have been formally set down. The features that provide this rigidity, as well as ensuring political stability, are the fact that Parliament is sovereign, in that it is free to make and unmake any laws that it chooses, and the concept of the rule of law, which says that all governments are subject to the laws which Parliament makes, as interpreted by the courts. The queen is one part of the trinity of Parliament, the other parts being the two legislative and debating chambers, the House of Lords and the House of Commons. Since becoming a member of the European Union (EU) the supremacy of the UK Parliament has been challenged by the superior laws of the EU and it has become clear that, as long as it continues in membership, domestic legislation can in certain circumstances be overridden by that of the EU as a whole. Since 1997 control over the setting of interest rates has been conceded to the independent Bank of England, while other powers have been devolved to the new 'national assemblies' in Scotland, Wales, and Northern Ireland.

The House of Lords has three main kinds of member: those who are there by accident of birth, the hereditary peers; those who are there because of some office they hold; and those who are appointed to serve for life, the life peers. There are around 750 hereditary peers and peeresses and they include dukes, marquesses, earls, viscounts, and barons. Among those sitting because of the position they hold are two archbishops and 24 bishops of the Church of England and nine senior judges, known as the law lords. The rest, numbering over 470, are the appointed life peers, who now include about 100 women, or peeresses. Around 20 hereditary peers and 150 life peers align with the Labor Party; most of the rest support the Conservatives, or are independent. The Labor government that assumed power in 1997 announced plans for a major reform of the House of Lords, in the interest of greater democracy. The immediate aim is to remove the voting rights of hereditary peers, who are for the most part Conservatives or independent 'cross-benchers'. The longer-term aim is to create a democratically elected second chamber.

The House of Commons has 659 members, elected by universal adult suffrage, by a simple plurality voting

system, from single-member geographical constituencies, each constituency containing on average about 65,000 electors. Although the House of Lords is termed the upper house, its powers, in relation to those of the Commons, have been steadily reduced so that now it has no control over financial legislation and merely a delaying power of a year over other bills. Before an act of Parliament becomes law it must pass through a five-stage process in each chamber – first reading, second reading, committee stage, report stage, and third reading – and then receive the formal royal assent. Bills, other than financial ones, can be introduced in either House, but most begin in the Commons.

The monarch appoints the prime minister on the basis of support in the House of Commons and he or she, in turn, chooses and presides over a cabinet. The simple voting system favors two-party politics and both chambers of Parliament, are physically designed to accommodate two parties, the government, sitting on one side of the presiding speaker, and the opposition on the other. No matter how many parties are represented in Parliament only one, that with the second largest number of seats in the Commons, is recognized as the official opposition, and its leader is paid a salary out of public funds and provided with appropriate office facilities within the Palace of Westminister, as the Houses of Parliament are called.

A proportional representation system of election was used for the first time in the UK in the June 1999 European Parliament eections.

Political parties

There are currently more than 50 active political parties but this number is subject to variation, particularly when elections are taking place. Parties are not required to register and the only restriction on their operations is the requirement that parliamentary candidates make a deposit of £500, which will be forfeited if less than 5% of the total votes cast in the constituency are obtained. There are also restrictions on the amount that can be spent by candidates during an election campaign.

Despite the number of parties in existence, the simple plurality voting system, combined with a number of social, economic, and demographic factors, has invariably resulted in two-party politics, the two major groups being the Conservative and Unionist Party and the Labor Party. There is one other national party currently represented in the House of Commons: the Liberal Democrats.

Contesting only in Scottish constituencies is the Scottish Nationalist Party (SNP), and only in Welsh constituencies, the Welsh Nationalist Party (Plaid Cymru). There are also four Northern Ireland parties represented at Westminster: the Official Ulster Unionist Party (OUUP), the Democratic Unionist Party (DUP), the Social Democratic Labor Party (SDLP), the United Kingdom Unionist Party (UKUP). Sinn Féin was represented until 1992.

The Conservative Party dates from the Tories of the 17th century who supported the Duke of York's claim to the English throne against the Whigs. They were regarded as 'conservators' because of their belief in traditional values and came to be called the Conservatives in the early 1830s. The title Unionist was added to indicate their support for the union of Ireland and England. In its present form, the party was established in 1870. It has a right-of-center orientation and is led by William Hague. It has a membership of 350,000.

The Labor Party was founded in 1900 following a meeting of trade unionists and representatives of a number of socialist organizations. Prior to this there had been an Independent Labor Party and, later, a Labor Representation Committee. It has both individual members and affiliated members, through membership of trade unions or other affiliated bodies. The party has a moderate left-of-center orientation and is led by Tony Blair. It has a membership of 330,000.

The Liberal Democrats were formed in 1988 by a merger of the Liberal Party and a majority of members of the Social Democratic Party (SDP). The Liberals can trace their origins back to the Whigs of the 17th century, when they were the main opponents of the Tories. They changed their name to the Liberal Party in the 1850s. The SDP was formed in 1981 by four leading dissidents from the Labor Party. The party has a center-left orientation and was led by Paddy Ashdown until mid-1999. It has a membership of 100,000.

The rump of the SDP consists of the minority of members of the party formed in 1981 who chose not to merge with the Liberal Party. It no longer operates as a national party.

Three additional minor parties of some significance operate across the United Kingdom: the environmentalist Green Party (established in 1973 as the Ecology Party); the UK Independence Party, which opposes UK membership of the European Union and the recently formed Referendum Party, which campaigned for a UK referendum on European integration.

The SNP was formed in 1934 with the aim of securing the recognition of an independent Scotland, with its own elected assembly. It favors Scotland's independence within the European Union and is led by Alex Salmond.

Plaid Cymru was formed in 1925 with aims for Wales similar to those of the SNP for Scotland. The two parties have cooperated from time to time in pursuit of their common purposes. It is led by Dafydd Wigley.

The OUUP was formed in 1905 and for a long time supported the policies of the Conservative Party. However, since the signing of the Anglo-Irish Agreement in 1985, and subsequent developments in the search for a lasting peace in Northern Ireland, differences have arisen between them. The OUUP is the largest single party in the province. It is led by David Trimble.

The DUP was formed in 1971 by dissident Ulster Unionists who adopted a less moderate and more rightwing stance than the OUUP, and bitterly opposed the Anglo-Irish Agreement and the 1998 'Good Friday' agreement on power sharing. It is led by the Rev. Ian Paisley.

The SDLP was formed in 1970 and has strong links with the Labor Party, which has never contested seats in Northern Ireland. The party has a moderate left-of-center orientation and was a strong supporter of the Anglo-Irish Agreement and the reconciliation of all views and opinions in Northern Ireland. It is led by John Hume.

Sinn Féin was formed in 1970 and is the political wing of the Irish Republican Army (IRA). It has a strongly pro-United Ireland stance but has demonstrated its wish to secure a united Ireland through peaceful political channels. It is led by Gerry Adams.

The UKUP, led by Robert McCartney, has opposed the 1998 'Good Friday' peace agreement for the province.

Political leaders since 1970

1970–74 Edward George Heath (Conservative), 1974–76 James Harold Wilson (Labor), 1976–79 Leonard James Callaghan (Labor), 1979–90 Margaret Hilda Thatcher (Conservative), 1990–97 John Major (Conservative), 1997– Tony Blair (Labor)

Latest elections

The results of the May 1997 general election were as follows:

United Kingdom latest election results

Party	% votes	House of Commons seats
Labor	43.1	418
Conservatives	30.6	336
Liberal Democrats	16.7	46
Other	9.6	30*

* OUUP, ten seats; SNP, six seats; Plaid Cymru, four seats; SDLP, three seats; DUP, two seats; Sinn Fein, two seats; UKUP, one seat.

The election saw a 10% swing from the Conservatives to Labor, which returned to power after 18 years in opposition, with its greatest number of seats, and a parliamentary majority of 179, a 20th-century record. The Liberal Democrats, despite the fact that their share of the vote fell slightly, won 46 seats, their best performance since 1929, and the Conservatives found themselves squeezed in multi-party races. In Scotland and Wales, the Conservatives failed to win any seats for the first time ever, and the rout was so extreme that seven cabinet ministers lost their seats. The rightwing anti-European Referendum and UK Independence parties drew away some of the Conservatives' support, winning 3% of the British vote. Many other Conservative supporters stayed at home, with turnout slumping to 71% (down 7% on April 1992). In Scotland, the SNP won 22% of the Scottish vote, and in Wales, Plaid Cymru secured 10% of the Welsh vote.

Political history

1. The start of a monarchy to Callaghan

England has been a monarchy since the 10th century, apart from the brief period of the commonwealth between 1649 and 1660, and Wales a united principality since the 11th century. The two nations were united in 1535. Scotland has been a kingdom since the 9th century and joined England and Wales, to form the state of Great Britain, in 1707. Northern Ireland was originally joined to Great Britain, as part of the single nation of Ireland, in 1801. In 1921 Southern Ireland broke away to become the Irish Free State, and eventually the Republic of Ireland, while six of the nine northern counties of Ulster remained in the United Kingdom of Great Britain and Northern Ireland.

By exploration, commercial enterprise, and force of arms, on land and sea, a great empire was created, particularly during the 18th and 19th centuries, which covered a quarter of the world's surface and included a quarter of its population. In 1945 the United Kingdom was still at the hub of this empire and, although two world wars had gravely weakened it, many of its citizens, and some of its politicians, still saw it as a world power. The reality of its position soon became apparent in 1945 when the newly elected Labor government, led by Clement Attlee (1883–1967), confronted the problems of rebuilding the damaged economy. This renewal was greatly helped, as in other Western European countries, by support from the United States in the shape of the Marshall Plan.

The period of Labor government, from 1945 to 1951, saw the carrying through of an ambitious program of public ownership and investment and the laying of the foundations of a national health service and welfare state which became the envy of the world. During the same period a civilized dismemberment of the British Empire, restyled the British Commonwealth, was started. It was a process which was to continue through to the 1980s.

In 1951 the Conservative Party returned to power under Sir Winston Churchill (1874–1965) and, although there were changes in emphasis in domestic and foreign policies, the essential features of the welfare state and the public sector were retained. Both administrations, Labor and Conservative, however, missed an opportunity to seize the leadership of Europe so that by the mid-1950s the framework for the European Community had been created, with the United Kingdom an onlooker rather than a participant. In 1955 Sir Winston Churchill, now in his 81st year, handed over to his heir apparent, the distinguished foreign secretary, Sir Anthony Eden (1897–1977).

In little more than a year Eden found himself confronted by what he perceived to be a threat as great as that from Germany in the 1930s, but now it was from the president of Egypt, Gamal Nasser, who had taken possession of the Suez Canal. Eden's perception of the threat posed by Nasser was not shared by everyone, not even within the Conservative Party. The invasion of Egypt, in conjunction with France and Israel, brought widespread criticism and was abandoned in the face of pressure from the United States and the United Nations. Eden resigned, on the grounds of ill health, and the Conservatives chose Harold Macmillan (1894–1986) as their new leader and prime minister.

Macmillan skilfully and quickly repaired the damage caused within the party, and internationally, by his predecessor's ill-judged adventure and, with a booming economy and rising living standards, had by the early 1960s won himself the reputation of 'Super Mac'. Internationally, he acquired a reputation for wise statesmanship, establishing a close working relationship with his United States contemporary, President Dwight Eisenhower and then the relatively youthful John F Kennedy. He also did much to cement the unique voluntary partnership of nations which the Commonwealth had become. He was, nevertheless, sufficiently realistic to see that the United Kingdom's long-term economic and political future lay in Europe. The Conservatives won the 1959 general election with an increased majority and in 1961 the first serious, if belated, attempt was made to join the European Community, only to have it blocked by the French president, Charles de Gaulle.

Despite rising living standards, the UK's economic performance was not as successful as that of many of its competitors, particularly Germany and Japan. It was against this background that Macmillan unexpectedly resigned in 1963, on the grounds of ill health, and was succeeded by the foreign secretary, Lord Home (1903–1995), who immediately renounced his title to become Sir Alec Douglas-Home.

In the general election in the following year, the Labor Party was returned with a slender majority and its leader, Harold Wilson (1916–95), became prime minister. The election had been fought on the issue of the relative decline of the economy and the need to regenerate it. Wilson's immediate prescription was institutional change. He created a new Department of Economic Affairs (DEA), to challenge the short-term conservatism of the Treasury, and brought in a leading trade unionist to head a new Department of Technology. In an early general election in 1966 Wilson increased his Commons majority appreciably but his promises of fundamental changes in economic planning, industrial investment, and improved work practices were not fulfilled. The DEA was disbanded in 1969 and in the same year an ambitious plan for the reform of industrial relations was also dropped in the face of trade union opposition.

In 1970 the Conservatives returned to power under Edward Heath (b. 1916), who was as much committed to economic and industrial reform as his Labor predecessor. He, too, saw institutional change as one way of achieving the results he wanted and created two new central 'super-departments', Trade and Industry and Environment, and a high-powered 'think-tank' to advise the government on long-term strategy, the Central Policy Review Staff (CPRS). He chose to change the climate of industrial relations through legislation, introducing a long and complicated Industrial Relations Bill. He also saw entry into the European Community as the 'cold shower of competition' which industry needed and membership was successfully negotiated in 1972. Heath's 'counter revolution', as he saw it, was frustrated by economic events. Powerful trade unions thwarted his industrial relations reforms

and the European 'cold shower', combined with the sharp rise in oil prices in 1973, forced a drastic U-turn in economic policy. Instead of 'lame ducks' being forced to seek their own salvations, he found it necessary to take ailing industrial companies, such as Rolls Royce, into public ownership. The introduction of a statutory incomes policy precipitated a national miners' strike in the winter of 1973–74 and Heath decided to challenge the unions by holding an early general election in 1974.

The result was a 'hung' Parliament, with Labor winning the biggest number of seats but no single party having an overall majority. Heath tried briefly to form a coalition with the Liberals and, when this failed, resigned. Harold Wilson returned to the premiership, heading a minority government, but in another general election later the same year won enough additional seats to give him a working majority. He had taken over a damaged economy and a nation puzzled and divided by the events of the previous years. He turned to Labor's natural ally and founder, the trade union movement, for support and jointly they agreed a 'social contract'. The government pledged itself to redress the imbalance between management and unions which had resulted from the Heath industrial relations legislation and the unions promised to cooperate in a voluntary industrial and incomes policy. Wilson was, at the same time, faced with opposition from within his party and in March 1976, apparently tired and disillusioned, he decided to retire in midterm, arguing that it was a move he had always planned.

He was succeeded by James Callaghan (b. 1912), his senior by some four years. Callaghan was now leading an increasingly divided party and a government with a dwindling parliamentary majority. Meanwhile, there had been changes in the other two parties, Edward Heath being unexpectedly ousted by the relatively inexperienced Margaret Thatcher (b. 1925), and the Liberal Party leader, Jeremy Thorpe (b. 1929), resigning after an unsavoury personal scandal and being succeeded by the young Scottish MP, David Steel (b. 1938). Callaghan and his strong cabinet team decided to continue along the path of solid consensual economic recovery, built around the 'social contract' incomes policy and then, in 1976, their plans were upset by an unexpected financial crisis arising from a drop in confidence in the overseas exchange markets, a rapidly falling pound, and a drain on the country's foreign reserves. After a soul-searching debate within the cabinet, it was decided to seek help from the International Monetary Fund (IMF) and submit to its stringent economic policies. Within weeks the crisis was over and within months the economy was showing clear signs of improvement. Whether or not the storm could have been weathered without IMF help was a matter debated for some time afterwards. Then in 1977, to shore up his slender parliamentary majority, Callaghan entered into an agreement with the new leader of the Liberal Party, David Steel, the 'Lib-Lab Pact'. This lasted for some 18 months, resulting in Labor pursuing moderate nonconfrontational policies in consultation with the Liberals, who, in turn, voted with the government. During this period the economy improved dramatically and by the summer of 1978 it seemed certain that Callaghan would call a general election with every chance of winning it. Without apparently consulting his cabinet colleagues, he decided to continue until at least the spring of 1979 but in the winter events turned destructively against him. The Lib-Lab Pact had effectively finished by the autumn and soon afterwards the social contract with the unions began to disintegrate. The government was faced with widespread and damaging strikes in the public sector, with essential services badly affected. Callaghan's pre-election period became the 'winter of discontent'. At the end of March 1979 he lost a vote of confidence in the House of Commons and was forced into a general election.

2. Thatcher to Blair

The Conservatives returned to power under the United Kingdom's first woman prime minister, Margaret Thatcher. She had inherited a cabinet containing a majority of Heath politicians and it was nearly two years before she made any major changes. She had also inherited a number of inflationary public sector pay awards which were a residue of the winter of discontent. The honouring of these, plus a budget from the chancellor, Sir Geoffrey Howe (b. 1926), which doubled the rate of value-added tax (VAT), resulted in a sharp rise in the price level and interest rates. As the Conservatives had come into power pledged to reduce inflation, this became the government's main, if not sole, economic target and, in pursuing it, by mainly monetarist policies, the level of unemployment rose from 1.3 million to 2 million in the first year. Thatcher had little experience in government, being a cabinet minister in only one department, but it was in foreign affairs where she was least equipped. She relied strongly, therefore, on the foreign secretary, Lord Carrington (b. 1919) and it was under his influence that the independence of Zimbabwe (Rhodesia) was achieved bloodlessly in 1980.

Meanwhile, important changes were taking place in the other parties. Callaghan resigned the leadership of the Labor Party in 1980 and was replaced by the left-winger, Michael Foot (b. 1913), and early in 1981 three Labor shadow cabinet members, David Owen (b. 1938), Shirley Williams (b. 1930), and William Rodgers (b. 1928), with the former deputy leader, Roy Jenkins (b. 1920), broke away to form a new center-left group, the Social Democratic Party (SDP). The new party made an early and spectacular impression, winning a series of by-elections within months of its creation.

Unemployment continued to rise, passing the 3 million mark in January 1982, and the Conservatives, and their leader in particular, were receiving low ratings in the public opinion polls. A fortuitous and unforeseen event rescued them, the Argentine invasion of the Falkland Islands. Margaret Thatcher's determined decision to launch an invasion to recover the islands, in the face of apparently appalling odds, finally confirmed her as the resolute conviction politician she claimed to be. The general election of 1983 was fought with the euphoria of the Falklands victory still in the air and the Labor Party, under its new leader, divided and unconvincing. The Conservatives had a landslide victory, winning more Commons seats than any party since 1945, and yet with appreciably less than half the popular vote.

Thatcher was now able to firmly establish her position, making changes which meant that more than half her original cabinet had been replaced. The next three years were, however, marked by a sequence of potentially damaging events: rising unemployment; a dispute at the government's main intelligence gathering station, GCHQ; a bitter and protracted miners' strike; increasing violence in Northern Ireland; an attempted assassination of leading members of the Conservative Party during their annual conference; riots in inner city areas; embarrassing prosecutions under the Official Secrets Act; and the resignations of two prominent cabinet ministers. Meanwhile, the violence in Northern Ireland continued and, in 1985, in an effort to secure some improvement, an agreement was signed with the Irish government, providing for greater cooperation in security matters, including the exchange of intelligence. The Anglo-Irish Agreement was strongly opposed by Unionist parties in the province. On the positive side, the inflation rate continued to fall and by the winter of 1986–87 the economy was buoyant enough to enable the chancellor to allow a pre-election spending and credit boom.

Meanwhile, there had been leadership changes in two of the other parties. Michael Foot was replaced by his young Welsh protégé, Neil Kinnock (b. 1942), and Roy Jenkins was smoothly replaced by David Owen as SDP leader. Despite the unemployment figures and criticisms of Margaret Thatcher's increasingly authoritarian style of government, the Conservatives won the June election with virtually the same share of the popular vote as they had secured four years earlier, but with a slightly reduced parliamentary majority. Although the Labor Party had run what was generally considered to have been a very good campaign, its share of the popular vote showed only a marginal improvement and its seat tally only a modest gain. The Liberal-SDP Alliance had experienced a poor election, its vote share dropping and its seat count remaining virtually static.

The main political parties reacted differently in the aftermath of the 1987 general election. Margaret Thatcher regarded the result as a vindication of her earlier policies and strengthened her control of the party and her government, at the same time pressing ahead with an expansive privatization program. Her stated aim was to obliterate all traces of socialism from the British political scene. The Labor Party, stung by the jibes of its opponents that it was 'unelectable', embarked upon a massive reassessment of its policies and structure. The Liberal leader, David Steel, disillusioned with the election result and tired of being the dog wagged by the tail of the SDP leader, David Owen, made an immediate call for a full merger of the two parties. This was eventually agreed, amid considerable acrimony and some confusion, and in 1988 the new party of the Social and Liberal Democrats, or the Liberal Democrats, as they became, was born, with a new leader, the youngish Member for Yeovil, Paddy Ashdown (b. 1941). Not all of the SDP members chose to join the new grouping. Three MPs, led by David Owen, and a few thousand followers, stayed together and retained the SDP label, but this group eventually lost its leader and its role as a political party and in 1990 it was formally wound up.

Divisions within the Conservative Party, particularly over European policy, forced a leadership election in November 1990, Mrs Thatcher being challenged by her former cabinet colleague, Michael Heseltine (b. 1933). After an inconclusive first ballot Mrs Thatcher withdrew and John Major (b. 1943), the chancellor of the Exchequer, was elected party leader and prime minister. Throughout 1991 the economy deteriorated and Major postponed asking for a dissolution of parliament until April 1992. Contrary to many expectations and opinion poll predictions, the Conservatives won the election, with an overall majority of 21 seats. The Labor Party leader announced his intention to resign and, in July 1992, he was succeeded by the Scottish MP, John Smith (1938–94).

During the remainder of 1992 divisions within the Conservative Party, centerd on Europe and the Maastricht Treaty on closer union, resurfaced while the state of the economy worsened. In September the pound was devalued and the United Kingdom withdrew from the Exchange Rate Mechanism (ERM). The standing of the prime minister, and his chancellor, had fallen to an all-time low. During 1993 the government's problems increased and its popularity continued to wane, the Conservatives faring badly in local and parliamentary by-elections.

In May 1994 the nation was stunned by the sudden death of the Labor Party leader, John Smith, resulting in an almost unprecedented display of cross-party sadness and concern. His successor, the young articulate lawyer, Tony Blair (b. 1953), proved to be an even greater threat to the government's likelihood of regaining its popularity rating. As the leader of a 'New Labor', as he described it, Blair sought to recast the image and policy stance of his party so as to attract the wider middle-class electorate as well as traditional supporters and, despite some opposition from die-hard elements, he was largely successful.

The one redeeming feature of the government's policies was its success in moving closer to an all-party agreement on Northern Ireland. Even this success had been won at the expense of the possibility of losing the guaranteed support of Unionist MPs in Parliament. At the same time, the debate about Britain's future relationship with its partners in the European Union continued, causing rifts not only in the parliamentary party but within the government itself.

The divisions within the Conservative Party together with allegations of 'sleaze' produced a climate for change, which resulted in a landslide victory for Labor in the May 1997 general election. The new government immediately embarked on its prepared program of social, constitutional, and economic change, although after one year in office, economic indicators began to look unfavorable. However, Tony Blair and his Northern Ireland secretary, Mow Mowlam, scored a notable success in building on the work of former prime minister, John Major, and securing all-party agreement on Good Friday 1998 to a power-sharing peace plan and a cessation of violence in the province. Nevertheless, there were still dissident, breakaway groups, notably the 'Real

IRA' which threatened the future of the peace process.

Constitutional referenda were held successfully in September 1997, in Scotland and Wales, to establish devolved assemblies, elected on the basis of the additional member system of proportional representation, and also in May 1998, to establish a directly elected London mayor. The Blair government, which has sought to follow a new 'third way' of caring free-market capitalism and constitutional liberalism, also set up a commission to review the electoral system and put forward, in December 1998, legislation to reform the House of Lords, seeking to create an interim second chamber comprising life peers and 91 hereditory peers. It maintained high approval ratings throughout 1997–99.

In January 1999 Paddy Ashdown, the Liberal Democrat leader, announced that he would step down in the summer of 1999, after 11 years at the party's helm. Elections were held to the Scottish parliament and Welsh assembly. Labour finished in first position in both contests, with 38% of the vote. However, it fell short of assembly majorities, as a result of the proportional representation voting system used. The voting turnouts were 59% in Scotland and 46% in Wales and the nationalist parties, SNP and Plaid Cymru, both polled strongly, each attracting 28% of the vote. The Conservative Party secured only 15% of the both in each contest, one point ahead of the Liberal Democrats. After these elections, Labour formed a coalition government with the Liberal Democrats in Scotland, with the outgoing UK secretary of state for Scotland, Donald Dewar, becoming First Minister. In Wales Labour formed a minority administration, under Alun Michael, the outgoing secretary of state for Wales.

The Labour Party polled less impressively in the June 1999 European Parliament elections, held for the first time in England, Scotland, and Wales using proportional representation, with party lists. Labour's share of the national vote slumped to 28%, whereas the Conservatives, running a strongly 'Eurosceptic' campaign, recovered to 36% national support, while the anti-European UK Independence Party attracted 7% support, and the Greens, 6%. However, turnout was only 24%: the lowest of any country in the EU

In July 1999 there was a major setback for the peace process in Northern Ireland. The government's plans to devolve power to a Northern Ireland executive drawn from the province's elected assembly appeared to have collapsed when the Ulster Unionists, including 'First Minister' designate David Trimble, refused to share ministries with Sinn Fein, the IRA's political wing, without cast-iron guarantees about the decommissioning of weapons.

VATICAN CITY STATE

Temporal State of the Bishop of Rome
Stato della Città del Vaticano

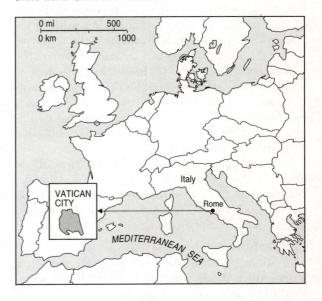

Capital: Vatican City, Rome

Social and economic data
Area: 0.45 sq km/0.15 sq miles
Population: 1,000[*]
Pop. density per sq km/sq mi: 2,500/6,666[*]
Literacy rate: N/A
GDP: N/A; per-capita GDP: N/A
Government spending on defense (% of GDP): N/A
Economy type: high income
Labor force in agriculture: N/A
[*] 1995.

Religions
Roman Catholicism is the sole religion.

Political features
State type: theocracy
Date of state formation: 1377/1929
Political structure: unitary
Executive: absolute (theocratic)
Assembly: none

Party structure: none
Human rights rating: N/A

Head of state
His Holiness Pope John Paul II, since 1978

Head of government
Cardinal Angelo Sodano, since 1990

Political system

The Vatican City State came into being through the Lateran Treaty of February 1929, under which the king of Italy recognized the sovereignty of the pope over the city of the Vatican. The pope, the supreme pontiff of the Roman Catholic Church, is elected for life by 120 members of the Sacred College of Cardinals. He appoints a Pontifical Commission (PC), headed by a president, to administer the state's affairs on his behalf and under his direction. The PC comprises seven cardinals, each appointed for a five-year period, served by lay staff headed by a Special Delegate. Routine Vatican administration has been entrusted since 1984 to the secretary of state.

In the Vatican, the central administration of the Roman Catholic Church throughout the world is also conducted by 11 Congregations, each under the direction of a cardinal, three secretariats, and numerous committees, councils, and commissions.

Political history

The Vatican City State is a direct successor to early papal states which had ruled much of the central Italian peninsula during the millennium between the era of Charlemagne and the unification of Italy in 1870–71. The Vatican Palace in Rome had served as the papal residence since 1377 and remained so during the period between 1871 and 1929 when the Vatican was formally absorbed within the new Italian state. Under the terms of the 1929 Lateran Agreement, signed by Benito Mussolini (1883–1945) and Pope Pius XI (1857–1939), full sovereign jurisdiction over the Vatican City State was restored to the Holy See, which is the formal title of the bishopric of Rome. The new state was declared a neutral and inviolable territory.

This treaty was reaffirmed in the Italian constitution of 1947. Under the terms of a Concordat, also agreed in 1929, Roman Catholicism became the state religion in Italy, enjoying special legal privileges. This status was also reaffirmed in 1947. However, a new Concordat was signed in February 1984, and subsequently ratified in June 1985, under which Catholicism ceased to be the Italian state religion.

The present (266th) pope, John Paul II (b. 1920), formerly Cardinal Karol Wojtyła, took up his office in October 1978. Born in Poland and having previously served as archbishop of Kraków in Poland, he is the first non-Italian pope since 1522. In May 1981 and May 1982 he survived two assassination attempts and has since established himself as a vigorous and influential leader. As head of a church claiming more than 750 million adherents worldwide, 26% of whom live in Europe, 53% in the Americas, and the remaining 21% in Africa, Asia, and Oceania, Pope John Paul II has travelled extensively, drawing large audiences wherever he visits. Probably his most notable journey was to communist Cuba, in 1998, and his most emotional – his return to Poland, in 1999.

Oceania

The region we have called Oceania occupies a total land area of nearly 9 million sq km/3.5 sq miles, equivalent to around 7% of the world total, but, as its name implies, the total land–sea coverage is considerably greater. It extends from 47 degrees south, at the foot of New Zealand, to 21 degrees north, at the top of the Philippines. The southern part enjoys a cool temperate climate while the central and northern areas are subtropical or tropical. Above all, it is a region of water and islands. Some of the islands are small and uninhabited, others are large, and the biggest of all, Australia, is twice the size of India and large enough to be regarded as a continent. The number of islands defies comprehension – in the Philippines alone, for example, there are more than 7,000.

Within the region are 15 sovereign states, three of which (Belau, the Federated States of Micronesia, or FSM, and the Marshall Islands) were formerly United Nations (UN) Trust Territories until the early 1990s. The largest in areal size is Australia and the largest in population, the Philippines. Oceania is very much a region of contrasts. For example, Australia has a population density of two people per square kilometre, while tiny Nauru has 523. Many countries are still undeveloped, or only partly developed, while others have well established secondary and tertiary industries and sophisticated infrastructures. Three of the 15 nations within Oceania have low per-capita GDPs, whereas those of Australia, Nauru, and New Zealand are high. Overall, the region comprises less than 2% of both the world's population and GDP, with average GDP in the region standing at $4,950 in 1995.

Until comparatively recently much of the region was one of the most isolated and inaccessible parts of the world. The nearest neighbor to Nauru, for example, is Kiribati, over 300 kilometres away. Before World War II, the journey from Europe to Australia was, for most people, a matter of weeks, rather than days. Now it can be accomplished, by scheduled airlines, in hours. The same can be said of most other parts of the region. The earlier isolation, which led to the region being used as a nuclear testing ground for the United States (on Bikini atoll), Britain (on Christmas Island), and France (on Mururoa atoll), is now being removed, not just for a wealthy minority, but for an increasing number of people of comparatively modest incomes. All this has meant not only that Europeans and Americans are wanting – and getting – to know more about the region, but that the inhabitants of Oceania are becoming less inward-looking themselves.

Despite many other differences, most of the 15 states in the region share certain common cultural and political features. Christianity, which was introduced, along with initially debilitating Western diseases, by European missionaries to the Pacific island states, is the predominant religion. The constituent states generally display high levels of representative government. As Table 61 shows, 13 are established liberal democracies, one we have defined as an emergent democracy, and only one, Tonga, does not have a pluralist political system. Eight have parliamentary executives, on the British model, and six have limited presidential executives, on the lines of that in the United States. Tonga, with its virtually unique system of hereditary paternalistic monarchs, is, again, the exception to the rule. Even their voting methods show a high degree of uniformity, ten of the 15 employing the simple plurality system.

This comparative uniformity in political processes can be largely explained by the historical backgrounds of the 15 nations. Eleven of them were, at one time or another, under British control and are still active members of the Commonwealth. The 'non-British' exceptions are the Philippines, which was a United States, possession for nearly 50 years until it achieved full independence in 1946, and the three ex-UN Trust Territories, which were under US tutelage from the end of World War II until they secured independence under the terms of 'Compacts of Free Association' with the United States. The links between the United Kingdom and the other Commonwealth countries in the region, and those between the Philippines and the three former UN Trust Territories and the United States, are still strong, although the former are not nearly as strong as they were in earlier decades. Britain's membership of the European Union has done much to force countries such as Australia and New Zealand to realign their attitudes and establish closer links with their neighbors and with the dominant economic force lying on the region's periphery, Japan. Nine of the states of the region have no independent armed forces of their own, being reliant on external 'great powers' for their ultimate defense.

The United States, in the 19th century and the early part of the 20th century, was described as the 'New World'. Today that epithet could, more appropriately, be applied to parts of Oceania, and particularly Australia and New Zealand. Australia is no longer regarded as a cultural backwater, but rather a leader in

Oceania: social, economic, and political data

Country	Area (sq km/sq mile)	c. 1995 Population (million)	c. 1995 Pop. density per sq km/sq mile	c. 1992 Adult literacy rate (%)	World ranking	Income type	c. 1991 Human rights rating (%)
Australia	7,686,850/2,967,908	18.424	2/6	99	8	high	91
Fiji	18,376/7,095	0.784	43/111	79	109	middle	N/A
Kiribati	861/332	0.077	89/232	90	80	low	N/A
Marshall Islands	180/69	0.054	300/783	95	59	middle	N/A
Micronesia	700/270	0.104	149/385	95	59	middle	N/A
Nauru	21/8	0.011	523/1,375	99	8	high	N/A
New Zealand	267,844/103,415	3.643	14/35	99	8	high	98
Palau (Belau)	508/196	0.017	33/87	N/A	–	middle	N/A
Papua New Guinea	462,840/178,703	3.997	9/22	52	146	middle	70
Philippines	300,000/115,831	67.038	223/579	94	66	middle	72
Samoa	2,831/1,093	0.164	58/150	98	34	low	N/A
Solomon Islands	27,556/10,639	0.366	13/34	60	131	low	N/A
Tonga	748/289	0.098	131/339	99	8	middle	N/A
Tuvalu	26/10	0.009	346/900	95	59	low	N/A
Vanuatu	12,190/4,707	0.165	13/35	66	123	middle	N/A
Total/average/range	8,781,531/3,390,567	94.951	11/28	52–99	–	–	70–98

A = appointed, AMS = additional member system, AV = alternative vote, E = elected, F = Federal, PR = proportional representation, SB = second ballot, SP = simple plurality, U = unitary, Lib-dem = liberal democratic, Em-dem = emergent democratic, Lim-pres = limited presidential, Trans = transitional.

the arts of literature, drama, music, and film-making. Although much of its interior will probably remain undeveloped for many years to come, the potential for development is undoubtedly there. Many of the smaller Oceanic countries will be handicapped by geographical factors and a lack of natural resources which has meant that their economies are heavily reliant on foreign aid. But, as they work together more in joint endeavours and develop new activities, notably tourism, they too have the capacities to improve their circumstances. However, a major threat to the very existence of several of the region's small low-lying island states is the likely rise in the sea level if 'global warming' continues.

A final point should be made. Oceania, in the form we have defined it, is a somewhat artificial entity and its proximity to the fast growing economies in parts of neighboring Asia should not be forgotten. If we include in our calculations the 'Pacific Rim' states of Japan, which during World War II ruled nearly a thousand Pacific islands, China, Taiwan, the Koreas, Thailand, Malaysia, and Hong Kong, then we are looking at a highly dynamic and potentially very important part of the world.

Recommended reading

Dommen, E C and Hein, P L (eds.) *States, Micro-states and Islands*, Croom Helm, 1985

Dorney, S *Papua New Guinea: People, Politics and History since 1975*, Random House (Australia), 1990

Jaensch, D *The Politics of Australia*, Macmillan (Australia), 1992

Linder, S B *The Pacific Century*, Stanford University Press, 1986

Marsh, I *Beyond the Two-Party System: Political Representation, Economic Competitiveness, and Australian Politics*, Cambridge University Press, 1995

Winchester, S *The Pacific*, Hutchinson, 1994

Table 61

World ranking	Date of state formation	State structure	State type	Executive type	Number of assembly chambers	Party structure	Lower house electoral system
20	1901	F	Lib-dem	Parliamentary	2	two	PR-AV
–	1970	U	Em-dem	Parliamentary	2	multi	SP
–	1979	U	Lib-dem	Lim-pres	1	two	SB
–	1990	U	Lib-dem	Lim-pres	1	none	SP
–	1986	F	Lib-dem	Lim-pres	1	none	SP
–	1968	U	Lib-dem	Lim-pres	1	none	SP
4	1853	U	Lib-dem	Parliamentary	1	multi	PR-AMS
–	1994	U	Lib-dem	Lim-pres	2	none	SP
47	1975	U	Lib-dem	Parliamentary	1	multi	SP
43	1946	U	Lib-dem	Lim-pres	2	multi	SP
–	1962	U	Lib-dem	Parliamentary	1	multi	SP
–	1978	U	Lib-dem	Parliamentary	1	multi	SP
–	1831/1970	U	Absolutist	Absolutist	1	trans	mixed-E/A
–	1978	U	Lib-dem	Parliamentary	1	none	SP
–	1980	U	Lib-dem	Parliamentary	1	multi	PR-PL
–	–	–	–	–	–	–	–

AUSTRALIA

Commonwealth of Australia

Capital: Canberra

Social and economic data
Area: 7,686,850 sq km/2,967,908 sq miles
Population: 18,424,000[*]
Pop. density per sq km/sq mi: 2/6[*]
Urban population: 85%[**]
Literacy rate: 99%[**]
GDP: $337,910 million[*]; per-capita GDP: $18,720[*]
Government defense spending (% of GDP): 2.5%[*]
Currency: Australian dollar
Economy type: high income
Labor force in agriculture: 5%[**]
Unemployment rate: 8.5%[*]
[*] 1995.
[**] 1992.

Head of state
Queen Elizabeth II, represented by Sir William Deane since 1996

Head of government
Prime Minister John Howard, since 1996

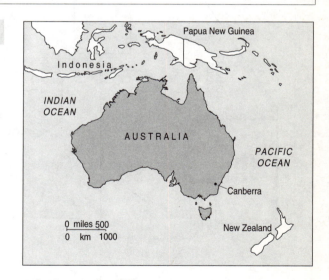

Ethnic composition
About 99% of the population is of European descent – British, Maltese, Italian, Greek, Dutch, and Polish, in that order. The remaining 1% is Aborigine or Asian. By 1993 around 23% of the population were born outside Australia. Non-Europeans, who were largely excluded until the 'White Australia' policy was abandoned in 1973, form the majority of recent immigrants. English is the official language.

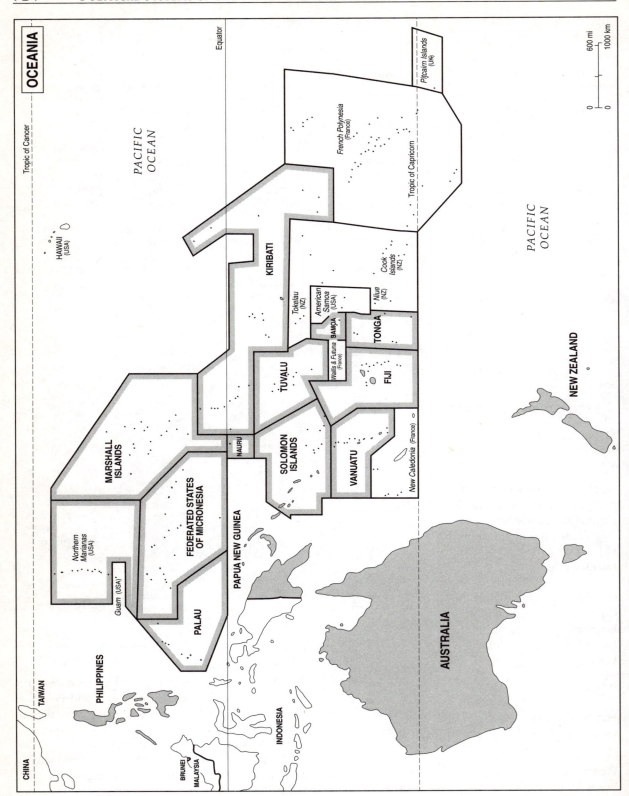

OCEANIA

PACIFIC OCEAN

PACIFIC OCEAN

Tropic of Cancer

Equator

Tropic of Capricorn

HAWAII (USA)

Pitcairn Islands (UK)

French Polynesia (France)

KIRIBATI

Cook Islands (NZ)

Tokelau (NZ)

American Samoa (USA)

Niue (NZ)

SAMOA

TONGA

TUVALU

Wallis & Futuna (France)

FIJI

MARSHALL ISLANDS

NAURU

SOLOMON ISLANDS

VANUATU

New Caledonia (France)

NEW ZEALAND

Northern Marianas (USA)

FEDERATED STATES OF MICRONESIA

PAPUA NEW GUINEA

Guam (USA)

PALAU

PHILIPPINES

TAIWAN

AUSTRALIA

INDONESIA

CHINA

BRUNEI

MALAYSIA

600 mi
1000 km

Religions

About 30% of the population is practising Anglican and 25% is Roman Catholic.

Political features

State type: liberal democratic
Date of state formation: 1901
Political structure: federal
Executive: parliamentary
Assembly: two-chamber
Party structure: two-party
Human rights rating: 91%
International affiliations: AG (observer), ANZUS, APEC, CP, CW, IAEA, IBRD, IMF, IWC, NAM (guest), OECD, SPC, SPF, UN, WTO

Local and regional government

Australia is a federal nation, consisting of the six states of New South Wales, Victoria, Queensland, Western Australia, South Australia, and Tasmania; and the Northern Territory, Australian Capital Territory, and Jervis Bay Territory.

The states are modern-day equivalents of the 19th-century colonies which were federated to become a single nation. State identification therefore remains a strong feature of Australian life. This aspect is accentuated by the size of the country and the distribution of the population. Most communities are in coastal areas, and particularly the east and south coasts, and around the major cities of Sydney, Melbourne, Brisbane, Perth, Adelaide, and the capital, Canberra.

The federal system is modelled on that of the United States, with each state having its own governor, representing the queen, and its own executive, legislative, and judicial system, but the detailed arrangements for each state vary.

New South Wales has a two-chamber assembly consisting of a Legislative Council of 42 members, directly elected for the duration of two federal parliaments, with half retiring every four years, and a Legislative Assembly of 99 members, directly elected for a four-year term.

Victoria has a similar arrangement, with 44 members in the Legislative Council, elected for six years, half retiring every three years, and a Legislative Assembly of 88, elected for three to four years.

The Queensland assembly has a single chamber of 89 members, directly elected for a three-year term.

South Australia has a two-chamber assembly consisting of a Legislative Council of 22 members, elected by proportional representation for a six-year term, half retiring every three years, and a House of Assembly of 47 members, directly elected for three years.

Western Australia also has a Legislative Council and a Legislative Assembly. The Council has 34 members elected for six years, half retiring every three years, and the Assembly has 57 members elected for three years.

Tasmania has a two-chamber arrangement, with 19 members in the Legislative Council elected for six years, retiring in rotation, and 35 members in the House of Assembly, elected for four years.

The Northern Territory has a single-chamber assembly, the Legislative Assembly, with 25 members elected for a four-year term, and the Australian Capital Territory, in Canberra, has an elected House of Assembly of 18 members, with essentially an advisory function on matters affecting the territory itself.

Jervis Bay Territory is governed under the terms of the Jervis Bay Territory Administration Ordinance of 1990, issued by the governor general.

Political system

Australia is an independent sovereign nation within the Commonwealth, retaining the British monarch as head of state, and a governor general as her representative. The constitution was adopted in 1900 and came into effect on 1 January 1901. As in the United Kingdom, there is a parliamentary executive, in the shape of the prime minister and cabinet, drawn from the federal assembly and answerable to it.

The federal assembly consists of two chambers: an elected Senate of 76 (12 for each of the six states, two for the Australian Capital Territory, and two for the Northern Territory) and a House of Representatives of 148, elected by universal adult suffrage. Senators serve for six years and members of the House of Representatives for three years. Voting is compulsory and the majoritarian system of the alternative vote is used for elections to the House, and proportional representation, via the single-transferable vote, for elections to the Senate. One-half of the Senate seats are contested every three years.

In March 1986 the United Kingdom parliament removed the last relics of British legislative control over Australia.

Political parties

There are more than 70 active national and regional political parties, the most significant being the Australian Labor Party (ALP), the Liberal Party of Australia, the National Party of Australia, and the Australian Democrats Party. Although now all national organizations, there are still clear local divergences and parts of the country where each party is particularly strong or weak.

The ALP was founded in 1891 and is Australia's oldest party. It is moderately left-of-center, supporting the democratic socialization of industry, production, distribution, and exchange. It is led by Kim Beazley.

The Liberal Party of Australia dates from 1944, although its origins go back towards the beginning of the 20th century when free traders and protectionists fused together and were later joined by breakaway groups from the ALP. In its modern form it is largely the achievement of the notable Australian politician, Sir Robert Menzies. It advocates free enterprise, social justice, and individual initiative and liberty, and is led by John Howard.

The National Party of Australia was formed in 1916 as the Country Party to represent the interests of farmers. Its orientation is centrist, with an emphasis on the needs of people outside the metropolitan areas. It is led by Tim Fischer.

The Democrats, formed in 1977, are a centrist party with important representation in the Senate.

In March 1997 Pauline Hanson, an independent MP criticized for her openly racist comments, announced the formation of a new party, 'One Nation'.

Political leaders since 1970

1968–71 John Gorton (Liberal Party), 1971–72 William McMahon (Liberal-Country Party coalition), 1972–75 Gough Whitlam (ALP), 1975–83 Malcolm Fraser (Liberal-Country Party coalition), 1983–91 Bob Hawke (ALP), 1991–96 Paul Keating (ALP), 1996– John Howard (Liberal-National Party coalition)

Latest elections

The most recent elections to the House of Representatives and Senate were held on 3 October 1998 with the following result:

Political history

Although Australia was visited by Europeans as early as the 17th century, the main immigration came towards the end of the 18th century when Captain James Cook (1728–79) claimed New South Wales as a British colony. Exploration of the interior began in the next century when there was rapid expansion, aided by gold discoveries. With this growth other colonies were developed. A depression in the 1890s prompted the growth of trade unionism and the foundation of the Australian Labor Party. By the end of the century the movement towards a federation and self-government had developed sufficiently for the establishment of the Commonwealth of Australia in 1901, with Canberra to be created as the federal capital.

Since 1945 Australia has strengthened its ties with India and other Southeast Asian countries and this realignment was accelerated following Britain's entry into the European Community in 1973. The links with its original founder are now more emotional and historic than economic or political.

Politically, the immediate postwar years were dominated by the Liberal Party which, under Robert Menzies (1894–1978), held power for 17 years. He retired in 1966 and was succeeded by Harold Holt (1908–67). Holt died in a swimming accident the following year and in 1968 John Gorton (b. 1911) took over the premiership. In 1971 he lost a vote of confidence in the House and resigned, to be succeeded by William McMahon (b. 1908), heading a Liberal-Country Party coalition.

Then, at the end of 1972, the Liberal hegemony was broken and the Australian Labor Party, led by Gough Whitlam (b. 1916), took office. A general election in 1974 gave the Labor Party a fresh mandate to govern, although its majority in the House was reduced and it had lost control of the Senate. In 1975 the Senate blocked the government's financial legislation and,

Australia latest election results

| Party | House of Representatives | | Senate | |
	% of Vote	Seats	% of Vote	Seats
ALP	40.0	66	37.7	29
Liberals	34.1	64	37.3	31
National Party	5.3	16	[in above]	3
One Nation	8.4	0	9.0	1
Democrats	5.1	0	8.5	9
Others	7.1	2	7.5	3

with Whitlam unwilling to resign, the governor general, Sir John Kerr (1914–90), took the unprecedented step of dismissing him and his cabinet and inviting Malcolm Fraser (b. 1930) to form a Liberal-Country Party coalition caretaker administration. The wisdom of the governor general's action was widely questioned and eventually, in 1977, he himself resigned.

In the 1977 general election the coalition was returned with a reduced majority and this became even smaller in 1980. In the 1983 general election the coalition was eventually defeated and the Australian Labor Party, under Bob Hawke (b. 1929), again took office. Hawke immediately honoured an election pledge and called together leaders of employers and unions to agree a prices and incomes policy and to deal with the problem of growing unemployment. He called a general election in December 1984, 15 months earlier than necessary, and was returned with a reduced majority.

After taking office, Hawke developed a distinctive foreign policy for Australia, placing even greater emphasis than his predecessors on links with Southeast Asia and, in 1986, boldly imposing trading sanctions against South Africa as a means of influencing its dismantling of the system of apartheid.

In 1988 it was surprisingly announced that Bill Hayden (b. 1933), the foreign minister in Bob Hawke's administration, was to be Australia's next governor general, in February 1989, and, in accepting the post, Hayden announced that he would not also accept the customary knighthood.

In the 1990 general election the Liberal Party improved its position in the House and, with a decline in its fortunes and a deteriorating economy, in December 1991 the ALP chose a new leader, the former finance minister, Paul Keating (b. 1954). Bob Hawke immediately announced his withdrawal from active politics. Keating continued with his predecessor's market-centerd economic reforms, including privatization. Although unemployment rose to 11%, the ALP won an unprecedented fifth term in the March 1993 House of Representatives elections, Keating describing the result as the 'sweetest victory ever'.

Within two years the leadership of the Liberal Party changed hands twice, John Hewson resigning as leader of the opposition in May 1994 and his successor, Alexander Downer, being replaced by John Howard in January 1995.

In the March 1996 general election, the ALP was defeated after 13 years in government. There was a 6% national swing against the ALP, and one-third of the cabinet lost their seats. ALP support particularly fell in its New South Wales heartland. With 48% of the vote (up 4% on 1993), the Liberal-National coalition won 94 of the 148 House seats, to Labor's 49 (with 39% of the vote). Keating, whose abrasive style helped contribute to the ALP's defeat, acknowledged the result graciously and announced his retirement from politics. He was replaced as ALP leader by the former finance minister, Kim Beazley. The Liberal Party leader, John Howard, became the new prime minister, leading a Liberal-National coalition government. He enjoyed a period of improving economic growth, but faced a new challenge from the 'One Nation' party, formed in 1997 by Pauline Hanson, which campaigned against Asian immigration. In February 1998 a 152-member constitutional convention, comprising appointed and elected members, voted to call a referendum in 1999 on whether or not Australia should become a republic. The latter option appeared to be gathering public support. In the general election of October 1998, the ruling Liberal-National coalition held on to power, but with a much reduced majority, receiving around 40% of the vote, the same as the ALP. The 'One Nation' party attracted 8% support, although its leader, Pauline Hanson, failed to hold on to her seat. The new Howard government pledged to introduce a new 10% Goods and Services Tax (GST) on consumer items, including food.

The attorney-general announced, in December 1998, that a referendum would be held in November 1999 on whether Australia should become a republic.

FIJI

Republic of Fiji
Matanitu Koviti

Capital: Suva (on Viti Levu)

Social and economic data
Area: 18,376 sq km/7,095 sq miles
Population: 784,000[*]
Pop. density per sq km/sq mi: 43/111[*]
Urban population: 37%[**]
Literacy rate: 79%[**]
GDP: $1,895[*]; per-capita GDP: $2,440[*]
Government defense spending (% of GDP): 1.5%[*]
Currency: Fiji dollar
Economy type: middle income

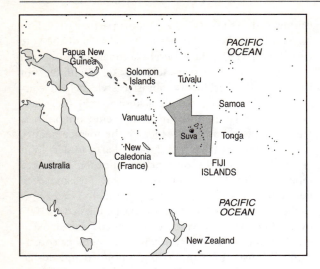

Labor force in agriculture: 44%[**]
Unemployment rate: 5.4%[*]
[*] 1995.
[**] 1992.

Head of state
President Ratu Sir Kamisese Mara, since 1994

Head of government
Prime Minister Mahendra Chaudhry, since 1999

Ethnic composition
Fiji is one of the few countries in the world where the native population is in a minority. Fijians, who are ethnically a mixture of Melanesians and Polynesians, comprise only 48% of the population, while about 51% are Asians who were brought to the country from India as indentured laborers during the period of British colonial rule. Fijian and Hindi are the official languages but English is widely spoken.

Religions
Most ethnic Fijians are Christians, mainly Protestant, while the Asian majority are Hindus, Muslims, or Sikhs.

Political features
State type: emergent democratic
Date of state formation: 1970
Political structure: unitary
Executive: parliamentary
Assembly: two-chamber
Party structure: multiparty
Human rights rating: N/A
International affiliations: ACP, CP, CW, IBRD, IMF, PC, SPF, UN, WTO

Local and regional government
For administrative purposes, the country consists of four divisions.

Political system
Fiji was a constitutional monarchy within the Commonwealth, with the British monarch as the formal head of state, until a military coup in 1987 established a republic. The system of government retains much of its British origins, with a two-chamber parliament, comprising a Senate and a House of Representatives, and a parliamentary executive, consisting of a prime minister and cabinet, drawn from and responsible to the House of Representatives.

In 1990, however, the interim government established after the military coup amended the constitution so as to effectively to guarantee a majority in both chambers of the assembly for the Melanesian population.

The Senate has 34 members, 24 elected for five years by the Great Council of Fijian Chiefs, nine appointed members, and one appointed on the advice of the Council of Rotuma Island, which is a Polynesian dependency of Fiji.

The House of Representatives has 71 members, elected for five years through a two-ballot majoritoria voting system in single-seat constituencies. Twenty-three seats are reserved for indigenous Fijians, 19 for Indians, three for other races, one for a representative of Rotuma, and 25 are open to all. Until the constitution was amended in 1997, the prime minister had to be Melanesian, as had to be the president, who is elected by the Great Council of Fijian Chiefs.

Political parties
There are some 15 political parties, the most significant being the Fijian Political Party (FPP), the National Federation Party (NFP), the Fijian Labor Party (FLP), and the General Voters' Party (GVP).

The FPP was formed in 1990 as the political vehicle for Sitiveni Rabuka. It has a right-of-center orientation and is now led by Ratu Inoke Kubuabola.

The NFP was formed in 1960 by the merging of the multiracial, but chiefly Indian, Federation Party and the National Democratic Party. Its orientation is moderate left-of-center. It contested the 1999 general election in coalition with the FPP.

The FLP dates from 1985. It is a left-of-center party, drawing most of its support from the Indian community. The GVP was founded as an ally of the FPP and has a similar orientation.

Political leaders since 1970
1970–87 Kamisese Kapaiwai Tuimacilai Mara (AP), 1987 Lieutenant Sitiveni Rabuka (military), 1987–92

Kamisese Kapaiwai Tuimacilai Mara (AP), 1992–99
Major General Sitiveni Rabuka (FPP), 1999– Mahendra
Chaudhry (FLP)

Latest elections

In the most recent general election, held on 8 and 15
May 1999, the FLP won 37 of the 71 House of
Representatives' seats, while the FPP won only eight.
The Fijian Association Party (FAP) finished second
with ten seats and the Fijian Party of National Unity
(PANU) fourth, with four seats. Three other parties
secured representation. Voting was compulsory, but
turnout was only 89% and after the election the police
asked for extra funding to prosecute the 45,000 people
who had failed to vote.

Political history

A British possession since 1874, Fiji achieved full independence within the Commonwealth in 1970. Before
independence there had been racial tensions between
Indians, descended from workers who had been
brought to Fiji in the late 19th century, and Fijians, so
the constitution incorporated an electoral device which
would help to ensure racial balance in the House of
Representatives. The leader of the Alliance Party (AP),
Ratu Sir Kamisese Mara, became prime minister at the
time of independence and held office until there was a
brief military coup in 1987.

The AP was traditionally supported by ethnic Fijians
and the National Federation Party (NFP) by Indians.
The main divisions between the two centerd on land
ownership, with the Fijians owning more than 80% of
the land and defending their traditional rights, and the
Indians claiming greater security of land tenure. The
Fijian Labor Party (FLP) was formed in 1985 and in the
April 1987 general election gained power in association
with the NFP. This provoked an unsuccessful coup the
following month, led by Lieutenant Colonel Sitiveni
Rabuka (b. 1948). In September 1987 a second coup
succeeded and Rabuka announced that he had abrogated the constitution and assumed the role of head of
state. After some indecision and confusion Fiji was
declared a republic, the British queen ceasing to be
head of state and the country automatically leaving the
Commonwealth.

In December 1987 a civilian government was
restored, with Mara resuming as prime minister, and
Rabuka retaining control of the security forces as minister for home affairs. The former governor general, Sir
Penaja Ganilau, resumed his role as head of state, now
in the position of Fiji's first president.

Rabuka prepared for the future by forming the Fijian
Political Party (FPP) as the vehicle for his political
ambitions, and in the 1992 general election his party
won 30 seats, allowing him to form a coalition government with the General Voters' Party (GVP).

In November 1993 the government's budget was
rejected by parliament so Prime Minister Rabuka
announced that there would be a general election in early
1994. President Ganilau died in December 1993 and was
succeeded by his deputy, Ratu Sir Kamisese Mara.

In the February 1994 general election the FPP, supported by the GVP and two independents, secured a
parliamentary majority and Rabuka began a second
term as prime minister.

In May 1997 the prime minister tabled amendments
to the constitution to remove some of its more racist
provisions, saying that he hoped that readmission to
Commonwealth membership would come soon. Kiji
was formally readmitted in August 1997. During its
period under suspension, Fiji had continued to maintain the Union Flag as part of its national emblem, and
had been the only country officially to celebrate the
birthday of the Prince of Wales.

In January 1999 Ratu Sir Kamisese Maru was
endorsed for a further five-year term as president by
Fiji's General Council of Chiefs. Earlier, in December
1998, a new governing coalition was formed in
December 1998 by the ruling FPP, the Indian-dominated National Federation Party (NFP), and the United
General Party (UGP), ahead of the May 1999 general
election. However, this failed to prevent Prime Minister
Rabuka's FPP from being swept from power in this
election, being defeated by a coalition of parties led by
the ethnic Indian-dominated FLP. The FLP's leader,
Mahendra Chaudhry, became Fiji's first ethnic Indian
prime minister, but, concerned to defuse racial tensions, he chose to form a broad-based government.
This included Melanesian (indigenous Fijian) members
of the Fijian Association Party (FAP), the Fijian Party of
National Unity (PANU) and the Christian Democratic
Alliance (CDA). Rabuka resigned as leader of the FPP,
immediately after the election.

KIRIBATI

Republic of Kiribati

Capital: Bairiki (on Tarawa Atoll)

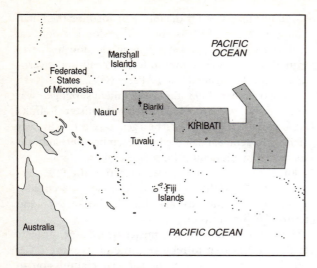

Social and economic data
Area: 861 sq km/332 sq miles
Population: 77,000*
Pop. density per sq km/sq mi: 89/232*
Urban population: 36%*
Literacy rate: 90%*
GDP: $73 million*; per-capita GDP: $920*
Government defense spending (% of GDP): 0%**
Currency: Australian dollar
Economy type: low income
Labor force in agriculture: N/A
* 1995.
** Kiribati has no armed forces.

Head of state and head of government
President Teburoro Tito, since 1994

Ethnic composition
The population is predominantly Micronesian, with a Polynesian minority also to be found, as well as a few Europeans and Chinese. I-Kiribati (Gilbertise) is the local language, with English being used for official business.

Religions
The islands adhere both to the Protestant, chiefly Congregational, and Roman Catholic faiths in almost equal proportions. Traditional beliefs and practices also survive.

Political features
State type: liberal democratic
Date of state formation: 1979
Political structure: unitary
Executive: limited presidential
Assembly: one-chamber
Party structure: two-party*
Human rights rating: N/A
International affiliations: ACP, ADB, CW, ESCAP**, IBRD**, ICAO**, IDA**, IFC**, IMF**, ITU**, PC, SPEC, SPF, UNESCO**, UPU**, WHO**

* However, many deputies are elected as independents.
** UN bodies of which Kiribati is a member, although it is not formally a member of the UN.

Local and regional government
The islands are divided into seven administrative districts: Banaba, Northern Gilbert Islands, Central Gilbert Islands, Southern Gilbert Islands, Southeastern Gilbert Islands, Line Islands, and the Phoenix Group, with a district officer in charge of each. In addition, elected councils function on each of the 21 inhabited islands, enjoying considerable autonomy.

Political system
Kiribati is an independent republic within the Commonwealth, with a constitution which dates from independence in June 1979. It provides for a president, known as the Beretitenti, and a 41-member single-chamber assembly, the Maneaba ni Maungatabu. The president combines the roles of head of state and head of government, and is elected by universal adult suffrage, for a four-year term. After each general election the Maneaba nominates from among its members three or four candidates for president, who then stand in a national contest.

The Maneaba itself comprises 39 popularly elected members, one nominated representative of the inhabitants of the island of Banaba, and, if he is not an elected member, an attorney general who serves in an *ex officio* capacity. All members serve a four-year term, and the assembly is subject to dissolution during that period.

The president governs with the help of a vice president (Kauoman ni Beretitenti) and a cabinet composed of up to eight additional ministers, chosen from and responsible to the Maneaba. At present, the president holds the portfolios of foreign affairs and international trade. A Council of State, composed of the speaker of the Maneaba, the chief justice, and the chairperson of the Public Service Commission, carries out the functions of the president and Maneaba during the period between dissolution and the holding of fresh elections.

Since 1995, a constitutional review committee has been conducting research throughout the islands on public opinion concerning possible amendments to the constitution.

Political parties

Traditionally, all candidates for the Maneaba have fought as independents, but in recent years an embryonic party system has emerged. In 1985 an opposition party, the Christian Democratic Party, was formed by Maneaba members opposed to the policy strategy of President Tabai. Led by Teburoro Tito, it is now known as the Maneaban Te Mauri (MTM) party and has been the dominant force in parliament since July 1994. Tito leads a 'Christian-democratic' faction of the MTM, and the vice president Tentoa a 'liberal faction'.

The formerly dominant grouping, the National Progressive Party (NPP), led by Teatao Teannaki, though not constituting a formal political party, had effectively ruled Kiribati since independence.

Political leaders since 1970

1974–78 Naboua Ratieta (independent), 1978–91 Ieremia T Tabai (independent), 1991–94 Teatao Teannaki (NPP), 1994 Council of State, 1994– Teburoro Tito (MTM)

Latest elections

The most recent Maneaba elections were held on 23 and 30 September 1998. As usual, contests were fought in multimember constituencies, with a second run-off ballot among the three leading candidates in constituencies where no candidate obtained the requisite 50% of the votes cast. Teburoro Tito's MTM and the opposition NPP lost a significant number of seats to independent candidates. The MTM finished with 14 seats. Teburoro Tito was re-elected president for a second term on 27 November 1998, securing 52% of the vote. He defeated Harry Tong, who won 46% of the vote, and Ambreroti Nikora.

Political history

Kiribati comprises three groups of 33 low-lying coral atolls plus Banaba, a raised volcanic atoll in the west. The whole group is situated in the southwest Pacific Ocean and scattered over an area of 5 million square kilometres. In the center, lying on the equator, are the 16 Gilbert Islands; to the east are the eight uninhabited Phoenix Islands; and to the north lie eight of the 11 Line Islands, the remaining three being uninhabited dependencies of the United States. Thirty-three per cent of the population lives on Tarawa Atoll, principally at the port and town of Bairiki, in the Gilbert group.

Kiribati was visited by the Spanish in 1606, before being officially 'discovered' by the British navy during the late 18th century. Designated the Gilbert Islands, in 1892 they were joined with the Ellice Islands, now called Tuvalu, to the south, to form a British protectorate. They became a formal colony in 1916, under the designation Gilbert and Ellice Islands Colony (GEIC). A resident commissioner was based at Tarawa Atoll, although supreme authority rested with the Western Pacific High Commission (WPHC), which had its headquarters in Fiji. The colony was extended to embrace Ocean Island, Christmas Island, or Kiritmati, three of the Line Islands, and the eight Phoenix Islands, then uninhabited, between 1916 and 1937.

The GEIC was invaded and occupied by the Japanese in 1942, during World War II, but, following fierce fighting on Tarawa Atoll, which caused great and lasting damage, they were removed by US naval forces in 1943 and British control was restored. During the 1960s, as a means of preparing the islands for self-government, a succession of legislative and executive bodies was established, culminating in the creation of a House of Assembly in May 1974. This comprised 28 elected members and three official members. Naboua Ratieta was elected from among these members as the GEIC's first chief minister, and chose a four- to six-member ministerial cabinet.

In October 1975, following a referendum, the Polynesian-peopled Ellice Islands, fearing domination in an independent GEIC from the Micronesian Gilbert Islands majority, broke away to form the separate territory of Tuvalu. This reduced the size of the Gilbert Islands' House of Assembly by eight elected members. During the mid-1970s, a separatist movement also developed among the people of Ocean Island, or Banaba, an atoll which was rich in phosphate resources, producing more than 80% of the country's export earnings and 50% of government tax revenue. Opencast phosphate mining was in the hands of the British Phosphate Commission, who exported the produce to Australia and New Zealand as fertilizer. The mining, which ceased in 1979, had adversely affected Banaba's environment, necessitating the resettlement of the local population on Rabi Island, 2,600 kilometres away in the Fiji group. Banaba's leaders, the Rabi Council of Leaders, pressed for large-scale compensation for this damage and opposed the distribution of revenue derived from phosphate mining over the whole Gilbert Islands territory. They, therefore, campaigned for the constitutional separation of the island. They eventually accepted a British government *ex gratia* compensation offer in April 1981, but, during recent years, have continued to campaign for separation.

The Gilbert Islands were granted internal self-government in January 1977 and the number of elective members in the House of Assembly was increased to 36. After the general election of February 1978 the opposition leader, Ieremia Tabai, was chosen as the new chief minister. In July 1979 the islands were finally granted full independence as a republic within the Commonwealth under the designation Kiribati. The House of Assembly was also now renamed the Maneaba ni Maungatabu and Chief Minister Tabai became the country's first president. He was re-elected after parliamentary and presidential elections in March and May 1982. Within seven months of the elections, however, as a result of the Maneaba's rejection of proposals to raise civil servants' salaries, the assembly had to be dissolved and fresh parliamentary and presidential elections were held in January and February 1983. President Tabai was again returned to office.

During 1985 opposition to the Tabai government began to mount when a controversial fishing agreement was negotiated with a Soviet state-owned company, Sovrybflot. The move prompted the formation of the country's first political party, the Christian Democratic Party, by the opposition leader, Harry Tong, and 15 members of the Maneaba. The 12-month fishing agreement, which expired in October 1986, was not, however, renewed, the Soviet company claiming that the fees charged by the government had been too high. Following this, Tabai was elected for a fourth term as president in May 1987.

Having served the maximum mandate permitted by the constitution, Tabai was succeeded as executive president in July 1991 by the former vice president, Teatao Teannaki. Charged by opposition deputies with the misuse of public funds, Teannaki's government was brought down in May 1994 after a vote of no confidence was carried. A three-member Council of State held power pending fresh elections. These parliamentary and presidential elections, which were held in July and September 1994, resulted in victory for candidates of the former opposition, the Maneaban Te Mauri (MTM), ending 15 years of rule by the National Progressive Party (NPP). Teburoro Tito was sworn in as president on 1 October 1994.

Despite the 1985–86 Soviet fishing incident, Kiribati has generally pursued a moderate pro-Western foreign policy. In September 1979 a treaty of friendship was signed with the United States, under which the United States relinquished its claims to the Line and Phoenix Islands, including Canton and Enderbury. This was followed in October 1986 by the signing of a five-year agreement by the South Pacific Forum (SPF), of which body Kiribati is an influential member, to grant US tuna boats the right to fish within the 'exclusive economic zones' of the Forum's member states. In return, the United States paid Kiribati US$5.7 million in 1992. In the same year a new agreement was signed with South Korea, allowing its fishing vessels to operate within Kiribati waters for an annual fee of US$2 million. A significant factor behind this pro-Western policy approach has been Kiribati's heavy dependency on foreign development aid, particularly since the closure of the Banaba phosphate works in 1979. Nevertheless, the new administration of President Tito has pledged to reduce the country's dependence on foreign aid. In September 1995 diplomatic relations were severed with France in protest against the resumption of French nuclear weapons-testing at Mururoa Atoll.

Kiribati is faced with problems of a high rate of population growth (2% per year), and over-population on South Tarawa, which has led to recent resettlement on outlying atolls, the depletion of its important tuna fish stock as a result of the use of drift nets by Asian fleets, and the threat that rising sea levels brought about by the 'greenhouse effect' could well submerge a country where none of the land is more than two metres above sea level. It has a limited export base and needs to import virtually all essential commodities. However, tourism is being developed to bring in foreign exchange and currently generates a fifth of GDP.

MARSHALL ISLANDS

Republic of the Marshall Islands (RMI)

Capital: Dalap-Uliga-Darrit Municipality (on Majuro Atoll)

Social and economic data
Area: 180 sq km/69 sq miles
Population: 54,000[*]
Pop. density per sq km/sq mi: 300/783[*]
Urban population: N/A
Literacy rate: 95%[*]
GDP: $88 million[*]; per-capita GDP: $1,630[*]
Government defense spending (% of GDP): 0%[**]
Currency: US dollar
Economy type: middle income

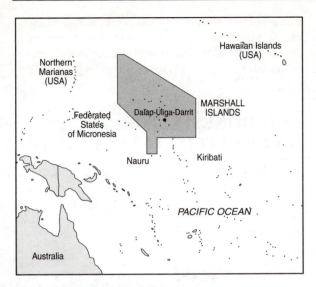

Labor force in agriculture: N/A
* 1995.
** The United States is responsible for the Marshall Islands' defense.

Head of state and head of government
President Imata Kabua, since 1997

Ethnic composition
Ninety-seven per cent of the population is Marshallese, of predominantly Micronesian ethnic stock. English (official) and Marshallese are spoken.

Religions
The main religion is Christianity, including Roman Catholicism and various Protestant churches, notably the Assembly of God, Jehovah's Witnesses, Seventh-Day Adventist, and the Church of Jesus Christ of Latter-Day Saints (Mormons).

Political features
State type: liberal democratic
Date of state formation: 1990
Political structure: unitary
Executive: limited presidential*
Assembly: one-chamber
Party structure: none
Human rights rating: N/A
International affiliations: AsDB, ESCAP, IBRD, IMF, PC, SPEC, SPF, UN

* But with parliamentary features.

Local and regional government
There is a rudimentary system of local government on each inhabited atoll, with elected magistrates and munic-ipal councils, and a traditional form of village government.

Political system
Under the terms of the May 1979 constitution, the Republic of the Marshall Islands has a parliamentary form of government. Legislative authority rests with the 33-member Nitijela, from whose ranks a president, who heads an 11-member cabinet, is elected. The term of the Nitijela is four years, and members are elected directly from 25 districts. There is a 12-member consultative Council of Chiefs (Iroij), comprising traditional leaders, for matters relating to land and custom.

Political parties
There is no organized party system, but in June 1991 the Ralik Ratak Democratic Party (RRDP) was founded by Tony DeBrum, a former foreign minister and protégé of President Kabua, to oppose the group which Kabua led.

Political leaders since 1970
1979–96 Amata Kabua (independent), 1997– Imata Kabua (independent)

Latest elections
Nitijela elections were held in November 1995, producing a pro-Kabua legislature which re-elected Amata Kabua, for the fourth time, as president. In the legislative elections, eight incumbent members of the Nitijela were defeated. Imata Kabua was elected president on 13 January 1997, winning 20 Nitijela votes and defeating the speaker, Kessai Note, and a former ambassador, Wilfred Kendall, who each secured six votes.

Political history
The Marshall Islands comprise two parallel groups of island chains, the Ratak (Sunrise) and Ralik (Sunset), comprising 34 atolls and 870 reefs in the west Pacific Ocean region of northeast Micronesia, 3,200 kilometres/2,000 miles southwest of Hawaii and 2,100 kilometres/1,250 miles southeast of Guam. Thirty-seven per cent of the population lives on Majuro Atoll.

The islands were visited by the Spanish navigator Miguel de Saavedra in 1529 and remained under Spanish influence until being annexed and colonized by Germany in 1885. At the start of World War I, in 1914, the Japanese occupied the islands, afterwards administering them under the terms of a League of Nations' mandate between 1920 and 1944, when they were removed by US forces.

After the war the islands were placed under US administration as part of the United Nations (UN) Trust Territory of the Pacific Islands. Part of the area was used for testing US atomic and hydrogen bombs, necessitating abandonment of Bikini and Enewetak atolls, while a large missile range was built at Kwajalein. (In 1997 a group of Bikini Islanders returned to the atoll to assist in a project for its rehabilitation.) In moves towards autonomy set in train by the US Carter administration, the Marshall Islands District adopted its own constitution in May 1979 and in October 1982 a 'compact of Free Association' was signed by the United States. Under the terms of this compact, the islands secured full independence, but the United States remained responsible for their defense and was allowed to retain its military bases for at least 15 years. In return, it pledged to provide annual aid of $30 million. It was also required to set up a $150-million trust fund to compensate for claims made against the US government in connection with contamination caused by the nuclear tests of the 1940s and 1950s. There was also a 'rent' payment for land still used for missile tracking.

The compact was approved in a plebiscite on the islands in September 1983 and, following endorsement by the UN Trusteeship Council, came into effect in October 1986. The UN trusteeship was terminated in December 1990 and the islands became a full member of the United Nations on 17 September 1991. Amata Kabua, who became president in 1979, was re-elected in 1983, 1987, 1991, and 1995. He sought to promote the development of tourism, on Majuro, and a tuna-fishing industry in an economy which is heavily dependent on US aid. In February 1994 a US court ruled that Amata Kabua had legal title to the position of paramount chief (*Iroijlaplap*) of the Marshall Islands, a post that had been claimed by his uncle, Kabua Kabua.

In 1996 there were cabinet divisions and church opposition over legislation introducing gambling, to generate additional state revenue, forcing repeal in April. In December 1996 Amata Kabua died, at the age of 68, and he was succeeded as president in January 1997, following a contested ballot, by his cousin, Imata Kabua. As the traditional chief of Kwajalein Atoll, which received annual rental payments of $7 million from the USA for its use as a missile tests facility, Imata Kabua was one of the richest of the Marshall Islanders. He retained all members of the previous cabinet and pledged to maintain the status quo.

Along with other low-lying island groups in Oceania, the Marshall Islands are threatened with submergence by 2030 if sea-levels continue to rise as a result of the 'greenhouse effect'. During recent years, the economy has been growing at an annual rate of 3%; and in 1996,

in conjunction with other Oceania states, the Marshall Islands helped set up a new Council of Micronesian Government Executives, to promote economic cooperation and development across the region.

MICRONESIA, THE FEDERATED STATES OF (FSM)

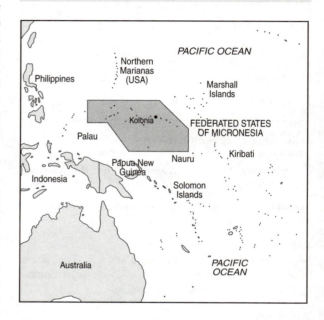

Capital: Kolonia (on Pohnpei)

Social and economic data
Area: 700 sq km/270 sq miles
Population: 104,000*
Pop. density per sq km/sq mi: 149/385*
Urban population: N/A
Literacy rate: 95%*
GDP: $215 million*; per-capita GDP: $2,067*
Government defense spending (% of GDP): 0%**
Currency: US dollar
Economy type: middle income
Labor force in agriculture: N/A
* 1995.
** The United States is responsible for the FSM's defense.

Head of state and head of government
President Leo Falcam, since 1999

Ethnic composition
The main ethnic groups are Trukese (41%) and

Pohnpeian (26%), both Micronesian. English is the official language.

Religions

The main religion is Christianity, predominantly Roman Catholicism, but with Protestant churches also represented, including the Assembly of God, Jehovah's Witnesses, and Seventh-Day Adventists.

Political features

State type: liberal democratic
Date of state formation: 1986
Political structure: federal
Executive: limited presidential*
Assembly: one-chamber
Party structure: none
Human rights rating: N/A
International affiliations: AsDB, ESCAP, IBRD, IMF, PC, SPEC, SPF, UN

* But with parliamentary features.

Local and regional government

Below the state legislatures there are elected magistrates, municipal councils, and traditional village governments.

Political system

Under the terms of the May 1979 constitution, each of the constituent states of the FSM has its own assembly, elected for a four-year term, governor, and constitution. In Chuuk the legislature is bicameral, comprising a ten-member Senate and 28-member House of Representatives; while in Kosrae, Pohnpei, and Yap the legislatures are unicameral, comprising 14 members, 27 members, and ten members respectively. Four of the representatives of the Yap assembly are elected from its outer islands of Ulithi and Woleal. There is also a federal assembly, termed the Congress of the FSM. This contains 14 members, termed senators. Each state elects one 'Senator at Large' to serve a four-year term, while the remaining ten members serve two-year terms and are elected from constituencies designed to reflect the relative populations of the states. An executive president and vice president are elected by the Congress after each general election from among the four 'senators at large' on a rotational basis, with by-elections being held to fill the places vacated. The president works with a cabinet of, in 1998, 14 members. The constitution provides for a review of the governmental and federal system every ten years.

Political parties

There are no organized political parties.

Political leaders since 1970

1987–91 John Haglegam (independent), 1991–97 Bailey Olter (independent), 1997–99 Jacob Nena (independent), 1999–   Leo Falcam (independent)

Latest elections

Following elections to the Congress of the FSM in March 1999, Leo Falcam, formerly the vice-president, was elected president by the chamber in May 1995. Redley Killion was elected the new vice-president.

Political history

The FSM comprises four states, Yap, Chuuk (formerly Truk), Pohnpei (formerly Ponape), and Kosrae, which form, together with Belau, the archipelago of the Caroline Islands, situated in south-central Micronesia in the west Pacific Ocean, 800 kilometres east of the Philippines. There are more than 600 islands in the archipelago, 40 of which are of some size and inhabited. Fifty per cent of the population lives in Chuuk state, 31% in Pohnpei, 12% in Yap, and 7% in Kosrae. The population growth rate is 3% per year.

The islands have a similar history to the Marshall Islands, although they did not come under German control until 1898, when they were purchased, under the designation of the Caroline Islands, from Spain. After World War II they were placed, by the United Nations, under United States administration and, until 1979, were governed by a local administrator appointed by the US president. In May 1979, however, a constitution was adopted, establishing the 'Federated States of Micronesia'. In October 1982 a 'Compact of Free Association' was signed with the United States, under which the FSM became independent, though the United States remained responsible for their defense and security. This compact was approved in a plebiscite held in June 1983 and came into effect in October 1986, following its endorsement by the United Nations Trusteeship Council. This established the FSM as a 'sovereign, self-governing state'. In December 1990 the trust status was terminated and in September 1991 the FSM became a full member of the United Nations. Currently, nearly nine-tenths of FSM budget outlays are funded from US economic aid, but attempts are being made to develop tourism and tuna processing. The economic and defense provisions of the November 1986 Compact with the United States are renewable after 15 years.

Bailey Olter, who had become president in May 1991 and had been re-elected in May 1995, suffered a stroke in July 1996. The vice president, Jacob Nena, took over as acting president while Olter convalesced and, in May

1997, was formally sworn in as the new president. A succession of typhoons and drought caused considerable physical and economic damage between 1996 and 1998, forcing a state of emergency to be declared briefly in early 1998. The annual GDP growth rate has dropped to 1% per year despite the adoption of an economic reform program in 1995. The FSM joined other states in the region to set up, in 1996, a Council of Micronesian Government Executives to promote regional economic cooperation and development.

NAURU

Republic of Nauru

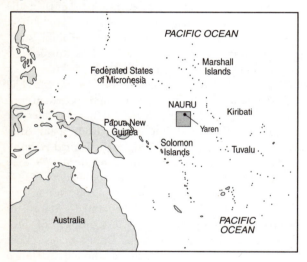

Capital: Yaren*

* *De facto*, although there is no official capital.

Social and economic data
Area: 21 sq km/8 sq miles
Population: 11,000*
Pop. density per sq km/sq mi: 523/1,375*
Urban population: N/A
Literacy rate: 99%*
GDP: $175 million*; per-capita GDP: $16,000*
Government defense spending (% of GDP): 0%**
Currency: Australian dollar
Economy type: high income
Labor force in agriculture: N/A
* 1995.
** Nauru has no armed forces, Australia being responsible for the country's defense.

Head of state and head of government
President Rene Harris, since 1999

Ethnic composition
Fifty-eight per cent of the population are indigenous Nauruans of mixed Polynesian, Micronesian, and Melanesian descent, 26% are Tuvaluans/Kiribatians, 8% are Chinese, and 8% are a mixture of Australians and New Zealanders. Nauruan is the national language, with English also being widely understood.

Religions
Fifty-eight per cent of the population are Protestants, belonging to the Nauruan Protestant Church, 24% are Roman Catholics, and 8% (the Chinese community) are Confucians and Taoists.

Political features
State type: liberal democratic
Date of state formation: 1968
Political structure: unitary
Executive: limited presidential*
Assembly: one-chamber
Party structure: none
Human rights rating: N/A
International affiliations: CW (special status), ESCAP**, ICAO**, ITU**, PC, SPEC, SPF, UPU**, WHO**

* But with parliamentary features.
** UN bodies to which Nauru belongs, although it is not formally a member of the UN.

Local and regional government
The country is divided into 14 districts which are grouped, for electoral purposes, into eight divisions. Elected local councils function at the district level.

Political system
The constitution dates from independence in January 1968. It provides for a single-chamber parliament of 18 members, elected by universal adult suffrage, for a three-year term, and a president who is both head of state and head of government. Voting in parliamentary elections is compulsory for those over 20 years of age. The president and cabinet are elected by Parliament, from among its members, and are responsible to it. Although the president has broad powers, Parliament is, nevertheless, empowered to pass bills without his or her formal assent. The size of the country allows for a very intimate style of government, with the president, combining several portfolios, including external affairs and island development and industry, in a cabinet of only six.

Political parties

Traditionally, members of Parliament have been elected as independents, but have grouped themselves into majority and minority pro- and anti-government factions. In February 1987, however, a formal political party, the Democratic Party of Nauru (DPN), was formed by the opposition leader, Kennan Adeang. It is a loose grouping, comprising around eight parliamentary members. The party declares its principal aim to be the curtailment of presidential powers and the promotion of democracy. It is effectively a successor to the Nauru Party (NP), which, formed by Lagumot Harris and Bernard Dowiyogo in December 1976, no longer functions.

Political leaders since 1970

1968–76 Hammer DeRoburt (independent), 1976–78 Bernard Dowiyogo (NP), 1978 Hammer DeRoburt (independent), 1978 Lagumot Harris (NP), 1978–86 Hammer DeRoburt (independent), 1986 Kennan Adeang (independent), 1986 Hammer DeRoburt (independent), 1986 Kennan Adeang (independent), 1987–89 Hammer DeRoburt (independent), 1989 Kenas Aroi (independent), 1989–95 Bernard Dowiyogo (independent) 1995–96 Lagumot Harris (independent), 1996 Bernard Dowiyogo (independent), 1996 Kennan Adeang (DPN), 1996–97 Reuben Kun (independent), 1997–98 Kinza Clodumar (independent), 1998–99 Bernard Dowiyogo (independent), 1999– Rene Harris (independent)

Latest elections

The most recent parliamentary elections were held on 8 February 1998. All members were elected as independents, and four new members were elected. Parliament elected Kinza Clodumar as president; he defeated Lasumot Harris by nine votes to eight. Clodumar was defeated on a no-confidence motion and replaced as president by Bernard Dowiyogo on 17 June 1998.

Political history

Nauru is a small isolated island, composed of phosphatic rock, in the west central Pacific Ocean, lying 42 kilometres south of the equator and 4,000 kilometres/2,500 miles northeast of Sydney, Australia. The population lives in small, scattered, coastal settlements. There is no urban center as such and the island, being low-lying, is in danger of being submerged if the 'greenhouse effect' results in a substantial rise in the sea level.

The island was discovered in 1798 by the British whaler, Captain John Fearn, and was called 'Pleasant Island'. Between the 1830s and 1880s it became a haven for white runaway convicts and deserters, before being placed under German rule in 1888, when the western Pacific was partitioned into British and German 'zones of influence'. The Germans discovered and intensively exploited the island's high grade phosphate reserves. After Germany's defeat in World War I, however, Nauru was placed under a joint British, Australian, and New Zealand mandate by the League of Nations, and was then administered on the other trustees' behalf by Australia.

During World War II, Nauru was invaded and occupied by the Japanese between 1942 and 1945 and was devastated. Two-thirds of the population were deported to Chuuk (Truk) Atoll, 1,600 kilometres/1,000 miles to the northwest, situated today in the Federated States of Micronesia, and all the mining facilities were destroyed. It was reoccupied by Australian forces in 1945 and the Nauruans were repatriated from Chuuk. After the war Nauru was designated a United Nations (UN) Trust Territory, subject to the continuing administration of the former mandatory powers. As part of a process of preparation for self-government, and in response to local community pressure, a local governing council was established in 1951 and an elected assembly in January 1966. Two years later, in January 1968, full independence was achieved. Nauru became a republic and was designated a 'special member' of the Commonwealth, which meant that, because of its small size, it did not have direct representation at meetings of heads of government.

Hammer DeRoburt (1923–92), who had held the position of head chief of Nauru since 1956, was elected the country's first president in May 1968 and was re-elected in May 1971 and December 1973. Criticisms of his personal style of government led to his replacement in December 1976 by Bernard Dowiyogo, leader of the Nauru Party grouping. However, mounting assembly opposition to Dowiyogo by DeRoburt supporters forced his resignation in April 1978 and the recall of DeRoburt. president DeRoburt was duly re-elected in December 1978, December 1980, and in May and December 1983. Parliamentary opposition to the government's annual budget forced DeRoburt's resignation in September 1986 and his replacement as president by the opposition leader, Kennan Adeang. Within a fortnight, however, following a successful 'no-confidence' motion, Adeang was ousted. DeRobert returned as President, but briefly lost power again to Adeang following the general election of December 1986. Fresh elections in January 1987 gave DeRoburt an effective majority and prompted the defeated Adeang to form the Democratic Party of Nauru as a formal opposition grouping.

In 1989 a vote of no confidence forced DeRoburt's resignation. He was initially replaced by Kenas Aroi, a former finance minister. However, Aroi soon resigned because of ill health and, after the general election of December 1989, Parliament elected Bernard Dowiyogo as the new president by ten votes to DeRoburt's six. This was DeRoburt's final challenge for the presidency. He died in July 1992 and was given a state funeral. Dowiyogo was re-elected president in November 1992, defeating his challenger, Buraro Detudamo, by ten votes to seven. He was replaced as premier by Lagumot Harris in November 1995, following a general election contested by a record 67 candidates.

In November 1996 Harris was narrowly defeated, by eight votes to seven, in a no-confidence motion, and was replaced as president by his predecessor, Dowiyogo. However, within a month, Dowiyogo was forced to resign, after also losing a parliamentary vote of no confidence and, by nine votes to eight, Kennan Adeang became president. He formed a cabinet chiefly comprising supporters of Harris, but, in December 1996, there was the third change of government within two months, when Adeang also lost a no-confidence motion. Reuben Kun, formerly finance minister, now became president, on the understanding that an early general election would be called. At this election, held on 8 February 1997, four incumbent deputies were removed. It was hoped that this might break the recent political stalemate. On 13 February 1997, the veteran Kinza Clodumar, who was backed by Dowiyogo, became president, defeating Harris by nine votes to eight. Adeang became parliamentary speaker and Dowiyogo was included in the government. However, in June 1998 Clodumar, who had promoted economic reform, was defeated in a no-confidence motion and was replaced by Dowiyogo as prime minister.

In April 1999 Dowiyogo was forced out of office when he was defeated by 10 votes to seven in a parliamentary vote of no-confidence. He was replaced as prime minister by Rene Harris, a member of Parliament since 1977 and a former chairman of the Nauru Phosphate Corporation. His new cabinet included Kinza Clodumar as finance minister.

Nauru achieved economic independence in 1970 when the company called the British Phosphate Commissioners, which had been in charge of the phosphate industry during the period of Australian rule, was nationalized and renamed the Nauru Phosphate Corporation. However, with the island's phosphate reserves set to run out between 1995 and 2010, recent attempts have been made to reinvest the substantial profits, which hitherto enabled the people to enjoy a high standard of living and welfare provision, in a Royalties Trust to fund new shipping, aviation, and off-shore banking ventures. In addition, in August 1993 the Australian government agreed to pay Nauru US$73 million in compensation for damage inflicted by phosphate mining during the pre-independence period which has left 80% of Nauru agriculturally barren. In 1997 a Rehabilitation Corporation was set up to oversee a 23-year-long program of rehabilitation.

In its external relations, Nauru has sought to pursue an independent course, remaining outside the United Nations, although links with Australia, Britain, and New Zealand remain close. It is a member of the South Pacific Forum (SPF), which has negotiated fisheries management treaties with Western and Southeast Asian nations with the aim of reducing excessive exploitation of tuna stocks and securing large foreign currency payments for fishing licences.

In May 1999 Nauru joined the Commonwealth as its 53rd full member. It has formerly been an associate member.

In 1995 Nauru was particularly critical of France's resumption of nuclear weapons-testing in the South Pacific and suspended diplomatic relations between 1995 and 1998. Along with other low-lying islands in Oceania, Nauru is threatened with submergence by 2030 if sea levels continue to rise as a result of global warming.

NEW ZEALAND

Capital: Wellington

Social and economic data
Area: 267,844 sq km/103,415 sq miles
Population: 3,643,000[*]
Pop. density per sq km/sq mi: 14/35[*]
Urban population: 84%[**]
Literacy rate: 99%[**]
GDP: $51,655 million[*]; per-capita GDP: $14,340[*]
Government defense spending (% of GDP): 1.7%[*]
Currency: New Zealand dollar
Economy type: high income
Labor force in agriculture: 10%[**]

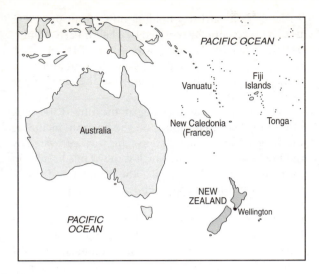

Unemployment rate: 6.3%[*]

[*] 1995.

[**] 1992.

Head of state
Queen Elizabeth II, represented by Governor General Sir Michael Hardie Boys, since 1996

Head of government
Prime Minister Jenny Shipley, since 1997

Ethnic composition
About 87% of the population is of European origin, mostly British, about 10% Maori, and about 2% is Pacific Islander. English is the official language and Maori is also spoken.

Religions
There are about 895,000 Anglicans, 495,000 Roman Catholics, 170,000 members of other Christian denominations, and 30,000 Maoris.

Political features
State type: liberal democratic
Date of state formation: 1853/1947
Political structure: unitary
Executive: parliamentary
Assembly: one-chamber
Party structure: multiparty
Human rights rating: 98%
International affiliations: ANZUS (membership suspended), APEC, CP, CW, IAEA, IBRD, IMF, IWC, NAM (guest), OECD, PC, SPF, UN, WTO

Local and regional government
For planning and civil defense purposes, the country is divided into 22 regions. For other administrative purposes there are counties, boroughs, and urban and rural districts, based broadly on the British system of local government. Each unit has an elected council.

Political system
As a constitutional monarchy, New Zealand's system of government displays many features found in that of the United Kingdom, including the absence of a written constitution. As in Britain, the constitution is the progressive product of legislation, much of it passed by the parliament in London. The governor general represents the British monarch as formal head of state and appoints the prime minister who chooses a cabinet, all of whom are drawn from and collectively responsible to the single-chamber assembly, the House of Representatives. Until 1996, it had 99 members, including four Maoris, elected by universal adult suffrage from single-member constituencies, by a simple plurality voting system. It has a maximum life of three years and is subject to dissolution within that period.

In November 1993 it was agreed, following a national referendum, that from 1996 the size of the House would be increased to 120 and voting would be by the semi-proportional representation additional member system, 55 of the members being directly elected by simple plurality in single-member constituencies, and half drawn from party lists by proportional representation, with a 5% cut-off limit for representation. The other five seats are reserved for Maori voters and are returned by the first-past-the-post system.

Political parties
Of around 15 active and six significant political parties, two have dominated the political scene for most of the time since New Zealand has been an independent state. They are the Labor Party and the New Zealand National Party, but in recent years there has been a significant realignment and three other parties have been formed in an effort to break the two-party system. They are the Alliance Party, the New Zealand First Party (NZFP), and the United New Zealand Party (UNZ).

The Labor Party was formed in 1916. It has a moderate left-of-center orientation and advocates democratic socialist policies. It is led by Helen Clark.

The New Zealand National Party was founded in 1936 as an anti-Labor party during the period of economic depression. It has a center-right free-enterprise orientation and is led by Jenny Shipley.

The Alliance Party is an alliance of five left-of-center

parties, including Maori and ecologist (Green) parties, formed in 1993 by the former Labor Party president, Jim Anderton. It is led by Jim Anderton.

The NZFP was also formed in 1993 by Winston Peters, a former member of Jim Bolger's cabinet. It has a centrist orientation and attracts many Maori votes.

The UNZ was formed in 1995 as a centrist breakaway from the Labor Party and National Party.

The new electoral system has encouraged the formation of new smaller parties.

Political leaders since 1970

1969–72 Keith Holyoake (National), 1972–74 Norman Kirk (Labor), 1974–75 Wallace Rowling (Labor), 1975–84 Robert Muldoon (National), 1984–89 David Lange (Labor), 1989–90 Geoffrey Palmer (Labor), 1990 Michael Moore (Labor) 1990–97 Jim Bolger (National), 1997– Jenny Shipley (National)

Latest elections

The results of the 12 October 1996 general election were as follows:

New Zealand latest election results

Party	% of vote	Seats
National Party	34	44
Labor Party	28	37
NZFP	13	17
Alliance Party	10	13
Others	15	9[*]

[*] Eight for the rightwing Association of Consumers and Taxpayers (ACT), and one for the UNZ.

Fought under the new semi-proportional voting system, it resulted in the return of a record number of Maori (14) and women (35) MPs, who had been placed high on parties' lists.

Political history

New Zealand was a dependency of the colony of New South Wales, Australia, until 1841, when it became a separate British colony. It was made a Dominion in the British Empire in 1907 and then granted full independence by the Statute of Westminster of 1931. Independence was formally accepted by the New Zealand parliament in 1947.

It has been in the forefront of democratic government, being, for example, the first country in the world to give women the right to vote, in 1893. It also has a record of great political stability, with the centrist New

Zealand National Party holding office from the 1930s until it was eventually replaced by a Labor Party administration, led by Norman Kirk (1923–74), in 1972. During this period of stability, New Zealand built up a social security system which became the envy of the world.

The economy was thriving at the time Kirk took office but there were clouds on the horizon, including the danger of growing inflation. This was aggravated by the 1973–74 energy crisis which resulted in a balance of payments deficit. Meanwhile, the Labor government was following a more independent foreign policy line, to some extent influenced by Britain's decision to join the European Community, with its possible effects on New Zealand's future exports. It began a phased withdrawal from some of the country's military commitments in Southeast Asia and established diplomatic relations with China. Norman Kirk died in August 1974 and was succeeded by the finance minister, Wallace Rowling (b. 1927).

The state of the economy worsened and in the 1975 general election the National Party, led by Robert Muldoon (1921–92), was returned to power with a clear working majority. However, the economy failed to revive and in the 1978 general election Muldoon's majority was greatly reduced. In 1984 he introduced controversial labor legislation which was widely opposed by the trade unions. To renew his mandate, he called an early election and was swept out of office by the Labor Party, now led by David Lange (b. 1942).

The Labor Party had fought the election on a non-nuclear defense policy, which Lange immediately put into effect, forbidding any vessels carrying nuclear weapons or powered by nuclear energy to enter New Zealand's ports. This put a great strain on relations with the United States. In 1985 the trawler *Rainbow Warrior*, the flagship of the environmentalist pressure group Greenpeace, which was monitoring nuclear tests in French Polynesia, was mined, with loss of life, by French secret service agents in Auckland harbour. The French prime minister eventually admitted responsibility and New Zealand subsequently demanded compensation.

In 1984 Sir Robert Muldoon, as he now was, was defeated in elections for the leadership of the National Party by James McLay but he, in turn, was replaced in 1986 by Jim Bolger (b. 1935). Muldoon died in 1992, at the age of 70. In August 1987 Lange was re-elected with a majority of 17 but his 'free-enterprise' economic policies created tensions within the Labor

Party, resulting in the creation of a small breakaway party, the New Labor Party (NLP), in 1989. In the same year Lange resigned and was replaced by his deputy, Geoffrey Palmer (b. 1942). The National Party won a decisive victory in the 1990 general election and its leader, Jim Bolger, became prime minister. The new government introduced austerity packages to reduce the budget deficit.

During 1993, in anticipation of the next general election, there were substantial party realignments, the New Zealand First Party (NZFP) being formed by dissident National Party members and the Alliance Party founded on the basis of the coming together of left-of-center politicians disenchanted with the Labor Party.

Although Bolger's hard-nosed economic policies had proved unpopular, the National Party won a narrow victory in the November 1993 general election and Bolger continued in office, with a one-seat majority. Voters also approved, in a national referendum, a change in the future from the first-past-the-post to an additional member system (AMS) form of proportional representation, on the German model. In September 1994 one of Prime Minister Bolger's junior ministers, Ross Meurant, resigned to form a new Right of Center Party (ROC), initially threatening the government's position. Eventually Bolger managed to continue by entering a working relationship with the ROC.

During 1995 there were further party changes, Jim Anderton resigning the leadership of the five-party Alliance and a new Labor Party breakaway grouping being formed, the United New Zealand Party (UNZ).

New Zealand's relations with France, which had been soured by the sinking of the *Rainbow Warrior* in 1985, deteriorated further in 1995 when the French government announced its intention to resume nuclear tests in the Pacific. The New Zealand government said it would test the legality of the French decision in the international courts.

Following the inconclusive October 1996 general election, held under the new semi-proportional representation voting system, and two months of negotiations, Prime Minister Jim Bolger formed a coalition with the New Zealand First Party (NZFP), led by Winston Peters. Twelve months later he was challenged for the National Party leadership by Jenny Shipley, and in November 1997 he resigned. Shipley was elected NP leader and in December was sworn in as New Zealand's first female prime minister.

PALAU (BELAU)

Republic of Palau

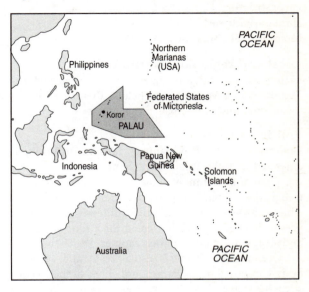

Capital: Koror (on Koror island)

Social and economic data
Area: 508 sq km/196 sq miles
Population: 17,000[*]
Pop. density per sq km/sq mi: 33/87[*]
Urban population: N/A
Literacy rate: N/A
GDP: $30 million[*]; per-capita GDP: $1,765[*]
Government defense spending (% of GDP): 0%[**]
Currency: US dollar
Economy type: middle income
Labor force in agriculture: N/A
[*] 1995.
[**] The United States is responsible for Palau's defense.

Head of state and head of government
President Kuniwo Nakamura, since 1992

Ethnic composition
The population is predominantly Micronesian, with English and Palauan being spoken.

Religions
The main religion is Christianity, chiefly Roman Catholicism.

Political features
State type: liberal democratic
Date of state formation: 1994

Political structure: unitary
Executive: limited presidential
Assembly: two-chamber
Party structure: two-party
Human rights rating: N/A
International affiliations: PC, UN

Local and regional government

Each of the republic's 16 states has its own elected legislature and governor, and, below, there are elected magistrates and municipal councils.

Political system

Under the terms of the January 1981 constitution, as amended in 1992, Palau has a democratic representative form of government, which blends elements of the indigenous system of hereditary female chiefs with American democracy. Executive authority is held by a president, who is directly elected for a four-year term and heads an eight-member cabinet, which includes the vice president. There is also a presidential advisory body, composed of the paramount chiefs of the 16 constituent states. The legislature, or Palau National Congress (Olbiil era Kelulau), is a two-chamber body, comprising a 14-member Senate, or upper house, and a 16-member House of Delegates, or lower house. Senators are elected from demographically based constituencies, four being returned from northern Palau, nine from Koror, and one from the southern islands. Delegates are elected from each of the 16 states which comprise the republic: Kayangel, Ngerchelong, Ngaraard, Ngardmau, Ngaremlengui, Ngiwal, Melekeok, Ngchesar, Ngatpang, Aimeliik, Airai, Koror, Peleliu, Angaur, Sonsorol, and Tobi. Each state has its own elected legislature and governor.

Political parties

During the later 1980s two political coalitions were formed, the Ta Belau Party and the Coalition for Open, Honest and Just Government, to respectively support and oppose the Compact of Free Association. These were not formally organized political parties. The Ta Belau Party has survived and is led by President Nakamura. It is now opposed by the Palau Nationalist Party, led by Johnson Toribiong.

Political leaders since 1970

1984–85 Haruo Remeliik (independent), 1985–88 Lazarus Salii (independent), 1988 Thomas Remengesau (independent), 1988–92 Ngiratkel Etpison (independent), 1992– Kuniwo Nakamura (independent Ta Belau Party)

Latest elections

The most recent legislature and presidential elections were held on 5 November 1996. President Kuniwo Nakamura was re-elected, securing 62% of the national vote, defeating Yukata Gibbons, who attracted 38% support, in the run-off round. In the first round, held in September 1996, Nakamura had won 52% of the vote, finishing ahead of Johnson Toribiong (who later withdrew) who gained 34% of the vote, and Gibbons, who gained 14%.

Political history

Palau comprises more than 350 (mostly uninhabited) islands, islets and atolls in the West Micronesia Caroline Islands group, lying in a 650-kilometre/406 mile-long chain in the West Pacific Ocean, 960 kilometres/600 miles east of the Philippines and 7,150 kilometres/4,468 miles southwest of Hawaii. Fifty-eight per cent of the population lives in the capital, Koror.

Palau has a similar history to the Federated States of Micronesia with which it forms part of the Caroline Islands group. A republic was proclaimed in January 1981 when, following its approval in a referendum held in July 1979, a locally drafted constitution came into effect. Later, in August 1982, a Compact of Free Association was signed with the United States, providing for Palau's independence, though the United States remained responsible for the republic's defense and security.

This compact was approved by 60% of those who voted in a referendum held in February 1983. However, fewer than the required 75% supported the proposal to amend the Republic's constitution so as to allow the transit, storage, or disposal of nuclear, chemical, or biological weapons, which, otherwise, was outlawed by one of its clauses. The United States government viewed this constitutional change as essential if it was to fulfil its defense obligations and thus refused to endorse the compact. A new compact was framed in 1986, in which the US, anxious to make use of Palau's ports as a possible naval alternative to its Philippines bases, agreed to provide, over a 15-year period, $421 million in economic assistance to the islands. However, after the failures of plebiscites held in February 1986, October 1986, and June 1987 to secure the necessary 75% majority support to change the constitution, the compact was unratified.

Following pressure from pro-nuclear supporters of the compact, an effort was made to break this impasse, in a new referendum held in August 1987. This proposed changing the plebiscitary majority required for amending the constitution from 75% to only 51%. Support for this proposed change was achieved, the required majority for both the compact and constitutional nuclear clause change being obtained in an ensuing referendum. However, in April 1988, the Supreme Court of Palau ruled these changes unconstitutional. Five months later, in August 1988, the Republic's president, Lazarus Salii, was found dead with a gunshot wound to his head. Initial reports suggested that, like Palau's first president, Haruo Remeliik in June 1985, he had been assassinated by political opponents. Later evidence suggested, however, that the president had committed suicide because of both policy failures and pending corruption charges.

A further referendum in 1990 failed to resolve the compact issue. This left Palau as the only surviving part of the Trust Territory of the Pacific Islands which had not either formally achieved 'independence' or become a US commonwealth Territory and prompted the United States to declare in May 1991 that if Palau did not soon adopt the Compact it should consider commencing independence negotiations. However, in November 1992 the requirement for the approval of constitutional amendments was reduced, by referendum, to a simple majority. This margin was achieved comfortably in November 1993 when, in an eighth referendum, 68% of voters approved a constitutional amendment designed to pave the way for implementation of the compact with the United States. Full independence was achieved on 1 October 1994, after all legal challenges by the compact's opponents had been dismissed, and in November 1994 Palau became a member of the United Nations.

Kuniwo Nakumura, who had become president in 1992, was re-elected in November 1996. This election was held at a time of economic difficulties, caused by the collapse of the bridge linking the capital, Koror, with the country's international airport, on Babeldaob island. A state of emergency was declared briefly, and construction of a new bridge was made an immediate priority of the new government.

There have been efforts during recent years to develop small-scale industries and expand tourism, which generates employment for a tenth of paid workers and attracts vital foreign exchange. These attempts have been hampered by a shortage of investment capital and a large budget deficit. However, with the compact approved, Palau became eligible for a $141 million initial grant from the United States, as well as $23 million per year for 14 years. In 1996, along with other states in the region, Palau established a new regional organization, the Council of Micronesian Government Executives, which sought to promote greater regional economic cooperation and find ways of reducing the high costs of shipping essential items between the islands.

PAPUA NEW GUINEA

The Independent State of Papua New Guinea

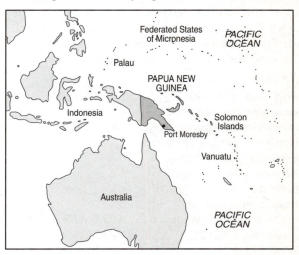

Capital: Port Moresby

Social and economic data
Area: 462,840 sq km/178,703 sq miles
Population: 3,997,000[*]
Pop. density per sq km/sq mi: 9/22[*]
Urban population: 16%[**]
Literacy rate: 52%[**]
GDP: $4,976 million[*]; per-capita GDP: $1,220[*]
Government defense spending (% of GDP): 1.3%[*]
Currency: kina
Economy type: middle income
Labor force in agriculture: 66%[**]
[*] 1995.
[**] 1992.

Head of state
Queen Elizabeth II, represented by Governor General Sir Silas Atopare since 1997

Head of government
Prime Minister Mekere Moranta, since 1999

Ethnic composition

The population is mainly Melanesian, particularly in the coastal areas. Further inland, on New Guinea and on the larger islands, Papuans predominate. On the outer archipelagos and islands mixed Micronesian-Melanesians are to be found. A small Chinese minority, numbering 3,000, also exists. The official language is pidgin English, but about 750 indigenous languages are spoken locally among what is an intensely regionalized population.

Religions

More than half the population is nominally Christian, of whom 60% are Roman Catholic and 40% belong to the Evangelical Lutheran Church. The rest mainly follow traditional magico-ritual pantheistic beliefs and practices.

Political features

State type: liberal democratic
Date of state formation: 1975
Political structure: unitary*
Executive: parliamentary
Assembly: one-chamber
Party structure: multiparty
Human rights rating: 70%
International affiliations: ACP, AsDB, APEC, ASEAN (observer), CW, CP, ESCAP, INRD, IMF, NAM, SG, PC, SPEC, SPF, UN

* Although considerable authority has been devolved to the provinces.

Local and regional government

As part of a decentralization program launched in 1978, 19 directly elected provincial assemblies and governments were established in the provinces and National Capital District and enjoy a substantial measure of autonomy. However, legislation was passed controversially in June 1995 abolishing the provincial government system. It established, instead, non-elected regional bodies composed of national parliamentarians and local councillors, and headed by appointed governors. Within the regions there is a range of district, town, and village councils.

Political system

Papua New Guinea is a constitutional monarchy within the Commonwealth, with the British Crown represented by a resident governor general as formal head of state. The constitution dates from independence in September 1975 and provides for a parliamentary system of government, broadly based on the Westminster model. There is a single-chamber assembly, the National Parliament, which consists of 109 members elected by universal adult suffrage, for a five-year term through a simple plurality voting system. The age of majority is 19 years. Eighty-nine members represent 'open', or local, single-member constituencies, 20 provincial constituencies, and there is provision in the constitution, though, as yet, unfulfilled, for a further three members to be nominated and appointed on a two-thirds majority vote of parliament. Each elector has two votes, one of which is cast for the local and one for the provincial seat. The National Parliament is subject to dissolution within its term.

The governor general formally appoints a prime minister and National Executive Council (NEC), or cabinet, whose 28 members, the maximum number (equivalent to one-fifth of the parliament) permitted under the constitution, are drawn from and responsible to the National Parliament. The government needs parliament's approval for its legislative proposals and may be removed by a vote of no confidence, without fresh elections necessarily being required. Under the terms of a recently adopted convention, a no-confidence vote may not be called until at least 18 months after a government's formation. Currently, the prime minister is also minister for foreign affairs and trade.

The governor general, who must be a 'mature' and 'respected' citizen of Papua New Guinea, is appointed by the British monarch on the recommendation of the prime minister. He or she serves a six-year term and is eligible for reappointment once only, requiring a two-thirds parliamentary majority to secure a second term. The principal role of governor general, as a result of the shifting coalition character of politics in faction-ridden Papua New Guinea, is as 'government-maker'. To amend the constitution, a two-thirds majority of the National Parliament members is required twice in succession, within a period of six weeks.

Political parties

Political parties in Papua New Guinea are weak organizations, dominated by personalities, patronage, and regional differences. They lack the formal policy-making and membership structures of the Western European kind. Their assembly members are frequently persuaded to 'cross the floor' and temporarily join other groupings in the National Parliament. Ideological differences between them are limited.

Of the 16 parties which currently function, the most important eight, in terms of parliamentary representation, are the Papua New Guinea Party (Pangu Pati: PP), the People's Democratic Movement (PDM), the National Party (NP), the Melanesian Alliance (MA), the National Alliance (NA), the People's Action Party (PAP), the People's National Congress (PNC), and the People's Progress Party (PPP).

The centrist PP, currently led by Chris Haiveta, is the country's oldest and most influential party, having been founded in June 1967 to campaign for internal self-government and eventual independence and for the adoption of pidgin as the official language. It has a strong urban base in north New Guinea and the coast, and is the best organized party in the country, with more than 75 local branches. Its former leader, Michael Somare (b. 1936), governed the country for eight of the first ten years after independence. However, the formation of the PDM in 1985, by 15 of its former parliamentary representatives, including Paias Wingti (b. 1951), undermined the PP, siphoning away crucial support. Despite this, under the leadership of Rabbie Namaliu, it succeeded in returning to power as the governing party between 1988 and 1992.

The NA was formed in 1996 by Somare and ten deputies, to campaign for 'ethical standards in government'.

The NP is a highlands-based party. It was formed in May 1978, under the designation the People's United Front (PUF), by Iambakey Okuk, a former member of the once influential United Party (UP). The UP was formed in 1969 initially to oppose independence and has fought since for maintaining close links with Australia. The NP is a generally conservative grouping and, following the death of Sir Iambakey Okuk in November 1986, has been led by Michael Mel.

The MA had its origins in a secessionist movement which, in September 1975, declared the ethnically distinct, eastern, copper-producing island of Bougainville the 'Independent Republic of the North Solomons'. A year later this movement, after securing the granting of greater autonomy for the region, accepted the island's position within Papua New Guinea. It subsequently transformed itself into a political party, originally called the Bougainville Pressure Group, and contested seats in the 1977 general election. It later adopted the designation Alliance for Progress and Regional Development (APRD), but is commonly known as the MA. Led since its inception by Father John Momis, the party is regarded as a left-of-center socialist body, demanding 'liberation from foreign domination' and favoring greater local participation in economic decision-taking. The MA draws the bulk of

its support from Bougainville dock and copper industry workers and white-collar professionals.

The PAP was formed in 1985 and is a conservative force, led by Ted Diro. The PNC, later renamed the PNG First Party, was formed more recently and is led by Bill Skate, governor of the National Capital District and speaker, before he became prime minister in 1997.

The PPP is a much older party, dating back to 1970. A conservative non-highlands based grouping, it was led by Sir Julius Chan until 1997. The party enjoys strong support in the islands north of New Guinea – New Ireland, New Britain, and the North Solomons.

In May 1995 a new political party, the Movement for Greater Autonomy (MGA), was founded by the premiers of several northern provinces who opposed the government's plans to abolish the provincial government system.

Political leaders since 1970

1972–80 Michael Somare (PP), 1980–82 Sir Julius Chan (PPP), 1982–85 Michael Somare (PP), 1985–88 Paias Wingti (PDM), 1988–92 Rabbie Namaliu (PP), 1992–94 Paias Wingti (PDM), 1994–97 Sir Julius Chan (PPP), 1997 John Giheno (PPP), 1997 Sir Julius Chan (PPP), 1997–99 Bill Skate (PNC), 1999– Mekere Morauta (PDM)

Latest elections

In the most recent National Parliament elections, held between 14–28 June 1997, the results were as follows:

Papua New Guinea latest election results

Party	Seats
People's Progress Party (PPP)	16
Pangu Pati (PP)	13
People's Democratic Movement (PDM)	10
National Alliance (NA)	6
People's Action Party (PAP)	6
People's National Congress (PNC)	6
Melanesian Alliance (MA)	4
National Party (NP)	1
Movement for Greater Autonomy (MGA)	1
Other minor parties	4
Independents	42
Total	**109**

Many of the 'independents' were expected to later align with one of the established parties.

As usual, because of the remoteness and ruggedness of much of the country, the election process extended over two weeks. In addition, illiterate voters were allowed to cast 'whispering votes', quietly intimating their choices in the ear of the presiding election officer who then proceeded to mark the ballot paper accordingly. The election campaign was dominated by allegations of government corruption and, as in 1992, many incumbents lost their seats, including the two preceding prime ministers, Sir Julius Chan and John Giheno, and the PDM leader, Paias Wingti. There was violence in the highlands during the campaign and riots at rallies, claiming several lives. This forced the government to impose a temporary evening curfew and a ban on the sale of alcohol. At the opening session of the new parliament on 2 July 1997, Bill Skate defeated Sir Michael Somare for the premiership by 71 votes to 35.

Political history

Papua New Guinea is an extensive island grouping in the southwest Pacific Ocean, 160 kilometres/100 miles northeast of Australia. It comprises the eastern half of the large island of New Guinea; the volcanic Bismarck (Mussau, New Britain, New Hanover, and New Ireland) and Louisiade archipelagos; the Trobriand and D'Entrecasteaux Islands; and an assortment of smaller groups. The country shares a 777-kilometre/485-mile-long border with Indonesia (Irian Jaya) to the west and is skirted by the Solomon Islands in the east.

New Guinea had been inhabited by indigenous Melanesians for more than 9,000 years before it was first visited by a European, the Portuguese navigator Jorge de Menezes, in 1526. Dutch merchants later made regular trips to the island during the 17th century, before the Dutch East India Company established control over the western portion of the island, incorporating it into the Netherlands East Indies in 1828. More than half a century later, under the terms of the Anglo-Dutch Agreement of 1885, Britain took possession of the southern portion of New Guinea and adjacent islands, while Germany assumed control of the northeast, which included New Britain, New Ireland, and Bougainville.

In 1901 Britain transferred its rights to Australia, which proceeded to rename the territories Papua in 1906. Then, in 1914, during World War I, Australia invaded and established control over German New Guinea. From the merged territories, Papua New Guinea was formed. It was designated, first, a Mandate Territory by the League of Nations between 1921 and 1946 and then, from 1947, a Trust Territory by the United Nations

(UN), and placed under Australian guardianship. The two territories were administered jointly by Australia, but formally retained their separate status.

During World War II, parts of Papua New Guinea were invaded and occupied by the Japanese between 1942 and 1945. The territory was reunited, however, after the war and Australia, under the terms of its UN agreement, began to prepare it for self-government. In November 1951 a Legislative Council was established and then, in June 1964, an elected House of Assembly. The state was formally named Papua New Guinea in July 1971 and secured internal self-government in December 1973. Finally, in September 1975, full independence within the Commonwealth was achieved, with the House of Assembly redesignated the National Parliament.

The first prime minister after independence was Michael Somare, leader of the nationalist Pangu Pati (PP). He had been chief minister in the interim government since 1972. Despite allegations of governmental inefficiency and discrimination against the Highland provinces, Somare remained in office until 1980. At first he headed a PP and People's Progress Party (PPP) coalition and then, from October 1978, a PP and United Party (UP) alliance. However, Somare, following a corruption scandal, was eventually defeated on a confidence vote in the National Parliament in March 1980 and a new government was formed by the PPP leader and former deputy prime minister, Sir Julius Chan.

In the general election of June 1982 the PP won 47 National Parliament seats, compared with 39 in 1977, and the UP ten, compared with 38, enabling Somare to return to power the following August, leading a coalition with the UP and nine independents. In March 1985, however, the deputy prime minister, Paias Wingti, resigned from the PP and, forming a tactical alliance with PPP leader, Chan, proceeded to challenge Somare for the premiership. Somare quickly responded by forming a new coalition with the National Party (NP) and Melanesian Alliance (MA) and successfully fought off, by 68 votes to 19, a no-confidence challenge in parliament. Fourteen dissident members, who had been expelled from the PP by Somare, immediately set up a new opposition party, the People's Democratic Movement (PDM), under the leadership of Wingti.

Later, in August 1985, Iambakey Okuk's NP departed from the government coalition. This, coupled with mounting opposition to Somare's tax-raising budget strategy, fatally weakened the government and in

November 1985 Somare was eventually defeated by 58 votes to 51 in a no-confidence motion. Wingti took over as prime minister, at the head of a five-party coalition comprising the PDM, PPP, NP, UP, and MA, with Chan as deputy prime minister, and set about instituting a new program of public spending economies as a means of tackling the economic crisis. At the general election of June – July 1987, Wingti's PDM secured 18 seats, losing two, and formed the core of a new coalition government which incorporated the People's Action Party (PAP), whose leader, Ted Diro, was brought into the cabinet as 'minister without portfolio'. In November 1987, however, following charges of misappropriation of election funds, Diro was forced to resign.

Faced with a no-confidence motion in April 1988, Wingti, requiring the PAP's support, brought Diro back into the National Executive Council. This controversial move created a constitutional crisis, precipitating shifts in coalition alliances. Three months later, in July 1988, Wingti was defeated, by 58 votes to 50, on a no-confidence motion. He was replaced as prime minister by the former foreign minister, Rabbie Namaliu, who had been elected leader of the PP in succession to Michael Somare in May 1988. Namaliu established a new six-party coalition government which comprised the PP, MA, PAP, Papua Party, NP, and the recently formed League for National Advancement (LNA), with Michael Somare serving as foreign minister.

The new government was faced by a deteriorating internal law and order situation. In Port Moresby soldiers rioted in February 1989 over inadequate pay increases and in June 1989 a state of emergency had to be imposed on Bougainville island because of the growing strength of the Bougainville Revolutionary Army (BRA), a separatist movement concerned with issues of land rights and environmental damage, led by Francis Ona, which had forced the closure of the island's important Panguna copper mine a month earlier. This mine had provided 20% of the government's revenue and 44% of export earnings. In March 1990 government forces were evacuated from the island under a ceasefire agreement after the conflict had escalated, claiming several hundred lives. An economic blockade was then imposed on BRA-controlled Bougainville, prompting Ona to make a unilateral declaration of independence. This embargo was lifted after the Honiara Accord was signed in January 1991 by the BRA and Namaliu government, but was soon reimposed when the agreement broke down. Refusing to countenance the grant of independence, a military solution was sought to the conflict.

In the 1992 general election support for the PP declined and the largest gains were made by the PAP and the PPP. Following this result the National Parliament narrowly restored Wingti as prime minister, leading a PDM, PPP, and LNA coalition. The new administration instituted a drive against political corruption and crime, which had both increased during recent years, introduced a conservative new internal security law, and proposed significant reform of the regional and local government structure. However, in August 1994 Wingti was replaced as prime minister by Sir Julius Chan (PPP), formerly deputy prime minister and foreign minister. This followed a Supreme Court ruling that a snap re-election in September 1993, contrived by Wingti in order to prolong the government's period of immunity from a vote of no confidence for a further 18 months, was invalid. Chan's government negotiated a ceasefire in October 1996 in the six-year secessionist guerrilla war on Bougainville. The terms of the agreement included the holding of peace talks with the BRA, a lifting of the blockade on the island, and the deployment of a multinational peacekeeping force. However, the guerrilla war resumed after a breakdown in the peace talks. A decision in June 1995 to abolish the system of provincial government led to a split in the cabinet and the dismissal of five dissenting ministers.

During 1996–97 there were intermittent peace talks with the BRA, which controlled the south and center of Bougainville, but the murder by government soldiers in October 1996 of Theodore Miriung, the premier of the Bougainville 'transitional government', formed in 1995, and a former legal adviser to the BRA leader, Francis Ona, was an unpromising development. The BRA, which had refused to participate in the 'transitional government', intensified its insurgency, leading to the government's re-imposition of a military blockade in March 1996. As the fighting escalated, there were reports, in February 1997, that the government was seeking secretly to engage, at a cost of $30 million, British (Sandline International) and South African mercenaries to train and bolster the government's forces. This created a political outcry and on 16 March the defense forces' commander, Brigadier General Jerry Singirok, criticized the policy and demanded Chan's resignation. Chan dismissed Singirok, but the armed forces remained loyal to Singirok and there were riots and looting in Port Moresby. On 26 March 1997 Chan narrowly survived a no-confidence vote in the Parliament, but outside there were more than 15,000 demonstrators. This persuaded Sir Julius to resign on

27 March. John Giheno, the mining and petroleum minister, took over as caretaker prime minister, but, in early June 1997, after an inquiry into the mercenary affair reported that Chan had not been guilty of misconduct, Sir Julius was re-instated.

Nevertheless, the PPP lost considerable support in the June 1997 general election and Sir Julius was not reelected. There was a strong challenge from the National Alliance, which had been recently formed by Sir Michael Somare to campaign against corruption, and from the People's National Congress (PNC), which was led by Bill Skate, the governor of the National Capital District. Subsequently, Skate defeated Somare to become prime minister and constructed a five-party coalition government which included the PNC, PP, PDM, and PPP and some independents. Sir Rabbie Namaliu became a senior minister of state, while the PP leader, Chris Haiveta, continued as the deputy prime minister.

In November 1997, Silas Atopare became the new governor, defeating Sir Getake Gam, head of the Evangelical Lutheran Church, by 54 National Parliament votes to 44. In the same month, the government was rocked when a videotape shown on Australian television seemed to suggest that Prime Minister Skate had connections with Port Moresby's notorious 'raskol' criminal gangs and alleged that he had authorized bribes. Skate claimed that he had been drunk at the time of the filming and dismissed the demand, made by Somare, for his resignation. He also claimed that the PP and PPP's leaders had conspired against him, and dismissed them from the government. However, Skate's government was able to survive after four PP ministers decided to remain with the coalition, as did the PPP, under its new leader, Michael Nali, who now became the deputy prime minister.

In October 1997 an interim truce was agreed in Bougainville with the BRA. This developed, in January 1998, into a permanent ceasefire agreement, effective from May 1998 and amnesty for the secessionist rebels, ending an eight-year-old conflict which had claimed 20,000 lives since 1989. Government troops withdrew from Bougainville in June 1998.

An interim Bougainville Reconciliation Government (BRG) was established in December 1998, headed by former rebel leader Joseph Kabui and Bougainville Transitional Government leader Gerald Sinato. This was followed, in May 1999, by the direct election of a Bougainville People's Congress (BPC). The new Congress elected Kabui as its president.

Earlier, Prime Minister Skate's ruling coalition was weakened when, in October 1999, Michael Nali and colleagues from the PPP left the government, charging Skate with having mismanaged the economy. Skate eventually decided to resign, in July 1999, and was replaced as prime minister by Mekere Morauta, of the PDM.

In its external relations, despite continuing border demarcation disputes, Papua New Guinea has maintained close diplomatic ties with Australia since independence, receiving, in return, substantial economic aid. The country, as a result of its relative size, has also been able to establish itself as the leader of the group of small island states in the South Pacific which have achieved independence during recent decades. It is a founder member of the South Pacific Forum (SPF) and, together with Vanuatu and the Solomon Islands, a leader of the 'Spearhead Group' (SG), which was set up in March 1988 with the aim of preserving Melanesian cultural traditions and securing independence for the French Overseas Territory of New Caledonia. Relations with Papua New Guinea's western neighbor, Indonesia, have traditionally been strained as a result of the latter's maltreatment of Melanesians in Irian Jaya, the western part of New Guinea. In 1963 Indonesia foiled an independence bid by Irian Jaya and, in more recent years, has been involved in fighting guerrillas of the Free Papua Movement (OPM) and with importing Javanese settlers into the territory, the so-called 'transmigration program'. These actions have prompted the flight of more than 10,000 Melanesian refugees into Papua New Guinea. Despite these tensions, a Treaty of Mutual Respect, Friendship and Cooperation was signed by the two countries in October 1985, providing for the settlement of disputes by peaceful means. In 1999 Papua New Guinea controversially extended diplomatic recognition to Taiwan.

During the 1980s Papua New Guinea experienced mounting economic difficulties as a result of both rapid population growth, 2.3% per year, and falling world prices for its copra, coffee, and cocoa exports. However, the discovery of substantial gold and oil reserves has made the country's economic prospects more promising, with real GDP growing by 5% per year between 1993 and 1997, although there was severe drought in 1997. The country is now the world's third biggest gold producer, and gold provides a quarter of all export earnings.

THE PHILIPPINES

Republic of the Philippines
Repúblika ng Pilipinas

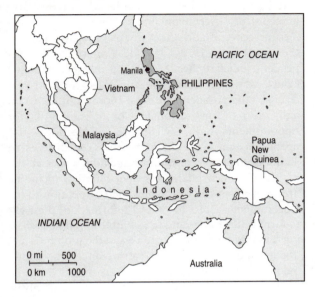

Capital: Manila

Social and economic data
Area: 300,000 sq km/115,831 sq miles
Population: 67,038,000[*]
Pop. density per sq km/sq mi: 223/579[*]
Urban population: 44%[**]
Literacy rate: 94%[**]
GDP: $71,865 million[*]; per-capita GDP: $1,050[*]
Government defense spending (% of GDP): 1.6%[*]
Currency: Philippine peso
Economy type: middle income
Labor force in agriculture: 44%[**]
Unemployment rate: 8.4%[*]
[*] 1995.
[**] 1992.

Head of state and head of government
President Joseph Estrada, since 1998

Ethnic composition
The Philippines is a pluralistic society, comprising more than 50 ethnic communities. However, a sense of national unity imbues these communities, with 95% of the population designated 'Filipinos', an Indo-Polynesian ethnic grouping. The official language is Pilipino, based on Tagalog, with 72 local dialects and languages also being spoken.

Religions
Eighty-four per cent of the population adheres to the Roman Catholic faith, 4% to Islam, 4% to the Aglipayan or Independent Philippine Christian Church, and 4% to the Protestant Church.

Political features
State type: liberal democratic
Date of state formation: 1946
Political structure: unitary
Executive: limited presidential
Assembly: two-chamber
Party structure: multiparty
Human rights rating: 72%
International affiliations: AsDB, APEC, ASEAN, CP, ESCAP, G-24, G-77, IBRD, ICFTU, IMF, LORCS, NAM, OIC (observer), WTO

Local and regional government
The country is divided into 12 regions, 75 provinces headed by governors, 1,550 cities and municipalities governed by mayors, and 41,818 neighborhoods. Local government is by citizens' assemblies (*barangays*), with autonomy granted to any region if it is endorsed by referendum. Since January 1988 governors and mayors have been popularly elected, as have advisory councils. An active decentralization program is underway, with, in November 1989, Muslim Mindanao, comprising four provinces, with an area of 13,122 sq km/5,066 sq miles and a population of 1.83 million, being granted autonomy.

Political system
The present constitution which, following approval by a national referendum, became effective in February 1987, replaced the earlier one of 1973 which had been amended in 1984. It provides for a US-style limited presidential system in which the executive works in tandem with an influential two-chamber legislature, Congress.

The upper chamber of Congress, the Senate, comprises 24 members who are directly elected by universal adult suffrage, initially for a special five-year term, but thereafter for a six-year term. Senators must be at least 35 years of age and may serve no more than two consecutive terms. They are elected in national-level contests. Terms are staggered, so that one-half of the Senate is elected every three years for a six-year term.

The lower chamber, the House of Representatives, comprises a maximum of 254 members, 204 of whom are directly elected at the district level, and, until 1998, up to 30 were appointed by the president from 'lists of nominees proposed by indigenous, but nonreligious, minority groups, such as the urban poor, peasantry, women and youth'. From 1998 these 'top-up' seats have been directly elected from national party lists. A minimum national support of 2% is needed to secure representation, and the maximum permitted representation is three seats per party. Representatives must be at least 25 years of age and are restricted to a maximum of three consecutive three-year terms.

As in the United States, the Congress is a powerful legislative institution, enjoying substantial autonomy vis-à-vis the executive. Bills originate within Congress, the approval of both chambers being required for their passage. Joint 'conference sessions' are convened to iron out differences when they arise. The Senate has special authority over foreign affairs, two-thirds approval from it being required for the ratification of all international treaties and agreements.

Executive authority resides with the president, who serves as head of state, chief executive of the republic and commander in chief of the armed forces. The president, together with a vice president, who automatically assumes the presidency for the remainder of the unexpired term in the case of the president's death or resignation, is popularly elected in a direct national contest for a nonrenewable six-year term. The office holder must be at least 40 years of age, a native-born literate citizen, and must have resided in the country for at least ten years prior to the election. The president appoints an executive cabinet of around 25–35 members to take charge of departmental administration. He or she also appoints ambassadors, military officers, and government department chiefs. These appointments are subject, however, to the approval by majority vote of the Commission on Appointments (COA), a 25-member body consisting of 12 senators and 12 representatives, elected from the political parties represented in each chamber on the basis of proportional representation. The COA is chaired, *ex officio*, by the president of the Senate.

The president and his or her cabinet cannot directly introduce legislation into Congress. They are expected, however, to set the 'policy agenda' and ensure that suitable legislation is introduced by their party supporters within Congress. To become law, all bills that have been approved by Congress must also be signed by the president before they can become law. The president can veto such measures, but this veto can be overridden by a two-thirds majority in Congress. Finally, in an emergency, the president may proclaim martial law or suspend the writ of habeas corpus for a period of up to 60 days. However, these actions may be revoked by Congress by majority vote.

The 1987 constitution is a determinedly liberal and democratic document, building in substantial checks and balances between the legislative and executive branches of government in an effort to prevent the recrudescence of authoritarian executive rule that was the feature of the 1972–86 period. A substantially independent judiciary, headed by a 15-member Supreme Court, whose members are appointed for four-year terms by the president, with the approval of the COA, and four Constitutional Commissions – for Appointments, Audit, Civil Service, and Elections – also operate as a means of checking abuses of privileges. In addition, the 1987 constitution includes a special 'Bill of Rights' which guarantees civil liberties, including 'freedom of speech, of the press and of petition to the Government'; access to official information; the right to form trade unions and to assemble in public gatherings'; the right of habeas corpus; and the prohibition of 'the intimidation, detention, torture or secret confinement of apprehended persons'.

Proposals to amend the constitution may initially be made either by a vote of three-quarters of the members of Congress; or by a Constitutional Convention, convened by a vote of two-thirds of the members of Congress; or through a public petition signed by at least 12% of the country's registered voters. Proposed amendments are then submitted to the people in a national plebiscite and, to become valid, must secure a majority of the votes cast.

Political parties

Political parties were banned between 1972 and 1978 but permitted in the 1984 elections, since when, inspired by the events of 1986–87, a new 'party system', based on broad government and opposition groupings, has begun to develop. In general, however, political parties in the Philippines, compared with those of Western Europe, are weak affairs, and based primarily on personalities and local patronage ties. Internally they are highly factionalized and formal organizational structures remain inchoate. Instead, fluid opportunistic and ephemeral tactical alliances are effected between 'vote controlling' bosses at the local level.

Currently, the three most important groupings are: the center-right Lakas ng EDSA (Power of Edasa)-National Union of Christian Democrats (NUCD), or Lakas-NUCD; the right-of-center Laban ng Makabayang Masang Pilipino (Struggle of Nationalist

Filipino Masses), or LaMMP; and the Liberal Party.

The Lakas-NUCD was formed in 1992 as an alliance to support the presidential candidacy of General Fidel Ramos, and it is now led by Jose de Venezia and Gloria Macapagal Arroyo, the Philippines' vice president from 1998 and the social welfare secretary in the new Estrada cabinet.

The LaMMP, led by President Estrada and by Edgardo Angara (who contested unsuccessfully for the vice presidency in May 1998), was formed in 1997 through the merger of the center-right Laban ng Demokratikong Pilipino (LDP: Democratic Filipino Struggle Party), the rightwing Nationalist People's Coalition (NPC) and the Partido ng Masang Pilipino (PMP). The LDP was formed in 1987 to support President Corazon Aquino, and provided early backing to President Ramos.

The Liberal Party originated in 1946 and is a centrist body which has traditionally supported the LDP.

The two main conservative opposition parties are the Nationalist (Nacionalista) Party and the New Society Movement. The Nationalist Party, first founded in 1907, is a rightwing grouping which was resurrected in 1987 by Corazon Aquino's opponents, Salvador Laurel and Juan Ponce Enrile. The party split into contending factions during 1991–92 as its three leading figures, Laurel, Enrile, and Eduardo Cojuangco, the estranged cousin of Corazon Aquino, vied for its presidential nomination. Conjuangco's faction became known as the NPC and supported the Ramos administration in a 'rainbow coalition' with the Liberal Party and LDP defectors from June 1992. The New Society Movement (NSM: Kilusan Bagong Lipunan), founded in 1978, is a conservative pro-Marcos family force, led by Vincente Mellora and Imelda Marcos, who returned to the Philippines in November 1991, despite facing law suits for alleged embezzlement during her late husband's years in power, and was elected to the House of Representatives in May 1995. Another important opposition party is the People's Reform Party (PRP), which was set up in 1991 to support the presidential candidacy of Miriam Defensor Santiago.

Also opposed to the government, and officially banned until September 1992, is the National Democratic Front, an umbrella alliance of 14 leftwing groups, the two most important of which are the 15,000-member Communist Party of the Philippines (CPP; estd. 1968) and the New People's Army (NPA). The NPA is the Maoist CPP's 2,500-member guerrilla wing. It was founded in 1969 and currently exercises *de* facto control over a sixth of the country's villages. Its leader, Romulo Kintanar, was arrested in August 1991 but released in August 1992 as a conciliatory gesture by the new Ramos administration(LaMMP).

Political leaders since 1970

1965–86 Ferdinand Marcos (Nationalist Party/New Society Movement), 1986–92 Corazon Aquino (People's Power Movement), 1992–98 Fidel Ramos (Lakas-NUCD), 1998– Joseph Estrada (LaMMP)

Latest elections

The most recent presidential election, held on 11 May 1998, was contested by ten candidates and won by the vice president, Joseph Estrada, representing the LaMMP. When the results were finally collated on 29 May, Estrada had secured 46% of the vote, while his closest rival, Jose de Venezia, representing the Lakas-NUCD of the outgoing President Ramos, attracted 17% of the vote. The other candidates included: Paul Roco (11.9%), of the Democratic Action Party; General Renato de Villa (4.6%), the former defense secretary who was a close associate of Ramos and had formed his own Party for Democratic Reform (Reporma) after unsuccessfully contesting the Lakas-NUCD nomination; Alfredo Lim (7.4%), the mayor of Manila and former head of the Manila police department, who was supported by Corazon Aquino and the Liberal Party; Lito Osmena (8.6%), formerly the economics adviser to President Ramos, who led the Progressive Movement for Devolution of Initiatives (PROMDI); Juan Ponce Enrile (1.4%), a rightwing former defense minister in the mid-1980s; and Miriam Defensor Santiago (1.5%), a former judge who had finished second in the May 1992 presidential election. Imelda Marcos, the widow of the former dictator, Ferdinand Marcos, who faced a 12-year prison sentence for corruption, which was later rescinded in 1998, withdrew from the contest in April 1998, having attracted little support. Seventy-two other candidates were initially registered to contest the election, but were subsequently disqualified by the Election Commission (Comelec).

There were concurrent elections to the vice presidency, won by the Lakas-NUCD-allied Gloria Macapagal Arroyo (the daughter of a former president, Diosdado Macapagal), with 50% of the vote, and also for the House of Representatives, 12 of the 24 Senate seats, provincial governorships, and local government posts. Overall turnout was 80% and despite violence during the campaign, notably in Mindanao in the south, which claimed 51 lives, the elections were viewed as generally orderly and fair. The LaMMP won seven of the Senate seats contested and the Lakas-NUCD the other five. However, the Lakas-NUCD had greatest success in the House elections. By June 1998 it had won 111 of the 202 seats for which results had been declared, while the LaMMP won 59 seats, the Liberal Party 15; the NPC seven; Reporma four; and PROMDI four. Seats remained to be allocated under the new party-list elections for up to 50 seats. Ten organizations had cleared the stipulated national minimum support hurdle of 2% and seemed set to be allocated the maximum permitted representation of three seats each.

Political history

1. Early settlings to Corazon Aquino

The Philippines consist of an archipelago of more than 7,100 islands and islets, of which around 700 are inhabited, extending 1,851 kilometres/1,157 miles between the southeast and the northwest. Eleven islands, Luzon, Mindanao, Samar, Negros, Palawan, Panay, Mindoro, Leyte, Cebu, Bohol, and Masbate, account for 93% of the land area and population, the two most important, Luzon and Mindanao, contributing two-thirds. More than half the country's total area is forested.

The islands of the Philippines were subject to successive waves of Malay, Indonesian, and Chinese settlement before being 'discovered' by Ferdinand Magellan (c. 1480–1521) and subsequently conquered by Spanish forces in 1565. Roman Catholicism was introduced during the reign of Philip II (1527–98), after whom the islands were named, replacing the Muslim religion which had been spread by Arab traders and missionaries. Under Spanish rule a sugar, tobacco, rubber, and coffee based plantation economy was established, with rigid socio-economic stratification developing between the darker skinned, Malay-origin, peasantry (indios) and the fairer skinned, estate-owning, 'mixed blood' (mestizo) elite, of Spanish and Chinese origin. A series of armed nationalist revolts broke out during the 19th century and continued after the islands were ceded by Spain to the United States in December 1898, after the war the two countries fought over Cuba. This resulted in the concession of increasing degrees of internal self-government to the Philippines, in 1916 and 1935.

During World War II the Philippines were occupied by the Japanese, between 1942 and 1945, before becoming a fully independent republic in July 1946. A succession of presidents drawn from the islands' wealthy estate-owning elite followed between 1946 and 1965: Manual Roxas (1946–48), Elpidio Quirino (1948–53),

Ramón Magsaysay (1953–57), Carlos García (1957–61), and Diosdado Macapagal (1961–65). They did little to improve the lot of the ordinary peasant. A partial exception, between 1953 and 1957 was the honest humble-born Ramón Magsaysay. During Magsaysay's presidency, the Philippines enjoyed a period of extended economic growth which temporarily established the country as the richest per capita, after Japan, in Asia. The internal menace posed by the communist Hukbalahap guerrillas, an insurgency grouping which had originally been formed to fight the Japanese but which had continued its operations after independence, was suppressed through a skilful combination of force and incentives. However, following Magsaysay's death in an air crash in 1957, the country rapidly retrogressed under the corrupt and lacklustre stewardships of García and Macapagal.

In the presidential election of November 1965, Diosdado Macapagal (1910–97), leader of the Liberal Party, was eventually defeated by Ferdinand Marcos (1917–89), the dynamic young leader of the Nationalist Party. Marcos, promising a new start, initiated a program of rapid economic development, based on import-substituting industrialization and infrastructural investment. He was re-elected in 1969, but during his second term encountered growing opposition from new communist insurgents, the New People's Army (NPA), in Luzon in the north, and from Muslim separatists, the Moro National Liberation Front (MNLF), in Mindanao island in the south. In September 1972, 14 months before his second, and constitutionally his last, term had been completed, and with the economy deteriorating rapidly and the communist insurgency growing in strength, Marcos declared martial law, suspended the constitution, and began to rule by decree. The birth of a 'New Society' was proclaimed.

The following year, President Marcos announced a return to democratic government. A new constitution, providing for a single-chamber National Assembly (Batasang Pambansa), a constitutional president and an executive prime minister, elected by the assembly, was formally promulgated. However, Marcos proposed that, for the time being, he should remain in office and continue to rule by decree. Referenda in July 1973, February 1975, and October 1976 approved these actions, allowing him to retain power. Criticisms of Marcos' authoritarian and corrupt leadership were, however, growing and in November 1977 the main opposition leader, Benigno Aquino, was sentenced to death, for alleged subversion, by a military tribunal.

In April 1978 martial law was relaxed and elections for an interim National Assembly held, resulting in an overwhelming victory for Marcos and his supporters' party, the New Society Movement, a party which had been specially formed for the election by former Nationalist Party members. Soon afterwards Aquino, who was a sick man, was temporarily released from prison to travel to the United States for medical attention. In January 1981, martial law was lifted completely and hundreds of political prisoners released. Marcos then won approval, by referendum, for a partial return to democratic government, with himself as president for a new six-year term, working with a prime minister and Executive Council. Political and economic conditions deteriorated, however, as the NPA guerrilla insurgency escalated. With GDP growth now negative, unemployment climbed to over 30% and, following the sudden rise in the international oil price between 1979 and 1982, national indebtedness, and debt-serving problems increased sharply.

In August 1983 the opposition leader, Benigno Aquino, returned from the United States and was immediately shot dead on his arrival at Manila airport. A commission of inquiry reported 11 months later that Aquino had been killed by the military guard escorting him as part of a broader conspiracy. This act had momentous repercussions for the Marcos regime, serving to unite a previously disunited opposition. National Assembly elections were held in May 1984, amid violence and widespread claims of corruption, and although they resulted in success for the government party, which captured 68% of the 183 elective seats, they also registered significant gains for the opposition. Then, early in 1986, the main anti-Marcos movement, the United Nationalist Democratic Organization (UNIDO), chose Aquino's widow, Corazon Aquino (b. 1933), despite her political inexperience, to contest new elections for the presidency which Marcos had been persuaded to hold, as a means of maintaining American economic and diplomatic support.

The presidential campaign of December 1985 – February 1986 proved violent, resulting in more than 150 deaths, and widespread electoral fraud was witnessed by international observers. On 16 February 1986, following polling a week earlier, the National Assembly declared Marcos the winner by 54% to 46%. This result, however, was immediately disputed by an independent electoral watchdog, the National Citizens' Movement for Free Elections (Namfrel). Corazon Aquino began a nonviolent protest, termed 'People's Power', which gathered massive popular support, particularly from the Roman Catholic Church. President Marcos also came under strong international pressure, particularly from his former ally, the United States, to step down. On 22 February 1986 the army, led by Chief of Staff Lieutenant General Fidel Ramos (b. 1928) and Defense Minister Juan Enrile, declared its support for Corazon Aquino and on 25 February 1986 Marcos, given guarantees of safe passage, left, with his wife Imelda, for exile in Hawaii.

On assuming the presidency, Corazon Aquino immediately dissolved the pro-Marcos National Assembly and announced plans for the framing of a new 'freedom constitution'. She proceeded to govern in a conciliatory fashion, working with an emergency coalition cabinet team, comprising a broad cross-section of radical, liberal, and conservative opposition politicians and senior military figures. Five hundred political prisoners were freed and an amnesty granted to the NPA's communist guerrillas, in an effort to bring an end to the 17-year-old insurgency. She also introduced a major rural employment economic program. The new administration was faced, however, during the summer and autumn months of 1986, with a series of attempted coups by pro-Marcos supporters, as well as internal opposition from Defense Secretary Enrile, resulting in his dismissal in November 1986.

In February 1987 a new constitution was overwhelmingly approved by 76% of the voters in a national plebiscite. This gave Aquino a mandate to rule as president until 30 June 1992 and paved the way for elections to the new two-chamber Congress in May 1987.

The congressional elections resulted in a huge majority for the supporters of President Aquino. In August 1987, however, the government was rocked by another attempted military coup, the most serious thus far, led by Colonel Gregorio Honasan, an army officer linked closely with Enrile, in which 53 people were killed in intense fighting in Manila and Cebu. Facing accusations of 'policy drift', President Aquino responded by organizing a major cabinet reshuffle in September 1987. This involved the replacement of vice president Laurel as foreign affairs secretary by Senator Raúl Manglapus, and the sacking of Finance Secretary Jaime Ongpin and the president's 'leftist' executive secretary, Joker Arroyo. These changes signalled a shift to the right for the Aquino administration, which, concerned to maintain internal order and prevent further coup attempts by the disaffected military, proceeded to approve a series of tough measures to deal with the

NPA insurgency and a more conservative economic and social program. Included in the latter was an important, though diluted, land reform act, which was passed by Congress in June 1988 and which included favorable compensation terms for substantial estate holders. A regional referendum, proposing the merging of 13 southern provinces which had been at the center of a 20-year-old Muslim separatist struggle, was rejected in nine of the provinces, resulting in autonomy, as Muslim Mindanao, for just four provinces.

During her presidency Corazon Aquino enjoyed firm backing from the United States. The Philippines received $1.5 billion of economic and military aid between 1985 and 1989 and in December 1989 American air support was provided to help foil a further coup attempt planned by Honasan and the rightwing Young Officers Union (YOU). However, despite Aquino's advocacy of renewal of the US leases to the important Subic Bay naval and Clark Field air bases, the Philippines Senate voted, in September 1991, to reject renewal. A US pull-out duly occurred, with the bases, in any case, having been badly damaged by a major eruption of the long-dormant Mount Pinatubo volcano in June 1991, killing 343 people and rendering 200,000 homeless. Subic Bay has subsequently developed into a successful export-processing zone.

2. Fidel Ramos to Joseph Estrada

Corazon Aquino stepped down as president at the end of June 1992, being replaced by her chosen heir, Fidel Ramos, who won the May 1992 direct presidential election and formed a cabinet which included six members from the Aquino administration. With seven candidates contesting, including Imelda Marcos, whose husband had died in exile in Hawaii in September 1989, Ramos, a liberal Protestant and former general, was able to secure just 24% of the national vote. This left him with a much weaker popular mandate than had been enjoyed by Aquino. The new president was forced to work with a Senate in which he lacked majority support. In the House of Representatives, Ramos put together what became known as a 'rainbow coalition', comprising members of the Liberal Party, the Nationalist People's Coalition (NPC), and 55 'Laban' defectors from the LDP. During his first two years in power the economy, hit by power shortages and fiscal constraints, stagnated. However, from 1994 an economic upturn commenced, with annual GDP growth more than 5% between 1994 and 1997. This was largely due to structural reforms, including the dismantling of protectionist legislation and a program of privatiza-

tion. Internal order also improved as a result of a series of imaginative initiatives by Ramos, including the formation in August 1992 of a National Unification Commission (NUC) to consult with rebel groups, the legalization of the formerly proscribed CPP, the conditional release of communist leaders and rebel soldiers, and the disarming of the private armies maintained by provincial landlords and politicians. During 1993 and 1994 peace talks were held with both the communist NPA and the Muslim-secessionist MNLF and Moro Islamic Liberation Front (MILF) and a number of temporary ceasefires were negotiated. President Ramos' promising early record secured endorsement in the midterm congressional elections of May 1995 when the ruling pro-Ramos coalition parties won around 80% of House and Senate seats and governorships contested.

From February 1996 the position of President Ramos became weakened when the LDP, which opposed new anti-terrorist legislation, withdrew from the ruling two-party coalition in the Senate, leaving the Lakas-NUCD in a minority. In September 1996 a peace deal was signed with Nur Misuari, leader of the MNLF, to end its 25-year-long insurrection in Mindanao, the traditional homeland of the Philippines' five-million strong Muslim minority, but where there was now a large Christian immigrant majority community. This civil war had claimed more than 100,000 lives. The agreement provided for the establishment of a Southern Philippines Council for Peace and Development, led by Misuari, to oversee 14 of the 25 Mindanao provinces for three years, and the integration of 5,500 of the MNLF's 17,000 guerrillas into the Philippines army and 1,500 into the police. After three years, there was to be a referendum to decide which provinces wished to join the existing four-province Autonomous Muslim Region in Mindanao of which Misuari was elected governor in September 1996. However, the pact was not endorsed by the more radical, 45,000-strong, MILF.

During 1997 politics were dominated by mounting financial difficulties and manoeuvring for the 1998 presidential election. The authorities raised interest rates sharply, but were unable to prevent devaluation of the peso, in July 1997, as it came under attack from international speculators: it fell by a third against the US dollar by the year's end. The stock market also fell sharply and inflation increased. Nevertheless, the Philippines economy performed better than most others in the region, with GDP growing by 5% in 1997. After considering amending the constitution to allow himself to run again in November 1997, President Ramos made clear that he would not seek a second term. In December 1997 he selected Jose de Venezia, the president of Lakas-NUCD and House speaker, as the party's candidate for the state presidency, but also remained close to General Renato de Villa, who left the Lakas-NUCD to form a new party to fight the election.

De Venezia, who had helped forge the Lakas-NUCD into a powerful nationwide force, was eclipsed in the presidential election by the charismatic, populist vice president, Joseph Estrada, a former film star and reformed playboy, with a power-base among the poor. Despite opposition to his candidacy from the Roman Catholic church and the business and political elite, Estrada won a clear victory in May 1998. He inherited a worsening economy, with a growing budget deficit and rising unemployment, but pledged to continue with the market-centerd reform program initiated by Ramos and appointed the banker, Edgardo Espiritu, as finance secretary. However, during his campaign, Estrada had also promised to alleviate poverty, reduce crime levels and, ambitiously, establish peace and order across all the Philippines, including Mindanao, within six months. During the early months of the Estrada presidency, there were indications of a return to influence of some former associates of the late President Marcos. This persuaded Imelda Marcos to seek to start a campaign for the burial of her late husband's body, currently being kept in cold storage in his home town of Batac, in Heroes' Cemetery, in Manila.

SAMOA (FORMERLY WESTERN SAMOA)

Ole Malo Tutoatasio Samoa
The Independent State of Western Samoa

Capital: Apia

Social and economic data
Area: 2,831 sq km/1,093 sq miles
Population: 164,000[*]
Pop. density per sq km/sq mi: 58/150[*]
Urban population: 27%[**]
Literacy rate: 98%[**]
GDP: $184 million[*]; per-capita GDP: $1,120[*]
Government defense spending (% of GDP): 0%[***]
Currency: tala, or Samoa dollar
Economy type: middle income

Labor force in agriculture: 60%[**]
[*] 1995.
[**] 1992.
[***] Western Samoa, which has no army, relies on New Zealand for its defense.

Head of state
King (O le Ao O le Malo) Susuga Malietoa Tanumafili II, since 1962

Head of government
Prime Minister Tuila'epa Sa'ilele Malielegaoi, since 1998

Ethnic composition
Ninety per cent of the population is of Samoan, or Polynesian, ethnic stock and 10% Euronesian, or mixed European and Polynesian. Samoan, a Polynesian dialect, and English are the official languages.

Religions
Ninety-nine per cent of the population is Christian. Forty-five per cent belongs to the Congregational Christian Church in Samoa, which was established in 1830 as the London Missionary Society; 22% is Roman Catholic; 19% belongs to the Methodist Church in Samoa, which was founded in 1828; 8% follows the Church of Jesus Christ of Latter-Day Saints (Mormons), established in 1888; and 4% belongs to the Seventh-Day Adventist Church, which was founded in 1895. The constitution guarantees freedom of religion, but there is increasing concern over the spread of US evangelical forms of Christianity, promoted by television, which are undermining traditional Samoan Christianity.

Political features
State type: liberal democratic
Date of state formation: 1962
Political structure: unitary
Executive: parliamentary
Assembly: one-chamber
Party structure: two-party
Human rights rating: N/A
International affiliations: ACP, AsDB, CW, ESCAP, G-77, IBRD, ICFTU, IMF, LORCS, PC, SPEC, SPF, UN

Local and regional government
The country is divided into 24 districts for development and law and order administration. However, the real units of local government are the villages (*nu'u*) and sub-villages (*pitonu'u*), where extended family (*aiga*) heads (*matai*) gather in assemblies (*fonos*), each headed by a chief (*ali'i*). These local assemblies direct the use and distribution of family land and assets and supervise welfare provision.

Political system

Samoa (known as Western Samoa until 1997) is an independent state within the Commonwealth. The constitution dates from independence in January 1962 and provides for a parliamentary system of government, with a constitutional head of state (O le Ao O le Malo), a single-chamber Legislative Assembly (fono), and a prime minister and cabinet drawn from and responsible to the Assembly. The head of state is normally elected by the Assembly for a five-year term from among the holders of the country's four paramount titles. However, the present holder of the office has been elected for life.

The Assembly has 49 members. Forty-seven of these are Samoans, who, until 1991, were elected by holders of Matai titles, or elected clan chiefs. There were about 16,000 of such chiefs, but the system was undermined by the purchasing of Matai titles by those seeking election. Thus, following a referendum held in October 1990, a switch to universal adult suffrage was made for these seats. The remaining two members are non-Samoans elected by people, mainly Europeans, who appear on the individual voters' rolls. The Assembly has traditionally had a life of three years, but it has been extended to five years since 1993. Only members of the Matai are eligible to stand for election.

The head of state appoints the prime minister and a cabinet of around 12 further Fono members, on the basis of Assembly support. In 1998, prime minister Tofilau Eti Alesana, held three additional ministerial portfolios: foreign affairs, broadcasting, and police and prisons. Cabinet decisions are subject to review by an Executive Council, which is composed of the head of state and cabinet. A stress on consensus and the blending of both traditional and modern representative forms, in a conservative manner, the 'Samoan Way' (fa'a Samoa), permeates and distinguishes the political system.

Political parties

Prior to 1979 there were no formal political parties, all candidates for election standing as independents. Then, in February 1979, the Human Rights Protection Party (HRPP) was formed by opposition Fono deputies, led by Va'ai Kolone, a former chairperson of the Public Accounts Committee. The party opposed the rapid economic development plans of the Tupuola Taisi Efi government and emerged, under the leadership of Tofilau Eti Alesana, as the dominant party between 1982 and 1985. In 1985 it was weakened by the breakaway of a faction supporting former leader, Va'ai Kolone. This breakaway group later became, through the union of the Va'ai Kolone Group (VKG) and the Christian Democratic Party (CDP; estd. 1985), led by Tupuola Taisi Efi, the Samoan National Development Party (SNDP), which is jointly led by Kolone and Tupuola Efi.

In 1998 three other smaller parties were also in operation.

Political leaders since 1970

1970–73 Tupua Tamasese Lealofi (independent), 1973–75 Fiame Mata'afa Mulinu'u (independent), 1975–76 Tupua Tamasese Lealofi (independent), 1976–82 Tupuola Taisi Efi (independent), 1982 Va'ai Kolone (HRPP), 1982 Tupuola Taisi Efi (independent), 1982–85 Tofilau Eti Alesana (HRPP), 1985–88 Va'ai Kolone (VKG), 1988 Tupuola Taisi Efi (CDP), 1988–98 Tofilau Eti Alesana (HRPP), 1998– Tuila'epa Sa'ilele Malielegaoi (HRPP)

Latest elections

Following the most recent Fono elections, held on 26 April 1996, and post-election recruitment of independents, the HRPP captured 28 seats, the SNDP 14, and independents 7. These were the second elections held under universal adult suffrage, with an estimated 80,000 voters becoming newly enfranchised. The votes took three weeks to count, and there were reports that during the campaign voters had demanded gifts and favors from candidates in return for their support.

Political history

Samoa is a volcanic island grouping in the southwest Pacific Ocean, 2,575 kilometres/1,600 miles northeast of Auckland, New Zealand, and between 13 and 15 degrees south of the equator. It comprises two large inhabited islands, Upolu and Savaii, which are 11 miles apart, two much smaller inhabited islands, Apolima and Manono, and four tiny uninhabited islands, Fanuatapu, Nuutele, Nuula, and Nuusafee. The inland portions of the inhabited islands are mountainous, covered with extinct volcanoes, and agriculturally barren. The bulk of the population therefore lives in scattered coastal villages, with 72% of the total on Upolu island.

The islands of Samoa were first, 'discovered', by Dutch and French traders during the 1720s, but had been previously inhabited by Polynesians for more than 2,000 years. During the early 19th century, Christian missionaries began to settle here and from that time Germany, Britain, and the United States vied with each other for their control, intriguing with local paramount chiefs in a series of mid-century civil wars. Eventually, in 1899, a treaty was signed between the three Western powers, recognizing American paramountcy over the islands east of 171 degrees longitude west, which were to be called American Samoa, and German supremacy over the other islands, named Western Samoa. Britain was given control of Tonga and the Solomon Islands as part of this agreement. German control lasted, however, barely a decade. On the outbreak of World War I in 1914, New Zealand took over Western Samoa and thereafter administered the islands, first as a League of Nations Mandated Territory, between 1919 and 1945, and then, from 1946, as a United Nations (UN) Trust Territory.

During the interwar years, New Zealand rule was challenged by a nationalist organization, the Mau, which resorted to civil disobedience. After World War II, as part of its trusteeship agreement, New Zealand began to promote self-government, introducing a cabinet form of government in 1959 and a provisional constitution in October 1960. This paved the way for the achievement of full independence as Western Samoa, within the Commonwealth, on 1 January 1962, after the holding of a UN-sponsored plebiscite. Initially, the office of head of state in the newly independent country was held jointly by two traditional rulers. However, on the death of one of them, in April 1963, the other, Malietoa Tanumafili II, became the sole head, for life, serving as a constitutional monarch. Effective executive power was held by the prime minister, who, at the time of independence, was Fiame Mata'afa Mulinu'u. He had occupied that position since 1959.

Mata'afa lost power to Tupua Tamasese Lealofi in the general election of 1970. He regained it, however, in 1973, after fresh elections, and continued to serve as prime minister until his death in May 1975. Tamasese briefly succeeded him, before being replaced by his cousin Tupuola Taisi Efi, the first prime minister not of royal blood, in the March 1976 general election. Tupuola Efi held power for six years, being re-elected by the Legislative Assembly in March 1979. At the general election of February 1982, however, the opposition groupings, who had combined in 1979 to form the Human Rights Protection Party (HRPP), won a narrow majority and their leader, Va'ai Kolone, became prime minister. Within seven months, however, he was forced to resign, after charges of electoral malpractice, including impersonation of the dead. Tupuola Efi briefly returned to power for three months, but, when his budget proposal was voted down in the Fono in December 1982, resigned to be replaced by the HRPP leader, Tofilau Eti Alesana.

The HRPP won a decisive victory in the February 1985 general election, substantially increasing its Fono majority, by securing 31 of the 47 seats, and Tofilau Eti continued as prime minister. At the end of the year, however, he resigned because of opposition within the Assembly to his budget plan and the defection from the HRPP grouping of supporters of Va'ai Kolone. The head of state refused to call another general election and Va'ai Kolone was appointed as the new prime minister, putting together a coalition of 'independents' and members of the newly formed Christian Democratic Party (CDP), led by former prime minister, Tupuola Taisi Efi. Va'ai held power until the general election of February 1988. This resulted in a disputed 'hung parliament' after which Tupuola Efi was first chosen as prime minister and, then, from April 1988, the HRPP leader, Tofilau Eti. Meanwhile, Kolone's supporters joined with the CDP after the election to form a new opposition group, the Samoan National Development Party (SNDP).

Voters narrowly accepted government proposals for a switch from indirect elections by Matai chiefs to universal adult suffrage in a referendum held in October 1990 and opposed by the SNDP. A linked proposal to create a second chamber comprising Matai chiefs was rejected. The HRPP won the April 1991 general election and Tofilau Eti continued for what he declared would be his final term as prime minister. Tupuola Taisi Efi lost his seat and Fiame Naomi, the daughter of Samoa's first prime minister, became the first female cabinet minister.

The life of the Fono was extended by two years in 1993 and its size increased by two seats by the government. This led to opposition protests, but the HRPP won the two new seats, which were contested in 1992.

There were also widespread demonstrations, during 1994–95, against the unpopular imposition of value-added tax on goods and services.

Despite deteriorating health, Tofilau Eti fought and won the April 1996 general election. Shortly before the election, Matatumua Naimoaga, one of two female Fono deputies, had left the HRPP to form a small new party, the Samoa All-People's Party, but it had little electoral success. In May 1996 Tofilau Eti was re-elected prime minister by the Fono, securing 34 votes to 14 for opposition leader Tuiatua Tupua Tamasese of the SNDP.

The country's name was officially changed from Western Samoa to Samoa in July 1997, despite protests from American Samoa, which considered that it would undermine its identity. One reason for the change was that 'Samoa' had been used by the United Nations (UN) ever since its entry in 1976. In late 1997 and early 1998 there was a rising wave of anti-government protest and calls for Tofilau Eti to resign. This was triggered by general concern about political corruption and the government's increasing intolerance of media criticisms.

In November 1998 the 74-year-old Tofilau Eti Alesana resigned as prime minister, on health grounds, and was replaced by Tuila'epa Sa'ilele Malielegaoi, of the Human Rights Protection Party HRPP, who had been deputy prime minister. Tofilau became senior minister without portfolio, but later died in March 1999.

Samoa has maintained close links with New Zealand since independence, entering into a Treaty of Friendship in 1962. Samoa has a free-enterprise economic system, encouraging inward foreign investment, but remains predominantly subsistence-based and is highly dependent on remittances sent home by its nationals working overseas and on foreign development aid. In December 1991 the country was struck by the worst cyclone in living memory, 'Cyclone Val'. Considerable damage was inflicted both to the infrastructure and to the main export crop, taro, and a state of emergency was declared. Australia and New Zealand immediately provided substantial assistance. Further cyclone damage since 1991 and an outbreak of taro leaf blight from 1991 has meant that, despite the promotion of tourism and 'offshore banking', there has been little improvement in per-capita GDP during the 1990s. In 1995 there were large demonstrations in Apia protesting against France's decision to resume nuclear weapons-testing in French Polynesia, and the Samoan government banned visits by French warships and aircraft.

SOLOMON ISLANDS

Capital: Honiara (on Guadalcanal)

Social and economic data
Area: 27,556 sqkm/10,639 sq miles
Population: 366,000[*]
Pop. density per sq km/sq mi: 13/34[*]
Urban population: 8%[**]
Literacy rate: 60%
GDP: $341 million[*]; per-capita GDP: $920[*]
Government defense spending (% of GDP): 0%[***]

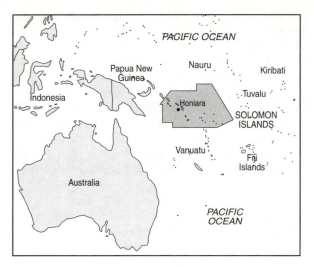

Currency: Solomon Islands dollar
Economy type: low income
Labor force in agriculture: 30%[**]
[*] 1995.
[**] 1992.
[***] The Solomon Islands have no defense forces.

Head of state
Queen Elizabeth II, represented by Governor General Sir Moses Puibangara Pitakaka since 1994

Head of government
Prime Minister Bartholemew Ulufa'alu, since 1997

Ethnic composition
Ninety-three per cent of the population is Melanesian, 4% Polynesian, 1.5% Micronesian, 0.7% European, and 0.2% Chinese. The official language is English, although many local languages are also spoken.

Religions
Ninety-five per cent of the population is Christian: 34% adhering to the Church of Melanesia (Anglican), 19% to the Roman Catholic Church, 17% to the South Seas Evangelical Church, 11% to the United Church, and 10% to the Seventh-Day Adventist Church. Traditional ancestor worship also prevails.

Political features
State type: liberal democratic
Date of state formation: 1978
Political structure: unitary
Executive: parliamentary
Assembly: one-chamber
Party structure: multiparty
Human rights rating: N/A

International affiliations: ACP, AsDB, CW, ESCAP, G-77, IBRD, IMF, IWC, SG, PC, SPEC, SPF, UN, WFTU

Local and regional government

The country is divided into four districts, within which there are nine elected local government councils. Seven of them have provincial assemblies, Western, Guadalcanal, Central, Malaita, Santa Isabel, Eastern, and San Cristobal, and one, Honiara, has a town council.

New legislation was passed in August 1996 to transfer the legislative and administrative powers of the nine provincial governments to 75 area assemblies and councils, with complete financial control resting with the central government. In February 1997 the High Court declared the legislation invalid, but this ruling has been appealed against.

Political system

The most recent constitution dates from independence in July 1978. This established the state as a constitutional monarchy within the Commonwealth, in which a resident governor general represents the British Crown as head of state. The governor general, who must be a Solomon Islands citizen, is appointed for a renewable five-year term on the recommendation of the assembly. This is called the National Parliament and is a single-chamber body of 50 members elected by universal adult suffrage, on a simple plurality basis, in single-member constituencies. The parliamentary system adheres closely to the Westminster model, with the governor general formally appointing a prime minister who is elected by MPs and a cabinet of about 15 members, on the prime minister's recommendation, drawn from and collectively responsible to the assembly, which is subject to dissolution within its four-year term.

Political parties

Political parties in the Solomon Islands are loose, personality- regional- and patronage-based groupings, rather than disciplined and ideologically united units. Currently parties are aligned in two opposing blocks: the Alliance for Change (AfC) and the Group for National Unity and Reconciliation (GNUR).

The AfC, formed in 1997, is the successor to the National Coalition Partners (NCP), which was formed after the May 1993 general election to force the GNUR leader, Solomon Mamaloni, from power. It was a loose coalition comprising independents and six parties: the Labor Party (LP; estd. 1988), led by Joses Tuhanuku; the National Action Party of the Solomon Islands (NAPSI; estd. 1993), led by Francis Saemala; the federalist

People's Alliance Party (PAP), led by David Kausimae; the centralist National Party (estd. 1996), formerly the Solomon Islands United Party (SIUPA/UP; estd. 1973), led by the former prime minister, Ezekiel Alebua until 1997; the rural-interest orientated Nationalist Front for Progress (NFP; estd. 1985), led by Andrew Nori; and the Christian Fellowship Group (CFG). The SIUPA/UP, a conservative party, originated as an outgrowth of the Civil Servants Association, and was the dominant force in Solomon Islands politics for much of the period between 1976 and 1989. A faction, led by Andrew Nori, split from the SIUPA in October 1985, and, known as the NFP, established itself as an 'open forum' for those wishing to discuss land disputes. The PAP, which was the governing party, though in coalitions, between 1976 and 1981 and from 1984 to 1986, is a center-left force. It was formed in 1973 under the designation People's Progressive Party (PPP), before uniting with the Rural Alliance Party, which was established in 1977, to form the PAP in 1979. The PAP favors greater decentralization of power and the strengthening of regional Melanesian alliances. At the center of the new AfC is the centrist Solomon Islands Liberal Party (SILP), led by Bartholemew Ulufa'alu.

Opposed to the AfC is the GNUR, a party formed in 1993 by the then prime minister, Solomon Mamaloni, leader of the PAP until 1990, to contest the general election. It became the governing party in 1994–97. Since Mamaloni's retirement after the August 1997 general election, the GNUR has been led by Danny Philip. The Coalition for National Advancement, led by Job Dudley Tausinga, became, in April 1998, the largest single opposition party to the AfC.

Political leaders since 1970

1974–76 Solomon Mamaloni (PPP), 1976–81 Peter Kenilorea (SIUPA), 1981–84 Solomon Mamaloni (PAP), 1984–86 Sir Peter Kenilorea (SIUPA), 1986–89 Ezekiel Alebua (SIUPA), 1989–93 Solomon Mamaloni (PAP/independent), 1993–94 Francis Billy Hilly (independent/NCP), 1994–97 Solomon Mamaloni (GNUR), 1997– Bartholemew Ulufa'alu (SILP)

Latest elections

In the most recent elections, held on 6 August 1997, the Alliance for Change coalition, under the leadership of the SILP, won 26 of the 50 National Assembly seats and the GNUR the other 24. Those elected included 19 incumbents. As usual, the election was characterized by instances of attempted 'vote buying'. Already, in mid-1996, one year before the poll, there were reports of candidates buying gifts of canoes and outboard motors in an effort to influence voting, with members using the Constituency Development Fund, which entitled each member to $66,000, for this purpose.

Political history

The Solomon Islands are an archipelago of several hundred small islands, situated in the south Pacific Ocean, scattered between Papua New Guinea in the northwest and Vanuatu in the southeast. The six principal islands are Choiseul, Guadalcanal, Malaita, New Georgia, San Cristobal, and Santa Isabel. The bulk of the population resides in dispersed settlements along the coasts and is involved in subsistence agriculture or work on copra and palm oil plantations.

The islands, which at the time were inhabited by Melanesians, were 'discovered' by the Spanish navigator Alvaro de Mendaña in 1568, but were not visited again by Europeans until the later 18th century. The Northern Solomon Islands became a German protectorate in 1885 and the Southern Solomon Islands a British protectorate in 1893. Five years later Germany ceded its possessions to Britain and, in 1900, a unified British Solomon Islands Protectorate (BSIP) was formed. This was placed under the jurisdiction of the Western Pacific High Commission (WPHC), whose headquarters were in Fiji. A resident commissioner was placed in charge of day-to-day administration. During World War II, the islands were invaded by Japan in 1942, but recaptured by the United States a year later.

After the war the islands remained under British control, the WPHC moving its headquarters to Honiara. Elected island councils began to be established and, under a constitution adopted in October 1960, legislative and executive councils were established. These were amalgamated into a single elected Governing Council, based on a ministerial system, under the terms of the March 1970 constitution, as amended in 1973. In April 1974, following the adoption of a new constitution, the islands became substantially self-governing, a 24-member Legislative Assembly being established, from whose members a chief minister, who enjoyed the right to appoint a cabinet, or Council of Ministers, was selected. Solomon Mamaloni, leader of the newly formed People's Progressive Party (PPP), was chosen as the country's first chief minister in August 1974.

The BSIP was renamed the Solomon Islands in June 1975 and in January 1976 became fully self-governing, when the chief minister was allowed to preside over the Council of Ministers in place of the British-appointed governor. After new Legislative Assembly elections, in June 1976, Peter Kenilorea (b. 1943) was chosen as the new chief minister. He was redesignated prime minister, and the Legislative Assembly the National Parliament, when full independence, within the Commonwealth, was granted in July 1978. Kenilorea was re-elected in August 1980, following fresh parliamentary elections, but the following year was defeated on a motion of no confidence in the National Parliament and replaced by former chief minister, Solomon Mamaloni. The main factor behind Kenilorea's downfall had been his resistance to growing pressure, which was particularly strong in the commercially developed Western District, to decentralize and devolve powers to the regions. In contrast, his successor, Mamaloni, warmly supported the idea and one of his first actions as prime minister was to create five ministerial posts specifically for provincial affairs.

By the time of the October 1984 general election, support for Sir Peter Kenilorea, as he had become, had risen and he was put back into office, at the head of a coalition government. He immediately abolished the five provincial ministries, restoring the balance between central and regional power. Support for the governing party soon began to wane, however. Kenilorea narrowly survived no-confidence votes in Parliament in September 1985 and July 1986 and was forced to reconstitute his coalition when the Solomons Ano Sagufenua (SAS) Party withdrew its support. Following allegations that he had secretly accepted US$47,000 of French aid to repair cyclone damage to his home village in Malaita province, and faced with a fresh no-confidence motion, Kenilorea eventually resigned as prime minister in December 1986. He was replaced, following three secret ballots in parliament, by the deputy prime minister and fellow Solomon Islands United Party (SIUPA) member, Ezekiel Alebua. Kenilorea continued, however, to hold ministerial office, serving, first, as natural resources minister and then, from February 1988, as joint foreign minister and deputy prime minister, while Alebua continued to adhere to the existing policy course. However, at the general election of February 1989 support for the SIUPA slumped, its seat tally being halved, and the PAP, led by Mamaloni, re-emerged as the dominant political party. In March 1989 Mamaloni became head of a new PAP government which was determined to reduce the influence of 'foreign aid personnel' and which promised to reform the constitution so as to establish a republic.

In October 1990, encountering mounting criticism at a time of financial crisis, Mamaloni gave up the leadership of the PAP, but despite protests, carried on as prime minister. He headed a government of 'national unity' which included, as foreign affairs minister, Sir Peter Kenilorea. Mamaloni's actions created splits both within the PAP and the opposition. He held on to power until June 1993 when, following a general election, a coalition of opposition legislators ensured that Francis Billy Hilly, an independent, became the new prime minister. However, the new administration was weakened by the resignation of several ministers in November 1993, and in October 1994, having lost his parliamentary majority, Hilly was dismissed as premier by Governor General Moses Pitakaka. Solomon Mamaloni, as leader of the GNUR, the largest grouping within parliament, returned as prime minister in November 1994, defeating Sir Baddeley Devesi, a former governor general, by 29 parliamentary votes to 18.

Mamaloni's government controversially reversed the policy of the preceding administration, which, for conservationist reasons, had placed stricter controls on logging activities. Despite opposition protests, virtually unrestrained logging by foreign companies was now allowed, and on Pavuvu island there was compulsory resettlement to vacate land. In protest, the Australian government and the European Union reduced their annual aid to the Solomon Islands from 1996. The Mamaloni government and the bureaucracy faced criticisms of corruption, with 25 Finance Ministry officials being suspended in May 1996 following the disappearance of $10 million.

A new general election was called in May 1997 and was held in August 1997. It was fought between new political leaders: Mamaloni having retired as GNUR leader, being replaced by Danny Philip, and Alebua having stepped down as leader of the National Party (successor to the SIUPA), being replaced by Edward Hunuehu. The elections brought a victory for the Alliance for Change (AfC) coalition, centerd around the Solomon Islands Liberal Party (SILP), led by Bartholomew Ulufa'alu, who was elected prime minister on 27 August 1997, defeating Philip by 26 votes to 22. Sir Baddeley Devesi became deputy prime minister and minister for transport. In October 1997 the new government secured passage of structural economic and administrative reforms, which involved a streamlining of government (reducing the number of ministries from 16 to ten, and civil servant numbers by 1,000) and stimulation of the private sector, but with controls over logging. In addition, in an effort to establish greater political stability, there were proposals to force by-elections on deputies who sought to change parties.

During late 1998 and early 1999 there was rising ethnic tension on Guadalcanal, between locals and immigrants from other parts of the Solomons, particularly from Malaita province. This was spearheaded by the illegal Guadalcanal Revolutionary Army (GRA), whose leader was assassinated in December 1998, but was also stimulated by a demand by Ezekiel Alebua, the province's prime minister, who had demanded financial compensation from the national government for accommodating the capital, Honiara, on the island. The crisis was resolved in May 1999 when the national government made an interim compensation payment of SI$500,000.

Since the 1960s the broad strategy of successive governments has been to diversify the Solomons' economic base, reducing dependence on copra exports, by encouraging tuna, timber, palm kernel, and cocoa exports. This has been successfully achieved. Nevertheless, the country was adversely affected by the decline in world commodity prices during the early 1980s, resulting in a decline in GDP and a sharp rise in inflation and a widening balance of payments deficit. The current rapid rate of population growth, around 3.5% per annum, has not helped matters. As a consequence, although per-capita GDP has grown during the 1990s, the country remains dependent on economic aid for 15% of its GDP.

In its external relations the Solomon Islands, under the SIUPA administrations, pursued a moderate, pro-Western course. This contrasted with the more radical approach of the PAP between 1981 and 1984, when relations with the United States were strained by the government's refusal to allow nuclear-powered warships within the Solomons' territorial waters and by the seizure of an American fishing boat in June 1984, for violating its claimed 320-km/200-mile sea limit. In March 1988 the Solomon Islands, as part of a new, broader 'Pacific strategy', joined Vanuatu and Papua New Guinea to form the 'Spearhead Group' (SG), with the aim of preserving Melanesian cultural traditions and campaigning for New Caledonia's independence. In 1994 the Group took its first steps towards establishing intra-regional free trade.

TONGA

The Kingdom of Tonga
Pule'anga Fakatu'i 'o Tonga

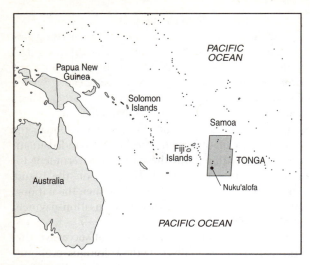

Capital: Nuku'alofa

Social and economic data
Area: 748 sq km/289 sq miles
Population: 98,000[*]
Pop. density per sq km/sq mi: 131/339[*]
Urban population: 21%[**]
Literacy rate: 99%[**]
GDP: $170 million[*]; per-capita GDP: $1,700[*]
Government defense spending (% of GDP): 0%[**]
Currency: Pa'anga or Tongan dollar, which is pegged to the Australian dollar
Economy type: middle income
Labor force in agriculture: 44%[**]
[*] 1995.
[**] 1992.
[***] Tonga has no army, but has a national police force.

Head of state (executive)
King Taufa'ahau Tupou IV, since 1965

Head of government
Prime Minister Baron Vaea of Houma, since 1991

Ethnic composition
Ninety-eight per cent of the population is of Tongan ethnic stock, a Polynesian group with a small mixture of Melanesian. The remainder is European and part-European. Tongan (Tongatabu) is the official language, with English and Polynesian subdialects also being widely spoken. In 1996, 7,000 Tongan citizenships were made available to purchase by Hong Kong Chinese.

Religions
The population is almost entirely Christian. Forty-seven per cent and 9% respectively adhere to the Methodist Free Wesleyan Church of Tonga and Church of Tonga, 15% to Roman Catholicism, and 14% to the Church of Jesus Christ of Latter-Day Saints (Mormon).

Political features
State type: absolutist
Date of state formation: 1970
Political structure: unitary
Executive: absolute
Assembly: one-chamber
Party structure: in transition[*]
Human rights rating: N/A
International affiliations: ACP, AsDB, CW, ESCAP[**], FAO[**], G-77, IBRD[**], ICAO[**], ICFTU, IDA[**], IFAD[**], IFC[**], IMF[**], ITU[**], LORCS, PC, SPEC, SPF, UNCTAD[**], UNESCO[**], UNIDO[**], UPU[**], WFTU, WHO[**]

[*] Tonga's first formal party was established in 1994.
[**] UN bodies which Tonga belongs to, although it is not formally a member of the UN.

Local and regional government
For administrative purposes, the country is divided into three districts – Vava'u, Ha'apai, and Tongatapu – corresponding to its three island groups. The first two districts are administered by governors who are *ex officio* members of the Privy Council. For Tongatapu, the king acts as governor. Below, there is a small network of town and district officials who have been popularly elected since 1965.

Political system
Tonga is an independent hereditary monarchy within the Commonwealth. Its constitution dates from 1875, having been most recently revised in 1970, and provides for a king who is both head of state and head of government. He appoints and presides over a Privy Council, which also serves as a cabinet, and consists of himself and ten ministers appointed for life. The cabinet is led by the prime minister and includes, as *ex officio* members, the governors of Ha'apai and Vava'u. Between 1965 and 1991 Prince Fatafehi Tu'ipelehake, the king's younger brother, was prime minister. He was replaced in August 1991 by the king's cousin, Baron Vaea. There is a single-chamber Legislative Assembly of around 30 members, who include the king, the Privy Council, nine hereditary nobles, elected by the 33 hereditary nobles of Tonga, and nine representatives of the people, elected by universal adult suffrage (for all adults over 21 years of age). The Assembly has a life of three years and meets at least once a year, usually for a session which lasts between two to four months. Legislation, in the form of ordi-

nances, passed by the executive is subject to review by the Assembly.

Political parties

Traditionally there have been no official political parties in Tonga, 'People's Representatives' being elected as independents. However, within the Legislative Assembly informal pro- and anti-government groupings do form from time to time. In 1992 the Pro-Democracy, or People's Democratic, Movement opposition group was unofficially founded and in August 1994 the People's Party, led by a business executive, Huliki Watab and the commoner Akilisi Pohiva, and supported by four other commoner MPs, became the country's first formal political party. It was later renamed the Human Rights and Democracy Movement (HRDM).

Political leaders since 1970

1965– King Taufa'ahau Tupou IV

Latest elections

In the most recent Legislative Assembly elections, held 10–11 March 1999 the nine 'People's Represent-atives', or commoners, who were elected included five members of the reformist HRDM.

Political history

Tonga is an island chain in the southwest Pacific Ocean, 2,250 km/1,398 miles northeast of New Zealand and 640 km/398 miles east of Fiji, between 18 and 22 degrees south of the equator. It comprises 133 inhabited and 36 uninhabited volcanic and coral islands divided into three main groups, Vava'u in the north, Ha'apai in the center, and Tongatapu-Eua in the south. Sixty-eight per cent of the population resides on the main island of Tongatapu, on which the capital of Nuku'alofa is situated.

The first European visitor to Tonga was the Dutch explorer, Abel Tasman (1603–59) in 1643. More than a century later, in 1773, the islands were charted by Captain James Cook (1728–79) and dubbed the 'Friendly Islands'. The contemporary Tongan dynasty was founded in 1831 by Prince Taufa'ahau Tupou, who took the name King George Tupou I when he ascended the throne. He consolidated the kingdom by conquest, encouraged the spread of Christianity, and, in 1875, granted a constitution. In 1900 his great-grandson, King George Tupou II, signed a Treaty of Friendship and Protection under which Tonga formally became a British protectorate. Tonga retained its independence and substantial internal autonomy, but handed over control of its foreign policy and defense to the United Kingdom. This position was broadly reaffirmed in revised treaties which were signed in 1958 and 1967, under which Tonga was granted increased control over its internal affairs.

Queen Salote Tupou III (1900–65), who had ascended the throne in 1918, died in December 1965 and was succeeded by her son, Prince Tupouto'a Tungi (b. 1918), who had been prime minister since 1949. He assumed the title King Taufa'-ahau Tupou IV and appointed his brother, Prince Fatafehi Tu'ipelehake, as the new prime minister. Full independence, within the Commonwealth, was finally achieved in June 1970, giving the nation control over its foreign affairs. The country's foreign policy approach since independence has, however, changed little, the country remaining the strongest supporter of the Western powers in the Pacific region, particularly close links being maintained with Britain, Australia, and New Zealand. Tonga remains dependent on foreign development aid for more than a fifth of its current GDP and is still heavily reliant on its traditional cash crop exports of coconuts, vanilla, and pumpkins, and despite recent lucrative growth in the tourist and fishing industries, unemployment remains high, inducing substantial emigration. In recent years, popular demands for constitutional reforms have grown. In February 1990 three prodemocracy candidates were elected to the Legislative Assembly and in 1992 an unofficial political party, the People's Democratic Movement, was founded to campaign for democratization. Led by Akilisi Pohiva, a magazine editor and reform-minded legislator, and supported by Fr Seluini 'Akau'ola, a Catholic priest, it won six of the nine commoner seats contested in the 1993 and 1996 general elections and became known as the People's Party in August 1994. The king has firmly resisted reform of the Legislative Assembly so as to provide for an elected majority. However, Crown Prince Tupouto'a, the foreign affairs and defense minister, has expressed support for the establishment of political parties and a formalized political structure.

In September 1996 Pohiva was imprisoned for a month for contempt of the legislature and, in June 1997, his newspaper's editor was charged with sedition for publishing a letter that questioned government policy. Unlike other Pacific states, Tonga did not condemn France's resumption of nuclear weapons-testing in the South Pacific in 1995. However, in May 1996 it was announced that Tonga would adopt, at last, the South Pacific Nuclear-Free-Zone Treaty.

TUVALU

South West Pacific State of Tuvalu

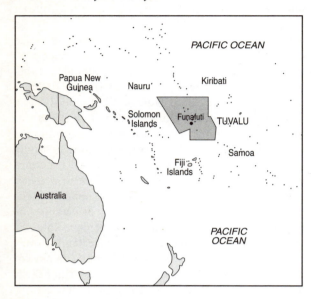

Capital: Fongafale (on Funafuti Atoll)

Social and economic data

Area: 26 sq km/10 sq miles
Population: 9,000[*]
Pop. density per sq km/sq mi: 346/900[*]
Urban population: 30%[**]
Literacy rate: 95%[**]
GDP: $7 million[*]; per-capita GDP: $780[*]
Government defense spending (% of GDP): 0%[***]
Currency: Tuvalu dollar, which is pegged to the Australian dollar
Economy type: low income
Labor force in agriculture: N/A
[*] 1995.
[**] 1992.
[***] Tuvalu has no army.

Head of state

Queen Elizabeth II, represented by Governor General Sir Tulaga Manuella since 1994

Head of government

Prime Minister Ionatana Ionatana, since 1999

Ethnic composition

The population is almost entirely of Polynesian stock, maintaining close ties with the Samoans and Tokelauans to the south and east. Tuvaluan and English are the principal languages.

Religions

Ninety-eight per cent of the population adheres to the Protestant Church of Tuvalu (Ekalesia Tuvalu) which was established in 1861. It is a Congregationalist body derived from the London Missionary Society. In 1991 Parliament approved legislation to establish the Church of Tuvalu as the State Church and prohibit new religions from the islands.

Political features

State type: liberal democratic
Date of state formation: 1978
Political structure: unitary
Executive: parliamentary
Assembly: one-chamber
Party structure: no parties
Human rights rating: N/A
International affiliations: ACP, CW (special status), ESCAP[*], PC, SPEC, SPF, UNESCO[*], UPU[*], WHO[*]

[*] UN bodies which Tuvalu belongs to, although it is not formally a member of the UN.

Local and regional government

For local government, each of the nine inhabited atolls has its own six-member island council, headed by a president. The councils meet in large council halls (*maneabas*), which are also used to sleep as many as 1,000 people during the annual communal feasts, which last for several weeks.

Political system

The constitution dates from October 1978 when Tuvalu became an independent state within the Commonwealth, accepting the British monarch as head of state, represented by a resident governor general. The system of government contains elements of the British, Westminster, model, with a single-chamber Parliament of 12 members and a prime minister and cabinet, of four additional ministers, elected by and responsible to it. The governor general must be a citizen of Tuvalu and is appointed on the recommendation of the prime minister for a four-year term. The prime minister also currently holds the portfolio of foreign affairs. Members of Parliament are elected by universal adult suffrage, through a simple plurality voting system, for a four-year term. The Parliament is subject to dissolution during its term. Four atolls, Nanumea, Niutao, Vaitupu, and Funafuti, each send two representatives to Parliament, with Niulakita being regarded, for electoral purposes, as part of Niutao. The remaining four atolls return one member each.

Political parties

There are no political parties. Members are elected to Parliament as independents, but alliances are subsequently established within the legislature based on clan loyalties and family connections.

Political leaders since 1970

1975–81 Toaripi Lauti (independent), 1981–89 Dr Tomasi Puapua (independent), 1989–93 Bikenibeu Paeniu (independent), 1993–96 Kamuta Laatasi (independent), 1996–99 Bikenibeu Paeniu (independent), 1999– Ionatana Ionatana (independent)

Latest elections

The most recent parliamentary elections were held on 26 March 1998, 12 independents being returned, with an average of three candidates contesting each seat. Seven members of the previous parliament were returned to office.

Political history

Tuvalu is a small island grouping in the southwest Pacific Ocean, 1,050 km/650 miles north of Fiji and 4,020 km/2,500 miles northeast of Sydney, Australia. It comprises the low-lying coral atolls of Funafuti, on which 34% of the population resides, Vaitupu, with 15%, Nanumea, 11%, Niutao, 11%, Nukufetau, 8%, Nanumanga, 7%, Nui, 7%, Nukulailai, 4%, and Niulakita, 1%, and extends 560 kilometres from north to south.

The islands were invaded and occupied by Samoans during the 16th century. In the mid-19th century, between 1850 and 1875, European slave traders visited Tuvalu and captured the indigenous Melanesians for forced labor in the guano mines and on the coffee plantations of South America. As a result of both these activities and the importation of European diseases, the islands' population fell markedly from an estimated 20,000 to barely 3,000.

In 1877, when the British established the Western Pacific High Commission (WPHC), with its headquarters on Fiji, Tuvalu, which at this time was known as the Ellice, or Lagoon, Islands, was placed under its charge. Fifteen years later, in 1892, the islands were officially declared a British Protectorate and were linked, for administrative purposes, with the larger, Micronesian-peopled, Gilbert Islands, known today as Kiribati. From 1916 the protectorate was ruled formally as a colony under the designation Gilbert and Ellice Islands Colony (GEIC), a resident commissioner being based on Tarawa Atoll in the Gilbert group.

During World War II the GEIC was invaded and occupied by Japan in 1942. A year later, the Japanese were removed by American naval forces and British control was re-established. After the war a succession of advisory and legislative councils were set up, paving the way for self-government. This culminated, in May 1974, in the establishment of a House of Assembly, comprising 28 elected members, eight from the Ellice Islands, and three official members. The assembly elected a chief minister and between four to six cabinet ministers, one of whom had to be from the Ellice Islands. The British seemed, at this time, to be preparing the way for granting independence to the GEIC as a constituent whole. This, however, was strongly opposed by the Ellice Islanders, who feared domination by the Micronesians of the Gilbert Islands. They therefore pressed for separate status and in a referendum held on the Ellice Islands in August – September 1974 they voted overwhelmingly, by a 90% majority, for this option. Thus, in October 1975, reverting to their traditional name of Tuvalu, meaning 'eight standing together', the Ellice Islands became a separate British dependency. The eight Ellice Islands representatives of the former GEIC House of Assembly constituted themselves as a new Tuvalu House of Assembly and elected Toaripi Lauti as their first chief minister.

In the House of Assembly elections of August 1977, the number of elective seats was increased to 12 and a year later, in October 1978, following the framing in London of a constitution, Tuvalu became fully independent as a 'special member' of the Commonwealth. This meant that, because of its small size, it did not participate in heads of government meetings. Lauti became the country's prime minister and the House of Assembly was redesignated Parliament.

In the first post-independence parliamentary elections, of September 1981, Lauti, who had been involved in an alleged investment scandal, was replaced as prime minister, following a 7–5 parliamentary vote against him. His successor was Dr Tomasi Puapua (b. 1938), who was re-elected in July 1985. During 1986 constitutional changes designed to reduce the authority of the governor general, and in particular his or her right to reject the advice of the incumbent government, were mooted. However, in February 1986, in a national poll held to decide whether Tuvalu should remain a constitutional monarchy or become a republic, only one atoll supported republican status.

The September 1989 general election saw the replacement of Dr Puapua by Bikenibeu Paeniu. However, the general election of September 1993 resulted in a Parliament split evenly between supporters of Paeniu and ex-premier, Puapua. Governor General Toaripi Lauti was thus forced to dissolve Parliament and call fresh elections in November 1993. With the support of Dr Puapua, the new legislature elected on 10 December 1993, as prime minister, Kamuta Laatasi, who defeated Paeniu by seven votes to five. In July 1994 Prime Minister Laatasi controversially forced Governor General Toomu Sione, who was only seven months into his four-year term, to resign on the grounds that his appointment, by Paeniu, had been politically motivated. Tulaga Manuella became the new governor general.

In 1995 Tuvalu removed the Union Jack from its national flag. This move, influenced by the reduced amount of economic aid supplied by Britain, although unpopular, was seen as the first step towards the removal of the British queen as head of state and the declaration of a republic. A three-member committee was formed in 1995 to consider this possible change.

In December 1996 Prime Minister Laatasi was defeated on a no-confidence motion, after the deputy prime minister, Otinielu Tausi, and the parliamentary speaker, Dr Tomasi Puapua, withdrew their support from the government, which had lost public popularity. Bikenibeu Paeniu was elected prime minister, by seven votes to five, and, in February 1997, his new government restored the country's original flag. Paeniu was re-elected prime minister, by ten votes to two, after the general election of March 1998. This election campaign had been particularly torrid, with Paeniu and Laatasi trading allegations of sexual and financial misconduct. Unexpectedly, Laatasi was not voted back to the Parliament.

In April 1999 Prime Minister Paeniu was forced from office, when his government lost of parliamentary vote of confidence by seven votes to four. The vote had been triggered by allegation of misconduct in Paeniu's private life and criticisms that he had failed to carry out government pledges. He was replaced as prime minister by Ionatana Ionatana, a former education and health minister

As a result of its scanty resource base, with much of the soil too poor to make cultivation feasible, economic development has been slow in Tuvalu. Rapid population growth, currently at 3.4% per annum, the closure of the phosphate mines in neighboring Kiribati in 1979, where many Tuvaluans worked, and cyclone damage have made matters worse, depressing living standards in recent years. As a consequence, the country has become highly dependent on overseas development aid, more than a quarter of its GDP being derived

from this source. Efforts to develop the tourist industry have been hampered by the country's remoteness. To generate extra revenue, the sale of Tuvaluan passports commenced in 1996.

In its conduct of foreign relations, close links have been maintained with Britain and the United States. Tuvalu has, however, been a strong opponent of the French nuclear weapons testing program based at Mururoa Atoll, in French Polynesia, and has urged Western governments to take action to combat the 'greenhouse effect' which threatens the country's very existence if sea levels continue to rise.

VANUATU

Ripublik Blong Vanuatu
The Republic of Vanuatu
La République de Vanuatu

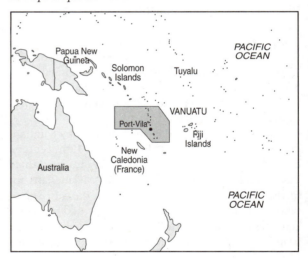

Capital: Port-Vila

Social and economic data
Area: 12,190 sq km/4,707 sq miles
Population: 165,000[*]
Pop. density per sq km/sq mi: 13/35[*]
Urban population: 27%[**]
Literacy rate: 66%[**]
GDP: $202 million[*]; per-capita GDP: $1,210[*]
Government defense spending (% of GDP): N/A[***]
Currency: vatu
Economy type: middle income

Labor force in agriculture: 60%**

* 1995.

** 1992.

*** Vanuatu has only a small, 300-member paramilitary force.

Head of state
President Father John Bernard Bani, since 1999

Head of government
Prime Minister Donald Kalpokas, since 1998

Ethnic composition
Ninety-five per cent of the population is Melanesian, 3% European or mixed European, and 2% Vietnamese, Chinese, or from other Pacific islands. Bislama (ni-Vanuatu pidgin English) is the official language, with English and French also being widely understood.

Religions
Thirty-three per cent of the population belongs to the Presbyterian Church of Vanuatu, 13% to the Church of the Province of Melanesia, 13% to the Roman Catholic Church, and 10% to other Christian churches, including the Apostolic, Churches of Christ, Assemblies of God, and Seventh-Day Adventists. Nine per cent adheres to traditional animist beliefs.

Political features
State type: liberal democratic
Date of state formation: 1980
Political structure: unitary
Executive: parliamentary
Assembly: one-chamber
Party structure: multiparty
Human rights rating: N/A
International affiliations: ACP, AsDB, CW, ESCAP, G-77, IBRD, ICFTU, IMF, NAM, SG, PC, SPEC, SPF, UN, WFTU

Local and regional government
The country is divided into four administrative regions, with headquarters at Lenakel (Tanna), Vila, Lamap (Malakula), and Espíritu Santo. Considerable power has been constitutionally devolved to six regional councils, which replaced 11 local government councils in 1994, and are Malampa, Penama, Sanma, Shefa, Tafea, and Torba.

Political system
Vanuatu is an independent republic within the Commonwealth. The constitution dates from independence in July 1980. It provides for a president, who functions as a ceremonial head of state and is elected for a five-year term in a secret ballot, by what will be a 58-member electoral college consisting of parliament and the presidents of the country's regional councils. A two-thirds majority is required in this election. Parliament consists of a single chamber of, from 1998, 52 members, elected by universal adult suffrage, through a system which embraces an element of proportional representation, for a four-year term. A prime minister is elected from among the members of Parliament, who then appoints and presides over a 9–11-member Council of Ministers. In June 1998 the prime minister, Donald Kalpokas, also held the public service, foreign affairs, and ministerial portfolios, overseeing a comprehensive reform program. There is a National Council of Chiefs, comprising custom chiefs elected by District Councils of Chiefs, which is empowered to make recommendations to Parliament on subjects connected with the preservation and promotion of traditional culture and languages.

Political parties
The Vanuaaku Parti (VP: 'Party of Our Land') was formed in 1972 as the New Hebrides National Party (NHNP). Led by Donald Kalpokas, it promotes a unique 'Melanesian socialist' program, founded on nonalignment overseas and, domestically, the transfer of lands held by non-natives to the indigenous population. The VP was the ruling party from 1980, but its national support, drawn predominantly from English-speaking Melanesian Protestant groups, declined significantly in the general elections of 1979 and 1983 and it was defeated in 1991. It returned to power in 1998. Its former leader, Father Walter Lini, founded the center-left National United Party (NUP) in 1991, but the NUP subsequently split into two opposed factions. In May 1994 the NUP's congress expelled 16 members, including Deputy Prime Minister John Sethy Regenvanu, who defied party instructions to withdraw support from the Maxime Carlot Korman government. These expelled members immediately formed the new People's Democratic Party.

The ruling party 1991–98 was a Francophone umbrella grouping, the Union of Moderate Parties (UMP), led by Serge Vohor. The conservative UMP was associated with the 1980 Espíritu Santo rebellion and enjoys strong Roman Catholic support. In January 1998 Maxime Carlot Korman, leader of an important UMP party, broke away to form the Vanuatu Republican Party (VRP).

The other main parties are the Melanesian Progressive Party (MPP), founded in 1988 by VP dissidents, notably Barak Sope; the John Frum Movement (JFM), representing the interests of the southern island of Tanna; the Tan Union, representing rural interests; the Fren Melanesian Party (FMP), a splinter group based in Espíritu Santo and Malekula, formed when the UMP superseded the New Hebrides Federal Party in 1982; and the Na-Griamel (NG) Movement, led by Franky Stephens, the son of Jimmy Stephens, leader of the 1980 Espíritu Santo revolt, who died in 1994.

Political leaders since 1970

1978–80 Father Gerard Leymang (independent), 1980–91 Father Walter Lini (VP), 1991 Donald Kalpokas (VP), 1991–95 Maxime Carlot Korman (UMP) 1995–96 Serge Vohor (Unity Front), 1996 Maxime Carlot Korman (UMP), 1996–98 Serge Vohor (UMP), 1998– Donald Kalpokas (VP)

Latest elections

In the most recent parliamentary elections, held on 6 March 1998, the VP won 18 seats, the UMP, 12, the NUP, 11, the MPP, 6, the JFM, 2, the URP, 1, and independents, 2.

The most recent presidential election was held on 24 March 1999 and was won by Father John Bernard Boni, on the second round of votes.

Political history

The Republic of Vanuatu, formerly known as the New Hebrides, is an irregular Y-shaped chain of 13 volcanic islands and 70 islets in the southwest Pacific Ocean lying between Fiji and New Caledonia. Sixty per cent of the population resides on the four main islands of Efate, Espíritu Santo, Malakula, and Tanna. The bulk of the inland portions of the islands are densely forested, settlements being concentrated on the coastal fringes.

The islands were first visited by the Portuguese navigator Pedro Fernandez de Queiras in 1606, before being charted and named the New Hebrides by the British explorer, James Cook (1728–79), in 1774. During the 19th century they were disputed by both Britain and France until 1887, when a joint naval commission was placed in charge of their administration. From 1906, the New Hebrides (Nouvelles-Hébrides) were placed under a joint Anglo-French condominium, with each power being responsible for its own citizens, governing in its own language, and having its own forces and institutions. British and French missionaries, planters, and traders subsequently settled in the country, which escaped occupation by Japan during World War II.

After the war an indigenous political grouping, Na-Griamel (NG) began to develop, and was formally

established in 1963. It campaigned against the acquisition of native land by Europeans, more than a third of the country's land being owned by foreigners by the 1960s. Later, in 1972, the New Hebrides National Party (NHNP) was formed, enjoying the support of Protestant missions and British interests. It was opposed by the Union of New Hebrides Communities (UNHC), a body which had been established by pro-French groups. Discussions began in London in 1974 about eventual independence and they resulted in the creation of a 42-member Representative Assembly, 29 members being directly elected in November 1975. This body superseded an Advisory Council which had been operating since 1957.

Negotiations for establishing a timetable for a gradual move towards independence, planned for 1980, were hampered by objections by the National Party, renamed the Vanuaaku Party (VP) in January 1977, which pressed for immediate independence. Eventually, however, a Government of National Unity was formed in December 1978, with Father Gerard Leymang as chief minister and the VP leader, Father Walter Lini (1942–99), a former Anglican priest, as his deputy. A further delay was caused in 1980 when French settlers and pro-NG plantation workers on the island of Espíritu Santo revolted, after a sweeping victory in the Representative Assembly elections of November 1979 by the VP. Jimmy Stevens, leader of the NG, proclaimed Espíritu Santo independent under the designation 'State of Vemarana' in June 1980, allegedly receiving financial support from the Phoenix Foundation, a rightwing group in the United States. The revolt was, controversially, put down by British, French, and Papua New Guinean troops after several days of fighting and Stevens was imprisoned for 11 years.

Agreement was finally reached about independence in July 1980, with the new sovereign state remaining within the Commonwealth and its name being changed to the Republic of Vanuatu. The first president was the former deputy chief minister, George Kalkoa, who adopted the name Sokomanu, or 'leader of thousands', and the first prime minister was Father Lini. In the November 1983 general election the VP was re-elected, with a slightly reduced majority, and Father Lini continued as prime minister.

Lini proceeded to pursue a controversial left-of-center nonaligned foreign policy, which included support for the Kanak National Liberation Front (KNLF) which was fighting for independence in French-ruled New

Caledonia, and the possible establishment of diplomatic relations with the USSR and Libya. This soured relations with France and provoked mounting parliamentary opposition, the government's actions being viewed as likely to discourage both inward foreign investment and the expansion of the tourist industry, with consequential adverse effects on the country's economic development. During 1986 three anti-government opposition parties, the National Democratic Party (NDP), the New People's Party (NPP), and the Vanuatu Labor Party (VLP), were formed. However, in the general election of November 1987, the VP retained its assembly majority and Lini, despite ailing health, was re-elected prime minister.

Nevertheless, opposition to Lini's domestic and external policies continued to grow during 1988. In response, in July 1988 the prime minister expelled from Parliament his intra-party rival Barak Sope, together with four supporters, as well as 18 opposition MPs who had boycotted Parliament in protest. Five months later, in December 1988, Lini was dismissed as prime minister and Parliament dissolved by President Ati George Sokomanu, who appointed his nephew, Sope, head of an interim administration. Within days, however, following a Supreme Court ruling that these actions had been unconstitutional, security forces loyal to the former prime minister arrested both the president and Sope, reinstating Lini in power. Fred Timakata, formerly the minister of health, was elected the new president in January 1989, with, two months later, Sokomanu, Sope, and Carlot each being initially sentenced to between five and six years' imprisonment for their seditious actions in December 1988. The Court of Appeal quashed these sentences in April 1989.

Despite suffering a heart attack, Lini clung to office, still dismissing colleagues who disagreed with him, until, in August 1991, as opposition within the VP mounted, he lost the leadership of the party and was then dismissed as prime minister. He was replaced by the VP's general secretary, Donald Kalpokas. The general election of December 1991 produced an inconclusive result, but eventually the UMP leader, Maxime Carlot Korman, formed a coalition with the Anglophone NUP, which had been set up in 1991 by ex-premier, Walter Lini. In August 1993 the NUP split between a pro-government faction, led by the deputy prime minister, John Sethy Regenvanu, and including three other colleagues, and an opposition faction, led by Lini. The six-member Lini faction left the governing coalition whose popularity declined as a combination

of the damage inflicted in March 1993 by 'Cyclone Prema' and falling copra prices produced hardship during 1992–93, while Regenvanu and 15 colleagues were expelled from the NUP and formed the new government-aligned People's Democratic Party in May 1994. Na-Griamel switched allegiance to the government in 1995. The November 1995 general election brought an inconclusive victory for the VP-dominated Unity Front, which won 20 of the 49 seats in parliament.

Serge Vohor, the UMP president who led a faction which was opposed to Carlot Korman, became prime minister in December 1995, forming a UMP-National United Party (NUP) coalition administration. However, in February 1996, faced with certain defeat in a no-confidence vote, Vohor resigned and was replaced as prime minister by Carlot Korman, who was supported by seven dissident members of the UMP and by the VP-dominated Unity Front, which also included the Melanesian Progressive Party (MPP), the Tan Union, and Na-Griamel. This new coalition government's standing was damaged from July 1996 by the revelation of a massive financial scandal, relating to the issue of large bank guarantees, and in August 1996, following the dismissal of its leader, Barak Sope, as finance minister, the MPP withdrew from the Unity Front and formed a new alliance, called the MTF, with the Tan Union and the French Melanesian Party (FMP). Consequently, on 30 September 1996, the Carlot government was defeated in a no-confidence vote and was replaced by a new Vohor-led coalition government, which included his faction of the UMP, the NUP, led by Walter Lini, and the MTF, with Sope back as deputy prime minister.

In November 1996 the country was shaken by a mutiny, over pay levels, by half of the 300-strong paramilitary defense force (VMF), who briefly kidnapped President Leye. Sope, who had expressed sympathy with the VMF's demands, was dismissed and the MTF expelled from the ruling coalition. The VP took its place, with its leader, Donald Kalpokas, becoming deputy prime minister and education minister, while the NUP's Lini became justice minister. The coalition government was reshaped in May 1997 when some UMP supporters of Carlot Korman were brought into the cabinet – but not Carlot Korman himself, who declined to become foreign minister – and Barak Sope was brought back in as deputy prime minister. The coalition now comprised the UMP, MPP, FMP, and Tan Union, but no longer the VP, which had attracted five defectors from the NUP and been expelled. Sope returned as deputy prime minister, despite being described by the national ombudswoman as 'unfit for public office'.

These changes failed to ensure stability for the government, and in November 1997, when faced by the tabling of another no-confidence motion by Carlot Korman, President Leye dissolved the legislature and called fresh elections. In January 1998, followed rioting in Port-Vila, by angry investors who were seeking to withdraw savings from a fund that had been misused by politicians, a two-week state of emergency was imposed. The March 1998 general election saw a fall in support for the UMP, which won only 12 (down five) of the 52 seats in the newly enlarged parliament. After the election, the VP and NUP, which jointly controlled 29 seats, put aside their past differences to form a coalition government, with Donald Kalpokas as prime minister and foreign minister, and Lini as deputy prime minister and justice and internal affairs minister. The coalition was also supported by Carlot Korman, who headed a new one-deputy strong Vanuatu Republikan Pati (VRP), and an independent.

In October 1998 a new coalition government was formed by Prime Minister Kalpokas (VP) with a faction of the UMP and the John Frum Movement (JFM). This followed the expulsion of deputy prime minister Walter Lini and his NUP from the government, after it had drafted a no-confidence motion. Willie Jimmy of the UMP became deputy prime minister. Lini later died in February 1999, at the age of 56.

Externally, Vanuatu's relations with France reached a low point in October 1987, when the French ambassador was expelled from the country for providing 'substantial financial assistance' to opposition parties. However, diplomatic relations were restored in October 1992 by the new Francophone administration of Maxime Carlot Korman. Indeed, in 1995 the Carlot government was one in the region that did not condemn France's resumption of nuclear weapons-testing in French Polynesia. Relations with the United States improved after Vanuatu's signing of a five-year fishing agreement in October 1986, under which American trawlers were granted licences to fish for tuna within the country's 'exclusive fishing zone'. The general thrust of Vanuatu's foreign policy since independence has, however, been to promote greater cooperation between the small states of the Pacific region. As part of this strategy, Vanuatu joined Papua New Guinea and the Solomon Islands in forming, in March 1988, the 'Spearhead Group' (SG), whose aim is to preserve Melanesian cultural traditions and campaign for New Caledonia's independence.

In 1994 the group took the first tentative steps towards establishing intra-regional free trade. With rapid population growth, averaging 2.7% per annum, real per-capita GDP fell annually by 1% between 1990 and 1996. The tourist sector and 'offshore banking' continue to grow in importance, and in 1997 a comprehensive reform program was adopted by the new Kalpokas government.

South America

The region of South America extends from the Panamanian border in the north to Cape Horn in the south, and is bounded to the east by the Atlantic Ocean and to the west by the Pacific Ocean. The total land area is nearly 18 million square kilometres, almost five times greater than Northern and Western Europe and only slightly smaller than the North American half-continent of the United States and Canada. Its total population, at 308 million in 1995, is greater than that of the United States and Canada combined but, like them, it has a relatively low population density.

The fact that it is frequently referred to as Latin America, or Spanish America, reveals its colonial origins. Most of the present modern states were settled by Spanish explorers in the heyday of Spain's imperial supremacy, and most achieved independence during the 19th century. The major exception is Brazil, whose origins are Portuguese, rather than Spanish.

All 12 states in the region are liberal, or emergent democracies, some having recently emerged from overt or covert military rule. The South American military have always tended to be near, or just below, the surface of political activity in most states, so that the region is now enjoying its strongest period of democratic government.

Whereas the Caribbean states virtually universally adopted the Westminster style of political system, those of South America have been modelled more on that of the United States. All of them have favored a limited presidential executive and a quarter are federal states.

Although democratic systems now predominate, the human-rights records of some countries in the region are still not good and there is always a danger that representative institutions will be overthrown in some unpredictable coup. Parts of South America are rife with drug trafficking and this had impacted strongly, in some states, on political processes, making apparently fair elections fraudulent. However, pluralist democracy, restored to Brazil in 1985, has proved sufficiently robust to successfully accommodate the peaceful removal of a president, Collor de Mello, for impeachment on charges of embezzlement.

Spanish influence, or Spanishness (*hispanidad*) as it is often called, waned significantly during the years of the Franco regime in Spain but, with the return of the monarchy and the revival of pluralist politics in their 'home country', South Americans are showing a great resurgence of interest in Spain and are forging, or reforging, links with it.

Now that Spain is a member of the European Union (EU), connections with its former South American colonies promise to give it more weight in discussions with other Union members than its previous solitary position might have credited. For the South American states there is an attraction, even in the case of Brazil, in Spain becoming an important power in the region again, particularly as US influence has been showing signs of a decline. How the administration in Washington would react to such a challenge to its leadership is difficult to judge.

As Spain relinquished most of its South American colonies during the 19th century, France began to fill the cultural gap and Britain the economic one. In the 20th century, of course, the United States has been the rising influence. However, US interference in Latin American domestic affairs has often had a boomerang effect and not realized its original purpose. It has merely succeeded in irritating, or antagonizing, the proudly independent South American states.

Despite their long histories of political independence, and despite the wealth of natural resources in many areas, the economies of the 12 South American countries do not have a particularly good record (see Table 62). Nine fall into the 'middle income' category; two, Bolivia and Guyana, achieve only 'low income' status; and only Argentina has a 'high income'. The international indebtedness of most of them continues to grow, and some, notably Brazil, have battled with enormously high levels of inflation, but the future is not entirely bleak.

Political changes in Europe will, increasingly, have their impact on South America. The resurgence of Spain has already been noted but it is also interesting to speculate about the future position of Castro's Cuba, in the neighboring region of Central America and the Caribbean, now that it has lost its former Soviet patron. Many observers of the political and economic scene saw the 1980s as an era of lost opportunities, during which the countries in the region might have raised their levels of investment and living standards, but failed to do so. There are hopeful prospects, however, for the new millennium and the North American Free Trade Agreement (NAFTA), which has already expanded beyond Canada, the United States, and Mexico to Chile, might suggest a way forward for the nations of the south.

SOUTH AMERICA

NICARAGUA

COSTA RICA PANAMA

Aruba (Neth)

Netherlands Antilles (Neth)

BARBADOS

GRENADA

TRINIDAD & TOBAGO

ATLANTIC OCEAN

VENEZUELA

GUYANA

FRENCH GUIANA

COLOMBIA

SURINAME

ECUADOR

Equator

PERU

BRAZIL

BOLIVIA

PARAGUAY

Tropic of Capricorn

CHILE

PACIFIC OCEAN

URUGUAY

ARGENTINA

ATLANTIC OCEAN

Falkland Islands (UK)

0   600 mi

0   1000 km

Recommended reading

Calvert, P (ed.) *Political and Economic Encyclopaedia of South America and the Caribbean*, Longman, 1991

Corradi, J E *The Fitful Republic: Economy, Society and Politics in Argentina*, Westview Press, 1985

Diamond, L, Linz, J, and Lipset, S M (eds.) *Democracy in Developing Countries*, Vol. 4 *Latin America*, Lynne Rienner, 1989

O'Donnell, G, Schmitter, P C, and Whitehead, L (eds.) *Transitions from Authoritarian Rule: Prospects for Democracy*, Vol. II *Latin America*, Johns Hopkins University Press, 1986

Masterson, D M *Militarism and Politics in Latin America: Peru from Sanchez Cerro to Sendero Luminoso*, Greenwood Press, 1991

McDonald, R and Ruhl, J M *Party Politics and Elections in Latin America*, Westview Press, 1989

Pocket Latin America, Economist Books, 1997

Przeworski, A *Democracy and the Market: Political and Economic Reforms in Eastern Europe and Latin America*, Cambridge University Press, 1991

Stepan, A *Rethinking Military Politics: Brazil and the Southern Cone*, Princeton University Press, 1988

South America: social, economic, and political data

Country	Area (sq km/sq mile)	c. 1995 Population (million)	c. 1995 Pop. density per sq km/sq mile	c. 1992 Adult literacy rate (%)	World ranking	Income type	c. 1991 Human rights rating (%)
Argentina	2,766,889/1,068,301	34.180	12/32	95	59	high	84
Bolivia	1,098,600/4,241,72	7.237	7/17	63	128	low	71
Brazil	8,512,000/3,286,500	153.725	18/47	75	112	middle	69
Chile	756,950/292,260	13.994	18/48	94	66	middle	80
Colombia	1,138,994/439,768	34.520	30/78	87	89	middle	60
Ecuador	270,670/104,506	11.221	41/107	80	105	middle	83
Guyana	215,000/83,012	0.825	4/10	92	76	low	N/A
Paraguay	406,750/157,047	4.700	12/30	88	84	middle	70
Peru	1,285,220/496,226	23.088	18/47	82	99	middle	54
Suriname	163,265/63,027	0.418	3/7	65	124	middle	N/A
Uruguay	176,215/68,037	3.167	18/47	94	66	middle	90
Venezuela	912,050/352,144	21.177	23/60	85	94	middle	75
Total/average/range	17,702,603/6,335,010	308.252	17/45	63–95	–	–	54–90

F = Federal, PL = party list, PR = proportional representation, SP = simple plurality, Lib-dem = liberal democratic, Em-dem = emergent democratic, Lim-pres = limited presidential, U = unitary.)

ARGENTINA

Republic of Argentina
República Argentina

Capital: Buenos Aires

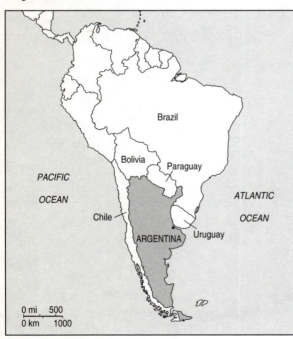

Social and economic data

Area: 2,766,889 sq km/1,068,301 sq miles
Population: 34,180,000[*]
Pop. density per sq km/sq mi: 12/32[*]
Urban population: 87%[**]
GDP: $278,430 million[*]; per-capita GDP: $8,150[*]
Government defense spending (% of GDP): 1.7%[*]
Currency: peso
Economy type: high income
Labor force in agriculture: 13%[**]
Unemployment rate: 13%[**]
[*] 1995.
[**] 1992.

Head of state and head of government

President Carlos Saúl Menem, since 1989

Ethnic composition

About 85% of the population is of European descent, mainly Spanish, and 15% are mestizos, offspring of Spanish-American and American-Indian parents. The almost universally used language is Spanish.

Religions

About 90% of the population adheres to the Roman Catholic faith, which is a quasi-state religion. The constitution, for example, requires the president to be a Roman Catholic.

Table 62

World ranking	Date of state formation	State structure	State type	Executive type	Number of assembly chambers	Party structure	Lower house electoral system
28	1816	F	Lib-dem	Lim-pres	2	two	SP
45	1825	U	Lib-dem	Lim-pres	2	multi	SP
49	1822	F	Lib-dem	Lim-pres	2	multi	PR-PL
36	1818	U	Em-dem	Lim-pres	2	multi	SP
60	1830	U	Lib-dem	Lim-pres	2	multi	SP
30	1830	U	Lib-dem	Lim-pres	1	multi	PR-PL
N/A	1966	U	Lib-dem	Lim-pres	1	two	PR-PL
47	1811	U	Em-dem	Lim-pres	2	multi	PR-PL
69	1824	U	Lib-dem	Lim-pres	1	multi	PR-PL
N/A	1975	U	Em-dem	Lim-pres	1	multi	SP
21	1825	U	Lib-dem	Lim-pres	2	multi	PR-PL
40	1830	F	Lib-dem	Lim-pres	2	multi	PR-PL
–	–	–	–	–	–	–	–

Political features

State type: liberal democratic
Date of state formation: 1816
Political structure: federal
Executive: limited presidential
Assembly: two-chamber
Party structure: two-party
Human rights rating: 84%
International affiliations: AG (observer), ALADI, BCIE, G-11, G-15, G-24, IAEA, IBRD, IMF, IWC, Mercosur, OAS, RG, SELA, UN, WTO

Local and regional government

Argentina is a federal state comprising the Federal District (Buenos Aires), 22 provinces, and the National Territory of Tierra del Fuego. Each province has its own elected governor and assembly, responsible for all matters which have not been specifically entrusted to the federal government. Each governor serves a four-year term and is either directly elected by popular vote or through an electoral college. Two-thirds of the provincial assemblies have single chambers and the other third have two. In most provinces the governor appoints the city mayors, but the mayor of Buenos Aires is popularly elected.

Political system

The 1994 constitution, which substantially amended the original of 1853, provides for a US-style president, who is head of state and head of government, presid-ing over an appointed cabinet. There is a two-chamber legislature, the Congress (Congreso), consisting of the Senate and the Chamber of Deputies. The president is elected by universal adult suffrage for a four-year term, renewable once only. To gain a victory, a candidate must win at least 45% of the vote, or 40% with a 10% lead. The Senate has 72 members, two nominated by each provincial assembly and the Federal District as general representatives and the remaining third representing minorities. Senators serve a six-year term. The Chamber of Deputies has 257 members, directly elected by universal adult suffrage for a four-year term, with half the seats renewable every two years. There is a nine-member Supreme Court.

Political parties

There are many political parties and groups, the four most significant being the Radical Union Party (UCR), the Justice (Justicialist) Party (PJ), the Front for a Country in Solidarity (Frepaso), and the Movement for Dignity and Independence (Modin). The 1.4 million-member UCR was formed in 1890 and has a moderate centrist orientation. The PJ represents the present-day Peronist movement and was founded in 1945. It is a populist force which operates through three factions and claims 3 million members. Modin is a righwing body formed in 1991. Frepaso, a center-left coalition of socialists, communists, and Christian Democrats, was formed in 1994.

Political leaders since 1970

1966–1973 (military), 1973 Héctor Cámpora (Justice-Peronist Party), 1973–74 Juan Perón (Peronist), 1974–76 Isabel Perón (Peronist), 1976–78 General Jorge Videla (military), 1978–81 General Roberto Viola (military), 1981–82 General Leopoldo Galtieri (military), 1982–83 General Reynaldo Bignone (military), 1983–89 Raúl Alfonsín Foulkes (UCR), 1989– Carlos Saúl Menem (PJ)

Latest elections

In the May 1995 presidential election President Menem was re-elected with 49.8% of the vote, defeating José Bordón (29%) of Frepaso and Horacio Massaccesi (17%) of the U.C.R. In the October 1997 Chamber of Deputies elections the PJ lost its overall majority, winning only 118 of the 257 elective seats. Frepaso and the UCR, who fought the election in alliance, won 110 seats and 46% of the vote, against 36% for the PJ.

Political history

Colonized by Spain in the 16th century, Argentina achieved independence in 1816. The country experienced a series of internal conflicts, peace only being achieved through strong, often dictatorial, governments. The first relatively free and democratic elections took place in 1916 and were won by the UCR, which had been formed 26 years earlier. In 1930 the first of what were to be a series of military coups ousted the civilian government. Two years later there was a return to civilian rule, but a second military coup, in 1945, saw the arrival of Lieutenant General Juan Domingo Perón (1895–1974), who, with his widely popular first wife, Eva (Evita) Duarte Perón (1919–52), created the Peronista Party, favoring policies of extreme nationalism and social improvements. Perón admired Franco's Spanish brand of fascism and set about expanding and strengthening the urban working class, at the expense of the agricultural community. He relied heavily on the military for support.

Evita Perón died in 1952 and, with her death, her husband's popularity faded. Three years later he was forced to resign and a civilian government was restored. Perón went into exile in Spain from where he continued to oversee his party's affairs. Another coup in 1966 brought back military rule and then, in 1973, the success of the Justice (Peronist) Party brought Dr Héctor Cámpora to the presidency, essentially to pave the way for Perón's return. Cámpora resigned after three months and was replaced by Perón, this time with

a new wife, María Estela Martínez de Perón, 'Isabelita' (b. 1931), as vice-president. A year later Perón died and his widow took over.

Isabelita did not enjoy the same degree of popularity as Evita had done nor was her government successful in managing the economy. It was not surprising, therefore, that two years after her succession she was ousted in yet another military coup, led by Lieutenant General Jorge Videla. The constitution was amended, political and trade union activity banned, and a policy of harsh repression of leftwing elements was pursued, during which it is estimated that between 6,000 and 15,000 people 'disappeared'. Although he had been confirmed in office until 1981, in 1978 General Videla announced his retirement and was succeeded by General Roberto Viola, who promised a speedy return to democratic government. Three years later Viola died of a sudden heart attack and was replaced by the commander in chief of the army, General Leopoldo Galtieri (b. 1926).

During the next two years the state of the economy worsened and Galtieri, following the examples of many political leaders, sought to divert attention from internal problems by creating an external diversion. In April 1982 he ordered the invasion of the Islas Malvinas, or Falkland Islands (see *Chapter 8*), over which Britain's claims to sovereignty had long been disputed. After a short, undeclared, war, during which 755 Argentinians lost their lives, the islands were reoccupied by British forces and, with the defeat, Galtieri's stock fell and he was forced to resign in a bloodless coup. He and other members of the military junta he led were later declared by a military commission of inquiry to be responsible for the Falklands failure and were given prison sentences.

General Reynaldo Bignone took over the government and announced that the 1853 constitution would be revived and democratic elections held. The ban on political and trade union activity was lifted and in presidential and assembly elections in October 1983 the UCR, led by Dr Raúl Alfonsín Foulkes (b. 1927), secured the presidency and a narrow victory in the Chamber of Deputies. The new president announced a radical reform of the armed forces, leading to the retirement of more than half of the senior officers, and the setting up of a National Commission on the Disappearance of Persons (CONADEP) to investigate the events of the 'dirty war' between 1976 and 1983, when thousands of 'disappearances' had taken place. A report by CONADEP in 1984 gave details of the deaths of more than 8,000 people and named 1,300 army officers who had been involved in the campaign of repression.

The Alfonsín administration was, however, soon faced with economic problems, forcing it to seek help from the International Monetary Fund (IMF) and the adoption of an austerity program, described by Alfonsín as an 'economy of war'. The government's popularity fell and a swing to the right in the September 1987 assembly elections gave the smaller parties in the Chamber of Deputies the balance of power, although the UCR remained the largest single block.

Externally, Alfonsín set about improving Argentina's international reputation by undertaking a six-nation tour in 1986. The re-establishment of normal relations with the United Kingdom continued to elude him, however, the British prime minister, Margaret Thatcher showing no obvious signs of wanting a rapprochement.

Alfonsín was limited by the constitution to one term as president and in elections for his successor, in May 1989, the PJ candidate, Carlos Saúl Menem (b. 1935), was victorious. Although Menem had spoken belligerently about regaining the Falklands during the election campaign, soon after his assumption of the presidency there were signs of improving relations between Argentina and Britain, and this improvement developed quietly rather than dramatically, consular ties eventually being restored. Domestically, Menem embarked on an extensive privatization program, often in the face of leftwing opposition. He also succeeded in bringing down the level of inflation from 200% a month in 1989 to 11% per annum in 1994 and in 1991 Argentina joined Brazil, Uruguay, and Paraguay to form Mercosur, the 'Common Market of the Southern Cone'. Since 1991 the peso has been pegged to the US dollar.

In 1993 the PJ won a comfortable majority in the Chamber of Deputies and in 1994 the constitution was amended to allow the president to seek another term of office. Despite undergoing a heart operation in October 1993, Menem fought the 1995 presidential election and won convincingly. The PJ also secured a majority in the Chamber of Deputies in concurrent elections.

In April 1995, in the wake of the Mexican economic crisis, an austerity program was introduced, leading to a sharp economic slowdown and rising levels of unemployment. IMF pressures for further reductions in public spending as a condition of new loans forced Menem to assume additional executive powers in 1996 in order to force through budget cuts. This led to a 36-hour general strike in September 1996. In the October 1997 midterm elections, the PJ lost its Chamber of Deputies majority and was outpolled by the center-left opposition alliance.

The economy remained depressed during 1998 and 1999, with GDP forecast to fall by 1.5% in 1999, forcing further budget cuts. Nevertheless, in May 1999 all the main candidates who were vying to succeed Carlos Menem as president in the October 1999 election ruled out the possibility of any change in the country's fixed (to the US$) exchange rate. In June 1999 opinion polls gave the opposition Alliance a ten point lead over its likely PJ rival, Eduardo Duhalde, the governor of Buenos Aires who was vying with President Menem for control of the PJ. However, the polls remained volatile.

BOLIVIA

Republic of Bolivia
República de Bolivia

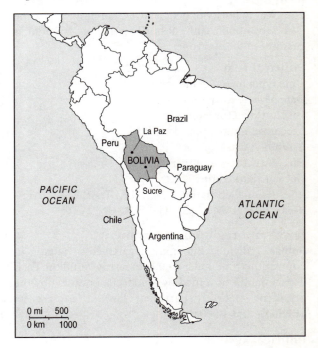

Capital: Sucre (legal capital and seat of the judiciary); La Paz (seat of government)

Social and economic data
Area: 1,098,600 sq km/424,172 sq miles
Population: 7,237,000*

Pop. density per sq km/sq mi: 7/17[*]
Urban population: 52%[**]
Literacy rate: 63%[**]
GDP: $5,900 million[*]; per-capita GDP: $815[*]
Government defense spending (% of GDP): 2.6%[*]
Currency: boliviano
Economy type: low income
Labor force in agriculture: 46%[**]
Unemployment rate: 3.6%
[*] 1995.
[**] 1992.

Head of state and head of government

President General (retired) Hugo Bánzer Suárez, since 1997

Ethnic composition

The population comprises 30% Quechua Indians, 25% Aymara Indians, 25–30% of mixed race, and 5–15% of European descent. The official languages are Spanish, Quechua, and Aymara.

Religions

The great majority of people, over 5 million, follow the Roman Catholic faith, although religious freedom is guaranteed for everyone.

Political features

State type: liberal democratic
Date of state formation: 1825
Political structure: unitary
Executive: limited presidential
Assembly: two-chamber
Party structure: multiparty
Human rights rating: 71%
International affiliations: AG, ALADI, AP, G-11, IAEA, IBRD, IMF, NAM, OAS, RG, SELA, UN, WTO

Local and regional government

Bolivia is divided into nine departments, ranging in population from under 43,000 to nearly 2 million. Each department is governed by a prefect, appointed by the president. Below department level, there are 94 provinces and 1,000 cantons.

Political system

Bolivia became an independent republic in 1825 after nearly 300 years of Spanish rule. It adopted its first constitution in 1826 and since then a number of variations have been produced, the present one being based on that of 1947. After years of abrogation, it was revived, after a *coup d'état*, in 1964. It provides for a two-chamber National Congress consisting of a 27-member Senate and a 130-member Chamber of Deputies, both elected for four years, by universal adult suffrage, through a simple plurality voting procedure. Three senators are elected from each of the country's nine departments. The president is also directly elected for a five-year term, which cannot be renewed immediately, and combines the roles of head of state and head of government. The president chooses and appoints the cabinet. If no candidate obtains a clear majority in the presidential election, the president is chosen by Congress from between the two leading candidates.

Political parties

There is a large number of political parties, the most significant being the National Revolutionary Movement (MNR), the Nationalist Democratic Action Party (ADN), the Movement of the Revolutionary Left (MIR), the Solidarity and Civic Union (UCS), and the Conscience of the Fatherland (Condepa).

The 700,000-member MNR was founded in 1942 by Victor Paz Estenssoro. Its orientation is right-of-center. The ADN is a rightwing grouping, formed in 1979 and led by Hugo Banzer. The MIR is a leftwing party formed in 1971. The UCS is a populist, free-market party formed in 1989, and Condepa is another populist party, formed in 1988.

Political leaders since 1970

1970–71 General Juan Torres Gonzáles (military), 1971–80 Colonel Hugo Bánzer Suárez (military), 1980–81 General Luis García (military), 1981–82 General Celso Torrelio Villa (military), 1982 General Guido Vildoso (military), 1982–85 Hernan Siles Zuazo (MNR), 1985–89 Victor Paz Estenssoro (MNR-Izquierda), 1989–93 Jaime Paz Zamora (MIR), 1993–97 Gonzalo Sanchez de Lozada (MNR), 1997– Hugo Bánzer Suárez (AND)

Latest elections

The June 1997 presidential election was won by the ADN candidate, Hugo Bánzer Suárez. As neither he nor any of his nine rivals had won an absolute majority, the final choice was passed to the National Congress. Bánzer secured 22% of the vote, against 18% for Juan Carlos Durán of the MNR,and 17% for Jaime Paz Zamora of the MIR.

The results of the concurrent congressional elections were as shown in the table below.

Bolivia latest election results

Party	Senate seats	Chamber of Deputies seats
ADN	13	33
MNR	3	26
MIR	6	25
UCS	2	21
Condepa	3	17
Others	2	8

Political history

Bolivia became a Spanish colony in 1538 and took its name from Simón Bolívar (1783–1830), the legendary figure who liberated it in 1825. Since then it has had a very chequered political history, experiencing more than 60 revolutions, 70 presidents, and 11 constitutions. Distracted by its internal problems, Bolivia lost large tracts of land to its three neighbors, Chile in 1884, Brazil in 1903, and Paraguay in 1938.

In 1951 Dr Victor Paz Estenssoro (b. 1907), who had founded the MNR in 1942, returned from exile in Argentina to fight the presidential election. He failed to get an absolute majority and the sitting president transferred power to an army junta. However, a popular uprising, supported by the MNR and a section of the army, demanded the return of Paz, who assumed the presidency the following year and immediately embarked on a program of social reform.

Paz lost the 1956 election to an MNR colleague who was to become a bitter rival, Hernán Siles Zuazo, but was returned to power in 1960. In 1964, following strikes and civil disorder, a coup led by the vice president, General René Barrientos, overthrew the Paz government and a military junta was installed. Two years later Barrientos fought for and won the presidency. He met great opposition from leftwing groups and in 1967 a guerrilla uprising, led by Ernesto ('Che') Guevara (1928–67) was only put down with US help. In 1969 President Barrientos was killed in an air crash and replaced by the vice-president. He, in turn, was replaced by General Alfredo Ovando, who, after a military power struggle, was ousted by General Juan Torres, who was also to be removed in 1971 by a fellow officer, Colonel Hugo Banzer.

Banzer announced a return to constitutional government but another attempted coup in 1974 prompted him to postpone elections, ban all trade union and political activity, and proclaim that there would be military government until at least 1980. Succumbing to mounting pressure for a return to a more democratic form of government, Banzer agreed to elections in 1978. There were allegations of widespread electoral fraud, prompting, in the same year, two more military coups. Elections were eventually held in 1979 and the two ex-presidents who had been rivals before, in 1956, Dr Siles and Dr Paz, received virtually identical votes. An interim administration was installed, pending fresh elections. An election in 1980 proved equally inconclusive and was followed by the 189th military coup in Bolivia's 154 years of independence.

General Luis García was installed as president but forced to resign the following year after allegations of involvement in drug trafficking. He was replaced by General Celso Torrelio who promised to fight corruption and return the country to democratic government within three years. In 1982 a mainly civilian cabinet was appointed but rumours of an impending coup resulted in Torrelio's resignation. A military junta, led by the hardliner, General Guido Vildoso, was installed. Because of the worsening economic situation, the junta decided to ask Congress to elect a president and Dr Siles, who had won most votes in the close elections of 1979 and 1980, was chosen to head a coalition cabinet. Economic aid from the United States and Europe, which had been cut off in 1980, resumed but the economy continued to deteriorate. There was widespread opposition to the government's austerity measures and, in an attempt to secure national unity, President Siles even embarked on a five-day hunger strike.

A general strike and another abortive army coup followed in 1985, prompting President Siles to resign. Again, the election was inconclusive, with no candidate winning an absolute majority. The veteran MNR leader, Dr Paz, at the age of 77, was chosen by Congress as the new president. Despite strict austerity measures, including a wage freeze, to attempt to curb inflation, which had reached 23,000% in 1985, Bolivia's economy worsened.

In the 1989 presidential election there was no conclusive result, the eventual new president, Jaime Paz Zamora (MIR), being determined by the National Congress in August 1989. After negotiations, he formed a coalition government with the ADN and Christian Democrats.

The 1993 presidential election was decided in a similar fashion, Gonzalo Sánchez de Lozada (b. 1930), representing the MNR, eventually being elected. In the concurrent National Congress elections the MNR won most seats but not an overall majority. A government was eventually formed with the support of the UCS and the small centrist Free Bolivia Movement (MBL). By

1994 the annual inflation rate had been brought down to single figures and the Sánchez administration was encouraging foreign inward investment in the country's state-owned industry.

The June 1997 presidential election saw candidates from the five main parties each secure between 16% and 22% of the vote, and the former dictator, the rightwing Hugo Bánzer, was elected by the National Congress. The 71-year-old Bánzer pledged to continue with the MNR's free-market reforms and pursue its war against cocaine manufacturing and trafficking.

BRAZIL

The Federative Republic of Brazil
A República Federativa do Brasil

Capital: Brasília

Social and economic data
Area: 8,512,000 sq km/3,286,500 sq miles
Population: 153,725,000[*]
Pop. density per sq km/sq mi: 18/47[*]
Urban population: 77%[**]
Literacy rate: 75%[**]
GDP: $579,800 million[*]; per-capita GDP: $ 3,770[*]

Government defense spending (% of GDP): 1.5%[*]
Currency: real
Economy type: middle income
Labor force in agriculture: 29%[**]
Unemployment rate: 6.2%[*]
[*] 1995.
[**] 1992.

Head of state and head of government
President Fernando Henrique Cardoso, since 1995

Ethnic composition
There is a wide range of ethnic groups, including about 55% of European origin, mainly Portuguese, Italian, and German, about 38% of mixed parentage, and about 6% of Black African origin, as well as Native Americans and Japanese. The official and almost universally used language is Portuguese. English and Spanish are also spoken.

Religions
Nearly 90% of the population is Roman Catholic, the rest being Protestant or Spiritualist.

Political features
State type: liberal democratic
Date of state formation: 1822
Political structure: federal
Executive: limited presidential
Assembly: two-chamber
Party structure: multiparty
Human rights rating: 69%
International affiliations: AG (observer), ALADI, AP, G-11, G-15, G-24, IAEA, IBRD, IMF, IWC, Lusophone, Mercosur, NAM (observer), OAS, RG, SELA, UN, WTO

Local and regional government
Brazil is divided into five geographical regions, central-west, northeast, north, southeast, and south. The regions are subdivided into 23 states, three territories, and a federal district (Brasília). The populations of the states range from about 300,000 to over 25 million, the federal district has a population of nearly 1.2 million, and the populations of the territories vary from just over 1,000 to nearly 80,000. Each state has a constitution modelled on that of the federal constitution, with an elected single-chamber assembly and governor. The governor of the federal district is appointed by and directly responsible to the president.

The powers and duties of the federal government are set out in the constitution and include responsibility for external affairs, defense, and nationwide services, such as communications, education, agriculture, and maritime and labor law. The residue of powers and duties is left with the states.

Below state level there are municipalities with elected councils and mayors.

Political system

The 1988 constitution provides for a federal system, based broadly on the US model, with a two-chamber National Congress consisting of a Senate of 81 members and a Chamber of Deputies of variable size. The number of deputies is determined by the population of each state and each territory is represented by one deputy. The Chamber of Deputies had 513 members in 1994. Senators are elected on the basis of one per state for an eight-year term, at four-year intervals for one-third and two-thirds of the seats alternatively. Deputies are elected for a four-year term. Elections to the lower chamber are by universal adult suffrage, through a party list system of voting, while Senate elections are by simple plurality voting. Voting is compulsory for people between the ages of 18 and 69 and optional for people younger than 18, or older than 69, or illiterate. Senators must be at least 35 and deputies 21 years of age.

The constitution also provides for a president to be elected by universal adult suffrage for a five-year term, governing through a cabinet of his or her own choosing. The constitution was amended in May 1994 to reduce the presidential term to four years, and in 1997 to allow for re-election.

The 1988 constitution which replaced that of 1969, which had been amended several times, transferred considerable power from the president to Congress, placing the executive somewhere between a limited presidential and a parliamentary one. In a national referendum held in 1993, there was a vote in favor of the current presidential system and against a parliamentary system or restoration of the monarchy.

Other novel features of the constitution include the extension of the franchise to 16-year-olds and an unusual legal device, the *habeas data*, which gives people the right of access to personal files held by the National Intelligence Agency.

Political parties

Historically, Brazilian political parties were built on the power of landowners who were also the local political bosses. As the country experienced its succession of military and civilian rulers, in the period after 1945, so the parties adapted to the changing political scene, regularly regrouping. In 1965 all political parties were banned except for two which were given official recognition, one as the government party and one as the opposition. The practice of operating controlled parties was ended in 1979 and for a period other parties were permitted to operate under strictly controlled conditions. In 1985 all restrictions were removed and the free formation of parties was allowed.

Among 20 now operating, the most significant are the National Reconstruction Party (PRN), the Social Democratic Party (PSDB), the Brazilian Democratic Movement Party (PMDB), the Liberal Front Party (PFL), the Democratic Labor Party (PDT), the Workers' Party (PT), the Brazilian Labor Party (PTB), and the Brazilian Progressive Party (PPB).

The PRN was formed in 1989 to promote the candidacy of Fernando Collor de Mello for the presidency. It has a right-of-center orientation.

The PSDB was formed in 1988 by dissidents from six other parties. It has a generally moderate centrist stance and is led by President Cardoso.

The PMDB was formed in 1980 as a direct descendant of an older party, the Brazilian Democratic Movement (MBD) which, between 1965 and 1979, was the official opposition party. It retained most of the moderate elements of the old MBD and in 1982 merged with the Popular Party (PP). Its orientation is center-left.

In 1984 some Social Democratic Party (PDS) members joined with others from the PMDB to fight the 1985 presidential election and formed the moderate center-right PFL, led now by Ricardo Fiuza. The PDT is another moderate left-of-center grouping and was formed in 1980.

The PT was the first independent labor party and also dates from 1980. Its orientation is left-of-center and it is led by Luis Inácio 'Lula' da Silva.

The PTB is a moderate center-left force, formed in 1980. The PPB was formed in September 1995 through the merger of three progressive rightwing parties. It has been the ally of the PSOB, PFL, and PMDB in the pro-Cardoso governing coalition.

Political leaders since 1970

1969–74 General Emilio Garrastazu Medici (military), 1974–78 General Ernesto Geisel (military), 1978–85 General João Baptista de Figueiredo (military), 1985 Tancredo Neves (PFL), 1985–89 José Sarney Costa (PDS), 1989–92 Fernando Collor de

Mello (PRN), 1992–94 Itamar Franco (PRN), 1995– Fernando Henrique Cardoso (PSDB)

Latest elections

The October 1998 presidential election resulted in the re-election of the PSDB candidate, Fernando Henrique Cardoso, who, with 53% of the vote, secured victory in the first round. His chief challenger, as in 1994, was the PT's Lula da Silva, who attracted 31% of the vote. Turnout was 80%.

The results of the concurrent Chamber of Deputies elections were as follows:

Brazil latest election results

Party	Seats
PFL*	112
PSDB*	101
PMDB*	82
PPB*	60
PT	55
PTB*	31
PDT	24
Others	48

* Members of governing coalition.

Political history

Brazil became a Portuguese colony from 1500 and in 1808 the king of Portugal, in the face of a French invasion of his country, moved the capital from Lisbon to Salvador in Brazil. He returned to Lisbon in 1821 leaving his son, Crown Prince Pedro (1798–1834), as regent. In 1822 Pedro declared Brazil an independent kingdom and assumed the title Emperor Pedro I. He was succeeded by his son, Pedro II (1825–91), who persuaded large numbers of Portuguese to emigrate, resulting in a rapid development of the center of the country, largely on the basis of slavery. In 1888 slavery was abolished, in 1889 a republic was established, and in 1891 a constitution for a federal state was adopted.

The 1920s saw great social unrest and the world economic crisis of 1930 produced a major revolt which brought Getúlio Vargas (1883–1954) to the presidency. He continued in office and, in the role of a benevolent dictator, influenced by the Italian leader, Benito Mussolini, set up a profascist state known as 'Estado Novo', until ousted by the army in 1945. General Eurico Dutra was elected president and a new constitution was adopted. In 1950 Vargas returned to power but in 1954, faced with the threat of impeachment, he committed suicide. He was succeeded by Juscelino Kubitschek. Six years later the capital was moved from Rio de Janeiro to Brasília.

In 1961 Janio Quadros won the presidency but resigned after seven months, to be succeeded by the vice president, João Goulart, who was suspected by the army of having leftwing leanings. They forced an amendment to the constitution, restricting presidential powers and creating the office of prime minister. However, a referendum in 1963 brought back a fully presidential system, with Goulart choosing his own cabinet.

Dissatisfaction with the civilian administration resulted in a bloodless coup in 1964, which brought General Humberto Castelo Branco to power. He immediately banned all political parties, then gave recognition to two artificially created groups on which he felt he could rely, the progovernment National Renewal Alliance (ARENA) and an opposition party, the Brazilian Democratic Movement (MBD). This heralded a 21-year period of military rule (1964–85) during which the Brazilian economy expanded rapidly, but social and political rights were severely restricted.

In 1967 Branco named Marshal Artur da Costa e Silva as his successor and a new constitution was adopted. In 1969, however, da Costa resigned because of ill health and a new military junta took over. In 1974 General Ernesto Geisel was chosen as president, under the terms of the constitution, by an electoral college and he continued in office until succeeded by General João Baptista de Figueiredo in 1978. The following year legislation was passed to allow a return to a multiparty operation, but under strictly controlled conditions. President Figueiredo continued in office until 1985, the last few years of his presidency witnessing a deterioration in the state of the economy with strikes and mass rallies calling for the return of full democratic government.

In 1985 restrictions on political activity were removed and Tancredo Neves became the first civilian president for 21 years, amid a nationwide wave of optimism. He died within months of assuming office and was succeeded by the vice-president, José Sarney Costa (b. 1930). The constitution was amended to provide for the election of the president by direct universal adult suffrage and a new constitution, creating a near-parliamentary executive, was adopted in October 1988.

In December 1989 Fernando Collor de Mello (b. 1949), governor of the state of Alagoas, emerged from comparative obscurity to be elected president at the age of 40. However, within a year of his taking office, disenchantment with his economic policies grew and in

September 1992, following allegations of past corruption, he was removed from office, prior to his impeachment. He was replaced by the vice president, Itamar Franco (b. 1931). A referendum held in 1993 rejected a move to a parliamentary system and restoration of the monarchy.

Franco's popularity declined as inflation continued to soar to over 2,000%, and he was also criticized for indiscreet behaviour during the 1994 Rio carnival. In a surprisingly successful attempt to control inflation, in July 1994 a new currency was introduced, the real, at parity with the US dollar.

In November 1994 the PSDB candidate, Fernando Cardoso, was elected president and his PSDB-PFL coalition won most seats, but not an overall majority, in the concurrent congressional elections. As the former finance minister, Cardoso had been the architect of the 'real plan'. In the following month the former president, Collor, was acquitted on charges of corruption because of insufficient evidence.

Financial pressures, caused by economic crises in Mexico in 1995 and in Asia in 1997–98, meant that President Cardoso was forced to raise interest rates sharply (to 50% in 1998) and cut government spending, to defend the value of the real. This led to labor unrest and opposition from within his own PSDB, as he backtracked on measures to relieve poverty and promote land reform. However, inflation, which was 7% in 1997, was kept under tight control, privatization was promoted, and foreign inward investment encouraged. Cardoso was re-elected in October 1998 amid a new financial crisis.

After the election, the crisis worsened, forcing, on 13 January 1999, a 9% devaluation of the currency, the real. Meanwhile, on 1 January 1999, President Cardoso put together a new broad-based cabinet, including ministers from the PFL, the PSDB, the PMDB, the PPB and the PTB, which together controlled around three-quarters of the seats in the Chamber of Deputies. By mid-1999, the economic situation had begun to stabilize, with interest rates being cut and the forecasts of GDP contraction during the years were halved to –2%. Nevertheless, President Cardoso's approval had fallen sharply amidst these economic difficulties.

CHILE

The Republic of Chile
República de Chile

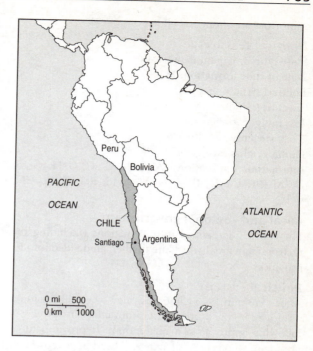

Capital: Santiago (the legislature meets at Valparaíso)

Social and economic data
Area: 756,950 sq km/292,260 sq miles
Population: 13,994,000[*]
Pop. density per sq km/sq mi: 18/48[*]
Urban population: 85%[**]
Literacy rate: 94%[**]
GDP: $59,150 million[*]; per-capita GDP: $4,230[*]
Government defense spending (% of GDP): 3.8%[*]
Currency: Chilean peso
Economy type: middle income
Labor force in agriculture: 19%[**]
Unemployment rate: 4.7%[*]
[*] 1995.
[**] 1992.

Head of state and head of government
President Eduardo Frei Ruiz-Tagle, since 1994

Ethnic composition
The population is fairly homogeneous, consisting of about 65% mestizos (offspring of Spanish American and Native American parents), and 30% European, the remainder being mainly Indian. Class is a more divisive factor than race. The official language is Spanish.

Religions
Roman Catholicism was the established religion until 1925 and it remains the dominant faith, being practised by about 80% of the population. Among the religious

minorities are about 30,000 Jews.

Political features

State type: emergent democratic
Date of state formation: 1818
Political structure: unitary
Executive: limited presidential
Assembly: two-chamber
Party structure: multiparty
Human rights rating: 80%
International affiliations: ALADI, APEC, G-11, G-15, IAEA, IBRD, IMF, IWC, NAM, OAS, RG, SELA, UN, WTO

Local and regional government

The country is divided into 13 regions (including the metropolitan area) which are further subdivided into 51 provinces.

Political system

After a coup in 1973 Chile was ruled by a military junta until a new constitution came into effect in July 1989, following approval in a referendum. It provides for a president, who is head of state and head of government, and a two-chamber assembly (or Congress) of a Senate and Chamber of Deputies. The president is elected by universal adult suffrage for a six-year term and appoints a cabinet of ministers, headed by a prime minister. Immediate re-election as president is prohibited. The Senate has 47 members, 38 popularly elected and nine appointed by the outgoing government and the Supreme Court. They serve an eight-year term, with one-half being elected every four years. The Chamber of Deputies has 120 members, popularly elected for a four-year term. Voting is compulsory.

Political parties

Of over 30 parties, the most significant are the Christian Democrat Party (PDC), the Socialist Party of Chile (PS), the Party for Democracy (PPD), the Party of National Renewal (RN), the Independent Democratic Union (UDI), the Union of the Center-Center (UCCP), and the Communist Party of Chile (PCCh).

The Coalition of Parties for Democracy (CPD) was formed in 1988 to oppose the Pinochet regime and includes the PDC, PS, PR, PPD, and other centrist and left-of-center groupings.

The PDC was formed in 1957. It has within it leftwing and centrist factions, but is predominantly a center-right force. The PS was formed in 1933. It has a leftwing orientation. The PPD is a left-of-center party within the CPD. The RN was founded in 1987 and is a rightwing party. The UDI is another rightwing party, formed in

1989. The UCCP is another rightwing grouping. The PCCh achieved legal status in 1990.

Political leaders since 1970

1970–73 Salvador Allende (Unidad Popular), 1973–90 General Augusto Pinochet (military), 1990–94 Patricio Aylwin (PDC), 1994– Eduardo Frei (PDC)

Latest elections

In the December 1993 presidential election the PDC candidate, Eduardo Frei, was a clear winner, with 58% of the vote.

In the December 1997 congressional elections, where turnout was 86%, the results were as follows:

Chile latest election results

Party	Senate seats	Chamber of Deputies seats
PDC	10	39
RN	2	23
UDI	3	17
PPD	0	16
PS	1	11
Others	0	14

Political history

The first European to sight Chile was Ferdinand Magellan (c. 1480–1521), in 1520, at which time the country was under Inca rule. It became part of the Spanish Empire 21 years later. It won its independence from Spain in 1818 and soon became a dominant power in western Latin America. Through most of the 20th century, however, there have been struggles between left- and rightwing political factions.

Between 1964 and 1970 the Christian Democrats, under Eduardo Frei (b. 1943), were in power, followed by a leftwing coalition led by Dr Salvador Allende (1908–73), who was the world's first democratically elected Marxist head of state. He promised to create social justice by constitutional means and embarked upon an extensive nationalization program, which included the US-owned copper mines. Allende was seen by the CIA in Washington as a pro-Cuban communist and opposition to him within Chile was encouraged. The culmination of this movement to overthrow him was an attack on the presidential palace in 1973 by the army, led by General Augusto Pinochet (b. 1915). The government was ousted and Allende killed, the new regime claiming he committed suicide. Pinochet became president and any opponents were imprisoned, after torturing, or just made to 'disappear'.

In 1976 Pinochet established what he called an

'authoritarian democracy', all political parties being banned, despite UN condemnation, and in 1978 he secured an endorsement of his policies through a referendum. In 1980 a new constitution was announced, as a 'transition to democracy' by 1989, but reports of imprisonments and tortures continued to be received by the world outside.

Opposition to the Pinochet regime grew, with widespread demands for a return to democratic government, and when in 1986 Pinochet, at the age of 71, announced that he was considering serving another eight-year term, opposition groups decided to work together to oppose him in the 1988 plebiscite to ratify him as the sole nominee for the presidency. The result of the plebiscite, answering the question whether or not Pinochet should continue for another term, was a 'No' vote of 55% and a 'Yes' vote of 43%. The general said he would honour the result but declined to step down before the end of his current term of office.

Eventually, in June 1989 the general agreed to constitutional changes which would permit fully pluralist politics, the amendments to be put forward for approval in a national plebiscite. The result was an overwhelming vote for change and in December 1989 Patricio Aylwin Azocár (b. 1915), leader of the Christian Democrats (PDC), was elected president.

His party also won the greatest number of seats in the House of Deputies but not an overall majority. However, he was able to form a stable government, founded on a multiparty Coalition for Democracy (CPD). The December 1993 presidential election was won by the CPD nominee, Eduardo Frei, and his Christian Democrat party was also successful in the congressional elections. A CPD coalition government was formed, and in the December 1997 assembly elections, the PDC-led government maintained majority in both chambers. In March 1998 Pinochet retired from the army and was made 'senator for life' despite earlier attempts to block the appointment. Later in the year the Spanish government attempted to extradite him, while on a visit to Britain, to put him on trial for war crimes against humanity.

This extradition order was granted by the British government in April 1999.

Faced with a sluggish economy, in June 1999, President Frei announced a package of public spending measures which were designed to reduce the level of unemployment. A month earlier, in May 1999, the ruling Concertacíon (CPD) coalition held a primary for the presidential election, due to be held in December 1999. Ricardo Lagos Escobar, a moderate social-democrat of the Socialist Party (PS), won a clear victory, defeating Andres Zaldivar of the PDC and thus emerging as the clear favourite to win in December 1999.

COLOMBIA

Republic of Colombia
República de Colombia

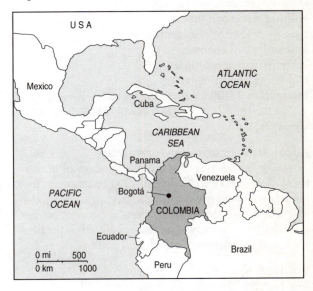

Capital: Bogotá

Social and economic data
Area: 1,138,994 sq km/439,768 sq miles
Population: 34,520,000[*]
Pop. density per sq km/sq mi: 30/78[*]
Urban population: 69%[**]
Literacy rate: 87%[*]
GDP: $70,260 million[*]; per-capita GDP: $2.035[*]
Government defense spending (% of GDP): 2.0%[*]
Currency: Colombian peso
Economy type: middle income
Labor force in agriculture: 28%
[*] 1995.
[**] 1992.

Head of state and head of government
President Andrés Pastrana Arango, since 1998

Ethnic composition
Although the main ethnic groups are of mixed Spanish,

Indian, and African blood, Colombia is one of the most Spanish of all South American countries and Spanish customs and values predominate. Spanish is the national language.

Religions
About 95% of the population is Roman Catholic and Roman Catholicism is sufficiently strong to be regarded as the quasi-state religion.

Political features
State type: liberal democratic
Date of state formation: 1830
Political structure: unitary
Executive: limited presidential
Assembly: two-chamber
Party structure: multiparty
Human rights rating: 60%
International affiliations: ACS, AG, ALADI, AP, G-3, G-11, G-24, IAEA, IBRD, IMF, NAM, OAS, RG, SELA, UN, WTO

Local and regional government
Although it does not have a federal system of government, the country is divided into 23 departments, four intendencies, and five commissaries, enjoying considerable autonomy. Below these levels are municipalities. Each department has a governor appointed by the president and there are regional elected assemblies.

Political system
The July 1991 constitution, which, with 397 articles, is one of the longest in the world, provides for a president who is head of state and head of government and a two-chamber Congress, consisting of a 102-member Senate and a 163-member House of Representatives.

The president is directly elected by universal adult suffrage for a four-year non-renewable term, by the majoritarian second-ballot system. Members of Congress are elected in the same way for the same term length. Of the 163 members of the House of Representatives, there must be two from each of the 23 national departments. Two seats in the House and in the Senate are reserved for ethnic minority groups. The president appoints a cabinet over which he or she presides.

Political parties
There are some 20 political parties, the most significant being the Liberal Party (PL), the Conservative Party (PSC), the April 19th Movement (ADM-19), and the National Salvation Movement (MSN). The PL and the

PSC have dominated the political scene for most of the 20th century but this dominance is being increasingly challenged.

Although there are strong democratic traditions, politics in Colombia have long been stained by violence between the two ruling parties and from leftwing opposition groups and the drug lords, based in Colombia's second city, Medellín, and in Cali.

The Liberal Party was founded in 1815. It is divided into two factions, the official group and the independent group, who call themselves New Liberalism. The party has a centrist orientation.

The Conservative Party was formed in 1849. It too has a history of internal factionalism but this is not as clearly defined as in the Liberal Party. Its political stance is right-of-center and claims nearly 3 million members.

The ADM-19 was a leftwing guerrilla group which reformed itself into a legitimate party in 1991.

The MSN is a right-of-center coalition which has come together in recent years after a breakaway, in 1990, from the PSC.

Political leaders since 1970
1970–74 Misael Pastrana Borrero (PSC), 1974–78 López Michelsen (PL), 1978–82 Julio Cesar Turbay Ayala (PL), 1982–86 Belisario Betancur Cuartas (PSC), 1986–90 Virgilio Barco Vargas (PL), 1990–94 Cesar Gaviria Trujillo (PL), 1994–98 Ernesto Samper (PL), 1998– Andrés Pastrana Arango (PSC)

Latest elections
The June 1998 presidential election was won by the PSC candidate, Andrés Pastrana Arango, with 50.6% of the second-round votes. He defeated Horacio Serpa Uribe of the PL. Turnout was 60%.

In the March 1998 congressional elections, where turnout was 45%, the results were as follows:

Colombia latest election results

Party	Senate seats	House of Representatives seats
PL	58	98
PSC	28	52
ADM-19	16	11

Political history
Colombia became a Spanish colony in the 16th century and obtained its independence in 1819, as part of a union with Ecuador, Panama, and Venezuela. In 1903 it became entirely independent. Since then two main political parties, the Conservatives and the Liberals,

have dominated Colombian politics. Between 1860 and 1884 the Liberals were in power, between 1884 and 1930 it was the Conservatives, between 1930 and 1946 the Liberals, and between 1946 and 1953 the Conservatives. In 1948 the leftwing mayor of the capital city, Bogotá, was assassinated and there followed a decade of near civil war, 'La Violencia', during which it is thought that well over a quarter of a million people died. The legacy of this war was the continuation of leftwing guerrilla activity through to the 1980s.

In 1957, in an effort to halt the violence, the Conservatives and Liberals agreed to form a National Front, with the presidency alternating between them. In 1970, the National Front was challenged by the National Popular Alliance (ANAPO), with a special appeal to the working classes, but the Conservative-Liberal cooperation continued and when in 1978 the Liberals won majorities in both chambers of Congress and the presidency they kept the National Front accord.

In 1982 the Liberals retained their majorities in Congress but Belisario Betancur won the presidency for the Conservatives. He sought a truce with the leftwing guerrillas by granting them an amnesty and freeing political prisoners. He also embarked upon a radical program of public works expenditure. His plans suffered a major blow in 1984 when his minister of justice, who had been using harsh measures to curb drug dealing, was assassinated. Betancur's reaction was to strengthen his anti-drug campaign.

In the May 1986 elections the presidency changed hands again, going to the Liberal, Virgilio Barco Vargas, by a record margin. In 1990 the presidency was again won by the Liberals.

The new young president, Cesar Gaviria, embarked on further constitutional reform and an effort of reconciliation with the guerrilla groups who were opposing him. In 1991, as a new constitution came into effect, most, including the April 19th Movement (ADM-19), abandoned their struggle and converted themselves into political parties. However, the Colombian Revolutionary Armed Forces (FARC) and the National Liberation Army (ELN) remained active throughout the 1990s, sabotaging oil pipelines.

The Liberals dominated the first elections under the new constitution, winning the presidency and a majority in both congressional chambers. Meanwhile, the war against the drug lords continued, with Pablo Escobar (1949–93), leader of the Medellín ring, being killed in December 1993 while attempting to avoid arrest after escaping from prison in 1992. However, another drugs cartel, based in Cali, remained a serious threat.

In the March 1994 elections the Liberals retained their control of Congress, but with a reduced majority, and the party's candidate, Ernesto Samper (b. 1951), won the presidency.

In 1995 President Samper decreed a state of emergency to fight the rising wave of violence and guerrilla activities and in the summer of 1995 six of the top seven Cali drugs cartel leaders were arrested and imprisoned. However, there were concurrent allegations that the 1994 Samper presidential campaign had received at least $6 million in 'dirty money' from the Cali cartel. This led to mounting calls for the president to resign and investigations by a committee of Congress.

The PL secured 56% of the vote in the March 1998 congressional elections, to 25% for the PSC and 19% for the ADM-19. However, in June 1998 the PSC candidate, Andrés Pastrana Arango won the presidency, ending 12 years of PL rule. Pastrana, whose father had been president 1970–74, was a center-right advocate of free-market reforms.

During the spring of 1999 President Pastrana sought to promote peace negotiations with the left-wing FARC and ELN guerrillas who remained active, particularly in northern Colombia, in killings, kidnappings, and confrontations with right-wing paramilitaries. However, his efforts were thwarted by the FARC continuing to launch large and bloody offensives. Consequently, with guerrilla violence continuing, the economy in recession and the currency, the peso, having to be devalued by 10% in June 1999, Pastrana's public approval rating plunged.

ECUADOR

Republic of Ecuador
República del Ecuador

Capital: Quito

Social and economic data
Area: 270,670 sq km/104,506 sq miles
Population: 11,221,000[*]
Pop. density per sq km/sq mi: 141/107[*]
Urban population: 58%[**]
Literacy rate: 80%[**]
GDP: $15,995 million[*]; per-capita GDP: $1,425[*]
Government defense spending (% of GDP): 3.4%[*]
Currency: sucre

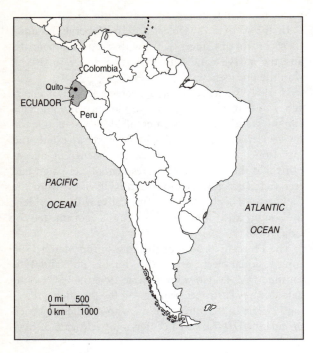

Economy type: middle income
Labor force in agriculture: 38%**
Unemployment rate: 7.1%*
* 1995.
** 1992.

Head of state and head of government
President Jamil Mahuad Witt, since 1998

Ethnic composition
The population is about 55% mestizo (offspring of Spanish American and Native American parents), 25% Indian, 10% Spanish, and 10% African. The official language is Spanish but Quecha and other indigenous languages are spoken.

Religions
About 90% of the population is Roman Catholic. There are also other Christian and Jewish minorities.

Political features
State type: liberal democratic
Date of state formation: 1830
Political structure: unitary
Executive: limited presidential
Assembly: one-chamber
Party structure: multiparty
Human rights rating: 83%
International affiliations: AG, ALADI, AP, G-11, IAEA, IBRD, IMF, IWC, NAM, OAS, RG, SELA, UN

Local and regional government
Ecuador is not a fully federal state, but has a devolved system of 21 provinces, including the Galápagos Islands, each administered by an appointed governor.

Political system
The 1979 constitution underwent reform in 1998. It provides for a president, elected by universal adult suffrage for a nonrenewable four-year term, and a single-chamber National Congress, the Chamber of Representatives, with 121 members. Voting in presidential elections is by the majoritarian system of second ballot, with a second-round run-off needed if the leading candidate fails to secure at least 45% of the vote, and for the Congress by the party list system of proportional representation. There are 20 deputies elected from national lists and 105 from two- or multi-seat constituencies. The Chamber's term is four years and voting is compulsory. In November 1997 a 70-member Constitutional Assembly was elected to frame amendments to the constitution.

Political parties
There are some 18 political parties, the most significant being Popular Democracy (PD), the Democratic Left (ID), the Social Christian Party (PSC), the Conservative Party (PCE), the Ecuadorean Roldosist Party (PRE), and the Alfarista Radical Front (FRA).

The ID was formed in 1970 as a result of a split in the Liberal Party (PLR: estd. 1895). It has a moderate socialist orientation. The PSC is a rightwing party formed in 1951 and led by León Febres Corero. The PCE is Ecuador's oldest party, having been established in 1855, and has a rightwing orientation. The PRE is a populist party formed in 1982. DP is a Christian Democrat center-right party formed in 1978. FRA is a small centrist party established in 1972. It is led by Fabián Alarcón.

Political leaders since 1970
1968–72 José María Velasco (PLR), 1972–76 General Guillermo Rodríguez Lara (military), 1976–79 General Alfredo Poveda Burbano (military), 1979–81 Jaime Roldos Aguilera (Coalition of Popular Forces: CFP), 1981–84 Osvaldo Hurtado Larrea (CFP), 1984–88). Febres Cordero (PSC), 1988–92 Rodrigo Borja Cevallos (ID), 1992–96 Sixto Durán Ballén (PUR), 1996–97 Abdala Bucaram Ortiz (PRE), 1997–98 Fabián Alarcón Rivera (FRA), 1998– Jamil Mahuad Witt (DP).

Latest elections
In the May 1998 elections for the National Congress, seats were won as follows:

Ecuador latest election results

Party	National Congress seats
DP	29
ID	17
PRE	16
PSC	13
Others	46

The 1998 presidential election was won by the DP candidate, Jamil Mahuad Witt. He secured 35% of the first-round vote, finishing ahead of five other candidates, and 51% of the second-round vote, defeating Alvaro Noboa Ponton of the PRE. Turnout was 64%, and 14% of first-round votes lost were either blank or invalid.

Political history

Under Spanish rule from the 16th century, Ecuador became part of Gran Colombia in 1822 and then a fully independent state in 1830. From independence onwards the political pendulum has swung from the Conservatives to the Liberals, from civilian to military rule, and from democratic to dictatorial government. By 1948 some stability was evident and eight years of Liberal government ensued.

In 1956 Camilo Ponce became the first Conservative president for 60 years. Four years later a Liberal, José María Velasco, who had been president in 1933–35, 1944–47 and 1952–56, was re-elected. He was deposed in a 1961 coup by the vice-president, who, in the following year, was himself dismissed and replaced by a military junta. In 1968 Velasco returned from exile and took up the presidency again. Another coup in 1972 put the military back in power until, in 1979, when it seemed as if Ecuador had returned permanently to its pre-1948 political pattern, a new, democratic constitution was adopted.

The 1979 constitution has survived, even though a deteriorating economy has resulted in strikes, demonstrations, and, in 1982, a state of emergency. In the 1984 elections no party or coalition of parties won a clear majority in the National Congress, and León Febres Cordero won the presidency for the PSC, on a promise of 'bread, roofs and jobs'. With no immediate support in Congress, his policies seemed likely to be blocked but in 1985 he won a majority there when five opposition members decided to change allegiance and support him. At the end of his term of office, Cordero was succeeded by one of the leaders of the leftwing Progressive

Democratic Front coalition, Rodrigo Borja. However, President Borja's austerity measures failed to find public favor.

In July 1992 Sixto Durán Ballén (b. 1922), representing the conservative coalition led by the Republican Unity Party (PUR), won the presidency and in the Congress the PSC emerged as the largest party, followed by the PRE and PUR. Lacking an overall majority in Congress, Duran called for a 'national consensus' and formed a coalition which included PSC members and others from the business sector. A privatization program was launched and Ecuador, which had been a significant oil producer since the 1970s, withdrew from OPEC in November 1992 to enable it to increase its output levels. In February 1995 a long-running border dispute with Peru was finally resolved. In September 1995, the Durán Ballén administration was rocked by Parliament's dismissal of three key ministers, including the vice president and finance minister, who were accused of masterminding the country's biggest corruption scandal.

In July 1996 Abdalá Bucaram Ortiz of the PRE was elected president on a populist platform to help the poor. However, faced with a budget deficit, he switched to a free-market program, including privatization, and instituted a 300% rise in utility prices and an austerity budget. This, along with government corruption, provoked unprecedented, violent, nationwide strikes in February 1997. Congress declared the eccentric Bucaram, who was known as 'El Loco' ('the madman') as mentally unfit for office, thus removing him without the need for impeachment proceedings. The speaker, Fabián Alarcón, was made president in February 1997 for an 18-month interim term, heading a center-left government, and pledging to undertake political reforms. He established an anti-corruption commission and constitutional changes were made, including the abolition of midterm congressional elections. In July 1998 the Popular Democracy (DP) candidate, Jamil Mahuad, the mayor of Quito, was elected president.

In March 1999 a state of emergency was briefly imposed by President Mahuad and banks were temporarily closed, as the country faced a currency collapse and anti-austerity strikes by public sector workers. Tough measures by the government to cut the budget deficit helped stabilise the currency, but, in July 1999, further strikes by transport workers, triggered by rising fuel prices, led to the president's fresh imposition of a 60-day national state of emergency.

GUYANA

The Cooperative Republic of Guyana

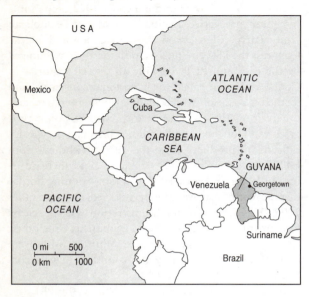

Capital: Georgetown

Social and economic data
Area: 215,000 sq km/83,012 sq miles
Population: 825,000*
Pop. density per sq km/sq mi: 4/10*
Urban population: 34%**
Literacy rate: 92%**
GDP: $495 million*; per-capita GDP: $600*
Government defense spending (% of GDP): 1.1%*
Currency: Guyana dollar
Economy type: low income
Labor force in agriculture: 20%*
* 1995.
** 1992.

Head of state (executive)
President Janet Jagan, since 1997

Head of government
Prime Minister Sam Hinds, since 1992

Ethnic composition
About 51% of the population are East Indians, descended from settlers from the subcontinent of India, and about 43% are Afro-Indian. There are also small Native American, Chinese, and European minorities. Racial tensions led to violence in 1964 and 1978. English is the official language but Hindi, Urdu, and Amerindian dialects are also spoken.

Religions
There are about 430,000 Hindus, 125,000 Anglicans, 120,000 Muslims, and 94,000 Roman Catholics.

Political features
State type: liberal democratic
Date of state formation: 1966
Political structure: unitary
Executive: limited presidential
Assembly: one-chamber
Party structure: two-party
Human rights rating: N/A
International affiliations: ACP, ACS, AP, CARICOM, CW, IBRD, IMF, NAM, OAS, SELA, UN, WTO

Local and regional government
The country is divided into ten regions, each with an elected Regional Democratic Council, which is represented on the National Assembly by one member. Day-to-day administration is by an appointed commissioner.

Political system
Guyana is a sovereign republic within the British Commonwealth. The 1980 constitution provides for a single-chamber National Assembly of 65 members, 53 elected by universal adult suffrage, through a party list system of proportional representation, and 12 elected by the regions. They serve a five-year term. The executive president is the nominee of the party winning most votes in the National Assembly elections and serves for the life of the Assembly. The president appoints a cabinet which is collectively responsible to the Assembly, and is headed by a prime minister, who is known also as a first vice president. The political system therefore represents an adaptation of a parliamentary to a limited presidential executive.

Political parties
Although there are some 14 active parties and a proportional representation system of voting is used, a two-party system effectively operates, the main parties being the People's National Congress (PNC), the People's Progressive Party (PPP), and the Civic Party.

The PNC was formed in 1955 by dissidents from the PPP. Its supporters are mainly Afro-Indians. It has a centrist orientation.

The PPP dates from 1950. It is a leftwing reformed-Marxist party and draws its support mainly from people of Indian descent.

The Civic Party, which aligned itself with the PPP in the 1997 general election, is a grouping of business executives and professionals. Its leader is Sam Hinds.

Political leaders since 1970

1964–85 Forbes Burnham (PNC), 1985–92 Desmond Hoyte (PNC), 1992–97 Cheddi Jagan (PPP), 1997– Janet Jagan (PPP)

Latest elections

In the December 1997 general election the PPP, together with the Civic Party, won 36 of the 53 seats. The PNC won 26 seats. The PPP-Civic Party secured 56% of the vote and the PNC 42%.

Political history

Guyana was originally a Dutch colony which was seized by Britain in 1814. It became a colony of the British Empire, as British Guiana, with large numbers of Indian and Chinese laborers imported to work on sugar plantations. It achieved full independence, within the Commonwealth, in 1966.

The move from colonial to republican status was gradual and not entirely smooth. In 1953 a constitution, providing for free elections to an assembly, was introduced and the leftwing People's Progressive Party (PPP), led by Dr Cheddi Jagan (1918–97), won the popular vote. Within months, however, the United Kingdom government suspended the constitution and put in its own interim administration, claiming that the PPP threatened to become a communist dictatorship.

In 1957 a breakaway group from the PPP founded a new party, the People's National Congress (PNC), which was socialist, rather than Marxist – Leninist. A revised constitution was introduced at the end of 1956 and fresh elections were held in 1957. The PPP won again and Jagan became chief minister. Internal self-government was granted in 1961 and, with the PPP again the successful party, Jagan became prime minister.

A system of proportional representation, based on party lists, was introduced in 1963 and in the 1964 elections, under the new voting procedures, the PPP, although winning most votes, did not have an overall majority so a PPP-PNC coalition was formed, with the PNC leader, Forbes Burnham (1923–85), as prime minister. This coalition took the country through to full independence in 1966.

The PNC won the 1968 election and in 1970 legislation was passed to make Guyana a 'Cooperative Socialist Republic' within the Commonwealth. The PNC was again successful in the 1973 general election, but the PPP, dissatisfied with the results, claiming that there had been ballot-rigging, decided to boycott the Assembly. Then, in 1976, it partly relented, offering the government its 'critical support'. Discussions began about framing a new constitution and in 1980, after a referendum, a new version was adopted. It turned a parliamentary executive into a limited presidential one, making the president both head of state and head of government.

The 1981 elections, which were declared fraudulent by the opposition parties, made Burnham the new executive president. The following years of his administration were marked by a deteriorating economy and cool relations with the United States, whose invasion of Grenada he condemned. He died in August 1985 and was succeeded by Desmond Hoyte (b. 1929).

Hoyte faced problems with the economy, which led the government to promote inward investment. This had a measure of success, with GDP growing by 7% per year during 1992 and 1993. Hoyte was also confronted with criticisms of unnecessary delays in producing accurate electoral lists. This resulted in a delay in the holding of a general election, which was due in December 1991. When the election was eventually held, in October 1992, the PPP, led by the veteran politician, Cheddi Jagan, won a clear victory and the contest was generally considered to have been the fairest since independence. In 1993 a program of privatization was approved by parliament.

In March 1997 President Jagan died after a suspected heart attack, and Sam Hinds was made his interim replacement. The late president's wife, Janet Jagan, a former US citizen, replaced Hinds as prime minister, before, following parliamentary elections, they switched positions in December 1997. The 77-year-old Jagan became the country's first female and first white president. She had helped found the PP, with her late husband, in 1950.

In 1998 the Caribbean Community-brokered an agreement between the PPP/CIVIC and the PNC parties to reform the 1998 constitutional and during 1999 a 20-member Constitutional Reform Commission gathered together ideas for presentation to the National Assembly.

PARAGUAY

The Republic of Paraguay
La República del Paraguay

Capital: Asuncil

Social and economic data

Area: 406,750 sq km/157,047 sq miles

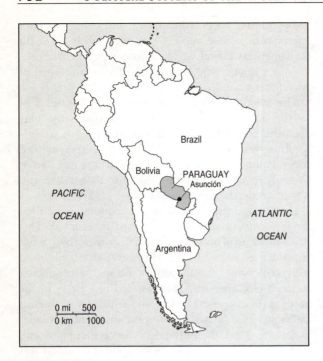

Population: 4,700,000*
Pop. density per sq km/sq mi: 12/30*
Urban population: 49%**
Literacy rate: 88%*
GDP: $8,160 million*; per-capita GDP: $1,735*
Government defense spending (% of GDP): 1.4%*
Currency: guaraní
Economy type: middle income
Labor force in agriculture: 49%**
Unemployment rate: 4.4%*
* 1995.
** 1992.

Head of state and head of government
President Luis Angel González Macch, since 1999

Ethnic composition
Paraguay is unusual in that, instead of the Spanish colonizers assimilating the indigenous population, the reverse has happened, so that now less than 5% of the population can be said to be clearly Spanish or Indian. The overwhelming majority are, therefore, mixed-race mestizos. Spanish is the official language but the majority of people speak Guarani, an indigenous Indian language.

Religions
Roman Catholicism is the established religion and 90% of the population practises it, but religious freedom for all is guaranteed in the constitution. There are also Anglican and Baptist minorities.

Political features
State type: emergent democratic
Date of state formation: 1811
Political structure: unitary
Executive: limited presidential
Assembly: two-chamber
Party structure: multiparty
Human rights rating: 70%
International affiliations: AG (observer), ALADI, IAEA, IBRD, IMF, Mercosur, OAS, RG, SELA, UN, WTO

Local and regional government
The country is divided into 19 departments, each administered by a governor appointed by the president. The departments are further subdivided into municipalities, each with a small elected board. The largest municipalities have appointed mayors.

Political system
The 1992 constitution provides for a president, who is head of state and head of government, and a two-chamber assembly, the National Congress, consisting of a Senate and Chamber of Deputies. The president is elected by universal adult suffrage for a five-year non-renewable term. The 45-member Senate and 80-member Chamber are also elected by universal adult suffrage, through a regionally based party list system of proportional representation, and serve a five-year term. The president, who has veto powers, is assisted by an elected vice president and appoints and leads the cabinet, which is called the Council of Ministers. Voting is compulsory.

Political parties
For many years there was a 'model' two-party system of Conservatives versus Liberals but now there are some 13 active parties, the most significant being the National Republican Association (ANR-PC), also known as the Colorado Party; the Authentic Radical Liberal Party (PLRA); the National Encounter (EN); the Radical Liberal Party (PLR); and the Liberal Party (PL).

The ANR-PC was founded in 1887 and was in power continuously until 1904 and returned to power from 1946 to the present day. It has traditionally received the support of the military and contains two major factions, the militants and the traditionalists, and three smaller factions. Its overall orientation is right of center and it has over 900,000 members.

The PLRA is the major surviving part of the old Liberal Party which was originally formed in 1887. It has a center-left orientation.

The Liberal Party also exists in its own right (PL) and in another form, the PLR. Both have centrist orientations.

The EN is a coalition formed by supporters of the former president, General Stroessner. It has a right-of-center orientation.

Political leaders since 1970

1954–89 General Alfredo Stroessner Mattiauda (military), 1989–93 General Andrés Rodríguez (ANR-PC), 1993–98 Juan Carlos Wasmosy (ANR-PC), 1998– Raúl Cubas Grau (ANR-PC), 1999– Luis Angel González Macchi (ANR-PC)

Latest elections

The May 1998 presidential election was won by the Colorado Party candidate, Raúl Cubas Grau. He secured 54% of the vote, defeating Domingo Laíno of the PLRA-EN 'Democratic Alliance'. Turnout was a record 85%.

The results of the concurrent congressional elections were as follows:

Paraguay latest election results

Party	Senate seats	Chamber of Deputies seats
ANR-PC	24	45
PLRA-EN	20	35
Other parties	1	0

Political history

Paraguay was first colonized by Spain in 1537 and soon became a major settlement, the Jesuits arriving to convert the Indians in 1609. It achieved full independence in 1811, but, under the dictator General José Francia, became isolated between 1814 and 1840. As a landlocked country, it needed access to the sea and this involved it in a violent and damaging war with Brazil, Argentina, and Uruguay between 1865 and 1870, which resulted in the loss of half its people and much territory. The two main political parties, Conservative and Liberal, were both founded in the late 1880s. There then followed a period of political instability until the Liberal leader, Edvard Schaerer, came to the presidency in 1912 and formed an administration which gained foreign confidence and attracted foreign investment. This relative stability continued, even though many of the presidencies were

short-lived, until the Chaco Wars erupted with Bolivia between 1929 and 1935. Paraguay was the victor but, again, the cost was great on both sides.

After 1940 Paraguay was mostly under the control of military governments led by strong autocratic leaders. General Morinigo was president from 1940 to 1947 and General Alfredo Stroessner (b. 1912), the commander in chief from 1951, became president in a coup in 1954. He was re-elected in 1958, 1963, 1968, 1973, 1978, 1983, and 1988. During the 1977–81 US presidency of Jimmy Carter, the repressive Stroessner regime came under strong criticism for its violation of human rights and this resulted in some tempering of the general's ruthless rule. Criticism by the succeeding rightwing 1981–89 US administration of President Ronald Reagan was less noticeable. Stroessner maintained his supremacy by ensuring that the armed forces and business community shared in the spoils of office and by preventing any opposition groups from coalescing into a credible challenge.

From 1984 onwards there was increased speculation about the eventual succession to the presidency. There was a division of opinion within his own party, the militant faction favoring Stroessner seeking an eighth term, with his son, Gustavo, then succeeding him, and the traditionalists believing that he should retire in 1988. The general, however, decided to stay on and in February 1988 was re-elected for yet another term. Early in 1989, however, he was overthrown and forced into exile in Brazil by General Andrés Rodríguez, who replaced him. He promised early elections, which he and the Colorado Party won in 1989.

A new constitution was adopted in 1992 and under its terms the country's first genuinely free elections were held in May 1993. The presidency was won by the Colorado candidate, Juan Carlos Wasmosy (b. 1939), and his party also secured most seats in Congress, but not an overall majority. Without that majority, the new president tried to agree a 'governability pact' with the main opposition parties, but they were reluctant to support him without a promise of greater constitutional reform. Eventually a cabinet was appointed, criticized by the opposition as being too reactionary.

The Colorado Party was again successful in the May 1998 presidential election. Its presidential candidates General (retired) Lino César Oviedo had been banned, in April 1998, from standing for election after being sentenced to ten years' imprisonment for attempting a military coup in 1996. Consequently his running-mate, Raúl Cubas Grau, a wealthy engineer who had prospered during the Stroessner era, was elected instead. Cubas pledged to grant Oviedo a presidential pardon. In the May 1998 congressional elections, the Colorado Party regained the majority in both chambers which it had lost in 1990.

In August 1998 President Cubas issued a decree to commute General Oviedo's prison sentence. However, in December 1998 the Supreme Court declared this decree to be unconstitutional and ordered that Oviedo be returned to prison. Cubas sought to defy this verdict, declaring that the president was not subordinate to the Supreme Court. This prompted the attorney-general to recommend, in February 1999, that impeachment proceedings should be started against President Cubas. A power struggle then developed within the ruling Colorado Party, which culminated, on 23 March 1999, in Vice-President Argaña, who was fighting against the Cubas-Oviedo faction, being assassinated in Asunción by three men in military uniform, allegedly with connections to General Oviedo. Facing popular demonstrations and workers' strikes calling for his resignation and impeachment charges, on 28 March 1999 President Cubas resigned and fled to Brazil, where he was granted political asylum. Oviedo, meanwhile, fled to Argentina, while the Senate's president, Luis González Macchi took over as state president. The Supreme Court ruled, in April 1999, that Macchi could remain in office until 2003, serving out the remainder of Cubas's presidential term. In the same month, President Macchi carried out a major reshuffle of the military's leadership and appointed a new 'government of national unity'. It was dominated by the ruling Colorado Party, but also included ministers from the PLRA-EN opposition parties.

PERU

Republic of Peru
República del Perú

Capital: Lima

Social and economic data
Area: 1,285,220 sq km/496,226 sq miles
Population: 23,088,000[*]
Pop. density per sq km/sq mi: 18/47[*]
Urban population: 71%[**]
Literacy rate: 82%[**]
GDP: $55,020 million[*]; per-capita GDP: $2,380[*]

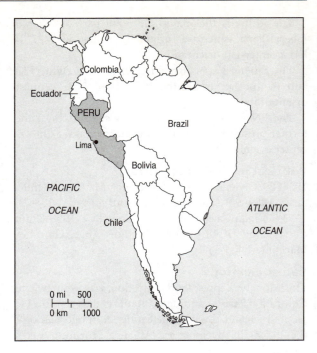

Government defense spending (% of GDP): 1.6[*]
Currency: new sol
Economy type: middle income
Labor force in agriculture: 35%[**]

Unemployment rate: 7.1%[*]

[*] 1995.
[**] 1992.

Head of state (executive)
President Alberto Keinya Fujimori, since 1990

Head of government
Prime Minister Victor Joy Way Rojas, since 1999

Ethnic composition
About 45% of the population is South American Indian, about 37% mestizo (offspring of Spanish American and Native American parents), 15% European, and 3% African. The three official languages are Spanish, Quecha, and Aymara.

Religions
Roman Catholicism is the official religion and about 90% of the population practises it, but all beliefs are tolerated.

Political features
State type: liberal democratic
Date of state formation: 1824

Political structure: unitary
Executive: limited presidential
Assembly: one-chamber
Party structure: multiparty
Human rights rating: 54%
International affiliations: AG (observer), ALADI, AP, G-11, IAEA, IBRD, IMF, IWC, NAM, OAS, RG, SELA, UN, WTO

Local and regional government

The country is divided into 11 regions, the constitutional province of Callao, and 24 departments. Each department is administered by an appointed prefect. Within the departments are provinces and districts administered by sub-prefects and governors respectively.

Political system

The 1993 constitution provides for an executive president, who is head of state, and a single-chamber 120-member National Congress. The president is elected by universal adult suffrage, using the second-ballot majoritarian system, for a five-year term, renewable once only. The National Congress is also elected by universal adult suffrage, from a national party list, for the same term length. The president appoints a prime minister and a Council of Ministers. Voting is compulsory for citizens aged 18–70.

Political parties

In the 1980s two groups dominated Peruvian politics, the American Popular Revolutionary Alliance (APRA) and an alliance of six leftwing parties called the Unified Left (IU). This dominance was challenged and disturbed in the 1990s and now, of some 30 groupings, the most significant, in addition to APRA and the IU, are Change '90 (Cambio '90), the New Majority, (Nueva Mayoría: NM), the Popular Christian Party (PPC), and the Union for Peru (UPP).

APRA was founded in 1924 in Mexico by Victor Raúl Haya de la Torre, who had been exiled from Peru by the military regime. It was originally formed to fight imperialism throughout South America but Peru was the only country in which it became established. Haya de la Torre returned in 1930 and APRA became the first popular party to challenge the Peruvian establishment and its rivalry with the military leadership has been a constant feature since the 1930s. It has a moderate leftwing orientation and a membership of 700,000.

The IU was formed in 1980 as an alliance of ten leftwing groups combining to fight the subsequent elections.

Cambio '90 was formed by a group of independent politicians to fight the 1990 presidential election. It has a right of center orientation and supports Alberto Fujimori.

The NM has a similar background and orientation but dates from 1992, when it joined Cambio '90 for the 1992 congressional elections.

The PPC was formed in 1966 by dissidents from the Christian Democratic Party (PDC), which was founded ten years earlier. It has a right-of-center orientation and 120,000 members.

The UPP is a new centrist grouping which supported the candidacy of the former United Nations secretary general, Javier Pérez de Cuéllar, for the presidency.

Political leaders since 1970

1968–75 General Juan Velasco Alvarado (military), 1975–78 Francisco Morales Bermúdez (military), 1978–80 Victor Raúl Haya de la Torre (APRA), 1980–85 Fernando Belaúnde Terry (AP), 1985–90 Alan García Pérez (APRA), 1990– Alberto Keinya Fujimori (Cambio '90)

Latest elections

Alberto Fujimori was re-elected in April 1995, securing 64.4% of the popular vote. His nearest rival, Javier Pérez de Cuéllar, obtained 21.8%.

In the May 1995 congressional elections, the results were as follows:

Peru latest election results

Party	Seats won
Cambio '90/Nueva mayoría	67
UPP	17
APRA	8
Other parties	28

Political history

From the 12th century Peru was the center of the South American Indian Inca empire, which extended during the 15th century from Quito in Ecuador to beyond Santiago in southern Chile. Its capital was at Cuzco in the Andes. The relatively advanced Inca civilization was destroyed by Spanish conquistadores, led by Francisco Pizarro (c. 1475–1541) in 1532–33, seizing and murdering the Inca king, Atahualpa (c. 1502–33). Thereafter, Spain had a firm grip on Peru and the people had to fight long and hard to obtain their independence. They were eventually victorious in 1824.

There was progress between 1844 and 1862 under the rule of General Ramón Castilla, but the country lost some territory to Chile after a war between 1879 and

1883, fought in alliance with Bolivia. At the start of the 20th century civilian governments held power, but from the mid-1920s rightwing dictatorships dominated. Amazonian territory was secured from Ecuador after victory in a brief war (1941) and in 1945 free elections returned. Although APRA was the largest party in Congress it was constantly thwarted by smaller conservative groups, anxious to protect their business interests. In 1948 a group of army officers, led by General Manuel Odría, ousted the elected government, banned APRA, and installed a military junta. Odría became president in 1950 and remained in power until 1956. In the meantime APRA had become a more moderate party and the ban on it had been lifted.

In 1963 military rule ended and Fernando Belaúnde Terry (b. 1913), the joint candidate of the Popular Action (AP) and Christian Democrat (PDC) parties, won the presidency, while APRA took the largest share of the Chamber of Deputies seats. Following economic problems and industrial unrest, Belaúnde was deposed in a bloodless coup in 1968 and the army returned to power with an all-military Council of Ministers, led by General Velasco. This instituted a populist program of land reform. Another bloodless coup in 1975 brought in General Morales Bermúdez, who judged that the time for a return to constitutional government had come.

Fernando Belaúnde was re-elected in May 1980 and embarked upon a program of agrarian and industrial reform but at the end of his presidency, in 1985, the country was in a state of economic and social crisis. Peru's fragile democracy somehow survived and Belaúnde became the first civilian president to hand over power to another constitutionally elected civilian, the young Social Democrat, Alan García Pérez (b. 1949).

García promised to end internal terrorism, which was being spearheaded by the extreme leftwing Sendero Luminoso ('Shining Path') guerrilla movement, which also exploited the illegal cocaine drugs trade, and to halt the decline in the economy. He declared his support for the Sandinista government in Nicaragua and criticized US policy throughout Latin America. He then embarked on a program of cleansing the army and police of the 'old guard'. By February 1986 about 1,400 had elected to retire. After trying to expand the economy, while controlling inflation with price and exchange controls, he announced his intention of nationalizing the banks and insurance companies. Meeting considerable opposition from the business community, the decision was postponed. By the middle of 1988 the economy had still not revived and García came under widespread pressure to

seek help from the IMF, as inflation reached the rate of 400% per month in 1990.

In the April 1990 presidential election a late entrant, a Catholic Japanese-born immigrant, Alberto Fujimori (b. 1938), sponsored by a group of independents, Cambio '90 (Change '90), defeated the Democratic Front candidate, the novelist Mario Vargas Llosa (b. 1937), a former communist who had moved to the center-right.

With the economy showing little sign of improvement, despite the launching of a privatization program, public unrest with the government grew and in April 1992 Fujimori decided to ally himself with the military, to avoid a potential coup. He suspended the constitution, detained opposition leaders, and temporarily ruled by decree. Accused of becoming a dictator, he said he would return the country to fully democratic government in 1993. In August of that year the Congress agreed to allow Fujimori an additional term, in 1995, and in December 1993, following approval in an October referendum, a new constitution was adopted.

In February 1994 Alfonso Bustamente, who had been appointed prime minister under the new constitution and had enjoyed considerable success in managing the economy, resigned following a disagreement with the president over his handling of a human rights issue. He was replaced by the foreign minister, Efrain Goldenberg Schreiber. In August 1994 President Fujimori revealed that he was removing his wife, Susana Higuchi, as first lady because of her political disloyalty. In the following month she announced that she had formed a new party, Harmony 21st Century, and that she would fight the next presidential election under its banner. However, her application to register as a candidate was rejected by the National Election Board (JNE) because she had not obtained the necessary minimum of 100,000 valid supporters. Meanwhile, there were sporadic outbreaks of violence by the Maoist Shining Path and Tupac Amaru Revolutionary Movement (MRTA) guerrillas. However, these were not seen as serious threats by the president. In 1992, Abimael Guzman Renoso, leader of the Shining Path, was captured and during 1994 more than 6,000 of the organization's guerrillas surrendered to the authorities.

With the economic situation improving rapidly, GDP growing by 12% in 1994, and inflation under control, Fujimori was challenged in the 1995 presidential election by the former UN secretary general, Javier Pérez de Cuéllar (b. 1920), whom he easily defeated, as well as his supporting party grouping. The New Majority alliance was successful in the concurrent congressional elections. In June 1995 President Fujimori controversially promulgated an amnesty for people who had previously been convicted of human rights crimes. His critics accused him of trying to win favor with the military, some of whom would benefit from the amnesty. In July 1995 Dante Cordova, the former education minister, was made prime minister. In March 1996 he resigned, following a disagreement with President Fujimori, and was replaced by Alberto Pandolfi Arbulu.

Between December 1996 and April 1997 MRTA guerillas sought to secure the release of 400 imprisoned comrades by holding several hundred hostages at the Japanese ambassador's residence in Lima. However, the 127-day siege by government commandos, ended on 22 April 1997 when all 14 rebels were shot dead. This decisive action briefly improved Fujimori's popularity. However, there was broader public concern at the influence of the military intelligence and at government corruption. In June 1998 Javier Valle Riestra, a human rights lawyer and a critic of the authoritarian features of the Fujimori regime, unexpectedly became the new prime minister, but he resigned after two months in office.

His replacement, in August 1998, Alberto Pandolfi Arbulu, was soon dismissed by Fujimori in January 1999, as the president sought to revive his flagging popularity. He chose as the new prime minister Victor Joy Way Rojas, the current president of Congress and a former industry minister, as part of a broader government reshuffle. During 1999 the government had successes with the capture of senior military leaders of the Maoist Shining Path guerrilla group, including Juan Carlos Rios, in January 1999, and Oscar Ramirez, in July 1999. However, there was great opposition to the prospect of Fujimori running for re-election in 2000, with trade unions launching a one-day protest general strike on 28 April1999 and opposition parties contemplating forming an anti-Fujimori united front in 2000.

SURINAME

Republic of Suriname
Republiek Suriname

Capital: Paramaribo

Social and economic data
Area: 163,265 sq km/63,037 sq miles

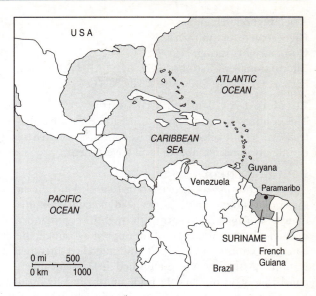

Population: 418,000[*]
Pop. density per sq km/sq mi: 3/7[*]
Urban population: 43%[**]
Literacy rate: 65%[**]
GDP: $1,300 million[*]; per-capita GDP: $3,110[*]
Government defense spending (% of GDP): 3.9%[*]
Currency: Suriname guilder
Economy type: middle income
Labor force in agriculture: 20%[**]
Unemployment rate: 12.7%[*]
[*] 1995.
[**] 1992.

Head of state and head of government
President Jules Wijdenbosch, since 1996

Ethnic composition
There is a very wide ethnic composition, including Creoles, East Indians, Indonesians, Africans, Amerindians, Europeans, and Chinese. Most people speak the native Creole language, Sranang Tongo, known as Negro English or taki-taki. Chinese, English, French, and Spanish are also spoken.

Religions
About 45% of the population is Christian, 28% Hindu, and 20% Muslim.

Political features
State type: emergent democratic
Date of state formation: 1975
Political structure: unitary
Executive: limited presidential

Assembly: one-chamber
Party structure: multiparty
Human rights rating: N/A
International affiliations: ACP, ACS, AP, CARICOM, IBRD, IMF, NAM, OAS, SELA, UN, WTO

Local and regional government

The country is divided into nine administrative districts, each controlled by a district commissioner. There is little or no representative local government.

Political system

The constitution was suspended in 1980 and in 1982 an interim president took office as head of state, with ultimate power held by the army, through its commander in chief who was also chair of the Supreme Council, the country's controlling group. A nominated 31-member National Assembly was established in January 1985, consisting of 14 military, 11 trade union, and six business nominees, and given 27 months in which to prepare a new constitution. This was approved in September 1987.

The 1987 constitution provides for a National Assembly of 51 members, elected by universal adult suffrage, through a simple plurality voting system for a five-year term. Once elected, the assembly then elects a president, who is both head of state and head of government, to serve a similar term. It describes the army as the 'vanguard of the people'.

Political parties

There are some 15 political parties, the main groupings being the New Front (NF), the National Democratic Party (NDP), and the Democratic Alternative 1991 (DA '91).

The NF, formerly called the Front for Democracy and Development (FDD), is a coalition of three parties: the Suriname National Party (NPS), the Progressive Reform Party (VHP), and the Suriname Labor Party (SPA). It was originally formed in 1987 to fight the election, and then recast in 1991.

The NPS began in 1946 and has largely Creole support. The VHP is a predominantly Indian party, and the SPA is a multiracial grouping. The NF has a left-of-center orientation.

The Party for National Unity and Solidarity (KTPI), which dates from 1947, was a member of the NF until after the 1996 general election and draws its support mainly from the Indonesian population.

The NDP was formed in 1987 by Desi Bouterse, mainly to legitimize his regime. It is based on Standvaste, a mass movement which resulted from the coup of 1982. It has a leftwing and military orientation.

The DA '91 is an alliance of three left-of-center parties, formed to fight the 1991 elections. It split after the 1996 general election, with part joining the NDP-led government.

Political leaders since 1970

1969–73 Jules Sedney (VHP), 1973–80 Henck Arron (NPS), 1980–82 Henk Chin A Sen (PNR), 1982–88 Lieutenant Colonel Desi Bouterse (military/NDP), 1988–90 Ramsewak Shankar (FDD), 1990–91 Johan Kraag (NPS), 1991–96 Ronald Venetiaan (NF), 1996– Jules Wijdenbosch (NDP)

Latest elections

The results of the May 1996 general election were inconclusive, with the NF winning most seats – 24 against 16 for the NDP – but fewer than the two-thirds majority needed to elect the president. In September 1996, in accordance with the constitution, the United People's Congress (UPC), comprising National Assembly members and regional and district councils, elected Jules Wijdenbosch, deputy leader of the NDP, president. He secured 438 votes, against 407 for Ronald Venetiaan of the NF.

Political history

Britain was the first European power to establish a settlement in Suriname, in 1651. In 1667 the Dutch took over, only to be removed by the British in 1799. The colony was finally restored to the Netherlands in 1819. As Dutch Guiana, it became in 1954 an equal member of the Kingdom of the Netherlands, with internal self-government. Full independence was achieved in 1975, with Johan Ferrier as president and Henck Arron, leader of the mainly Creole Suriname National Party (NPS), as prime minister.

In 1980 Arron's government was overthrown in an army coup but President Ferrier refused to recognize the military regime and appointed Henk Chin A Sen, of the Nationalist Republican Party (PNR), to head a civilian administration. Five months later the army staged another coup and President Ferrier was replaced by Chin A Sen. The new president announced details of a draft constitution which would reduce the role of the military, whereupon the army, led by Lieutenant Colonel Desi Bouterse, dismissed Chin A Sen and set up a Revolutionary People's Front.

There followed months of confusion in which a state of siege and then martial law were imposed. Between February 1980 and January 1983 there were no fewer than six attempted coups by different army groups.

Because of the chaotic conditions, aid from the Netherlands and the United States was stopped and Bouterse was forced to look elsewhere for assistance, making agreements with Libya and Cuba. The partnership between the army, the trade unions, and business, which had operated since 1981, eventually broke up in 1985 and Bouterse turned to the traditional parties which had operated prior to the 1980 coup.

The ban on political activity was lifted in anticipation of the adoption of a new constitution based on civilian rule. Leaders of the Creole, Indian, and Indonesian parties were invited to take seats on a Supreme Council, with Wym Udenhout, a former colleague of Bouterse, as interim prime minister. In September 1987 a new constitution was approved and elections to the National Assembly were held in November. The combined opposition parties, which had formed an alliance under the umbrella name Front for Democracy and Development (FDD), won an overwhelming victory and then elected Ramsewak Shankar as the new president. In December 1990 the military, under the direction of Commander in Chief Lieutenant Colonel Bouterse, persuaded Shankar to 'resign' and Johan Kraag, of the minority NPS, took over as interim president.

For the May 1991 general election the FDD was reformed into a coalition, the New Front (NF), which contained the Party for National Unity and Solidarity (KTPI), the Suriname National Party (NPS), the Suriname Labor Party (SPA), and the Progressive Reform Party (VHP). Eventually, the newly elected Congress chose Ronald Venetiaan, a former education minister, as president. In 1992 a peace agreement was reached between government troops and guerrillas who had destabilized the state. The May 1996 general election was inconclusive, and President Venetiaan declined to form a coalition with Bouterse. The NDP deputy leader, Jules Wijdenbosch, became president in September 1996, after the KTPI broke away from the NF to become allied to the NDP.

From the spring of 1999 a series of events rocked the governing coalition and led to mounting pressure for President Wijdenbosch's resignation. In April 1999 the president sacked Desi Bouterse, leader of the NDP, as his senior adviser, in response to the opening, in the Netherlands, of a trial (in absentia) in which the former dictator was charged with smuggling 1.5 tonnes of cocaine. A month later, the government endured a financial crisis, as the currency fell by a third in value and the inflation rate began to spiral beyond 10% a month. This provoked antigovernment street protests and led to calls from members of the ruling five-party coalition for Wijdenbosch to step down. However, although on 1 June 1999 a majority – 27 of the 51 – of National Assembly deputies supported the president's resignation, this fell short of the two-thirds majority required by the constitution. Wijdenbosch offered to call early elections, but there did not exist a clear alternative candidate to replace him as president.

URUGUAY

The Eastern Republic of Uruguay
La República Oriental del Uruguay

Capital: Montevideo

Social and economic data
Area: 176,215 sq km/68,037 sq miles
Population: 3,167,000*
Pop. density per sq km/sq mi: 18/47*
Urban population: 89%**
Literacy rate: 94%**
GDP: $16,460 million*; per-capita GDP: $5,200*
Government defense spending (% of GDP): 2.6%*
Currency: new Uruguayan peso
Economy type: middle income

Labor force in agriculture: 15%[**]
Unemployment rate: 10.2%
[*] 1995.
[**] 1992.

Head of state and head of government
President Julio María Sanguinetti, since 1995

Ethnic composition
The great majority of the population is of European descent, about 54% Spanish, and about 22% Italian. There are minorities from other European countries. Spanish is the national language.

Religions
All religions are tolerated but most of the population (58%) is Roman Catholic.

Political features
State type: liberal democratic
Date of state formation: 1825
Political structure: unitary
Executive: limited presidential
Assembly: two-chamber
Party structure: multiparty
Human rights rating: 90%
International affiliations: AG (observer), ALADI, G-11, IAEA, IBRD, IMF, Mercosur, NAM (observer), OAS, RG, SELA, UN, WTO

Local and regional government
The country is divided into 19 departments or regions, ranging in population from less than 24,000 to nearly 1.3 million. Each department has an elected governor and legislature. Cities have elected councils and mayors.

Political system
The 1966 constitution provides for a president, who is head of state and head of government, elected by universal adult suffrage for a five-year term, and a two-chamber assembly, consisting of a Senate and a Federal Chamber of Deputies. The Senate has up to 30 members (excluding the vice president) and the Chamber of Deputies, 99, all elected by universal adult suffrage through a modified party list system of proportional representation, which ensures that there are at least two deputies representing each of the republic's 19 departments. Both chambers serve a five-year term. The president is assisted by a vice president and presides over a Council of Ministers. There is a lower age limit of 25 years for deputies, and 30 years for senators. Voting is compulsory.

Political parties
There are over 20 active political groupings, the most significant being the Colorado Party (PC), the National (Blanco) Party (PN), the New Space (NE), and Progressive Encounter (EP).

The PC was formed in 1836, following a successful revolt against the oppressive government of Fructuoso Rivera. It took the name of Colorado, or red, from the color of the headbands of the revolutionaries who fought in the civil war. It now has a progressive center-left orientation and comprises four factions.

PN supporters had white headbands, hence the name Blanco. It, too, began in 1836 in similar circumstances to the birth of the PC, but on the opposite side in the civil war. The PN has a traditionalist right-of-center orientation and comprises four factions.

The NE was formed in 1989 by Amplio Front (FA) dissidents. It, also, has a moderate social-democratic stance.

The EP is an alliance of leftwing parties.

Political leaders since 1970
1967–72 Jorge Pacheco Areco (PN), 1972–76 Juan María Bordaberry Arocena (PC), 1976–81 General Aparicio Méndez Manfredini (military), 1981–85 General Grigorio Alvárez Armellino (military) 1985–90 Julio María Sanguinetti (PC coalition), 1990–95 Luis Alberto Lacalle Herrera (PN coalition), 1995– Julio María Sanguinetti (PC coalition)

Latest elections
The PC candidate, Julio María Sanguinetti, was narrowly elected president in November 1994, with his presidency taking effect from March 1995. He had secured 32% of the vote, against 31% for Alberto Volonté of the PN and 30% for Tabaré Vázquez of the EP.

Uruguay latest election results
The results of the concurrent assembly elections were as follows:

Party	Senate seats	Chamber of Deputies seats
PC	11	32
PN	10	31
EP	9	31
NE	1	5

Political history
Uruguay was under Portuguese rule in the 17th century and under Spanish control for the next 100 years. It

achieved full independence in 1825. The period that followed saw a series of local disturbances, leading to a civil war in 1836. After that the country enjoyed relative peace so that Uruguay gained a reputation for being not only the smallest but the most politically stable of all South American republics. Under the presidencies of José Battle (between 1903 and 1907 and from 1911 to 1915), a successful ranching economy and the rudiments of a welfare state were established. However, during the 1930s depression there was a reversion to a military dictatorship.

Between 1951 and 1966 there was a collective leadership called 'collegiate government' and then a new constitution was adopted and the Blanco candidate, Jorge Pacheco Areco, was elected as a single president. His presidency was marked by high inflation, labor unrest, and growing guerrilla activity by leftwing sugar workers, the Tupamaros.

In 1972 Pacheco was replaced by the Colorado candidate, Juan María Bordaberry Arocena. Within a year the Tupamaros had been crushed and all other leftwing groups banned. Bordaberry now headed a repressive regime, under which the normal democratic institutions had been destroyed. When, in 1976, he refused any movement towards constitutional government, he was deposed by the army and Aparicio Méndez Manfredini was made president.

Despite promises to return to democratic government, the severe repression continued and political opponents were imprisoned. In 1981 the deteriorating economy made the army anxious to return to constitutional government and a retired general, Gregorio Alvárez Armellino, was appointed to serve as president for an interim period until full constitutional government was restored. Discussions between the army and the main political parties failed to reach agreement on the form of constitution to be adopted and civil unrest, in the shape of strikes and demonstrations, grew. By 1984 anti-government activity had reached a crisis point and eventually all the main political leaders signed an agreement for a Program of National Accord.

The 1966 constitution, with some modifications, was restored and in 1985 a general election was held. The Colorado Party won a narrow majority and its leader, Julio María Sanguinetti (b. 1936), became president. The army stepped down and by 1986 President Sanguinetti was presiding over a government of National Accord in which all the main parties were represented.

The November 1989 presidential and assembly elections produced a PN president, Luis Alberto Lacalle

Herrera (b. 1941), and a PN-PC coalition government and the earlier signs that Uruguay was returning to the form of government which, historically, had made it a model democracy, were confirmed. The Lacalle administration concentrated on fighting inflation and promoting the development of a more competitive private sector. The economy began to grow strongly from 1992, with inflation down to 50% per year. However, the government's planned privatization initiative had to be halted when, in December 1992, 78% of the public voted against the measure in a national referendum. In March 1995 the PC candidate, the former president, Julio María Sanguinetti, returned to office. Earlier, in November 1994, his party won a plurality of seats in assembly elections which were characterized by the strong showing of the recently formed left-of-center Progressive Encounter (EP), which ended the two-party dominance of the PN and PC. The new president said he would appoint a broad-based cabinet, based around the PC and PN, to ensure 'governability'.

In April 1999 the three main parties selected as their candidates to contest the October 1999 presidential election three veteran politicians: ex-President Luis Alberto Lacalle, for the PN; Jorge Battle Ibáñez, for the PC; and Tabaré Vázquez, for the EP.

VENEZUELA

The Republic of Venezuela
La República de Venezuela

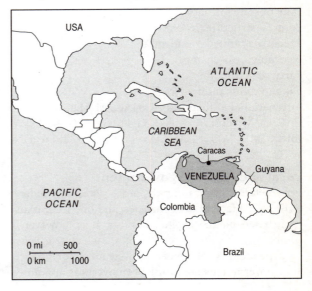

Capital: Caracas

Social and economic data
Area: 912,050 sq km/352,144 sq miles
Population: 21,177,000[*]
Pop. density per sq km/sq mi: 23/60[*]
Urban population: 91%[**]
Literacy rate: 85%[*]
GDP: $65,380 million[*]; per-capita GDP: $3,090[*]
Government defense spending (% of GDP): 1.1%[*]
Currency: bolívar
Economy type: middle income
Labor force in agriculture: 12%[**]
Unemployment rate: 10.3%
[*] 1995.
[**] 1992.

Head of state and head of government
President Hugo Rafael Chávez Frias, since 1999

Ethnic composition
About 67% of the population are mestizos (offspring of Spanish-American and Native American parents), 21% Europeans, 10% Africans, and 2% Indians. Spanish is the official language.

Religions
Roman Catholicism is the state religion and the great majority of the population (92%) practise it. There is, however, complete freedom of worship for all denominations.

Political features
State type: liberal democratic
Date of state formation: 1830
Political structure: federal
Executive: limited presidential
Assembly: two-chamber
Party structure: multiparty
Human rights rating: 75%
International affiliations: ACS, AG, ALADI, AP, BCIE, CARICOM (observer), G-3, G-11, G-15, G-24, IAEA, IBRD, IMF, IWC, NAM, OAS, OPEC, RG, SELA, UN, WTO

Local and regional government
Venezuela is a federal nation of 22 states, one federal territory, 72 federal dependencies, and one federal district, based on the capital, Caracas. It is, however, a comparatively weak system because each state is heavily dependent on the federal government for finance. State governments are headed by governors appointed by the president and have elected assemblies. For administrative purposes, they are further subdivided into electorates and then municipalities.

Political system
The 1961 constitution contains features similar to those of the United States and provides for a president, who is head of state and head of government, and a two-chamber National Congress, consisting of a Senate and a Chamber of Deputies. The president is elected by universal adult suffrage for a five-year term and may not serve two consecutive terms. The Senate has 48 members elected by universal adult suffrage, on the basis of two representatives for each state, Federal Territory, and the Federal District, plus all living ex-presidents, *ex officio*. The Chamber has 189 deputies, elected by universal adult suffrage, through a party list system of proportional representation using multimember constituencies. Both chambers serve five-year terms. The president appoints and presides over a Council of Ministers (cabinet).

Political parties
There are more than 20 political parties, the most significant being the Democratic Action Party (AD), the Christian Social Party (COPEI), the National Convergence (CN), the Movement towards Socialism (MAS), the Radical Cause (LCR), Project Venezuela (PRVZL), and the Fifth Republic Movement (MVR).

The AD was formed in 1936 as the National Democratic Party and adopted its present name in 1941. It has a moderate left-of-center orientation and membership of 1.4 million.

COPEI was founded in 1946 by the leader of the Catholic Student Movement. It adopts a Christian center-right stance and claims 1.5 million members.

The center-right CN is a wide-ranging spectrum of 17 parties, formed in 1993, and including some former COPEI members.

The MAS dates from 1971 and was formed by members of the Communist Party who broke away after the Soviet invasion of Czechoslovakia. It has a left-of-center orientation and 220,000 members.

The LCR is another nontraditional party, with a left-wing orientation.

The PRVZL is a party which was formed to support the 1998 presidential candidacy of Henrique Salas Romer.

The MVR was also formed in 1998, to support the populist presidential candidate, Lieutenant-Colonel Hugo Chávez Frías.

Political leaders since 1970

1969–74 Rafael Caldera Rodríguez (COPEI), 1974–79 Carlos Andrés Pérez Rodríguez (AD), 1979–84 Luis Herrera (COPEI), 1984–89 Jaime Lusinchi (AD), 1989–93 Carlos Andrés Pérez Rodríguez (AD), 1993 Octavio Lepage (interim), 1993–94 Ram). Ramón José Velásquez (AD-COPEI interim), 1994–99 Dr Rafael Caldera Rodríguez (CN), 1999– Hugo Rafael Chávez Frías (MVR)

Latest elections

In the 6 December 1998 presidential election Lieutenant-Colonel Hugo Chávez Frías, candidate of his recently formed MVR, was successful with 56.2% of the vote. His closest rival, Henrique Salas Romer, an independent who was endorsed by the country's two major parties, the AD and COPEI, secured 40% of the vote.

In the 8 November 1998 assembly elections, the results were as follows:

Venezuela latest election results

| Party | Chamber of Deputies | | Senate | |
	% of vote	Seats	% of votes	Seats
AD	21.7	55	24.4	19
MVR	21.3	49	19.8	12
COPEI	10.7	27	12.2	7
PRVZL	12.3	24	10.2	1
MAS	8.7	17	9.1	5
Others	25.3	17	24.3	4

Political history

Venezuela was first colonized by Spain in the 16th century and from then until independence was achieved, in 1830, there were repeated rebellions against Spanish rule. In the 19th century the independence movement was led by Francisco Miranda (1752–1816) and Símon Bolívar (1783–1830). The latter established, in 1823, the state of Gran Colombia, which included the area of present-day Colombia, Ecuador, and Venezuela, driving out the Spanish royalist forces. Venezuela became an independent republic when Gran Colombia was dissolved in 1830. Between 1870 and 1889 the caudillo (military leader), Antonio Guzmán Blanco (1829–99), ruled as a benevolent dictator, modernizing the infrastructure and developing agriculture and education.

From 1909 to 1935 the country suffered under the harsh dictatorship of General Juan Vicente Gómez (1864–1935), who developed Venezuela's rich oil resources, making it the world's largest exporter of petroleum, but passed little of the wealth on to the ordinary inhabitants. The first free elections were held in 1947 but were soon followed by another period of repression, this time under General Marcos Pérez Jiménez. Venezuela had to wait until 1959 before the democratically elected government of Rómulo Betancourt came to power.

A new constitution was adopted in 1961 and three years later Betancourt became the first president to complete his full term of office. He was succeeded in 1964 by Raúl Leoni and then, in 1969, Rafael Caldera Rodríguez (b. 1916) was elected as Venezuela's first Christian Social Party (COPEI) president. He did much to bring economic and political stability, although underground abductions and assassinations still occurred. In 1974 Carlos Andrés Pérez Rodríguez (b. 1922) of the Democratic Action Party (AD) came to the presidency and the movement towards greater stability continued. In 1979 Luis Herrera, leader of the Christian Social Party (COPEI), was elected, but without a working majority in Congress so he was dependent on the other parties for legislative support.

Against a background of growing economic problems, the 1983 general election was contested by 20 parties and 13 presidential candidates. It was a bitterly fought campaign and resulted in the election of Jaime Lusinchi (b. 1924) as president and a win for the AD in Congress. President Lusinchi's austere economic policies were unpopular and throughout 1985 he worked hard to try to conclude a social pact between the government, trade unions, and business. He also reached an agreement with the government's creditor bankers for a rescheduling of Venezuela's large public debt. In the 1988 presidential election Lusinchi was decisively defeated by his AD rival, the former president, Carlos Andrés Pérez Rodríguez, who embarked upon a strict austerity program in return for IMF loans, resulting in protest riots in Caracas.

The public unrest continued in 1992 and in February the government had to deal with an attempted coup by a group of army officers led by the populist Lieutenant-Colonel Hugo Chávez. As his unpopularity grew, the president promised constitutional reforms but in May 1993 he was accused by the Senate of corruption and the embezzlement of government funds, and this charge was endorsed by the Supreme Court. Pérez was suspended from office and the chairperson of the Senate, Octavio Lepage, was made interim president. The following month the Congress elected Senator Ramón José Velásquez to serve the remaining eight months of Pérez's presidency, and he was given special powers to introduce economic and financial measures by decree. In August 1993 Pérez was permanently suspended and made ineligible for public office again.

In the December 1993 presidential election the voters turned their backs on the two traditional parties and elected as the new president the veteran COPEI politician and former head of state, Rafael Caldera Rodríguez, who now headed the National Convergence (CN) coalition which had campaigned against government corruption and had promised to suspend a planned privatization initiative. The concurrent congressional elections resulted in a sharing of the Senate and Chamber of Deputies seats by all the main political parties. During 1996, as the state of the economy worsened, President Caldera was forced to seek IMF assistance and, subsequently, to introduce austerity measures. These resulted in violent public demonstrations in 1997 as real incomes fell sharply.

The December 1998 presidential election was won by the left-wing populist, Lieutenant-Colonel Hugo Chávez, who had served two years' imprisonment between 1992-94, following his role in the February 1992 attempted coup. Chávez's newly formed Fifth Republic Movement (MVR) also polled strongly in the legislature elections, held a month earlier. Drawn from outside the country's political establishment, based around the AD and COPEI parties, Chávez advocated radical economic and political changes, including a threat to dissolve the legislature, suspend foreign debt payments and revise recent privatization contracts. His election was widely viewed as marking a new trend in South America, as witnessed in Bolivia and Peru, away from corrupt bipartisan politicians towards populist 'strongmen'.

Chávez was sworn in as president in February 1999, but within two months faced a constitutional crisis as the Congress refused, initially, to grant him emergency economic powers. Chávez reacted by announcing plans to establish a new 131-member Constituent Assembly to reform the constitution and also, he threatened, to possibly take over the work of the Congress. However, the Supreme Court objected to the latter proposal. Nevertheless, in a referendum held in April 1999, voters overwhelmingly approved the convening of the Constituent Assembly, although turnout was only 39%, and in July 1999 the Assembly was elected. It had the brief of drawing up a new constitution which would be put before voters for their approval in 2000. Also, in July 1999, President Chávez launched a $935 million plan designed to create jobs and stimulate the country's sluggish economy.

3

Towards One World

CHAPTER 8

The Relics of Empire – Colonies, Dependencies, and Semi-Sovereign States

8.1 The building of the colonial empires: 1492–1919

Nine-tenths of the contemporary sovereign states outside Western Europe have, at one time or another during the two centuries before 1945, been subject to external rule by the 'great' colonial powers of Europe, the United States, or Japan. The notable exceptions have been Japan itself, China, apart from Manchuria and the coastal 'treaty port' enclaves, Afghanistan, until 1979–89, Iran, Saudi Arabia, (North) Yemen, Liberia, since 1847, Thailand, Bhutan, and Nepal. 'Informal' external influence was, however, strong in many of these states, Nepal and Bhutan, for example, being bound by strict treaty obligations to Britain until 1947.

The process of modern colonization occurred in a series of distinct phases. It began in the late 15th and early 16th centuries, with the conquest of Southern and Central America, including the Caribbean, by Spain and Portugal, the indigenous Amerindian civilization being destroyed and replaced by a new mixed, white-creole-black, plantation and mining economy. This was

---

The initial wave of colonial expansion – The Americas, 1496–1903 (22 states)　　　Table 63

Country	Date of colonization	Original colonizing power	Date of independence	Country	Date of colonization	Original colonizing power	Date of independence
Argentina	1516	Spain	1816	Guatemala	1524	Spain	1839
Bolivia	1530s	Spain	1825	Haiti	1697	France	1804
Brazil	1532	Portugal	1822	Honduras	1523	Spain	1821/38***
Canada	1604	France and UK	1851-67*	Mexico	1521	Spain	1821
Chile	1541	Spain	1818	Nicaragua	1552	Spain	1838
Colombia	1538	Spain	1821/30**	Panama	1513	Spain	1821/1903****
Costa Rica	1563	Spain	1821	Paraguay	1537	Spain	1811
Cuba	1511	Spain	1899	Peru	1533	Spain	1824
Dominican Republic	1496	Spain	1844	United States of America	1607	United Kingdom	1776
Ecuador	1532	Spain	1821/30**	Uruguay	1624	Spain	1825
El Salvador	1525	Spain	1821/38***	Venezuela	1567	Spain	1821/30**

* Canada was not fully freed from the supremacy of Acts of the UK Parliament until 1931, while Newfoundland remained under British administration until 1949.

** These states formed part of a federation between 1821 and 1830.

*** Part of a federation of Central American States until 1838.

**** Part of Colombia until 1903.

followed, during the 17th century, by the Netherlands' assertion of supremacy over the East Indies' 'spice islands', and the creation of British and French settlements in coastal North America.

The majority of the early colonies on the mainland of the Americas were, following revolts by the settlers, to secure their independence during the late 18th and early 19th centuries, as Table 63 shows. Elsewhere in the world, however, European interests multiplied, an extensive new chain of dependencies being established across South and Southeast Asia, Australasia, Africa, and the Caribbean during what was the dominant era of imperial expansion, between the 1770s and the 1920s. The lead in this second phase of colonialism was taken by Britain and France. Also involved in the process were the rising nations of central, eastern, and southern Europe, notably Germany, tsarist Russia, and Italy, the ambitious small kingdom of Belgium, the old imperial states of the Netherlands, Spain, and Portugal, and the emergent world powers of the United States and Japan.

Imperial expansion during this 'mature' phase usually took the form of the imposition of a ruling body, or person, on indigenous peoples, or even indirect control, rather than the emigration and settlement of white colonists. The exceptions were the settler colonies of Australia and New Zealand, upland parts of southern and eastern Africa, and the tea and rubber planter belts of Southeast Asia. The expansion was at its maximum, in areal terms, at the time of the Versailles Settlement of 1919, when nearly all of Africa, South and Southeast Asia, Oceania, and the Caribbean, as well as much of West Asia and the Middle East, had been politically incorporated into the imperial nexus.

8.2 The decolonization process: 1920–98

During the interwar years, the first halting steps towards decolonization were taken, beginning in the Middle East, where, in 1922, Britain, prompted by the outbreak of serious nationalist riots, transferred full sovereignty in Egypt. It continued to maintain, however, a strategic military presence to protect its Suez Canal interests. Then, in 1932 and 1944 respectively, Britain and France, which had been administering the territories under League of Nations mandates since 1920, conceded independence to Iraq and Lebanon. During the same period the 'white settler' dominions of

Canada and South Africa, which had experienced a substantial measure of self-government from as early as the mid-19th century, became effectively fully independent with the passage of the Statute of Westminster, in 1931. Australia and New Zealand, the other two overseas dominions, delayed accepting the terms of this legislation until 1942 and 1947 respectively. These cases were, however, the exceptions. Elsewhere, the 1920s and 1930s were a period of imperial consolidation, and even some further expansion by countries such as fascist Italy, militarist Japan, and, finally, remotivated to imperial ambitions, Nazi Germany.

Matters changed dramatically after World War II, the process of decolonization now gaining an unstoppable momentum. The initial factor behind this change was the strain imposed on ruler – colony relations by the war itself. For example, in the case of India, where a powerful nationalist movement had already won significant political concessions during the interwar period, the British government was forced, in 1940, to offer the carrot of Dominion Status as a means of securing civilian cooperation in the war effort. By the end of the war, however, the popular desire for full independence had become irresistible, with the result that full sovereignty, on a partitioned basis, was transferred in August 1947. The adjacent South Asian countries of Ceylon (Sri Lanka) and Burma (Myanmar) soon followed suit and were granted independence in 1948. The loss of the Indian subcontinent, the linchpin of the British imperial system, was to have far-reaching consequences, undermining its whole economic and strategic rationale.

Further to the east, in Southeast Asia, the French and Dutch colonies in 'Indochina' and the 'East Indies' had been even more seriously affected by the events of World War II. Between 1942 and 1945 both had been occupied by Japan, which had sponsored new puppet nationalist governments. The reimposition of European colonial rule proved highly unpopular and was fiercely resisted. Full autonomy was thus granted to the Dutch 'East Indies', now Indonesia, in 1949 and substantial semi-autonomy, within the 'French Union', to France's possessions in Indochina: Vietnam, Cambodia, and Laos. They achieved full independence some five years later after a prolonged military struggle.

During the later 1940s and mid-1950s, the British- and French-administered states of North Africa and the Middle East were also granted independence: Syria in 1946; Israel, formerly Palestine, in 1948; Libya in 1951; and Sudan, Morocco, and Tunisia, all in 1956. In addition, the 'informal colony' of Oman regained full sovereignty in foreign and defense affairs, in 1951, and Eritrea was handed over to Ethiopian control in 1952. It was not, however, until the Suez and Algerian crises of 1956 and 1958 that the pace of decolonization decisively quickened. Both events had profound repercussions on the internal political dynamics of the two leading imperial nations, and on their global outlooks, resulting in the accession to power of the realistic decolonizers, Harold Macmillan (1894–1986; prime minister 1957–63), in the United Kingdom, and General Charles de Gaulle (1890–1970; president 1959–69), in France. These crises also transformed public opinion, adding a new moral imperative to a decolonization process which had now gained an irresistible momentum.

The first indication of this changed perspective was the granting of full independence to the British West African colony of Ghana, known as the Gold Coast, in March 1957, by the handing over of power to the popular radical socialist, Kwame Nkrumah (1909–72). Ushering in, what the British prime minister, Harold Macmillan, termed, a 'wind of change' across black Africa, 33 African states secured independence during the next ten years. In one year alone, 1960, 17 new African states were proclaimed. Independence was also granted during this hectic decolonization phase, between 1957 and 1968, to nine small island states in the Caribbean, Oceania, and East Asia, as Tables 64 and 65 show.

By the early 1970s, Britain and France, playing the leading roles in the decolonization process, as can be seen in Table 64, had divested themselves of their principal mainland-based colonial possessions. They were now left mainly in control of small island dependencies in the Caribbean and Oceania, as well as treaty protectorates in the Gulf region. These were slowly 'set free', at an average rate of two per year, during the 1970s and early 1980s.

Ironically, the last substantial European overseas empire was maintained during this period by Portugal, the pioneer of European imperial expansion. Comprising Guinea-Bissau in West Africa, Angola in southwestern Africa, Mozambique in southeastern Africa, and the offshore islands of Cape Verde and São Tomé e Príncipe, this empire covered more than 2,000 square kilometres and had been under Portuguese rule for almost 500 years. With its still untapped mineral wealth and energy reserves, it remained, moreover, of considerable economic value to the colonial power, attracting extensive white settlement during the 1960s.

Portuguese rule and immigration were, however, becoming increasingly unpopular with the indigenous population, fuelling a powerful guerrilla resistance movement, which was supplied with modern arms by the Soviet Union's Cuban and East German proxies. This eventually had calamitous repercussions for the Lisbon regime, provoking a leftwing coup by disaffected army units which succeeded in bringing down the conservative dictatorship of Marcello Caetano (1906–80), in April 1974. In the immediate wake of this power change, Portugal's African dependencies pressed for independence. Unable and unwilling to resist, the new Lisbon regime hastily acceded to the requests, and within the space of 14 months, between October 1974 and November 1975, the empire was dissolved.

This left, during the 1980s, only one major land-based European overseas empire that dated back to the pre-1945 period, the one established by tsarist Russia in Central Asia between 1846 and 1895. It was an empire inherited by the 'anti-colonial' Soviet Union, but which it had firmly consolidated and incorporated within its federal structure. After the war the Soviet Union also established an informal hegemony over its East European neighbors, although the economic relationship by no means corresponded to a classic imperial one in terms of the nature of the goods interchanged, the USSR exporting mineral and energy products westwards and importing manufactured items. In addition, Afghanistan was invaded by the Soviet Red Army in 1979 and a puppet regime installed. Two other major communist powers, China, in the case of Tibet, and Vietnam, in relation to Laos and Cambodia, also maintained both formal and quasi-formal imperial control over neighboring regions.

These communist informal and formal empires disintegrated dramatically between 1989 and 1991 as a result of economic problems at the center, the consequence both of overly rigid central-planning systems and of the crippling defense burden, and of the growth in nationalist sentiment in the colonized territories. The latter was particularly evident in the Soviet 'satellite states' of Central and Eastern Europe and the voicing of this sentiment was made possible by the *glasnost* ('political openness') initiative instituted by the reformist Mikhail Gorbachev (b. 1931), who became the Communist Party leader in the Soviet Union in 1985. Abandoning the existing imperialist 'Brezhnev doctrine', which had held that the Soviet Union would always intervene militarily to ensure that 'correct' socialism was upheld within its 'sphere of influence',

The changing pace of decolonization between 1920 and 1998 — Table 64

Number of countries 'freed'*

Period	Under British control	Under French control	Under Dutch control	Under Belgian control	Under Portuguese control	Under US control	Under Russian/USSR control	Under control of other states	Total
1920–45	5	1	–	–	–	–	–	1	7
1946–50	6	1	1	–	–	2	–	2	12
1951–55	2.7	3.3	–	–	–	–	–	–	6
1956–60	7.5	16.5	–	1	–	–	–	–	25
1961–65	13	1	–	2	–	–	1	–	17
1966–70	9	–	–	–	–	–	–	2	11
1971–75	5	1	1	–	5	–	–	2	14
1976–80	7.5	1.5	–	–	–	–	–	–	9
1981–85	4	–	–	–	–	–	–	–	4
1986–90	–	–	–	–	–	–	1	1	2
1991–98	1	–	–	–	–	3	14	–	18
1920–98	60.7	25.3	2	3	5	5	15	9	125
% share of total	48.6	20.2	1.6	2.4	4.0	4.0	12.0	7.2	100

Regional distribution of 'freed' countries

Period	Central & Southern Africa	Middle East & North Africa	Asia	Central America & the Caribbean	South America	North America	Oceania	Western Europe	Central, Eastern, & Southern Europe	Total
1920–45	2	3	–	–	–	1	1	–	–	7
1946–50	–	3	8	–	–	–	1	–	–	12
1951–55	1	2	3	–	–	–	–	–	–	6
1956–60	20	2	2	–	–	–	–	1	–	25
1961–65	10	2	1	2	–	–	1	1	–	17
1966–70	5	1	–	1	1	–	3	–	–	11
1971–75	6	4	–	2	1	–	1	–	–	14
1976–80	1	1	–	3	–	–	4	–	–	9
1981–85	–	–	1	3	–	–	–	–	–	4
1986–90	1	–	1	–	–	–	–	–	–	2
1991–98	–	–	6	–	–	–	3	–	9	18
1920–98	46	18	22	11	2	1	14	2	9	125
% share of total	36.8	14.4	17.6	8.8	1.6	0.8	11.2	1.6	7.2	100

* Where control was shared between two or more colonial powers, the number of 'freed' countries is shown proportionately.

Gorbachev sanctioned the withdrawal of the Red Army from Afghanistan in 1989 and permitted the overthrow of entrenched communist regimes in Bulgaria, Czechoslovakia, East Germany, Hungary, Poland, and Romania during 1989–90. Also during 1989, Vietnam, partly responding to Soviet prompting and partly influenced by its own economic considerations, withdrew all its forces stationed in Cambodia and Laos.

Gorbachev fought harder to preserve communist and Russian control over the formally colonized 14 republics that formed constituent parts of the Soviet Union. However, the dynamics of his *glasnost* and *perestroika* ('economic restructuring') reform program were such that the unbottling of previously suppressed nationalist sentiment, particularly in the Baltic republics, Georgia, west Ukraine, and parts of Soviet

The decolonization process, 1922–98

Table 65

Year of decolonization or transfer of sovereignty	State	Last colonizing power	Date of establishment of control
1922	Egypt	Britain	1882
1931	Canada*	Britain (France 1604–1763)	1713–63
1932	Iraq	Britain (M)	1920
1934	South Africa*	Britain (Netherlands 1652–1795)	1795–1824
1941	Ethiopia	Italy (MO)	1936
1942	Australia*	Britain	1788
1944	Lebanon	France (M)	1920
1946	Jordan	Britain (M)	1920
1946	Mongolia	China	1689
1946	Philippines	United States (Spain 1565–1898)	1689
1946	Syria	France (M)	1920
1947	India and Pakistan (including E Pakistan, later Bangladesh)	Britain	late 18th–early 19th century
1947	New Zealand*	Britain	1840
1948	Myanmar (Burma)	Britain (Japan 1942–45)	1824–86
1948	Israel (formerly W Palestine)	Britain (M)	1920
1948	Korea, North	Soviet Union (OZ) (Japan 1910–45)	1945
1948	Korea, South	United States (OZ) (Japan 1910–45)	1945
1948	Sri Lanka (Ceylon)	Britain	1798
1949	Indonesia	Netherlands (Japan 1942–45)	1595
1951	Libya	70% Britain and 30% France (Italy 1912–42)	1942
1951	Oman	Britain (MP)	1891
1952	Eritrea	Britain (Italy until 1941)	1941
1954	Cambodia (Kampuchea)	France (Japan 1941–45)	1863
1954	Laos	France (Japan 1940–45)	1893
1954	Vietnam	France (Japan 1940–45)	1867–83
1956	Morocco	France	1912
1956	Sudan	Britain	1899
1956	Tunisia	France	1881
1957	Ghana	Britain	1901
1957	Malaysia	Britain (Portugal 1511–1641, Netherlands 1641–1795)	1795–1888
1957	Singapore	Britain	1819
1958	Guinea	France	1898
1960	Benin	France	1892
1960	Burkina Faso (Upper Volta)	France	1896
1960	Cameroon	80% France and 20% Britain (M) (Germany 1884–1916)	1919
1960	Central Africa Republic	France	1901
1960	Chad	France	1900
1960	Congo	France	1910
1960	Cyprus	Britain	1914
1960	Gabon	France	1890
1960	Côte d'Ivoire	France	1893
1960	Madagascar	France	1885
1960	Mali	France	1881–99
1960	Mauritania	France	1904–12
1960	Niger	France	1901
1960	Nigeria	Britain	1861–99

continues

The decolonization process, 1922–98   Table 65

Year of decolonization or transfer of sovereignty	State	Last colonizing power	Date of establishment of control
1960	Senegal	France	1659–1840
1960	Somalia	Britain (Italy 1908–41)	1884–86
1960	Togo	66% France and 34% Britain (M) (Germany 1884–1914)	1914
1960	Zaire	Belgium	1885–1908
1961	Kuwait	Britain (MP)	1899
1961	Sierra Leone	Britain	1808
1961	Tanzania	Britain (M) (Germany 1885–1914)	1914
1962	Algeria	France	1830
1962	Burundi	Belgium (M) (Germany 1895–1916)	1916
1962	Jamaica	Britain (Spain 1509–1655)	1655
1962	Rwanda	Belgium (M) (Germany 1894–1916)	1916
1962	Trinidad and Tobago	Britain (Spain 1552–1797)	1797–1820
1962	Uganda	Britain	1888
1962	Western Samoa (now Samoa)	New Zealand (M) (Germany 1900–14)	1914
1963	Kenya	Britain (Portugal 1498–1699)	1888–95
1964	Malawi	Britain	1887–92
1964	Malta	Britain	1814
1964	Zambia	Britain	1891–1923
1965	Gambia	Britain	1816
1965	Maldives	Britain	1887
1965	Rhodesia (later Zimbabwe: UDI)	Britain	1897–1923
1966	Barbados	Britain	1624
1966	Botswana	Britain	1885
1966	Guyana	Britain (Netherlands 1616–1796)	1796–1814
1966	Lesotho	Britain	1868
1967	South Yemen	Britain	1839
1968	Equatorial Guinea	Spain (Portugal 1494–1778, Spain 1778–81, Britain 1781–1843)	1858
1968	Mauritius	Britain (Netherlands 1598–1710, France 1715–1810)	1810
1968	Nauru	Australia (M) (Germany 1888–1914, Japan 1942–45)	1914
1968	Swaziland	Britain (South Africa 1894–1902)	1881
1970	Fiji	Britain	1874
1970	Tonga	Britain	1900
1971	Bahrain	Britain (MP)	1861
1971	Qatar	Britain (MP) (also temp 1868–72)	1916
1971	United Arab Emirates	Britain (MP)	1892
1973	Bahamas	Britain	1629
1974	Grenada	Britain (France 1674–1762)	1762
1974	Guinea-Bissau	Portugal	late 15th century
1975	Angola	Portugal	1491
1975	Cape Verde	Portugal	late 15th century
1975	Comoros	France	1912
1975	Mozambique	Portugal	1505
1975	Papua New Guinea	Australia (50% German 1885–1914, and 50% Britain 1885–1901)	1901
1975	São Tomé e Príncipe	Portugal	1471
1975	Spanish Sahara (W Sahara)	Spain	1912
1975	Suriname	Netherlands (Britain 1651–67, 1779–1802, and 1804–16)	1816

continues

The decolonization process, 1922–98

Table 65

Year of decolonization or transfer of sovereignty	State	Last colonizing power	Date of establishment of control
1976	Seychelles	Britain (France 1768–1814)	1814
1977	Djibouti	France	1859
1978	Dominica	Britain (France 1778–83)	1763
1978	Solomon Islands	Britain (50% Germany 1885–1900)	1885
1978	Tuvalu	Britain	1875
1979	Kiribati	Britain	1892
1979	St Lucia	Britain (France 1651–1803)	1803
1979	St Vincent and the Grenadines	Britain (France 1779–83)	1783
1980	Vanuatu	Britain and France (JT)	1887
1981	Antigua and Barbuda	Britain	1632
1981	Belize	Britain	17th century–1862
1983	St Kitts and Nevis	Britain	1623
1984	Brunei	Britain	1888
1989	Afghanistan	Russia (USSR) (MO)	1979
1990	Namibia	South Africa (Britain 1884–1915, Germany 1884–1915)	1915
1991	Armenia	Russia (USSR) (Turkey 1639–1918, West Armenia; Persia 1639–1828, East Armenia; Independent 1918–20)	1828
1991	Azerbaijan	Russia (USSR) (Independent 1918–20)	1805
1991	Belarus	Russia (USSR) (Independent 1918–19, Germany 1941–44)	1795
1991	Estonia	Russia (USSR) (Independent 1919–40, Russia 1940–41, Germany 1941–44)	1721
1991	Georgia	Russia (USSR) (Independent 1918–21)	1801
1991	Kazakhstan	Russia (USSR)	early 18th century
1991	Kyrgyzstan	Russia (USSR)	1876
1991	Latvia	Russia (USSR) (Russia 1918–19, 1939–41, Independent 1919–39, Germany 1941–44)	late 18th century
1991	Lithuania	Russia (USSR) (Germany 1915–18 1941–44, Russia 1918–19, 1939–41, Independent 1919–39)	1795
1991	Marshall Islands	United States (TT) (Spain 1529–1885, Germany 1885–1914, Japan 1914–45)	1945
1991	Micronesia, Federated States of	United States (TT) (Spain 16th century–1898, Germany 1898–1914, Japan 1914–45)	1945
1991	Moldova	Russia (USSR)	1812
1991	Tajikistan	Russia (USSR)	late 19th century
1991	Turkmenistan	Russia (USSR)	1870s
1991	Ukraine	Russia (USSR) (Independent 1917–20, Germany 1941–44)	1654
1991	Uzbekistan	Russia (USSR)	1876
1994	Palau (Belau)	United States (TT)	1945
1997	Hong Kong	Britain	1842

* The white-settler colonies of Australia, Canada, New Zealand, and South Africa achieved *de facto* independence from British control at earlier dates than those shown. The separate Australian states, for example, enjoyed a substantial measure of autonomy as early as 1855–68; the Canadian colonies between 1851 and 1867; and New Zealand and Cape Colony in South Africa as early as 1853. These powers were extended in 1907 when Dominion status was conferred. Not until the dates shown, however, following the passage of the Statute of Westminster, 1931, were these territories fully freed from the supremacy of Acts of the United Kingdom parliament.

JT = joint condominium, MO = military occupation, MP = independent and fully internally self-governing, but dependent on British military protection, much in the same way as Bhutan and Nepal, M = League of Nations 'mandate' territory, OZ = occupied zone, TT = UN Trust Territory, UDI = unilateral declaration of independence.

Central Asia, proved to be corrosive of the entire Union. In September 1991, following the failure of an anti-Gorbachev coup in Moscow by nationalist-communist hardliners, the independence of the three Baltic republics of Estonia, Latvia, and Lithuania was reluctantly recognized by Moscow. Three months later, the USSR was itself dissolved.

8.3 Remaining colonial possessions and dependencies in the world today

There currently exist, on the broadest count, 44 regularly inhabited colonies or dependencies, controlled by 13 colonial powers. These territories and the controlling nations are set out, in an aggregated form, in Tables 66, 67, and 68. They total fewer than 11 million people, a number that corresponds to less than 0.2% of the global population. This compares with the situation in 1945 when almost a third of the world's population lived in colonies or dependencies or with early 1960, when the proportion stood at 5%.

Included in these figures are the occupied territory of Western Sahara, the Chinese 'Autonomous Region' of Xizang (Tibet), and the French internal 'Collective Territory' of Corsica. These areas do not always feature in textbook dependency categories. They have, however,

been included in this chapter so as to provide more detailed treatments of their political structures and histories. Taken together, they embrace 2.7 million people, a figure that is equivalent to 26% of the colonies/dependencies total.

In the remaining colonial territories and dependencies, there are fewer than 8 million people. Almost half of this total is accounted for by the United States' dependency of Puerto Rico, with, as Table 68 shows, the majority of the other 'colonial relics' being relatively tiny communities, with populations below 100,000. The territories still held by eight of the colonial powers, Australia, Denmark, Finland, New Zealand, the Netherlands, Norway, Portugal, and Spain, are particularly small. Only two of them, controlled by the Netherlands and Portugal, are the residue of earlier, and greater, empires. Instead, there are three powers, the United States, France, and the United Kingdom, which dominate any record of contemporary colonial holdings, the territories still under their control embracing, respectively, 40%, 23%, and 4% of the total colonial/dependency population. The territories they administer are spread across the world. There is, however, a notable numerical concentration in Oceania and the Caribbean, many of the dependencies being island communities, too small to have an independent political and economic viability. In a few cases, most notably in some of the French Oceania dependencies, colonial

Contemporary colonies, dependencies, and external territories — Table 66

Controlling state	Number of inhabited colonies, dependencies, and external territories	Area ('000 sq km/'000 sq mile)	Population (million) (c. 1995)	% share of total colonial population
Australia	3	0.18/0.07	0.004	0.0
China	1	1221.60/471.66	2.260	21.5
Denmark	2	2177.00/840.54	0.099	0.9
Finland	1	1.48/0.57	0.025	0.2
France	10*	128.27/49.52	2.444	23.3
Morocco	1	252.12/97.34	0.208	2.0
Netherlands	2	0.99/0.38	0.295	2.8
New Zealand	3	0.51/0.20	0.023	0.2
Norway	1	62.92/24.29	0.004	0.0
Portugal	1	0.02/0.008	0.395	3.8
Spain	2	0.03/0.016	0.129	1.2
United Kingdom	12	14.49/5.59	0.410	3.9
United States	5	10.52/4.06	4.193	40.0
Total	*44*	*3870.13/1494.26*	*10.489*	*100.0*

* Including Corsica.

Regional distribution of contemporary colonies, dependencies, and external territories
Table 67

	Oceania	Central America & Caribbean	North America	South America	Asia	Middle East & North Africa	Central & Western Europe	Southern Africa
Number	13	12	2*	2	2	3	7**	3
Area (thousand sq km)	25.50	14.28	2175.84	102.17	1221.62	252.15	75.26	3.20
(thousand sq mile)	9.85	5.57	840.01	39.45	471.67	97.36	29.06	1.24
Population (million)	0.744	5.163	0.062	0.147	2.655	0.336	0.567	0.814
% share of total colonial population	7.1	49.2	0.6	1.4	25.3	3.2	5.4	7.8

* Includes Greenland in the Arctic.
** Includes Svalbard in the Arctic.

Distribution of contemporary colonies, dependencies, and external territories by population size
Table 68

(> = less than.)

	Below 10,000	>10,000– 50,000	>50,000– 100,000	>100,000– 500,000	>500,000– 1 million	1 million– 6 million	Total
Number of colonies, dependencies, and external territories	10	10	9	12	1	2	44

control has been maintained against the wishes of a significant proportion of the indigenous population. In general, however, in the bulk of the other, still dependent, territories no discernible independence movement is visible and, colony – colonizer cultural and economic ties remain strong.

8.4 Profiles of existing colonies and dependencies

In the pages that now follow we shall try to sketch a profile of each of the countries which still remain within the category of colony or dependency, following

Australia's external territories
Table 69

(– = not applicable.)

Territory	Date of first coming under Australian administration	Area (sq km)	Area (sq mile)	Population (c. 1995)
The Ashmore and Cartier Islands	1931	5	2	uninhabited
The Australian Antarctic Territory	1936	6,112	2,360	uninhabited
Christmas Island	1958	135	52	1,275
Cocos (Keeling) Islands	1955	14	5	647
Coral Sea Islands	1969	22*	8	uninhabited
Heard Island and McDonald Islands	1947	412	159	uninhabited
Norfolk Island	1913	35	14	1,772
Total	–	*6,735*	*2,600*	*3,694*

* This figure is the area of land only. The islands cover one million sq km of ocean.

a similar approach to that taken in Part 2: in other words, on the bases of their political structures and recent histories.

8.4.1 Australia's dependencies

Australia's dependencies are called External Territories, of which, as Table 69 shows, there are seven. Five of them are within the Oceania region, two of which are uninhabited. The other two, both uninhabited, are within Antarctica. Details of the political structures and histories of the inhabited regions are given below.

CHRISTMAS ISLAND

Location
Oceania. In the Indian Ocean 360 km/220 miles south of Java and 1,400 km/870 miles north-west of Australia.

Social and economic data
Area: 135 sq km/52 sq miles
Population: 1,275[*]
Pop. density per sq km/sq mile: 9[*]/25
Economy type: high income (c. $15,000 per capita)
Currency: Australian dollar
[*] 1991.

Ethnic composition
Around 58% of the population are ethnic Chinese, 25% Malay, and 12% 'European'. English is the official language.

Religions
Fifty-five per cent of the population, chiefly the Chinese community, are Buddhists.

Political system
The island, which became an Australian Territory in October 1958, is governed by an administrator appointed by the governor general of Australia and responsible to the minister for territories. For municipal government, a Christmas Island Shire Council was established in 1992. Elections to the nine-member assembly were last held in December 1998. There are no political parties, so only independents were elected.

Political history
Discovered on Christmas Day in 1643 by Captain W Mynars, the island, then uninhabited, was annexed by Britain in 1888, and administered as part of the Straits Settlement Crown Colony, together with Singapore, Malacca, Penang, and the Cocos Islands. During World War II it was occupied by Japan. In 1958, following the grant of independence to Singapore, under whose direct responsibility it had been placed since 1900, Britain transferred its sovereignty to Australia. Since then it has been ruled as part of the Northern Territory. The island's economy has traditionally been dependent on the recovery of phosphates, for which Chinese workers were imported. In 1987 the phosphate mine was closed because of industrial unrest, but it was reopened by private operators in 1990. Efforts are also now being made to develop the island for tourism. A nine-member advisory Island Assembly was formed in 1985, with annual elections by proportional representation. It was dissolved in 1987, but a new Shire Council was established in 1992. In an unofficial referendum, held on 7 May 1994 and organized by the Christmas Islands Workers' Union, the option of secession from Australia was rejected, but 85% of those participating called for greater autonomy. Since 1981 the island's residents have been able to claim Australian citizenship.

COCOS (KEELING) ISLANDS

Location
Oceania. In the Indian Ocean, southwest of Christmas Island and 3,685 km/2,290 miles west of Darwin.

Social and economic data
Area: 14 sq km/5 sq miles
Population: 647[*]
Pop. density per sq km/sq mile: 46[*]/129
Economy type: middle income (c. $3,000 per capita)
Currency: Australian dollar
[*] 1991.

Ethnic composition
The principal island, Home Island, is peopled by local Cocos Malays, who form 58% of the islands' total population, while the other major island, West Island, is settled chiefly by Europeans.

Religions
Around 57% of the population, comprising chiefly the ethnic Malay community, are Muslims, and 22% are Christians.

Political system
The Australian government is represented on the islands by an administrator, appointed by the governor

general of Australia and responsible to the minister of territories. Most local government functions are, however, undertaken by a Cocos Islands Shire Council. Modelled on local government in Western Australia, it was formed in 1992 to replace the Cocos Islands Council, which was established in July 1979 and whose authority was expanded in 1984. Following the islands' vote in April 1984 to become fully integrated with Australia, the islanders now enjoy the rights and privileges of ordinary Australian citizens, including voting rights in Australian parliament elections.

Political history

The Cocos Islands, a group of low-lying coral atolls thickly covered with coconut palms, were discovered in 1609 by Captain William Keeling of the East India Company. They were originally settled by Malays brought to the islands by Alexander Hare and John Clunies-Ross, in 1826–27. They were annexed to the British Crown in 1857 and incorporated in the Settlement of Singapore from 1903, although their economic interests, which were mainly the extraction of copra from coconuts, had been granted to the Clunies-Ross family in 1886. In November 1955 administration was transferred to Australia and in 1978 the Australian government bought out the Clunies-Ross family's interests and established a Cocos Malay cooperative to manage the copra plantation. In April 1984 the islands' residents voted to become part of Australia.

NORFOLK ISLAND

Capital: Kingston

Location

Oceania. In the Western Pacific 1,488 km/925 miles northeast of Sydney, off eastern Australia, and almost midway between Australia and New Zealand.

Social and economic data

Area: 35 sq km/14 sq miles
Population: 1,772*
Pop. density per sq km/sq mile: 51*/127
Economy type: middle-high income (c. $6,000–7,000 per capita)
Currency: Australian dollar
* 1996.

Ethnic composition

The population comprises descendants of those who migrated from Pitcairn in the mid-19th century, and who speak Tahitian, and more recent 'mainlander' immigrants from Australia, New Zealand, and Britain, who speak English.

Religions

The inhabitants are predominantly Christians (71%), belonging to the Church of England (38%), the Uniting Church (16%), and the Roman Catholic Church (11%).

Political system

The Australian government is represented on the island by an administrator, appointed by the governor general of Australia and responsible to the minister for territories. Since the passage of the Norfolk Island Act in 1979, there has been a progression towards a form of responsible legislative and executive self-government, founded on an elected nine-member Legislative Assembly, from which is drawn a five-member ministerial Executive Council, headed by a president of the Legislative Assembly, a position analogous to that of a chief minister. In 1985 the powers of the Assembly and Council were extended to cover such matters as civil defense and public works and services. Legislative Assembly elections are held every three years and are determined by an unusual 'cumulative method of voting', in which electors are allowed to cast as many votes as there are vacancies, subject to the proviso that they may not give more than four votes to any one candidate.

Latest elections

Following the April 1997 general election, which was contested by 22 candidates, George Smith became president of the Legislative Assembly.

Political history

The island, which was then uninhabited, was first visited by Captain James Cook (1728–79) in 1774 and originally served as a British penal settlement, between 1788 and 1814 and 1826 and 1855. After 1856 there was an influx of people from over-populated Pitcairn Island, some of them descendents of those who had settled there after the 'Mutiny of the Bounty', in 1789. In 1913 Norfolk Island became an Australian 'external territory', forming part of the New South Wales colony. Since 1979 it has been substantially self-governing and its economy has become increasingly reliant on tourism, although there are prospects of developing offshore oil and gas production. In December 1991 the island's population overwhelmingly rejected an Australian government proposal that it be included in the Australian federal electorate.

8.4.2 China's dependencies

China's has two dependencies: Xizang, or Tibet, is one of the country's five Autonomous Regions.

TIBET (XIZANG)

Capital: Lhasa

Location

Asia. In a mountainous region in southwest China, bordered to the south by Bhutan, India, and Nepal, to the west by India, to the east by Sichuan province, China, and to the north by Xinjiang autonomous region, China. The country is one of immense strategic importance to China, with between 50,000 and 100,000 troops, and a major nuclear missile base at Nagchuka.

Social and economic data

Area: 1,221,600 sq km/471,662 sq miles
Population: 2,260,000[*]
Pop. density per sq km/sq mile: 2[*]/5
Economy type: low income
Currency: Chinese renminbi or yuan
[*] 1993.

Ethnic composition

Predominantly Tibetan, with a growing Han Chinese immigrant minority.

Religions

The Tibetans adhere to Tibetan (yellow sect) Buddhism, in the form of Lamaism. There are, however, barely 1,000 lamas, or Buddhist monks/priests today, compared with 110,000, in 6,000 monasteries and temples, prior to 1959. The construction of further monasteries was banned in 1994.

Political system

Xizang constitutes one of the five Autonomous Regions of the People's Republic of China (PRC) and has its own People's Government and Local People's Congress. The controlling force in Tibet is the Communist Party of China (CPC), headed by a local party first secretary. As an Autonomous Region, Xizang is allowed to conduct its government's affairs in its own language and uphold local customs and culture. It enjoys, however, little real political autonomy, being required to adhere to decisions made in Beijing (Peking) by the leadership of the ruling CPC.

Political history

Xizang was an independent kingdom from the 5th century AD, with the Dalai Lama, popularly viewed as a reincarnation of the Compassionate Buddha, emerging as its spiritual and temporal ruler, or 'god king', from 750 AD onwards. The country was conquered and ruled by the Mongols between 1279 and 1368 and came under nominal Chinese sovereignty between about 1700 and 1912. However, independence was regained, under the Dalai Lama's leadership, after a revolt in 1912. China's rule over Xizang was nominally re-established in 1950 and Tenzin Gyatso (b. 1935), who had been designated in 1937 by the monks of Lhasa as the 14th Dalai Lama, was forced to flee to Chumbi in south Xizang and the Buddhist monks, who constituted a quarter of the population, were forced out of their monasteries. The Dalai Lama negotiated an autonomy agreement with the Chinese authorities in 1951, enabling him to return as nominal spiritual and temporal head of state, but the Chinese People's Liberation Army (PLA) had effective control over the country.

In 1959, a Tibetan uprising spread from bordering regions to Lhasa and was supported by the Xizang local government. The rebellion was, however, brutally suppressed by the PLA. As a result, the Dalai Lama and 9,000, subsequently mounting to 100,000, Tibetans were forced into permanent exile in Dharamsala, in India, where an alternative, democratically-based government was formed. The Chinese proceeded to dissolve the Xizang local government, abolish serfdom, collectivize agriculture, and suppress Lamaism.

In 1965 Xizang became an Autonomous Region of China. Industrialization, based on the production of textiles, chemicals, and agricultural machinery, was encouraged and 200,000 Han Chinese settled in the country. Chinese rule continued to be resented, however, and the economy languished, thousands dying from famine. From 1979 the new leadership in Beijing, dominated by Deng Xiaoping (b. 1904), adopted a more liberal and pragmatic policy towards Xizang. Traditional agriculture, livestock, and trading practices were restored, under the 1980 slogan 'relax, relax and relax again', a number of older political leaders and rebels were rehabilitated or pardoned, and the promotion of local Tibetan cadres was encouraged. In addition, a more tolerant attitude towards Lamaism was adopted, with temples damaged during the 1965–68 Cultural Revolution being repaired, and attempts were made to persuade the Dalai Lama to return from exile. However, the violent pro-independence demonstrations by Buddhist monks, which

Danish outlying territories

Table 70

Territory	Date of first coming Danish under administration	Area (sq km)	Area (sq mile)	Population (c. 1995)
Faroe Islands	1380	1,399	540	43,700
Greenland	985*	2,175,600**	840,004	55,70
Total	–	2,176,999	840,544	99,400

* Formally in 1917.

** 80% covered by ice-cap.

erupted in Lhasa in September and October 1987, in March and December 1988, and in March 1989, which were forcibly suppressed by Chinese troops, at the cost of hundreds of lives, exhibited the continuing strength of nationalist feeling. Since 1989 security in the Autonomous Region has been subject to stricter control from Beijing, with human rights abuses being routinely recorded by Western monitors. Between March 1989 and May 1990, when martial law was in force, it is believed that more than 2,000 opponents of the Chinese regime were executed. In 1989 the Dalai Lama was awarded the Nobel Peace Prize for his commitment to the nonviolent liberation of his homeland. In May 1995, a six-year-old boy was designated the new reincarnation of the Panchem Lama, second ranking in the country's spiritual hierarchy, by the Dalai Lama. However, in December 1995 he was detained in Beijing by the Chinese authorities, who enthroned their own choice. Since 1995 there has been an upsurge in terrorism in Xizang and continuing anti-Chinese demonstrations.

8.4.3 Denmark's dependencies

Denmark has two dependencies, described as Outlying Territories. Their political structures and histories follow.

FAROE ISLANDS

Capital: Torshavn

Location

Western Europe. A group of 21 volcanic islands, 18 of which are inhabited, in the North Atlantic between Iceland and the Shetland Isles, some 320 km/200 miles to the southeast. They are situated 1,000 km/620 miles away from Denmark. The largest islands are Stromo and Ostero.

Social and economic data

Area: 1,399 sq km/540 sq miles
Population: 43,700*
Pop. density per sq km/sq mile: 31*/81
Economy type: high income (c. $12,000 per capita)
Currency: Danish krone
* 1995.

Ethnic composition

The inhabitants are predominantly ethnic Faroese. Five per cent of the work force are immigrants. The main language is Faroese, but Danish is a compulsory school subject.

Religions

The population is predominantly Christian, in the form of the Evangelical Lutheran Protestant Church of Denmark.

Local governmnent

Power has been decentralized to 50 local authorities.

Head of government

Prime Minister Anfinn Kallsberg, since 1998

Political system

An elected assembly (Logting) of 32 members has operated since 1852. Twenty-seven of its seats are filled by direct election, under universal adult suffrage (minimum voting age 18 years), on the basis of proportional representation in seven multimember constituencies. There are a further five supplementary seats, which are dependent upon the numbers of people voting. The parliamentary term is four years. A six-member cabinet (Landsstyri), headed by a chairperson, or prime minister (Logmadur), is responsible to the chamber. This assembly has, since 1948, been devolved full authority for internal affairs, but the Danish government, which is represented on the islands by a High Commissioner, has responsibility for foreign affairs and regulates education, social welfare, civil, criminal, and church affairs, and currency matters. The islands elect two representatives to the Danish parliament (Folketing), having been represented there since 1851.

Political parties
Eight main political parties currently operate in the Faroes. They are the Social Democratic Party (SDP: Javnaoarflokkurin), the Union (or Coalition) Party (UP), the Republican Party (RP), the Faroese People's Party (FPP: Folkaflokkurin), the Home Rule Party (HRP), the Christian People's Party-Progressive and Fishing Industry Party (CPP-PFIP), the allied Center Party (CP), and the Workers' Front (WF; estd. 1994) of trade unionists.

The left-of-center SDP was established in 1928, and has a membership of about 1,000. It has frequently participated in coalition governments, with the UP, RP, FPP, and HRP, since 1958 and is social democratic in outlook. The UP was founded in 1906. It is a conservative party which stands for close links with the Danish Crown and dominated the Logting before 1958. The RP dates from 1948. It favors secession from Denmark and the establishment of a fully independent republic. It has participated in government coalitions, with the HRP, CPP-PFIP, SDP, and FPP, since the early 1960s.

The FPP was established in 1940 and is a liberal-conservative, right-of-center party, in favor of free enterprise and greater economic autonomy. It has also participated in government coalitions, with the RP, SDP, HRP, and CPP-PFIP, since the early 1960s.

The HRP was formed in 1906 and now has a membership of about 1,700. It is a centrist party, originally formed to press for greater legislative devolution. It was a regular member of government coalitions between 1948 and 1970. The CPP-PFIP is a minor center-right party, formed in 1954, which favors increased internal self-government.

Latest elections
The most recent Logting elections were held on 30 April 1998 and resulted in the RP, with 24% of the vote, doubling its representation to eight seats. The FPP, with 21% of the vote, also won eight seats; the SDP, seven and 22% of the vote; and the UP, six seats and 18% of the vote. The HRP, won two seats and the CP one seat, but the CPP-PFIP and WF failed to win any seats. Turnout was 86%.

Political history
The islands were settled by the Norse during the 8th–9th centuries and became part of the Kingdom of Norway in the 11th century. They passed to Denmark in 1380, when Queen Margrethe I (1353–1412) inherited Norway. However, the Faroes were not finally separated administratively from Danish-ruled Norway until 1709, when a Danish royal trade monopoly was established. During World War II, following the German invasion of Denmark, they were temporarily occupied by British troops. Home rule was granted in 1948. Fishing is the principal industry, employing a quarter of the labor force, and is the chief export earner; although stocks are now declining as a consequence of overfishing. Danish subsidies account for a sixth of GDP and provide nearly 30% of government revenue. Although Denmark joined the European Community in 1973, the Faroes remained outside.

Following the November 1984 general election, a four-party center-left coalition government, consisting of the SDP, HRP, RP, and CPP-PFIP, and headed by the SDP's leader, Atli Dam, was formed. The Social Democratic coalition lost its majority, however, in the general election of November 1988, when there was a swing to the right, with the FPP emerging as the new dominant force. The FPP's leader, Jogvan Sundstein, became the new Logmadur (prime minister), heading a center-right coalition, including the HRP, RP, and CPP-PFIP and pledging to support the fishing industry, while pursuing an economic austerity program in an effort to tackle a mounting level of governmnent debt. There was a new early general election in November 1990, after the FPP's coalition partners withdrew their support. The SDP re-emerged as the largest single party, with ten Logting seats to the FPP's seven, and a 'grand coalition' was formed by the SDP and FPP, headed by Atli Dam. The coalition was restructured in April 1993 to comprise the SDP, RP, and HRP. Led by Marita Petersen, the prime minister since January 1993, the SDP lost support in the July 1994 general election, winning just five seats, and the opposition right-of-center UP emerged as the largest single party. In September 1994 a broad-based coalition was formed embracing the UP, SDP, HRP, and new WF, with Edmund Joensen, leader of the UP, the new prime minister. During the early 1990s the Faroes' economy, crippled by huge trade and public-spending deficits and depletion of the fish stock, went into severe recession, with the unemployment rate climbing to 20% and nearly a tenth of islanders emigrating. Since 1995 there has been gradual economic recovery, helped by large subsidies from the Danish government, worth $147 million a year.

In 1996 the SDP withdrew from the ruling coalition and was replaced by the FPP, with there being evidence of growing support for increased autonomy. The rightwing UP, FPP, and RP coalition remained in power after the April 1998 general election, with an increased number of seats, and Anfinn Kallsberg of the FPP took over as prime minister. Later in 1998, with Denmark's coalition government requiring support from the Faroes' two deputies to stay in office, the Faroes' government opened negotiations with the government in Copenhagen on the territory's constitutional future. It hoped to secure what was known as the 'Iceland solution', becoming a sovereign nation under the Danish crown for a period of around 25 years, as Iceland had in 1917, before later becoming fully independent.

GREENLAND

Kalaallitt Nunaat

Capital: Godthaab (Nuuk)

Location

Arctic. Greenland is the second largest island in the world, after Australia. It is situated in the North Atlantic and Arctic Oceans, northeast of Canada. The interior is covered by an ice-sheet, with only 16% ice-free and 5% habitable by humans.

Social and economic data

Area: 2,175,600 sq km/840,004 sq miles
Population: 55,700[*]
Pop. density per sq km/sq mile: 0.2[**]/0.07
Economy type: high income (*c.* $10,000 per capita)
Currency: Danish krone
[*] 1995.
[**] Based on ice-free area.

Ethnic composition

The population is predominantly Inuit (Eskimo), with Danish mixtures. Greenlandic, an Inuit (Eskimo) language, and Danish are the official languages.

Religions

Chiefly Shamanism and Evangelical Lutheran Christianity.

Local government

There are 18 municipality councils responsible for local affairs.

Head of government

Prime Minister Jonathan Motzfeldt, since 1997

Political system

In 1979 a new parliament (Landsting) was set up to replace the existing Greenland Provincial Council. It consists of 31 members, elected for four-year terms, by universal adult suffrage (minimum age 18 years) on the basis of proportional representation. A seven-member government (Landsstyre) is drawn from the Landsting, being based on the strength of the parties, and is headed by a prime minister. Denmark is represented on the island by a high commissioner (Rigsom budsmand) and has control over foreign affairs, defense, monetary policy, and constitutional matters. Greenland also sends two representatives to the Danish Folketing and used to elect one Euro-MP.

Political parties

There are five political parties: the Forward (Siumut) Party; the Feeling of Community/Solidarity (Atassut) Party; the Eskimo/Inuit Brotherhood (Inuit Ataqatigiit: IA); the Center Party (Akulliit Partiiat, or CP); and the Polar Party (Issitrup-partii: IP).

The Siumut is the most important of the five, regularly drawing support from nearly 40% of the electorate. Although originating as a movement in 1971, it was formally established as a party in 1977 and has a current membership of 5,000. It is a center-left body which spearheaded the movement for self-rule and opposed Greenland's European Community entry terms. Drawing its support from the fishing and hunting community, the Siumut, led by a Lutheran pastor, Jonathan Motzfeldt, formed Greenland's first home-rule government in 1979. The Atassut, a center-right conservative grouping which dominated the pre-autonomy Council, is the second most important party, normally able to attract around 30% of the vote. The IA leftwing party which was founded in 1978 and advocates full independence for Greenland. The CP is a liberal party, formed in 1991, which supports the open-sea fishing industry. The right-of-center IP, formed in 1987, favors a reduced state role in the economy, including privatization of the state's trawler fleet.

Latest elections

The most recent general election was held on 16 February 1999. Siumut attracted 35% of the territory's vote and captured 11 Landsting seats, while its coalition partner, Atassut won 25% of the vote and eight seats. The IA with 22% of the vote won seven seats, while the independent Katassegstigiit attracted 17% of the vote to win seven seats.

Political history

The island was settled by seal-hunting Inuit from North America *c.* 2,500 BC and colonized by the Danish king, Erik the Red, in 985 AD. The southwest of the island was colonized by Danes between the 12th and 15th centuries, but these colonies were later abandoned. New settlements were founded in the 17th century and a Danish colony was set up in 1721. Danish sovereignty extended over the whole island in 1917. An agreement for the joint defense of Greenland, within the North Atlantic Treaty Organization (NATO), was signed with the United States in 1951 and an American air base and, later, a radar station, were established at Thule in the far north. In 1953 the island became fully part of Denmark, returning two members to the Danish parliament (Folketing). Following a referendum supported by 70% of voters, it was granted home-rule in 1979.

On 1 February 1985, after a referendum held in February 1982 had resulted in a 53% majority in favor of withdrawal, Greenland left the European Community, which it had joined, with Denmark, in 1973. There had been an overwhelming, 71% to 29%, vote against entering in October 1972. Greenland, as a territory 'in association', has subsequently retained preferential access to European Union markets. Following the May 1987 general election, a new Siumut–IA coalition was formed, with Jonathan Motzfeldt, prime minister since 1979, remaining in office. The coalition broke down in June 1988 and

Siumut found a new governing partner in the Atassut party. However, after the March 1991 general election the Siumut-IA coalition was reformed, and Siumut's new leader, Lars Emil Johansen, became prime minister. The Siumut-IA was re-elected in March 1995, but in September 1997 Jonathan Motzfeldt (Siumut) took over as prime minister. He headed a new coaalition with Atassut, which was re-elected, with a reduced majority, in the February 1999 general election. Fishing, especially cod, is the principal industry, but a very high proportion of the island's GDP, and nearly half of the government's annual revenue, is derived from annual subsidies from Denmark. Depletion of the fish stocks led to GDP decline in the early 1990s, but since 1994, helped by the development of tourism, there has been an upturn.

8.4.4 Finland's dependency

Finland has one dependency, described as an External Territory. Its political structure and history follow.

THE ALAND ISLANDS

Capital: Mariehamn

Location
Western Europe. A group of 6,554 islands in the Baltic Sea, at the southern extremity of the Gulf of Bothnia, situated between Finland and Sweden. Only 60 are inhabited. The largest island in the group is Aland, on which the capital is situated.

Social and economic data
Area: 1,481sq km/572 sq miles
Population: 25,257[*]
Pop. density per sq km/sq mile: 17[*]/44
Economy type: high income
Currency: Finnish markka
[*] 1996.

Ethnic composition
The great majority of the population, around 95%, are Swedish-speaking. Swedish is the official language.

Religions
The population is predominantly Christian, in the form of the Evangelical Lutheran Church of Finland.

Head of government
Prime Minister Roger Jansson, since 1995

Political system

Under the current 1991 constitution, there is a 30-seat legislature, the Lagting, whose members are directly elected by proportional representation every four years. From the Lagting is formed a five- to seven-member executive council (Landskapsstyrelse), or government, headed by a chairperson (Landtrad), who is the equivalent of a prime minister. The government of Finland is represented on the islands by a governor, who is appointed by the Finnish president, with the agreement of the speaker of the Lagting.

Political parties

There are six party groupings in the Aland Islands: the centrist Center Party (CP); the centrist Liberal Party (LP); the center-right Moderate Party (Freethinking Cooperation: MP); the left-of-center Social Democratic Party (SDP); the environmentalist Green Party; and the conservative Non-aligned Rally/Independents.

Latest elections

At the most recent general election, held on 15 October 1995, the CP, with 28% of the vote, won nine of the Lagting seats and the LP, with 27% of the vote, eight. A further six seats were won by the MP (20% of the vote), four by the SDP (15%), and three by independents (10%).

Political history

For reasons of geography, the islands were long associated with Sweden and the population became Swedish-speaking. However, when Sweden was forced to cede Finland to Russia in 1809 the islands were incorporated, as the 'County of Aland', within the Finnish Grand Duchy. The islanders tried to secede from Finland and rejoin Sweden when, in 1917, Finland declared its independence from Russia. Finland responded by conceding the islands' autonomy in 1920 and a provincial parliament, Landsting, was elected in 1922. Meanwhile, the League of Nations approved Finland's continuing sovereignty on condition that the islands be neutral and non-fortified. Increased powers of self-government and control over internal and economic affairs were conceded in the Autonomy Acts of 1951 and 1991; while the principle of majority parliamentary government was established by constitutional reforms in 1988. A succession of coalition governments held power during the last decade. They comprised the Center Party (CP), Moderate Party (MP), and the Liberal Party (LP) between 1987 and 1991; the CP, MP, and Social Democratic Party (SDP) between 1991 and 1995; and a center-right coalition made up of the CP and MP and

one independent since 1995, with Roger Jansson (MP) head of government. The islands became a member of the Nordic Council in 1970. In January 1995, following a referendum in November 1994, in which 74% voted in favor of accession, the Aland Islands joined the European Union (EU), along with Finland. To protect the tourist and ferry industries, the islands have been granted special exemption from tax union with the EU.

8.4.5 France's dependencies

The French dependencies consist of four Overseas Departments, two Overseas Collective Territories, four Overseas Territories, and one Internal Collective Territory, as listed in Table 71.

FRENCH OVERSEAS DEPARTMENTS

Overseas Departments, which form integral parts of the French Republic, have an administrative structure similar to that of the Departments of metropolitan France, although the former have their own Courts of Appeal. Prior to the decentralization reforms of 1982, each Overseas Department was administered by a central government-appointed prefect, assisted by a directly elected General Council and an indirectly elected Regional Council. After the reforms the prefect was renamed Commissaire de la République (government commissioner), his or her formal executive power being transferred to the General Council, while the powers of the Regional Council, which was now directly elected, were considerably increased in the social, economic, and cultural spheres. An earlier plan to merge the two councils into one was blocked by a decision of the French Constitutional Council in December 1982. French Overseas Departments also send representatives to the French national parliament and participate in French presidential elections.

FRENCH GUIANA

La Guyane Française

Capital: Cayenne

Location

South America. French Guiana lies between Suriname, to the west, and Brazil, to the east and south, on the

French overseas departments, territories, and collective territories · Table 71

Name	Date of first coming under French administration	Area (sq km)	Area (sq mile)	Population (c. 1995)	French National Assembly (NA) and Senate (S) seats
Overseas Departments					
French Guiana	1817	90,000	34,749	144,009	2NA, 1S
Guadeloupe	1613	1,780	687	414,000	4NA, 2S
Martinique	1635	1,100	425	381,000	4NA, 2S
Réunion	1642	2,512	970	675,000	5NA, 3S
Overseas Collective Territories					
Mayotte	1843	376	145	131,000	1NA, 1S
St Pierre and Miquelon	17 c/1816	242	93	6,600	1NA, 1S
Overseas Territories					
French Polynesia	1842	4,200	1,622	230,000	2NA, 1S
French Southern and Antarctic Territories	–	7,567*	2,921	210**	–
New Caledonia	1853	19,103	7,375	197,000	2NA, 1S
Wallis & Futuna Islands	1842	274	106	15,000	1NA, 1S
Total	–	*127,154*	*49,094*	*2,193,810*	*22NA, 13S*
Internal Collective Territory					
Corsica	1768	8,680	3,351	250,000	–

* Excludes 500,000 sq km of the uninhabited mainland of Antarctica.
* Scientific mission workers.

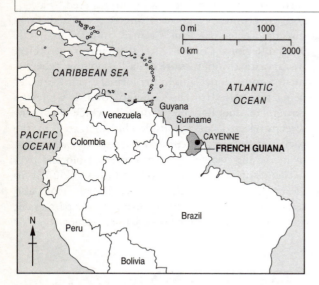

north coast of South America. It is the site of the European Space Agency's satellite-launching center.

Social and economic data
Area: 90,000 sq km/34,749 sq miles
Population: 144,000*
Pop. density per sq km/sq mile: 1.6*/4

Literacy rate: 83%
Economy type: middle income (c. $3,000 per capita)
Currency: French franc
* 1995.

Ethnic composition
The population is a mixture of Creoles, Europeans, Amerindians, and Africans. French is the official language, but a creole dialect is also spoken.

Religions
Seventy-eight per cent of the population is Roman Catholic.

Local government
The country is divided into two districts of Cayenne and Saint Laurent du Maroni.

Political system
French Guiana is administered by an appointed French government prefect, who is assisted by a two-chamber body comprising the 19-member General Council (Conseil Général) and the 31-member Regional Council (Conseil de Région). Both are directly elected for six-year terms and exercise a number of local pow-

ers. Additionally, the inhabitants elect two members to the French National Assembly and send, through indirect elections, one representative to the Senate. The Department is also represented at the European Parliament in Strasbourg.

Political parties

The principal political parties are the two conservative groups, the Rally for the Republic (RPR) and Guyanese Union for French Democracy (UDF); the Guiana Socialist Party (PSG); the leftist Guyanese Democratic Action Party (Action Démocratique Guyanaise: ADG); the Guyanese Democratic Force (Forces Démocratiques Guyanaises: FDG); and the separatist Guyanese Popular National Party (Parti National Populaire Guyanais: PNPG). The FDG was set up in 1989 by Georges Othily, who had been expelled from the PSG in June 1989 for working too closely with opposition parties. The PNPG was established in 1985, before which it was known as the Union of Guyanese Workers (UTG). Walawari is a leftwing party led by a dissident independent socialist, Christiane Taubira-Delannon.

Latest elections

The most recent elections to the Regional Councils were held on 15 March 1998 and were won by the PSG, which captured 11 Regional Council seats. Antoine Karam of the PSG remained president of the Regional Council. The RPR won six seats; Walawar, two; various leftwing candidates, nine; and independents, three. In the May – June 1997 elections to the French National Assembly, the RPR retained its seat, while the other was held by Christiane Taubira-Delannon.

Political history

First settled by France in 1604, the area was, successively, under Dutch, English, and Portuguese rule during the 17th and 18th centuries before French control was re-established and recognized in 1817. It was used as a penal colony during the 19th century, including the notorious Devil's Island, and remained economically undeveloped, possessing few natural resources except timber. In 1946 French Guiana became an Overseas Department of the French Republic, making it subject to the same laws and system of government as France's mainland departments. Such departmental status was opposed during the 1970s by leftwing groups, led by the Guiana Socialist Party (PSG), who demanded greater internal autonomy and called for increased priority to be given to economic development. In response, the French government introduced an indirectly elected Regional Council in 1974,

which became directly elected and was given increased authority in 1983. In addition, France provided substantial amounts of economic aid. After five years of growth, the economy began to slow down from 1991 and unemployment began to rise, leading to a general strike in October 1992.

The PSG has been the dominant force in the Regional Council since the latter's inception. Georges Othily, who was then PSG leader, was re-elected president of the Council following the elections of March 1986. He was later expelled from the party in June 1989, but, nevertheless, took the Department's one seat in the French Senate in September 1989. The PSG, led by Antoine Karam, held on to power after the March 1992 elections. However, facing accusations that its domination of French Guiana had become corrupt, its majority was greatly reduced and the FDG, a new party formed by Othily, polled strongly.

Christiane Taubira-Delannon, an independent socialist candidate, was elected to the European Parliament, in June 1994, as representative of the 'Radical Energy' grouping, which attracted 36% of the vote: while in the French presidential elections of May – June 1995 Jacques Chirac, the candidate of the right, attracted 57% of the second-round vote. This reflected declining popularity for the PSG, as the unemployment rate rose to 22% in mid-1996 leading to social problems and violent riots in Cayenne, involving students, unemployed youths, and separatists, in October 1996 and April 1997. Paramilitary forces had to be flown in from France in November 1996 to quell the disturbances. In the May – June 1997 French National Assembly elections, candidates from pro-independence parties attracted 10% of the vote. Nevertheless, the PSG held on to power, though with a reduced share of the vote and seats, after the March 1998 regional council elections.

GUADELOUPE

Capital: Basse-Terre

Location

Central America. Guadeloupe consists of a group of islands in the central Lesser Antilles, of the eastern Caribbean, lying between Dominica, to the south, and Antigua and Montserrat, to the northwest. The two principal islands are Basse-Terre and Grande-Terre, on which 43% and 48%, respectively, of the total population live.

Social and economic data
Area: 1,780 sq km/687 sq miles
Population: 414,000[*]
Pop. density per sq km/sq mile: 233[*]/603
Literacy rate: 90%
Economy type: middle income (*c.* $8,000 per capita)
Currency: French franc
[*] 1995.

Ethnic composition
Ninety per cent of the population are of African descent or mulattos, 5% Caucasians, and 4% East Indians. French, spoken in a creole dialect, is the main and official language. English is the main language on St Martin island.

Religions
Ninety-five per cent of the population is Roman Catholic.

Local government
The islands are divided into three districts (*arrondissements*), which are subdivided into 34 communes.

Political system
The country is administered by an appointed French government prefect, who is assisted by a two-chamber body comprising the 42-member General Council (Conseil Général) and the 41-member Regional Council (Conseil de Région). Both are elected for a period of up to six years and exercise a number of local powers. The Regional Council is responsible for economic and social planning and the General Council for internal executive power. In addition, Guadeloupe elects four members to the French National Assembly and sends two, indirectly elected, representatives to the Senate. The Department is also represented at the European Parliament in Strasbourg.

Political parties
The principal political parties are the two conservative groups, Rally for the Republic (RPR) and Union for French Democracy (UDF); the left-of-center Guadeloupe Socialist Party (Fédération Guadeloupéenne du Parti Socialiste: FGPS) and Socialist Party-Dissidents (FRUI-G); the Guadeloupe Communist Party (PCG), which was established in 1944, and the Guadeloupean Progressive Democratic Party (PPDG), which was formed in 1991 by a breakaway group of PCG militants; and the Popular Union for the Liberation of Guadeloupe (UPLG), a pro-independence force formed in 1978.

Latest elections
The most recent elections to the Regional Council were held on 15 March 1998. They were won by the RPR, which captured 25 of the 41 seats. The FGPS won 12 seats and various rightwing candidates, two seats. Lucette Michaux-Chévery, of the RPR, who had become president of the Regional Council in March 1992 with FRUI-G support, retained the position and also represented Guadeloupe in the French Senate. Dominique Larifla, leader of the FRUI-G, remained president of the General Council. The PPDG, a FGPS 'dissident', the RPR, and a leftwing independent won the Department's other French National Assembly seats in May-June 1997.

Political history
Discovered by Christopher Columbus (1451–1506) in 1493, the islands of Guadeloupe were occupied by France in 1635. They became renowned for sugar production and remained under French rule for the next three centuries, apart from brief British occupations in the 18th and early 19th centuries. The country became an Overseas Department of the French Republic in 1946. During the 1960s opposition to the monopoly of economic power by white (Creole) settlers and to the restrictions imposed by the status of being a Department, led to a movement for greater internal autonomy, spearheaded by the Guadeloupe Communist Party (PCG). In response to these demands, an indirectly elected Regional Council was established in 1974. This body became directly elected, with increased powers, from February 1983. A small extremist minority, led by the Popular Movement for an Independent Guadeloupe (Mouvement Populaire pour une Guadeloupe Indépendante: MPGI) and the outlawed Caribbean Revolutionary Alliance (Alliance Révolutionnaire Caraïbe: ARC), a leftwing extremist group, continued to seek full independence during the 1980s. The ARC, which is now disbanded, resorted to terrorist bombing outrages. However, despite a deterioration in economic conditions from the 1970s, caused by the steady decline of the sugar industry, which sent the unemployment rate to above 25%, electoral support for pro-independence parties remained below 5%. There was, however, a gradual shift in support away from the parties of the right and center towards those of the pro-autonomy 'conventional left', the Guadeloupe Socialist Party (FGPS) and PCG. This persuaded the formerly pro-independence UPLG to moderate its stance and to declare, in March 1990, that it would henceforth participate in elections and seek associated status for Guadeloupe.

The FGPS, with support from the PCG, won control of the General Council and Regional Council following the elections of March 1985 and 1986, with the party's leader, Dominique Larifla, becoming president of the General Council. Larifla, by now a dissident member of the FGPS, remained president of the General Council after the March 1992 elections, but the RPR captured the presidency of the Regional Council, with the support of FGPS dissidents. The left retained control of the General Council following cantonal elections in March 1994 and the socialist candidate, Lionel Jospin, attracted 55% of the second-round vote in the May 1995 French presidential election. However, the RPR retained control over the Regional Council after the March 1998 elections. Hurricanes Luis and Marilyn caused extensive damage in 1995 and in 1997 the unemployment rate had risen to 27%.

MARTINIQUE

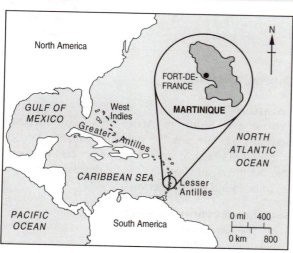

Capital: Fort-de-France

Location

Central America and the Caribbean. Martinique is one of the Windward Islands in the eastern Caribbean, situated between Dominica, to the north, and St Lucia, to the south.

Social and economic data

Area: 1,100 sq km/425 sq miles
Population: 381,000[*]
Pop. density per sq km/sq mile: 347[*]/896
Literacy rate: 93%

Economy type: high income (c. $11,700 per capita in 1994)
Currency: French franc
[*] 1994.

Ethnic composition

Ninety per cent of the population are of African and African-Caucasian-Indian descent. French is the official language, with a creole dialect widely spoken.

Religions

Ninety per cent of the population is Roman Catholic.

Local government

The island is divided into three districts (*arrondissements*), which are subdivided into 34 communes.

Political system

Martinique is administered by an appointed French government prefect, assisted by a two-chamber body comprising the 45-member General Council (Conseil Général) and the 41-member Regional Council (Conseil de Région). Both are elected for a term of up to six years and exercise a number of local powers. In addition, Martinique elects four members to the French National Assembly and sends, through indirect election, two representatives to the French Senate. The Department is also represented at the European Parliament in Strasbourg.

Political parties

The principal political parties are the two conservative groups, the Rally for the Republic (RPR) and Union for French Democracy (UDF); the left-of-center Progressive Party of Martinique (Parti Progessiste Martiniquais: PPM), which was established in 1957, and the Martinique Socialist Federation (Fédération Socialiste de la Martinique: FSM), which is a local branch of the mainland Socialist party; the Martinique Communist Party (PCM), which was formed in 1920 and was affiliated to the French Communist Party until 1957; and the secessionist Martinique Independence Movement (Mouvement Indépendentiste Martiniquais: MIM), formed in 1978 and also known as Patriotes Martiniquais.

Latest elections

In the most recent Regional Council election, held on 15 March 1998, the MIM won 13 of the 41 seats, the PPM, seven, the RPR, six, the UDF, five, and FSM, three seats. Various rightwing (divers droit) candidates won three seats and others four. The PPM hold control of the General Council. In the May – June 1997 French National Assembly elections, the RPR won two seats, and the PPM and an independent, one seat each.

Political history

Martinique was discovered by Spanish navigators in 1493 and became a French colony in 1635. Famed for its sugar production and as the birthplace of Napolion's wife, the Empress Josephine (1763–1814), the island became an Overseas Department of the French Republic in 1946. Despite the country's close cultural integration with France, a nationalist movement emerged during the 1950s and 1960s, spearheaded by the Progressive Party of Martinique (PPM) and the Martinique Communist Party (PCM), which opposed the concentration of economic power in the hands of white settler families (*békés*). In response to this movement, consultative General and Regional Councils were created in 1960 and 1974 respectively. The Regional Council became directly elected and was granted additional powers, including greater control over taxation, local police, and economic affairs, in 1983, as part of the metropolitan Socialist government's decentralization initiative. The PPM and PCM continue to seek greater autonomy, but only a small, though growing, minority of the population, less than 5%, support a campaign for full independence from France.

This extreme policy has been championed by the Martinique Independence Movement (MIM) and the outlawed, and now disbanded, Caribbean Revolutionary Alliance (ARC) terrorist organization. The island's economy has been in a depressed condition during recent years, the sugar industry continuing to decline, and growth in new export lines, for example bananas, has been adversely affected by the European Union's new competitive regime for exports to its single market, and by periodic cyclones. More than a quarter of the labor force are currently unemployed and emigration to France and French Guiana is now at a level of 15,000 per annum. However, tourism has developed into a significant sector.

Following the March 1986 elections, the parties of the left (PPM, FSM, and PCM) retained control of the Regional Council, with 21 seats, after forming a 'Union of the Left' and the PPM's leader, Aimé Césaire, was re-elected Council president. The center-right RPR-UDF, although a minority, controlled the administration of the General Council after the elections of March 1985. However, the PPM captured the Council's presidency in March 1992 and Emile Capgras, of the PCM, concurrently became president of the Regional Council. In the May 1995 presidential election, the socialist candidate, Lionel Jospin, secured 59% of the second-round vote. Following the elections to the Regional Council in March 1998, Alfred Marie-Jeanne of the MIM became the Council's new president.

RÉUNION

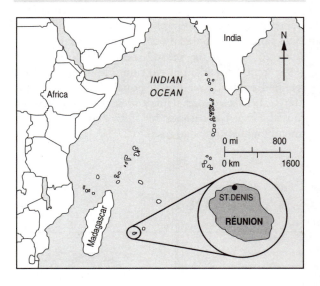

Capital: Saint-Denis

Location

Central and Southern Africa. Réunion, formerly Bourbon, island lies in the Indian Ocean, 800 km/500 miles east of Madagascar. Thirty-five per cent of its area is under forest, and both active and dormant volcanoes are to be found in the interior.

Social and economic data

Area: 2,507 sq km/968 sq miles
Population: 675,000[*]
Pop. density per sq km/sq mile: 269[*]/697
Literacy rate: 79%
Economy type: high income (*c.* $9,300 per capita in 1994)
Currency: French franc
[*] 1997.

Ethnic composition

The population comprises a mixture of people of European, African, Indian, and Chinese descent. There are also more than 3,000 French troops based on the island, which serves as the headquarters of French military forces in the Indian Ocean. The official language is French.

Religions

Ninety per cent of the population is Roman Catholic.

Local government

The island is divided into four districts *arrondissements*, which are subdivided into 24 communes and 36 cantons.

Political system

The island is administered by an appointed French prefect, assisted by a two-chamber body consisting of the 47-member General Council (Conseil Général) and the 44-member Regional Council (Conseil de Région). Both are directly elected for six-year terms and exercise a number of local powers. In addition, Réunion elects five members to the French National Assembly, and sends, through indirect election, three representatives to the French Senate and one to the Economic and Social Council. The Department is also represented at the European Parliament in Strasbourg.

Political parties

The principal political parties are the two right-of-center groups, the Rally for the Republic (RPR) and the Union for French Democracy (UDF); the Réunion Communist Party (PCR), which was founded in 1959; and the Socialist Party (PS). The pro-autonomy Movement for an Independent Réunion (MIR) was formed in 1981.

Latest elections

The most recent General Council elections were held on 20 and 27 March 1994, and resulted in the PS winning control from the RPR and Christophe Payet, from the PS, being elected Council president in April 1994. The left-of-center PS, and PCR draw the bulk of their support from poor Creole (Afro-Asian) urban and rural workers who seek improved labor conditions. Regional Council elections were last held on 15 March 1998. The UDF won eight seats; the PCR, seven; various rightwing candidates 15; and various leftwing candidates five seats. In the May – June 1997 elections to the French National Assembly, the PCR won three seats and the PS and UDF, one apiece.

Political history

Discovered by the Portuguese in 1513, Réunion was annexed by France in 1642, serving initially as a penal colony and then, from 1665, as a post of the French East India Company. During the 18th century the island was developed into a major coffee exporter, this crop being replaced by sugarcane during the 19th century. Réunion was designated an Overseas Department of the French Republic in 1946 and was given the additional status of a region in 1974. Despite calls on the part of the Organization of African Unity (OAU) for the island's 'liberation', there is majority support on Réunion for continued French control. The leftwing parties, however, favor enhanced autonomy. Réunion's economy, which remains heavily dependent on the sugar industry, has been depressed during recent years. As a consequence, despite growth in the tourist sector, the unemployment rate has risen to nearly 40%, forcing the island to draw increasingly on the mainland for development grants. Discontent with the island's social and economic conditions provoked riots in February and March 1991 when the broadcasting transmitters of the unauthorized television service, Tele Free-DOM, were seized by the French authorities. The director of Tele Free-DOM, Camille Sudre, was subsequently elected president of the Regional Council in March 1992, with PCR support, after independent candidates representing Tele Free-DOM polled strongly. In March 1994 Eric Boyer of the RPR, the president of the General Council and a senator, was sentenced to two years' imprisonment for corruption. Further politicians and business executives were later arrested for corruption. In the May 1995 second round of the French presidential election, Lionel Jospin, the socialist candidate, secured 56% of the vote in Réunion and leftwing candidates also dominated the May – June 1997 National Assembly elections. Paul Vergès, of the PCR, who was elected to the French Senate in April 1996, also became the new president of the Regional Council, after elections in March 1998.

FRENCH OVERSEAS COLLECTIVE TERRITORIES

The status of a Collective Territory (CT) is intermediate between that of an Overseas Department and an Overseas Territory. CTs constitute integral parts of the French Republic. They are administered by an appointed government commissioner (Commissaire de la République), who works with an elected General Council, and they send representatives to the French parliament and participate in French presidential elections.

MAYOTTE (MAHORE)

Capital: Dzaoudzi

Location
Central and Southern Africa. Mayotte consists of a volcanic island group that forms part of the Comoro archipelago, between Madagascar and the African mainland. The two main islands are Grande Terre and La Petite Terre.

Social and economic data
Area: 374 sq km/144 sq miles
Population: 131,000[*]
Pop. density per sq km/sq mile: 350[*]/910
Economy type: low income (*c.* $700 per capita in 1991)
Currency: French franc
[*] 1997.

Principal languages
French is is the official dialect and Mahorian, a Swahili dialect is used.

Religions
Ninety-eight per cent of the population adheres to Islam.

Local government
Mayotte is divided into 17 communes.

Political system
The islands are administered by an appointed French government prefect , who works with the assistance of an elected 19-member General Council (Conseil Général). In addition, Mayotte elects one member to the French National Assembly and one representative to the French Senate.

Political parties
Five main political parties operate on the islands, including branches of the mainland Union for French Democracy (UDF), Rally for the Republic (RPR), and the Socialist Party (PS). The RPR branch is termed the Mayotte Federation of the Rally for the Republic (FMRPR).

The dominant political party on the islands is the Mayotte People's Movement (Mouvement Populaire Mahorais: MPM). The MPM led the movement for Mayotte's exclusion from the independent Republic of the Comoros and has since campaigned for full departmental status within France. Its leader, Younoussa Bamana, is president of the General Council. The Party for the Democratic Rally of Mayotte (PRDM), formed in 1978, seeks unification with the Federal Islamic Republic of the Comoros.

Latest elections
The most recent elections to the General Council were held on 20 and 27 March 1994 with further by-elections for nine seats on 23 March 1997. The MPM retained control of the Council, holding eight seats; the FMRPR held five, the PS one and the indpendents five. The May – June 1997 election to the French National Assembly saw the re-election of the Martinique-born Henry Jean-Baptiste, of the UDF-Center of Social Democrats. The September 1995 election to the French Senate saw the re-election of Marcel Henry (MPM).

Political history
The most populous of the Comoros group of islands in the Indian Ocean, Mayotte, together with its sister islands, was a French colony from 1843, and attached to Madagascar from 1914. Later, in 1947, the Comoros Islands were designated a French Overseas Territory, and granted internal autonomy within the French Republic in 1961. It was agreed, in 1973, that eventual independence would be secured in 1979. However, when the Comoran parliament declared unilateral independence in July 1975, Mayotte refused to join the new state, preferring to remain formally linked to France. The French government granted Mayotte special status as a Collective Territory of the French Republic in December 1976, a decision which was reaffirmed by the French National Assembly in December 1979 and October 1984. They rejected, however, the Mayotte People's Movement's demands for full departmental status, because of the island's economic backwardness. The Comoran government continues to claim sovereignty over Mayotte and is supported in this view by the United Nations General Assembly and the Organization of African Unity (OAU), officially representing Mayotte in the UN. A referendum to determine the future of the island has been postponed indefinitely. Immigration from the Comoros in recent years has caused tension in Mayotte, with a population increase of nearly 40% between 1991 and 1997. Yet more than a third of the population is unemployed and the country relies heavily on French aid. Nevertheless, the islands' relative prosperity led, in July 1997, to the Comoran Islands of Mwali and Nzwani to declare their independence and demand the restoration of French rule.

ST PIERRE AND MIQUELON (SPM)

Iles Saint-Pierre-et-Miquelon

Capital: Saint-Pierre

Location

North America. It consists of a small group of eight rocky islands, lying 25 km/15 miles south of Newfoundland, in the North Atlantic Ocean. Ninety per cent of the population lives on Saint-Pierre Island.

Social and economic data

Area: 242 sq km/93 sq miles
Population: 6,600*
Pop. density per sq km/sq mile: 27*/71
Literacy rate: 99%
Economy type: high income
Currency: French franc
* 1996.

Principal language

The principal language is French.

Religions

Ninety-seven per cent of the population is Roman Catholic.

Political system

The islands are administered by an appointed French government prefect, who is assisted by a 19-member General Council (Conseil Général), which is elected for a six-year term. Fifteen of the General Council's members are elected from St Pierre and four from Miquelon. In addition, the islands elect one member to the French National Assembly and one representative to the French Senate and one to the Economic and Social Council.

Political parties

The main political parties are the left-of-center Socialist Party (PS); the right-of-center Union for French Democracy (UDF), and the Rally for the Republic (RPR).

Latest elections

In the most recent General Council elections, on 20 March 1994, candidates of the UDF-RPR secured 15 seats and the PS, four. The September 1995 and the May – June 1997 elections to the French National Assembly were won by candidates of the RPR and UDF parties.

Political history

The islands, which were first visited and settled by Breton and Basque fishermen during the 16th and 17th centuries, constitute the remnants of the once extensive French empire in North America. They were formally designated French territory in 1816 and gained departmental status in the French Republic in July 1976. This move, tying the local economy into the remote institutions of metropolitan France and the European Community, disrupted economic relations with neighboring Canada and was opposed by local politicians and trade unionists. In 1978 and 1980 there were general strikes in protest and in the March 1982 General Council election, Socialist candidates, campaigning for a change in the islands' status, swept the board. This persuaded the French government to grant them special status as a Collective Territory, in June 1985. The islands continue to serve as the center for French Atlantic cod fishing, although this industry has been in steady decline since the mid-1970s, seriously depressing the local economy. During recent years, a dispute has developed between the French and Canadian governments over cod quotas and territorial limits, France claiming a 13,000-square-nautical-mile 'exclusive economic zone' in the waters around St Pierre and Miquelon. This conflict, which was heightened by recent offshore gas and petroleum exploration, was resolved, to Canada's advantage, by the International Court of Justice, which set the 'exclusive economic zone' at only 2,537 square nautical miles. Since the late 1980s, there have been efforts to develop the tourism industry, but the islands remain highly dependent on French financial assistance. In the May 1995 second round of the French presidential election, Jacques Chirac won 67% of the second-round vote.

FRENCH OVERSEAS TERRITORIES

Territoires d'Outre-Mer

Overseas territories, which form integral parts of the French Republic, are administered by an appointed high commissioner or chief administrator, who works with an elected Territorial Assembly or Congress. They send representatives to the French parliament and participate in French presidential elections.

FRENCH POLYNESIA

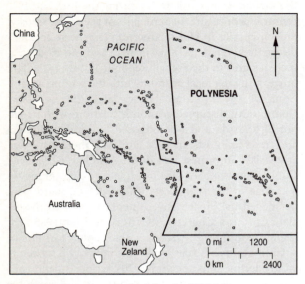

Capital: Papeete, on the island of Tahiti

Location
Oceania. French Polynesia comprises five scattered volcanic and coral island groups in the southeastern Pacific Ocean, between the Cook Islands, to the west, and Kiribati to the northeast. The largest island, on which 75% of the population lives, is Tahiti.

Social and economic data
Area: 4,167 sq km/1,609 sq miles
Population: 230,000*
Pop. density per sq km/sq mile: 55*/143
Literacy rate: 95%
Economy type: high income (*c.* $19,700 per capita in 1994)
Currency: Pacific franc
* 1996.

Ethnic composition
Seventy per cent of the population is Polynesian, 18% Chinese, and 12% European. French is the official language, but Polynesian languages are spoken by the indigenous population.

Religions
About 55% of the population is Protestant and 35% is Roman Catholic.

Local government
Under the terms of constitutional changes adopted in 1990, five consultative Archipelago Councils have been established, comprising territorial and municipal elected representatives.

Political system
Under the terms of the 1984 constitution, as amended in 1990 and 1996, an appointed French high commissioner controls defense, foreign policy, justice, and monetary affairs; while a 41-member Territorial Assembly (Assemblée Territoriale), which is directly elected for a five-year term, appoints, from its own ranks, a president and six- to 12-member Council of Ministers (COM). The COM has considerable autonomy in internal policy matters. French Polynesia also elects two members to the French National Assembly and one each to the French Senate and Economic and Social Council. The territory is also represented at the European Parliament in Strasbourg.

Political parties
Around a dozen political parties function. The five principal ones are the right-of-center Rally for the Republic/Popular Union Party (RPR/Tahoeraa Huiraatira); the New Land Party (Ai'a Api); the Tavini Huiraatira/Polynesian Liberation Front (Front de Libération de la Polynésie: FLP); Alliance 2000; and New Star (Fe'tia Api).

The RPR/Tahoeraa Huiraatira was established in 1958, and is led by Gaston Flosse. It supports the maintenance of close links with France, though with enhanced internal autonomy. The party split in 1987 after Flosse was forced to resign as president of the COM, following corruption charges, and Alexandre Leontieff formed the breakaway Te Tiaraama. The New Land Party dates from 1982, being formed after a split in the United Front Party (Te E'a Api). The FLP campaigns for independence and is led by Oscar Temaru. Alliance 2000 favors independence. New Star is led by Boris Léontieff.

Latest elections
The most recent Territorial Assembly elections were held on 13 May 1996 and resulted in the RPR winning a majority of seats, 22 out of 41, with 39% of the vote; while the FLP, with 25% of the vote, won ten seats; and the New Land Party, with 16% of the vote, won five seats. Four other parties each won a seat, including New Star and Alliance 2000. Gaston Flosse remained president of the COM, a position he had filled during 1986–87, and since June 1991. The territory's two French National Assembly seats were won in May – June 1997 by the RPR and the New Land Party.

Political history

The islands of French Polynesia were visited by Spanish and Portuguese explorers in the late 16th century and by the French and British in the 1760s. Tahiti became a French protectorate in 1842, the remaining islands being annexed between 1880 and 1900. In 1957 French Polynesia was made an Overseas Territory of the French Republic, ruled by an appointed governor and an advisory Territorial Assembly. During the mid-1970s, a separatist movement, spearheaded by Francis Sanford, leader of the United Front Party (Te E'a Api), gained strength. France responded by devolving greater authority to the Territorial Assembly and its Council of Ministers under new constitutions of 1977, 1984, 1990, and 1996.

Mururoa Atoll, in the Tuamotu Archipelago, has been a controversial nuclear test site since 1966. However, despite the adverse environmental aspects, its use has brought an influx of French military personnel into the territory, 3,800 being stationed in French Polynesia in 1997, and provided economic opportunities in the service and construction industries. Between 1992 and 1995 the French government of President François Mitterrand suspended its nuclear testing program, while compensating French Polynesia for the associated financial losses. However, in June 1995 the new French president, Jacques Chirac, announced that testing would resume at Mururoa Atoll from September 1995. This led to anti-nuclear and anti-colonial riots in Papeete in September 1995 and international condemnation of the French government. Six tests were eventually carried out, before testing was halted in January 1996.

As the Territory achieves an increasing degree of independence from metropolitan France, it has begun to develop closer ties with leading states in Asia and the Pacific, notably Australia, New Zealand, South Korea, Japan, and Taiwan.

Income tax was imposed in French Polynesia for the first time in 1994, as a means of funding infrastructural improvements, but the immediate consequence was widespread disorder, forcing 100 police officers to be flown in from France in October 1994. Value-added tax was introduced in 1997.

In April 1992 the Territorial Assembly president, Gaston Flosse, of the RPR, was found guilty of fraud, in connection with the sale of government land. He received a six-month suspended prison sentence, but this was overturned on appeal and he remained as Assembly president. The territory's voters supported the RPR candidate, Jacques Chirac, in the May 1995 French presidential election, giving him 61% of the second-round vote. However, while the RPR secured a majority of seats in the May 1996 Territorial Assembly elections, there was a surge in support for the pro-independence Tavini Huiraatira party, which was attributed to local hostility to French nuclear testing during 1995. French Polynesia is a member of the Pacific Community regional organization.

NEW CALEDONIA

Nouvelle Calédonie

Capital: Nouméa

Location

Oceania. New Caledonia comprises the large, mountainous island of Grande Terre, or New Caledonia, the adjacent Loyalty Islands and, 400 km/250 miles to the northwest, the uninhabited Chesterfield Islands. They are situated in the South Pacific Ocean, 1,500 km/900 miles east of Queensland, Australia. Forty-one per cent of the population lives in the capital, Nouméa, on Grande Terre.

Social and economic data

Area: 19,103 sq km/7,376 sq miles
Population: 197,000[*]
Pop. density per sq km/sq mile: 10[*]/27
Literacy rate: 91%
Economy type: high income (*c.* $18,600 per capita in 1994)
Currency: Pacific franc
[*] 1996.

Ethnic composition

Forty-three per cent of the population is Melanesian, 37% European settlers, termed Caldoches, 8% Wallisian, 4% Polynesian, 4% Indonesian, and 2% Vietnamese. Between 1989 and 1997 the immigration rate of Europeans to the territory increased tenfold. France maintains a force of 3,900 military personnel in New Caledonia. The official language is French, but the indigenous Kanak community also speaks Melanesian languages.

Religions

About 60% of the population is Roman Catholic.

Local government

The territory is divided into three provinces and subdivided into 32 communes, administered by locally elected councils and mayors. There are also eight Regional Consultative Custom Councils, for the maintenance of Kanak traditions.

Political system

Following the 'Fabius plan' of April 1985, New Caledonia has enjoyed a considerable degree of autonomy. A high commissioner represents the French government's interests in the islands and retains control over defense, foreign policy, finance, external trade, secondary education, and justice. New Caledonia is divided into three provinces, North, South, and the Loyalty Islands, each of which has the status of a self-governing territorial unit and has its own directly elected assembly of 32, 15, and seven members respectively, each headed by a president. Assembly terms are up to six years. The three assemblies together constitute the Territorial Congress (Congrès Territorial), which sits under the French High Commissioner. The Territorial Congress is responsible for the budget, fiscal affairs, primary education, and infrastructure, while the provincial assemblies are responsible for cultural affairs, land reform, and local economic development. The territory also elects two deputies to the French National assembly, one senator and one Economic and Social Councillor, and is represented in the European Parliament at Strasbourg.

Political parties

Many parties operate, but there are five principal political parties in New Caledonia. Two of them, the extreme rightwing National Front (FN) and the right-of-center Rally for Caledonia within the Republic (Rassemblement pour la Calédonie dans la République: RPCR), led by Jacques Lafleur, are settler-orientated bodies which favor retaining French control over the islands. One, the Caledonia For All party (NCPT) is a moderate, non-racial party formed in 1995 by a Nouméa business executive, Didier Leroux. Three parties press for full independence: the Melanesian-orientated Kanak Socialist National Liberation Front (Front de Libération Nationale Kanake Socialiste: FLNKS), a five-party alliance created in 1984, including the Caledonian Union (UC) and the Kanak Liberation Party (Palika), and led by Paul Neaoutyine; the Loyalty Islands-based Kanak Socialist Liberation Party (Libération Kanake Socialiste: LKS); and its offshoot, the National Union for Independence (UNI) . The LKS withdrew from the Matignon Accord in April 1991. The Federation of pro-Independent Coordinating Committees (FCCI) is a breakaway from the FLNKS.

Latest elections

The most recent legislature elections were held on 9 May 1999 and resulted in the FLNKS, heading pro-independence alliances, retaining control of the North and Loyalty Islands provincial assemblies and the RPCR the South assembly. For the Territory as a whole, in the general election of May 1999, the RPCR captured 24 of the 54 Territorial Congress seats, the FLNKS won 18 seats; the FN won four seats, the Federation of pro-Independent Coordinating Committes (FCCI), four seats, others, three seats; and the LK one seat. The territory's two French National Assembly seats were both retained by the RPCR during May and June 1997, but the FLNKS and LKS boycotted the poll.

Political history

Discovered by James Cook (1728–79) in 1774, New Caledonia was annexed by France in 1853, and was initially used, between 1871 and 1898, as a penal settlement. It became an Overseas Territory of the French Republic in 1946. Friction developed between the urban-based French settlers (*Caldoches*) and the local Melanesians (*Kanaks*) during the 1970s. Many of the Caldoches had been attracted to the Territory during the 1960s nickel boom, New Caledonia being the world's third largest nickel producer. The Kanaks, however, constituted a majority in rural areas. In response to Kanak demands for self-government, the authority of the locally elected Territorial Assembly, which had been established in 1956, was increased in December 1976. Direct 'Commissioner rule' had to be imposed in 1979 when pro-independence parties gained control of the Assembly's Council of Government and in September 1981 tensions were heightened, following the assassination of Pierre Declercq, leader of the separatist movement. Further cultural and political reforms were suggested by France's socialist Mitterrand administration after 1981, including proposals, in January 1985, for independence 'in association with' France, subject to a referendum. The holding of a national referendum, planned for July 1985, was violently opposed, however, by the Kanak Socialist National Liberation Front (FLNKS), forcing the declaration of a state of emergency.

The poll was shelved and a new 'Fabius plan' of regional devolution adopted instead. Regional councils were elected in September 1985 and a referendum on independence was held in September 1987. In this poll, 98% of those who voted gave approval to New Caledonia remaining part of the French Republic. Turnout was only 59%, however, with the bulk of the Melanesian community adhering to the advice of the

FLNKS and boycotting the poll. Soon after the referendum, Bernard Pons, the minister for overseas departments and territories in France's conservative (RPR) Chirac administration, submitted an administrative reorganization plan to New Caledonia's Territorial Assembly. This settler-biased scheme was accepted by Rally for Caledonia within the Republic (RPCR) Assembly members, but was strongly criticized by the FLNKS. This prompted a renewed outbreak of Kanak violence by militant factions during the run-up to the French presidential and new regional elections, in April – May 1988.

The return of the Socialists to power in Paris in June 1988 was swiftly followed by a fresh initiative by Michel Rocard (b. 1930), the new French prime minister. After two weeks of negotiations in Paris, a compromise settlement was agreed by the FLNKS and RPCR leaders, Jean-Marie Tjibao and Jacques Lafleur, in late June. The outcome was a decision to delay the holding of another referendum on independence until 1998, and, instead, to establish, in June 1989, a new system of local government based on the division of the territory into three self-governing provinces: one in the south for white settlers, and two, in the north and outer islands, for Kanaks. This scheme, which was planned to bring to an end a year of direct administration from Paris, was approved in a national referendum held throughout the French Republic in November 1988. It was accompanied by a generous, new economic development program, targeted at poor Kanak rural areas. However, its long-term success in securing communal peace remains to be proven. External pressure for decolonization has increased during recent years, particularly since the United Nations General Assembly decision, in December 1986, to reinscribe New Caledonia on the UN list of non-self-governing territories. Internal Kanak disquiet with the June 1988 Matignon Accord surfaced in May 1989 with the assassination of Tjibaou by a separatist extremist. High levels of youth unemployment among the Melanesian community were a factor behind riots in Nouméa in the spring of 1992. Provincial elections held in July 1995 produced once again pro-independence Kanak majorities in the North province and Loyalty Islands, while the South province remained dominated by white, pro-French settlers. In total, over a third of the population supported separatist parties. On-off talks between the French government and the RPCR and FLNKS were held between 1995 and 1998, culminating in April 1998 in the Noumea Accord, an agreement to postpone, for at least 15 years, the independence referendum due in 1998. In the interim, there would be further decentralization of authority, with a sharing of sovereignty. In November 1998 voters approved the Noumea Accord in a referendum, with 72% supporting the government's proposals: turnout was 74%. Elections to the legislature, the Territorial Congress, in May 1999, resulted once again in no single party securing an overall majority. However, Simon Loueckhote (RPR) was re-elected as the Congress's president, heading an RPCR-led coalition. The Congress subsequently elected Jacques Leques (RPCR) as New Caledonia's first president (elected government leader) under the increased autonomy terms of the Noumea Accord. New Caledonia is a member of the Pacific Community regional organization.

WALLIS AND FUTUNA ISLANDS (WFI)

Capital: Mata-Utu, on Wallis Island

Location

Oceania. The Territory comprises two groups of islands, the Wallis (Uvea) and the Futuna and Alofi. They are situated in the south-central Pacific Ocean to the northeast of Fiji and west of Western Samoa. Sixty-five per cent of the population lives on Wallis Island.

Social and economic data

Area: 274 sq km/106 sq miles
Population: 15,000*
Pop. density per sq km/sq mile: 55*/142
Economy type: middle income (c. $3,000 per capita in 1994)
Currency: Pacific franc
* 1996.

Ethnic composition

The population is almost predominantly Polynesian. French and Wallisian (Uvean), a Polynesian language, are spoken.

Religions

The population is almost entirely Roman Catholic.

Local government

Each kingdom has a traditional hierarchy of village chiefs and districts.

Political system

The islands are administered by an appointed French chief administrator, who is assisted by a 20-member Territorial Assembly (Assemblée Territoriale), which is directly elected for five-year terms on a common roll and elects its own president. The Territory elects one member to the French National Assembly and one representative to the Senate. The three traditional kingdoms, one on Wallis, Sigave on north Futuna, and Alo on south Futuna and Alofi, from which the territory was formed retain a number of limited powers and have their own council of ministers. The three kings and their own council of ministers, along with three appointed members of the Territorial Assembly, form a six-member Council of the Territory which advises the chief administrator. The islands are represented at the European Parliament in Strasbourg.

Political parties

The main political parties are the right-of-center Rally for the Republic (RPR); the Taumu'a Lelei (Bright Future); and the center-right Union for French Democracy (UDF). The Futuna-based Local Popular Union (Union Populaire Locale: UPL), formed in April 1985 by the Territorial Assembly's then president, Falakiko Gata, a former member of the RPR, places emphasis on local issues.

Latest elections

The most recent Territorial Assembly elections, held on 16 March 1997, were won by the RPR, which secured 14 of the 20 seats. Leftwing candidates and independents won the remaining six seats. Victor Brial of the RPR became the Assembly's president and was also elected to the French National Assembly in June 1997.

Political history

The Futuna island group was discovered by Dutch explorers in 1616 and the Wallis islands by the British in 1767. They were later settled by French missionaries in the early 19th century, becoming a French dependency in 1842 and protectorate in 1888. Following a local referendum in December 1959, the WFI was designated an Overseas Territory of the French Republic in July 1961. In contrast to the French Pacific territories of French Polynesia and New Caledonia, there is no secessionist movement at present on the islands. However, there have been calls by the kings of Futuna for two separate (Wallis and Futuna) Overseas Territories to be created. Lacking

natural resources, the WFI exports little and is heavily dependent on economic aid from France and remittances sent home by the 14,000 nationals employed in New Caledonia and Vanuatu.

At the March 1992 Territorial Assembly elections, the rightwing RPR lost the majority it had held continuously since 1964 to the newly formed Bright Future party. New elections in December 1994 produced a 'hung Assembly', with no overall majority for a single party. But after elections in March 1997, the RPR secured a solid majority. The islands belong to the Pacific Community regional organization.

FRENCH 'INTERNAL' COLLECTIVE TERRITORY

This category is a special one, since Corsica is so close to France that it is not usually thought of as an 'overseas' dependency. Prior to the decentralization reforms of 1982, it constituted the 22nd region of metropolitan France. It was then, however, elevated to the status of a Collective Territory and given a parliament with substantive powers, thus distinguishing it from the other 21 regions of metropolitan France.

CORSICA

Corse

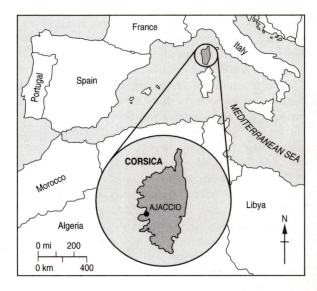

Capital: Ajaccio

Location

Western Europe. Corsica is an island in the Mediterranean Sea, west of Italy and north of Sardinia.

Social and economic data

Area: 8,680 sq km /3,351 sq miles
Population: 250,000[*]
Pop. density per sq km/sq mile: 29[*]/75
Economy type: high income
Currency: French franc
[*] 1990.

Ethnic composition

More than half the population are native Corsicans.

Religions

The population is predominantly Roman Catholic.

Local government

The island is divided into two departments (Haute-Corse and Corse-du-Sud), five districts (*arrondissements*), 52 cantons, and 360 communes.

Political system

Corsica forms an integral part of the French Republic. Since 1982, however, it has been given the special status of a Collective Territory, with its own directly – elected, 51-member parliament. This has the power to scrutinize bills passed by the French National Assembly and propose amendments applicable to the island. The 'Joxe plan' autonomy bill approved by the French National Assembly in 1992 gives the island still greater autonomy in the education, training, transport, and tourism sectors.

Political parties

The principal political parties are the moderate Radical Party, based principally in the north (Haute-Corse); the Bonapartist Party, based in Ajaccio; the center-right Rally for the Republic (RRR) and Liberal Democracy (DL), based especially in the far south (Corse-du-Sud); the Communist Party (PCF); the Socialist Party (PS); the nationalist Corsica Nazione, the Union for the Corsican People, a moderate autonomist movement; and the Corsican Movement for Autodetermination (MCA), the political wing of the Corsican National Liberation Front (FNLC), a separatist, extremist organization, which was banned in 1983. Political activity is clan-based and intensely localized.

Latest elections

The most recent elections to the 51-seat regional assembly were held in two rounds on 7 and 14 March 1999: party lists had to obtain at least 5% of the first round vote in order to participate in the second round. No single party or alliance achieved an assembly majority. The results are shown below:

Party	% of 2nd round round vote	Assembly seats
RPR-DL (centre right)	27.3	17
PS-PCF-Greens (left)	22.7	11
Corsica Nazione (nationalist)	16.8	8
New Corsica (centre right)	9.4	4
Corsica Social Democrats (left)	9.7	5
Movement for Corsica (centre)	7.7	3
Another Future (centre-left)	6.4	3

Political history

The island, which had earlier been ruled by the Phocaeans of Ionia, the Etruscans, the Carthaginians, the Romans, the Vandals, and the Arabs, came under Genoa's control during the 14th century, before being sold to France in 1768. Under French rule it remained underdeveloped, but its people made their mark in metropolitan France and the French empire as eminent soldiers and administrators. The most notable of these was Napoléon Bonaparte.

During World War II, Corsica was occupied by Italy between 1942 and 1943. Since 1962 French *pieds noirs* (refugees from Algeria) settled on the island, largely as vineyard owners. Their relative prosperity fuelled a radical separatist movement, involving the bombing of 'colonial targets', by the Corsican National Liberation Front (FNLC). The annual level of bombings increased from 200 in 1975 to a peak of 800 in 1982. The French socialist Mitterrand administration responded by granting considerable autonomy to the island, to be exercised through a directly-elected regional parliament. Elections to this body were held in 1982 and 1984, but, under the proportional representation system used, failed to produce a clear party or coalition majority. Terrorism has continued since 1982 at a reduced level, although only 5% of the population support the Corsican Movement for Autodetermination (MCA) or the FNLC extremists, and 25% supported independence candidates in the 1992, elections. In January 1987 the MCA itself was banned and dissolved by the French government, but from mid-1989 the FLNC resumed its bombing and assassination campaign, targeting banks and other financial institutions. In the 1992 elections 25% of the island's residents supported independence candidates. During 1994–95 the FNLC split into two antagonistic wings. This resulted in a fratricidal war and a new level of violence, with drug-running and crime syndicates involved. The FLNC suspended its terrorist activities between January and August 1996. In October 1996 a faction known as the FLNC-Historic Wing bombed the town hall in Bordeaux in southwestern France. FLNC bombing increased in Corsica and southern France in early 1997 after the arrest of Francois Santoni, a hardline leader. In February 1998 the French prefect French (the state's highest representative on the island), Claude Erignac, of Corsica was assassinated, but the FLNC condemned the incident which may have been the work of organized crime syndicates.

In April 1999 Bernard Bonnet, Erignac's replacement as prefect, was arrested and dismissed after allegedly encouraging an arson attack on an illegally-built seafront restaurant near Ajaccio. Bonnet had been responsible for instituting a crackdown on lawlessness, which resulted, after his departure and replacement by Jean-Pierre Lacroix, in the arrest, in May 1999, of four Corsican nationalists charged with the murder in 1998 of Erignac. The Bonnet scandal had repercussions in mainland France, with Prime Minister Jospin facing, in May 1999, a related vote of censure in the National Assembly, which he survived. The March 1999 regional assembly elections resulted in the nationalist Corsica Nazione, with eight seats and a sixth of the vote, holding the balance of power, as parties of the centre-right and centre won 24 of the 51 seats and the left and centre-left, 19.

8.4.6 Morocco's dependency

Western Sahara, which Morocco has controlled in one way or another since the early 1950s, is in strict legality an occupied territory, rather than a colony or dependency, and its future has yet to be finally determined. Details of its political structure and history are given below.

WESTERN SAHARA

Capital: Laâyoune (El Aaiún) Cal A'ayuni

Location
Middle East and North Africa. It is situated in north-west Africa, between Morocco, to the north, and Mauritania, to the south, with the Atlantic Ocean to the west. The bulk of the territory is desert.

Social and economic data
Area: 252,120 sq km/97,344 sq miles
Population: 208,000[*]
Pop. density per sq km/sq mile: 0.8[*]/2
Currency: Morrocan dirham
[*] 1994.

Ethnic composition
The territory is peopled predominantly by nomads. The main language is Arabic (Moroccan and Hassaniya).

Religions
The principal religion is Sunni Islam.

Local government
For administrative purposes, the territory is divided into the provinces of La'youn, Oued Eddahab, Es-Semara, and Boujdour.

Political system and parties
Since 1976, as a result of the territory's disputed status, Western Sahara has had two competing governments, both of which claim legitimacy. The Moroccan-controlled area is divided into the four provinces noted above and administered by Moroccan officials. The nationalist Polisario Front (PF), which was set up in 1973, also, however, claims to rule this territory and has its own Saharan Arab Democratic Republic (SADR), 'government in exile', headed by a president, Mohammed Abdel Aziz, the secretary general of Polisario, and prime minister, Mahfoud Ali Larous Beiba. It also includes a seven-member Executive Council, a 25-member Political Bureau and a 101-member, elected legislative, Saharawi National Assembly. At the most recent elections, held in October 1995, only Polisario members were elected. In the territory's refugee camps in south – western Algeria, there is also a rudimentary form of local government, based on people's councils. The PF is a socialist organization, campaigning for the establishment of a fully independent and non-aligned Arab-Islamic state.

Political history
The 1,000-kilometre/600 mile-long Saharan coastal region between French-dominated Morocco and Mauritania was designated a Spanish 'sphere of influ-

ence' in 1884, being situated opposite the Spanish-ruled Canary Islands. However, Morocco had long laid claim to this border region and when it secured independence from France, in 1956, re-activated its claim by invading Spanish Sahara, only to be repulsed by Spanish troops. From 1965, after the discovery of rich phosphate resources at Bu Craa, in the heart of the territory, Moroccan interest was rekindled, but in a peaceful manner. Meanwhile, within Spanish Sahara, nationalist sentiment began to awaken and in 1973 the Yema'a, a council of local elders and elected officials, pressed for self-determination. A more radical nationalist group, the Polisario Front (Frente Popular de Liberación de Sakiet el Hamra y Río de Oro), was also formed, in May 1973, to fight for independence.

These calls were rejected by neighboring Morocco and Mauritania, who soon after the death of the Spanish ruler, General Franco, had moved in to divide the territory between themselves. This partition was finally effected during 1975–76, when Spain withdrew completely. Morocco secured two-thirds of the land area, including the phosphate mines, and Mauritania the rest. The Polisario nationalist forces, however, refused to accept this division and, declaring the establishment of their own Saharan Arab Democratic Republic: SADR República Arabe Saharaui Democrática, proceeded to wage a guerrilla war against both Morocco and Mauritania, benefiting from indirect support provided by Algeria and Libya.

Polisario was successful in its struggle with Mauritania and forced its recognition of the SADR in August 1979. The SADR was also accepted, in February 1982, as a full member of the Organization of African Unity (OAU). However, Morocco, by establishing an 'electronic defensive wall', which was a 2,500-kilometre/1,500-mile-long sand barrier, 2.75 metres/9 feet high, on which modern electronic surveillance devices were put, and by the receipt of support from the United States, remained impregnable. It kept control of the key towns and phosphate mines of Western Sahara, while conceding most of the surrounding, largely unpopulated, desert interior to Polisario. It also occupied much of the Mauritania-conceded area in the south.

With an army of more than 100,000 stationed in the territory and faced with a Polisario force of barely 8,000, the Moroccans gradually began to gain the upper hand, during the mid-1980s, and progressively extended their defensive wall outwards. They were boosted by Libya's decision to end its support for Polisario, in 1984, and by a gradual calming of Algeria's socialist revolutionary ardour, culminating, in May 1988, in the formal re-establishment of Algerian – Moroccan diplomatic relations. Three months later, in August 1988, a United Nations-sponsored settlement of the 'Western Saharan dispute' was effected in Geneva, when representatives from Morocco and the Polisario Front accepted a plan to hold a referendum, based on 1974 voting rolls, in Western Sahara, to decide whether the territory's political future should be independence or integration with Morocco. As part of this agreement, a UN special representative was to be appointed to serve as a temporary pro-consul to run the civil administration and ensure order and political neutrality during the run-up to the planned referendum. A ceasefire was agreed between Morocco and Polisario in 1991. However, the referendum failed to be held, as anticipated, in 1992 and, although the Polisario Front and Moroccan government held direct talks for the first time in July 1993, problems over voter identification were so great that doubts were expressed as to whether the referendum would ever be held. In July 1995 the United States warned both sides that it would withdraw its support for the UN operation, the UN Mission for the Referendum in Western Sahara (MINURSO), if a referendum was not soon forthcoming. In March 1997, James Baker, a former US secretary of state, was appointed special UN envoy to Western Sahara, reflecting a new determination at the UN to achieve real progress. He visited the Polisario Front's base in Algeria in April 1997 and mediated face-to-face talks between the Moroccan and Western Saharan governments in London and Lisbon, between June and August 1997. Agreement was reached, in September 1997, on the process of identifying eligible voters for a referendum to be held in December 1998. Identification, which had begun in 1994, was renewed from December 1997 and landmines were cleared from the area between February and April 1998. By 31 May 1998, the deadline set for voter registration, 117,285 people had been registered. However, it was decided in June 1998 to delay the referendum. In May 1999 the UN Security Council extended the mandate of MINURSO until later in 1999 so as to enable resumption of the process of identifying the voters eligible to take part in the referendum on self-determination. A new date of 31 July 2000 was set for this referendum.

8.4.7 Netherlands' dependencies

The two dependencies of the Netherlands represent the residue of what was once a considerable colonial empire, dating back to the 17th century, which had been built up on the basis of trade and exploration. They are known as Overseas Territories. Details of the political structures and histories of these remaining overseas possessions are given below.

ARUBA

Capital: Oranjestad

Location
Central America and the Caribbean. Aruba is the westernmost island of the Lesser Antilles group, situated in the southeastern Caribbean, 30 km north of Venezuela.

Social and economic data
Area: 193 sq km/75 sq miles
Population: 87,971*
Pop. density per sq km/sq mile: 456*/1,173
Economy type: high income (c. $9,400 per capita in 1995)
Currency: Aruban guilder (or florin)
* 1996.

Principal languages
Dutch is the official language, with Papiamento (a local form of creole) spoken by the majority of the population. Spanish and English are also used.

Religions
Eighty per cent of the population is Roman Catholic.

Head of government
Prime Minister Henny Eman, since 1994

Political system
There is a 21-member single chamber assembly, termed the Island Council (Staten), elected by universal adult suffrage for a 4-year term and subject to dissolution during that time. Executive authority for internal affairs is wielded by an 8–10-member Council of Ministers, headed by a prime minister and reponsible to the Staten. Dutch interests are overseen by a crown-appointed governor, who serves a six-year term as commander in chief of the island's armed forces and has executive authority in external matters. To be carried, any proposal for full independence needs approval in a referendum and the support of a two-thirds majority in the Staten.

Political parties
Dutch is the official language, with Papiamento (a local form creole) spoken by the majority of the population. Spanish and English are also used. Seven political parties operate in Aruba. The three principal parties are: the People's Electoral Movement (MEP); the Aruba People's Party (AVP); and the Aruban Liberal Organization (OLA). The MEP was established in 1971, has a current membership of 1,200, and is led by Nelson Oduber, who was prime minister 1989–94. It is a secular, cross-race, social democratic party which dominated the Staten until 1985 and between 1989 and 1994. The AVP was formed in 1942, led by Henny Eman. Like the MEP, it campaigned for separation from Curaçao during the 1970s, but boycotted the MEP-induced referendum on the subject, in 1977. With minority party support, it gained a majority in the Staten following the elections of November 1985, when Eman became the island's first prime minister. Among the minor parties, the Aruban Patriotic Party (PPA), which was formed in 1949, and opposes full independence, and National Democratic Action (ADN), formed in 1985, are the most influential.

Latest elections
In the most recent Staten elections, held on 12 December 1997, following the collapse of a AVP-OLA coalition government, the AVP, won ten seats and 41% of the vote, the MEP, nine seats with 39% popular support, and the OLA, two seats and 9% of the vote.

Political history
The island was colonized by Holland in 1636 and became a member of the Netherlands Antilles autonomous federation in 1954. The economy developed significantly from the 1930s, following the establishment of a large oil refinery at St Nicolaas in 1929. This created growing resentment at the island's political dominance by adjacent Curaçao and the redistributive drain of wealth to other poorer islands in the federation. During the 1970s the People's Electoral Movement (MEP) exploited this sentiment by campaigning for Aruba's secession from the federation. A referendum on the issue was forced in March 1977, 82% of the electorate voting for withdrawal and independence. Formal separation from the federation was finally achieved on 1 January 1986, following the report of a commission on the subject. The Netherlands

remains responsible for the defense and external relations of the island. Full independence was planned for 1996, but in March 1994 the island shelved the idea and opted instead for special status. Henry Eman, of the People's Party (AVP), became the island's first prime minister in 1986. MEP-dominated coalitions held power during 1989–94, but Eman became prime minister again following the July 1994 general election. The island's economy in recent years has been in a depressed condition, following the closure of the oil refinery in March 1985, but an economic recovery began in 1988, based on tourism. During recent years, Aruba has improved its relations with the other Netherlands Antilles, entering into a cooperative economic union from 1987, and with neighboring Caribbean and Latin American states, including Venezuela, which has traditionally claimed the Dutch Leeward Islands, including Aruba. In 1990 the oil refinery was re-opened and, helped by continued expansion of tourism and development of a data-processing industry, annual GDP growth has exceeded 4% during the 1990s.

THE NETHERLANDS ANTILLES

Capital: Willemstad, on Curaçao

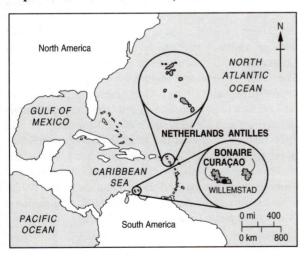

Location

Central America and the Caribbean. The Netherlands Antilles consists of two island groups, 800 km/500 miles apart, in the southeastern Caribbean. The main group is the 'Leeward Islands', which includes Curaçao, Bonaire, and, formerly, Aruba. It is 60 km/40 miles north of Venezuela. The other group is the 'Windward Islands' and consists of the three small volcanic islands of St Eustatius, Saba, and St Maarten situated to the north east.

Social and economic data

Area: 800 sq km/309 sq miles
Population: 207,175 *
Pop. density per sq km/sq mile: 259*/670
Literacy rate: 92%
Economy type: high income (*c.* $8,800 per capita in 1994)
Currency: Netherlands Antilles guilder (or florin)
* 1996.

Ethnic composition

Eighty-five per cent of the population is of mixed black descent. Dutch (official on the Leeward Islands), Papiamento (a local form of creole), Spanish, and English (official on the Windward Islands) are the main languages.

Religions

Roman Catholicism is the predominant religion, especially on the Leeward Islands and Saba. Protestantism is strong on St Eustatius and St Maarten in the Windward Islands.

Head of Government

Prime Minister Susanne Camelia-Römer, since 1998

Local government

Each of the five island territories has its own Island Council, Executive Council, and lieutenant governor to manage local affairs in what is, effectively, a federal system.

Political system

A crown-appointed governor serves for a six-year term as head of state and oversees Dutch interests, having control of the islands' defense and external affairs. The governor is assisted by an Advisory Council. Executive authority for internal affairs rests with a ten-member Council of Ministers, responsible to an elected assembly, the Staten. This is composed of 22 members elected by universal adult suffrage, for a four-year term and subject to dissolution within this period. Each island group forms an electoral district for election purposes, Curaçao returning 14 members, Bonaire and St Maarten three each, and Saba and St Eustatius, one member each. A proportional representation system is used in the cases of the multimember districts.

Political parties

The principal political party is the Curaçao-based Restructured Antilles Party (PAR), formed in 1993 by Miguel Pourier, who was prime minister 1994–98. It is a 'social-Christian' body, as is the Curaçao-based National People's Party (PNP), founded in 1948 and led until 1994 by Maria Liberia-Peters, the prime minister from 1984 to 1985 and from 1988 to 1993. The third significant party is the socialist New Antilles Movement (MAN), formed in 1979 and led by Dominico (Don) Martina, who was prime minister between 1979 – 84 and 1985–88. Other significant parties are the liberal-socialist Democratic Party (DP), which was established in 1944. It is divided between Curaçao, Bonaire, and St Maarten branches. Other parties include the Bonaire Patriotic Union (UPB); the Socialist Workers' Liberation Front of 30 May, (FOL; estd. 1969); and the Workers' Popular Crusade Party (PLKP; estd. 1997).

Latest elections

In the most recent Staten elections, held on 30 January 1998, the PAR attracted 19% of the vote and captured four of the 22 seats. The PNP won 15% of the vote and three seats; the PLKP, 14% of the vote and three seats; the FOL, 10% of the vote and two seats; the MAN 8% of the vote and two seats; the DP 8% of the vote and four seats; and the St Maarten Patriotic alliance, the UPB, the St Eustatius Alliance, and the Sabah-based Windward Islands People's Movement, one seat apiece.

Political history

Originally claimed by Spain, the Netherlands Antilles were colonized by Holland during the 1630s, Curaçao developing into a prosperous entrepôt for the Caribbean trade. Sovereignty was periodically contested by France and Britain during the 18th century, before the islands were finally confirmed as Dutch territories in 1816. The abolition of slavery in 1863 ushered in a period of economic depression which was only ended during the 1920s by the establishment of petroleum refineries on Aruba and Curaçao islands. In 1954 the island group was granted full autonomy over domestic affairs, while remaining within the Kingdom of the Netherlands.

During the 1960s and 1970s internal politics were characterized by intense inter-island rivalries, most notably between Curaçao and Aruba, and policy-making was paralysed by the coalition nature of the governments returned. Arguments over revenue sharing and rights to prospective offshore oil reserves eventually led to the withdrawal of Aruba from the Netherlands Antilles fed-

eration in 1986. In recent years, the economy, which is heavily dependent on the refining of oil imported from Venezuela, for export to the United States, tourism, and 'offshore' financial services, has been in a depressed condition, forcing unpopular budgetary retrenchment. There have also been charges of government corruption. The 'metropolitan' Dutch government envisages the Netherlands Antilles eventually adopting a commonwealth structure, with the 'Antilles of Five' forming themselves into two parts: Curaçao and Bonaire; and St Maarten, Saba, and St Eustatius. However, in a November 1993 referendum, electors in Curaçao rejected the government plan for separate status and voted overwhelmingly for continuance of the current Antillean federation. In referenda held in October 1994, between 85–90% of electors in Bonaire, St Eustatius, and Saba voted to remain within the Antillean federation, but only 60% in St Maarten voted likewise.

Between July 1992 and September 1995 the Dutch 'metropolitan' government placed St Maarten island under 'higher supervision', restricting the local government's powers in expenditure areas, following problems with corruption. A center-right coalition, with Miguel Pourier of the Restructured Antilles Party (PAR) as prime minister, took office following the February 1994 general election. Economic growth remained sluggish, at around 1% per annum, and, with economic assistance from the Netherlands being reduced, there was a growing budget deficit. Efforts were made to diversify the economy, but in September 1995 Hurricanes Luis and Marilyn caused extensive damage and in 1996 the government was forced to agree a structural adjustment program with the IMF. The austerity measures included a 'wage freeze' during 1996–97, the imposition of new taxes, and cut-backs in civil service numbers. This led to the unemployment rate rising to above 14% in 1996 and to support for the PAR halving to 19% at the January 1998 general election. After this election, a new five-party center-left coalition government was formed, headed by Susanne Camelia-Römer of the National People's Party (PNP), with support from the Democratic (DP) and the new Workers' Popular Crusade Party (PLKP).

8.4.8 New Zealand's dependencies

New Zealand's four dependencies were acquired 'second hand', all having been British possessions but, after it had achieved full independence, being more sensibly

New Zealand's overseas (associated) territories — Table 72

Territory	Date of first coming under New Zealand administration	Area (sq km)	Area (sq mi)	Population (c. 1992)
Cook Islands	1901	237	92	19,000
Niue	1901	259	100	2,321
Ross Dependency	1923	414	160	Uninhabited
Tokelau	1925	12	5	1,700
Total	–	922	356	23,021

administered by New Zealand than by the 'mother country'. The Ross Dependency is uninhabited, so only the political structures and histories of the other three are set out below.

COOK ISLANDS

Capital: Avarua, on Rarotonga Island

Location
Oceania. The islands are situated in the South Pacific Ocean, 2,600 km/1,600 miles northeast of Auckland, New Zealand. There are six large and nine small volcanic and coral islands in the Cook group, scattered widely across almost 2 million square kilometres/800,000 square miles of the South Pacific. The highest-lying and most important island is Rarotonga, which is in the southern island group.

Social and economic data
Area: 237 sq km/92 sq miles
Population: 19,000*
Pop. density per sq km/sq mile: 80*/207
Literacy rate: 92%
Economy type: middle income (c. $2,000 per capita)
Currency: New Zealand dollar
* 1995.

Ethnic composition
Eighty-one per cent of the population is Polynesian; 8% mixed Polynesian and European; 8% mixed Polynesian and other races; and 2% European. English is the official language, but Cook Islands' Maori is also spoken.

Religions
Seventy per cent of the population belongs to the Cook Islands (Congregational) Christian Church and 16% is Roman Catholic.

Local government
Each of the main islands, except Rarotonga, has an elected mayor and appointed government representative. Rarotonga is divided into three tribal districts (*vaka*).

Political system
There is a 25-member Legislative Assembly, which is elected for a five-year term, by universal adult suffrage. Ten deputies represent the main island of Rarotonga, 14 represent constituencies on the other 14 islands, and one represents Cook Islanders resident in New Zealand. The Assembly selects from its ranks a prime minister, who oversees an eight-member cabinet of his or her choosing and also holds a wide range of functional portfolios. Hereditary island chiefs are represented in a second assembly chamber, the House of Ariki, comprising up to 15 members. This body, however, has no legislative powers. An appointed high commissioner represents the British Crown as the islands' formal head of state, and the New Zealand government has a representative on Rarotonga.

Political parties
There are three principal political parties: the Cook Islands Party (CIP), which was formed in 1965 and, under the leadership of Sir Albert Henry, held power continuously between 1965 and 1978; the Democratic Party (DP), established in 1971, and the dominant party between 1978 and 1989; and the Alliance Party (AP), formed in 1992.

Latest elections
In the most recent general election, held on 16 June 1999, the CIP, led by Prime Minister Sir Geoffrey Henry, a cousin of Sir Albert Henry, won only 10 of the 25 available seats, as against 20 in 1994. The Centrist Democratic Alliance (DA) won 11 seats and the New Alliance (NA) four vote shares were CP 40%, DA 44%, and NA 13%.

Political history
The islands, which were first visited by Captain James Cook (1728–79) in 1773, and subsequently named after him, were annexed by Britain in 1888, but were later transferred to New Zealand, in 1901. In 1965 they became internally self-governing in 'free association' and with common citizenship with New Zealand, which retains responsibility for defense and foreign affairs. Their chief importance lies in their coconut, pineapple, and citrus fruit production, fruit processing constituting

the main industry, and as a growing tourist center. However, the islands have a huge trade deficit and rely on substantial aid to sustain their living standards. Three-quarters of this aid is supplied by New Zealand and currently amounts to $12 million, or $630 per year for each of the dwindling number of inhabitants. In late 1991 Cyclones Val and Wasa struck the islands, causing damage estimated at $2 million. In 1997 Cyclone Martin killed eight, and destroyed crops and the islands' infrastructure. In March 1994 the islanders voted in a referendum to reject the adoption of a Maori name for the islands. In 1995 a financial crisis on the islands led to withdrawal of the Cook Islands' dollar, government default on a $100 million debt to an Italian bank, and to retrenchment, including a sharp cutback in civil service staff numbers and the closure of many diplomatic missions overseas. After the June 1999 general election, the CIP lost its assembly majority, but Sir Geoffrey Henry remained as prime minister. This was after he had arrived at a 'gentleman's agreement' with Norman George of the New Alliance Party (NAP). The Cook Islands are a member of the South Pacific Forum and favor the establishment of a South Pacific 'nuclear-free zone'. In 1995 the government strongly criticized France's resumption of nuclear testing in the South Pacific.

NIUE

Capital: Alofi

Location
Oceania. Niue is a coral island situated in the South Pacific Ocean west of the Cook Islands and 2,140 km/1,330 miles northeast of New Zealand. The population lives in small coastal villages, with a concentration in Alofi.

Social and economic data
Area: 259 sq km/100 sq miles
Population: 2,321[*]
Pop. density per sq km/sq mile: 9[*]/23
Literacy rate: 94%
Economy type: low–middle income (*c.* $1,500–2,000 per capita)
Currency: New Zealand dollar
[*] 1994.

Ethnic composition
The inhabitants are predominantly Polynesian and mixed Polynesian. English is the official language, but Niuean is also spoken. Some 10,000 Niueans live in New Zealand.

Religions
Three-quarters of the population belong to the Ekalesia Niue, a Protestant organization.

Political system
There is an elected, 20-member Legislative Assembly, comprising 14 village representatives and six members elected on a common roll. Government is in the hands of a cabinet of four, headed by a prime minister, and drawn from the Assembly's ranks. The New Zealand government has a high commissioner on the island, stationed at Alofi.

Political parties
Until recently, candidates for election to the Assembly have stood as independents. To contest the general election of March 1987, however, the island's first political party, the Niue People's Action Party (NPAP), was founded by Young Viviani. It has been highly critical of the government's record of economic management. Viviani briefly became prime minister during 1992–93.

Latest elections
The most recent Assembly elections were held on 19 March 1999, with the NPAP securing 14 seats and independents six. Following the contest, Sani Lakatoni was elected prime minister.

Political history
The island, when visited by Captain James Cook (1728–79) in 1774, was already inhabited. Its indigenous population, who were at first hostile to Europeans, were converted to Christianity by missionaries during the 19th century and, following petitioning by the islanders, a British protectorate was established in 1900. In the following year Niue was annexed by New Zealand. Full internal self-government, in 'free association' with New Zealand, was granted in October 1974, with New Zealand retaining reponsibility for the island's defense and external affairs. The economy is founded upon passion fruit, copra, and handicraft exports, but, despite this, is heavily dependent on foreign aid and support from New Zealand.

In 1991 the New Zealand government announced it was reducing its aid allocation by 10% in an effort to compel the Niue government to reduce the public sector labor force and spend more on development. There have subsequently been efforts to develop 'offshore banking'. In December 1992 the island was rocked by the death of Sir Robert Rex, who had dominated politics in Niue, being its prime minister since the early 1950s. He was succeeded in 1993 by Frank Lui, who was re-elected in 1996. In 1999 Sani Lakatani became prime minister after

Lui failed to secure re-election to parliament and the NPAP polled strongly. Niue then retired from politics. Niue is a member of the South Pacific Forum.

TOKELAU

Capital: Nukunonu

Location
Oceania. Tokelau consists of three coral atolls, Atafu, Fakaofo, and Nukunonu, situated in the South Pacific Ocean, 480 km/300 miles north of Western Samoa and 3,500 km/2,175 miles north-northeast of New Zealand.

Social and economic data
Area: 12 sq km/5 sq miles
Population: 1,700*
Pop. density per sq km/sq mile: 142*/340
Literacy rate: 97%
Economy type: low income (*c.* $1,000 per capita)
Currency: New Zealand dollar
* 1995.

Ethnic composition
The population is wholly Polynesian, enjoying close family and cultural links with Western Samoa. English is the second language. Around 2,300 inhabitants have migrated to New Zealand, sending home earnings for their families.

Religions
The majority of people belong to the Roman Catholic or Congregational Church.

Political system
The islands are governed directly by a resident administrator of the New Zealand Ministry of Foreign Affairs. In practice, much of the executive work is delegated to an official secretary, based at Tokelau. At the local level,

however, the islands are substantially self-governing. On each atoll there is a Council of Elders (COE, or Taupulega), comprising the heads of family groups plus two members elected triennially by universal adult suffrage: the minimum voting age is 21 years. One is the Faipule, or commissioner, who presides over the Council and represents the atoll in its dealings with the New Zealand administration, and the other is the Pulenuku, who is responsible for village affairs. Twice a year, 15 delegates from each atoll COE convene in a General Fono, or meeting, chaired by one of the islands' three Faipules. The General Fono has limited, but increasing, legislative power.

Political history
Tokelau is an association of three autonomous atoll communities. The islands were made a British protectorate in 1877 and formed part of the Gilbert and Ellice Islands colony, together with Kiribati and Tuvalu, from 1916. In 1925 they were transferred to New Zealand, becoming formally part of New Zealand in 1949. Copra is the principal revenue-earning product and the sale of licences to foreign fleets to fish in its exclusive economic zone is another important source of income, but 80% of the island's annual budget expenditure is paid for from a subsidy provided by New Zealand.

In 1994 the General Fono approved a ten-year National Strategic Plan, setting out plans for progression towards increased self-determination and, eventually, possible 'free association'. New Zealand's House of Representatives voted, in May 1996, to grant the General Fono increased legislative powers, effective from August 1996.

8.4.9 Norway's dependencies

Norway has five dependencies, all situated in the Arctic or Antarctic regions, and most of them uninhabited.

Norwegian dependencies			Table 73
Dependency	Date of first coming under Norwegian administration	Area (sq km/sq miles)	Population (1994)
Bouvet Island	1928	60/23	uninhabited
Jan Mayen Island	1929	380/147	uninhabited
Peter I Island	1931	180/69	uninhabited
Queen Maud Island	1939	(Antarctic Territory)	uninhabited
Svalbard	1920	62,924/24,295	3,700
Total	–	*63,544/24,538*	*3,700*

The one inhabited possession, Svalbard, was finally secured by an international treaty after its sovereignty had been contested by other European powers.

SVALBARD

Capital: Long Year City (Longyearbyen) on Spitsbergen

Location

Arctic. Svalbard is an archipelago composed of nine main islands, the most important being Spitsbergen. It is situated in the Arctic Ocean, 650 km/400 miles north of Norway.

Social and economic data

Area: 62,924 sq km/24,295 sq miles
Population: 3,700*
Pop. density per sq km/sq mile: 0.06*/0.15
* 1994.

Ethnic composition

Sixty-two per cent of the population is Russian and 36% is Norwegian.

Political system

The island is administered by a Norwegian governor (*Sysselmann*) resident at Longyearbyen.

Political history

The island group was discovered by the Dutch seafarer Willem Barents (*c.* 1550–1597) in 1596 and briefly served as a center for whale hunting during the 17th century, with its sovereignty being contested by Denmark, Norway, Britain, and the Netherlands. Interest in the islands was reawakened during the early 20th century with the discovery of coal deposits. In 1920 Norway's sovereignty claims were upheld in an international agreement, the Svalbard Treaty, formally ratified in 1925. In return, Norway agreed to allow free scientific and economic access to other nations. Norway and Russia currently maintain permanent mining settlements on the islands, while Poland has a small research station. Three-quarters of state revenue is derived from Norway and the rest from the sale of fishing licences.

8.4.10 Portugal's dependency

Portugal was once one of the world's leading colonial powers, and one of the last to concede sovereignty to

the local communities. It now has only one possession and that will pass to Chinese control at the end of the century.

MACAU

Macau

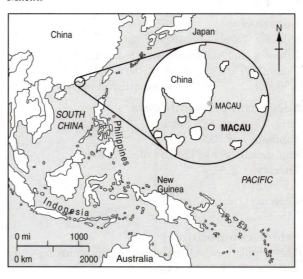

Capital: Macau

Location

Asia. The territory consists of the coastal peninsula of Macau and the two small islands of Taipa and Coloane, situated on the Zhujiang or Pearl River delta in southeast China, 64 km/40 miles west of Hong Kong.

Social and economic data

Area: 17 sq km/7 sq miles
Population: 393,000*
Pop. density per sq km/sq mile: 23,235*/56,143
Literacy rate: 79%
Economy type: middle–upper income (*c.* $6,000–7,000 per capita)
Currency: pataca
* 1995.

Ethnic composition

Ninety-nine per cent of the population is Chinese, speaking Cantonese, which is the joint official language, alongside Portuguese.

Religions

The people are predominantly (45%) Buddhists, with 15% adhering to Roman Catholicism.

Political system

Designated a Special Territory of Portugal, executive power is held by a governor, appointed by the president of Portugal, who is assisted by a cabinet of seven Portuguese-appointed under secretaries. Foreign affairs are controlled by the president of Portugal. The governor works in consultation with a local Legislative Assembly, which comprises 23 members, eight of whom are elected directly by universal adult suffrage, eight elected indirectly by business associations, and seven appointed by the governor. The members serve four-year terms and elect a president from among themselves. The governor also presides over a Superior Council of Security, which comprises seven under secretaries appointed by the president of Portugal, and a Consultative Council, five of whose members are indirectly elected by local administrative bodies and interest groups.

Political parties

There are no formal political parties in Macau. However, six civil associations are represented in the Legislative Assembly.

Latest elections

The most recent Legislative Assembly elections, held in September 1996, saw 62 candidates from 12 groupings contest the eight directly-elected seats. The business-orientated Association for the Promotion of Macau's Economy secured two of these eight seats, and 17% of the vote; the Convergence for Development and the General Union for the Development of Macau, one seat each; the pro-Beijing candidates of the Union for the Promotion of Progress, two seats and 15% of the vote; and the Union for Development, one seat and 14% of the vote. The pro democracy Association of the New Democratic Macau won one seat. Turnout was 64% of the registered electorate, corresponding to 16% of the population. In May 1999 Edmund Ho Hao Wah defeated Stanky Au Choy Kit, by 163 votes to 34, to be elected the first chief executive of the Special Administration Region by a 200-member Selection Committee.

Political history

Macau was first established as a Portuguese missionary and trading post in 1537, before being leased by China in 1557. Later, in 1849, it was annexed by Portugal and formally recognized as a colony by the Chinese government under the terms of an 1887 treaty. The colony's commercial importance steadily diminished during the later 19th and early 20th centuries, as Macau harbour silted up and trade was diverted to the British center of Hong Kong and other Treaty Ports. It was forced, instead, to concentrate on the local 'country' trade, as well as on gambling and tourism.

In 1951 Macau became more closely integrated with mainland Portugal, and was designated a Portuguese Overseas Province. This entitled it to send an elected representative to the Lisbon parliament. However, after the Portuguese revolution of 1974, the colony, redesignated a 'Special Territory', was granted greater autonomy, based upon the adoption, in February 1976, of an 'organic statute' which established the present political structure.

In June 1986; the Portuguese and Chinese governments began negotiations over the question of the return of Macau's sovereignty, under similar 'one country, two systems' terms as had been agreed in 1984 by Britain and China for Hong Kong. These negotiations were successfully concluded in March 1987, when the 'Macau Pact' was signed. Under the terms of this concord, Portugal has agreed to formally hand over sovereignty to the People's Republic on 20 December 1999. In return, the People's Republic has undertaken to maintain the capitalist economic and social system of the port enclave for at least 50 years thereafter. Under Chinese rule, Macau will be redesignated a 'Special Administrative Region' (SAR) and will have its own assembly which, with a similar basis of representation to the current Legislative Assembly, will contain 'a majority of elected members'. To overseee the transfer of power, a Sino-Portuguese Joint Liaison Committee has been established. In July 1991 the Draft Basic Law of the Macau SAR was published. It provides for the future chief executive of the SAR to be selected by a 300-member electoral college.

Real GDP grew at an annual rate of more than 4% between 1993 and 1997; however, population has grown by more than 3.5% per annum. Increasing competition from the neighboring 'Special Economic Zone' (SEZ) of Zhuhai (low tax and low labor costs) in the People's Republic, has led to a number of factories re-locating. In December 1995 the opening of an airport helped enhance Macau's role as a point of entry to China. However, it has been followed by an explosion in criminal activity by 'organized crime' triad gangs, who were responsible for 34 murders in the first quarter of 1997 alone. This has discouraged tourism. In May 1998 a Preparatory Committee for the Establishment of the Macau SAR was formed. It comprised representatives from China and Macau and would oversee the transfer of sovereignty. By this date, nearly four-fifths of 'leading and directing' posts in the Macau civil service were held by local, as opposed to Portuguese-expatriate, officials.

In May 1999 a 200-member Nomination Committee elected Edmund Ho Hau Wah, a banker, to become the SAR's chief executive.

8.4.11 Spain's dependencies

Once the possessor of a large overseas empire, Spain is left now with two tiny dependencies, described as External Territories, situated in North Africa. Their political structures and histories follow. Spain's off-shore possessions, the Balearic Islands (Majorca, Minorca, Ibiza, Cabrera, and Formentera) and the Canary Islands (Tenerife, Palma, Gomera, Hierro, Gran Canaria, Lanzarote, and Fuerteventura) form two of the 17 Autonomous Communities, or regions, of Spain.

CEUTA

Capital: Ceuta

Location
North Africa. Ceuta forms an enclave within Moroccan territory on the north African coat, opposite Gibraltar.

Social and economic data
Area: 20 sq km/8 sq miles
Population: 68,796[*]
Pop. density per sq km/sq mile: 3,492[*]/8,600
Economy type: high income (c. $8,500 per capita)
Currency: Spanish peseta
[*] 1996.

Ethnic composition
The population comprises a mixture of North Africans and Europeans. Spanish is the official language.

Religions
The European population is predominantly Christian and the North African population is chiefly Muslim.

Head of government
Mayor/President Jesus Cayetano Fortes Ramos, since 1996

Political system
Ceuta has an elected, 25-member local assembly (Council), which has control over such areas as public works, agriculture, culture, tourism, and internal trade, and also a mayor/president. The Council's powers are akin to those of a municipal council in mainland Spain and are much less than those of the assemblies of Spain's 17 Autonomous Communities, or regions. Ceuta is an integral part of Spain and sends one deputy to Spain's Congress of Deputies and two representatives to the Senate. Spanish civil authority is exercised by a government delegate, who is responsible to the Spanish interior ministry.

Political parties
More than a dozen political parties operate in Ceuta. These include branches of the major Spanish parties: the right-of-center Popular Party (PP); and the center-left Socialist Workers' Party (PSOE). Four other significant parties, with representation in the Council, are: the Progress and Future of Ceuta (PFC) party; the nationalist United Ceuta (CEU) party; the Socialist Party of the People of Ceuta (PSPC), a breakaway group of PSOE dissidents; and the Social and Democratic Party of Ceuta (PDSC), which is orientated towards the Muslim community.

Latest elections
At the most recent Council elections, held on 28 May 1995, the PP, won nine of the 25 seats; the PFC, six; the CEU, four, the PSOE, three, the PSPC, two, and the PDSC, one seat. The deputies and representatives sent to the Spanish Cortes are all drawn from the PP. Turnout was 57%.

Political history
An ancient port and walled city, Ceuta came under Spanish control in medieval times. It developed as a military center during the 19th century, when Spain controlled parts of North Africa. It was retained by Spain on Morocco's independence in 1956, but Morocco has subsequently claimed sovereignty, drawing parallels between continued Spanish control over the enclave and British control over Gibraltar. In 1983, Morocco blocked the passage of goods and people to Ceuta and since the mid-1980s there has been unrest among the territory's Muslim community and demand for greater autonomy. In October 1994, 20,000 people demonstrated in Ceuta for autonomy; there was a general strike in October 1994; and in April 1995 two bomb explosions, attributed to the Organization of the 21st August for the Liberation of the Usurped Moroccan Territories, a terrorist group which receives assistance from within Morocco.

At the local elections of May 1995, Mustafa Mizzian

Ammar, leader of the Social and Democratic Party of Ceuta (PDSC), became the territory's first ever elected Muslim deputy. A coalition comprising the Progress and Future of Ceuta (PFC), nationalist United Ceuta (CEU) and the Socialist Party (PSOE), held power after the election. It was headed, as mayor/president, by Basilio Fernandez Lopez (PFC), until July 1996, when Jesus Fortes Ramos of the Popular Party (PP), took over, leading a new, conservative coalition. He called on the Spanish government to consider giving the enclave the status of a full autonomous region. In April 1998, when Spain's new PP prime minister, Jose Maria Aznar, visited Morocco the Moroccan government requested that Spain review its policy on Ceuta and Melilla. The other burning issue in Ceuta (and Melilla) during recent years has been that of illegal immigration from Africa, with the enclave having become an attractive entry point to the European Union (EU) since the EU Schengen Agreement, allowing the free movement of persons across signatory countries (which included Spain) from March 1995. In 1997–98, for example, around 4,500 illegal immigrants were expelled from Ceuta.

MELILLA

Capital: Melilla

Location

North Africa. Mellila forms an enclave within Moroccan territory on the north African coast, situated in a peninsula. Penon de Velez de la Gomera, a small fort on the Mediterranean coast, and two groups of islands, Penon de Alhucemas and the Chafarinas, are attached to Melilla for administrative purposes.

Social and economic data

Area: 13 sq km/5 sq miles
Population: 59,576[*]
Pop. density per sq km/sq mile: 4,766[*]/11,915
Economy type: high income (*c.* $8,500 per capita)
Currency: Spanish peseta
[*] 1996.

Ethnic composition

The population comprises a mixture of North Africans and Europeans. Spanish is the official language.

Religions

The European population is predominantly Christian

and the North African population, numbering around half the population is chiefly Muslim. More than 10,000 Moroccans commute daily to work in the enclave.

Head of government

Mayor/President Enrique Palacios, since 1997

Political system

Melilla has an elected, 25-member local assembly (Council), which has control over such areas as public works, agriculture, culture, tourism, and internal trade, and also a mayor/president. The Council's powers are akin to those of a municipal council in mainland Spain. Melilla sends one deputy to Spain's Congress of Deputies and two representatives to the Senate. Spanish civil authority is exercised by a government delegate, who is responsible to the Spanish interior ministry.

Political parties

More than a dozen political parties operate in Melilla. These include branches of the major Spanish parties: the right-of-center Popular Party (PP); and the center-left Socialist Workers' Party (PSOE). Two other significant parties, with representation in the Council, are: the Coalition for Melilla (CM), a new Muslim grouping; and the rightwing Union for Melilla People (UPM). The Nationalist Party of Melilla (PNM) is a more extreme rightwing nationalist party which has traditionally been allied to the PP.

Latest elections

At the most recent Council elections, held on 28 May 1995, the PP, won 14 of the 25 seats, the PSOE,, five, the CM, four, and the UPM, two seats. The deputies and representatives sent to the Spanish Cortes are drawn from the PP,. Turnout was 62%.

Political history

Melilla was founded as a Spanish port in 1497 and during the 19th century developed into an important military center for surrounding areas of Spanish North Africa. At the beginning of the Spanish Civil War in 1936, Melilla was the first Spanish town to rise up against the Popular Front government. It was retained by Spain on Morocco's independence in 1956. Morocco has subsequently maintained claims to sovereignty over the territory, but has discounted the use of force as a means of settling the dispute. A formal Moroccan claim to Ceuta and Melilla was presented to the UN General Assembly in October 1988. Since the mid-1980s there has been periodic unrest among the enclave's Muslim community and calls for full autonomy by the territory's political leaders. However, unlike in Ceuta, the Spanish government's 1995 'limited autonomy' package, setting up a 25-member local assembly in addition to a municipal council, was broadly accepted in Melilla.

At the local elections of May 1995, the conservative Popular Party (PP) strengthened its position, winning a majority of seats and Ignacio Velazquez, of the PP and rightwing Nationalist Party of Melilla (PNM), remained as mayor/president. He was later ousted, in March 1997, following defeat on a censure motion, engineered by two opposition PP councillors. One of the latter, Enrique Palacios, who had accused Velazquez of financial mismanagement, became the new mayor/president. In March 1996, the Coalition for Melilla (CM), a Muslim grouping, organized a large demonstration to protest against the community's 'marginalization'.

8.4.12 United Kingdom's dependencies

The British Empire began when the first successful English colony was founded at Jamestown, Virginia, in 1607. At its peak, at the end of the 19th century, it covered a quarter of the world's land surface and included a quarter of its peoples. It had spread over every continent to every race. Now most of the greatest empire history has ever recorded consists of separate, independently sovereign, states, banded together, as much by sentiment and history as other ties, within the Commonwealth. This global body is described, with other world and regional groupings, in *Chapter 9*. What is left of the British Empire today consists of a number of states which still enjoy the protection of the British Crown. Their political structures and histories are given below.

UNITED KINGDOM CROWN DEPENDENCIES

These islands, although lying offshore, do not form integral parts of the United Kingdom. Instead they are designated as Crown Dependencies, enjoying effective self-government in internal affairs.

United Kingdom crown dependencies and British dependent territories			Table 74
Name	Date of first coming under British administration	Area (sq km/sq miles)	Population (c. 1996)
UK Crown Dependencies			
Channel Islands	1066	196/76	146,000
Isle of Man	1765	572/221	71,100
British Dependent Territories			
Anguilla	1650	96/37	10,300
Bermuda	1612	53/20	63,000
British Antarctic Territory	1908	1,710,000/660,234	uninhabited*
British Indian Ocean Territory	1965	60/23	uninhabited*
British Virgin Islands	1666	153/59	18,000
Cayman Islands	1670	259/100	33,600
Falkland Islands	1765/1833	12,173/4,700	2,564
Gibraltar	1704	6/2	27,000
Montserrat	1632	102/39	12,500
Pitcairn Islands	1790	36/14	49
St Helena and Dependencies	1659	308/119	7,900
South Georgia and the South Sandwich Islands**	1775	3,903/1,507	uninhabited*
Turks and Caicos Islands	1765	430/166	18,000
Total	–	*1,728,347/667,318*	*410,013*

* With the periodic exception of scientific or military personnel.
** Dependencies of the Falkland Islands between 1908 and 1985, with the Falklands' governor continuing to serve as their administrative commissioner.

THE CHANNEL ISLANDS

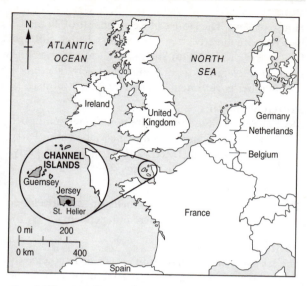

Capitals: St Helier, on Jersey, and St Peter Port, on Guernsey

Location

Western Europe. The Channel Islands comprise the islands of Guernsey (Area: 78 sq km/30 sq miles; Population: 62,000 in 1995), Jersey (Area: 116 sq km/45 sq miles; Population: 85,000 in 1995), Alderney (Population: 2,300), Sark (Population: 600), Herm, Jethou, Brechou, and Lihou, and lie in the English Channel off the northwest coast of France. Fifty-eight per cent of the population lives on Jersey and 40% on Guernsey.

Social and economic data

Area: 196 sq km /76 sq miles
Population: 150,000*
Pop. density per sq km/sq mile: 765*/1,974
Literacy rate: 100%
Economy type: high income (*c.* $16,000 per capita)
* 1996.

Religions

The population is Christian, mainly Church of England and Roman Catholic.

Political system

The Channel Islands are internally self-governing. However, the United Kingdom is responsible for their defense and international relations, with Queen Elizabeth II serving as head of state. For the purposes of government, the islands are divided into the Bailiwick

of Jersey and the Bailiwick of Guernsey, the latter embracing Guernsey island, as well as Alderney, Sark, and the remaining smaller islands. In each Bailiwick the Crown is represented by a lieutenant governor who appoints bailiffs from the ranks of the local legal community, to serve as presidents of the representative assemblies, termed the States of Deliberation (SD), and the judicial bodies, or Royal Courts.

Government on the islands is conducted by Committees appointed by the SD. On Jersey, the SD comprises 12 senators, who are elected for six-year terms, half retiring every three years. At the local and at-large levels, respectively, there are 12 constables and 29 deputies, directly elected for three-year terms. On Guernsey, the SD consists of 12 conseillers, who are indirectly elected by the States of Election, a 108-member body comprising local political and judicial officers, for six-year terms, half retiring every three years; plus 33 people's deputies directly elected for four-year terms, ten Douzaine representatives, elected by their respective parishes, and two Alderney representatives. In Alderney, the SD is a 12-member body, directly elected for a three-year term. Finally, in Sark, the assembly, called the Chief Pleas, consists of 12 popularly elected members plus 40 tenants nominated by the feudal suzerain of the island, the seigneur.

Political parties

Members sit in the SDs usually as independents, although the Jersey Democratic Movement has occasionally held a number of seats.

Political history

The islands were granted to the Duke of Normandy in the 10th century, being attached to the Crown of England in 1066. They are the only part of Normandy to have remained under British rule since 1204 and were the only British possession to have been occupied by Germany during World War II. The islands enjoy tax sovereignty and, with imports exempt from British value-added tax, and local income tax levels low, they have developed into 'tax haven' finance centers in recent decades.

THE ISLE OF MAN

Capital: Douglas

Location

Western Europe. The Isle of Man lies in the Irish Sea,

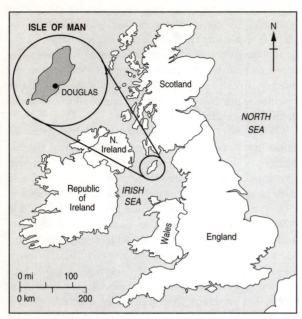

ISLE OF MAN

DOUGLAS

Scotland

N. Ireland

NORTH SEA

Republic of Ireland

IRISH SEA

Wales

England

0 mi 100
0 km 200

equidistant from Scotland, to the northeast, England, to the east, and Northern Ireland, to the west.

Social and economic data
Area: 572 sq km/221 sq miles
Population: 71,100[*]
Pop. density per sq km/sq mile: 124[*]/1,322
Literacy rate: 100%
Economy type: high income (*c.* $13,000 per capita)
[*] 1996.

Religions
The population is Christian, adhering especcially to the Church of England.

Head of government
Chief Minister Donald Gelling, since 1996

Political system
Queen Elizabeth II is head of state, under the designation 'Lord of Man', and has ultimate responsibility for the island's good government, being represented on the island by an appointed lieutenant governor. The Isle of Man is dependent on the United Kingdom for its defense and external relations. In internal matters, however, it is substantially self-governing, having its own legislative assembly, the Court of Tynwald, and legal and administrative systems, as well as control over direct taxation. The Court of Tynwald, which traces its roots back to Scandinavian times, is a two-chamber body, comprising the Legislative Council, or Upper House, and the House of Keys, or Lower House. The

Legislative Council consists of the lieutenant governor, a president, the lord bishop of Sodor and Man, the attorney general and eight members elected by the House of Keys. The House of Keys consists of 24 members who are directly elected by universal adult suffrage for five-year terms. Both chambers sit together as one body in the legislature, but vote separately. There is a ten-member government, headed by a chief minister.

Political parties
Most members sit as independents, although a number of political parties, most notably the Manx Labor Party and the Sons of Man (Mec Vannin) nationalist party, have won seats from time to time.

Latest elections
The last general election was held on 21 November 1996. All members elected were independents.

Political history
The Isle of Man (Euan Vannin) was ruled successively by the Welsh, during the 6th to 9th centuries, the Vikings/Norwegians, from the 9th century to 1266, and the Scots, between 1266 and 1765, before being purchased by the British government, in 1765. Because of its independent fiscal policies, the island has, like the Channel Islands, become something of a tax haven in recent years.

BRITISH DEPENDENT TERRITORIES

These are overseas territories enjoying a colonial status, with varying degrees of internal autonomy.

ANGUILLA

Capital: The Valley

Location
Central America and the Caribbean. Anguilla is an island in the Eastern Caribbean, the most northerly of the Leeward Islands, and situated 112 km/70 miles northwest of St Kitts and Nevis, and 8 km/5 miles north of St Maarten.

Social and economic data
Area: 96 sq km/37 sq miles
Population: 10,300[*]
Pop. density per sq km/sq mile: 107[*]/278

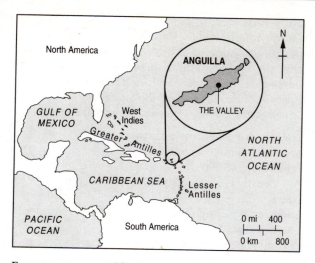

Economy type: middle income (*c.* $6,500 per capita in 1995)

Currency: East Caribbean dollar

* 1995.

Ethnic composition

The population is predominantly of black or mixed race and European descent. Around 4,000 Anguillans live in the US Virgin Islands and 10,000 in the UK. English is the official language.

Religions

The population is mainly Christian, especially Anglican and Methodist, with a Roman Catholic minority.

Head of government

Chief Minister Hubert Hughes, since 1994

Political system

Under the terms of the 1982 constitution, as amended in 1990, the British Crown is represented on Anguilla by an appointed governor who is responsible for external affairs, defense, the judiciary, the 'offshore' banking sector, and internal security, and presides over meetings of the Executive Council and House of Assembly. The Executive Council, or cabinet, comprises a chief minister, with whom the governor works closely, and three other ministers drawn from the House of Assembly, as well as two *ex officio* members, the attorney general and the permanent secretary for finance. The House of Assembly consists of seven members directly elected for five-year terms, as well as two nominated and two *ex officio* representatives.

Political parties

Five political parties, all broadly center-right, currently operate: the Anguilla National Alliance (ANA), which was known as the People's Progressive Party (PPP) prior to 1980 and dominated politics until 1994, with Sir Emile Gumbs as chief minister 1984–94; the Anguilla Democratic Party (ADP), which was known as the Anguilla People's Party (APP) prior to the resignation of Ronald Webster as party leader in 1984; the Anguilla United Party (AUP), which, originally formed in 1979, was revived in 1984 by Webster and is now led by Chief Minister Hubert Hughes; The Angullans For Good Government (AGG), led by Webster; and the Party For Anguilla's Culturation and Economy (PACO).

Latest elections

In the 4 March 1999 general election the ANA won 43% of the vote; the ADP 33% and two seats; and the AUP 15% and two seats. The AUP-ADP coalition government, headed by Hubert Hughes, retained power.

Political history

Anguilla was first colonized by English settlers from overcrowded St Kitts in 1650. It became more closely tied with St Kitts in 1825 and was later formally incorporated in the colony of St Kitts-Nevis-Anguilla (SNA). In February 1967 this colony, together with others in the Eastern Caribbean, became an internally self-governing state in association with the United Kingdom, Britain retaining responsibility for its defense and external affairs.

However, in May 1967, under the leadership of Ronald Webster, a local business executive and leader of the People's Progressive Party (PPP), Anguilla, alleging domination by its larger associated islands, revolted, refusing to accept rule from St Kitts. After attempts to reach a compromise had failed and Anguilla had voted to cut all ties with the UK and declare independence, British troops were sent there, in March 1969. A crown-appointed British commissioner was installed and a truce signed. Subsequently, in July 1971, Anguilla was designated a dependency of Britain and two months later all troops were withdrawn.

A new constitution was framed in 1976, providing for a government of elected representatives, and in December 1980 the island was formally separated from the SNA. Ronald Webster served as the island's chief minister between 1976 and 1977 and between 1980 and 1984, but, after being replaced as the party's leader in February 1977 by Emile Gumbs, left the PPP to form the Anguilla United Party (AUP), and the Anguilla People's Party (APP), in 1979 and 1981 respectively. In the March 1984 general election, however, Webster's

APP was heavily defeated, its leader losing his seat. Gumbs, who had earlier served as chief minister between 1977 and 1980, returned to office, as leader of the Anguilla National Alliance (ANA), the successor party to the PPP. He proceeded to implement a policy program geared towards revitalizing the economy, unemployment standing at 40% in 1984, by encouraging tourism, international banking, and foreign inward investment. By 1995 tourism contributed a third, and 'offshore finance' an eighth of GDP and the unemployment rate had fallen to 5%. Gumbs, who was later knighted, remained as chief minister until his retirement from politics in February 1994.

The new chief minister, Hubert Hughes of the AUP, strained the island's relations with the British government, which he criticized for inadequate investment in Anguilla's development projects; its slow response to the devastation caused by Hurricane Luis, which resulted in East Caribbean $72 million of damage to the island in October 1995; and its lack of consultation with Anguilla when appointing officials. When Hughes raised the issue of independence, the British government proposed, in 1997, to re-introduce reserve powers for the governor, enabling legislation approved by the local legislature to be vetoed, worsening the tension between Britain and the island. The proposal was made in the light of British concerns over the possible abuse by criminals and drug-traffickers of Anguilla's secretive 'offshore finance' sector.

BERMUDA

Capital: Hamilton, on Main Island, or Great Bermuda

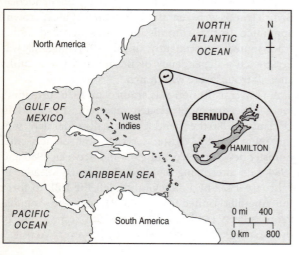

Location
Central America and the Caribbean. Bermuda is an archipelago consisting of 138 low-lying coral islands and islets stretching 35 km/22 miles east and west and 22 km/14 miles north and south, and lying in the Atlantic Ocean 917 km/570 miles off the coast of South Carolina, United States. Twenty of the islands are inhabited.

Social and economic data
Area: 53 sq km/20 sq miles
Population: 63,000[*]
Pop. density per sq km/sq mile: 1,190[*]/3,150
Literacy rate: 98%
Economy type: high income (*c.* $28,000 per capita in 1995)
Currency: Bermuda dollar (equivalent to US dollar)
[*] 1995.

Ethnic composition
Two-thirds of the population are of African descent, the remainder being of British or Portuguese stock. English is the official language, but some Portuguese is also spoken.

Religions
The poulation is Christian, with 42% of the people Anglicans and 16% Roman Catholics.

Local government
The country is divided into nine parishes, with St George and Hamilton constituting two municipalities.

Head of government
Premier Jennifer Smith, since 1998

Political system
Bermuda is internally self-governing. However, Britain remains, under the terms of the 1968 constitution, as amended in 1973 and 1979, responsible for the islands' external affairs, defense, and internal security, including the police, with British interests being represented by a crown-appointed governor (J Thorold Masefield since June 1997). The islands' assembly has two chambers: the 11-member Senate and the 40-member House of Assembly. Three of the Senate's members are appointed by the governor, five by the prime minister and three by the leader of the opposition. The members of the House of Assembly are all directly elected by universal adult suffrage for five-year terms, standing in 20 two-member constituencies. The minimum voting age was lowered from 21 years to 18 years in 1990. From the majority grouping in the House of Assembly, the governor appoints a prime minister to preside over a cabinet of

around 14 ministers of his or her own choosing. At least six cabinet ministers must be drawn from the assembly, to which the cabinet itself is collectively responsible. There is also a Governor's Council which is used by the governor and ministers for consultative purposes.

Political parties

Three political parties currently operate in Bermuda. The most important is the United Bermuda Party (UBP; estd. 1964), led by Pamela Gordon, the prime minister during 1997–98. It held power continuously from 1968. It is liberal-conservative in outlook and supports multiracialism and free enterprise. The main other party is the Progressive Labor Party (PLP; estd. 1963), led by Jennifer Smith. The PLP is a social-democratic force which advocates the 'Bermudianiz-ation' of the economy, electoral reform, and eventual independence. The third minor party, the National Liberal Party (NLP), is a centrist grouping led by Charles Jeffers, and was formed in August 1985 by breakaway members from the PLP.

Latest elections

At the November 1998 general election the PLP broke a run of eight successive election victories by the UBP. It won 26 seats in the House of Assembly, with 54% of the popular vote. The UBP, with 44% of the vote, won 14 seats.

Political history

The islands were discovered by and named after the Spanish mariner, Juan de Bermudez, in 1515. They were later colonized by British settlers in 1612, forming part of the Virginia Company's charter, before being transferred to the British Crown, in 1684. During the 17th century the economy was based on tobacco growing, whaling, and ship building. Bermuda also served as a penal settlement, until 1862, and a naval station, before developing into an Atlantic trading entrepôt during the 19th century. The islands were granted a new constitution, conceding internal autonomy and establishing a new ministerial system.

Popular politics were to be characterized, however, by intense rivalry between the moderate, though predominantly white, United Bermuda Party (UBP) and the more radical, black-led, pro-independence Progressive Labor Party (PLP). The general election of May 1968, which was won by the UBP, was accompanied by serious race riots. This was followed by a wave of murders in 1972–73, including that of the governor, Sir Richard Sharples. Further race riots broke out in December 1977, after two blacks were hanged for com-

plicity in the 1972–73 incidents. This forced the despatch of British troops to restore order. To investigate the causes of this racial tension, a Royal Commission was set up, in February 1978. This later recommended, in its report of August 1978, a redrawing of constituency boundaries to improve the PLP's prospects of capturing seats. However, despite implementation of this recommendation, the UBP continued to win Assembly majorities in the elections of December 1980, February 1983, October 1985, February 1989, and October 1993.

The 1978 Royal Commission also recommended early independence for Bermuda, but the majority of the population oppose this. This was evidenced by a referendum held in August 1995 when, with a turnout of 59%, only 26% voted in favor of independence. Sir John Swan, the prime minister since 1982, and seven of his black colleagues in the UBP had advocated independence, while the party's remaining 14 members, including all its white deputies, had opposed it. The opposition PLP, which favored independence in principle, urged its predominantly black supporters to abstain, arguing that electoral reform must come first. Defeat in the plebiscite brought Swan's resignation as premier and UBP leader. Swan was replaced by David Saul, formerly the finance minister, who had remained neutral during the independence referendum. However, Saul encountered growing divisions within the UBP and government and, after surviving a censure vote in June 1996, stepped down as premier and retired from politics in March 1997. Pamela Gordon became the new UBP leader and premier. However, the UBP suffered its first ever defeat in the November 1998 general election to the PLP, led by Jennifer Smith, who became prime minister. She pledged to make Bermuda more attractive to international business aand not change its tax status.

The country currently has one of the highest per-capita GDPs in the world, having developed, in recent decades, with the British guarantee of security, into a major center for tourism and financial services, as well as as an offshore 'tax shelter' for more than 8,000 exempted international companies. Bermuda is the world's largest insurance market and has the fifth largest 'free flag' shipping fleet in the world. The United States' air base on the islands at Kindley Field was closed, along with British and Canadian military bases, in 1995. A sharp drop in tourist arrivals in 1991 provoked the government into passing a bill classifying the hotel business as an 'essential industry' since it employs a third of the workforce and contributes 35% of GDP.

THE BRITISH VIRGIN ISLANDS

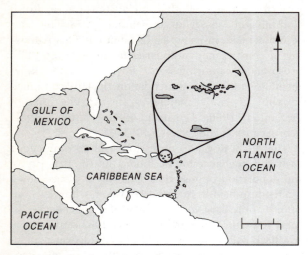

Capital: Road Town, on Tortola island

Location

Central America and the Caribbean. The British Virgin Islands consist of 60 mountainous islands and islets situated at the north end of the Leeward Islands, or Lesser Antilles, chain, 90 km/55miles east of Puerto Rico and adjoining the US Virgin Islands. Sixteen of the islands are inhabited, 83% of the population living on Tortola island and 13% on Virgin Gorda.

Social and economic data

Area: 153 sq km/59 sq miles
Population: 18,000*
Pop. density per sq km/sq mile: 118*/305
Literacy rate: 98%
Economy type: high income (*c.* $15,000 per capita in 1995)
Currency: US dollar
* 1995.

Ethnic composition

The population is predominantly of African or mixed race and European descent. English is the official language.

Religions

The population is Christian, especially Protestant, with a Roman Catholic minority.

Head of government

Chief Minister Ralph O'Neal, since 1995

Political system

Under the terms of the 1977 constitution, the British Crown is represented on the Virgin Islands by an appointed governor who has sole responsibility for external affairs, defense, judicial, and internal security matters. The governor also serves as chairperson of a six-member Executive Council, or cabinet, and possesses reserve legislative powers. There is also a 15-member Legislative Council, which comprises nine members directly elected from single-member constituencies, four elected (since 1994) from a single national constituency, an appointed speaker and one *ex officio* member, the attorney general. From the majority grouping in the Legislative Council is drawn a chief minister and three other ministers who work with the governor and attorney general in the Executive Council. The minimum voting age has been 18 years since 1979.

Political parties

Four political parties currently function on the islands: the Virgin Islands Party (VIP), led by Chief Minister Ralph O'Neal; the National Democratic Party (NDP); the United Party (UP), led by Conrad Maduro; at the Concerned Citizens' Movement (CCM), formed in 1994 as the successor to the Independent People's Movement (IPM; estd. 1989). The CCM is led by Walwyn Brewley, who is the official leader of the opposition.

Latest elections

The most recent elections to the Legislative Council, held on 17 May 1999, saw the VIP re-elected. It won 38% of the vote and seven seats, the NDP, with 37% of the vote, won five seats, while the UP and CCM secured 8% and 4% of the vote respectively.

Political history

Tortola was originally settled by the Dutch in 1648. It was colonized by British planters in 1666 and formally annexed by Britain in 1672. A form of constitutional government was granted in 1774 and in 1834 slavery was abolished. From 1872 the islands formed part of the British federal colony of the Leeward Islands, before later becoming a separate Crown Colony, in July 1956. They received their own appointed administrator, known as governor from 1971, in 1960 and a constitution was promulgated in 1967 which provided for a ministerial system. This was superseded by a new constitution in June 1977 which extended the degree of internal self-government.

Politics have been characterized since 1967 by the alternation in power of the Virgin Islands Party (VIP), led until his death in 1995 by H Lavity Stoutt, and a coalition of United Party (UP) and independent deputies. Cyril Romney, an independent councillor, served as chief minister from November 1983, but lost power to Stoutt in September 1986, after his reputation had been damaged by his alleged connection with a company which was under investigation by the British police and US Drug Enforcement Administration.

The Stoutt administration introduced, in 1990–91, tighter regulation of the 'offshore finance' sector, as concern grew over its abuse by drug-traffickers. His government was re-elected in November 1990 and February 1995, holding on to power after the last election with the support of an independent deputy. On Stoutt's unexpected death in May 1995, the deputy chief minister, Ralph O'Neal, took over as prime minister. In July 1996 the new British governor, David Mackilligin, caused controversy by suggesting that the islands should join other British Dependent Territories and end the use of corporal punishment as a judicial sentence.

Since the mid-1970s, the islands' economy has developed rapidly, principally as a result of a boom in tourism, the number of annual visitors having tripled to more than 340,000. The tourist industry now contributes nearly 50% of GDP and one-third of employment, but there is increasing concern over its damage to the local environment. Following the passage of the Business Companies Act by the Legislative Council in 1984, which simplified procedures for company registrations, the Virgins have also attracted much foreign 'offshore capital', more than 210,000 international companies being registered by 1997, utilizing the islands as a 'tax shelter'. The business sector contributes a quarter of GDP. The population has doubled since the mid-1980s, with large-scale immigration from other Caribbean Islands as well as the USA, and the UK.

CAYMAN ISLANDS

Capital: George Town, on Grand Cayman

Location

Central America and the Caribbean. The Cayman Islands consist of the islands of Grand Cayman, Cayman Brac, and Little Cayman, and lie in the Western Caribbean, 290 km/180 miles northwest of Jamaica and 240 km/150 miles south of Cuba. Ninety-three per cent of the population lives on Grand

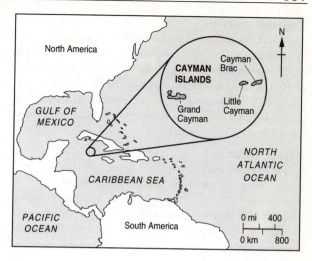

Cayman and 6% on Cayman Brac.

Social and economic data

Area: 259 sq km/100 sq miles
Population: 33,600*
Pop. density per sq km/sq mile: 130*/336
Literacy rate: 97%
Economy type: high income (c. $28,000 per capita in 1995)
Currency: Cayman Islands dollar
* 1995.

Ethnic composition

Sixty per cent of the population are of mixed descent. English is the official language.

Religions

Christianity is the chief religion, predominantly of the Anglican and Baptist churches, with a Roman Catholic minority.

Head of government

Governor John Owen, since 1995

Political system

Under the terms of the 1959 constitution, as revised in 1972, 1992, and 1994, the British Crown is represented on the Caymans by an appointed governor who has sole responsiblity for external affairs, defense, judicial, public service, and internal security matters. The governor also serves as chairperson of the Executive Council, or cabinet, which comprises three appointed *ex officio* members, including a chief secretary, and five elected representatives drawn from the Legislative Council. The latter five serve as ministers. The Legislative Assembly consists of three official representatives and 15 members elected by universal adult suffrage, from six electoral districts, for a four-year term.

Political parties

Party politics collapsed in the 1960s and, until 1991 and the formation of the Progressive Democratic Party (PDP), candidates contested elections both as independents and in loose 'teams', the most important of which has been the 'National Team'. All candidates favor the Caymans' continued dependent status and liberal-conservative economic strategy.

Latest elections

In the 20 November 1996 general election, the 'National Team' grouping, which includes the nucleus of the PDP, won nine of the 15 Legislative Assembly seats. Independent candidates won three seats, while two new groupings, the Democratic Alliance and the anti-government Team Cayman, won two seats and one seat respectively.

Political history

The Caymans were first visited by Christopher Columbus (1451–1506) in 1503, but were never settled by the Spanish. They were subsequently ceded, with Jamaica, to Britain under the terms of the 1670 Treaty of Madrid. Grand Cayman island was later colonized by British military deserters from Jamaica, from where it was administered. The islands of Cayman Brac and Little Cayman were permanently settled only from 1833, and until 1877 were not administratively connected with Grand Cayman. On Jamaica's independence in 1962, the islands were made a separate British Crown Colony and have subsequently grown into an important center for tourism, currently attracting almost half a million visitors annually and providing employment for half the work force, as well as for oil transhipment and as an offshore 'tax shelter' for foreign businesses and banking companies. During the 1990s, there has been concern about possible abuse of the islands' financial services sector by drug-traffickers and increasing levels of drug-related crime. A stock exchange was opened in 1996. In 1997, fierce opposition from the business community forced the government to retreat from plans to substantially raise taxes and duties.

FALKLAND ISLANDS (MALVINAS)

Capital: Port Stanley, on East Falkland Island

Location

South America. The Falkland Islands consist of two

large islands, East and West Falkland, and around 200 smaller islands, all situated in the South Atlantic Ocean, 770 km/480 miles northeast of Cape Horn. Seventy per cent of the population live in the capital.

Social and economic data

Area: 12,173 sq km/4,700 sq miles
Population: 2,564[*]
Pop. density per sq km/sq mile: 0.2[*]/0.5
Economy type: high income (*c.* $8,500 per capita)
Currency: Falkland Islands pound (equivalent to pound sterling)
[*] 1996.

Ethnic composition

Most of the population are of British descent. English is the official language.

Religions

Christianity is the recognized religion, based on the Anglican, Roman Catholic, and United Free Churches.

Head of government

Governor Richard Ralph, since 1996

Political system

Under the terms of the October 1985 constitution, the Falkland Islands are administered by a crown-appointed governor, who works with an advisory Executive Council composed of two, non-voting, *ex officio* members, a chief executive, and a financial secretary, and three representatives elected by the Legislative

Council. The Falkland Islands' Legislative Council comprises eight directly elected members and the two, non-voting, *ex officio* representatives.

Political parties

Members of the Legislative Council are elected as independents, although one political party was formed in 1988: the Desire the Right Party (DRP). The DRP favors a limited rapprochement with Argentina and has 100 members.

Latest elections

Legislature elections were most recently held on 9 October 1997 and saw the sole return of independent candidates, all of whom opposed sovereignty negotiations with Argentina.

Political history

The Falklands were first visited by the English navigator, John Davis (c. 1550–1605), in 1592 and in the late 17th century were named after Lord Falkland, treasurer of the British Navy. East Falkland was colonized by French settlers from St Malo in 1764 and given the name Iles Malouines, and West Falkland by British settlers in 1765. From 1767, however, the Spanish, who took over the French settlement, gradually gained the upper hand, ejecting the British in 1774. British sovereignty was never ceded, however. During the early 19th century, Spanish influence waned, its garrison being withdrawn in 1811, and, following a brief period of occupation, between 1826 and 1831, by the Republic of Buenos Aires, Britain reasserted her possession in 1833. Formal annexation of the Falkland Islands and their dependencies took place in 1908 and 1917, a modest, sheep-raising, settler economy being established.

Argentina, however, never relinquished its claim over the islands ('Islas Malvinas') and in 1966, at the instigation of the United Nations, negotiations to resolve the continuing dispute were started. During the early 1970s, relations thawed. Britain's Heath administration (1970–74) signed a communications agreement which effectively gave Argentina control over air access to the islands. Following this, the Buenos Aires government extended the Port Stanley airstrip, enabling tourists to visit the Falklands and islanders to make use of Argentinian schools and hospitals. The British government appeared anxious to foster closer socio-economic links between the Falklands and the Argentinian mainland, but consistently refused, in intergovernment talks, to countenance any transfer of sovereignty against the wishes of

the inhabitants, who consistently favored maintaining their British connection.

After the accession to power, in 1976, in Buenos Aires, of a nationalist-minded military junta, led by Lieutenant General Jorge Videla, Anglo-Argentinian relations deteriorated. In December 1977 a military invasion was threatened and, in response, the British Callaghan administration (1976–79) despatched a hunter-killer submarine to the islands. Two years later, the new Conservative Thatcher administration (1979–90) recommended negotiations with the Argentinian government. However, the two compromise options suggested to resolve the dispute, condominium, or joint sovereignty and rule, or 'lease-back', the transfer of formal sovereignty to Argentina, who would, in turn, lease back the islands' administration to Britain, were overwhelmingly rejected when put before the islands' Council. A third, Argentinian-sponsored, option, designated 'most pampered region' status, which would involve the transfer of sovereignty in return for Argentinian guarantees to retain the existing democratic form of government and local legal and education systems, was also rejected. Two years later, on 2 April 1982, soon after the accession to power in Buenos Aires of another military leader, General Leopoldo Galtieri (b. 1926), Port Stanley was invaded by Argentinian troops. The British government immediately responded by despatching a naval 'task force' and a fierce conflict ensued in which 255 British, 755 Argentinian, and three Falklander lives were lost, before, on 14 June 1982, the 12,000 Argentinian troops on the islands surrendered and British control was restored.

After this war, the British government instituted a new 'Fortress Falklands' policy, based on establishing a large permanent garrison on the islands to deter future Argentinian aggression together with the construction of a new airport, for larger aircraft, in 1985. The cost to the British government to 1988 (including the war) exceeded $7.5 billion. A 278-kilometre-wide protection and fishing zone was declared, licences being sold to foreign trawler companies seeking to fish within it. New development schemes were also promoted by the islands' newly established Falklands Islands Development Agency, resulting in a boom in the islands' once moribund economy. Despite UN calls for a re-opening of negotiations to find a peaceful solution to the 'Falklands issue' and the accession to power of a new democratic administration in Argentina, the British government has declined to enter into talks and the islanders' right to self-determinantion was guaranteed in the Falklands' 1985 constitution. Full diplomatic relations between the United Kingdom and Argentina were restored in February 1990 and in September 1991 the two governments signed agreements substantially reducing military restrictions in the South Atlantic. By 1997 the size of the British military garrison on the Falklands had been halved to 2,000, with annual maintenance costs of £70 million. However, the discovery, in 1988, of offshore oil reserves has heightened international interest in the islands. Exploratory drilling began in 1997, with little initial success, but it was agreed in 1995 that royalties would be shared with Argentina for oil produced midway between the Falklands and the mainland. In May 1999 thee Falkland Islands agreed to hold their first direct talks with Argentina since the 1982 war. The talks covered air links, visits by Argentines, and economic co-operation.

GIBRALTAR

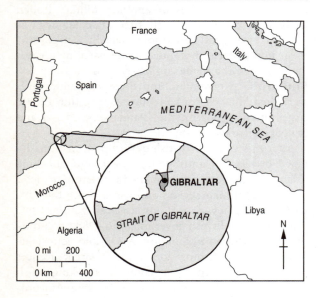

Capital: Gibraltar

Location

Western Europe. Gibraltar consists of a narrow peninsula connected to the southwest tip of Spain by an isthmus.

Social and economic data

Area: 6 sq km/2 sq miles
Population: 27,000*
Pop. density per sq km/sq mile: 4,153*/13,500
Literacy rate: 99%
Economy type: high income (*c.* $18,000 per capita in 1995)
Currency: Gibraltar pound (at par with sterling)
* 1997.

Ethnic composition

Seventy-six per cent of the population are Gibraltarians and 15% British. More than a thousand Moroccan laborers also work on 'The Rock'. English is the official language, but most of the population are bilingual in English and Spanish.

Religions

Three-quarters of the population are Roman Catholics, 8% members of the Church of England, 10% are Muslims, and 3% are Jewish.

Head of government

Chief Minister Peter Caruana, since 1996

Political system

Under the terms of the 1969 constitution, British interests in Gibraltar have been represented by a crown-appointed governor, who is advised by the Gibraltar Council, a body which comprises four *ex officio* and five elected members of the House of Assembly. The United Kingdom is responsible for the territory's defense and external affairs, as well as matters of internal security. Since 1969, full control over the remainder of internal affairs has been vested in the elected House of Assembly and a Council of Ministers, or cabinet, drawn from the majority grouping within the Assembly.

The House of Assembly consists of a speaker appointed by the governor, two *ex officio* representatives, the attorney general and the financial and development secretary, and 15 members who are popularly elected for four-year terms. The electoral system is unique, allowing each elector to vote for a maximum of eight candidates and the party with the largest share of the vote is restricted to a maximum of eight seats. The Council of Ministers, which constitutes the territory's 'internal executive', has seven ministers and a chief minister drawn from the House.

Political parties

Four political parties currently function. The two

most important are the moderate-socialist Gibraltar Socialist Labor Party (GSLP), which was established in 1976 and is led by its founder, José (Joe) Bossano, and the center-right Gibraltar Social Democrats (GSD), formed in 1989 and led by Peter Caruana. The GSLP, a strongly nationalist body, seeks to achieve full independence for 'The Rock' within the European Union, while the GSD supports the participation of Gibraltar in Anglo-Spanish negotiations. The Gibraltar Liberal Party (GLP), known before 1997 as the Gibraltar National Party (GNP), formed in 1991, advocates self-determination for Gibraltar. The center-right Gibraltar Labor Party-Associ-ation for the Advancement of Civil Rights (GLP-AACR), formed in 1942, dominated political affairs in Gibraltar prior to 1988, with its former leader, Sir Joshua Hasan, serving continuously as chief minister between 1964 and 1969 and between 1972 and 1987 and Adolfa Canepa as chief minister in 1987–88. However, opposition to the December 1987 Anglo-Spanish transport accord, which sanctioned joint civilian use of Gibraltar's air-port, caused a split in the GLP-AACR and, since its electoral defeat in March 1988, the GLP-AACR has been inactive.

Latest elections

In the general election of 16 May 1996, the GSD secured eight seats in the House of Assembly and the GSLP, seven, based on 48% and 39% shares of the popular vote. The GLP won 13% of the vote but no seats. Turnout was 88%.

Political history

Gibraltar has long served as a strategic promontory, commanding the western entrance to the Mediterranean and boasting excellent port facilities. Occupied by Arabs from 711 AD, it passed to the Moorish kingdom of Granada during the 15th century and subsequently fell under Spanish control. During the War of the Spanish Succession (1701–14), it was captured by an Anglo-Dutch force in 1704 and was for-mally ceded to Britain by Spain under the terms of the Treaty of Utrecht (1713). It was designated a Crown Colony in 1830 and, following World War II, during which it served as a strategic base for Allied naval forces, a Legislative Council was established in 1950. In 1963 the Franco government in Spain began to campaign for the territory's return to Spain, exerting diplomatic pressure through the United Nations and economic pressure, culminating in the closure of the frontier with Spain and the withdrawal of the Spanish

labor force. In accordance with a UN resolution which called for the interests of the people of Gibraltar to be taken into account, the British government held a referendum on the sovereignty question in September 1967 in which an overwhelming (95%) majority voted to retain the link with the United Kingdom. A new constitution was thus framed and adopted in 1969 in which full internal self-government was conceded, but in which the UK government undertook never to enter into arrangements to transfer the territory's sovereignty to another state against their freely and democratically expressed wishes.

Spain remained intransigent, continuing to claim Gibraltar's sovereignty and keeping the border closed until General Franco's death in November 1975. Thereafter Anglo-Spanish relations slowly thawed, beginning with the restoration of Gibraltar – Spain telephone links in December 1977 and culminating in the re-opening of the border in February 1985: a year before Spain's entry into the European Community. In March 1991 the British government withdrew the majority of its army personnel from Gibraltar because Spain's commitment to the EC and NATO had made the need for substantial defenses unnecessary. At the same time, it reassured Gibraltarians that no change in sovereignty would be contemplated without their agreement. Tourism and financial services are now the mainstay of the economy, in which the unemployment rate was 13% in 1997.

José Bossano, leader of the Gibraltar Socialist Labor Party (GSLP), became chief minister in March 1988 and sought to achieve self-determination within the European Union (EU). However, this was rejected by Spain, which continues to claim sovereignty and has been concerned at the apparent lack of action by the Gibraltar authorities to stop money laundering and drug smuggling occurring in its territory. This has led the Spanish government to periodically impose stringent border inspections. However, in July 1995 the government's confiscation of 60 speed launches, as part of a crackdown against smuggling, provoked two days of riots and looting. Bossano's GSLP fought the May 1996 general election on the platform of changing Gibraltar's status to one of 'free association' with the United Kingdom by 2000 and saw its share of the vote slump from 73% (achieved in January 1992) to 39%. This enabled the GSD, led by Peter Caruana and pledging to modernize the constitution and improve relations with Spain and Britain, to secure power. The new Caruana government proposed that, to 'strengthen and modernize' Gibraltar's relations with the United Kingdom, its status be changed from that of a Crown Dependency to a Crown Colony, analogous to the Channel Islands and the Isle of Man and also allow a referendum on self-determination. Meanwhile, Spain proposed that sovereignty over Gibraltar be shared with the United Kingdom for a hundred years, before full control then passed to Spain. Britain has rejected this idea. In January 1999 the Gibraltar government seized a Spanish fishing boat during a dispute over territorial waters. This led to a brief diplomatic crisis between Spain and the United Kingdom as Spain implemented a strict frontier control policy, causing long border delays.

MONTSERRAT

Capital: Plymouth

Location
Central America and the Caribbean. Montserrat is a volcanic island lying 43 sq km/7 miles southwest of Antigua in the Leeward Islands group of the Lesser Antilles in the Eastern Caribbean. Thirty per cent of the population lived in the capital before the major volcanic eruption in 1997.

Social and economic data
Area: 102 sq km/39 sq miles
Population: 12,500*
Pop. density per sq km/sq mile: 123*/321
Literacy rate: 97%
Economy type: middle income (*c.* $5,000 per capita in 1994)
Currency: East Caribbean dollar
* 1995 (In 1998, after a major volcanic eruption, the population fell to 2,850.)

Ethnic composition
The population is predominantly of mixed African and European descent. English is the official language.

Religions
The population is Christian, especially Anglican, with a Roman Catholic minority.

Head of government
Chief Minister David Brandt, since 1997

Political system
Under the terms of the 1960 constitution, as amended in 1977 and 1989, the British Crown is represented on the island by an appointed governor who is responsible for defense, foreign affairs, and internal security. The governor also serves as president of a seven-member Executive Council, or cabinet, which also includes a chief minister, three other ministers drawn from among the elected members of the legislature, and the attorney general and financial secretary, both *ex officio*. The legislature, or Legislative Council, is a 12-member body consisting of two official members, three nominated, including a speaker, and seven members directly elected for five years. The Executive Council's chief minister and ministers are chosen from the Legislative Council. The 1989 constitutional amendment provided for the island's right to self-determination.

Political parties
There are three main political parties currently operating. The most important is the right-of-center National Progressive Party (NPP), formed in 1991 by a former civil servant, Reuben Meade. The others are the Movement for National Reconstruction (MNR), led by Austin Bramble, and the centrist People's Progressive Alliance (PPA), both formed in 1996. The PPA, led by John Osbourne (chief minister between 1978 and 1991), is successor to the People's Liberation Movement (PLM), which campaigned for greater spending on development and for independence, when 'economically viable'.

Latest elections
In the most recent Legislative Council elections, held on 11 November 1996, the PPA, with 35% of the vote, won two of the seven elected seats; the MNR, with 22%, two seats; the NPP, 19% of the vote and one seat; and independent candidates, 23% of the vote and two seats. Altogether, 4,159 people voted: a turnout of 58%.

Political history
Montserrat was first visited in 1493 by Christopher Columbus (1451–1506), who named the island after the Abbey of Montserrat, near Barcelona. In 1632 it was colonized by English settlers, who had moved from the overcrowded Caribbean island of St Kitts (Christopher), and Irish political prisoners sent by Oliver Cromwell (1599–1658). They proceeded to establish a plantation economy based on slave labor. However, the island was not formally made a British Crown Colony until 1871. Between 1871 and 1956 Montserrat was administered as a division of the federal colony of the Leeward Islands. When the federation was dissolved, it became a separate colony, opting not to join the West Indies Associated States, which was

established in 1967. Since 1960 the island has had its own administrator, who was redesignated governor in 1971, and its own constitutional system.

The dominant political party from 1978 to 1991 was the People's Liberation Movement (PLM), a moderate, nationalist body, led by John Osbourne. The party supported the development of agriculture, cotton and peppers being important export crops, light manufacturing, 'offshore' finance, and the tourist industry, which contributed 25% of Montserrat's GDP in 1995. In September 1989 Hurricane Hugo caused widespread damage to the island and between 1989 and 1992 more than nine-tenths of 'offshore banks' were closed after a series of scandals and subsequent investigations by British inspectors.

The PLM, with the reputation of its leader, Osbourne, tarnished by charges of corruption on which he was later acquitted, was defeated in the October 1991 general election by the newly formed National Progressive Party (NPP), led by Reuben Meade. In August 1995 the southern half of the island was evacuated after a partial eruption of the Chances Peak volcano, which had been dormant for a century. A state of emergency and night curfew were declared. There were further evacuations in December 1995 and April 1996, as fears of a full eruption grew, leading to around 5,000 islanders leaving the territory by December 1996 and several thousand living in evacuation camps, in the north. In response, the British government granted Montserratians residency and the right to work in the UK for two years and announced, in August 1996, an over $40 million package of reconstruction assistance. However, there was dissatisfaction on the island with the government's handling of the crisis. This was reflected in the November 1996 general election, in which the NPP won only one seat (down three on 1991) and no party secured an overall majority. A coalition government was subsequently formed, with Bertrand Osborne the new chief minister and Meade as minister for agriculture, trade, and the environment, until March 1997.

In June 1997 a major eruption of the Soufriere Hills volcano destroyed the capital, Plymouth, killed 19 people, and left two-thirds of the island uninhabitable. The British government announced a further package of emergency aid, along with assisted passage and resettlement grants, of $4,000 for adults and $1,000 for minors, for those wishing to leave Montserrat and a five-year sustainable development plan for the 'safe area' in the north. However, islanders considered this response to be inadequate and, after four days of public protests, Osborne was replaced as chief minister on 21 August 1997 by David Brandt, an independent deputy. By February 1998 the island's population, which had been around 12,500 in 1995 had fallen to 2,850, with many having resettled elsewhere in the Caribbean (including more than 3,000 in neighboring Antigua), and in the UK. Since the start of the volcano crisis in 1995, the British government has committed $90 million in emergency and reconstruction aid.

PITCAIRN ISLANDS

Capital: Adamstown, on Pitcairn Island

Location
Oceania. The Pitcairn Islands consist of volcanic Pitcairn Island and the uninhabited atolls of Ducie, Henderson, and Oeno, all situated in the southeastern Pacific Ocean, east of French Polynesia.

Social and economic data
Area: 35.5 sq km/13.7 sq miles
Population: 49[*]
Pop. density per sq km/sq mile: 1.4[*]/3.5
Economy type: high income (*c.* $8,000 per capita)
Currency: Pitcairn dollar (equivalent to the New Zealand dollar)
[*] 1996.

Languages
Pitcairnese English is used

Religions
The population adheres to the Seventh-Day Adventist Church

Head of government
Governor Martin Williams, since 1997

Political system
As a Crown Colony, Pitcairn is administered by the British high commissioner in New Zealand. Under the terms of the 1940 constitution, as amended by the Local Government Ordinance of 1964, the High Commissioner governs in consultation with a ten-member Island Council, presided over by the island magistrate, who is elected for a three-year term. The ten-member Island Council consists of an *ex officio* representative, two appointees, and three members elected by the elected deputies. Elections are annual, held in December. No parties exist, so only independents are elected.

Political history

Pitcairn Island was discovered by the British navigator, Philip Carteret (d. 1796), in 1767 and was settled in 1790 by nine mutineers from HMS *Bounty*. It was annexed as a British colony in 1838, but by 1856 the population had outgrown the island's resources, forcing 194 inhabitants to move to Norfolk Island, off the east coast of Australia. Forty-three Pitcairn islanders later returned home, in 1864, and since then the island has remained permanently settled. In 1898 Pitcairn was brought within the jurisdiction of the high commissioner for the Western Pacific. It was later transferred to the Governor of Fiji, in 1952, but since Fiji's independence, in 1970, it has been governed by the British high commissioner in New Zealand. Despite the high costs involved in administering the island, Britain announced in 1993 that it would not abandon its responsibilities to the island since independence was not a viable option and no other state wanted to take over the administration.

ST HELENA AND DEPENDENCIES

Capital: Jamestown

Location

Central and Southern Africa. St Helena (Area: 122 sq km/47 sq miles; Population: 6,472) and its dependencies constitute a volcanic island grouping situated in the South Atlantic Ocean. St Helena lies 1,930 km/1,200 miles off the southwest coast of Africa. The dependency of Ascension island (Area: 88 sq km/38 sq miles; Population: 1,102) is 1,131 sq km/703 miles northwest of St Helena, while the dependency of Tristan da Cunha island (Area: 98 sq km/38 sq miles; Population: 288) lies 2,100 km/1,305 miles to the northeast.

Social and economic data

Area: 308 sq km/119 sq miles
Population: 7,900[*]
Pop. density per sq km/sq mile: 26[*]/66
Literacy rate: 97%
Economy type: middle income (*c.* $2,500 per capita)
Currency: St Helena pound
[*] 1996.

Religions

The population is Christian, principally Anglican, with a Roman Catholic minority.

Head of government

Governor David Smallman, since 1995

Political system

Under the terms of its 1989 constitution, St Helena is administered by a crown-appointed governor, who works with a Legislative Council and an advisory Executive Council. The Legislative Council comprises the speaker and the chief secretary, the financial secretary and the attorney general, as *ex officio* members, and 12 elected members. The Executive Council, or cabinet, presided over by the governor, also includes the three *ex officio* members noted above and five of the elected members of the Legislative Council. The task of the Legislative Council is to oversee the work of government departments.

The dependencies of Ascension and Tristan da Cunha are governed by appointed administrators. Tristan da Cunha also has an advisory Council, consisting of eight elected (including at least one woman) and three nominated members.

Political parties

Two political parties nominally exist. These are the St Helena Labor Party, which was established in 1975, and the St Helena Progressive Party, formed in 1973, which favors the retention of close economic links with Britain; both have been inactive since 1976.

Latest elections

The most recent elections in St Helena, on 9 July 1997, were contested on a non-partisan basis.

Political history

The island of St Helena was discovered by the Portuguese navigator Joao da Nova Castella in 1502 and subsequently became a port of call for ships en route to the East Indies. It was annexed and occupied by the British East India Company in 1659 and, before being brought under direct crown rule in 1834, gained fame as the place of Napoleon's exile between 1815 and 1821. The island, with meagre natural resources, has an unemployment rate of around 20% and relies heavily on British economic aid. The 1981 British Nationality Act removed the islanders' traditional right of residence in Britain. However, after legal protests, this right was restored in 1997. Since 1998, the British government has sought to develop St Helena's economy. The building of a civilian airstrip is planned, to aid the development of 'environmental tourism' on the island.

Ascension was discovered in 1501, but remained uninhabited until occupied by Britain in 1815. It was made a dependency of St Helena in 1922 and today serves as an important commercial and military communications center. During the Falklands War, of 1982, it also served as a crucial staging area for the naval 'task force' which had been sent to the South Atlantic. Around 750 St Helenians work on the island.

Tristan da Cunha, which has been occupied since 1816, is currently the site of a small crayfish processing plant operated by a subsidiary of the South Atlantic Islands Development Corporation. It was briefly evacuated, during 1961–63, after volcanic eruptions.

TURKS AND CAICOS ISLANDS

Capital: Cockburn Town, on Grand Turk island

Location

Central America and the Caribbean. The Turks and Caicos Islands consist of 30 islands, which form the southeastern archipelago of the Bahamas chain in the West Atlantic Ocean, 114 km/89 miles north of the Dominican Republic and Haiti, and 920 km/572 miles southeast of Miami. Eight of the islands are inhabited. Forty-two per cent of the population lives on Grand Turk, 19% on South Caicos, 17% on North Caicos, 13% on Providenciales, and 5% on Middle Caicos island.

Social and economic data

Area: 430 sq km/166 sq miles
Population: 18,000[*]
Pop. density per sq km/sq mile: 42[*]/108
Literacy rate: 98%
Economy type: middle income (c. $6,500 per capita in 1995)
Currency: US dollar
[*] 1995.

Ethnic composition

The population is predominantly of African descent. English is the official language.

Religions

The population is Christian, chiefly Baptist and Anglican.

Head of government

Chief Minister Derek Taylor, since 1995

Political system

Under the terms of the 1976 constitution, later amended in March 1988, executive power is exercised by a crown-appointed governor, who is responsible for defense, external affairs, internal security, and official appointments. The governor presides over an eight-member Executive Council, or cabinet, comprising three *ex officio* representatives and five chosen, including a chief minister, by the governor from among the elected members of the Legislative Council. The Legislative Council consists of seven appointed members and 13 representatives directly elected for four-year terms.

Political parties

Five political parties currently function, the most important two of which are the centrist People's Democratic Movement (PDM), which was formed in 1976 and is led by Derek Taylor, and the right-of-center Progressive National Party (PNP). Both parties are strong supporters of a free enterprise economy and favor continued development of the islands' tourist and financial services industries. The PDM favors eventual independence, which the PNP opposes. Before 1995 there were five electoral districts on the islands and thus a number of multimember constituencies. However, at the 1995 election all constituencies were single-member.

Latest elections

In the Legislative Council election, held on 4 March 1999, the PDM won 10 of the 13 contested seats, and 53% of the vote, while the once dominant PNP, three seats, with 40% of the vote.

Political history

The Turks and Caicos Islands were first linked administratively to the Bahamas in 1765, before being made dependencies of Jamaica, in 1874. They subsequently became a unit territory within the Federation of the West Indies in 1959 and, on Jamaica's independence in 1962, were made a Crown Colony. Under this new arrangement, the islands were first administered from the Bahamas, but in 1972 received their own governor.

The first elections under the new 1976 constitution were won by the People's Democratic Movement (PDM), a political party which was, initially, strongly committed to achieving independence. In 1980 Britain agreed to accede to this on the condition that the PDM again won a Legislative Council majority in the general election of November 1980. It failed to achieve this, however, being handicapped by the death of its leader and founder, J A G S McCartney, in an accident in June 1980. Instead, the Progressive National Party (PNP), which favored continued dependent status, secured a Legislative Council majority in both this and the subsequent May 1984 general election. As a consequence, the question of independence faded from the political agenda.

Instead, the islands' politics became dominated by a series of high-level scandals. These began in March 1985, when the chief minister and PNP leader, Norman Saunders, together with two senior colleagues, was forced to resign, after charges of drug smuggling into the United States. All three were later convicted and imprisoned. A year later, in July 1986, Saunders's replacement as chief minister, Nathaniel Francis (PNP), was also compelled to step down, after the publication of a report by a commission of inquiry found him, and two ministerial colleagues, guilty of unconstitutional behaviour and administrative malpractice. The government was immediately dissolved by the governor and a special five-member Advisory Council set up to take over the work of the Executive Council while the islands' political future was reviewed by a special constitutional commission. The recommendations subsequently made by this commission were accepted by the UK government, in March 1987, and formed the basis for an amended constitution, which came into force after the general election of March 1988 and which strengthened the reserve powers of the governor. This election was won by the PDM, with Oswald Skippings becoming chief minister. Power alternated again at the April 1991 election, won by the PNP-led by Washington Missick, and in January 1995 the PDM won and Derek Taylor became chief minister. Relations soon deteriorated between elected members of the Legislative Council and the governor, Martin Bourke, who had commented in a magazine interview that corruption and drugs-related crime were rife in the islands. In February 1996 a petition was signed requesting Bourke's removal. This was resisted by the British government, which deployed a frigate offshore, as a precautionary measure. Bourke's term of office ended in September 1996.

The islands' economy is dominated by tourism (concentrated on Providenciales), fishing, and an 'offshore' financial sector, with 12,000 foreign or exempt companies registered in the islands in 1996. The unemployment rate was 15% in 1996.

8.4.13 United States' dependencies

The dependencies of the United States have been acquired in a variety of ways. Guam and Puerto Rico were ceded, as part of the spoils of victory after a war;

the American Virgin Islands were purchased; others had been held as Trust Territories, on behalf of the United Nations; and many, particularly in the Pacific, form part of what the United States sees as its defensive shield. In total, including three military bases, there are eight territories in the anti-imperialist United States' 'mini-empire'.

FORMAL DEPENDENCIES ('UNINCORPORATED/EXTERNAL TERRITORIES')

AMERICAN SAMOA

Capital: Pago Pago, on Tutuila

Location
Oceania. American Samoa consists of five main volcanic islands and two coral atolls situated in the central South Pacific Ocean, 3,550 km/2,205 miles north-northeast of New Zealand. Ninety-three per cent of the population lives on the westernmost island of Tutuila.

Social and economic data
Area: 195 sq km/75 sq miles
Population: 59,600[*]
Pop. density per sq km/sq mile: 306[*]/795
Economy type: middle–high income (c. $8,000 per capita in 1992)
Currency: US dollar
[*] 1996.

Ethnic composition
The indigenous population is of Polynesian origin. English and Samoan, a Polynesian language, are spoken. Population growth is high, at 4% per year; around 85,000 American Samoans live on the US mainland or Hawaii.

Religions
Fifty per cent of the population adheres to the Christian Congregational Church and 20% is Roman Catholic.

Local government
The islands are divided, for administrative purposes, into 15 counties, which are grouped into Eastern, Western, and Manu'a districts.

Head of government
Governor Tauese Sunia, since 1997.

United States external territories | Table 75

Territory	Date of first coming under United States administration	Area (sq km/sq miles)	Population (c. 1996)
External territories			
American Samoa	1899/1922	195/75	59,600
Guam	1899	549/212	157,000
US Virgin Islands	1917	347/134	97,000
Commonwealth territories			
Northern Mariana Islands	1947	457/176	58,900
Puerto Rico	1898	8,959/3,459	3,820,000
Military bases			
Johnston Atoll	1898	2/1	330
Midway Islands	1867	5/2	50
Wake Islands	1898	8/3	300
Total	–	*10,522/4,063*	*4,193,180*

Political system

Under the terms of the 1967 constitution, executive power is exercised by a governor, who is directly elected for a four-year term, and is limited to two terms. The governor has the authority to appoint heads of government departments, subject to the approval of the assembly, and can veto legislation. The assembly, termed the Fono, is a two-chamber body, comprising an 18-member Senate, elected, according to Samoan custom, from among local male chiefs (*matai*) for four-year terms, and a 20-member House of Representatives, whose members are popularly elected every two years. Swain's Island, with a population of only 27, also sends one non-voting member to the House. The Fono meets twice a year, in January and July, for a maximum of 45 days a year. American Samoa has, since 1981, also sent a non-voting delegate to the US House of Representatives, who is elected every two years. Changes to the 1967 constitution were drafted in 1986 by a constitutional convention, but by 1998 these still awaited ratifcation by the US Congress. The amendments include increasing the size of the Senate and House of Representatives.

Political parties

Most candidates are elected as independents, though some stand as Democrats and Republicans, identifying with the mainland US parties.

Latest elections

The most recent elections to the Senate, held on 3 November 1998, concurrently with US congressional elections, saw the election of only non-partisans. Elections to the lower house were held on 3 November 1998, and to the governorship in two rounds, on 15 and 19 November 1996. In the gubernatorial contest, the Democrat vice-governor, Tauese Sunia, won the second-round run-off, with 51% of the vote, defeating Leala Peter Reid. The incumbent governor, AP Lutali, was defeated in the first round. Eni Faleomavaega, the islands' delegate to the US House of Representatives since 1988, was re-elected with 57% of the vote.

Political history

The islands of American Samoa were first visited by Europeans in the early 18th century and the London Missionary Society established a base there in 1830. They were ruled by local chiefs grouped together to form the independent Kingdom of Samoa. In 1878 the United States was given permission by the kingdom to establish a naval base at Pago Pago and, from 1899, when the Treaty of Berlin, signed by America, Britain and Germany, recognized US rights in the area, it gradually gained dominance over the region. In 1900 and 1904 the chiefs of the western and eastern islands, respectively, accepted US sovereignty and later, in 1922, after residual German claims had been removed, the islands were officially designated an 'unincorporated territory' of the United States.

American Samoa was, initially, between 1900 and 1951, placed under the administration of the US Department of the Navy and, thereafter, of the Department of the Interior, power being devolved to a resident governor. The governor was, for a long time, an American appointee, working, since 1948, with an advisory two-chamber assembly. Under the terms of the 1960 constitution, which was amended in 1967, the authority of this assembly was increased and in November 1977 direct elections for the governorship were introduced. Peter Coleman became the first governor, between 1978 and 1984. The Samoan economy, which is heavily dependent on the tuna-canning industry, is closely tied to the American economy. Many Samoans have emigrated to the United States in search of work during recent years and the country receives substantial economic aid from the mainland. The unemployment level was 13% in 1996. In September 1988, its delegate to the US House of Representatives, Fofo Sunia, was forced to resign his seat after being convicted of fraud over the use of his official expense account, and sentenced to five months' imprisonment. In December 1991 the islands were hit by Cyclone Val, which damaged 60% of dwellings and destroyed 95% of the subsistence crops; $87 million in financial compensation was received from a US insurance company.

American Samoa is a member of the Pacific Community regional organization and was fierce in its criticism of France, in September 1995, for its resumption of nuclear testing in the South Pacific. In 1998 the Fono passed legislation to reject the recent change of name of Western Samoa to 'Samoa' and banning (Western) Samoans from owning land in American Samoa, since the change was considered to have undermined American Samoan identity. In February 1999 the United States established an American Samoa Economic Advisory Commission, chaired by John Waihee, a former governor of Hawaii, to develop, with local business people, an economic plan to bring economic self-sufficiency to American Samoa. The budget deficit was currently $30 million.

In April 1999 legislation was proposed to provide for the introduction of capital punishment.

GUAM

Capital: Hagatna (formerly known as Aga'Samo

Location

Oceania. Guam is the largest and southernmost of the Mariana Islands, being situated in the West Pacific

Ocean, 5,920 km/3,680 miles west of Hawaii and 2,400 km/1,490 miles east of Manila.

Social and economic data
Area: 549 sq km/212 sq miles
Population: 157,000[*]
Pop. density per sq km/sq mile: 286[*]/741
Literacy rate: 96%
Economy type: middle income (*c.* $5,500 per capita)
Currency: US dollar
[*] 1996.

Ethnic composition
Forty-two per cent of the population are Chamorros, a mixture of Micronesian, Filipino, and Spanish, 24% Caucasians, and 21% Filipinos. Since 1993 Chamorro activists have campaigned for tighter controls on immigration and for full autonomy. Fifteen thousand US military personnel and their dependants also live on Guam. The official language is English, but Japanese and Chamorro, the local language, are also spoken.

Religions
Roman Catholicism is practised by about 90% of the population.

Head of government
Governor Carl Gutierrez, since 1995

Political system
Under the terms of the 1950 Guam 'Organic Act', or constitution, executive power is wielded by a governor, who is directly elected every four years. Legislative authority lies with a 15-member Legislature, whose members (senators) are elected biennially. It is empowered to pass laws regulating local affairs. A member, who may vote in committees but not on the floor, is elected to the the US House of Representatives every two years. However, residents of Guam, although classed as citizens of the United States, cannot vote in US presidential elections. In November 1996 a referendum was approved by voters to reduce the size of the Legislature to 15 senators, from November 1998, and to limit legislative expenses to a maximum of 25% of budget expenditure. A proposal to impose term limits on senators was rejected.

Political parties
Two political parties operate on the island, the Republican Party and the Democratic Party, both of which are mainland party affiliates.

Latest elections
Carl Gutierrez, a Democrat, was elected governor in

November 1998, with 53% of the vote, defeating the Republican, Joseph Ada. In the November 1998 elections the Republicans won 12 seats to the Democrats' three. Robert Underwood, a Democrat, was re-elected unopposed as Guam's delegate to the US House of Representatives, in November 1996.

Political history

Guam was 'discovered' by Ferdinand Magellan (c. 1480–1521) in 1521 and claimed by Spain in 1565. The native Micronesian population, which was estimated to be 100,000 in 1521, declined rapidly during the late 16th century and throughout the 17th and early 18th centuries, reaching a low of less than 5,000 in 1741, as a result of Spanish aggression and exposure to imported diseases. It later revived, however, through intermarriage with Spaniards and Filipinos. Spain ceded Guam to the United States after the Spanish – American war of 1898 and the country became an 'unincorporated territory' of the United States.

During World War II, the island fell under Japanese control, between December 1941 and July 1944. When American rule was re-established greater authority was progressively devolved to local inhabitants and its administration was transferred, in 1950, from the US Department of the Navy to the Department of the Interior. In 1970, the island's governor was directly elected for the first time and in September 1976 support for the maintenance of close ties with the United States was reaffirmed in a referendum. In November 1987, a referendum came out in support of the island negotiating a new relationship with the United States and discussions began in 1989 for a bill which would combine elements of free association with US citizenship and confer the status of commonwealth on the territory.

With a fine deep-water port at Apra, Guam has become one of the most important American naval and airforce bases in the Pacific. Currently, there are 7,300 US troops stationed on the island, and a third of its surface is covered by military installations. The island was used in September 1996 to launch a major US bombing raid on southern Iraq. Guam is also a commercial and financial entrepôt and growing tourist center, particularly for the Japanese. Its economy has, however, been in a depressed condition since the early 1970s. In August 1992 Typhoon Wake struck the island, causing damage estimated at $250 million and leaving 5,000 people homeless, and in August 1993 a powerful earthquake caused almost equal damage.

UNITED STATES VIRGIN ISLANDS

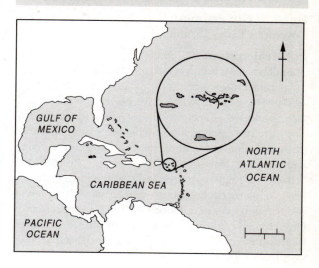

Capital: Charlotte Amalie, on St Thomas

Location

Central America and the Caribbean. The US Virgin Islands consist of more than 50 islands in the south and west of the Virgin Islands group, situated in the Caribbean Sea, 64 km/40 miles east of Puerto Rico. The two principal islands, accounting for 50% and 47% of the total population respectively, are St Croix and St Thomas. The island of St John is also inhabited.

Social and economic data

Area: 347 sq km/134 sq miles
Population: 97,000*
Pop. density per sq km/sq mile: 280*/724
Literacy rate: 90%
Economy type: high income (c. $12,000 per capita in 1990)
Currency: US dollar
* 1996.

Ethnic composition

Twenty to twenty-five per cent of the population are native-born, 35–40% come from other Caribbean islands, 10% from the US mainland, and 5% from Europe. Four-fifths of the population have African heratige. English is the official language, but Spanish and Creole are widely spoken.

Religions

The population is predominantly Protestant, with a 28% Roman Catholic minority.

Local government

The governor is represented on each of the three inhabited islands by an appointed administrator.

Head of Government

Governor Charles Turnbull II, since 1999

Political system

The islands have been granted a measure of self-government under the constitution of 1936, as amended in 1954, 1970, and 1973. Executive power is wielded by a directly-elected governor, who serves a four-year term. The governor appoints, on the advice of the assembly, the heads of government departments and is required to approve any legislation. The assembly, termed the Senate, is a single-chamber body, comprising 15 members, popularly elected for two-year terms, who represent two legislative districts. Since 1968 the US Virgin Islands have elected a non-voting delegate to the US House of Representatives. The islands' citizens are debarred, however, from voting in US presidential elections.

Political parties

The principal political parties are the Democratic Party of the Virgin Islands, the Republican Party, both of which are mainland affiliates, and the Independent Citizens Movement (ICM), a breakaway group from the Democratic Party.

Latest elections

In the last gubernatorial elections, held in November 1998, the incumbent Roy L Schneider of the Independent Citizens, was defeated by the Democrat, Charles Turnbull II, who attracted 59% of the vote. The Democrats won six seats, the ICM one, the Republicans two, and Independents five. The most recent Senate elections were held in November 1998.

Political history

Originally discovered by Christopher Columbus (1451–1506) in 1493, the islands passed, successively, into English, French, and Dutch control, before the Danish West Indies Company colonized St Thomas and St John islands in 1671. To these, the Danes added St Croix, which they had acquired from France in 1733, and established sugar plantations. Following a decline in the sugar trade, the United States, recognizing the islands' strategic importance in relation to the Panama Canal, took them over in 1917, purchasing them for US $25 million.

They became an 'unincorporated territory' of the United States and were originally placed under the administrative control of the US Department of the Navy, before being transferred to the Department of the Interior in 1931. The islanders were granted American citizenship in 1927 and have enjoyed increasing degrees of self-government since the 'Organic Law', which granted universal suffrage to all adults who could read and write English, was adopted in 1936. Popular election of the governor, who had previously been appointed by the US president, commenced in 1970. However, proposals for increased autonomy were rejected in referenda held in March 1979 and November 1981. In a referendum held in October 1993, 94% of electors voted for continued or enhanced territorial status and rejected the alternative options of independence or integration with the United States. However, the low turnout of just 27% invalidated the result of this plebiscite. Roy Schneider, of the Independent Citizens, a breakaway from the Democrats, served as governor from 1995, but was defeated by the Democrat, Charles Turnbull II, in the 1998 elections.

The islands have developed as a major center for tourism and have attracted, in growing numbers, white 'tax shelter' immigrants. St Croix is also an important center for petroleum refining. A succession of hurricanes, the first of which was Hurrican Hugo in 1989, have caused extensive damage to the islands' infrastructure.

COMMONWEALTH TERRITORIES

THE NORTHERN MARIANA ISLANDS

Commonwealth of the Northern Mariana Islands (CNMI)

Capital: Garapan, on Saipan

Location

Oceania. The territory consists of 16 islands and atolls in northern Micronesia in the West Pacific Ocean, 5,280 km/3,280 miles west of Hawaii and 2,800 km/1,740 miles east of the Philippines. Eighty-eight per cent of the population lives on the island of Saipan, 7% on Rota, and 5% on Tinian.

Social and economic data

Area: 457 sq km/176 sq miles
Population: 58,900[*]

Pop. density per sq km/sq mile: 129[*]/335
Economy type: middle income (*c.* $2,500 per capita in 1992)
Currency: US dollar
[*] 1995.

Ethnic composition

The population is predominantly Micronesian. There are around 20,000 foreign non-resident workers, two-thirds of which are Filipinos. English is the official language, but Chamorro, Carolinian, and Japanese are also spoken.

Religions

The population is predominantly Roman Catholic.

Head of government

Governor Pedro Tenorio, since 1998

Political system

Under the terms of the October 1977 constitution, the Northern Mariana Islands are internally self-governing as a US 'Commonwealth Territory'. Executive power is exercised by a governor who is directly elected for a four-year term, and legislative authority by a bicameral assembly (the Northern Marianas Commonwealth Legislature) composed of a nine-member Senate and an 18-member House of Representatives, elected biennially. The islands' inhabitants enjoy US citizenship. A non-voting representative is sent by the territory to the US Congress, being elected every four years.

Political parties

The principal political parties are the centrist Democratic Party, and the right-of-center Republican Party, mirroring the US two-party system.

Latest elections

In the most recent gubernatorial elections, held on 1 November 1997, the Republicans won back control of the office of governor, with Pedro Tenorio winning 46% of the vote, while the incumbent Democrat governor and lieutenant governor, Froilan Tenorio and Jesus Borja, won 27% and 26% respectively. The Republicans maintained substantial majorities in the Senate and House with eight and 13 votes respectively, after the November 1997 elections, and provided the territory's non-voting representative in the US Congress.

Political history

The islands of the Northern Marianas group were discovered by European explorers during the 1520s. They fell successively under Spanish (1565–1898), German (1899–1914), Japanese (1914–21 and 1941–44), and League of Nations (1921–41) control, before being liberated by US marines in 1944–45 and becoming, along with Palau (now Belau), the Federated States of Micronesia (FSM) and the Marshall Islands, part of the US' United Nations Trust Territory of the Pacific Islands, in 1947. Under the terms of this trusteeship agreement, the United States was given administrative control of the islands, but was charged with preparing them for eventual independence. Unlike the other UN Trust Territories, which chose to seek semi-independence under the terms of 'Compacts of Free Association' with the United States, in January 1978, following a referendum in June 1975, the Northern Marianas became a 'Commonwealth Territory' of the United States. As such they enjoyed considerable powers of internal self-government. In November 1986, the American administration conferred full US citizenship on the residents of the islands and this was recognized internationally, when the UN Trusteeship terminated in December 1990. Under the terms of the 1976 Commonwealth Covenant, substantial economic aid is provided anually by the US government. In return, the United States has acquired control of much land on Tinian island for military purposes.

Between 1979 and 1996 the population increased more than three-fold to 59,000, with the development of an export-orientated garment industry and important tourist sector. Large numbers of workers (chiefly Filipino) were attracted as immigrants, but in April 1995 the Philippines' government banned its nationals taking further unskilled jobs in the Northern Marianas, following reports of exploitation and abuse. In November 1993, after 12 years of Republican party control, the Democrats won the gubernatorial elections and Froilan Tenorio became governor in January 1994. However, in 1997 Tenorio fell out with the US Democrat president, Bill Clinton, after refusing to apply US minimum wage regulations on the islands. Despite receiving substantial corporate financial backing, the pro-business Froilan Tenorio was defeated in the November 1997 governorship elections by a Republican, Pedro Tenorio. However, there was subsequently a legal challenge since the latter had served two-terms as governor before 1990. The terms of the constitution stipulated a maximum of two gubernatorial terms for an individual, but this provision was introduced during Pedro Tenorio's second term in office. The Northern Mariana Islands is a member of the Pacific Community regional organization.

PUERTO RICO

Commonwealth of Puerto Rico (COPR)
Estado Libre Asociado de Puerto Rico

Capital: San Juan

Location

Central America and the Caribbean. Puerto Rico is the easternmost island of the Greater Antilles, situated between the Dominican Republic to the west and the US Virgin Islands to the east, and 1,600 km/1,000 miles southeast of Miami.

Social and economic data

Area: 8,959 sq km/3,459 sq miles
Population: 3,820,000*
Pop. density per sq km/sq mile: 426*/1,104
Literacy rate: 89%
Economy type: middle–high income (*c.* $7,000 per capita in 1990)
Currency: US dollar
* 1996.

Ethnic composition

The population is predominantly of European (Hispanic) descent. Spanish and English are the official languages.

Religions

Roman Catholicism is practised by about 85% of the population.

Local government

The island is divided into 78 'municipal districts', which include surrounding rural areas, each of which is governed by a mayor and municipal assembly, elected for a four-year term.

Head of Government

Governor Pedro Rosselló, since 1992

Political system

Under the constitution, called the 'Public Law', of 1952, Puerto Rico is a self-governing 'Commonwealth', voluntarily associated with the United States. Both states share a common currency and market, while the United States is responsible for the COPR's defense. However, Puerto Rico's position differs from that of a full member state in that its inhabitants, while officially designated US citizens and able to vote in national party primary elections, may not vote in presidential elections and are represented in the US Congress only by a resident commis-sioner, who, elected quadrennially, participates in House of Representatives' debates, but may only vote in committee. In addition, most US federal taxes, social security being an exception, are not levied in Puerto Rico.

Executive power is exercised by a governor, who must be at least 35 years old and is directly elected for a four-year term and works with a cabinet of around 15 secretaries. Legislative authority is held by a two-chamber Legislative Assembly, which is composed of a 28-member Senate and a 54-member House of Representatives, sitting each year between January and May. Assembly members are elected every four years, in November, at the same time as the US president, in accordance with an electoral procedure designed to ensure minority party representation. Sixteen senators are returned, two from each of the eight senatorial districts, and 40 representatives are elected in single-member constituencies, by a simple plurality voting system. The remaining places in each chamber are 'at large' seats elected by proportional representation, including a 'top up' to ensure the opposition have between a quarter and a third of the seats. Senators must be at least 30 years old and Representatives at least 25 years old. The legislative process is similar to that in the United States, the governor's approval being required for the enactment of bills. A veto can, however, be overridden by a two-thirds majority vote.

Political parties

Eight political parties operate in Puerto Rico. The three principal parties are the liberal, pro-Commonwealth, 660,000-member, Popular Democratic Party (PPD), which was established in 1938; the 225,000-member New Progressive Party (PNP), formed in 1967 and led by Governor Pedro J Rosselló, which favors federation as a constituent state within the United States; and the 60,000-member Puerto Rican Independence Party (PIP), dating from 1946 and with a social democratic, pro-separatist orientation. The PPD and PNP are the dominant forces, each regularly securing about 45% of the popular vote in what is essentially a two-party system. In 1997 a new pro-independence party, the Pro Patria National Union (PPNU) was formed. It encourages Puerto Ricans to renounce their US nationality.

Latest elections

The most recent gubernatorial and legislative elections, held on 5 November 1996, were won by the PNP. Its candidate for governor, Pedro Rosselló, was elected with 51% of the vote, with Hector Acevedo (PPD) securing 45% and David Rodriguez (PIP), 4%. In the legislature elections, the PNP, with 50% of the vote, won 217 House and 19 Senate seats. The PPD won sixteen and eight seats respectively and the PPD, one in each chamber.

Political history

Discovered by Christopher Columbus (1451–1506) in 1493, when known by the Arawak Indian name of Boriquen, Puerto Rico was annexed by Spain in 1509. The Spanish exploited gold and sugar resources during the succeeding centuries, during which period the indigenous Carib and Arawak Indians, newly exposed to European diseases, were virtually wiped out, and replaced by a new mixed-race population. Following the Spanish–American war of 1898, Puerto Rico was ceded to the United States, under the terms of the Treaty of Paris, in December 1898. It was declared an 'unincorporated territory' of the United States, administered by a US-appointed governor, working with an elected local assembly.

In March 1917, under the terms of the Jones–Shafroth Act, the island's inhabitants were granted US citizenship and in 1947 direct elections for the post of governor were introduced. In July 1952, following approval of a draft constitution in a referendum held a year earlier, the territory was given special status as a 'Commonwealth', 'freely associated' with the United States, enjoying extensive powers of self-government.

During the 1950s and 1960s, Puerto Rican politics were dominated by the Popular Democratic Party (PPD), who were strong supporters of the country's 'Commonwealth' status. A split occurred within the party's ranks, however, in 1967, leading to the formation of the New Progressive Party (PNP), following a referendum in which 60.5% of voters supported continued 'Commonwealth' status. Some 38.9% favored full incorporation within the United States as a constituent state and 0.6% favored independence. The PNP, led by Carlos Romero Barceló, held the governorship between 1977 and 1984 and pressed for Puerto Rico's inclusion as a state of the United States. This served to fan terrorist outrages by separatist extremists grouped in the Armed Forces for National Liberation (FALN) organization. Barcelo was, however, defeated by the PPD's Hernández Colón in the November 1984 governorship contest. Hernández Colón was re-elected in 1988, but did not contest the 1992 gubernatorial election, which was won by Pedro Rosselló of the PNP, with 49.9% of the popular

vote. A new, nonbinding referendum on the island's constitutional future was held in November 1993 and, despite Rosselló's advocacy of the statehood option, produced a narrow majority in favor of maintaining the current 'Commonwealth' status. 48% favored no change; 46% supported accession to statehood; and 4% supported full independence.

Rosselló was re-elected governor in November 1996 and in 1998 the US Congress passed legislation which provided for a referendum to be held in Puerto Rico in December 1998, on the 100th anniversary of its occupation by American troops, on whether it wished to become the 51st state of the USA. This plebiscite, held in December 1998, saw 47% of voters support the government–endorsed option of statehood, and 50.2% back the opposition PPD–endorsed option of no change in status. Turnout was 71%.

Since the launching of the program 'Operation Bootstrap' in 1948, there has been considerable industrial development on the island, most notably in the textiles and electrical equipment 'light industrial' sector. However, the pace of economic development slowed down from the mid-1970s. As a consequence, the unemployment rate was around 17% in 1992, with two-thirds of Puerto Rico's population living below the official US poverty line. In such circumstances, there has been considerable outmigration to the United States, and more than 2 million Puerto Ricans now live on the US mainland. The 1990s has seen an improving rate of expansion in the tourist industry, reducing the unemployment level to 13% in 1997.

Recommended reading

Fieldhouse, D K *The Colonial Empires: A Comparative Study from the Eighteenth Century*, 2nd edn., Macmillan, 1982

Holland, R F *European Decolonization, 1918–1981: An Introductory Survey*, Macmillan, 1985

Kennedy, K *The Rise and Fall of the Great Powers: Economic Change and Military Conflict from 1500 to 2000*, Fontana, 1988

Taylor, P J *Political Geography: World Economy, Nation-State and Locality*, Longman, 1985, Chap. 3

CHAPTER 9

The World Grows Smaller: International Cooperation

9.1 Competition or cooperation?

Ever since the birth of the nation-state, its history has been one of competition rather than cooperation. Nations have vied with each other in trade. One state has tried to impose its own religion on another. Empires have been created by strong countries dominating the weak. Where cooperation has occurred it has nearly always been on the basis of national self-interest and rarely in any altruistic, international sense.

International alliances have often been between major powers which have temporarily joined forces, in military terms, to attack, or defend themselves against, another opposing alliance. During the 19th and early 20th centuries the political maps of the world were drawn and redrawn as a result of treaties and agreements reached by victors in international disputes, the provisions of which were then imposed on the vanquished.

The two most significant examples of such international decision-making in the present century are the treaties signed at the end of the two World Wars, in 1918 and 1945. The terms of the Treaty of Versailles, of 1919, sowed the seeds of World War II, 21 years later, but its lessons were partially learned by the statespeople who had the responsibility of trying to secure lasting world peace after 1945.

Since 1945 there has been a virtually unending succession of regional conflicts but a global war has so far been avoided and there are encouraging prospects of greater, rather than less, international cooperation. A number of factors have contributed to this new sense of urgency and optimism in international affairs.

First, improvements in the ease and speed of communication have made the world shrink in physical terms.

Second, the complexities of production and distribution have resulted in international cooperation on a scale hitherto unknown, resulting in the growth of multinational, rather than national, corporations.

Third, there has been a growing realization that the economies of the major nation-states cannot be seen as discrete, separate entities, but are so intermeshed that the success or failure of one has its impact on the others.

Fourth, there has been a recognition in the years since 1945 that it is in the interests of the advanced world to assist the economic and social progress of the underdeveloped world by financial and technical means.

Fifth, the possibility of a nuclear holocaust has persuaded the major powers to step back from the brink of another global war.

The sixth, and ultimately the most significant, factor in the long term, is the increasing recognition of the fragility of the world's ecology, in other words, the 'green factor'.

Seventh, and last, have been the recent encouraging moves towards more pluralistic and democratic political systems in many states, including, of course, the major changes resulting from the demise of the Soviet Union in 1991 and the repercussions of these changes in other parts of the world.

There are encouraging signs, therefore, that in the years ahead, running into the 21st century, international cooperation, rather than competition, is likely to be the prevalent force. It would be unwise, however, to be overly optimistic. Political attitudes can quickly change and a regime favoring positive cooperation can easily be replaced by one based on negative self-interest. Nevertheless, there is already a widespread, and sometimes complex, array of global and regional cooperation planes already in place, some more successful than others, and those which have already proved their worth might well provide the foundation for yet greater future collaboration.

9.2 Global cooperation: the United Nations Organization

The United Nations (UN) originated from a conference held at Dumbarton Oaks, Washington, DC, between World War II allies, the Soviet Union, the United Kingdom, and the United States, at the end of September and the beginning of October, 1944. The name 'United Nations' was devised by Franklin Roosevelt and was first used in the Declaration by United Nations, on 1 January 1942, when representatives of 26 nations pledged their governments to continue fighting the Axis powers of Germany, Italy, and Japan. Its forerunner was the League of Nations, which had been established after World War I but had failed to fulfil its early promise, and had eventually been abandoned by the United States.

The Dumbarton Oaks conference produced a set of proposals which were put before a conference held in San Francisco on 25–26 June 1945 and, after certain amendments had been agreed, a charter was signed by 50 of the 51 founder members, on 26 June 1945. Poland, although a founder member, did not sign it at the time but did so at a later date. The United Nations officially came into being on 24 October 1945, which is now celebrated annually as United Nations Day. Membership is open to all peace-loving nations and in 1999 stood at 185. In 1999 Tonga applied to become the UN's 186th member. The names of member states and the dates of their admission are shown in Table 76.

The major declared aims of the United Nations are to maintain international peace and security, and to develop international cooperation in economic, social, cultural, and humanitarian problems, and, in pursuit of these aims, it has erected an impressive institutional structure of councils, commissions, committees, and agencies, as well as the International Court of Justice. Some institutions, such as the International Court, are developments of earlier bodies from the days of the League of Nations and before. Others are new creations.

Under the terms of Article 2(7) of its charter, the United Nations is precluded from interfering in the domestic affairs of states. However, Chapter VI permits its involvement in mediation and peacekeeping activities, with the consent of the parties, and Chapter VII, the use of force and imposition of mandatory sanctions. Between 1988 and 1995 the UN launched 23 new peacekeeping operations, compared to just 13 between 1945 and 1987. In 1997 the UN had 17 separate active peacekeeping operations, involving 24,000 military and civilian police personel. In 1999 it began an important new operation in Kosovo, Yugoslavia, where in June a UN administration was established to oversee the maintenance of peace.

9.2.1 Principal UN institutions

The principal UN institutions are the General Assembly, the Security Council, the Economic and Social Council, the International Court of Justice, and the Secretariat. The permanent headquarters of the UN are in the United Nations Plaza, in Manhattan, New York City. Meetings of its main organizations are usually held there, but they can be, and sometimes are, arranged elsewhere. The International Court of Justice is based in The Hague, in the Netherlands, and several other UN bodies have their headquarters in Geneva, Switzerland.

General Assembly

The General Assembly is the UN congress of which all nations are members, each having one vote. It meets once a year at the UN headquarters in New York in a session beginning on the third Tuesday in September, running through to the end of the year, or into the following year if business demands it. It can be summoned to meet at any time in an emergency session, and there have been over 25 such special sessions convened to date, covering such topics as peacekeeping in Lebanon, the Suez crisis, Afghanistan, Namibia, Bosnia-Herzegovina, and the economic situation in Africa. Below the main Assembly is a network of committees.

General Assembly decisions are made by simple majority voting but on certain important matters, such as the condemnation of an act by one of its members, a two-thirds majority is needed. If the Assembly feels that the Security Council is not fulfilling its chief responsibility of maintaining international peace satisfactorily it may take it upon itself to consider a special case, such as an act of aggression, or some other breach of the peace, and recommend action to be taken.

Security Council

The Security Council has a membership of l5. There are five permanent members, China, France, the Russian Federation (which assumed the Soviet Union's permanent seat in December 1991), the United Kingdom, and the United States, and the other ten are elected for two-year terms, by a two-thirds vote of the General

United Nations membership

Table 76

Country	Year of admission	1996 contribution to UN budget (%)	Country	Year of admission	1996 contribution to UN budget (%)
Afghanistan	1946	0.01	Egypt*	1945	0.07
Albania	1955	0.01	El Salvador*	1945	0.01
Algeria	1962	0.16	Equatorial Guinea	1968	0.01
Andorra	1993	0.01	Eritrea	1993	0.01
Angola	1976	0.01	Estonia	1991	0.04
Antigua and Barbuda	1981	0.01	Ethiopia*	1945	0.01
Argentina*	1945	0.48	Fiji	1970	0.01
Armenia	1992	0.05	Finland	1955	0.61
Australia*	1945	1.48	France*	1945	6.40
Austria	1955	0.86	Gabon	1960	0.01
Azerbaijan	1992	0.11	Gambia	1965	0.01
Bahamas	1973	0.02	Georgia	1992	0.11
Bahrain	1971	0.02	Germany**	1973/1990	9.04
Bangladesh	1974	0.01	Ghana	1957	0.01
Barbados	1966	0.01	Greece*	1945	0.38
Belarus*	1945	0.29	Grenada	1974	0.01
Belgium*	1945	1.00	Guatemala*	1945	0.02
Belize	1981	0.01	Guinea	1958	0.01
Benin	1960	0.01	Guinea-Bissau	1974	0.01
Bhutan	1971	0.01	Guyana	1966	0.01
Bolivia*	1945	0.01	Haiti*	1945	0.01
Bosnia-Herzegovina	1992	0.01	Honduras*	1945	0.01
Botswana	1966	0.01	Hungary	1955	0.14
Brazil*	1945	1.62	Iceland	1946	0.03
Brunei	1984	0.02	India*	1945	0.31
Bulgaria	1955	0.08	Indonesia	1950	0.14
Burkina Faso	1960	0.01	Iran*	1945	0.46
Burundi	1962	0.01	Iraq*	1945	0.14
Cambodia	1955	0.01	Ireland	1955	0.21
Cameroon	1960	0.01	Israel	1949	0.26
Canada*	1945	3.10	Italy	1955	5.19
Cape Verde	1975	0.01	Jamaica	1962	0.01
Central African Republic	1960	0.01	Japan	1956	15.43
Chad	1960	0.01	Jordan	1955	0.01
Chile*	1945	0.08	Kazakhstan	1992	0.20
China***	1945	0.73	Kenya	1963	0.01
Colombia*	1945	0.10	Korea, North	1991	0.05
Comoros	1975	0.01	Korea, South	1991	0.82
Congo, Democratic Republic of****	1960	0.01	Kuwait	1963	0.19
			Kyrgyzstan	1992	0.03
Congo, Republic of	1960	0.01	Laos	1955	0.01
Costa Rica*	1945	0.01	Latvia	1991	0.08
Côte d'Ivoire	1960	0.01	Lebanon*	1945	0.01
Croatia	1992	0.09	Lesotho	1966	0.01
Cuba*	1945	0.05	Liberia*	1945	0.01
Cyprus	1960	0.03	Libya	1955	0.20
Czech Republic	1993	0.26	Liechtenstein	1990	0.01
Denmark*	1945	0.72	Lithuania	1991	0.08
Djibouti	1977	0.01	Luxembourg*	1945	0.07
Dominica	1978	0.01	Macedonia	1993	0.01
Dominican Republic*	1945	0.01	Madagascar	1960	0.01
Ecuador*	1945	0.02			

continues

United Nations membership (continued)   Table 76

Country	Year of admission	1996 contribution to UN budget (%)	Country	Year of admission	1996 contribution to UN budget (%)
Malawi	1964	0.01	San Marino	1992	0.01
Malaysia	1957	0.14	São Tomé e Príncipe	1975	0.01
Maldives	1965	0.01	Saudi Arabia*	1945	0.72
Mali	1960	0.01	Senegal	1960	0.01
Malta	1964	0.01	Seychelles	1976	0.01
Marshall Islands	1991	0.01	Sierra Leone	1961	0.01
Mauritania	1961	0.01	Singapore	1965	0.14
Mauritius	1968	0.01	Slovakia	1993	0.08
Mexico*	1945	0.79	Slovenia	1992	0.07
Micronesia	1991	0.01	Solomon Isles	1978	0.01
Moldova	1992	0.08	Somalia	1960	0.01
Monaco	1993	0.01	South Africa*	1945	0.32
Mongolia	1961	0.01	Spain	1955	2.36
Morocco	1956	0.03	Sri Lanka	1955	0.01
Mozambique	1975	0.01	Sudan	1956	0.01
Myanmar (Burma)	1948	0.01	Surinam	1975	0.01
Namibia	1990	0.01	Swaziland	1968	0.01
Nepal	1955	0.01	Sweden	1946	1.23
Netherlands*	1945	1.59	Syria*	1945	0.05
New Zealand*	1945	0.24	Tajikistan	1992	0.02
Nicaragua*	1945	0.01	Tanzania	1961	0.01
Niger	1960	0.01	Thailand	1946	0.13
Nigeria	1960	0.11	Togo	1960	0.01
Norway*	1945	0.56	Trinidad and Tobago	1962	0.03
Oman	1971	0.04	Tunisia	1956	0.03
Pakistan	1947	0.06	Turkey*	1945	0.37
Palau	1994	0.01	Turkmenistan	1992	0.03
Panama*	1945	0.01	Uganda	1962	0.01
Papua New Guinea	1975	0.01	Ukraine*	1945	1.14
Paraguay*	1945	0.01	United Arab Emirates	1971	0.19
Peru*	1945	0.06	United Kingdom*	1945	5.31
Philippines*	1945	0.06	United States of America*	1945	25.00
Poland*	1945	0.34	Uruguay*	1945	0.04
Portugal	1955	0.27	Uzbekistan	1992	0.14
Qatar	1971	0.04	Vanuatu	1981	0.01
Romania	1955	0.15	Venezuela*	1945	0.34
Russian Federation†	1945	4.45	Vietnam	1977	0.01
Rwanda	1962	0.01	Yemen**	1947/67	0.01
St Kitts and Nevis	1983	0.01	Yugoslavia††	1945	0.10
St Lucia	1979	0.01	Zambia	1964	0.01
St Vincent and the Grenadines	1980	0.01	Zimbabwe	1980	0.01
Samoa	1976	0.01			

* Founder members.

** Represented by two countries until unification 1990.

*** Represented by the republic of China (Taiwan) to 1971 and by the People's Republic thereafter.

**** Formerly Zaire.

† Became a separate member upon the demise of the USSR which was a founder member 1945.

†† Founder member but suspended from membership 1993.

The sovereign countries that are not UN members are Kiribati, Nauru, Switzerland, Taiwan, Tonga, Tuvalu, and Vatican City.

Assembly in accordance with quotas for world regions. Retiring members are not eligible for immediate re-election. Any UN member may be invited to participate in its discussions if they bear on its interests, but only the permanent or elected members are permitted to vote. It has been argued in recent years that the Council's permanent membership should be updated to include former 'Axis' states, such as Japan and Germany, which, more than half a century after World War II, can justifiably claim to be leading members of the world community, and significant 'second' and 'third' world nations such as Brazil and India.

In pursuit of its responsibility for maintaining peace and security, the Council may call on armed forces, and other assistance, from member states. It has at its disposal a Military Staff Committee composed of the chiefs of staff of the countries of the permanent members. In June 1999 Britain and France made commitments to each supply up to 8,000 stand-by troops for use in UN peacekeeping operations. The lack of a military force was seen as having inhibited the UN in the past effectiveness in this. The presidency of the Security Council is held for a month at a time by a representative of a member state, in English language alphabetical order. The Council has two standing committees: a Committee of Experts and a Committee on the Admission of New Members.

Economic and Social Council

The Economic and Social Council is responsible for economic, social, cultural, educational, health, and related matters. It has 54 members, again elected by a two-thirds majority vote of the General Assembly, with membership being allocated by world regions. The Council has a large number of functional and regional commissions and committees working for it, as well as hundreds of nongovernmental agencies which have been granted consultative status. These commissions include the UN Commission on Human Rights.

International Court of Justice

The International Court of Justice is composed of independent judges, elected by the Security Council and the General Assembly, sitting separately, and chosen because of their competence in international law, irrespective of their nationalities. There are 15 judges, no two of whom can be nationals of the same state. Candidates for election are nominated by national groups and, once elected, serve for nine years, and may be immediately re-elected. Only states, not individuals, may be parties to cases before the Court.

The Court is based at The Hague, in the Netherlands, but may sit elsewhere if it chooses. It sits permanently, except for customary judicial vacations. Its official languages are English and French and it reaches its decisions by a majority of votes of the judges present. The president and vice president are elected by the Court itself and serve three-year terms. If the votes of judges are equal, the president has a casting vote. Judgements are final, and there is no appeal. At a special UN conference, held in Rome in July 1998, it was agreed to set up a permanent international criminal court to try individuals accused of war crimes, genocide, and crimes against humanity.

Secretariat

The United Nations Secretariat consists of the secretary general, who is its chief administrator, under and assistant secretaries general and a large international staff. The secretary general is appointed by the General Assembly for a five-year term, which can be renewed. The present occupant, Kofi Annan of Ghana, took up his appointment in 1997. The first holder of the post was Trygve Lie (1896–1968), of Norway (1946–53), and subsequent holders were Dag Hammarskjöld (1905–61), of Sweden (1953–61), U Thant (1909–74), of Myanmar (1961–71), Kurt Waldheim (b. 1918), of Austria (1972–81), and Javier Pérez de Cuéllar (b. 1920) of Peru (1981–1992), and Boutros Boutros Ghali (1992–97).

Being UN secretary general is clearly an important and prestigious job, but experience shows that its significance depends very much on what a particular holder makes of it. Trygve Lie and Dag Hammarskjöld, who was killed in an air crash while on UN business, became well known, even to ordinary people, as did U Thant, to a lesser degree. Hammarskjöld was awarded the Nobel Peace Prize for his efforts. Kurt Waldheim, on the other hand, made a less marked impression. Javier Pérez de Cuéllar became a popular, and even famous, international figure and did much to revive the standing of the UN, which had fallen to a low ebb during the 1970s. In 1991, a 28-nation UN military coalition, led by the United States, liberated Kuwait from Iraqi occupation, following the 'Operation Desert Storm' Gulf War. This provided an example of a new assertiveness for the UN in defense of the post-Cold War 'New World Order'.

The present holder of the post, Kofi Annan, like his predecessor, has served during one of the organization's most troublesome periods. In addition, UN finances have become strained by the cost of its 16,000 employed staff and 9,000 consultants and the burden of its peacekeeping missions. In 1995 more than 70,000 troops were deployed at an annual cost of nearly $4 billion in peacekeeping operations in 15 countries and disputed territories, namely: Angola, Cyprus, El Salvador, Georgia, India and Pakistan, Iraq and Kuwait, Israel's borders, the Lebanon, Liberia, Mozambique, Rwanda, Somalia, Western Sahara, and in Croatia and Bosnia-Herzegovina, where more than 55,000 troops were deployed.

Kofi Annan has proved to be a pro-active secretary general proposing, in July 1997, major reforms of the UN to facilitate a speedier response to world crises as well as urging the payment of overdue contributions to the UN budget, especially by major members such as the United States, which owed $1.5 billion in mid-1998. In June 1999 the US Senate agreed to pay $1 billion of the arrears owed by the USA.

9.2.2 UN specialized agencies

Working directly within the United Nations organizational structure are a number of specialized agencies, funded by the UN through contributions from the 185 member states. The scale of these contributions, which are based broadly on the principle of the 'ability to pay', are shown in Table 76. However, in 1994 the General Assembly vote had been withdrawn from 13 member states as a consequence of repeated failure to pay their agreed fees, while the United States and Russia were, respectively, $780 million and $500 million in arrears. The specialized agencies operate mainly from the headquarters in New York or from Geneva, in Switzerland.

International Atomic Energy Agency (IAEA)
The IAEA was established in 1957 to accelerate and enlarge the contribution of atomic energy to peace, health, and prosperity throughout the world and to prevent its diversion from peaceful purposes to military ends. It has negotiated safeguard agreements with over 160 individual states. The Agency is based in Vienna, Austria, and has 124 members. In the mid to late 1990s its inspectors were particularly active in Iraq and North Korea.

International Labor Organization (ILO)
The ILO predates the United Nations itself, having been originally created in 1919 by the League of Nations. It is an intergovernmental agency with a tripartite membership of government, employer, and worker representatives. It seeks to improve labor conditions, raise living standards, and promote productive employment through international cooperation. It became part of the UN in 1946 and in 1969 was awarded the Nobel Peace Prize. It conducts research into industrial relations and publishes conventions and recommendations. If a member state ratifies a convention it automatically agrees to bring its national law into line with it. Recommendations are not binding but all member states have a duty to consider them.

The ILO consists of the International Labor Conference, which is its supreme deliberative body and meets annually in Geneva, and the International Labor Office, which is also in Geneva. In 1960 it established the International Institute for Labor Studies and, in 1965, a training institution in Turin, Italy, particularly concerned with the needs of developing countries. Indeed, much of the ILO's work in recent years has been orientated towards the less developed parts of the world. It had 174 members in 1999.

Food and Agriculture Organization (FAO)
A conference in May 1943 at Hot Springs, Virginia, in the United States, provided the stimulus for the setting up of the FAO in October 1945. Its aims are to raise levels of nutrition and standards of living, to improve the production and distribution of food and agricultural products, to improve the living standards of rural populations, and, by accomplishing all these things, to eliminate hunger. Like many other UN agencies, the FAO tends to concentrate its efforts on the less developed parts of the world. It provides guidance on food production and can sponsor relief in emergency situations. It operates from Rome and has 157 members.

United Nations Educational, Scientific and Cultural Organization (UNESCO)
UNESCO came into being in 1946 as a result of a conference held in London, in November 1945, under the auspices of the UK and French governments. Its main purpose is to promote peace by encouraging international collaboration in education, science, and culture. It attempts to do this through teacher-training programs, the promotion of research, and the dissemination of information. Concerns over the organization's leadership led to the US and UK withdrawing in 1984–85, but the UK resumed membership in 1997. Its headquarters are in Paris and it has 186 members.

World Health Organization (WHO)
The World Health Organization was founded in April 1948. Its main purpose is to assist all peoples in attaining the highest possible levels of health. It does this by

research, teaching, and guidance through recommended standards of behaviour. For example, it has, in recent years, sponsored greater international cooperation in the prevention and treatment of AIDS and related infections. It has also made recommendations on the quality control of drugs. Its headquarters are in Geneva and it has regional offices in the Congo, Egypt, Denmark, the Philippines, India, and the United States. It has 191 members. Its director general, since 1998, is Gro Harlem Brundtland, the former Norwegian prime minister.

International Monetary Fund (IMF)

The inspiration for the IMF was the International Monetary Conference held at Bretton Woods, New Hampshire, in the United States, in July 1944, chaired by the US secretary to the treasury, Henry Morgenthau. Conference delegates, including the British delegation led by the celebrated economist John Maynard Keynes, agreed to the creation of a fund which would promote international monetary cooperation, establish a multilateral system of payments, and help remedy any serious disequilibrium in a country's balance of payments by allowing it to draw on the resources of the fund while it took measures to correct the imbalance. The IMF was established on 27 December 1945, as an independent organization, and began operating on 1 March 1947. It became associated with the UN, on the basis of mutual cooperation, on 15 November 1947.

IMF members subscribe to the Fund on a quota basis, determined by their ability to pay at the time of membership. The Fund itself can also borrow to supplement its resources. Most of the assistance given by the IMF is, naturally, to less developed countries but occasionally it is asked to provide temporary help to economically advanced nations. The United Kingdom, for example, had recourse to the Fund in 1976, and during 1997–99 the IMF made large loans to the newly industrialized countries (NICs) of south-east Asia and to Russia. When it is asked to assist, the IMF's representatives invariably impose conditions to ensure that the problem to be dealt with is only a temporary phenomenon. Such conditions are sometimes unacceptable to the sovereign states, particularly if they are pursuing socialist programmes, and can lead to a rejection of IMF loans, as occured in Zimbabwe in 1999. The headquarters of the IMF are in Washington, DC, and it also has offices in Paris and Geneva. Its membership is 189.

International Bank for Reconstruction and Development (IBRD)

The IBRD is often popularly known as the 'World Bank'. Like the IMF, it too was conceived at the Bretton Woods Conference. Its purpose is to provide funds and technical assistance to help the economies of the poorer nations of the world. It obtains its own funds from capital paid in by member countries, from loans, from repayments, from income from investments, and from fees paid for the technical services it provides. Its headquarters are in Washington, DC, where it also has a staff college, called the Economic Development Institute. It has 178 members.

International Development Association (IDA)

The IDA is an agency of the World Bank, concentrating on providing financial and technical help to the poorest nations. It came into existence in 1960 and has 155 members.

International Finance Corporation (IFC)

The IFC is affiliated to the World Bank and was established in 1956. It makes investments in companies, to assist their development, or provides loans. It is particularly active in helping new ventures or providing finance for established companies which wish to expand or diversify. It has 162 members.

International Civil Aviation Organization (ICAO)

The idea for creating the ICAO came from a conference on international aviation held in Chicago at the end of 1944. The Organization was formally set up on 4 April 1947. Its objectives are to establish technical standards for safety and efficiency in air navigation, to develop regional plans for ground facilities and services for civil aviation, and generally to provide advice to airline operators. Its headquarters are in Montreal, Canada. There are 185 members.

Universal Postal Union (UPU)

The UPU was established as long ago as 1875 when the Universal Postal Convention was adopted at a congress in Berne, Switzerland. It was originally called the General Postal Union and changed its name in 1878. Currently, 158 countries are members. Its aim is to improve the standards of postal services and promote international cooperation. Its headquarters are in Berne. There are 189 members.

International Telecommunication Union (ITU)

The aims of the ITU are to maintain and extend international cooperation in improving telecommunications of all kinds by promoting the development of technical skills and services and harmonizing national activities. It originated in 1932 when, at a conference in Madrid, it was decided to merge the Telegraph Convention of 1865 and the Radiotelegraph Convention of 1906 into a single convention and functioning organization. The ITU's headquarters are in Geneva. There are 187 members.

World Meteorological Organization (WMO)

The Directors of the International Meteorological Organization, which had been set up in 1873, met in Washington, DC, in 1947 and adopted a convention establishing the WMO. Its main aim is to facilitate worldwide cooperation in the creation and maintenance of a network of stations for making meteorological observations and to ensure the rapid exchange of information. The headquarters of the WMO are in Geneva. There are 179 members.

International Maritime Organization (IMO)

Known until 1982 as the Intergovernmental Maritime Consultative Organization (IMCO), the IMO was established as a specialized agency of the UN in 1948. It began to operate effectively in 1959. Its aim is to promote cooperation between governments on technical matters affecting merchant shipping, with the objective of improving safety at sea. It formulates and publishes conventions and regulations and has its headquarters in London. The UN Convention on the Law of the Sea came into force in 1994. There are 155 members.

World Trade Organization (WTO)

The World Trade Organization (WTO) came into operation on 1 January 1995 as the successor to the General Agreement on Tariffs and Trade (GATT). The GATT was negotiated in 1947 as a multilateral treaty, laying down a common code of conduct in international trade and providing a forum for discussion of trade problems, with the objective of reducing trade barriers. Part of its purpose was to help less developed countries, through its 'most-favored-nation' (MFN) treatment, which gave protection to 'infant economies'.

The WTO resulted from the Final Act of the Uruguay Round of the GATT which was formally approved in April 1994. This Final Act was the culmination of over seven years of negotiations, which had started at Punta del Este, Uruguay, in September 1986. When fully implemented in 2002, it will have reduced average duties in manufactured goods to 3%: they were 40% in the 1940s. The new organization is now a permanent trade-monitoring body, with a status commensurate with that of the International Monetary Fund (IMF) and the World Bank and has been given a wider remit than its prede-

cessor. A new round of WTO trade negotiations was launched in 1999, focusing on agriculture and services.

The WTO has a conference of finance ministers, attended by representatives of all its members, at least once every two years and a General Council to keep a continuing oversight of its affairs. The members of the GATT automatically became members of the WTO, and with subsequent additions, the total membership is 131, with a further 28 states seeking to join, including China. Membership entails acceptance of the results of the Uruguay Round, without exception. Like the GATT, it has its headquarters in Geneva.

World Intellectual Property Organization (WIPO)

WIPO was established in 1967 as the successor to the United International Bureau for the Protection of Intellectual Property. It became a UN specialized agency in 1974. Its primary purpose is to protect intellectual property, which, in general, means patents and trademarks, throughout the world. It is based in Geneva. It has 164 members.

International Fund for Agricultural Development (IFAD)

IFAD is the result of a recommendation of a World Food Conference which was held in 1974. The Fund began operating in 1977 with the prime objective of mobilizing funds for agricultural and rural development in developing countries. IFAD's headquarters are in Rome and it has 160 members .

9.2.3 UN Development Program (UNDP)

The UN Development Program was established in 1965 to promote higher standards of living in the poorer nations and to try to remedy the economic imbalance between industrialized and developing countries, to be achieved mainly by the economically advanced countries providing financial and technical help, and by adopting economic and commercial policies favoring the less advanced nations.

The UNDP is headed by an administrator who is responsible to a Governing Council. It has its headquarters in New York and operates through a number of regional commissions which are described later in this chapter.

The Commonwealth (53 states)   Table 77

Region/state	Year of independence	Date joined	Regime type	Head of state
Asia (8)				
Bangladesh	1971	1972	Em-dem	president
Brunei	1984	1984	Absolutist	local monarch
India	1947	1947	Lib-dem	president
Malaysia	1957	1957	Lib-dem	local monarch
The Maldives	1965	1982	Auth-nat	president
Pakistan	1947	1947/1989	Em-dem	president
Singapore	1965	1965	Lib-dem	president
Sri Lanka	1948	1948	Lib-dem	president
Central America and the Caribbean (11)				
Antigua and Barbuda	1981	1981	Lib-dem	British monarch
Bahamas	1973	1973	Lib-dem	British monarch
Barbados	1966	1966	Lib-dem	British monarch
Belize	1981	1981	Lib-dem	British monarch
Dominica	1978	1978	Lib-dem	president
Grenada	1974	1974	Lib-dem	British monarch
Jamaica	1962	1962	Lib-dem	British monarch
St Kitts and Nevis	1983	1983	Lib-dem	British monarch
St Lucia	1979	1979	Lib-dem	British monarch
St Vincent and the Grenadines	1979	1979	Lib-dem	British monarch
Trinidad and Tobago	1962	1962	Lib-dem	president
Central and Southern Africa (19)				
Botswana	1966	1966	Lib-dem	president
Cameroon	1960	1995	Em-dem	president
The Gambia	1965	1965	Em-dem	president
Ghana	1957	1957	Em-dem	president
Kenya	1963	1963	Em-dem	president
Lesotho	1966	1966	Em-dem	local monarch
Malawi	1964	1964	Em-dem	president
Mauritius	1968	1968	Lib-dem	British monarch
Mozambique	1975	1995	Em-dem	president
Namibia	1990	1990	Em-dem	president
Nigeria*	1960	1960	Em-dem	president
The Seychelles	1976	1976	Em-dem	president
Sierra Leone	1961	1961	Em-dem	president
South Africa	1931	1931/1994	Em-dem	president
Swaziland	1968	1968	Absolutist	local monarch
Tanzania	1961	1961	Em-dem	president
Uganda	1962	1962	Auth-nat	president**
Zambia	1964	1964	Em-dem	president
Zimbabwe	1980	1980	Nat-soc	president
North America (1)				
Canada	1931	1931	Lib-dem	British monarch
Northern and Western Europe (3)				
Cyprus	1960	1961	Lib-dem	president
Malta	1964	1964	Lib-dem	president
United Kingdom	–	1931	Lib-dem	British monarch

continues

The Commonwealth (53 states) (continued)   Table 77

Region/state	Year of independence	Date joined	Regime type	Head of state
Oceania (10)				
Australia	1931	1931	Lib-dem	British monarch
Fiji	1970	1970/97	Em-dem	president
Kiribati	1979	1979	Lib-dem	president
Nauru	1968	1999***	Lib-dem	president
New Zealand	1931	1931	Lib-dem	British monarch
Samoa	1962	1970	Lib-dem	president
Papua New Guinea	1975	1975	Lib-dem	British monarch
Solomon Islands	1978	1978	Lib-dem	British monarch
Tonga	1970	1970	Absolutist	local monarch
Tuvalu	1978	1978	Lib-dem	British monarch
Vanuatu	1980	1980	Lib-dem	president
South America (1)				
Guyana	1966	1966	Lib-dem	president

Note: Fiji was a Commonwealth member, with the British queen as head of state, until a republic was established in 1987; it was readmitted in 1997. Ireland withdrew from the Commonwealth, and Pakistan and South Africa withdrew in 1961 and 1972, but later rejoined in 1989 and 1994 respectively.

* Nigeria's membership was suspended in November 1995 until May 1999 because of its human rights record.

** Uganda also has a local tribal monarch, the King of Buganda, who was reinstated in 1993.

*** Nauru was an associate member from 1968.

Auth-nat = authoritarian nationalist, Lib-dem = liberal democratic, Nat-soc = nationalistic socialist.

9.3 Global cooperation: the Commonwealth

The Commonwealth is the modern successor to the British Empire. It is formally described as a free association of sovereign independent states. It has no charter, treaty, or constitution, the association being based on a desire for cooperation, consultation, and mutual assistance. The current membership is shown in Table 77. It comprises 53 sovereign countries, situated in seven of the world's nine regions and with a combined population of 1.6 billion, or nearly 30% of the global total. In addition, the more than 20 dependencies of Australia, New Zealand, and the United Kingdom, covered in *Chapter 8*, are regarded as 'Commonwealth countries'.

It has been described as the world's most unusual 'club' and is a singularly British institution, still echoing the United Kingdom's imperial past. In recent years, however, the influence of the 'mother country' has shown signs of weakening and there are indications that the leadership might be taken up by states such as India, Canada, or Australia. Nevertheless, it is inconceivable that the Commonwealth could survive in anything like its present form without Britain's active participation.

As the successor to the British Empire, the Commonwealth was effectively established in 1931, when the Statute of Westminster gave full autonomy to the white-settler dominions of Australia, Canada, New Zealand, and South Africa. The Commonwealth was initially based on allegiance to a common crown. However, in 1949, India chose to become a republic and from that date the modern Commonwealth was born, based now on the concept of the British monarch being a symbol, rather than a legal entity, and, as such, the 'Head of the Commonwealth'. At the moment 17 of the 53 members accept the British queen as their head of state, 31 are republics, and five have their own local monarchs.

Politically, 31, or 58%, of the sovereign states in the Commonwealth were liberal democracies in 1999, 16 were emergent democracies, three had absolutist regimes, two had authoritarian nationalist regimes, and one had a nationalistic socialist regime.

Heads of government of Commonwealth countries meet every two years to discuss international affairs and areas of cooperation. Finance ministers meet annually and other ministers as and when the need arises. The Commonwealth is not a mutual defense organization and most member countries are committed to regional treaties.

The Commonwealth is frequently criticized because it has little real power to influence world affairs. Its supporters would argue that its strength lies in its voluntary nature and that, should the need arise, its potentially immense resources could be put to considerable use. Britain's role as the originator of the Commonwealth would be crucial in this respect, but as it is increasingly committed to its role in Europe its place within the wider organization is put into some doubt.

The Commonwealth is serviced by a Secretariat which is based in Marlborough House, Pall Mall, London, and headed by the secretary general, Chief E Chukwuemeka Anyaoku, of Nigeria. The Secretariat's staff come from a wide range of member countries which also pay its operating costs.

Perhaps as an indication of its international standing, there have been, somewhat surprisingly, a number of recent enquiries about possible membership from countries which historically have not been associated with Britain or its empire. In 1995 Cameroon and Mozambique were the first members to be admitted which had not been fully under British rule. In April 1999 a think tank close to Britain's Labour government (The Foreign Policy Centre) proposed that a president from amongst the member countries be appointed to support the role of Queen Elizabeth II and that the secretariat be moved outside the UK, so as to make the body more truly international.

The French equivalent of the Commonwealth is la Francophonie, which is a biennial conference of heads of French-speaking states. The last summit, in Vietnam in 1997, was attended by 49 countries.

9.4 Global cooperation: the Non-Aligned Movement

The Non-Aligned Movement is an informal grouping of developing countries who meet triennially in an international conference to promote the interests of the poorer South, campaigning for a new international economic order. The origins of the movement can be traced back to the conference of Afro-Asian nations that was held in Bandung, Indonesia, in 1955, proclaiming anti-colonialism and neutrality between East and West power blocs during the Cold War era.

Its founding fathers were the Indian prime minister, Jawaharlal Nehru (1889–1964), Ghana's prime minister, Kwame Nkrumah (1909–1972), Egypt's president; Gamal Abdel Nasser (1918–1970), Indonesia's president Achmed Sukarno (1901–1970), and Yugoslavia's president Josip Broz, Tito (1892–1980), with the first official conference being held in Belgrade, Yugoslavia, 1961.

With the end of the Cold War, the chief issues promoted by the movement have been international action against poverty, environmental destruction, nuclear testing, and drug-trafficking. The most recent, 11th triennial conference held in October 1995 at Cartagena, Columbia, was attended by delegates and heads of states from 113 developing countries, including Nelson Mandela (b. 1918), the South African president, Fidel Castro (b. 1927), the Cuban president, and Yasser Arafat (b. 1929), the leader of the Palestine Liberation Organization (PLO). Its members hold more than half the world's population and, including in its ranks Saudi Arabia and Kuwait, 85% of oil resources, but only 7% of global GDP.

9.5 Global cooperation: Conference on Security and Cooperation in Europe/ Organization for Security and Cooperation in Europe (CSCE/OSCE)

The Helsinki Final Act was signed by 35 countries, including the then Soviet Union and the United States, at the end of a Conference on Security and Cooperation in Europe (CSCE) in 1975 during the era of East–West *détente*. The Act registered agreement on cooperation in a number of areas, such as security, economics, science, techology, and human rights. The competences of the CSCE were extended by the 1990 Charter of Paris for a New Europe, which was generally regarded as marking an end to the 'Cold War' between the Eastern European bloc and the West. In particular, it was agreed that fact-finding teams could be sent to investigate alleged human rights abuses in any member country and to monitor elections. In December 1994 members agreed to change the CSCE's title to the Organization for Security and Cooperation in Europe (OSCE), to denote its permanent status.

In addition to its original aims, the OSCE seeks to strengthen pluralist democracy and the settling of disputes between member states by peaceful means, including monitoring invasions. Its membership now includes all internationally recognized countries in Europe plus Canada and the United States: a total of 55, although Yugoslavia's membership was suspended in 1992. A Council of Foreign Ministers acts as its central decision-taking forum and a Committee of Senior Officials (CSO) implements these decisions. It has a Secretariat, which meets in Prague, a Conflict Prevention Center, and a Forum for Security and Cooperation, based in Vienna.

9.6 Global cooperation: Organization of the Islamic Conference (OIC)

The OIC was established in May 1971 following a conference of Muslim heads of state in Rabat, Morocco, in 1969, and meetings of Islamic foreign ministers in Jeddah and Karachi, in 1970. The main aim of the Organization is to promote Islamic solidarity and its members include 54 countries in the Middle East and North, Central and Southern Africa, and Asia, plus the Palestine Liberation Organization (PLO). The OIC has its headquarters and secretariat in Jeddah, Saudi Arabia.

9.7 Global cooperation: the Antarctic Treaty

The Antarctic Treaty was signed in 1959 by 13 countries which conduct scientific research in Antarctica. The membership has risen to 39, including ten consultative members. The main objective of the Treaty is to promote peaceful international scientific cooperation in the region.

9.8 Interregional cooperation

There are several examples of mutual cooperation between countries which cut across the regions we have defined for the purposes of this title. Some are sponsored by the United Nations, some by the European Community, some are the products of Commonwealth membership, some have been inspired by the United States, on the basis of enlightened self-interest, and some are examples of self-help by states in different, but physically adjacent, regions.

9.8.1 UN interregional groups

Within the United Nations organization there are four commissions intended to promote cooperation between under- or less-developed countries in various parts of the world.

Economic Commission for Africa (ECA)
ECA was founded by the UN in 1958. The total current membership consists of 50 states, representing virtually the whole of North, Central, and Southern Africa. The purpose of the commission is to promote and facilitate concerted action for the economic and social development of Africa, and it seeks to achieve this through research and the coordination of national policies.

Some examples of ECA's work are the establishment of the African Development Bank, in 1964, the creation of the Association of African Central Banks, in 1969, and the setting up of the Center for Mineral Resources Development at Dar es Salaam, Tanzania, in 1976. It is a regular publisher of largely statistical material, and operates from Addis Ababa, in Ethiopia.

Economic and Social Commission for Asia and the Pacific (ESCAP)
ESCAP was founded in 1947 as the Economic Commission for Asia and the Far East and changed its name in 1974. It currently has 35 full members and ten associate members. Most of the full members are states in Asia or Oceania but other countries with interests in the regions, such as the United States, the United Kingdom, the Russian Federation, France, and the Netherlands, also enjoy full membership. The associate members are the smaller countries of Asia and Oceania.

ESCAP performs a broadly similar role in Asia and Oceania to that of ECA in Africa. It, too, has had success in setting up a number of ventures and organizations, such as the Asian and Pacific Center for Development Administration, the Asian Clearing Union, and the Asian Development Bank. ESCAP has its headquarters in Bangkok, Thailand.

Economic Commission for Europe (ECE)
ECE was also founded in 1947 and includes all Western and Eastern European countries except Switzerland, which participates in a consultative capacity. The

United States, Canada, and Israel are also consultants. The Commission's role is to promote economic cooperation. It is based in Geneva.

Economic Commission for Latin America (ECLA)

ECLA was founded in 1948 with the object of raising the level of economic activity in Latin America, which, in the Commission's terms, includes what we have defined as Central America and the Caribbean and South America. It currently has 33 members. They include, in addition to the countries of the regions, Canada, France, the Netherlands, the United Kingdom, and the United States. Its headquarters are in Santiago, Chile.

Economic Commission for Western Asia (ECWA)

ECWA was founded in 1973 and operates from the UN building in Amman, Jordan. It was set up to provide a better service for countries previously catered for by the UN Economic and Social Office in Beirut. Its objectives are broadly similar to those of ECLA. The use of the term 'Western Asia' in its title is a little misleading since its 14 members, which include 13 countries plus the Palestine Liberation Organization (PLO), are all situated in the Middle East or North or Central Africa.

9.8.2 Commonwealth-inspired interregional cooperation

Colombo Plan for Cooperative Economic Development in South and Southeast Asia (CP)

The purpose of the Colombo Plan is to facilitate and coordinate economic and social development in the countries of South and Southeast Asia. It was set up in 1951 within the framework of the Commonwealth, on the initiative of the Commonwealth foreign ministers. Since that date it has lost much of its original Commonwealth character and most of its current members are not in the Commonwealth. They now total 26 and include, as well as the original Commonwealth states in the region, Afghanistan, Cambodia, Canada, Indonesia, Iran, Japan, South Korea, Laos, the Philippines, Thailand, the United Kingdom, and the United States. The Plan's headquarters are in Colombo, Sri Lanka.

9.8.3 Northern and Western European-inspired interregional cooperation

The Lomé Convention

The Lomé Convention takes its name from Lomé, the capital of Togo, in Africa, where, in 1975 the members of the European Community (EC) agreed to assist the less developed countries of Africa, the Caribbean, and the Pacific by establishing a 'special relationship' with them so that they would not suffer unduly from the tariff policies of the EC. The countries concerned include virtually all those in Central and Southern Africa, most of those in the Caribbean, and the smaller states of Oceania. Under the terms of the Convention the EC guarantees the 70 states who benefit from it virtually unrestricted access for their agricultural products to Western European markets. The 70 ACP (Asia-Caribbean-Pacific) countries, as they are called, may, for their part, operate varying degrees of protection of their own economies. Aid to the ACP nations is also provided from the European Development Fund. The original Convention was renewed in 1981, 1985 and 1990.

Organization for Economic Cooperation and Development (OECD)

The OECD is the expanded successor to the Organization for European Economic Cooperation (OEEC), which was set up in 1948, at the instigation of the United States, to promote economic recovery in postwar Europe. The new body was established in 1961 and now has 29 members, including the 15 members of the EU, plus Australia, Canada, the Czech Republic, Hungary, Iceland, Japan, Norway, Poland, Mexico, New Zealand, South Korea, Switzerland, Turkey, and the United States, plus representatives of the EU. In its expanded form its objective is to promote freer trade and to stimulate Western aid to undeveloped countries. An inner core of the seven most developed states, Canada, France, Germany, Italy, Japan, the United Kingdom, and the United States, forms the 'Group of Seven' (G7). Since 1975 the heads of governments of these countries have met for informal annual summits on major economic, monetary, and political problems. The presidents of the EU Commission and Russia have observer status at these meetings.

European Bank for Reconstruction and Development (EBRD)

The EBRD was founded in 1990 to assist the economic reconstruction of Central and Eastern Europe by financing industrial and economic expansion, using loan guarantees, equity investment, and underwriting, to promote the transition to free-market economies. The Bank was originally proposed by French President François Mitterrand, and his former adviser, Jacques Attali, became its first president. Its 60 members include Albania, Armenia, Australia, Austria, Azerbaijan, Belarus, Belgium, Bosnia-Herzegovina, Bulgaria, Canada, Croatia, Cyprus, the Czech Republic, Denmark, Egypt, Estonia, Finland, France, Georgia, Germany, Greece, Hungary, Iceland, Ireland, Israel, Italy, Japan, Kazakhstan, South Korea, Kyrgyzstan, Latvia, Liechtenstein, Lithuania, Luxembourg, Macedonia, Malta, Mexico, Moldova, Morocco, the Netherlands, New Zealand, Norway, Poland, Portugal, Romania, Russia, Slovakia, Slovenia, Spain, Sweden, Switzerland, Tajikistan, Turkey, Turkmenistan, the Ukraine, the United Kingdom, the United States, Uzbekistan, the Commission of the European Union, and the European Investment Bank. In 1995 it approved 134 projects totalling ECU 2,855 million. However, a number of its investments proved to be overgenerous and in 1998 the bank incurred losses of $225 million. Its headquarters are in London and its president, in 1999, was Horst Koehler.

9.8.4 Central, Eastern, and Southern European-inspired interregional cooperation

Central European Initiative (CEI)

This body, founded in 1989 as the five-member Pentagonal Group, adopted the designation CEI in 1992. Its objectives are improved relations between the states of Central Europe and with neighboring Western European countries, with the aim of eventual membership of the European Union. The 16 members are Albania, Austria, Belarus, Bosnia-Herzegovina, Bulgaria, Croatia, the Czech Republic, Hungary, Italy, Macedonia, Moldova, Poland, Romania, Slovakia, Slovenia, and Ukraine.

Commonwealth of Independent States (CIS)

The CIS was formed following the demise of the Soviet Union in December 1991 and was intended to replace it, but a number of former Soviet republics refused to join, preferring full independence. Eventually, its membership settled on 12 states: Armenia, Azerbaijan, Belarus, Georgia (from 1994), Kazakhstan, Kyrgyzstan, Moldova, the Russian Federation, Tajikistan, Turkmenistan, Ukraine, and Uzbekistan. It has a Council of Heads of State and a Council of Heads of Government, and the post of chairperson is rotated. Its administrative headquarters are at Minsk, Belarus, but with no firm political foundation and its members frequently divided on policy, its future is uncertain. However, in 1994 the CIS successfully negotiated ceasefires in Abkhazia, situated in Georgia, and the Nagorno-Karabakh dispute between Armenia and Azerbaijan, stationing peacekeeping forces in these regions, as well as in Tajikistan. An early objective of the CIS, the creation of a 'single economic space', or customs union, has been largely abandoned, although, in 1994, the three Central Asian states of Kazakhstan, Kyrgyzstan, and Uzbekistan created their own social, economic, and military union, and Belarus and Russia have established particularly close ties. At the September 1997 CIS summit the other members criticized Russia for dominating the organization, and refused to set up a 'crisis commission' to resolve intra-CIS disputes. In 1999 Georgia appeared unwilling to renew its membership. At the April 1999 CIS summit it was agreed to streamline the administration, to reduce the 2,000 strong staff by 50%, and to establish an executive committee to replace the executive secretarial and interstate economic committee. Yury Yarov, a Russian, became the new executive secretary of the CIS.

Council of Baltic Sea States (COBSS)

This interregional grouping, founded in March 1992, comprises 11 states from Northern and Western Europe and Central and Eastern Europe situated in the Baltic region: Denmark, Estonia, Finland, Germany, Iceland, Latvia, Lithuania, Norway, Poland, Russia, and Sweden. It seeks to increase cooperation between member states.

Danube Commission

The Danube Commission is based on a convention controlling navigation on the River Danube, which was signed in Belgrade in 1948. The convention confirmed that navigation from Ulm, in Germany, to the Black Sea was open and free to people, shipping, and merchandise of all states. The Commission, which ensures the convention's enforcement, is composed of representatives of all the seven states through which the Danube flows. The Commission comprises Austria, Bulgaria, Germany, Hungary, Romania, Russia, Slovakia,

Ukraine, and Yugoslavia (suspended). Its headquarters are in Budapest, Hungary.

9.8.5 Middle East-inspired interregional cooperation

Organization of Petroleum Exporting Countries (OPEC)

OPEC was formed in Baghdad, Iraq, in 1960, with five founder members: Iran, Iraq, Kuwait, Saudi Arabia, and Venezuela. Its membership later expanded to include, in addition to the founder members, Algeria, Indonesia, Libya, Nigeria, Qatar, and the United Arab Emirates. Ecuador withdrew in 1992 and Gabon in 1995. Its primary object is to coordinate the production and pricing policies of the major oil producers so as to guarantee stable prices and stable incomes, based on what the Organization would claim to be a fair return on capital invested. Despite its existence, oil prices on world markets have often been as much affected by changing economic conditions as by OPEC policies. It has, however, since coming into existence, done much to eliminate the worst examples of the exploitation of primary producing countries by the industrialized nations. The headquarters of OPEC are in Vienna, Austria. In March 1999, in response to a 34% fall in oil prices in 1998, OPEC agreed to cut members output by 7% to 24 billion barrels a day in effort to force up prices. However, in 1998 members had not fully complied with agreed cuts.

9.8.6 Central and Southern African-inspired interregional cooperation

African Development Bank (ADB)

The ADB was founded in 1963 to promote and finance economic development across the continent. Its members include 53 African and 24 non-African countries. Its headquarters are at Abidjan, in Côte d'Ivoire.

Organization of African Unity (OAU)

The OAU was founded in Addis Ababa in 1963, on the initiative of Emperor Haile Selassie of Ethiopia. Its main aims are to further African unity and solidarity; to coordinate political, economic, cultural, health, scientific, and defense policies; and to eliminate colonialism in Africa. A long-term goal (by 2025) is to create an African economic community. There are 53 countries in membership, representing virtually the whole of Central and Southern Africa, plus Algeria, Egypt, and Tunisia, in North Africa, and the Middle East. The Organization is headed by an Assembly of Heads of State and Government, which meets annually, and a Council of Ministers, which meets twice a year. It also has a Secretariat based in Addis Ababa. The elected post of OAU chairperson is a highly prestigious position in Africa. South Africa joined in 1994.

9.8.7 United States-inspired interregional cooperation

As a leading industrial and military power, and as part of a strategy of mutual defense and economic development, the United States has promoted or sponsored a number of interregional groups with European and North, Central and South American countries. Military groups are described later, in paragraph 9.10.

Organization of American States (OAS)

The OAS was founded in 1948 by a charter signed at Bogotá, Colombia, by representatives of 35 states in North, Central, and South America, and the Caribbean, including the United States. Its declared purpose is: 'To achieve an order of peace and justice, promoting solidarity among the American states; to defend their sovereignty, their territorial integrity and their independence; to establish new objectives and standards for the promotion of the economic, social and cultural development of the peoples of the Hemisphere, and to speed the process of economic integration.'

The origins of the OAS go back as far as 1826 when the First Congress of American States was convened by the Venezuelan revolutionary leader, Simón Bolívar. Since those early days the organization has become more formally institutionalized, with a general assembly a permanent council, consisting of one representative from each of the member states, and numerous other councils, commissions and committees. Although its objectives are clearly, and impressively, stated in its charter, and although its structure appears to be democratically representative of all the signatories, the OAS has become increasingly dominated by the United States, so that, in pursuit of the Monroe Doctrine, enunciated in 1823, which effectively warned off European powers from America's 'back yard', what is regarded as 'good' for the American continent is mostly what is seen as good in the eyes of the United States, and this is an attitude often resented by many of the

OAS members. The headquarters of the OAS are in Washington, DC.

Inter-American Development Bank (IADB)

The IADB was founded in 1959, at the instigation of the OAS, to finance economic and social development, particularly in the less wealthy regions of the Americas. Its membership of 46 states is wider than that of the OAS and includes Austria, Belgium, Canada, Croatia, Denmark, Finland, France, Germany, Israel, Italy, Japan, the Netherlands, Norway, Portugal, Slovenia, Spain, Sweden, Switzerland, and the United Kingdom, as well as the states of Central and Southern America, the Caribbean, and the United States. Its headquarters are in Washington, DC.

North American Free Trade Agreement (NAFTA)

The North American Free Trade Agreement was signed by the United States, Canada, and Mexico in August 1992 and ratified by the US Congress in November 1993. The first trade pact of its kind to link two highly-industrialized countries to a developing one, it created a free market of 375 million people, with a total GDP of US$6,800 billion, equivalent to 30% of global GDP. It was preceded, in 1989, by a bilateral agreement between Canada and the United States to form a free-trade zone aimed to rival the European Union. From January 1994, tariffs and restrictions on trade in manufactured goods and agricultural produce will be progressively eliminated over a ten to 15-year period and investment into low-wage Mexico by Canada and the United States progressively increased. Although the Agreement was initially viewed with caution by the Canadian government and opposed by US labor unions, it was welcomed by the European Union, provided it operated within agreed WTO rules. In December 1994 it was agreed to admit Chile into the Agreement.

9.8.8 Latin American-inspired interregional cooperation

In an effort to avoid overdependence on the United States, and to come out of the shadow of living in its 'back yard', some Latin American states have sought to pursue a more independent economic policy line.

Association of Caribbean States (ACS)

The Association of Caribbean States resulted from an agreement signed in Colombia in July 1994 by countries in the Caribbean basin to adopt a common approach to regional political policies and markets and to foster economic cooperation and eventual integration. Its 25 members include the states of the Caribbean and Central America, and the South American states of Colombia, Suriname, and Venezuela. Associate membership has been accepted by 12 dependent territories in the region. Seen as a reaction to the creation of the North American Free Trade Agreement (NAFTA) between the United States, Canada, and Mexico, observers doubt its viability in view of its much smaller potential market of 205 million.

Group of Rio

The Group of Rio was founded in 1987 from the Contadora Group, an alliance between Colombia, Mexico, Panama, and Venezuela to establish a general peace treaty for Latin America, as a 'permanent mechanism for joint political action'. To create the Group, the original Contadora members were joined by Argentina, Bolivia, Brazil, Chile, Ecuador, Paraguay, Peru, and Uruguay. The venues for its summit meetings rotate among member states. At its September 1995 Quito summit, the Group adopted a declaration of joint political objectives, including the strengthening of democracy, combatting drug-trafficking and corruption, and the creation of a Latin American and Caribbean free-trade area by 2005.

Group of Three

The Group of Three is a free-trade bloc formed in 1994 by Colombia, Mexico, and Venezuela who agreed to reduce and remove tariffs over a ten-year period.

Latin American Economic System (*Sistema Económico Latinoamericano*) (LAES/SELA)

LAES was founded by treaty in 1975 as the successor to the Latin American Economic Coordination Commission. The aim was to have a purely Latin American organization, with neither of the developed nations of North America involved. Its purpose is to create and promote multinational enterprises in the region, to provide markets, and to stimulate technological and scientific cooperation. Its membership has widened and now includes: Argentina, Barbados, Bolivia, Brazil, Chile, Colombia, Costa Rica, Cuba, the Dominican Republic, Ecuador, El Salvador, Grenada, Guatemala, Guyana, Haiti, Honduras, Jamaica, Mexico, Nicaragua, Panama, Paraguay, Peru, Spain, Suriname, Trinidad and Tobago, Uruguay, and Venezuela. Its headquarters are in Caracas, Venezuela.

Latin American Integration Association (*Asociación Latino-Americano de Integración*) (ALADI)

ALADI was formed in 1980 to replace the Latin American Free Trade Association (LAFTA). LAFTA encouraged trade by across-the-board tariff cuts while ALADI takes into account the different stages of economic development that individual countries have reached and so applies tariff reductions preferentially. The ultimate aim of the Association is to create a fully fledged common market. It has 12 member countries, all of them, except Mexico and Cuba (admitted in 1999), in South America. ALADI is based in Montevideo, Uruguay.

9.8.9 Asian-inspired interregional cooperation

Association of Southeast Asian Nations (ASEAN)

ASEAN is an association of traditionally noncommunist states in Southeast Asia which was formed in 1967 by the signing of the Bangkok Declaration. Its membership has been widened since 1995 to include 'reform-communist' states. The declared aims of the Association are to foster economic and social progress and cultural development and to promote peace in the region. Its ten members comprise Brunei, Cambodia (from April 1999), Indonesia, Laos (from 1997), Malaysia, Myanmar (from 1997), the Philippines, Singapore, Thailand, and Vietnam (from 1995). Its headquarters are in Jakarta, Indonesia. Russia has attended recent ASEAN meetings an observer. In 1992 ASEAN leaders reached agreement on a mutual tariff reduction scheme and the eventual goal of establishing an ASEAN Free Trade Area (AFTA) by the year 2008 (later brought forward to 2002). There is an ASEAN Regional Forum on security, which consists of the ASEAN states, the United States, Japan, Canada, Australia, South Korea, New Zealand, the European Union, China, Papua New Guinea, and Russia.

Asia-Pacific Economic Cooperation (APEC)

APEC was formed in 1989, on the initiative of the Australian prime minister, Bob Hawke, to promote multilateral trade in the Asia–Pacific region. In 1999, its 21 members comprised Australia, Brunei, Canada, Chile, China, Hong Kong, Indonesia, Japan, South Korea, Malaysia, Mexico, New Zealand, Papua New Guinea, Peru, the Philippines, Russia, Singapore, Taiwan, Thailand, the United States, and Vietnam. Together they account for more than half of the world's GDP. Operating within APEC, but excluding Australia and the United States, is the East Asian Economic Caucus (EAEC), which is dominated by members of ASEAN. APEC's permanent secretariat is based in Singapore. In 1998 Peru, Russia, and Vietnam were admitted as new members and a ten-year moratorium declared on further expansion. Meanwhile, in 1997 a 25-member Asia – Europe Meeting (ASEM) of finance ministers was set up, to promote greater economic interaction.

9.8.10 Oceania-inspired interregional cooperation

Rarotonga Treaty

The Rarotonga Treaty was signed in 1987 by Australia, Fiji, Indonesia, New Zealand, and the then Soviet Union, formally declaring the South Pacific a nuclear-free zone.

9.9 Intraregional cooperation

There are many examples of cooperation within our defined regions. Some are primarily political and cultural, such as the Arab League, many are essentially economic and at least one, the Palestine Liberation Organization (PLO), is intended to be an instrument for creating a new, independent state. To try to include every intraregional group currently operating would be a virtually impossible task, but those which are described below are seen as the most significant as well as being representative of their respective regions.

9.9.1 Northern and Western Europe

World War II had a profound and lasting effect on the countries of Northern and Western Europe, whether they were the 'victors' or the 'vanquished'. Above all else, it convinced the leading politicians of the countries which had experienced the war at first hand, France, Belgium, Luxembourg, the Netherlands, Germany, and Italy, that they should take steps to set up institutions which would make another war in Europe virtually impossible. The first practical step towards this end, in 1951, was the establishment of the European Coal and Steel Community (ECSC), in the belief that if the leading nations shared coal and steel-making facilities, which were seen as the basic raw materials of war, future conflicts would be avoided. The ECSC was followed, in 1955, by the European Investment Fund and then, two years later, in 1957, by the momentous signing in Rome of the treaties which established the European Economic Community (EEC) and the European Atomic Energy Community (Euratom). The preamble to the treaty setting up the EEC declared its objectives as: the establishment of the foundations of an ever-closer union among European peoples; the improvement of their working and living conditions; the progressive abolition of restrictions on trade between them; and the development of the prosperity of overseas countries. In 1986 the Single European Act provided for the establishment of a single market by 31 December 1992, entailing the free movement of goods, services, capital, and people between member states. The December 1991 Maastricht Treaty on European Union agreed to a series of objectives that included the establishment of a single currency in 1999, closer political union, and a more assertive role on the international scene. Maastrict sought to increase the role of the European Parliament; created new institutions such as the Committee of the Regions; set out a long-term goal of the framing of a common defense policy; included a 'social chapter' on fundamental social rights; and placed emphasis on 'subsidiarity', in which decisions are made at the lowest appropriate level, as the key governing principle of the Community. It was amended by the June 1997 Treaty of Amsterdam, which made maintaining a high level of employment a major new objective and incorporated a 1990 Schengen Agreement on freedom of movement of persons across member state borders into the Treaty. In 1999 a new post for EU foreign and security policy was created, being occupied by Javier Solana, former secretary general of NATO.

The founder members of the EEC were France, Germany, Italy, the Netherlands, Belgium, and Luxembourg. The United Kingdom, Ireland, and Denmark were admitted into membership in 1973, Greece in 1981, Spain and Portugal in 1986, and Austria, Finland, and Sweden in 1995. Norway was also set to join in 1995, but its referendum in November 1994 rejected membership. Applications for membership have also been made by Turkey, Cyprus, Morocco, and Malta, while the recently democratized states of Central Europe, including the Czech Republic, Hungary, Poland, Slovakia, Bulgaria, Estonia, Latvia,

Lithuania, and Romania, which are 'associate members', and Slovenia, aspire to full membership. Formal membership negotiations were opened in 1998 with the Czech Republic, Cyprus, Estonia, Hungary, Poland, and Slovenia. In May 1999 it was proposed by the European Commission that Albania and Macedonia be granted an association agreement as a means of bringing the region closer to the perspective of full intergration into EU structures. Expansion of the union eastwards has led to gradual reform of the financial structures, including farm subsidies, in an initiative known as Agenda 2000. Following the ratification in November 1993 of the Maastricht Treaty, the European Community became the European Union (EU). The EU's 15 member countries have a combined population of more than 370 million, far greater than that of the United States, and a GDP of $8,050 billion, equivalent to almost 30% of global GDP.

Other forms of Northern and Western European cooperation are important but all are overshadowed by the sheer size, economic and political importance, and enormous potential of the Union.

European Union (EU)

The main EU institutions are the Commission, the Council of Ministers, the Committee of the Regions, the Committee of Permanent Representatives (COREPER), the Economic and Social Committee, the Court of Justice, and the European Parliament.

The **European Commission** is at the heart of the Union's decision-making process. It consists of 20 members: two each from France, Germany, Italy, Spain, and the United Kingdom, and one each from Austria, Belgium, Denmark, Finland, Greece, Ireland, Luxembourg, the Netherlands, Portugal, and Sweden. The members are nominated by each state for a five-year, renewable, term of office. One member is chosen as president for a five-year, renewable, term. The post of president, occupied from May 1999 by Romano Prodi, Italy's former prime minister, is a mixture of head of government and head of the European civil service, and a highly respected appointment.

Although the commissioners are drawn proportionately from member states, each takes an oath on appointment not to promote national interests. They head a comparatively large bureaucracy, with 20 directorates-general, each responsible for a particular department. Critics often complain about the size of the EU permanent machine but it is not unduly large in relation to the scope of its activities and its workload. The Commission has a total staff of 15,000 civil servants.

In March 1999 a critical report by auditors, which claimed that fraud, nepotism, and mismanagement were prevalent in the commission, resulted in the resignation of all 20 commissioners, including the president, Jacques Santer. The new commission, appointed in July 1999, was brought more firmly under the control of the president, with commissioners agreeing to resign if asked by President Prodi. In addition, two commisioners have been designated vice-presidents.

The **Council of Ministers of the European Union** is the supreme decision-making body and consists of one minister from each of the 15 member countries. The actual representatives vary according to the subject matter under discussion. If it is economic policy it will be the finance ministers, if it is agricultural policy, the agriculture ministers. It is the foreign ministers, however, who tend to be the most active. The presidency of the Council changes hands at six-monthly intervals, each member state taking its turn. In certain areas, decisions are taken by 'qualified majority vote', and there are 87 votes in all. The number of votes each state has depends on its population, ranging from three to ten.

The **Committee of the Regions** debates and advises on the Union's regional policy. It comprises 222 appointed and indirectly elected representatives: 24 each from France, Germany, Italy, and the United Kingdom; 21 from Spain; 12 each from Austria, Belgium, Greece, the Netherlands, Portugal, and Sweden; nine each from Denmark, Finland, and Ireland; and six from Luxembourg. The members are drawn from both large regions and local authorities and the Committee meets five times a year for two days.

The **Committee of Permanent Representatives (COREPER)** is a subsidiary body of officials, often called 'ambassadors', who act on behalf of the Council. Its members are senior civil servants who have been temporarily released by member states to work for the Union.

The **Economic and Social Committee** is a consultative body consisting of 222 nominated representatives from member countries and covering a wide range of interests. For example, they may include employers, members of labor unions, professional people, farmers, and so on. The Committee advises the Council of Ministers and the Commission on draft legislation.

The **European Court of Justice** consists of 15 judges and officials appointed by the member states for six-year terms. Its task is to ensure that the Union treaties are fairly observed and that regulations and directives are followed. The Court can make rulings and impose fines on member states, but it has no powers of its own to enforce them. This is the responsibility of the individual member states in their own national courts.

Membership of the **European Parliament** is determined by the populations of member states. The total number of seats is 626, of which Germany, has 99, France, Italy, and the United Kingdom, 87 each, Spain, 64, the Netherlands, 31, Belgium, Greece, and Portugal, 25 each, Sweden, 22, Austria, 21, Denmark ,and Finland, 16 each, Ireland, 15 and Luxembourg, 6. Members are elected for five-year terms in large Euro-constituencies. Voting is by a system of proportional representation in all countries except the United Kingdom (excluding Northern Ireland). The party composition of the European Parliament in 1999 is shown in Table 78. Elections are held every five years, using proportional representation. The most recent elections were held in June 1999, and saw a swing away from the centre-left (Party of European Socialists) towards the centre-right (European People's Party). Turnout, which fell, ranged from 24% in the United Kingdom to 90% in Belgium. In July 1999 Nicole Fontaine, a French member of the European People's Party group, was elected preisident of the new parliament.

Around 70% of the deputies for the Socialist party group were supplied by five states: the United Kingdom (29), Germany (33), France (32), Spain (26), and Italy (15). Sixty-eight per cent of the deputies for the right-of-center European People's Party were drawn similarly

Party composition of the European Parliament 1999*	Table 78
Political groupings	Seats
Party of European Socialists	180
Group of the European People's Party	234
European Liberal Democrat and Reformist Party	50
Confederal Group of the European United Left–Nordic Green Left	42
Green Group	47
The Independent Europe of the Nations Group	21
Europe of Democracies and Differences	16
Non-attached or affiliation unknown	36
Total	*626*

*After June 1999 elections.

from these states, namely: Germany (53), Italy (22), France (21), Spain (27), and the United Kingdom (36).

EU operational methods. Policy is made and carried out within the Union in the following way. The Commission makes a particular proposal which will have first been worked on by one of the 20 directorates. The proposal is sent to the Council of Ministers who will initially pass it to COREPER for further examination. At the same time it will be passed to the European Parliament for consideration. The Parliament's role, although still mainly consultative, has been enhanced since the Maastricht Treaty. It has the right to reject the Union budget, to be consulted on the appointment of Commissioners and can dismiss the Commission if it has good grounds for doing so.

After examination by COREPER, with the addition of any views of the European Parliament, the proposal is formally considered by the Council of Ministers who decide whether or not action should be taken. Voting in the Council is weighted in favor of the larger member states, but votes are taken only rarely. Either there is a unanimous decision or, if one or more of the ministers argue that the policy would be against national interests, the proposal is likely to be shelved. Once the Council has agreed to a policy proposal it is passed back to the Commission for implementation.

A policy decision can take one of two forms. It can be a regulation or a directive. Both are legally binding, but a regulation applies to all member states, whereas a directive only relates to one or more specific countries.

Decision-making within the Union is only partially democratic and only marginally accountable to the electorates of the member states but, as the European Parliament becomes more firmly established, on broad European party lines, its influence, and eventually its powers, will undoubtedly grow.

In certain areas, the Parliament has a second reading of proposals, which if rejected can only be overturned by a unanimous decision of the Council.

Although a single European market, with all internal barriers to trade removed, has been created, the broader objective of agreeing common economic and foreign policies, eventually leading, as pro-Europeans would hope, to political union, is a much longer-term aim and some heads of government would clearly like to postpone its implementation indefinitely, or even summarily abandon it.

The Commission, the Council of Ministers, and COREPER are based in Brussels, the European Parliament meets in Luxembourg and Strasbourg,

France, and the European Court of Justice sits in Luxembourg.

The EU budget will amount, in 2000, to $90 billion, 45% of which is for agricultural support (the Common Agricultural Policy) and 35% for structural fund payments to less developed regions within the EU. Fifty-five per cent of the EU budget is contributed by three states: Germany; France; and the United Kingdom. The EU spends roughly 1% of EU GDP.

European Monetary Union (EMU). A European Monetary System (EMS) was established in 1979. Through its Exchange Rate Mechanism (ERM), it promoted stability in exchange rates by allowing member currencies to only fluctuate within a narrow band around a central rate, defined by a European Currency Unit (ECU) which was based on a basket of member currencies. Eight states joined the ERM at the outset, with Spain, the United Kingdom, and Portugal entering between 1989 and 1992, leaving only Greece outside. Financial difficulties forced the United Kingdom and Italy to withdraw in September 1992, but Italy rejoined in November 1996. As part of the Maastricht Treaty, a timetable for moving towards full EMU was agreed and a European Monetary Institute was set up in 1994. This was the precursor to a European Central Bank (ECB), which was formed in 1998 and based in Frankfurt, Germany, with Wim Duisenberg, from the Netherlands, as its president. The ECB regulates the operation of a European Single Currency (ESC), known as the 'euro', setting interest rates for member states. Eleven countries, which had achieved financial 'convergence criteria' stipulated in the Maastricht Treaty, joined the 'euro' at its launch in January 1999: Austria; Belgium; Finland; France; Germany; Ireland; Italy; Luxembourg; the Netherlands; Portugal; and Spain. Until June 2002, the ESC is to operate alongside national currencies, at a fixed exchange rate. Thereafter, Euro notes and coins will be introduced and national notes and coins cease to be legal tender.

Council of Europe

The Council of Europe was established in Strasbourg in 1949 to secure 'a greater measure of unity between the European countries', by the discussion of common interests and problems, and the discovery of new methods and areas of cooperation. In particular, it seeks to promote pluralist democracy and protect human and minority rights. Its membership is wider than that of the European Union, including: Albania, Andorra, Bulgaria, Croatia, Cyprus, the Czech Republic, Estonia, Georgia (admitted in 1999), Hungary, Iceland, Latvia,

Liechtenstein, Lithuania, Macedonia, Malta, Moldova, Norway, Poland, Romania, Russia, San Marino, Slovakia, Slovenia, Switzerland, Turkey, and Ukraine, as well as the 15 European Union members. It has a Consultative Assembly which meets annually and a Standing Committee to represent it when it is not in session.

The Council has been particularly active, and effective, in the field of human rights. Under the European Convention of Human Rights of 1950, it established the European Commission of Human Rights, also based in Strasbourg, to investigate complaints by states or individuals. The findings of the Commission are then considered by the European Court of Human Rights, in Strasbourg, which was formed in 1959. Many European states have recognized the jurisdiction of the Court by making its decisions binding nationally, and this has resulted in ordinary citizens who feel aggrieved by judgements in their own national courts, taking their cases, over the heads of governments, to Strasbourg.

Benelux

A customs union, to encourage trade between the three countries, was established by Belgium, the Netherlands, and Luxembourg in 1948 and was called Benelux. It was later overtaken by the creation of the European Economic Community (EEC), and the other bodies which now form part of the European Union (EU), but in 1960, by the Benelux Treaty, the economic union of the three states was formalized. This made them, in economic terms, a single unit, while retaining their political independence and their obligations to the European Union. The organization has a Committee of Ministers, comprising at least three ministers from each state, which meets every two months, and a Council of Economic Union which is an umbrella body with the task of coordinating the work of the many Benelux committees. The head of the permanent Secretariat, which is based in Brussels, is always Dutch and is assisted by two deputies from the other member states.

European Free Trade Association (EFTA)

EFTA was originally established in 1960 as a free-trade alternative to the European Economic Community (EEC). Its original members included Austria, Denmark, Norway, Portugal, Sweden, Switzerland, and the United Kingdom. Finland became an associate member in 1961 and Iceland a full member in 1970. It soon became clear that EFTA could never supplant the EEC and several members began to apply for entry into the Community. Denmark and the United Kingdom

left in 1972, Portugal in 1985, and Austria, Finland, and Sweden in 1994. EFTA now comprises Iceland, Liechtenstein, Norway, and Switzerland. It is essentially an economic association whereby import duties between the member countries have been abolished. It has its headquarters in Geneva.

In 1973 the EC signed agreements with EFTA members, setting up a combined free-trade area, and a further pact was signed in 1991 to create a European Economic Area (EEA) from 1994, giving EFTA greater access to the EU market. The EEA is based on four 'freedoms': circulation of goods, capital, services, and people. It covers 18 nations, comprising the EU 15 plus Iceland, Liechtenstein, and Norway, but not Switzerland, with a population exceeding 365 million.

Despite their reduced numbers, the remaining EFTA members agreed, in December 1994, to keep it, and the EEA, in existence.

Nordic Council

The Nordic Council was founded in 1952 by Denmark, Iceland, Norway, and Sweden as a consultative body to increase cooperation between them. They were joined in 1956 by Finland and between 1970 and 1984 by representatives from the Faroes, Aland Islands, and Greenland. Council members are elected by the parliaments of the member states. There are 87 voting members and two full sessions each year. There are secretariats in Stockholm and Copenhagen.

European Space Agency (ESA)

ESA is an organization to promote space research and technology for peaceful purposes. It was founded in 1975 and its members comprise Austria, Belgium, Denmark, Finland, France, Germany, Ireland, Italy, the Netherlands, Norway, Spain, Sweden, Switzerland, and the United Kingdom. ESA has developed a number of scientific and communication satellites, as well as the Ariane rocket.

European Organization for Nuclear Research (*Conseil Européen pour la Recherche Nucléaire*, renamed *Organisation Européenne pour la Recherche Nucléaire*; still known as CERN)

CERN was established in 1954 as a cooperative venture for research into nuclear energy for peaceful purposes. Its members include 19 major European countries who provide teams of scientists to work together at laboratories at Meyrin, near Geneva.

9.9.2 Central and Eastern Europe

Baltic Council

Originally in operation between 1934 and 1940, this body was revived in May 1990 by the three Baltic republics of Estonia, Latvia, and Lithuania, which were part of the Soviet Union until 1991. During 1990–91 the Council was used to coordinate the independence strategies of the three republics. It now promotes economic cooperation, with the aim of establishing a Baltic Common Market. In January 1998 the member states signed a US – Baltic Charter of Partnership with the United States, underpinning their commitment to democracy and free trade.

Black Sea Economic Cooperation Zone

This grouping was founded in 1992 to promote trade and economic cooperation and control pollution of the Black Sea. The 11 member states are: Albania, Armenia, Azerbaijan, Bulgaria, Georgia, Greece, Moldova, Romania, Russia, Turkey, and the Ukraine.

Visegrad Group

In October 1991, recently democratized Czechoslovakia, Hungary, and Poland signed the Visegrad cooperation treaty. This was extended in December 1992 by a Central European Free Trade Agreement (CEFTA). With the division of Czechoslovakia into the Czech and Slovak sovereign republics, the 'Visegrad Three' became the 'Visegrad Four' and in 1995 close ties were also developed with Slovenia. In 1999 Bulgaria joined the CEFTA.

9.9.3 Middle East and North Africa

Cooperation within the Middle East and North Africa is generally founded on a strong, and proud, sense of a common identity among Arabs, even though the region contains many races and religions. Israel has been excluded from virtually all the cooperative groups and associations and this has, undoubtedly, contributed to its sense of isolation and suspicions about neighboring states. Future harmony in the region depends greatly on whether the degree of mutual trust which has been established between Egypt and Israel can be extended to the wider Arab world.

League of Arab States (*Al Jamia al Arabiyyah*) or Arab League

The Arab League was founded in 1945 largely on the initiative of Egypt. It now has 22 members, comprising all the states of the Middle East and North Africa except Israel, plus the Comoros. Palestine is regarded as a member state. The League's declared purpose is 'to strengthen the close ties linking sovereign Arab States and to coordinate their policies and activities and direct them to the common good of the Arab countries'. It also acts as a mediator in disputes between Arab nations. The main body in the League is the Council which includes representatives of all the member states and usually meets twice a year, in March and September. Attached to it are 16 specialist, functional committees. There are a large number of agencies and bureaux operating with the League. The headquarters, with the secretariat, are in Cairo.

Arab Common Market

The Arab Common Market, providing for the abolition of customs duties on agricultural products, and reductions on other items, came into effect in 1965. Membership was open to all Arab League states but only Egypt, Iraq, Jordan, and Syria have signed the treaty which set it up.

Arab Monetary Fund (AMF)

The AMF was established in 1976 by 20 Arab states plus the PLO to provide a mechanism for promoting greater stability in exchange rates and to coordinate Arab economic and monetary policies. The Fund's headquarters are in Abu Dhabi, in the United Arab Emirates. It operates mainly by regulating petrodollars within the Arab community to make it less dependent on the West for the handling of its surplus funds.

Organization of Arab Petroleum Exporting Countries (OAPEC)

OAPEC was established in 1968 to safeguard the interests of its members and to encourage cooperation in economic activity within the petroleum industry. It currently has ten members: Algeria, Bahrain, Egypt, Iraq, Kuwait, Libya, Qatar, Saudi Arabia, Syria, and the United Arab Emirates. Its headquarters are in Kuwait.

Palestine Liberation Organization (PLO)

The PLO was founded in 1964 with the objective of

bringing about an independent state of Palestine. It contains a number of factions, the most important being *al-Fatah*, which is led by Yasser Arafat (b. 1929). To achieve its main aim it has pursued a mixed policy of diplomacy and guerrilla activity. Although it has long been recognized in the Arab world as a legitimate political body, its reputation among Western nations has not been good, some political leaders referring to it as a terrorist organization. However, in 1988, when Jordan announced its decision to relinquish its responsibility for the Israeli-occupied West Bank, and Arafat later publicly accepted the right of Israel to exist as an independent state, world opinion changed and the PLO became an organization which could be regarded as the legitimate representative of the Palestinians and, therefore, could provide the nucleus of an independent Palestine state.

Palestine National Authority (PNA)

The Palestine National Authority was appointed in 1994 to take over from Israel the management of Palestinian affairs in Gaza-Jericho, following the peace agreement between the PLO and Israel and the subsequent Israeli withdrawal. The PNA has jurisdiction over the whole of the formerly occupied areas, except for Israeli settlers and nationals. Israel retains responsibility for external defense and foreign affairs. The PNA held its first meeting in Gaza on 26 June 1994 and on 5 July 1994 the PLO leader, Yasser Arafat, formally swore in its members. It is intended to be an interim body, to be replaced by a more democratic, permanent one at a later date. On 5 December 1994 Israel extended the PNA's power to include the administration of health and the collection of taxes but, in the same month, the Israeli parliament, the Knesset, passed legislation that would allow Israel to close PNA offices which had been set up outside the self-rule areas, notably Orient House, in East Jerusalem. The occupants of Orient House said they would continue their political activities despite the new legislation. In July 1996 Yasser Arafat was elected PNA president.

Cooperative Council for the Arab States of the Gulf (CCASG)

The CCASG was established in 1981 as an exclusively Arab organization for promoting peace in the Persian Gulf area. Its declared purpose is 'to bring about integration, coordination and cooperation in economic, social, defense and political affairs among Arab Gulf states'. Its members include Bahrain, Kuwait, Oman, Qatar, Saudi Arabia, and the United Arab Emirates and its headquarters are at Riyadh, Saudi Arabia.

9.9.4 Central and Southern Africa

Cooperation in economic and social matters in Central and Southern Africa has been fragmentary and sometimes duplicated. Because of this, it has been less effective than in some other regions of the world. This lack of cohesion has arisen partly because of the sheer size of the continent and the poor communications within it, particularly between the east and west coasts, and partly because of tribal and language differences.

Cooperation is, therefore, frequently subregional and often influenced by the colonial histories of particular countries. Thus those states which used to form part of the French empire cooperate more naturally with other French-speaking countries, whereas former British colonies tend to link with countries where English is the principal language.

Southern African Development Community (SADC)

The SADC was formed at its first conference in Arusha, Tanzania, in July 1979, when representatives of Angola, Botswana, Lesotho, Malawi, Mozambique, Swaziland, Tanzania, Zambia, and Zimbabwe agreed to work more closely together to reduce their economic dependence on South Africa. Since then an organization has been formed with its headquarters in Gabarone, Botswana. Annual meetings of heads of state and heads of government are held and SADC ministers meet at least twice a year to formulate plans. The main areas that the organization has targeted as needing particular attention are transport and communications, energy and mining, and industrial production, and a number of sector units have been set up to implement proposals. Member states have agreed to share the scarce water that flows over their land. With the ending of apartheid in South Africa from 1991 and the establishment there of an all-race multiparty democracy in 1994, the SADC aims have changed and it is now a 14-member body, with the Democratic Republic of Congo (formerly Zaire), Mauritius, Namibia, Seychelles, and South Africa becoming new members. In August 1995 SADC leaders agreed to seek to create a Southern African economic community, with free trade by the year 2000, free movement of people, and, eventually, a single currency. The combined population of the SADC was 133 million in 1994 and the GDP $150 billion. However, South Africa dominates, with 31% of the population and 78% of the GDP. Currently, only 10% of Southern Africa's trade takes place within the region.

Organisation Commune Africaine et Mauricienne (OCAM)

OCAM was founded in 1965 as the *Organisation Commune Africaine et Malgache*. This was itself a successor to the *Union Africaine et Malgache de Coopération Economique*, which had operated between 1961 and 1965. In 1970 the name of *Organisation Commune Africaine, Malgache et Mauricienne* was adopted but when Madagascar withdrew from the Organization in 1975 the present name was adopted. The full membership now includes Benin, Burkina Faso, the Central African Republic, Côte d'Ivoire, Niger, Rwanda, Senegal, and Togo. The declared purpose of OCAM is to strengthen the solidarity and close ties between member states and to raise living standards and coordinate economic policies. Through the Organization, members share an airline, a merchant fleet, and a common postal and communications system. The headquarters of OCAM are at Bangui in the Central African Republic.

Council of the Entente (CE) (*Conseil de l'Entente*)

The CE was set up in 1959 by four states, Benin, Burkina Faso, Côte d'Ivoire, and Niger, to strengthen economic links and promote industrial development. Togo joined in l966 when a Mutual Aid and Loan Guarantee Fund was established. The headquarters of the Council are in Abidjan, Côte d'Ivoire.

Economic Community of West African States (ECOWAS) (*Communauté Economique des Etats de l'Afrique de l'Ouest*)

ECOWAS was established in 1975, by the Treaty of Lagos, to promote economic cooperation and development. Its 16 members comprise: Benin, Burkina Faso, Cape Verde, Gambia, Ghana, Guinea, Guinea-Bissau, Côte d'Ivoire, Liberia, Mali, Mauritania, Niger, Nigeria, Senegal, Sierra Leone, and Togo. Its headquarters are in Lagos, Nigeria. A revived ECOWAS treaty, effective from 1995, makes the prevention and control of regional conflicts, and provides for the creation of a regional parliament. ECOWAS peace-keeping forces have intervened to restore order in Liberia (1990–99), Sierra Leone (1997–), and Guinea-Bissau (1999).

Preferential Trade Area for Eastern and Southern African States (PTA)

The PTA was established in 1981 with the objective of increasing economic and commercial cooperation between member states, harmonizing tariffs and reducing trade barriers, with the eventual aim of creating a common market. The current members include: Burundi, the Comoros, Djibouti, Ethiopia, Kenya, Lesotho, Malawi, Mauritius, Rwanda, Somalia, Swaziland, Tanzania, Uganda, Zambia, and Zimbabwe. The headquarters of the PTA are in Lusaka, Zambia.

9.9.5 Central America and the Caribbean

Caribbean Community and Common Market (CARICOM)

CARICOM was founded in 1973 as a successor to the Caribbean Free Trade Association, as a vehicle for increasing political and economic cooperation and reducing trade barriers in the area. Its 14 members comprise: Antigua and Barbuda, Bahamas, Barbados, Belize, Dominica, Grenada, Guyana, Jamaica, Montserrat, St Kitts and Nevis, St Lucia, St Vincent and the Grenadines, Suriname, and Trinidad and Tobago. The headquarters of CARICOM are at Georgetown, Guyana. In 1994 CARICOM sponsored the formation of the Association of Caribbean States (ACS) trade group.

Central American Common Market (CACM)

The CACM is roughly the mainland equivalent of CARICOM. It was founded in 1960 with similar objectives and its members include Costa Rica, Guatemala, El Salvador, Honduras, and Nicaragua. It was suspended in the mid-1980s, but revived in the 1990s. Its headquarters are in Guatemala City.

Organization of Central American States (ODECA)

ODECA was founded in 1951 for the purpose of strengthening unity in Central America and fostering economic, political and social cooperation, with a view to avoiding overdependence on the United States and its dominance in the Organization of American States (OAS). ODECA's membership includes Costa Rica, El Salvador, Guatemala, Honduras, and Nicaragua. Its headquarters are in San Salvador.

9.9.6 South America

The Amazon Pact

The Amazon Pact is a treaty signed in 1978 by Bolivia, Brazil, Colombia, Ecuador, Guyana, Peru, Suriname, and Venezuela to protect and control the development of the Amazon River.

Andean Community of Nations

The Andean Community of Nations, also known as the Andean Group, was established under the Cartegena Agreement of 1969 to promote the balanced and harmonious development of member countries through economic integration. The members include Bolivia, Colombia, Ecuador, Peru, and Venezuela, with Mexico as a working partner since 1972. Chile was originally a member but left in 1976. The Group aims to harmonize policies on tariffs, the protection of intellectual property, such as patents and trademarks, and industrial and commercial development. Its institutions include a parliament and an executive commission and its headquarters are in Lima, Peru. In 1992 an Andean Pact was established to create a free-trade area.

URUPABOL

URUPABOL is a tripartite commission which was formed in 1981 by Bolivia, Paraguay and Uruguay to foster economic and commercial cooperation.

Mercosur (Southern Common Market)

Mercosur was founded in March 1991 by the Asunción Treaty signed by Argentina, Brazil, Paraguay, and Uruguay, to create a common market for the four member states. It was formally inaugurated on 1 January 1995. With a population of more than 197 million, it constituted the fourth largest free trade bloc after the North American Free Trade Area (NAFTA), 375 million people, the European Union (EU) 360 million, and the Association of Southeast Asian Nations (ASEAN), 340 million.

From 1 January 1995 tariffs among member states were removed for about 90% of traded goods and common tariffs, averaging 14%, were imposed on about 80% of goods imported from outside the market. On 23 January 1995 foreign ministers of the countries in the Andean Pact, Bolivia, Colombia, Ecuador, Peru, and Venezuela, agreed to seek a free-trade agreement with Mercosur. In 1996 Bolivia and Chile became associate members of Mercosur and signed a free trade agreement. In 1999 a trade dispute arose between Argentina and Brazil, following Brazil's January devaluation, which led to a flood of cheap exports to Argentina. This led the member countries to agree to contemplate common fiscal and monetary targets. In June 1999 the EU and Mercosur agreed to start talks to liberalize trade.

9.9.7 Asia

South Asian Association for Regional Cooperation (SAARC)

The forum was established in 1985 to foster cooperation between the seven South Asian states of Bangladesh, Bhutan, India, Maldives, Nepal, Pakistan, and Sri Lanka. An annual summit is held and in 1993 a South Asian Preferential Tariff Agreement was unveiled, with the goal of lowering or abolishing tariffs on intraregional trade.

9.9.8 Oceania

Pacific Community (PC)

Established as the South Pacific Commission (SPC) by an agreement signed in Canberra, Australia, in 1947, the PC's objective is to encourage economic and social cooperation in the region. Its 26 members include most of the states in Oceania, including the dependencies, plus France and the United States, which are involved because of their past and present interests in the region. The name Pacific Community was adopted to reflect the growing importance of north Pacific states within the PC body. The headquarters are in Nouméa, New Caledonia.

South Pacific Forum (SPF)

The SPF was created in 1971, as an offshoot of the SPC, to provide an opportunity for member states to meet annually to discuss common interests and develop common policies. The first meeting of the Forum's heads of government was held in New Zealand in 1971. The membership includes ,Australia, the Cook Islands, Fiji, Kiribati, the Marshall Islands, Micronesia, Nauru, New Zealand, Niue, Papua New Guinea, the Solomon Islands, Tonga, Tuvalu, Vanuatu, and Samoa. In 1985 the Forum adopted a treaty for creating a nuclear-free zone in the Pacific.

South Pacific Bureau for Economic Cooperation (SPEC)

SPEC was founded in 1973, following a meeting of the South Pacific Forum (SPF), as a practical scheme for stimulating economic cooperation and the development of trade. The headquarters of SPEC are in Suva, Fiji.

Spearhead Group of Melanesian Countries

This body was formed in 1988 by Vanuatu, Papua New Guinea, and the Solomon Islands to promote increased political and economic cooperation among the small Melanesian-peopled states of the Pacific Region. Annual leadership summits are held, with observers from Fiji and New Caledonia also attending. In 1996 a Council of Micronesian Government Executives (CMGE) was formed to promote further cooperation in the region.

9.10 Military cooperation

The examples of global, interregional, and intraregional cooperation described above are generally positive and peaceful in character. However, a number of military pacts and organizations have been established to provide what states and regions see as vital defenses against possible aggression. There are now hopeful signs that nations, and groups of nations, are beginning to talk more openly with each other, across the barriers that military organizations inevitably create.

ANZUS

This three-member defense alliance, comprising Australia, New Zealand, and the United States, was established in 1951 to coordinate defense policy and preserve peace in the Pacific region. The member states share defense and technical intelligence. Since 1984, joint ANZUS military services have been cancelled because of New Zealand's refusal to allow visits by nuclear-propelled or armed vessels. In 1986 the US suspended its security commitment to New Zealand, although senior-level contacts resumed in 1994.

North Atlantic Treaty Organization (NATO)

NATO was established under the North Atlantic Treaty of 1949, which was signed by Belgium, Canada, Denmark, France, Iceland, Italy, Luxembourg, the Netherlands, Norway, Portugal, the United Kingdom, and the United States. It is a mutual defense treaty by which it was agreed that 'an armed attack against one or more in Europe or North America shall be considered an attack against all'. Greece and Turkey joined the Organization in 1952, Germany was admitted in 1955, and Spain in 1982. France withdrew from the Organization's integrated military structure, but not the alliance, in 1966. Greece withdrew politically, but not militarily, in 1974, and its re-entry was opposed by Turkey in 1980. France rejoined the military committee in 1995. In March 1999 the Czech Republic, Hungary, and Poland joined to bring membership up to 19 states.

NATO's supreme body is the Council of Foreign Ministers of all the participating nations and its Secretariat is based in Brussels, where there is also a Military Committee composed of the chiefs of staff of the member countries. The military headquarters, Supreme Headquarters Allied Powers, Europe (SHAPE), are at Chièvres, near Mons, in Belgium. The two Supreme Allied Commanders, Europe and Atlantic, are US military officers. In 1990 it was agreed to form a permanent, multinational unit, called the Allied Rapid Reaction Corps (ARRC), to move immediately to any NATO country which appeared to be under threat. This mobile unit is based in Heidelberg, in Germany, and has a British commander.

NATO was originally formed to oppose a threat from the Soviet Union and its Warsaw Pact satellites and, although it has remained the keystone of Western defense for more than 40 years, relations between its members have not always been harmonious. The main areas of contention have been the degree of US dominance, the presence of nuclear weapons on European soil, and the respective levels of contribution by signatories to the Organization's upkeep.

The changed climate created by the demise of the Soviet Union in December 1991 added another dimension to NATO's role and in January 1994 a 'Partnership for Peace' program was launched. It invited former members of the Warsaw Pact, which was NATO's opposing organization in the 'Cold War' era, and ex-Soviet republics to take part in a wide range of military cooperation agreements, without the implication of imminent NATO membership. Partners train alongside NATO and open up their defense plans to NATO scrutiny and advice. Romania was the first to join, followed by Albania, Azerbaijan, the Czech Republic, Estonia, Finland, Georgia, Kazakhstan, Kyrgyzstan, Latvia, Lithuania, Poland, Sweden, Armenia, Austria, Bulgaria, Belarus, Hungary, Malta, the Russian Federation, Slovenia, Macedonia, Moldova, Turkmenistan, Ukraine, Uzbekistan, and Slovakia. Emerging out of the Partnership for Peace programme was the agreement, in January 1999, by six Balkan states – Albania, Bulgaria, Greece, Macedonia, Romania, and Turkey – to form a 4,000-strong 'Balkan brigade' regional peace-keeping force. Its headquarters are in Plovdiv, Bulgaria, and the troops would be available for UN humanitarian missions in southeastern Europe.

During the civil war in parts of the former Yugoslavia the United Nations Security Council made use of NATO's air resources to defend and support its own ground and naval units. In December 1995 Javier Solana became NATO secretary general, as 60,000 NATO troops were deployed in Bosnia-Herzegovina to replace a UN mission. The NATO stabilization force (S-FOR) had 32,000 troops in 1999. NATO forces also became involved in peacekeeping in Kosovo, Yugoslavia, in 1999, after a bombing campaign. A 50,000 strong Kosovo Force (K-FOR) was deployed in June 1999 to keep the peace, with dividing Kosovo into five sectors, each under the control of a member country. The UK provided 12,000 troops, Germany 8,500, and France and the USA 7,000 each. A number of NATO's 'partners', notably Finland, Austria, and Romania, also contributed troops.

In May 1997 a Founding Act on Mutual Relations, Cooperation and Security was signed by NATO and Russia. It established a new NATO – Russian Permanent Joint Council to consult and participate in security decisions and uphold equal status in peacekeeping operations. The Czech Republic, Hungary, and Poland joined NATO in April 1999, with Bulgaria, Romania, and Slovenia set to join within a few years. George Robertson, the former UK defence secretary, became secretary general of NATO in 1999.

Western European Union (WEU)

The WEU is based on the Brussels Treaty of 1948 and was established in 1955 as a forum for the discussion of defense issues by West European governments. Its members include Belgium, France, Germany, Greece, Italy, Luxembourg, the Netherlands, and the United Kingdom, and, since 1989, Portugal and Spain. There is an Assembly which meets twice yearly in Paris, and comprises 115 parliamentarians and a permanent Council, consisting of the representatives of member states, which meets weekly. There is a biannual meeting of foreign and defense ministers. The Union is pledged, under its charter, to work closely with NATO. Other EU members, who are not also in the WEU, are sometimes invited to attend Assembly meetings as observers and in May 1994 Bulgaria, the Czech Republic, Estonia, Hungary, Latvia, Lithuania, Poland, Romania, and Slovakia became associate partners.

Since 1995 the WEU has overseen a fully operational 50,000-strong 'Eurocorps', based on a Franco-German brigade, but also including Belgian, Luxembourg, and Spanish troops. In May 1999 the ten member countries of the WEU agreed in principle to merge with the EU at a future date. This would give the EU agreed in principle to merge new military rule.

Recommended reading

Berridge, G R *International Politics: States, Power and Conflict since 1945*, 2nd edn., Harvester Wheatsheaf, 1992

Brogan, P *World Conflicts: Why and Where they are Happening*, 2nd edn., Bloomsbury, 1992

Chan, S *The Commonwealth in World Politics: A Study of International Action 1965–1985*, Lester Crook Academic, 1988

Commonwealth Yearbook (annual), HMSO

Dinan, D *Ever Closer Union*, Macmillan, 1994

Faringdon, H *Strategic Geography: NATO, the Warsaw Pact and the Superpowers*, 2nd edn., Routledge, 1989

Hocking, B and Smith, M *World Politics: An Introduction to International Relations*, Harvester Wheatsheaf, 1990

Jacobs, F, Corbett, R, and Shackleton, M *The European Parliament*, Longman, 1992

Kaplan, L S *NATO and the United States: The Enduring Alliance*, Twayne, 1988

Kennedy, P *Preparing for the Twenty-First Century*, Harper Collins, 1993

Nicoll, W and Salmon, T *Understanding the New European Community*, Harvester Wheatsheaf, 1993

Osmanczyk, E J *Encyclopaedia of the United Nations and International Agreements*, 2nd edn., Taylor & Francis, 1990

Owen, R *The Times Guide to World Organizations*, Times Newspapers, 1996

Parsons, A *From Cold War to Hot Peace: UN Interventions 1947–1994*, Michael Joseph, 1994

Pinder, J *European Community: The Building of a Union*, Oxford University Press, 1991

Reynolds, P A *An Introduction to International Relations*, Longman, 1994

Righter, R *Utopia Lost: The United Nations and World Order*, The Twentieth Century Fund, 1995

Roberts, A and Kingsbury, B (eds.) *United Nations, Divided World: The UN's Role in International Relations*, 2nd edn., Clarendon Press, 1993

Segal, G *The World Affairs Companion: The Essential One Volume Guide to Global Issues*, 2nd edn., Simon & Schuster, 1991

United Nations *Basic Facts About the United Nations*, United Nations Publications, 1995

Appendices

China: leaders of the Communist Party

Term	Name
1935–76	Mao Zedong
1976–81	Hua Guofeng
1981–87	Hu Yaobang
1987–89	Zhao Ziyang
1989–	Jiang Zemin

France: presidents and prime ministers during the Fifth Republic

Term	Name	Party
Presidents		
1959–69	Gen. Charles de Gaulle	Gaullist
1969–74	Georges Pompidou	Gaullist
1974–81	Valery Giscard d'Estaing	Republican/Union for French Democracy
1981–95	François Mitterrand	Socialist
1995–	Jacques Chirac	Neo-Gaullist RPR
Prime ministers		
1959–62	Michel Debre	Gaullist
1962–68	Georges Pompidou	Gaullist
1968–69	Maurice Couve de Murville	Gaullist
1969–72	Jacques Chaban Delmas	Gaullist
1972–74	Pierre Messmer	Gaullist
1974–76	Jacques Chirac	Gaullist
1976–81	Raymond Barre	Union for French Democracy
1981–84	Pierre Mauroy	Socialist
1984–86	Laurent Fabius	Socialist
1986–88	Jacques Chirac	Neo-Gaullist RPR
1988–91	Michel Rocard	Socialist
1991–92	Edith Cresson	Socialist
1992–93	Pierre Beregovoy	Socialist
1993–95	Edouard Balladur	Neo-Gaullist RPR
1995–97	Alain Juppé	Neo-Gaullist RPR
1997–	Lionel Jospin	Socialist

Federal Republic of Germany: chancellors

Term	Name	Party
1949–63	Konrad Adenauer	Christian Democrat
1963–66	Ludwig Erhard	Christian Democrat
1966–69	Kurt Kiesinger	Christian Democrat
1969–74	Willy Brandt	Social Democrat
1974–82	Helmut Schmidt	Social Democrat
1982–98	Helmut Kohl	Christian Democrat
1998–	Gerhard Schröder	Social Democrat

India: prime ministers

Term	Name	Party
1949–64	Jawaharlal Nehru	Congress
1964–66	Lal Bahadur Shastri	Congress
1966–77	Indira Gandhi	Congress (I)
1977–79	Morarji Desai	Janata/coalition
1979–80	Charan Singh	Janata/Lok Dal/coalition
1980–84	Indira Gandhi	Congress (I)
1984–89	Rajiv Gandhi	Congress (I)
1989–90	Viswanath Pratap Singh	Janata Dal/coalition
1990–91	Chandra Shekhar	Janata Dal (Socialist)/coalition
1991–96	PV Narasimha Rao	Congress
1996	Atal Behari Vajpayce	BJP
1996–97	H D Deve Gowda	Janta Dal
1997–98	Inder Kumar Gujral	United Front
1998–	Atal Behari Vajpayce	BJP

Japan: prime ministers

Term	Name	Party
1945–46	Kijuro Shidehara	coalition
1946–47	Shigeru Yoshida	Liberal
1947–48	Tetsu Katayama	coalition
1948	Hitoshi Ashida	Democratic
1948–54	Shigeru Yoshida	Liberal
1954–56	Ichiro Hatoyama	Liberal/Liberal Democrat
1956–57	Tanzan Ishibashi	Liberal Democrat

continues

Postwar political leaders in the world's leading states (continued) — Appendix A

Term	Name	Party
1957–60	Nobusuke Kishi	Liberal Democrat
1960–64	Hayato Ikeda	Liberal Democrat
1964–72	Eisaku Sato	Liberal Democrat
1972–74	Kakuei Tanaka	Liberal Democrat
1974–76	Takeo Miki	Liberal Democrat
1976–78	Takeo Fukuda	Liberal Democrat
1978–80	Masayoshi Ohira	Liberal Democrat
1980–82	Zenko Suzuki	Liberal Democrat
1982–87	Yasuhiro Nakasone	Liberal Democrat
1987–89	Noboru Takeshita	Liberal Democrat
1989	Sosuke Uno	Liberal Democrat
1989–91	Toshiki Kaifu	Liberal Democrat
1991–93	Kiichi Miyazawa	Liberal Democrat
1993–94	Morihiro Hosokawa	Japan New/coalition
1994	Tsutomu Hata	Shinseito/coalition
1994–96	Tomiichi Murayama	Social Democrat/coalition
1996–98	Ryutaro Hashimoto	Liberal Democrat
1998–	Keizo Obuchi	Liberal Democrat

Soviet Union/Russia: leaders of the Communist Party*/Russian president**

Term	Name
1922–53	Joseph Stalin*
1953–64	Nikita Khrushchev*
1964–82	Leonid Brezhnev*
1982–84	Yuri Andropov*
1984–85	Konstantin Chernenko*
1985–91	Mikhail Gorbachev *
1990–	Boris Yeltsin**

United Kingdom: prime ministers

Term	Name	Party
1945–51	Clement Attlee	Labor
1951–55	Winston Churchill	Conservative
1955–57	Anthony Eden	Conservative
1957–63	Harold Macmillan	Conservative
1963–64	Alec Douglas-Home	Conservative
1964–70	Harold Wilson	Labor
1970–74	Edward Heath	Conservative
1974–76	Harold Wilson	Labor
1976–79	James Callaghan	Labor
1979–90	Margaret Thatcher	Conservative
1990–97	John Major	Conservative
1997–	Tony Blair	Labor

United States: presidents

Term	Name	Party
1945–53	Harry S Truman	Democrat
1953–61	Dwight D Eisenhower	Republican
1961–63	John F Kennedy	Democrat
1963–69	Lyndon B Johnson	Democrat
1969–74	Richard Nixon	Republican
1974–77	Gerald Ford	Republican
1977–81	Jimmy Carter	Democrat
1981–89	Ronald Reagan	Republican
1989–93	George Bush	Republican
1993–	Bill Clinton	Democrat

Glossary of abbreviations and acronyms — Appendix B

ACP	African, Caribbean and Pacific signatories to the Lomé Convention
ACS	Association of Caribbean States
ADB	African Development Bank
AFESD	Arab Fund for Social and Economic Development
AfDB	African Development Bank
AG	Andean Group
AL	Arab League
ALADI	Latin American Integration Association
AMF	Arab Monetary Fund
AMU	Arab Maghreb Union
ANZUS	Australian, New Zealand, United States Security Treaty
AP	Amazon Pact
APEC	Asia-Pacific Economic Cooperation
AsDB	Asian Development Bank
ASEAN	Association of Southeast Asian Nations
AT	Antarctic Treaty
BADEA	Arab African Economic Development Bank
BC	Baltic Commission
BCIE	Central American Economic Integration Bank
BDEAC	Central African States Development Bank
Benelux	Benelux Economic Union
BIS	Bank for International Settlements
BLEU	Belgo-Luxembourg Economic Union
BOAD	West African Development Bank
CACM	Central American Common Market
CARICOM	Caribbean Community and Common Market
CBSS	Council of Baltic Sea States
CCASG	Cooperative Council for the Arab States of the Gulf
CDB	Caribbean Development Bank
CE	Council of Europe
CEAO	West African Economic Community
CEEAC	Economic Community of Central African States

continues

Glossary of abbreviations and acronyms (continued)

Appendix B

CEI	Central European Initiative
CEPGL	Economic Community of the Great Lakes Countries
CERN	European Council for Nuclear Research
CILSS	Permanent Inter-State Committee on Drought Control in the Sahel
CIS	Commonwealth of Independent States
CP	Colombo Plan
CSCE	Conference on Security and Cooperation in Europe (renamed OSCE)
CW	Commonwealth
DDS	Damascus Declaration States
EADB	East African Development Bank
EBRD	European Bank for Reconstruction and Development
EC	European Community
ECA	Economic Commission for Africa
ECE	Economic Commission for Europe
ECLAC	Economic Commission for Latin America and the Caribbean
ECO	Economic Cooperation Organization
ECOWAS	Economic Community of West African States
ECWA	Economic Commission for Western Asia
EEA	European Economic Area
EFTA	European Free Trade Association
ESA	European Space Agency
ESCAP	Economic and Social Commission for Asia and the Pacific
ESCWA	Economic and Social Commission for Western Asia
EU	European Union
FAO	Food and Agriculture Organization
FLS	Front Line States
FZ	Franc Zone
GATT	General Agreement on Tariffs and Trade
G-3	Group of Three
G-5	Group of Five
G-7	Group of Seven
G-11	Group of Eleven (Cartegena Group)
G-15	Group of Fifteen
G-24	Group of Twenty-four
G-77	Group of Seventy-seven
GCC	Gulf Cooperation Council
GDP	Gross domestic product
Geplacea	Group of Latin American and Caribbean Sugar Exporting Countries
IADB	Inter-American Development Bank
IAEA	International Atomic Energy Agency
IBRD	International Bank for Reconstruction and Development (World Bank)
ICAO	International Civil Aviation Organization
ICC	International Chamber of Commerce
ICFTU	International Confederation of Free Trade Unions
IDA	International Development Association
IDB	Inter-American Development Bank

IEA	International Energy Authority
IFAD	International Fund for Agricultural Development
IFC	International Finance Corporation
IGADD	Inter-Governmental Authority on Drought and Development
ILO	International Labor Organization
IMF	International Monetary Fund
IMO	International Maritime Organization
IOC	Indian Ocean Commission
IsDB	Islamic Development Bank
ITU	International Telecommunication Union
IWC	International Whaling Commission
KBO	Kagera Basin Organization
LCBC	Lake Chad Basin Commission
LORCS	League of Red Cross and Red Crescent Societies
Mercosur	Southern Common Market
MRU	Mano River Union
NACC	North Atlantic Cooperation Council
NAFTA	North American Free Trade Agreement
NAM	Non-Aligned Movement
NATO	North Atlantic Treaty Organization
NC	Nordic Council
NEA	Nuclear Energy Authority
NIB	Nordic Development Bank
OAPEC	Organization of Arab Petroleum Exporting Countries
OAS	Organization of American States
OAU	Organization of African Unity
ODECA	Organization of Central American States
OECD	Organization for Economic Cooperation and Development
OECS	Organization of Eastern Caribbean States
OIC	Organization of the Islamic Conference
OMVG	Gambia River Development Organization
OMVS	Senegal River Development Organization
OPEC	Organization of Petroleum Exporting Countries
OSCE	Organization for Security and Cooperation in Europe
PC	Pacific Community
PFP	Partnership for Peace
PLO	Palestine Liberation Organization
PNA	Palestine National Authority
PTA	Preferential Trade Area for Eastern and Southern African States
RG	Rio Group
SAARC	South Asian Association for Regional Cooperation
SADC	Southern African Development Community
SELA	Latin American Economic System
SG	Spearhead Group
SPC	South Pacific Commission
SPEC	South Pacific Bureau for Economic Cooperation

continues

Glossary of abbreviations and acronyms (continued) Appendix B

SPF	South Pacific Forum	**UPU**	Universal Postal Union
UDEAC	Central African Customs and Economic Union	**VG**	Visegrad Group
UN	United Nations	**WCC**	World Council of Churches
UNCTAD	United Nations Conference on Trade and Development	**WEU**	Western European Union
		WFTU	World Federation of Trade Unions
UNESCO	United Nations Educational, Scientific and Cultural Organization	**WHO**	World Health Organization
		WIPO	World Intellectual Property Organization
UNIDO	United Nations Industrial Development Organization	**WMO**	World Meteorological Organization
		WTO	World Trade Organization

Data sources Appendix C

Annual Register (annual), Longman

Banks, A S, Day, A J, and Muller, TC (eds.) *Political Handbook of the World*, CSA Publications, 1997

Bogdanor, V (ed.) *The Blackwell Encyclopedia of Political Institutions*, Basil Blackwell, 1987

Central Intelligence Agency – The World Factbook, CIA, 1994

Collins Nations of the World Atlas, Harper Collins, 1996

Day, A J and Degenhardt, H W *Political Parties of the World: A Keesing's Reference Publication*, 3rd edn., Longman, 1988

Day, A J and Munro, D *A World Record of Major Conflict Areas*, Edward Arnold, 1990

Day, A J *et al.* (eds.) *Border and Territorial Disputes*, 3rd edn., Longman, 1992

Delury, G E (ed.) *World Encyclopedia of Political Systems*, Vols I–III, 2nd edn., Longman, 1987

The Economist (weekly), London

Pocket World in Figures, The Economist Publications, 1998

Europa Publications:

Africa South of the Sahara Yearbook (annual)

Europa Yearbook (annual)

Far East and Australasia Yearbook (annual)

Middle East and North Africa Yearbook (annual)

Evans, G and Newnham, J *The Dictionary of World Politics: A Reference Guide to Concepts, Ideas and Institutions*, Harvester Wheatsheaf, 1992

Facts on File, the Index of World Events, (weekly) Facts on File, 1940–

Gorvin, I (ed.) *Elections since 1945: A Worldwide*

Reference Companion, Longman, 1989

The Guardian (daily), London

Humana, C (ed.) *World Human Rights Guide*, Oxford University Press, 1992

The Hutchinson Encyclopedia, 11th edn., Helicon, 1998

The Hutchinson Guide to the World 3rd edn., Helicon, 1998

The Independent (daily), London

Keesing's Record of World Events (monthly), Longman, 1931–

Kidron, M and Smith, D *The New State of War and Peace: An International Atlas*, Grafton, 1991

Kurian, G T *Encyclopedia of the Third World*, Vols I–III, 4th edn., Facts on File, 1992

Kurian, G T *The New Book of World Rankings*, 3rd edn., Facts on File, 1991

Kurian, G T *Atlas of the Third World*, 2nd edn., Facts on File, 1992

Lawson, E (ed.) *Encyclopaedia of Human Rights*, Taylor and Francis, 1991

Lipset, S M (ed.), *The Encylopedia of Democracy*, 4 vols., Routledge, 1995

Mackie, T T and Rose, R *International Almanac of Electoral History*, 3rd edn., Macmillan, 1991

Magill, F N (ed.) *International Encyclopedia of Government and Politics*, 2 vols., Fitzroy Dearborn, 1996

Minority Rights Group Reports, MRG, London

Newsweek (weekly)

The Observer (weekly), London

Palmer, A *Who's Who in World Politics*, Routledge, 1996

continues

Data sources (continued)

Ransley, J (ed.) *Chambers Dictionary of Political Biography*, Chambers, 1991

South (monthly), South Publications

Statesman's Yearbook (annual), Macmillan, 1864–

Time Magazine (weekly)

The Times (daily), London

United Nations *Statistical Yearbook* (annual)

Whitaker's Almanac (annual)

The World Almanac and Book of Facts (annual)

The World Guide 1997/8, New Internationalist Publications, 1998

World Tables 1994, World Bank, 1994

Internet sources

Most of the states of the world now have their own official websites, which provide useful (though not always unbiased) information, on political structures and developments. Up-to-date news is available from the many news organization websites, with Reuters being particularly useful. In addition, there are a growing number of political websites which amass historical and current information on a wide range of political topics. The Keele Political Science Resources website, maintained by Richard Kimber, is the most useful 'gateway' to more specialist websites. Below are set out the web addresses of three particularly useful, and reliable, political websites.

The Electoral Website [Wilfred Derksen] at www.agora.stm.it/elections

Klipsan's Daily Election Notes at www.klipsan.com

Political Leaders Around the World [Robert Oritz de Zarate] at http://webjet.es/ziaorarr

Index

Please note

Names

In certain states in Asia, for example China and the Koreas, the family name (surname) precedes the personal name, for example Deng Xiaoping. In Latin American countries the family name usually appears in the middle, as in Ernesto Samper Pizano, shown in this index as Samper Pizano, Ernesto.

Country entries

The term 'country entry' indicates a full political, economic, and social profile of the respective state.